READINGS

■ PROFESSIONAL ESSAYS

■ STUDENT ESSAYS

Why Do You Need This New Edition?

6 good reasons why you should buy this new edition of *The Curious Writer*!

① 28 new readings (over half of the readings in the book) give you a wide range of fresh voices and styles. You'll find a fantasy tale by Ursula Le Guin, an essay on global warming by Michael Pollan, a new video game review, and many others.

② New writing projects: Chapters 1 and 2 introduce you to the idea of writing as discovery, beginning with two new reading and writing memoir projects, where you'll get to explore your own history and relationship with literacy as you have personally experienced it.

③ New *Writing in the Disciplines* and *Writing in Your Life* features: Ever wonder what your writing class has to do with your major, or your life? Two new features in each chapter show you how to apply skills you'll learn in this book to many other writing situations you'll encounter.

④ New kinds of writing and reading: Blog posts, PowerPoint slide presentations, photo essays, and even a review of *Grand Theft Auto IV*—all new readings and samples to offer the broadest possible picture of writing and composing in a digital age.

⑤ Updated documentation coverage: All sample papers and documentation examples are updated to reflect the 2009 editions of the MLA and APA style guides. You'll need this new information to produce accurate and current research papers!

⑥ You can use *The Curious Writer* with Pearson's unique MyCompLab—the gateway to a world of online resources developed specifically for you!

THE CURIOUS WRITER

THE CURIOUS WRITER

Third Edition

Bruce Ballenger

Boise State University

Longman

Boston   Columbus   Indianapolis   New York   San Francisco   Upper Saddle River
Amsterdam   Cape Town   Dubai   London   Madrid   Milan   Munich   Paris   Montreal   Toronto
Delhi   Mexico City   Sao Paulo   Sydney   Hong Kong   Seoul   Singapore   Taipei   Tokyo

Executive Editor: Suzanne Phelps Chambers
Senior Development Editor: Michael Greer
Editorial Assistant: Erica Schweitzer
Senior Supplements Editor: Donna Campion
Senior Media Producer: Stefanie Liebman
Senior Marketing Manager: Sandra McGuire
Production Manager: Eric Jorgensen
Project Coordination and Text Design: Elm Street Publishing Services
Electronic Page Makeup: Integra Software Services Pvt. Ltd.
Cover Design Manager: Nancy Danahy
Cover Design: Nancy Sacks
Cover Image: *Best Western,* © Joel Barr/SuperStock
Photo Researcher: Pearson Image Resource Center/Julie Tesser
Image Permission Coordinator: Craig A. Jones
Senior Manufacturing Buyer: Dennis J. Para
Printer and Binder: Courier/Kendallville
Cover Printer: Lehigh/Phoenix Color/Hagerstown

For permission to use copyrighted material, grateful acknowledgment is made to the copyright
holders on pp. CR-1 to CR-4, which are hereby made part of this copyright page.

Library of Congress Cataloging-in-Publication Data
Ballenger, Bruce P.
   The curious writer/Bruce Ballenger.—3rd ed.
     p. cm.
   Includes bibliographical references and index.
   ISBN 978-0-205-70764-5—ISBN 978-0-205-70765-2
     1. English language—Rhetoric—Handbooks, manuals, etc. 2. Interdisciplinary approach
in education—Handbooks, manuals, etc. 3. Academic writing—Handbooks, manuals, etc.
I. Title.
   PE1408.B37 2009b
   808'.042—dc22

2009030923

1 2 3 4 5 6 7 8 9 10—CRK—12 11 10 09

Longman
is an imprint of

www.pearsonhighered.com

Full (Hardcover) Edition
13-Digit ISBN: 978-0-205-70764-5
10-Digit ISBN: 0-205-70764-5

Brief (Softcover) Edition
13-Digit ISBN: 978-0-205-70765-2
10-Digit ISBN: 0-205-70765-3

BRIEF CONTENTS

DETAILED CONTENTS

PART 3

INQUIRING DEEPER   389

PREFACE

The "adventure of discovery" is what many of us love about writing. Our students often enter our composition classrooms with little experience using language as a tool of learning. Then we help them understand that writing can be a means for finding out what they didn't know they knew, and that the process of revision can lead to a fresh way of seeing things; pretty soon even some resistant writers welcome the invitation to sit down and write. They've discovered that they can write to learn.

What's New in This Edition?

This third edition represents a substantial revision from the previous edition. Building on suggestions and insight from teachers using the second edition, I have made revisions throughout with the overall aim of improving the book's "teachability" and appeal for students. Most visibly, a colorful new design highlights the importance of visual communication for today's students and showcases photographs and other visual texts. To get students into the process and writing sooner, I have streamlined Part One by merging the first three chapters into two; I've also given these chapters a more practical focus with the new reading and writing literacy memoir projects. I've made a number of other significant revisions that affect chapters throughout the book, including:

- **NEW reading selections:** More than half of the readings in the book are new to this edition. I was motivated by a desire to include a diverse range of authors, genres, and styles, and to include contemporary readings on timely topics alongside some recognized classics. Ursula Le Guin's sci-fi fantasy tale "The Ones Who Walk Away from Omelas," for example, provides a new centerpiece for Chapter 8 on the critical essay. Michael Pollan's "Why Bother?" brings a respected new environmental voice into Chapter 6 on proposals. In Chapter 5 on reviews, a new review of a Lotus sports car and a second new review of the video game "Grand Theft Auto IV" demonstrate the breadth of evaluative writing today and connect with popular cultural texts that may be part of many students' daily lives. Other authors whose work is new to this edition include Scott Russell Sanders, Sarah Vowell, Judith Ortiz Cofer, and Laura Zazulak.
- **NEW visual selections:** To provide illustrations of emerging visual forms and genres, I have added a range of new selections to help students discover ways in which images can make meaning and assert claims. A PowerPoint

presentation on "green dining" from a university dining services office, for example, and a photo essay proposing a change in bicycle storage policy on commuter trains both make effective case studies in the use of visual argument. A poster from the National Eating Disorders Association shows how visual rhetoric can enter the public sphere in effective ways.

- **NEW inquiry projects:** Chapters 1 and 2 are now built around two increasingly popular writing projects: the writing and reading literacy memoirs. These projects encourage students to apply the basic principles of inquiry and critical reading to their own histories as writers and readers.

- **NEW *Writing in the Disciplines* feature:** Each chapter includes a new "Writing in the Disciplines" feature designed to help students see how a particular genre is used across the disciplines. For example, in Chapter 7, a feature called "Argument in Academic Disciplines" helps students understand the different types of argument and forms of evidence valued in different academic fields.

- **NEW *Writing in Your Life* features:** Parallel to the "Writing in the Disciplines" features, new "Writing in Your Life" sections in each chapter connect work students are doing in a particular genre to similar writing situations they may find in their daily lives. For example, "Public Argument in a Digital Age" in Chapter 7 shows students the wide range of forms public argument now takes, including blogs, photo essays, and YouTube videos.

- **NEW genres:** The third edition includes a wider range of public, visual, and online genres than before, including PowerPoint proposals, blog posts, photo essays, and video game reviews.

- **Updated documentation coverage:** Both the MLA and the APA have published new editions of their style manuals in 2009. All sample papers, documentation coverage, and sample references and works cited have been revised to incorporate the latest style guidelines used by writers in the humanities and social sciences.

Inquiry in the Writing Classroom

Most of us already teach inquiry, although not all may realize it. For instance, our writing classes invite students to be active participants in making knowledge in the classroom through peer review workshops. When we ask students to fastwrite or brainstorm, we encourage them to suspend judgment and openly explore their feelings or ideas. And when we ask students to see a draft as a first look at a topic, and revision as a means of discovering what they may not have noticed, we teach a process that makes discovery its purpose. Indeed, most composition classrooms create a "culture of inquirers" rather than passive recipients of what their teachers know.

Historically, composition teachers have struggled to decide what besides reading and writing skills students can export to their other classes and, later, into their lives. Often we vaguely refer to "critical-thinking" skills. *The Curious Writer* offers a comprehensive approach for teaching inquiry.

For inquiry-based courses on any subject, there are five key actions I believe instructors should take:

1. Create an atmosphere of mutual inquiry. Students are used to seeing their teachers as experts who know everything that students need to learn. But in an inquiry-based classroom instructors are learners too. They ask questions not because they already know the answers but because there might be answers they haven't considered.

2. Emphasize questions before answers. The idea that student writers begin with an inflexible thesis or a firm position on a topic before they engage in the process of writing and thinking is anathema to inquiry-based learning. Questions, not preconceived answers, lead to new discoveries.

3. Encourage a willingness to suspend judgment. Student culture at most schools works against this. Papers get written at the last minute, multiple deadlines in multiple classes compete for students' time, and multiple-choice tests or lecture courses imply that there is one true answer and the teacher knows it. To suspend judgment demands that we trust the process that will lead us to new insights. This requires both faith in the process and the time to engage in it. The composition course, with its emphasis on process, is uniquely suited to nurture such faith.

4. Introduce a strategy of inquiry. It's not enough to simply announce that we're teaching an inquiry-based class. We have to introduce students to the strategy of inquiry we'll be using. In the sciences, the experimental method provides a foundation for investigations. What guidance will we give our students in the composition course? *The Curious Writer* features a strategy that is genuinely multidisciplinary, borrowing from science, social science, and the humanities.

5. Present inquiry in a rhetorical context. An essay, a research project, an experiment, any kind of investigation is always pursued with particular purposes and audiences in mind. In an inquiry-based class, the situation in which the inquiry project is taking place is always considered.

You'll find all of these elements of inquiry-based learning integrated in *The Curious Writer*. For example, each assignment in Part Two, "Inquiry Projects," leads students toward writing subjects that offer the most potential for learning. Rather than write about what they already know, students are always encouraged to choose a topic that they want to find out more about. In addition, the discussion questions that follow the student and professional essays are crafted to do more than simply test their comprehension of the piece or reduce it to a single theme. In many cases, questions are open ended and can lead students in many directions as they analyze a reading. *The Curious Writer* maintains a voice and persona throughout the book that suggests that I am working along with the students as a writer and a thinker, which is exactly the experience of mutual inquiry I try to create in my classes. Finally, *The Curious Writer* is organized around a strategy of inquiry that is present in every assignment and nearly every exercise. Introduced in Part One, "The Spirit of Inquiry," I call on the model often in every subsequent chapter. The inquiry strategy is the thematic core of the book.

The Inquiry Strategy of *The Curious Writer*

A strategy of inquiry is simply a process of discovery. In the sciences, this process is systematic and often quite formal. The model I use in this book borrows from science in some ways through its insistence on continually looking closely at the "data" (sensory details, facts, evidence, textual passages, and so on) and using it to shape or test the writer's ideas about a subject. But the heart of the model is the alternating movement between two modes of thinking—creative and critical—in a dialectical process. One way of describing this is shifting back and forth between suspending judgment and making judgments (see Figure A).

This inquiry strategy works with both reading and writing, but in Chapter 2, "Reading as Inquiry," I offer four categories of questions—those that explore,

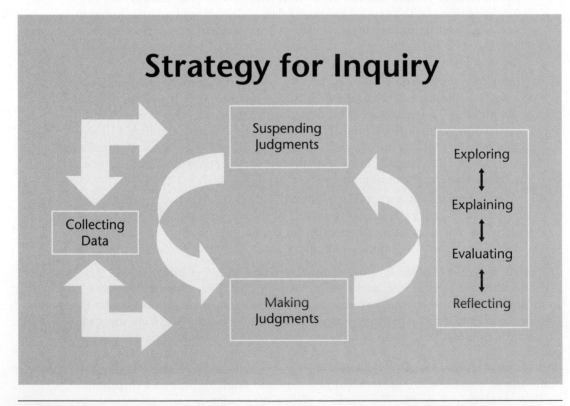

Figure A   In nearly every assignment in *The Curious Writer*, students will use this strategy of inquiry.

explain, evaluate, and reflect—that I think will help guide students in reading most texts more strategically. These types of questions will be most evident in the follow-up questions to the many readings throughout *The Curious Writer*.

Finally, a strategy of inquiry is useful only if it makes sense to students; I've tried very hard, particularly in the first section of the book, to make the model comprehensible.

Other Features

Because the inquiry-based approach is central to *The Curious Writer*, it's crucial for students to work through the first two chapters in Part One, "The Spirit of Inquiry." Part Two—the largest—focuses on "inquiry projects." The range of assignments in this part should satisfy the needs of most composition instructors. If your university is lucky enough to have a two-semester sequence, *The Curious Writer* includes assignments suitable for both courses, including personal, argument, and research essays. Also included is the ethnographic essay, a form that engages students in field research; *The Curious Writer* is the first major text to include ethnography.

The book's focus on genres of writing also makes it appealing for advanced composition courses. For example, assignments such as the profile, review, and proposal help students see how to apply what they've learned to distinct rhetorical situations and help them to understand how those situations shape the genres.

In recent years, I've become interested in reading strategies, a topic that I never mentioned as a novice teacher. There was simply so much to say about the writing process that I didn't think reading was a topic that should get much airtime. Yet, as in writing, students bring many prior beliefs and assumptions about reading into our classrooms, and because reading is always an important part of teaching writing, I've come around to talking more about it. *The Curious Writer* reflects this. Chapter 2, "Reading as Inquiry," is devoted to the topic. I've also expanded the discussion to reading images. This emphasis on visual rhetoric echoes the latest developments in composition in response to the growth of the Web and the growing visual literacy of our students.

Finally, the approach of *The Curious Writer* grows in part from my own scholarship on research writing, particularly the criticism that research is too often isolated in the writing course. Students understandably get the idea that research is reserved only for the research paper if they're asked to do it only when they're assigned a research project. This book makes research a part of every assignment, from the personal essay to the proposal, emphasizing that it is a useful source of information, not a separate genre.

This is the third textbook I've written with the "curious" moniker. Because all are inquiry-based, the word is a natural choice. And although I'm very interested in encouraging my students to be curious researchers, readers, and writers, I also hope to remind my colleagues who use the books that we should be curious, too. We should model for our students our own passion for inquiring into the world. We should also celebrate what we can learn from our students, and not just about writing, or the many topics they might choose to write about. I'm curious every time I walk into the writing classroom what my students will teach me about myself. That's a lifetime inquiry project for all of us, as teachers and as people.

Approaches to Teaching with the Book

The Instructor's Manual, written by my colleague Michelle Payne, will give you detailed suggestions about ways to teach *The Curious Writer*. Here are a few additional suggestions drawn with a much broader stroke.

I organized the book to span, if necessary, a two-semester composition course, though it can easily be adapted to one semester. Typically, in a two-semester sequence the first course focuses on the writing process, exposition, critical analysis, writing to learn, and so on. The second semester often focuses on argument and research. A single-semester composition course tries to combine them all. Fortunately, *The Curious Writer* is extremely flexible, with ample material to keep students busy for one or two semesters.

Sequence

Whether you use this book for one course or two, it's wise to introduce *The Curious Writer* to students by first working through Part One, "The Spirit of Inquiry," because this section lays the foundation for all that follows. The many exercises in these chapters will help students experience firsthand what we mean by inquiry. Part Two, "Inquiry Projects," is the heart of the book. I've organized chapters in an order that roughly follows typical composition courses, beginning with genres that draw heavily on students' personal experiences and observations and then moving them outward toward other sources of information and encounters with other people's experiences and ideas. In a one-semester course, for example, you might begin with the personal essay, and then move to the profile, followed by the review, and then the argument or research essay. This builds nicely by challenging students to work with more sources of information and leads to a more sophisticated understanding of persuasion and rhetoric. A two-semester course has the luxury of more assignments, of course, allowing you to potentially use most of the inquiry projects in Part Two.

Certain assignments clump together. For example, while arguably all writing is persuasive, the following genres are most explicitly so: proposal, review, argument, critical essay, and often the research essay. A course that focuses on argument might emphasize these assignments. A research-oriented course might exploit the wealth of material with a strong emphasis on outside sources, including the proposal, review, argument, research essay, and ethnography. A single-semester composition course that attempts coverage of critical thinking and writing as well as research and argument might move from personal essay to profile, and then cover persuasion through the review or critical essay, move on to the argument, and finish with the ethnographic and research essays.

Integrating the Research and Revision Sections

An unusual feature of the book is its treatment of research skills and revision. Research is an element of every assignment, but it receives special attention in Part Three, "Inquiring Deeper," in which students are introduced not only to the research essay but to research strategies and skills. I hope you will find that this section, particularly Chapter 11, "Research Techniques," is immediately relevant because students will be encouraged to consider research angles in every assignment they tackle. Consider assigning this chapter early in your course, particularly the sections on developing a working and focused knowledge of a subject.

Similarly, revision is an element of every assignment. That's hardly a novel idea, but what is unusual is that *The Curious Writer* devotes an entire section of the book—Part Four, "Re-Inquiring"—to revision. Like the section on research, the chapters on revision are relevant to students from their very first assignment. The first half of Chapter 13, "Revision Strategies," is a useful introduction to what it means to revise, and you might assign this material early on in your course. The chapter also features specific revision strategies that your students will use in every assignment.

Chapter 14, "The Writer's Workshop," can also be assigned at any time and in sections. Consider having your students read the first half of that chapter— an introduction to peer review—before the first class workshops. The second half of the chapter focuses on methods of responding, specific workshop formats that are most helpful for drafts at different stages in the writing process. Ask students who are responsible for presenting their work to read about the method of response they'll use in their workshop as preparation for it.

Using the Exercises

Learning follows experience, and the exercises in *The Curious Writer* are intended to help students make sense of the ideas in the text. I often plan the exercises as an in-class activity, and then assign the relevant reading to follow up that experience. Sometimes the discussion following these in-class exercises is so rich that some of the assigned reading becomes unnecessary. The students get it without having to hear it again from the author. More often, though, the reading helps students deepen their understanding of what they've done and how they can apply it to their own work.

However, assigning all of the exercises isn't necessary. Don't mistake their abundance in the book as an indication that you must march your students in lockstep through every activity, or they won't learn what they need to. *The Curious Writer* is more flexible than that. Use the exercises and activities that seem to emphasize key points that you think are important. Skip those you don't have time for or that don't seem necessary. If you're like me, you also have a few rabbits of your own in your hat—exercises and activities that may work better with the text than the ones I suggest.

For Instructors

The following resources are free to qualified adopters of Longman English textbooks.

The Instructor's Resource Manual

ISBN 0-205-75048-6
This manual includes several sample syllabi, as well as a helpful introduction that will offer general teaching strategies and ideas for teaching writing as a form of inquiry. It also gives a detailed overview of each chapter and its goals, ideas for discussion starters, handouts and overheads, and a large number of additional writing activities that teachers can use in their classrooms to supplement the textbook.

The NEW MyCompLab Website

MyCompLab empowers student writers and facilitates writing instruction by uniquely integrating a composing space and assessment tools with market-leading instruction, multimedia tutorials, and exercises for writing, grammar, and research.

Students can use MyCompLab on their own, benefiting from self-paced diagnostics and a personal study plan that recommends the instruction and practice each student needs to improve her writing skills. The composing space and its integrated resources, tools, and services (such as online tutoring) are also available to each student as he writes.

MyCompLab is an eminently flexible application that instructors can use in ways that best complement their course and teaching style. They can recommend it to students for self-study, set up courses to track student progress, or leverage the power of administrative features to be more effective and save time. The assignment builder and commenting tools, developed specifically for writing instruction, bring instructors closer to their student writers, make managing assignments and evaluating papers more efficient, and put powerful assessment within reach. Students receive feedback within the context of their own writing, which encourages critical thinking and revision and helps them to develop skills based on their individual needs.

Learn more at www.mycomplab.com.

Interactive Pearson eText

An e-book version of *The Curious Writer* is also available in MyCompLab. This dynamic, online version of the text is integrated throughout MyCompLab to create an enriched, interactive learning experience for writing students.

CourseSmart eTextbook

The Curious Writer is also available as a CourseSmart eTextbook. This is an exciting new choice for students, who can subscribe to the same content online and search the text, make notes online, print out reading assignments that incorporate lecture notes, and bookmark important passages for later review. For more information, or to subscribe to the CourseSmart eTextbook, visit www.coursesmart.com.

Acknowledgments

I owe the success of *The Curious Writer* to many people, particularly my Development Editors, Adam Beroud and Michael Greer, whose savvy judgments, sharp eyes, and imaginative thinking influenced me every step of the way. None of the Curious books would be possible if the Senior Vice President and Publisher of Longman, Joe Opiela, weren't a force behind them. I'm particularly indebted to Suzanne Phelps Chambers, my new editor at Pearson, who always seems to ask the right questions and whose enthusiasm for this book carried me through the days when "delete" was my favorite key.

I've also been fortunate to have the help of other bright and generous people, particularly my colleague and friend Michelle Payne, with whom I coauthored an inquiry book. Michelle developed the Instructor's Manual for this book and wrote the appendixes. I'm a lucky author to have a partner in these projects with such a rich understanding of what I'm trying to do, and what I might do better.

In addition to Michelle, I've benefited from the insights of other colleagues as well, including Devan Cook, Brock Dethier, Bonnie Sunstein, Elizabeth Chiseri-Strater, Mike Mattison, Karen Uehling, Gail Shuck, Lad Tobin, and many others in the field whose work informed my understanding of how writers get better.

My students always contribute to my work. Several whose own exemplary writing is featured here include Julia Arrendondo, Bernice Olivas, Sam Battey, Briana Duquette, Jon Butterfield, Gordon Seirup, Kersti Harter, Margaret Parker, Lana Kuchta, Amy Garrett-Brown, Julie Bird, Kelly Sundberg, Gina Sinisi, and Christy Claymore.

Reviewers of books like these can be crucial to their development. I was lucky enough to have some excellent reviewers for each edition, including the following folks who guided me on the first edition:

Jeffrey T. Andelora, Mesa Community College; Ken Autrey, Francis Marion University; Sandra Barnhill, South Plains College; Patrick Bizzaro, East Carolina University; Sara M. Blake, El Camino College; Pamela S. Bledsoe, Surry Community College; Libby Bradford Roeger, Shawnee Community College; Sharon Buzzard, Quincy College; Maria A. Clayton, Middle Tennessee State University; Dr. Keith Coplin, Colby Community College; Rachelle Darabi, Indiana University/Purdue University–Fort Wayne; Virginia B. Earnest, Holmes Community College–Ridgeland; Terry Engebretsen, Idaho State University; Shari Hammond, Southwest Virginia Community College; Anneliese Homan, State Fair Community College; David C. Judkins, University of Houston; Robert Lamm, Arkansas State University; James C. McDonald, University of

Louisiana–Lafeyette; Rhonda McDonnell, Arizona State University; Bryan Moore, Arkansas State University; John D. Moore, Eastern Illinois University; Margaret P. Morgan, University of North Carolina–Charlotte; Dr. Peter E. Morgan, University of West Georgia; Brigid Murphy, Pima Community College; Robin L. Murray, Eastern Illinois University; Dorothy J. Patterson, Oakwood College; Steven R. Price, Mississippi College; Mark Reynolds, Jefferson Davis Community College; David H. Roberts, Samford University; Elaine J. Roberts, Judson College; Robert A. Schwegler, University of Rhode Island; Dr. Bonita Selting, University of Central Arkansas; Vicki Stieha, Northern Kentucky University; Elizabeth A. Stolarek, Ferris State University; Lisa Tyler, Sinclair Community College; Marjorie Van Cleef, Housatonic Community College; Worth H. Weller, Indiana University Purdue University–Fort Wayne; Ann R. Wolven, Lincoln Trail College; and Richard T. Young, Blackburn College.

Reviewers for the second edition included Melissa Batai, Triton College; Jennifer Black, McLennan Community College; Mark Browning, Johnson County Community College; Jo Ann Buck, Guilford Technical Community College; Jason DePolo, North Carolina A&T State University; John Christopher Ervin, University of South Dakota; Greg Giberson, Salisbury University; Nels P. Highberg, University of Hartford; William Klein, University of Missouri–St. Louis; Mary C. Leahy, College of DuPage; Lynn Lewis, University of Oklahoma; Steve Luebke, University of Wisconsin–River Falls; Michael Lueker, Our Lady of the Lake University; Jacqueline L. McGrath, College of DuPage; Betty Porter, Indiana Wesleyan University; Kristie Rowe, Wright State University; Kathleen J. Ryan, University of Montana; and Heath Scott, Thomas Nelson Community College.

And for this latest, third edition, reviewers included Angela Cardinale Bartlett, Chaffey College; Jennifer Black, McLennan Community College; James C. Bower, Walla Walla Community College; Susan Butterworth, Salem State College; Donna Craine, Front Range Community College; Brock Dethier, Utah State University; Rosemarie Dombrowski, Arizona State University (DPC); Kevin Ferns, Woodland Community College; Michael Hammond, University of San Francisco; Vicki M. Hester, St. Mary's University; Charlotte Hogg, Texas Christian University; Shelly Horvath, University of Indianapolis; Dawn Hubbell-Staeble, Bowling Green State University; Tom Moriarty, Salisbury University; Jason E. Murray, University of South Dakota; Amy Ratto Parks, University of Montana; Susan Pesznecker, Clackamas Community College; Lynn Raymond, UNC Charlotte; Mark A. Smith, Lock Haven University of Pennsylvania; Ruthe Thompson, Southwest Minnesota State University; BJ Zamora, Cleveland Community College.

Finally, I want to thank my daughters, Rebecca and Julia, who allow themselves to be characters in all of my books. They are both actors, and like good theater people, they are more than willing to play their parts in these texts, no matter what role I assign. I'm especially grateful to Karen, my wife, who has endured multiple editions of these books and their hold on my attention, which has often come at her expense. She's the beacon I follow through this blizzard of words, always guiding me home.

BRUCE BALLENGER

THE CURIOUS WRITER

1

THE SPIRIT OF INQUIRY

Writing as inquiry is an invitation to wonder and discover again.

WRITING AS INQUIRY

Just the other night I was writing a card to my old friend Linda, someone I went to college with and haven't seen in twenty-five years. As I wrote, my words scribbled in a heavy black pen, she began to appear before me again. I saw her in geology class, a few rows up, wearing a black raincoat and rubber boots, carefully putting her straight black hair behind an ear so she could see her notes. I hadn't seen her so clearly in years, and the writing brought her back. Most of us have had this experience—the power of words to summon images, memories, and feelings—which is why we sometimes indulge, often with pleasure, in writing letters, cards, and e-mails to friends and family.

Yet many of us admit that we really don't like to write, particularly when forced to do it, or we clearly prefer certain kinds of writing and dislike others: "I just like to write funny stories," or "I like writing for myself, and not for other people," or "I hate writing research papers." I can understand this, because for years I felt much the same way. I saw virtually no similarities between my note to Linda and the paper I wrote for my philosophy class in college. Words that had power in one context seemed flimsy and vacant in another. One kind of writing was fairly easy; the other was sweating blood. How could my experience as a writer be so fundamentally different? In other words,

What You'll Learn in This Chapter

- Why it pays to spend time thinking about your writing process.
- Why learning to write well often involves *unlearning* things you already believe.
- How understanding rhetoric will help you analyze writing situations.
- What it means to be a writer who is motivated by a spirit of inquiry.
- How to harness both creative and critical ways of thinking to come up with new ideas.

what's the secret of writing well in a range of contexts *and* enjoying it more? Here's what I had to learn:

1. All writing can offer the joy of discovery, the opportunity to speak and be heard, and the satisfaction of earned insight.
2. A key to writing well is understanding the *process* of doing it.

They're not particularly novel ideas, but both were a revelation to me when I finally figured them out late in my academic career, and they changed the way I wrote for good. These two insights—that the pleasures of writing can span genres and situations, and that thinking about *how* we write matters—are guiding principles of this book. After they read *The Curious Writer,* I won't guarantee that haters of writing will come to love it, or that lovers of writing won't find writing to be hard work. But I hope that by the end of the book you'll experience some of the same pleasures I found writing to my friend Linda in most writing situations, and that you'll be able to adapt your own writing process to meet the demands of whatever situation you encounter.

The process of becoming a more flexible and insightful writer must begin by exploring what you already believe it means to write well and learning a bit about how we can talk about writing as a process. In this chapter, I'll also introduce you to an idea that will be at the heart of every activity and assignment in *The Curious Writer:* the habits of mind and practices that will encourage you to adopt the "spirit of inquiry" as a motive for writing. This may sound a bit lofty and abstract. But by chapter's end I hope you'll recognize some practical implications of this approach that will help you with any writing assignment.

MOTIVES FOR WRITING

Why write? You could probably build a long list of reasons in a minute or two, perhaps beginning facetiously: "Because I *have* to!" But as you consider the many situations that call for writing and the purposes for doing it, I suspect that most will fall under a broad and obvious category: to say something to someone else. I'm less confident that you will see another broad motive for writing, partly because it gets less attention: we write to *discover* what we want to say.

These two motives for writing—to *share* ideas with others and to *discover* what the writer thinks and feels—are equally important.

But both these motives may arise from a still deeper spring: a sense of wonder and curiosity or even confusion and doubt, a desire to touch other people, or an urge to solve a problem. These feelings can inspire what I call the *spirit of inquiry,* a kind of perspective toward the world that invites questions, accepts uncertainty, and makes each of us feel some responsibility for what we say. This inquiring spirit should be familiar to you. It's the feeling you had when you discovered that the sun and a simple magnifying glass could be used to burn a hole in an oak leaf. It's wondering what a teacher meant when he said that World War II was a "good" war and Vietnam was a "bad" war. It's the questions that haunted you yesterday as you listened to a good friend describe her struggles with anorexia. The inquiring spirit even drives your quest to find the best DVD player, an effort that inspires you to read about the technology and visit consumerreports.org.

BELIEFS ABOUT WRITING

Most of us have been taught about writing since the first grade. We usually enter college with beliefs about how best to write a paper, which rules govern school writing, and even how to improve at composing. As I mentioned earlier, I've learned a lot about writing since my first years in college, and a big part of that learning involved unraveling some of my prior beliefs about writing. In fact, initially, I'd say that my development as a writer had more to do with *unlearning* some of what I already knew than it did with discovering new ways to write. What do you believe about how people get better at writing? You have theories that arise from all those years of school writing. Take a moment to find out what they are and whether they still make sense.

EXERCISE 1.1

What Do You Believe?

STEP ONE: From the following list, identify *the one belief* about writing that you agree with most strongly, and *one* that you're convinced isn't true.

1. Writing proficiency begins with learning the basics and then building on them, working from words to sentences to paragraphs to compositions.

2. The best way to develop as a writer is to imitate the writing of the people you want to write like.

3. People are born writers. Either you can do it or you can't.

4. The best way to develop as a writer is to develop good reading skills.

5. Practice is the key to a writer's development. The more a writer writes, the more he or she will improve.

6. Developing writers need to learn the modes of writing (argument, exposition, description, narration) and the genres (essays, research papers, position papers, and so on).

> **RULES FOR FASTWRITING**
>
> 1. There are no rules.
> 2. Don't try to write badly, but give yourself permission to do so.
> 3. To the extent you can, think through writing rather than before it.
> 4. Keep your pen moving.
> 5. If you run out of things to say, write about how weird it is to run out of things to say until new thoughts arrive.
> 6. Silence your internal critic to suspend judgment.
> 7. Don't censor yourself.

7. Developing writers should start with simple writing tasks, such as telling stories, and move to harder writing tasks, such as writing a research paper.

8. The most important thing that influences a writer's growth is believing that he or she can learn to write well.

9. The key to becoming a better writer is finding your voice.

STEP TWO: Spend five minutes writing in your notebook or journal about *why* you agree with the one belief and disagree with the other. This is an open-ended "fastwrite." You should write fast and without stopping, letting your thoughts flow in whatever direction they go.

Journal Prompts

- *When* did you first start agreeing or disagreeing with the belief? Can you remember a particular moment or experience as a student learning to write that drove this home?

- *What* do you mean, exactly, when you say you agree or disagree with the belief? Can you explain more fully why you think the belief is true or false?

- *Who* was most influential in convincing you of the truth or falsity of the belief?

ONE STUDENT'S RESPONSE

Bernice's Journal

EXERCISE 1.1
STEP TWO

I used to be a firm believer in the idea of born writers—it was a genetic thing. People were gifted with the gold pen genes, or they weren't. Writing as a process involved a muse, inspiration, and luck. Things uncontrollable by the writer. Then I started writing, mostly for my 101 class, and I started to feel powerful when I put words on paper. In control. The idea of my voice, my words just being on the page and other people reading it and maybe liking it was a rush. I was always the girl who specialized in the art of being unnoticed, unseen, blending in. My Comp 101 prof. liked my writing and pushed really hard to work on my basics, to think about my process, to prewrite and revise. I started to see a clear distinction between how to write and what to write. How is all mixed up with the process, with discipline, with practice and perseverance.... The how isn't something you are born with; its something you develop, something you practice, a skill you hone.... Becoming a good writer takes learning how to write, figuring out a process that works for you, and then letting your voice be heard on the page.

INQUIRING INTO THE DETAILS

Journals

Throughout *The Curious Writer*, I invite you to write in a journal. Some people hate journals. These are usually students who were forced to keep a journal in some class and found it a chore, or who tried to keep a journal at home and had little to show from the experience but blank pages. If you suffer from this condition, use a notebook instead of a journal. The two terms are synonymous. It's not what you call it that counts—it's what you do inside it!

Why do I want you to use a journal? One reason is that it is easier to write freely in this medium than it is when confronting the first page of a rough draft. Also, it's okay to write badly in journals and, as you will see later in this chapter, that's a good thing.

What kind of journal should you use? That's up to you. Some students just use the ubiquitous spiral notebook, which works just fine. Others find the digital journal best. They may be able to write faster and with more ease using a keyboard instead of a pen; keeping a journal on the computer might even be required if you're taking your class in a computer lab.

Unlearning Unhelpful Beliefs

You shouldn't be surprised when I say that I have a lot of theories about writing development; after all, I'm supposedly the expert. But we are *all* writing theorists, with beliefs that grow out of our successes and failures as students who write. Because you don't think much about them, these beliefs often shape your response to writing instruction without your even knowing it. For example, I've had a number of students who believe that people are born writers. This belief, of course, would make any kind of writing course a waste of time because writing ability would be a genetic problem.

A much more common belief is that learning to write is a process of building on basics, beginning with words, and then working up to sentences, paragraphs, and perhaps whole compositions. This belief was very common when I was taught writing. I remember slogging my way through Warriner's *English Grammar and Composition* in the seventh and eighth grade, dutifully working through chapter after chapter, beginning with parts of speech, parts of sentences, sentences, and then paragraphs.

Along with a lot of experts on writing instruction, I don't think that this foundational approach to writing development is very effective. I know it didn't help me become a better writer, and while I can still diagram a sentence, that's never a skill I call on when I'm composing. As a matter of fact, fifty years of research confirms that teaching formal grammar separately from writing essays is largely a waste of time. Despite this, formal grammar instruction persists, testimony to the subversive power of common sense. (Isn't it common sense that we should always learn the basics first?)

> Unlearning involves rejecting common sense if it conflicts with what actually works.

Unlearning involves rejecting common sense *if it conflicts with what actually works.* Throughout this book, I hope you'll constantly test your beliefs about writing against the experiences you're having with it. Pay attention to what seems to work for you and what doesn't; mostly, I'd like you at least initially to play what one writing instructor calls the believing game. Ask yourself, *What do I have to gain as a writer if I try believing this is true?*

The Beliefs of This Book

One of the metaphors I very much like about writing development is offered by writing theorist Ann E. Berthoff. She said learning to write is like learning to ride a bike. You don't start by practicing handlebar skills, move on to pedaling practice, and then finally learn balancing techniques. You get on the bike and fall off, get up, and try again, doing all of those separate things at once. At some point, you don't fall and you pedal off down the street. Berthoff said writing is a process that involves *allatonceness* (all-at-once-ness), and it's simply not helpful to try to practice the subskills separately. This is one belief about writing development shared by this book.

Any number of beliefs—the importance of critical thinking, the connection between reading and writing, the power of voice and fluency, and the need to listen to voices other than your own—all guide the structure of this book. One belief, though, undergirds them all: *The most important thing that influences a writer's growth is believing that he or she can learn to write well.* Faith in your ability to become a better writer is key. From it grows the motivation to learn how to write well.

Faith isn't easy to come by. I didn't have it as a writer through most of my school career because I assumed that being placed in the English class for underachievers meant that writing was simply another thing, like track, that I was mediocre at. For a long time, I was a captive to this attitude. But then, as a college freshman, I wrote a paper I cared about and the writing started to matter, not because I wanted to impress my instructor but because I discovered something I really wanted to say, and say well. I didn't settle for mediocrity after that.

As someone who wasn't too keen on writing for a very long time, I know how difficult it is to develop compelling reasons to write, particularly when the writing is required. I had to learn, among other things, that my teacher wasn't responsible for supplying the motivation (though I acknowledge that deadlines can help). I had to find a way to approach a writing assignment that made it seem like an opportunity to learn something.

INQUIRING INTO THE DETAILS

Portfolios

One method for evaluating your development as a writer is to use a *portfolio,* which is a collection of work you assemble throughout a semester and submit to your instructor at the end of the course. If your instructor uses portfolios, he or she may grade some of your work as you go along, but will mainly assess your writing abilities by reviewing the total body of work in your portfolio. This means that until you hand in your final drafts, everything is pretty much a work in progress, and for much of the course you can focus on learning goals—say, finding new methods to begin and end your essays, or improving your editing skills. Performance goals, such as getting a decent grade, become a priority only at the end of the course. I'll have much more to say about portfolios later (see Appendix A).

WRITING SITUATIONS AND RHETORICAL CHOICES

Good writing is good writing, right? Well, it depends on the situation. For instance, here's what a friend of my daughter wrote as a comment on her blog the other day:

> im happy to be back w/ u guys it was a too long of a weekend- dancing friday then? u hailey and i runnin tomorrow- sounds fun 2 me

This isn't necessarily bad writing for Facebook and sites like it. The message uses online conventions that most of us are familiar with—text messaging abbreviations like "u" for *you* and "2" for *to*—and it possesses a level of informality and intimacy that seems appropriate for its context. Would it be good writing for a college essay? Obviously not.

Part of learning to write well, then, isn't simply learning how to craft transitions, organize information, and follow grammatical rules; it's learning to recognize that each writing situation asks you for something different. Actually, you know this already. You know, for example, that composing a letter to a landlord who refuses to return your security deposit will be fundamentally different from a letter to your sister describing your problem with the landlord. What you may not know is what to call this kind of knowledge: rhetoric.

One way of analyzing any writing situation is by using *the rhetorical triangle,* which reveals the dynamic relationships among the writer, the subject, and the reader (see Figure 1.1).

What the triangle implies is pretty straightforward—to write effectively, you must simultaneously address three main factors: your own perspective as the writer, the topic you are writing about, and the people you are writing for. The

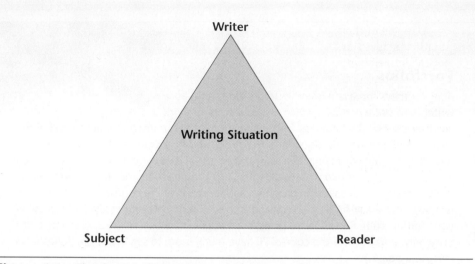

Figure 1.1   The rhetorical triangle

word *rhetorical,* of course, comes from *rhetoric,* the classical term for the study and practice of written and verbal communication. In fact, the rhetorical triangle has its origins in ancient Greece and the thinking of Aristotle, who first set down the principles of effective communication more than 2,000 years ago.

The three legs of the rhetorical triangle come together to shape the writing situation. The particularities of each leg—the writer, the subject, and the reader—determine the context of the writing situation. Consider again the security deposit problem. In that scenario, one thing is clear: Both of the proposed letters have a distinct—and different—*audience.* While the writer and the subject would seem to be the same for both letters, given the different audiences, the approach will be fundamentally different. In the letter to the landlord, the writer might adopt a formal, even legalistic, tone. The letter would be specific about what the writer is asking and when. The letter to the writer's sister would likely be informal, possibly more emotional. Its purpose would be to enlist a sibling's emotional support, not to persuade a landlord to return $500.

I'm pretty sure this is intuitively obvious to you. What may not be apparent is that you can use the same rhetorical knowledge to understand all kinds of writing situations, including academic ones. For example, consider next the opening two paragraphs from a writing assignment in Political Science 141: Contemporary Political Ideologies.

> This assignment aims to encourage students to connect the arguments being made by the thinkers in class to the issues and themes of our politics today. It aims to help students understand the relevance of political thinking for our political practice. Students are encouraged to share their judgments about the authors, only after they have shown that they understand the authors as the authors would understand themselves.

Use one of the following questions as the basis for a short essay. Your essay should be lucid and concise, and your argument should be thoroughly supported by relevant citations and allusions from the texts at hand. Grammar, spelling, punctuation, and syntax should be perfect.... Your paper is to be three to five pages in length, double-spaced, typed, and stapled in the upper left-hand corner. Please number your pages. A title page with an appropriate title must also be included, and all title pages should show what question the student is answering.

Using your own instincts about the rhetorical situation in this example, answer the following questions:

1. How would you characterize the instructor, and, based on that characterization, what kind of reader do you think he might be?

2. If you were in this class, how might your analysis of the rhetorical situation influence your approach to the writing assignment?

Writing well involves evaluating situations like these using your rhetorical knowledge.

HABITS OF MIND

When I first started teaching writing, I noticed a strange thing in my classes. What students learned about writing through the early assignments in the class didn't seem to transfer to later assignments, particularly research papers. What was I doing wrong, I wondered? Among other things, what I failed to make clear to my students was how certain "essential acts of mind" were present in every assignment, from the very first to the very last. What bound the writing course together was the idea of academic inquiry and the habits of mind—or *dispositions*, as one writer describes them—that lead students to see how writing can be a process of discovery.

Start with Questions, Not Answers

A lot of people think that writing is about recording what you already know, which accounts for those who choose familiar topics to write on when given the choice. "I think I'll write about _____," the thinking goes, "because I know that topic really well and already have an idea what I can say." Unfortunately, the result of writing about what you already know is too often an uninspired draft full of generalizations and clichés.

What do you do about this problem? *Make the familiar strange*. This means finding new ways to see what you've seen before. For years, I've asked some of my writing students to take photographs of any subject they want. Predictably, most students choose to take pictures of familiar things—their rooms or apartments, the trees outside the window, campus buildings, local landscapes—and they almost always take one picture of each subject. The result is that these photographs are rarely surprising. They see these familiar subjects in very familiar ways. But when I ask them to return to a single subject and take multiple pictures of it, there are almost always surprises and fresh ways of seeing the subject.

It's apparent that there are multiple ways of seeing the same thing, and of course this is one thing that we often admire about good writing—it offers a perspective on something familiar that we hadn't considered before. One of the ways writers accomplish this is by using questions. Questions shift a writer's perspective on a subject much as distance, angle, and light alter a photographer's ways of seeing. A shell is just a shell if you only look at it once and in one way. But if you want to see what you've seen before in a way you haven't seen it, you look again and again (see Figure 1.2). Questions are one way to keep shifting your gaze on any subject.

Therefore, in an inquiry-based approach to writing, you'll choose a writing topic that raises questions about how you think or feel over one that you have all figured out. Almost any topic can raise interesting questions. *There are no boring topics, only boring questions*. The key is to approach any topic with a sense of wonder and curiosity: *Why are houseflies so hard to kill? What distinguishes the cultures of skaters and snowboarders? When do most marriages fail and what can be done about it? Why do young people join gangs?*

Suspend Judgment

What's one of the most common problems I see in student writers? Poor grammar? Lack of organization? A missing thesis? Nope. *It's the tendency to judge too soon and too harshly*. A great majority of my students, including really smart, capable writers, have powerful internal critics, or as the novelist Gail Godwin once called them, "Watchers at the Gates." This is the voice you may hear when you're starting to write a paper, the one that has you crossing out that first sentence or that first paragraph over and over until you "get it perfect."

> It's okay to write badly. Resist the tendency to judge too soon and too harshly.

The only way to overcome this problem is to suspend judgment. In doing so, you essentially tell your Watchers this: *It's okay to write badly*.

I never try to write badly, of course, but whenever I'm stuck in the middle of something, or can't figure out what to say or where to begin, or even when I don't have a clue about my subject, I simply start writing. Sometimes it's absolutely horrible. But just as often, there's a glint of an idea, or direction, or topic, and away I go, trying to keep up with the vein of thought branching in all directions. The British novelist E. M. Forster once said, "How do I know what I think until I see what I say?" I've come to have a lot of faith in this idea. Rather than trying to use my journal the way I used to—to try to write beautiful, eloquent prose—I use the journal simply to think things through; that the prose sometimes stinks doesn't bother me anymore.

Figure 1.2   Good writing makes the familiar strange by offering multiple ways of seeing the same thing.

CONDITIONS THAT MAKE "BAD" WRITING POSSIBLE

1. Willingness to suspend judgment
2. Ability to write fast enough to out-run your internal critic
3. Belief that confusion, uncertainty, and ambiguity help thought rather than hinder it
4. Interest in writing about "risky" subjects, or those that you don't know what you want to say about until you say it

We know how powerful our internal critics can be, insisting that every word be spelled right, and every thought sharp. Our Watchers can't abide bad writing. One of the conditions that makes bad writing possible for me is that my Watchers are not voices I honor in my journal, at least not when I want to use my journal to think something through.

Now I know it must seem odd that a book on writing would talk about the virtues of writing badly, but it can be a useful tool for solving all kinds of writing problems. I encourage you to use this approach throughout *The Curious Writer*. I've seen bad writing turn slow writers into faster ones, procrastinators into initiators. I've seen bad writing help students who always wrote short papers begin to generate longer, more thoughtful essays. Best of all, I've seen bad writing transform students who once hated writing into people who see writing as a useful tool for thinking, and even a source of pleasure.

Search for Surprise

One of the key benefits of writing badly is *surprise*. This was a revelation for me when I first discovered the virtues of bad writing in graduate school. I was convinced that you never pick up the pen unless you know what you want to say, which may account for my struggles with journal writing. Suddenly I stumbled on a new way to use writing—not to *record* what I already knew about a subject, but to *discover* what I actually thought. This way of writing promised a feast of surprises that made me hunger to put words on the page.

EXERCISE 1.2

A Roomful of Details

STEP ONE: Spend ten minutes brainstorming a list of details based on the following prompt. Write down whatever comes into your mind, no matter how silly. Be specific and don't censor yourself.

Try to remember a room you spent a lot of time in as a child. It may be your bedroom in the back of the house at the edge of the field, or the kitchen where your grandmother kneaded bread or made thick red pasta sauce. Put yourself back in that room. Now look around you. What do you see? What do you hear? What do you smell?

STEP TWO: Examine your list. If things went well, you will have a fairly long list of details. As you review the list, identify one detail that surprises you the most, a detail that seems somehow to carry an unexpected charge. This might be a detail that seems connected to a feeling or story. You might be drawn to a detail that confuses you a little. Whatever its particular appeal, circle the detail.

STEP THREE: Use the circled detail as a prompt for a seven minute fastwrite. Begin by focusing on the detail: What does it make you think of? And then what? And then? Alternatively, begin by simply describing the detail more fully: What does it look like? Where did it come from? What stories are attached to it? How does it make you feel? Avoid writing in generalities. Write about specifics—that is, particular times, places, moments, and people. Write fast, and chase after the words to see where they want to go. Give yourself permission to write badly.

> **BRAINSTORMING**
>
> - Anything goes.
> - Don't censor yourself.
> - Write everything down.
> - Be playful but stay focused.

ONE STUDENT'S RESPONSE

Bernice's Journal

EXERCISE 1.2
STEP THREE

DETAIL: STAINLESS STEEL COUNTERS

When I was five or six my father and I made cookies for the first time. I don't remember what prompted him to bake cookies, he liked to cook but he didn't very well so he didn't like to use cook books. I remember sitting on the cold stainless steel, the big red and white cook book splayed over my lap. I was reading it out loud to my dad. The kitchen was warm but everything gleamed; it was industrial and functional. It was the only room in our house that still looked like it belonged to the "Old Pioneer School." My dad and uncles had renovated every other room into bedrooms, playrooms, family rooms. The place was huge but cozy, it was home. I remember reading off ingredients until I got to the sugar. It called for $3/4$ cup and I didn't understand the fraction. I thought it meant three or four cups. We poured so much sugar into the bowl. The cookies were terrible. Hard and glassy, too sweet and brittle. It wasn't until years later that I understood that my dad didn't understand the measurement either. He was persistent though. We pulled down every cook book in the house until we found one that described the measuring cups and what they meant. We started all over and our second batch was perfect. My dad is one of the smartest people I know, inventive, imaginative

(continued)

One Student's Response (*continued*)

but he only has a rudimentary education. He can read and write enough to get by, he's gifted with numbers, but I can't help looking back and wondering what he could have been, what he could have done for the world if just one person had taken him by the hand and showed him what he showed me. If just one person had told him not to give up, to keep trying, that in the end it will be worth all the work, I wonder who he could have been if one person had seen his curiosity and imagination and fostered it instead of seeing his muscles and capable hands and putting him to work. If just one person had told him that his mind was the greatest tool he possessed. If just one person baked cookies with him.

You may experience at least three kinds of surprise after completing a fast-writing exercise like the preceding one:

1. Surprise about *how much* writing you did in such a short time
2. Surprise about discovering a topic you didn't expect to find
3. Surprise about discovering a *new way of understanding or seeing a familiar topic*

The kind of surprises you encounter doing this sort of writing may not always be profound. They may not even provide you with obvious essay topics. With any luck, though, by hunting for surprises in your own work you will begin to experience the pleasure of writing *to learn*. That's no small thing, particularly if you've always believed that writers should have it all figured out before they pick up the pen.

INQUIRING INTO THE DETAILS

Invention Strategies

Perhaps without knowing it, you have already practiced some writing techniques designed to help you generate material. These *invention strategies* include fastwriting, listing, brainstorming, questioning, and even conversation. You can use these techniques in any writing situation when you need to gather more information, find a topic, or explore what you think. We call on these strategies often in the exercises and assignments that follow.

At first, spending time doing all this writing and thinking before you actually begin a draft may seem like a waste of time. After all, your goal is to finish the assignment. But if you want to find a focused topic that means something to you and write it with enough information, then invention strategies such as fastwriting will prove invaluable. They produce the raw material that can be shaped, like clay on a potter's wheel, into something with form and meaning. But really the best thing about invention strategies is that they often generate material that is ripe with surprise.

INVENTION STRATEGIES

- *Fastwriting:* The emphasis is on speed, not correctness. Don't compose, don't think about what you want to say before you say it. Instead, let the writing lead, helping you discover what you think.

- *Listing:* Fast lists can help you generate lots of information quickly. They are often in code, with words and phrases that have meaning only for you. Let your lists grow in waves—think of two or three items and then pause until the next few items rush in.

- *Clustering:* This nonlinear method of generating information, also called *mapping,* relies on *webs* and often free association of ideas or information. Begin with a core word, phrase, or concept at the center of a page, and build branches off it. Follow each branch until it dies out, return to the core, and build another. (See page 108.)

- *Questioning:* Questions are to ideas what knives are to onions. They help you cut through to the less obvious insights and perspectives, revealing layers of possible meanings, interpretations, and ways of understanding. Asking questions complicates things but rewards you with new discoveries.

- *Conversing:* Conversing is fastwriting with the mouth. When we talk, especially to someone we trust, we work out what we think and feel about things. We listen to what we say, but we also invite a response, which leads us to new insights.

- *Researching:* This is a kind of conversation, too. We listen and respond to other voices that have said something or will say something if asked about topics that interest us. Reading and interviewing are not simply things you do when you write a research paper but activities to use whenever you have questions you can't answer on your own.

- *Observing:* When we look closely at anything, we see what we didn't notice at first. Careful observation of people, objects, experiments, images, and so on generates specific information that leads to informed judgments.

WRITING AS A PROCESS

There is a process for doing almost anything—fixing a broken washing machine, learning how to play tennis, studying for the SAT, and, of course, writing. It might be hard to imagine, therefore, why some English teachers seem to make such a big deal out of the writing process. Here's why:

- The process of writing, like anything that we do frequently, is not something that we think about.

- When we focus, as we often do in writing, on *what* rather that *how,* on the product rather than the process, then when problems arise we don't see many options for solving them. We get stuck and we get frustrated.

- As we start to pay attention to how we write in a variety of situations, two things happen: We become aware of our old habits that don't always help, and that may actually hurt our success with writing. Second—and this is most important—we begin to understand that there are actually *choices* we can make when problems arise, and we become aware of what some of those are.

- The result of all of this is a simple yet powerful thing: The more we understand writing processes, the more control we get over them. Getting control of the process means the product gets better.[1]

Here's an example of what I mean. Chauntain summarized her process this way: "Do one and be done." She always wrote her essays at the last minute and only wrote a single draft. She approached nearly every writing assignment the same way: Start with a thesis and then develop five topic sentences that support the thesis with three supporting details under each. This structure was a container into which she poured all her prose. Chauntain deliberated over every sentence, trying to make each one perfect, and as a result she spent considerable time staring off into space searching for the right word or phrase. It was agony. The papers were almost always dull—she thought so, too—and just as often she struggled to reach the required page length. Chauntain had no idea of any other way to write a school essay. As a matter of fact, she thought it was really the *only* way. So when she got an assignment in her economics class to write an essay in which she was to use economic principles to analyze a question that arose from a personal observation, Chauntain was bewildered. How should she start? Could she rely on her old standby structure—thesis, topic sentences, supporting details? She felt stuck.

Not only did she fail to see that she had choices in this writing situation, she had no clue what those choices were.

That's why we study process. It helps us to solve problems like these. This must begin with a self-study of your own habits as a writer, identifying not just how you tend to do things but the patterns of problems that might arise when you do them.

EXERCISE 1.3

What Is Your Process?

Take a moment and analyze your own writing challenges. The following questions might help you develop a profile of your writing process in certain situations, and help you identify problems you might want to address by altering your process.

STEP ONE: Complete the Self-Evaluation Survey.

---

[1]There is considerable research in learning theory that confirms these conclusions; in particular, so-called "metacognitive thinking"—the awareness of how you do things—increases the transfer of relevant knowledge from one situation to another. In other words, what you learn about how to do something in one situation gets more easily activated in another.

Self-Evaluation Survey

1. When you're given a school writing assignment, do you wait until the last minute to get it done?

    Always———Often———Sometimes———Rarely———Never

2. How often have you had the experience of learning something you didn't expect through writing about it?

    Very often———Fairly often———Sometimes———Rarely———Never

3. Do you generally plan out what you're going to write before you write it?

    Always———Often———Sometimes———Rarely———Never

4. *Prewriting* describes activities that some writers engage in before they begin a first draft. Prewriting might include freewriting or fastwriting, making lists, brainstorming or mapping, collecting information, talking to someone about the essay topic, reading up on it, or jotting down ideas in a notebook or journal. How much prewriting do you tend to do for the following types of assignments? Circle the appropriate answer.

    - A personal essay:

        A great deal———Some———Very little———None———Haven't written one

    - A critical essay about a short story, novel, or poem:

        A great deal   Some   Very little   None   Haven't written one

    - A research paper:

        A great deal———Some———Very little———None———Haven't written one

    - An essay exam:

        A great deal———Some———Very little———None———Haven't written one

5. At what point in writing an academic paper do you usually get stuck? Check all that apply.
    - ❑ Getting started
    - ❑ In the middle
    - ❑ Finishing
    - ❑ I never get stuck (go on to Question 9)
    - ❑ Other _____

6. If you usually have problems getting started on an academic paper or essay, which of the following do you often find hardest to do? Check

all that apply. (If you don't have trouble getting started, go on to Question 7.)

❏ Deciding on a topic

❏ Writing an introduction

❏ Finding a good place to write

❏ Figuring out exactly what I'm supposed to do for the assignment

❏ Finding a purpose or focus for the paper

❏ Finding the right tone

❏ Other_____

7. If you usually get stuck in the middle of a paper, which of the following causes the most problems? (If writing in the middle of a paper isn't a problem for you, go on to Question 8.)

❏ Keeping focused on the topic

❏ Finding enough information to meet page length requirements

❏ Following my plan for how I want to write the paper

❏ Bringing in other research or points of view

❏ Organizing all my information

❏ Trying to avoid plagiarism

❏ Worrying about whether the paper meets the requirements of the assignment

❏ Worrying that the paper just isn't any good

❏ Messing with citations

❏ Other_____

8. If you have difficulty finishing an essay or paper, which of the following difficulties are typical for you? Check all that apply.

❏ Composing a last paragraph or conclusion

❏ Worrying that the paper doesn't meet the requirements of the assignment

❏ Worrying that the paper just isn't any good

❏ Trying to keep focused on the main idea or thesis

❏ Trying to avoid repeating myself

❏ Realizing I don't have enough information

❏ Dealing with the bibliography or citations

❏ Other_____

9. Rank the following list of approaches to revision so that it reflects the strategies you use *most often to least often* when rewriting academic

papers. Rank the items 1–6, with the strategy you use most often as a 1 and least often as a 6.

_____ I usually just tidy things up—editing sentences, checking spelling, looking for grammatical errors, and performing other proofreading activities.

_____ I mostly look for ways to reorganize existing information in the draft to make it more effective.

_____ I generally try to fill holes by adding more information.

_____ I do more research.

_____ I often completely change the focus or even the main idea in the revision, rewriting sections, adding or removing information, and rearranging the order of things.

_____ I rarely do any rewriting at all.

10. Finally, do you tend to impose a lot of conditions on when, where, or how you think you write most effectively? For example, do you need a certain pen, do you always have to write on a computer, must it be quiet or noisy, or do you often write best under pressure? Do you need to be in certain kinds of places to write effectively? Or can you write under a range of circumstances, with few or no conditions? Circle one.

Lots of conditions———Some———A few———No conditions

If you do impose conditions on when, where, or how you write, list some of those conditions here:

1.

2.

3.

4.

STEP TWO: In small groups, discuss the results of the survey. Begin by picking someone to tally the answers to each question. Post these on the board or a sheet of newsprint so they can be added to the class totals. Analyze the results for your group. In particular, discuss the following questions:

- Are there patterns in the responses? Do most group members seem to answer certain questions in similar or different ways? Are there interesting contradictions?
- Based on these results, what "typical" habits or challenges do writers in your class seem to share?
- What struck you most?

Thinking About Your Process

The survey you completed is the beginning of reflection on your own writing process. You will do this kind of reflection again and again throughout this book so that by the end you will have written a narrative of thought that tells the story of your reading and writing processes, and how you change those processes to produce better writing more efficiently. The reflective letter in your portfolio (see Appendix A) might be where you finally tell that story in full, perhaps beginning with what the survey revealed about your own habits, rituals, and challenges as you began this book.

However, now is a good time to begin telling yourself that story.

What do you remember about your own journey as a writer both inside and outside of school? One of my earliest, most pleasant memories of writing is listening to the sound of the clacking of my father's old Royal typewriter in the room down the hall as I was going to sleep. I imagine him there now, in the small study that we called the "blue room," enveloped in a cloud of pipe smoke. It is likely that he was writing advertising copy back then, or perhaps a script for a commercial in which my mother, an actress, would appear. I loved the idea of writing then. The steady hammering of typewriter keys down the hall sounded effortless, yet at the same time solid, significant. This all changed, I think, in the eighth grade when it seemed that writing was much more about following rules than tapping along to a lively dance of words.

Spend some time telling your own story about how your relationship to writing evolved.

EXERCISE 1.4

Literacy Narrative Collage

Generating Ideas

When you get a writing assignment, your habit is probably to sit down and simply write it, composing on the computer. This time, however, we'll begin by generating ideas (classical rhetoricians call this "invention").

To begin working toward a draft essay on your personal writing history, we'll start in your journal with a collage of moments, memories, or reflections. *For each prompt, write fast for about four minutes. Keep your pen moving and give yourself permission to write badly.* After you've responded to one prompt, skip a line and move on to the next one. Set aside about twenty minutes for this generating activity.

1. What is your earliest memory of writing? Tell the story.
2. We usually divide our experiences as writers into private writing and school writing, or writing we do by choice and writing we are required to do for a grade. Let's focus on school writing. Tell the story of a teacher, a

class, an essay, an exam, or other moment that you consider a *turning point* in your understanding of yourself as a writer or your understanding of writing.

3. Writing is part of the fabric of everyday life in the United States, and this is truer than ever with Internet communication. Describe a typical day for you in which writing plays a part, and think about how this has changed in your lifetime so far.

4. What is the most successful (or least successful) thing you've ever written in or out of school? Tell the story.

Congratulations. You've made a mess. But I hope this collage of your experiences as a writer is an interesting mess, one that brought some little surprises. As you look at these four fragments of fastwriting, you might sense a pattern between them. Is there a certain idea about yourself as a writer that seems to emerge in these various contexts for thinking about it? It's more likely that one or perhaps two of the prompts really took off for you, presenting trails you'd like to continue following. Or maybe nothing happened. For now, set your journal aside. We'll return to this material soon.

Writing Creatively, Writing Critically: A Process of Writing

Here was my writing process when I was in school:

1. Get the assignment. Find out when it was due and how long it was supposed to be.

2. Wait until the night before it was due and get started.

3. Stare off into space.

4. Eat ice cream.

5. Write a sketchy outline.

6. Write a sentence; then cross it out.

7. Stare off into space.

8. Write another sentence, and then squeeze out a few more.

9. Think about Lori Jo Flink, and then stare off into space.

10. Write a paragraph. Feel relief and disgust.

I would get the work done eventually, but the process was agonizing and the product mediocre. What did I conclude from this back then? That I wasn't good at writing, which was no big surprise because I pretty much hated it. Something happened to me to change that view, of course, because you hold my book in your hands. Among other things, I came to understand that the processes I was using for writing were really just habits I applied without thought no matter what the situation. I also was dedicated to the idea that I needed to know exactly what I was trying to say before I said it.

But more than anything, I thought writing was a process like this:

When it's really like this:

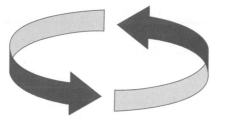

In other words, I had always thought that writing was a straight march forward from beginning to end; I had to wait for something to come into my head and then tried to get it down. At all costs, I avoided things like new ideas or other ways of seeing a topic—anything that might get in the way of the drive to the conclusion. If I thought about anything, it was trying to find the "perfect" way of saying things or worrying about whether I was faithfully following a certain structure. I rarely learned anything from my writing. I certainly never expected I should.

But this isn't the way experienced writers work at all. The writing process isn't a linear trajectory, but a looping, recursive process—one that encourages *thinking,* not simply recording the thoughts that you already have. Writing doesn't involve a series of steps that you must follow in every situation but is a much messier zigzag between collecting information and focusing on it, exploring things and thinking about them, writing and rewriting, reviewing and rearranging, and so on. The process is always influenced by the writing situation. For instance, experienced writers approach the process of writing an essay exam quite differently than they would a lab report. Some writers learn this flexibility slowly through experience. A faster way is to combine experience writing for all kinds of situations *and* monitoring the processes you use for each one and applying your knowledge of what works.

While there isn't a single writing process, I do think there are certain kinds of thinking that we can apply to most writing situations. Rather than read my explanation of it now, try the exercise that follows and maybe you'll see what I mean.

EXERCISE 1.5

Alternating Currents of Thought: Generating and Judging

Let's return to the subject you began writing about in Exercise 1.4—your experiences as a writer—but let's spend more time thinking about the third prompt in that exercise: your experience with writing technology.

Generating

STEP ONE: What are your earliest memories of using a computer for writing? Begin by telling the story and then let the writing lead from there. Keep your pen moving and allow yourself to write badly.

STEP TWO: Brainstorm a list of words or phrases that you associate with the word "literate" or "literacy."

Reread what you just wrote in your notebook or journal, underlining things that surprised you or that seem significant or interesting to you. Skip a line and respond in writing to the next set of prompts.

Judging

STEP THREE: Choose one of the following sentences as a starting point, and then write a paragraph about it. This time, compose each sentence thinking about what you want to say before you say it and trying to say it as well as you can.

> *What I understand now about my experiences with writing on computers that I didn't understand when I started out is* _____.
>
> *When they think about writing with computers, most people think* _____, *but my experience was* _____.
>
> *The most important thing I had to discover before I considered myself "computer literate" was* _____.

Reflecting

If you're like most people, then the parts of this exercise that involved generating felt different than the part where you judged what you had written. But *how* were they different? How would you distinguish between the experience of generating and judging? Talk about this or write about it in your journal.

Thinking and Writing Dialectically

At the heart of the strategy of inquiry, which is at the heart of *The Curious Writer* (see Figure A in the Preface), is the following model:

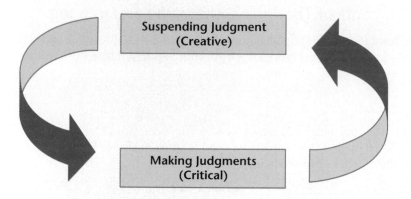

The two parts of Exercise 1.5, generating and judging, were designed to simulate this shift from suspending judgments and making judgments as you wrote about your early experiences using a computer for writing. In the first two steps, you spent some time fastwriting without much critical interference, trying to generate some information from your own experience. In the third step, which began with "seed" sentences that forced you into a more reflective, analytical mode, you were encouraged to look for patterns of meaning in what you generated.

> Suspending judgment feels freer, exploratory.... Making judgments shifts the writer into an analytical mode.

For many writers, these are two distinct ways of thinking. *Suspending judgment* feels freer, is exploratory, and may spark emotion. *Making judgments* shifts the writer into an analytical mode, one that might lower the temperature, allowing writers to see their initial explorations with less feeling and more understanding. Another way of distinguishing between these two modes of thought is to label the open-ended thinking we often associate with fastwriting as "creative" and the more closed-ended thinking we associate with judging or analyzing as "critical."

INQUIRING INTO THE DETAILS

Organizing Your Computer Files

In a writing class, you typically have lots of documents and frequently multiple versions of the same document. How do you make sure that you can find them? Take a little time to establish conventions for naming your files. Start by establishing a folder for your class, and then decide on what might be helpful naming categories to apply to each document. For example,

- Genre (e.g., essay, exercise, letter, response, and so on)
- Title of document
- Version number
- Date

Using the underscore key, separate each element when naming your document. For example, *essay_importanceofwritingbadly_v2_2008-December-12.* It takes a little more time to compose a more elaborate file name than *doc.1* but it ultimately saves time by helping you locate documents more easily.

Combining these two modes of thinking gives both thinking and writing more range and depth. Creative thinking creates the conditions for discovery—new insights or ways of seeing—while critical thinking helps writers refine their discoveries and focus on the most significant of them.

Figure 1.3 lists other ways you can visualize creative and critical thinking. In narrative writing, for instance (the kind of writing you likely did in the previous exercise), creative thinking helps you generate information about *what happened,* while critical thinking may lead you to insights about *what happens.* Likewise, in research writing, investigators often move back and forth between their *observations of* things and their *ideas about* them. More broadly speaking, when we think creatively we collect, and when we think critically we evaluate what we have collected.

Note that in Figure 1.3 double-ended arrows link the items in each pair. The process is *dialectical;* it consists of a back-and-forth movement between the two opposing modes of thought. Many writers do this instinctively. As they compose, they constantly shift between contrasting modes of thought, from collecting to focusing, from generating to criticizing, from showing to telling, from exploring to reflecting, from believing to doubting, from playing to judging.

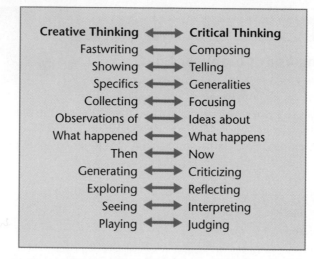

Figure 1.3   When writers use dialectical thinking, they move back and forth between two opposing modes of thought—the creative and the critical. One seems playful and the other judgmental; one feels open ended and the other more closed. Certain activities such as fastwriting or brainstorming promote one mode of thought, and careful composing or reflection promotes another.

Certain activities—such as fastwriting and composing—encourage one way of thinking or the other. Learning to balance these opposing forces is what dialectical thinking is all about. In practice, however, many beginning writers give too much emphasis to either one mode of thinking or the other, a tendency that accounts for many of the challenges these writers face within their own writing processes.

Spend too much time locked in the critical mode of thinking and your internal critic takes over. This voice pinches off the flow of material generated by creative thinking. The writing then comes slowly and painfully, and it rarely yields surprise. Topics are abandoned before the writer has fully explored their potential. Working from scarcity, the writer is compelled to use all the material he or she has at hand, often resulting in writing that feels forced, incomplete, or obvious.

On the other hand, give too much free rein to creative thinking and the artist runs wild. The problem here isn't scarcity but rather overabundance. It's a poverty of riches, for without a critical eye to provide shape and direction, the writer cannot present all of his or her material in a coherent and meaningful fashion.

Other challenges result when writers fail to move back and forth between creative and critical modes. One excursion into creative thinking followed by a second into critical thinking is rarely enough to produce good writing.

Writers need to move back and forth between the two modes until they come to see their topics in interesting ways that differ from what they might have creatively or critically thought about the topic when they started the writing process.

Put simply, the goal of this dialectical thinking is to address a question that ultimately all writing must answer:

So what?

So what? can be a pretty harsh question, and I find that some students tend to ask it too soon in the writing process, before they've fully explored their topic or collected enough information. That may have been your experience when you suddenly found yourself high and dry, forced to reflect on possible meanings of a moment you've written about for only eight minutes. When you can't come up with an answer to *So what?*, the solution is usually to generate more information.

There's another danger, too. In their enthusiasm to answer *So what?*, some writers seize on the first convenient idea or thesis that comes along. This abruptly ends the process of inquiry before they've had a chance to explore their subjects. These writers squander the opportunity to be surprised by what they discover.

Opening Questions

Using the dialectical thinking process is all well and good, but first you've got to have something to think about. The inquiry approach promoted by *The Curious Writer* is grounded in the idea that the writing process depends, more than anything else, on finding the right questions. What makes a question "right"? First and foremost, you must find it interesting enough to want to think and write about it for awhile.

I recently visited teachers in Laredo, Texas, and I told them that a good question can make even the most boring topic interesting. I would prove it, I said, and picked up a lemon that was sitting on a table and asked everyone, in turn, to ask a question about the lemon or about lemons. Twenty minutes later, we generated sixty questions, and in the process began to wonder how the scent of lemons came to be associated with cleanliness. We wondered why lemons appeared so often in wartime British literature. We wondered why the lime and not the lemon is celebrated in local Hispanic culture. We wondered a lot of interesting things that we never expected to wonder about because a lemon is ordinary. Questions can make the familiar world we inhabit yield to wonder.

The point is this: *There are no boring topics—just poor questions.*

Writing as inquiry, therefore, begins with questions and not answers. We pursue a subject because we want to find out what we think about it, and certain kinds of questions are much more likely to sustain our investigation than others. For example, I had a student once who really, really wanted to know whether Elvis was really dead. Yep, the King is gone. End of story. A better question for writing and thinking would have been to ask *why* we keep asking whether Elvis is dead. What is it about him that seems to sustain such a blind hope in his existence among certain people?

Learning to find the right question, one that will be worth spending time with, is an essential skill, and there are certain qualities that most good questions seem to share. Here are a few of them:

- The writer is genuinely interested in the question and the answers.
- People other than the writer have a stake in the answers to the question.
- It raises more questions; there isn't a simple answer.
- Something has been said already about the question. There's information out there.
- The question is a manageable size. It's isn't too broad ("What is the meaning of lemons?") or too specific ("What is the meaning of that lemon?").

QUESTIONS, CREATIVITY, AND CRITICAL THINKING: A STRATEGY FOR INQUIRY

If you combine the power of good questions with the back-and-forth process of writing creatively and critically discussed earlier in the chapter, you have a model for a strategy of inquiry that you can use for every assignment in this book (see Figure 1.4). Typically you begin exploring a subject, sometimes generating some initial thoughts through fastwriting, listing, or other invention methods. Subjects are like landscape shots in photography—they cover a huge amount of ground. You need to find a narrower topic, or some *part* of the landscape to look at more closely. Take popular music, for example. That's a huge subject. But as you write and read about it a little, you begin to see that the topic that interests you most is the blues, and maybe something about its influence on American popular music. Here's how it works:

- You start with a *subject* that makes you curious—music—and then work toward a *topic*—the influence of blues—that is beginning to focus your attention for a closer look.

Ultimately you are searching for a few questions about your topic that both interest you and will sustain your project. These are the questions that will help

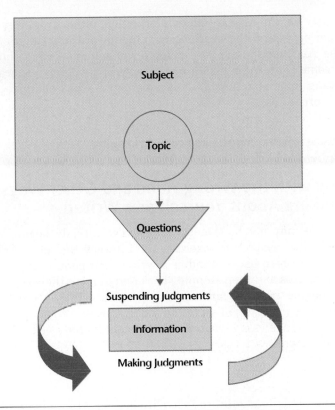

Figure 1.4   The process of inquiry first involves finding a topic in a larger subject that raises interesting questions, refining those questions, and then using them to collect information. Investigate the significance of what you've found by thinking creatively and critically—withholding judgments and then making judgments—working toward fresh understandings and new discoveries that lead you to what you want to say.

you focus your topic, that guide your research into yourself or other sources of information, and that may eventually become the heart of an essay draft on your topic. For example, you might arrive at a question like this one:

- Beginning with a topic—the influence of the blues on pop music—you work toward questions that might power your writing project—questions, say, like this: *What was the influence of Mississippi delta blues on white performers like Elvis who were popular in the fifties and sixties?*

An inquiry question may be no more than a train station in a longer journey. As you continue to write, you may find another, better question around which to build your project. But a good opening question will keep you on the tracks. This is enormously helpful as you collect information, either from research or from your own experiences and observations, working toward some answers to the questions you pose. And some of the best insights you get about what those answers might be will come from the alternating currents of thought—generating and judging, suspending judgment and making judgments—that energize your writing and thinking processes.

EXERCISE 1.6

Writing with the Wrong Hand and Other Ways of Thinking About Yourself as a Writer

Though you may not have noticed it, you've already begun using this inquiry strategy in this chapter. In Exercise 1.4 (Literacy Narrative Collage) you started exploring your own background as a writer, first generating material about your past experiences and then stepping back and judging their significance. I provided most of the questions. So far, everything you've written about your literacy narrative is in your journal. Let's use the inquiry process to shape the material into a three- to five-page essay draft. But before we do that, we'll continue with a little more journal work.

Generating

STEP ONE: This four-minute fastwrite begins strangely. If you're right-handed, put your pen in your left hand. If you're left-handed, put it in your right. Write the following phrase in your journal with your "wrong" hand: *Writing with my wrong hand reminds me of...* Now switch the pen to your writing hand, and in a fastwrite explore the connections you can make, if any, with the experience of writing with the wrong hand. Let the writing lead, especially to stories, particular people, specific memories, or times in your life.

Judging

STEP TWO: Based on what you wrote in step one, compose a brief answer to one or more of the following questions:

- What's the thing that surprised you most when you wrote about writing wrong-handed?

- If you were going to explain the significance of this experience to someone else, what would you say?

- If you were going to do this experiment with a friend, what would you ask him or her about it afterward?

Generating

STEP THREE: The information we generate from our experiences and observations is only one kind of information we can generate for writing. Reading is another. The passage that follows is the opening of an essay by David Bartholomae, a writing theorist, which begins his look at how students in their first years of college must adjust to writing in academic discourses. Carefully read the passage, and in your journal *copy at least three passages* from the Bartholomae excerpt that struck you. Maybe you agreed or disagreed with them, or you found them interesting or confusing, or they spoke in some way to your own experiences so far in college.

From "Inventing the University"
David Bartholomae

Every time a student sits down to write for us, he has to invent the university for the occasion—invent the university, that is, or a branch of it, like history or anthropology or economics or English. The student has to learn to speak our language, to speak as we do, to try on the peculiar ways of knowing, selecting, evaluating, reporting, concluding, and arguing that define the discourse of our community. Or perhaps I should say the *various* discourses of our community, since it is in the nature of a liberal arts education that a student, after the first year or two, must learn to try on a variety of voices and interpretive schemes—to write, for example, as a literary critic one day and as an experimental psychologist the next; to work within fields where the rules governing the presentation of examples or the development of an argument are both distinct and, even to the professional, mysterious.   1

The student has to appropriate (or be appropriated by) a specialized discourse, and he has to do this as though he were easily and comfortably one with his audience, as though he were a member of the academy or an historian or an anthropologist or an economist; he has to invent the university by assembling and mimicking its language while finding some compromise between idiosyncrasy, a personal history, on the one hand, and the requirements of convention, the history of a discipline, on the other hand. He must learn to speak our language. Or he must dare to speak it or to carry off the bluff, since speaking and writing will most certainly be required long before the skill is "learned." And this, understandably, causes problems.   2

STEP FOUR: Now fastwrite for four or five minutes about the Bartholomae excerpt, and begin by exploring your reactions to the passages you selected. This time, tell the story of your thinking as it develops in your bad writing by beginning with your first thoughts: *The first thing I think when I consider what Bartholomae is saying is…And then I think…And then.* Follow the writing.

Judging

STEP FIVE: Reread your fastwriting from the preceding step, and spend a full minute generating a list of questions, either about the Bartholomae excerpt or about your response to it.

STEP SIX: Finally, craft one or two strong sentences that might begin an essay you write in response to "Inventing the University." A strong first sentence is one that would make a reader want to read the next sentence and the one after that.

Writers are almost always better off when they work from abundance rather than scarcity. That makes choosing what to put in and what to leave out of a draft much easier and makes it much more likely that the resulting piece will have a strong focus. That's also why we've spent so much time in this chapter beginning to generate and shape material about your own experiences as a writer. If you go over your journal work on this topic, you should see some or all of the following, depending on what your instructor assigned:

- Your earliest memory of writing
- The story of a turning point in your sense of yourself as a writer or your understanding of writing
- Writing you do on a typical day
- The story of the most or least successful thing you've ever written
- Your earliest memory of writing with a computer
- Your definitions of the word "literate"
- Your exploration of the experience of writing with the wrong hand
- A response to an excerpt on how college students must "learn to speak the language" of the university by "compromising" their "personal history" as writers

That's a fair amount of writing, and most of it probably isn't very good. But now you're ready to try and shape some of that material into a first draft, writing that might make sense to someone other than you.

THE WRITING PROCESS

> ## INQUIRY PROJECT: THE WRITING LITERACY MEMOIR
>
> Drawing on the writing you've done on the topic so far and the writing you will continue to generate, compose a three- to five-page essay that is a memoir of your history as a writer. Like all inquiry projects, this essay should investigate some question about your writing experiences, and this question should be behind the stories you tell. To start with, look for a question that explores a relationship between two things in your writing life. For example, "What is the relationship between my success with online writing and my struggles with school writing?" Or something like this: "What is the relationship between my memories of earning praise about my writing from teachers and the lack of confidence in writing I've always felt, and still feel?"

mycomplab

For additional reading, writing, and research resources, go to www.mycomplab.com

Obviously, you've already started this assignment, and you have pages of writing in your journal from which to work. Let the inquiry question you come up with help you decide what to put in and what to leave out. As you are drafting, also consider opportunities to generate new information that will help to develop your essay. For example, there might be a key moment in your narrative that deserves particular emphasis because of its relevance to your question or its importance in developing what it is you might be trying to say. Use the "Explode a Moment" revision strategy on page 565 of Chapter 13 to help with this. This is a chapter you'll use often for many of the assignments in *The Curious Writer*. It's a toolbox of techniques that will help you develop your drafts, no matter what the subject.

As you compose your writing history, consider the following:

- Don't just tell one story. Tell several from different parts of your life that might illuminate your question.

- Does it make sense to tell your story out of order, in a structure that doesn't strictly follow chronology?

- Incorporate other sources. Nonfiction writers, no matter what the genre, can turn to four sources of information: personal experience, observation, interview, and reading. While this assignment will mine your personal experience most heavily, would it be useful to talk to a parent about your writing? Can you use any of the Bartholomae excerpt we read in Exercise 1.6? Might you find a relevant fact online?

■ SAMPLE STUDENT ESSAY

For the last thirty or so pages of this chapter, you've watched a student, Bernice Olivas, work alongside you, doing the exercises, generating material and then judging what she came up with. Here is her writing memoir draft:

Writing a New Path

Bernice Olivas

1   It's getting cold. The leaves have turned from green to gold and orange. A few weeks ago an unexpected snowstorm turned the world white for a few hours. Winter is coming, and with it the holiday season. As a child I lived for this time of year because it brought out the kid in my father. He decorated a tree, hung stockings, and the house was filled with the people we loved. In last five years that celebration has crumbled around us. My sisters treat each other like spun glass, afraid to reignite old fires over old arguments, afraid of what they might say if they speak, afraid of what they can't say out loud. My little brothers swagger in and out of my mother's house as if they owned the place, their young wives and children underfoot. They play house while my mother works herself haggard and my father slips in and out of the house, never staying at home for long.

2   We talk to each other in a way we'd never speak to a stranger, our voice filled with scorn, anger, and indifference. We disrespect each other, we belittle each other, and it's as if we've forgotten how much we love each other. The little ones, my boys, my nieces and nephews run around taking it all in as if such pain was normal. To them it is. I've perfected excuse after excuse to avoid the drive to Jerome because it hurts too much to watch.

3   We've grown up, we've grown apart, or maybe I've just lost the rose colored glasses that let me see a warm, loving home in a household scarred by poverty, and haunted by all the harsh realities of life for a Mexican American family trying to make it up north. Most days I console myself with the fact that my brothers are young, they'll grow up. I tell myself my sisters will come around, after all we're family. Occasionally things slip back into what they used to be and I tell myself time will heal the wounds but come Christmas time I find myself hard pressed to believe myself. I miss them. I miss who we used to be. I let myself wallow in just how much I miss them. Last year three little nieces and nephews joined the family and I couldn't stand the idea that these babies would never know the family the way we used to be.

4   I needed to get it all out of my head so I started writing short stories, memories really, of my siblings, my childhood. As I lost myself in retelling these family stories I recaptured something, a feeling, a sense of self and family I haven't felt in a long time. I wrote for days and finally when I was done I felt closer to my family than I had in years. I decided to make copies of these stories, have them bound, and give them as gifts to my family. As each of my siblings read them, and my mother cried over them, we shared a moment of just being together. It was quick, almost invisible, but for a moment, we were laughing together, leaning into each other, our bodies relaxed. It was good.

5   There were no spoken words that could have given us that little moment because our spoken language is heavy with years of family baggage. Putting it on paper lets each of us experience the camping trips, the smell of baking cookies, the inside jokes all over again. Such is the power of the written word. And it's a power that I had no idea existed until I was twenty-four, married, and the mother of two and going back to college.

I planned to get my teaching degree, work at a high school, and earn a little stability   6
for my children. It simply never occurred to me to want more. Just being at college was
more than I'd ever expected to achieve because people like me don't go to college. People
like me, and my family, work with our hands, and there is a deep sense of pride, almost a
reverence, attached to the conceptualization of ourselves as a strong, working class family.

My classes were amazing. I was learning so much and I loved the buzz and energy of   7
campus, but it was so hard. I'd been out of school for a long time, and even when I was in
high school no one ever asked me to write the way they were asking me to write in my college classes. My spelling sucked, my grammar was worse, and I was sure I'd fail my Comp
101 class. My Composition 101 teacher was ruthless, going over and over my drafts, pushing me to think on the page, to ask questions, to push myself past simply reporting information. I hated him for the first semester but found myself signing up for his early morning
class in the spring. Somewhere along the way I'd fallen in love with writing.

I'd found my voice and it felt good to write. I loved being able to write out all the noise   8
in my head; it was messy but once it was on the page I could work through it slowly, carefully,
untangling it until it was something new and exciting and all my own. The written word is a
language unto itself, a form of expression that opens up the world to be explored and navi-
gated in a way that is entirely unique. It was a language I wasn't fluent in. Like the rest of my
family, I could write enough to get by, in the same sense a beginning Spanish speaker gets by
in Latin America, and I had no idea how much of the conversation I was missing.

My grades improved and that nasty little voice that snuck up on me in the middle of   9
the night and whispered that I didn't belong, that there was no place amid all these
intellectuals for someone like me, disappeared. Four years later I'm a writing major, and
I'm headed to graduate school where I'll earn my PhD. After that I plan to write books,
and teach writing at a university. Finding my voice did more than just help me through
a few classes. It gave me a sense of power over my own life, a way to communicate with
the world at large. These days I go online and discuss politics with people in Australia,
London, and Quebec. I write my opinions to the school editor and occasionally they
print them. I'm slowly writing my way through my childhood and seeing it, myself, my
family, my people, and history in a whole new way. I'm writing a new path for my own
children.

Whenever I go to a family gathering someone asks me why I want to be a writer, why I   10
want to teach writing. They ask me why I don't do something more productive, more useful.
Nothing I say seems to make them understand. Nothing I can say satisfies them, and they
go away, still confused, reassuring themselves that I was always a little weird, a little off.
They remind each other that I was born left handed and my mom had to train me to use my
right hand. They remind themselves that I didn't start talking till I was almost four, and
then there was that nasty bump on the head that landed me in the hospital when I was six.

After all nobody else in the family writes. In fact Grandpa Domingo was illiterate,   11
could barely sign his own name, until the day he died. He did all right, built a trucking
company right up out of the ground and left Grandma the house, the land, and a healthy
savings account, and he never wrote a word.

(continued)

(continued)

12   How can I tell them that I write because it makes me more me, in a way I wasn't before. How can I tell them that being voiceless in the written word is dehumanizing in a way I cannot articulate verbally. How can I tell them how much I hurt to think of my grandfather navigating in this world, voiceless? How I can tell them that as a family, as a community, we are powerless without a voice on the page.

13   How can I make them feel the elation I feel when I write, when I learn something new? How can I tell them that writing is a powerful tool, which gave me the courage to step up and take on the responsibility of changing my life, the courage to offer my sons a life of more than backbreaking labor, and the audacity to dream of contributing on a wider scale to the world around me?

14   I can't; I have no words to tell them any of those things. They wouldn't understand if I tried. I don't have the right words to speak, but I can write them, explore them until they're filled with a power of their own, until I find truth within them. Then maybe my family can read them and understand me just a little better. Such is the power of the written word.

EXERCISE 1.7

Taking a Reflective Turn

After you've finished drafting your writing memoir, back away from the experience and think about how it went. Sadly, reflecting like this about something we've written is rare. But as I said earlier, this focus on *how* instead of *what* will do for you as a writer what a tennis coach can do for a player: help her to see that she's making often unconscious choices that affect her play. As a writer, you can see that in any writing situation you have a range of choices, not just one—but you can see this only if you make time to reflect on the choices you've made.

Let's do that with your writing memoir. In your notebook, use one or more of the following prompts for a fastwrite:

- What was different about how you approached the process of writing this essay from the way you approach other writing for school?

- Where did you run into problems? How might you have solved them if you had the chance to repeat the process of writing this essay?

- What did your writing memoir reveal to you about your writing habits, beliefs, and hopes? What do you see more clearly now that you didn't see before you wrote it?

You'll also have the chance to try out dialectical thinking, a process that may seem a little dizzying. In a way, it should, because both the writing process and dialectical thinking involve a great deal of back-and-forth movement, the sort of mental gymnastics you perform with the pen in your hand or your fingers on the keyboard.

Does it feel natural? Probably not. At least not yet. But I hope you'll find that your understanding of the writing process becomes more intuitive as you read further in the book. You may modify your writing process, add a step here or skip one there, prolong the process, or cut it short, depending on the writing situation and your rhetorical concerns. Whatever you do, though, you need to make choices based on an understanding of how they will influence your process. This is the key to making you a productive, confident writer.

USING WHAT YOU HAVE LEARNED

When I was in college I used to say this to anyone who asked how I felt about writing: *I don't like writing but I love having written.* What I meant, of course, is that I often felt satisfaction with the product of writing—the paper or essay—but didn't like the work that it took to produce it. This belief didn't help me improve as a writer because it prevented me from finding things about the process that could actually be okay, and even pleasurable: things like discovery. I never imagined surprise was possible. I hope this chapter initiated a reexamination of your own beliefs about writing. I hardly expect a revolution in your thinking, but maybe one or two things you once thought were true of writing may at least be in doubt, particularly if you think those beliefs get in the way of your progress. Carry that openness to revise your thinking into every assignment in this book and you may be surprised at what you can do.

You now know more about your writing process. You've identified what seems to go well and when you get into trouble. The habit of reflecting on your process will be invaluable as you face each new writing situation because each one presents different problems and choices. Understanding the basic rhetorical principles—considering how to present yourself to particular audiences on particular subjects—will help. You already know more than you think about rhetoric.

Reading to inquire opens a conversation with a text in which the words on the page are only part of the dialogue between the author and the reader.

READING AS INQUIRY

2

Here's what you might be thinking as you read this sentence: *This is a chapter about reading (in a textbook about writing) and I'm really hungry and could eat some potato chips and I already know about reading; I've been reading for years; this guy has a strange way of opening a textbook chapter, how does he know what I'm thinking, he probably doesn't want to know....* Okay, so I don't know exactly what you're thinking. But I do know that you're not simply sitting there decoding the meaning of each word I've written. For one thing, you're reading faster than that, looking at chunks of language. However, a lot of what is going on in your head isn't directly related to the words here. You're thinking about what kind of book you're reading—the textbook genre—and making mental predictions about what is going to come next. You're thinking about the subject—"reading as inquiry"—and considering what you may already know about it. And you're thinking about your purpose in reading these sentences or this book, trying to use that purpose as a guide to help you navigate my meaning and its relevance to you. However, I'm probably wrong about the potato chips.

I hope the image you get from reading this account is that what *you* bring to the reading situation is much more powerful than the words on the page. Experienced readers are aware of this, and like experienced writers, they can bring this knowledge to a range of reading situations and make choices about *how* to read. This rhetorical knowledge of reading is especially important in

What You'll Learn in This Chapter

- How your existing beliefs about reading might be obstacles to reading rhetorically.
- What connections exist between the writing and reading processes.
- How to use the double-entry journal to encourage dialectical thinking.
- How to apply some of the same strategies to reading pictures that you do to reading texts.
- How to understand the unique grammar of images.
- How to design the "look" of your writing.

college. First, you'll be reading a lot, and you'll be introduced, in classes across campus, to new genres and specialized writing that are entirely new to you. Sometimes you might feel as if you're in a wrestling match with texts whose moves are so novel that they threaten to pin you every time you confront them. But you can learn the moves, and in many cases you already know them.

My students fret about writing. But they don't seem to get very worked up about the challenges of reading. As you've seen, however, reading is complex, and in this chapter I'll show you how the writing process involves some of the same mental activities and even similar rhetorical choices used in reading. I'll also show you how writing can help you read better.

When we think of reading we usually associate the act exclusively with written texts, but so many of the images we encounter are, like written texts, crafted to communicate and persuade and so, whether we recognize it or not, we read images, too. In this chapter we'll use images as a metaphor to talk about all kinds of reading strategies, but we'll also focus on the unique grammar of visual literacy and how images work to influence a "reader."

MOTIVES FOR READING

Why read? In the case of best-selling popular fiction such as *The Da Vinci Code* or the Harry Potter books, the answer seems pretty clear: These are entertaining books. But pleasure is not a motive that seems to apply to most academic reading—we usually regard such reading as something we have to do to study for the test or write the paper. However, reading to inquire, while not always a source of pleasure, can offer the satisfaction of surprise and discovery, just as writing to inquire can. This is because what's behind an encounter with a text can be a desire to answer a question that interests you. Reading to inquire is, like writing to inquire, an open-ended process in which you set out to discover what you think, and along the way welcome confusion and ambiguity as a natural condition of the search. In other words, you never read just to collect information; you read to have a conversation with the information. You go back and forth between what an author says and what you think about what he or she says. *Does this help answer a question I've posed? Does it inspire me to see things differently? Does it complicate what I already believe?*

> Reading with the spirit of inquiry turns books, essays, and articles into one side of a dialog that you're having with yourself and an author.

Reading with the spirit of inquiry turns books, essays, and articles into one side of a dialog that you're having with yourself and an author. The meaning of a text (or an image) isn't fixed forever—engraved in stone tablets like a message from above—but worked out between the two of you, the author and the reader. This turns reading into a much more complicated intellectual activity, but it also makes reading more interesting because you create the conditions for surprise, for learning, and for discovery.

BELIEFS ABOUT READING

Most of us aren't very aware of our reading strategies and habits. Why should we be? After all, isn't reading just reading? How many ways can you do it? The way we go about learning how to read, however, is similar to the way we learn how to write. We start at an early age, perhaps even before we go to school. Along with the learning, we acquire beliefs that inform our response to *how* we read. These beliefs, though, can help or hinder our progress as readers. Once again, then, we need to assess our beliefs. Only by understanding *how* we read in certain situations can we acquire more control over what we get out of the reading experience.

EXERCISE 2.1

What Do You Believe?

STEP ONE: In your journal, draft a brief definition of a "good" reader. What exactly is a good reader able to do?

STEP TWO: Answer the following questions in your journal.

- Do you think you're a good reader? Why or why not?
- How would you describe your own reading habits and methods?

STEP THREE: It's helpful to think about the characteristics of a "good" reader in certain contexts. For example, what should a good reader be able to do when

- taking computerized exams like the ACT and the SAT?
- researching a paper for school?
- reading a textbook for an exam?
- analyzing a poem or short story?
- reading a text message?
- reading a friend's Facebook page?
- reading instructions on how to set up a new computer?
- reading a novel for pleasure?

Choose two of these reading situations (or two others that you can imagine), and in your journal write a definition of what a good reader should be able to do in each situation.

ONE STUDENT'S RESPONSE

Briana's Journal

STEP ONE:

Good readers read with an open mind and an open heart but cannot be too malleable. They have to be able to empathize and still be able to judge with some sense. They have to immerse themselves in the literature. I love when I read something and I feel something. Good readers have to be able to pick up a variety of materials at any given time and be able to have the skill to immerse themselves into that piece. They need to be able to get the full scope of the writing and see the big picture through the small details.

STEP THREE:

Reading a text message: Inflection is absent in this form of communication. And because it is a casual type of communication, we tend to text like we talk. You have to be able to recall the sender's personality and look at the words he or she has chosen and the order in which he or she has placed them; this takes a high level of analysis.

Most reading instruction seems to focus on comprehension—you know, the SAT- or ACT-inspired kind of situation in which you are asked to read something and then explain what it means. This often becomes an exercise in recall and vocabulary, an analytical challenge in only the most general way. Essentially, you train yourself to distinguish between specifics and generalities and to loosely follow the author's reasoning. In English classes, sometimes we are asked to perform a similar exercise with stories or poems—what is the theme or what does it mean?

> Only by understanding how we read in certain situations can we acquire more control over what we get out of the reading experience.

Questions such as these send students off on what is essentially an archaeological expedition where they must dig for hidden meaning. The "right" answers to the questions are in the text, like a buried bone; you just have to find them. Sometimes the expedition is successful, sometimes not. The trouble with this type of exercise has less to do with its success rate than with the belief that it tends to foster, which is that *all meaning resides in the text and the reader's job is merely to find it.* This belief limits the reader's interaction with the text. If meaning is fixed within the text, embedded like a bone in antediluvian mud, then all the reader has to do is dig to find that meaning. Digging isn't a bad thing, but reading can be so much more than laboring at the shovel and sifting through dirt.

READING SITUATIONS AND RHETORICAL CHOICES

You know those elaborate machines at the eye doctor's office that you look through while the optometrist tries various combinations of lenses, asking which make the fuzzy letters on the wall seem sharper? These devices are called phoropters (see Figure 2.1) and they immediately come to mind when I think about how we read. When we read anything—writing, images, graphics—we are looking through lenses. In a given situation, the right combination of lenses will help us to read better, and when we do we have found the right "prescription" for seeing a particular text for a particular purpose.

However, unlike the optometrist's phoropter, we can exercise more control over which lenses we use. Skillful readers are in command of the machine. This control comes from the same skill that gives writers more control: awareness of their own process and recognition of what each reading situation might demand. In Exercise 2.1 you began to think about both of these things, particularly

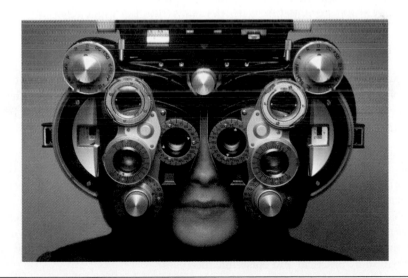

Figure 2.1   Reading is like looking through an optometrist's phoropter: The right combination of lenses will help us read better. Skillful readers are in command of the machine.

in Step 3, when you began to think about different contexts for reading, from SAT tests to text messages. Each situation demands different lenses that bring certain things—and not others—into sharper focus. The five most important types of lenses that influence how you see a text include the following:

- **Purpose:** Why are you reading?
- **Genre:** What do you know about this kind of text and what do you therefore expect?
- **Self-perception:** How good do you think you are at this kind of reading?
- **Knowledge:** What do you already know about the subject of the reading?
- **Rhetorical awareness:** What might be the purposes behind the text? What is it trying to do?

Imagine, for example, that you just purchased an iPhone and you're reading a page of instructions on how to use the video feature. Your purpose in reading in this case is entirely informational. You're motivated to learn how to use your new phone. You also probably have some experience with this genre—the instruction manual—because you've been buying electronics much of your life. Maybe you think you're a pretty good reader of the genre as a result. I know I'm not. I misread or misinterpret instructions, or ignore them altogether. I've also got a cell phone, but I've never used an iPhone, so I bring very little knowledge to my reading about how it works. If I were looking through the metaphorical phoropter, I'd start out with a pretty poor combination of lenses: difficulty with the genre, limited knowledge of the subject, and poor self-perception. If you were in my situation—or if you were advising me about how to be a better reader of this text—what would you do or say?

Let's look at an example of another kind of text. Last night I was reading a challenging piece on curiosity by two philosophers. It was published in the journal *Educational Theory*. The piece exemplifies a type of academic discourse that would be fairly typical in the discipline of philosophy. Here's an excerpt from the concluding paragraph of the article:

> In this article, we have characterized curiosity about a topic as attention to the topic giving rise to, and in turn sustained by, a motivationally original desire to know. Curiosity is biased by our practical and epistemic[1] interests. It is tenacious, typically involving a disposition to inquire into topics related to the topic of curiosity. And its motivational originality allows it to be some degree independent of practical and epistemic interests. The value of curiosity depends on these features. Its interest bias and tenacity together lead to deep inquiry than is motivated by practical and epistemic interests.[2]

---

[1]Of or related to knowledge.
[2]Schmitt, Fredrick F. and Reza Lahroodi. "The Epistemic Value of Curiosity." *Educational Theory* 58.2 (2008): 125–148.

This is pretty rough going for most readers. One of the problems has to do with purpose. Why are you reading this excerpt in the first place? I really didn't give you a reason. Now reread the passage once more, but this time your purpose is *to understand it well enough to write a two- or three-sentence summary of what you think the authors are saying.* After you're done, talk in class or in your journal about one or more of the following questions:

1. How competent do you think you are at reading this kind of writing? How did you feel when reading it? How do you often feel when reading difficult material?

2. You're probably not familiar with this genre of academic writing. What do you notice about its conventions: the language, the tone, the manner in which information is presented, and so on?

3. Curiosity is a condition of childhood, so we all bring some knowledge of it to this reading. Does this passage change anything about the way you think about your own curiosity? Does that make you think of a story?

4. What do you infer from reading this passage about the authors' purpose and audience for their article on curiosity? What exactly did you notice that inspired those inferences?

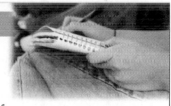

ONE STUDENT'S RESPONSE

Briana's Journal

READING ACADEMIC DISCOURSE

1. I feel like this piece is written for a certain kind of audience and that audience is not me. There are a lot of big words, some I am not sure what they mean and some I do but I have never heard or read them in that combination. As I read on I realize that it is not that difficult and they are really using a lot of words that people learn about that they are curious about. When I read difficult material I usually read the first sentence, then the second, realize that it is difficult and then sigh and then try and dig deeper and understand it and then I find that 4–5 sentences in I am not even paying attention and I usually altogether stop reading it.

2. It is not written plainly or for people that are not extremely knowledgeable in the subject; no one else would bother to read this. The info is presented in what I would consider a highly florid way; they are saying the same thing just in different ways and bringing in a minimum amount of new info.

(continued)

One Student's Response (*continued*)

3. It makes me think that when I find something interesting I will find all the books that I can on the subject and read them. Like I saw the movie *Marie Antoinette* and then I watched the special on the History channel and then I read her autobiography. Then my curiosity expanded to another queen, Queen Elizabeth. I watched the movies about her, and then I read her biography as well.

4. I am not sure what the authors' purpose is; I will presume it is to inform and I get the feeling that they also want to make others think that they are really smart. Like intellectual showoffs. I was under the assumption that that's what journals were for. But I am finding again that they are not saying a whole lot with all the words. This section is also a conclusion "we have characterized" part, maybe why it doesn't offer a lot of new information.

Figure 2.2 shows a genre that you might not be able to read very well.

Obviously, the electrical circuit diagram is a very specialized kind of text, and it presents tremendous challenges to novice readers. Even the most difficult academic discourse at least uses recognizable words, a symbol system that we've used most of our lives. But this is written in another language. Assume for a moment, though, that your assignment was to become a good

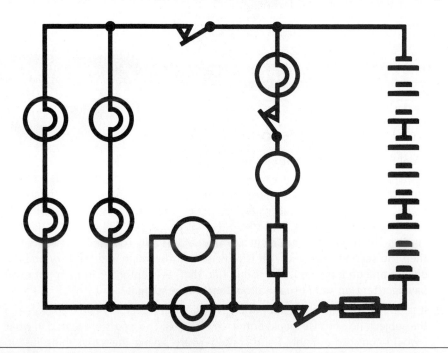

Figure 2.2   An electrical circuit diagram is a specialized kind of text that presents tremendous challenges to novice readers.

enough reader of this kind of text to be able to explain some of what this diagram is saying.

- How would you do that?
- What steps might you take?
- Might you generalize those steps or strategies to apply to any situation in which you're confronted with a difficult text?

Each of these three reading situations—an iPhone instruction manual, an excerpt from an academic journal, and an electrical circuit diagram—make different demands on you as a reader. One way of understanding these demands is to return to the rhetorical triangle we discussed in the last chapter (see Figure 2.3). Reading is a sometimes tricky negotiation between you, what you know, the subject and genre of the text, and the author's purpose behind it.

In the reader's rhetorical triangle, the reader moves to the apex of the triangle and the writer (or text's author, in this case) moves down to one of the lower legs (see Figure 2.3). The reader's portion of the triangle includes the reader's purpose for reading the text and knowledge of the subject and genre. Readers' self-perceptions—how competent they feel working with a particular text—strongly influence their motivation to wrestle with an unfamiliar work. The subject includes not only the main topic of the reading but the form or genre in which it is presented. The author's purpose shapes the third portion of the triangle. Combined, the three work to determine the context of each reading situation. The verbal SAT exam, for instance, in part involves reading short passages and answering multiple-choice comprehension questions. Speed is important. The significance of the test and the speed required to complete it influence the

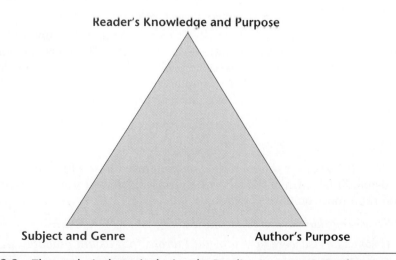

Reader's Knowledge and Purpose

Subject and Genre   **Author's Purpose**

Figure 2.3   The reader's rhetorical triangle. Reading is a negotiation between you, what you know, the subject and genre of the text, and the author's purpose.

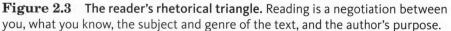

reader's portion of the triangle. So too does the subject, which is presented in the form of multiple-choice questions. The author's intent in composing the questions—to test comprehension—also shapes the reading situation.

Each reading situation, like each writing situation, presents you with a range of choices. Becoming a good reader, like becoming a good writer, involves learning to recognize those situations and being flexible about how you respond to them. The path to becoming a more sophisticated reader, like being a stronger writer, begins with a look at your history and habits dealing with texts.

EXERCISE 2.2

Reading Autobiography

How do you think of yourself as a reader? Let's explore that self-perception in your journal. As in the last chapter, you'll be working toward a memoir essay, but this time on yourself as a reader.

Generating

STEP ONE: Think back to an experience with reading—or being read to—that stands out in your memory. I immediately think about my father reading *Lassie Come Home* aloud to me as a child. My head was on his chest and I could feel the words vibrate, and once I caught him weeping. For five or six full minutes, tell your own story with as much detail as you can. This is a fastwrite, so give yourself permission to write badly.

STEP TWO: Skip a line, and then write about another experience with reading. Write for five minutes.

STEP THREE: Imagine that you've been given a reading assignment in a class. You must read the first three chapters in the textbook. There are hints about the material being on an exam. Describe yourself, in the third person, doing this reading. Write this as a scene. For example, *He is sitting at a cluttered desk with his earphones on in an otherwise darkened room staring at the open book before him. His eyes wander . . .*

Judging

STEP FOUR: Look over the material you generated in the first three steps. In your journal, finish each of the following phrases, follow it until the writing dies out, and then move on to the next one.

1. *The thing that surprised me most about what I wrote is . . .*
2. *If someone else were to read what I wrote, they would probably see . . .*
3. *Overall, the one thing my writing seems to say about me as a reader is . . .*

READING AS A PROCESS

The difference between novice readers and more experienced readers comes down to this: Experienced readers always keep their purposes for reading in mind. Generally, these purposes arise from these three questions:

- Will this give me pleasure?
- What can I *learn* from this?
- What can I *do* with this?

Obviously, an act of reading can involve a combination of these motives, but reading for inquiry is ultimately concerned with the last: How can what I'm reading be used to explore the questions that interest me? Learning and the pleasure that arises from chasing after the answers to questions that interest you is a wonderful byproduct of the inquiry process, but as a writer your reading goal is much more utilitarian: You want to see if you can *use* what you're reading in your writing.

Reading to Write

The process of reading to write is going to be different than, say, reading for pleasure. For example, I'm currently stuck in an odd obsession with reading Lincoln biographies. I just can't get enough of them. My motives are both learning and pleasure, but I really don't plan on writing anything about Lincoln, so I don't bother with things like taking notes, marking passages, mining the bibliography, and other things like that. I certainly think about what I'm reading, and sometimes I even talk about what I've learned and bore everybody to death who isn't a Lincoln fan. I am, in short, a much less active reader when I'm not worrying about what I can do with what I'm reading.

Lately, I've been working on an essay in which I am exploring why certain landscapes—usually the ones we know best from our childhoods—often get under our skins even if we no longer live in those places. My reading for this project has led me to all kinds of sources—articles in anthropology, history, and literary works. This reading is enjoyable, but it's also work. In the back of my mind, I'm always asking, *Does this relate to the questions I'm interested in?* It's a reading process that is much more directed by my goals, my interests, and my desire to use what I'm reading in my own writing.

Reading for inquiry is a process that looks something like Figure 2.4.

Prereading. Before I read to write, I'm thinking:

- What are my inquiry questions? What do I want to find out?
- How might this text provide new answers, extending or changing what I think now?

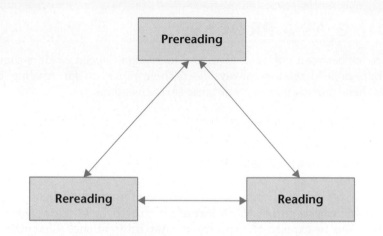

Figure 2.4 **A process for reading to write.** Reading, like writing, is a recursive process.

- What do I assume about the author's purposes?
- What do I know about how to read this kind of text?

Reading. When I read to write, I'm thinking:

- Is this relevant to what I want to know?
- Is this reliable?
- What does this say that I don't expect?
- What do I *think* about what it says?
- *How* might I use this in my writing?

Rereading. If the text seems relevant, I'll read it again, focused on not just the whole but also the parts, asking myself questions like these:

- What do I understand this to be saying?
- How does this connect with what I already know?
- Does it change the questions I'm asking?
- In my own words, what is the significance of this?
- How might the author's motives influence what this says?
- *Where* might I use this in my writing?

This process, like the writing process, is recursive. What I read may change the questions I'm asking, and every time I reread I'm also rereading my impressions from my first reading. But one thing doesn't change at any point in the process: My reading is always consciously goal-directed.

Goal-Directed Reading

Given a particular goal for reading, more experienced readers tend to agree on what's important. They learn to recognize certain patterns in a text that help them to use it more effectively. For example, I gave the following passage to sixty English majors. It's the concluding paragraphs of an essay by Christine Rosen[3] on the impact of social networking sites like Facebook on friendship. I then asked the students to assume that their purpose in reading the passage was to write a summary of what they understood Rosen to be saying about the effect of virtual relationships on human relationships, and I urged them to underline the words, phrases, or sentences in the excerpt that they thought would help them write it.

I've highlighted the sentences and phrases that my students consistently underlined the most. Keeping the goal of their reading in mind—to write a summary of this passage—what do you notice about the pattern of underlinings? What does this infer about where, in an article like this, readers can often find the most important information?

> We should also take note of the trend toward giving up face-to-face for virtual contact—and, in some cases, a preference for the latter. Today, many of our cultural, social, and political interactions take place through eminently convenient technological surrogates—Why go to the bank if you can use the ATM? Why browse in a bookstore when you can simply peruse the personalized selections Amazon.com has made for you? In the same vein, social networking sites are often convenient surrogates for offline friendship and community. In this context it is worth considering an observation that Stanley Milgram made in 1974, regarding his experiments with obedience: "The social psychology of this century reveals a major lesson," he wrote. "Often it is not so much the kind of person a man is as the kind of situation in which he finds himself that determines how he will act." To an increasing degree, we find and form our friendships and communities in the virtual world as well as the real world. These virtual networks greatly expand our opportunities to meet others, but they might also result in our valuing less the capacity for genuine connection.

> *(continued)*

---

[3]Rosen, Christine. "Virtual Friendship and the New Narcissism." *The New Atlantis* 2007 (Summer): 15–31.

(continued)

As the young woman writing in the *Times* admitted, "I consistently trade actual human contact for the more reliable high of smiles on MySpace, winks on Match.com, and pokes on Facebook." That she finds these online relationships more *reliable* is telling: it shows a desire to avoid the vulnerability and uncertainty that true friendship entails. Real intimacy requires risk—the risk of disapproval, of heartache, of being thought a fool. Social networking websites may make relationships more reliable, but whether those relationships can be humanly satisfying remains to be seen.

Sometimes we can learn the most about ourselves as readers by watching ourselves deal with a genre with which we're unfamiliar. Our knowledge about how the text works is limited so we're not quite sure where to direct our attention. We don't really trust ourselves to read the text "correctly." This may be exactly how you feel when you try to "read" a work of abstract art like the one by the artist Bridget Riley titled *Hesitate* (1964), shown in Figure 2.5. Riley was one of the most prominent artists in the short-lived Optical Art movement that began in the United States in the sixties.

Suppose you were asked by your art history professor to write a persuasive interpretation of *Hesitate*. Where would you begin? I would hope your instructor would have prepared your "reading" by helping you to understand how a painting like this one might be analyzed. What parts of this visual text should you pay attention to? How might you interpret the language of abstract art like this? One of the most important aspects of prereading is

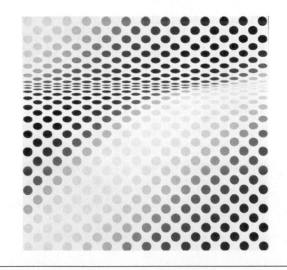

Figure 2.5 Where would you begin if you were asked to write a persuasive interpretation of a piece of abstract art like *Hesitate* (1964), by Bridget Riley?

tapping the knowledge you have about the subject, genre, and conventions of the text you're working with. If you don't have that knowledge, you're likely to read it pretty poorly. If you've never really read a painting or know little about "optical art," then you'll probably be at a loss when pressed to say anything insightful about *Hesitate*.

EXERCISE 2.3

What Do You Know and When Did You Know It?

What *do* you know about how to read certain kinds of texts?

Generating

STEP ONE: Think for a moment about what you *believe you read pretty well* and perhaps what you've always liked to read: science fiction, auto repair manuals, blogs, short stories, song lyrics, poetry, newspapers, recipes, comic books? In your journal, begin by telling yourself the story of how you came to enjoy that genre. What moments or situations come to mind? What were particularly influential encounters with that type of text? Write fast for at least three minutes.

Judging

STEP TWO: Reflect on the genre you wrote about in step one and finish the following sentence in your journal at least four times:

One of the things I learned about how to read_____ is that you should _____.

Our knowledge about reading comes to us accidentally, unexpectedly, and often unconsciously. We just do it, and eventually, if we're lucky, we get better at it. Eventually, we work tacitly from a series of assumptions about what it means to read something well, and we measure our success or failure against those assumptions. Perhaps several of those assumptions surfaced in this exercise. Examine them if they did. Do they still make sense? If you were going to teach someone else about how to read a recipe book, a comic book, or a poem, would these be the suggestions you might make?

Obviously, one way to become a more sophisticated reader is to expand this genre knowledge to other forms that you encounter with which you're less familiar, especially those you want to learn how to use in your writing.

ONE STUDENT'S RESPONSE

Briana's Journal

EXERCISE 2.3
STEP ONE: Generating

I read novels really well, but who doesn't? Generally they are easy reads and they are on topics of my personal choice. But I really get into them. When I read a suspenseful part I can feel my muscles clench. I once read a thriller book and my jaw hurt after I read a chapter or two everyday and I couldn't figure out why. Apparently I had been clenching my jaw the whole time. When there is a sad part I will feel my heart hurt and I will get mad at the person or event that caused the sadness on the inflicted's behalf. I have always been empathetic, so it goes to reason that it also extends to fictional things as well. Call me a bleeding heart.

I also love to read textbooks and nonfiction books. In between college when I was taking my seven-year break, I would find textbooks somewhere and appropriate them or buy them online; and read them from cover to cover. I think that it is really important to keep learning and growing as a human; don't let your brain be idle. Of course all the books I chose were on subjects that I was interested in: physics, history, biographies on infamous queens, music theory, Che Guevara, or Eastern European culture. I will get "stuck" on a subject and then have to learn everything about it. I want to know, so I pay close attention and will have great retention of the information.

STEP TWO: Judging

- ***One of the things that I learned about how to read*** textbooks ***is that you should*** really be interested in the subject that you are reading about.

- ***One of the things that I learned about how to read*** a novel ***is that you can*** skip the boring parts that you don't like and fill in the blanks (I pretty much skipped all of the Elvish poetry in *The Two Towers*).

- ***One of the things that I learned about how to read*** either novels or textbooks ***is that you should*** be interested in the subject, and if it is an area that you are not interested in and you have to read it, say for an assignment, then try and stay open-minded and try and find something that interests or intrigues you about it.

Inquiry Questions for Reading to Write

Writing to inquire, as you learned in the last chapter, begins with questions, not answers, and learning to craft a good question—one that will sustain your writing and thinking for some weeks—is an essential skill. Questions can also crack open a text and lead to new discoveries. To begin with, questions give you an initial reason for reading. I can imagine many kinds of questions that might

INQUIRING INTO THE DETAILS

Reading Perspectives

When we read, we always adopt certain perspectives toward a text, usually unconsciously. But one of the best ways to read strategically is to consciously *shift* our perspective while we read. Like changing lenses on a camera or changing the angle, distance, or time of day to photograph something, this shift in reading perspective illuminates different aspects of a text. Here are some of the perspectives you might take:

- *Believing:* What the author says is probably true. Which ideas can I relate to? What information should I use? What seems especially sound about the argument?

- *Doubting:* What are the text's weaknesses? What ideas don't jibe with my own experience? What are the gaps in the information or the argument? What isn't believable about this?

- *Updating:* What does this add to what I already know about the subject?

- *Hunting and gathering:* What can I collect from the text that I might be able to use?

- *Interpreting:* What might be the meaning of this?

- *Pleasure seeking:* I just want to enjoy the text and be entertained by it.

- *Connecting:* How does this information relate to my own experiences? What is its relationship to other things I've read? Does it verify, extend, or contradict what other authors have said?

- *Reflecting:* How was this written? What makes it particularly effective or ineffective?

- *Resisting:* This doesn't interest me. Why do I have to read it? Isn't *Survivor* on television right now?

guide your reading (also see "Inquiring into the Details: Reading Perspectives," above), but when you're reading to write, the following four categories of questions are the most common:

- Exploring questions
- Explaining questions
- Evaluating questions
- Reflecting questions

Questions in all four of these categories shift the way we see something. Years ago, I spent an afternoon taking photographs of an old wagon on a rolling New Hampshire hillside. I got up early on a September morning, hoping to take advantage of the slanting light and the shreds of mist that hung on the hayfield. I resolved to shoot an entire roll of film of the wagon, and I literally circled it, clicking away. By the fourth or fifth shot, I started to see the wagon in ways I'd never seen it, even though I had driven by it on my way to work for years. I saw how the beads of dew covered the bleached wood of the wagon's wheel. I saw how the ironwork of the driver's bench created a shadow on the grass that was a tangle of geometric shapes.

What I'm describing is the process of revision. But the anecdote also comes to mind now because it illustrates how different questions can shift your gaze on a topic. They help you to circle the wagon, changing your angle and revealing certain aspects of the subject. Behind each question is a different perspective on the subject. For example, take this finding from studies on computer literacy:

Boys generally outperform girls in knowledge and use of computers.

Suppose that you want to think about this. If you want to tap the power of questions, here are some that you might start with that fall into each of the four categories:

1. Do my own experiences and observations with computers tell me anything about what I think about this proposition? (Exploration)
2. How would I define "computer knowledge" in this context? (Explanation)
3. What have I seen, read, or experienced that provides support—or opposing evidence—for this idea? (Evaluation)
4. What do I notice about how each of the preceding questions shifts my way of seeing the claim about gender and computer use? (Reflection)

Can you see how each of these questions shifts your relationship to the topic and triggers different ways of thinking about it? Obviously, these aren't the only categories into which questions can be put, but they are very useful ones for reading to write.

You'll find exploring, explaining, evaluating, and reflecting questions (Figure 2.6) following readings throughout *The Curious Writer*. These form a launching point for your inquiry into the texts.

Exploration. To explore is to see a topic with wide-eyed wonder. *What might this mean to me? What do I feel or think about this?* Through questions like these, writers can openly investigate the things they read and there can be a big pay-off: You *discover* what you think. Obviously, exploratory questions about texts and the writing they inspire are most useful when you're writing about a topic that's relatively new to you. But you can also explore your existing beliefs, feelings, or ideas and you might also be surprised by what you find.

Here are some opening questions that might put you in an exploratory mode about any reading:

- What does this mean to me, or how do I think or feel about it?
- What are my first thoughts about this? And then what? And then?

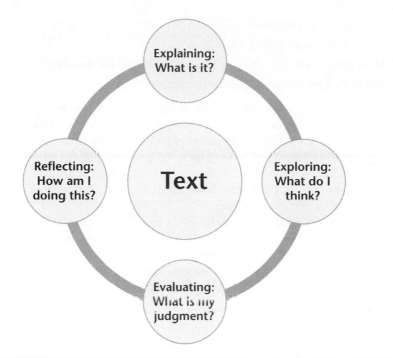

Figure 2.6   The four question categories—exploring, explaining, evaluating, and reflecting—will shift your gaze as a reader, encouraging you to see different things.

- What interests me most about this? What additional questions does it raise?
- What is the relationship between _____ and _____?
- How do my personal experiences and knowledge affect the way I feel and what I see?
- What surprises me about the way I see or think about this?

Explanation. We explain things all the time. Just a minute ago, Jim, the plumber who is working on our bedroom remodel, explained to me how the boiling water tap works on our sink. We use it for making tea, and it was sputtering and coughing and generally looking like it had symptoms of influenza. When we explain things, we usually have a particular audience in mind. We want audience members to *understand* something, but we are not merely reporting information. We're thinking about it too, trying to clarify in our own minds what we know or see and what we want to say about it.

   Some of the most common types of explanations involve defining, describing, categorizing, and comparing, often inspired by questions like these:

- What kind of text is this?
- What is its purpose?

- How is it put together?
- What is the text trying to do?
- How does it compare to something someone else has said?
- What do I understand this to be saying?

Evaluation. To evaluate something is to judge it or form an opinion about it. Evaluating things—restaurants, the quality of play in the NBA, the religious motives of Islamic extremists, the latest rap offering—is something we do all the time. These evaluations tend to lead us to do and say certain things and then to offer reasons and evidence that make them sound reasonable. If exploration is about *finding out* what we think about what we read, evaluation is often about using a reading to *prove our ideas*.

Don't misunderstand me, though. While we often have opinions about a topic, reading inquiry questions that move us to evaluate often inspire us to do more than simply find support for those opinions in what we read. We also evaluate the opinions themselves, and in the process we may begin to think differently.

Evaluation questions include the following:

- What's my opinion about what this reading seems to be saying, and what are my reasons?
- What is most convincing here? What is least convincing?
- What does the text assume to be true that might not be?
- What do I agree with? What do I disagree with?
- What does the author fail to see? How might it be seen differently?
- Who do I believe?

Reflection. If you did Exercise 2.3, you might have reflected on what you know about *how to read* the kinds of things you like to read. We often develop this kind of knowledge—knowledge about how to do things—slowly over time. But you can speed up the process by making time to ask yourself questions that encourage reflection.

You probably already have experience with this. We reflect on all kinds of processes that we want to get better at—things like playing golf, learning to act, and, of course, reading and writing. How am I executing that back swing? How might I do it differently? What new technique can I try that will deepen the emotional response of the character I'm playing? When we reflect like this on golf or acting, we discover other choices we can make that will help us perform better. The same is true when we reflect on how we think or write. The benefit of doing this is significant for everyone, but it's huge when you have problems with a process or you want to get better at it.

Inquiry questions that prompt reflection about how you read include:

- What do I notice about how I'm reading this?
- What assumptions do I bring to the reading that might influence what I think or how I feel about what it says?

- How do I compare how I approach this task with how I approach another one?
- When did I have the most problems with the text? What were they?
- How did this add to my knowledge about how to become a better reader?

READING DIALECTICALLY

Opening questions will give us goals for reading, as they do for writing, and we can also use the method of combining creative and critical thinking to help us get more out of what we read (see Figure 2.7). Remember the inquiry process described in Chapter 1 for combining creative and critical thinking?

You have already used this process extensively in the writing exercises so far, moving from suspending judgment when you generate ideas to making judgments when you analyze what you've generated. When we read to write, we can also use these alternate modes of thinking to ultimately answer the same question that all writing must answer: *So what?* What are you trying to say to others about what you've read that they might care to know? On the way to answering the "so what" question, we're trying to figure out what *we* think and, in particular, how a text helps us to think about the questions that moved us to look at it

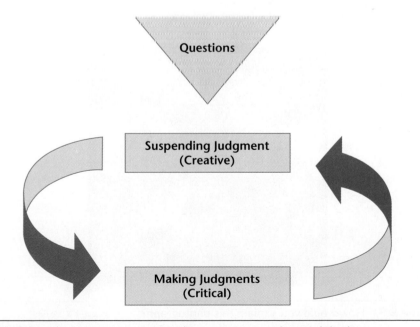

Figure 2.7   The inquiry process combines creative and critical thinking.

in the first place. Let's see how this might work with a visual text and then, later, a print text.

Suppose you were asked to *explain* the image in Figure 2.8, by famed American photographer Edward Weston, in a short response, offering your own idea about what it means based on particular things you see in the photograph.

You could approach this in two ways:

1. You could just make something up without thinking about it much and leave it at that. "Gee, this looks like, um, a bull's nostril."

2. You could withhold judgment and spend a little more time figuring out what you think.

The first option is a closed, cursory reading. It starts with answers rather than questions, and sidesteps any genuine inquiry into the text. The second option is more open-ended, and it requires that you look more closely at the text and *then* develop ideas about it. Reading dialectically is a method that can encourage that kind of inquiry.

When we read to write, we work from a question that gives our reading a goal. In the case of the photograph, we're asking an explaining question: "What is this image trying to do?" As you know, knowledge of *how* to read a kind of text with which we may not be familiar will really help us work toward a good reading

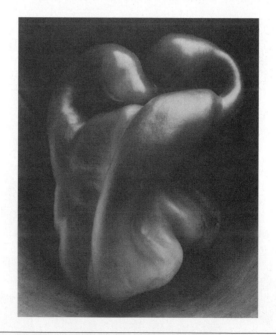

Figure 2.8   How would you explain this photograph?

(see "Inquiring into the Details: Visual Literacy: Reading Photographs, page 64). With this background knowledge, here's one way of finding an answer to our question:

- Start with two blank, opposing pages in a journal. Beginning on the left page, note your observations of the photograph. Writing fast, use your knowledge of how to read a photograph and explore what exactly you see in the image, describing this as specifically as you can.

- On the right page, compose your initial thoughts in response to the question, looking at the information you collected on the left page to help you think about what you are trying to say.

For example:

Observations of	Ideas about
What's interesting is that the setting of the image is stripped down and bare so that the green pepper is without question the most important visual subject here. The framing is so simple, really. All we need to know is before us. It's realistic and it's abstract at the same time. I can see the pepper, particularly the bruise in the bottom and the curving ribs of the thing, but the light seems to emphasize not the structure of the green pepper but the skin. The skin is amazing. The light has this amazing range reflecting on the skin—very dark at the top where the pepper turns into itself in contrast with the sheen on the edges. . . .	By stripping away any context and filling the frame with the image of a single green pepper, Weston's photograph emphasizes its abstract qualities. And yet, though we know it's a pepper, it's impossible to avoid seeing the play of the light on its skin as incredibly suggestive. It's sensuous and has some of the qualities of flesh, especially the curves and the muscular ridges.

Reading dialectically like this mimics the process you've already practiced in Chapter 1, moving back and forth from creative and critical, collecting and focusing, observations and ideas, specifics and generalizations. On the left page you are withholding judgment, trying to think through writing about what you see. On the right, you work toward making some kind of judgments about what you see. Obviously, this method—what writing theorist Ann Berthoff called the "dialogue journal" or double-entry journal—takes more time than just making a pronouncement like "It's a pepper!" or "It looks like two wrestling dinosaurs!" But by postponing the rush to a conclusion, you use the inquiry process to come up with better, more insightful, more informed ideas.

INQUIRING INTO THE DETAILS

Visual Literacy: Reading Photographs

As you know by now, it helps enormously when reading a new text to have some knowledge of *how* to read it. Here are some aspects to consider:

- *Framing:* As in writing, what the photographer chooses to leave in an image and what she chooses to leave out profoundly affect the story, idea, or feeling a photograph communicates.

- *Angle:* A front-on view of a subject creates a different effect than looking up—or down—at it.

- *Setting:* While good photographs emphasize certain visual elements and not others, some try, directly or indirectly, to communicate other information about where and when the photograph was taken. It's also significant when setting or context is missing.

- *Arrangement:* In writing, we give certain information emphasis by where we place it in a sentence, in a paragraph, or in the whole composition. Visual information also uses the physical arrangement of objects for emphasis, making some things larger or smaller, in the foreground or background, to one side or the other. Focus, or what is clear and what is fuzzy, is one way to manage visual arrangement.

- *Light:* What is most illuminated and what is in shadows—and everything in between—also influences what is emphasized and what is not. But since light is something we strongly associate with time and place, it also has an emotional impact.

EXERCISE 2.4

Reading Creatively, Reading Critically

Now that you've seen how the dialectical thinking approach can help analyze an image, let's try it with a more familiar kind of text. I published the essay "The Importance of Writing Badly" some years ago, but I think it still expresses several of the main ideas behind this book. I'd like you to read the piece critically, though, using the double-entry journal method we used when interpreting the pepper photograph.

As before, you'll use opposing pages of your journal. At the top of the left page write the word "Collecting," and at the top of the right page write the word "Focusing."

STEP ONE: Read the essay once through, and then once again. The second time through, carefully *copy* lines of passages from the essay on the left page of your notebook that:

- Connected with your own experience and observations
- Raised questions for you
- Puzzled you
- You thought seemed a key point
- You disagreed or agreed with or you think about differently
- You found surprising or unexpected

The Importance of Writing Badly
Bruce Ballenger

I was grading papers in the waiting room of my doctor's office the other day, and he said, "It must be pretty eye-opening reading that stuff. Can you believe those students had four years of high school and still can't write?"   1

I've heard that before. I hear it almost every time I tell a stranger that I teach writing at a university.   2

I also hear it from colleagues brandishing red pens who hover over their students' papers like Huey helicopters waiting to flush the enemy from the tall grass, waiting for a comma splice or a vague pronoun reference or a misspelled word to break cover.   3

And I heard it this morning from the commentator on my public radio station who publishes snickering books about how students abuse the sacred language.   4

I have another problem: getting my students to write badly.   5

Most of us have lurking in our past some high priest of good grammar whose angry scribbling occupied the margins of our papers. Mine was Mrs. O'Neill, an eighth-grade teacher with a good heart but no patience for the bad sentence. Her favorite comment on my writing was "awk," which now sounds to me like the grunt of a large bird, but back then meant "awkward." She didn't think much of my sentences.   6

I find some people who reminisce fondly about their own Mrs. O'Neill, usually an English teacher who terrorized them into worshipping the error-free sentence. In some cases that terror paid off when it was finally transformed into an appreciation for the music a well-made sentence can make.   7

But it didn't work that way with me. I was driven into silence, losing faith that I could ever pick up the pen without breaking the rules or drawing another "awk" from a doubting reader. For years I wrote only when forced to, and when I did it was never good enough.   8

(continued)

(continued)

9   Many of my students come to me similarly voiceless, dreading the first writing assignment because they mistakenly believe that how they say it matters more than discovering what they have to say.

10   The night before the essay is due they pace their rooms like expectant fathers, waiting to deliver the perfect beginning. They wait and they wait and they wait. It's no wonder the waiting often turns to hating what they have written when they finally get it down. Many pledge to steer clear of English classes, or any class that demands much writing.

11   My doctor would say my students' failure to make words march down the page with military precision is another example of a failed education system. The criticism sometimes takes on political overtones. On my campus, for example, the right-wing student newspaper demanded that an entire semester of Freshman English be devoted to teaching students the rules of punctuation.

12   There is, I think, a hint of elitism among those who are so quick to decry the sorry state of the sentence in the hands of student writers. A colleague of mine, an Ivy League graduate, is among the self-appointed grammar police, complaining often about the dumb mistakes his students make in their papers. I don't remember him ever talking about what his students are trying to say in those papers. I have a feeling he's really not that interested.

13   Concise, clear writing matters, of course, and I have a responsibility to demand it from students. But first I am far more interested in encouraging thinking than error-free sentences. That's where bad writing comes in.

14   When I give my students permission to write badly, to suspend their compulsive need to find the "perfect way of saying it," often something miraculous happens: Words that used to trickle forth come gushing to the page. The students quickly find their voices again, and even more important, they are surprised by what they have to say. They can worry later about fixing awkward sentences. First, they need to make a mess.

15   It's harder to write badly than you might think. Haunted by their Mrs. O'Neill, some students can't overlook the sloppiness of their sentences or their lack of eloquence, and quickly stall out and stop writing. When the writing stops, so does the thinking.

16   The greatest reward in allowing students to write badly is that they learn that language can lead them to meaning, that words can be a means for finding out what they didn't know they knew. It usually happens when the words rush to the page, however awkwardly.

17   I don't mean to excuse bad grammar. But I cringe at conservative educational reformers who believe writing instruction should return to primarily teaching how to punctuate a sentence and use *Roget's Thesaurus*. If policing student papers for mistakes means alienating young writers from the language we expect them to master, then the exercise is self-defeating.

18   It is more important to allow students to first experience how language can be a vehicle for discovering how they see the world. And what matters in this journey—at least initially—is not what kind of car you're driving, but where you end up.

STEP TWO: Now use the right page of your notebook to think further about what you wrote down on the left page. Remember these inquiry questions that can guide your thinking and writing:

- *Exploring:* What do I first notice about notes I took on "The Importance of Writing Badly?" And then what do I notice or think? And then?
- *Explaining:* What is it that I understand this to be saying?
- *Evaluating:* What is most convincing here? What is least convincing?

Write for five or six minutes without stopping.

STEP THREE: Reread what you've written. Again, on the right page of your notebook write your half of the dialog below with someone who is asking you about the idea of "bad writing."

Q: I don't understand how bad writing can help anyone write better. Can you explain it to me?

A:

Q: Okay, but is it an idea that makes sense to you?

A:

Q: What exactly (i.e., quotation) does Ballenger say that makes you feel that way?

A:

STEP FOUR: Finish the exercise by reflecting in your journal for five minutes on what, if anything, you noticed about this method of reading. In particular:

- How did it change the way you usually read an article like this?
- How might you adapt it for other situations in which you have to read to write?
- What worked well? What didn't?
- Do you think the method encouraged you to think more deeply about what you read?

ONE STUDENT'S RESPONSE

Briana's Journal

EXERCISE 2.4 READING CREATIVELY, READING CRITICALLY

STEP TWO:

I took pieces of the sentences, not necessarily writing down the whole sentence but the parts that were the most poignant. I mostly chose sentences that I found to be clever, amusing, or just liked the way they sounded...I also created a dichotomy,

(continued)

One Student's Response (*continued*)

focusing on two things: 1) the "proper" way of writing, which is English elitism, and is focusing on grammatical perfection and 2) the "artsy" way of writing, which focuses on writing as a thought process to help create understanding and growth. While I was writing down my notes and sentences, I was thinking that I have never had a Mrs. O'Neil. This has not been my experience. I write to write, and mostly to amuse myself or as a form of cheap therapy (also cheaper than cable). I also think that sometimes "grammatical imperfection" can add to the style and the voice of a piece. I also value voice and style over perfection…I see this piece as saying that writing is like a thinking process, like thinking out loud but you have an invaluable record of your thoughts. I also get that you need to write and write a lot. The more the better; it gives you more to work with. I also think that it helps you write better and enjoy it because you are getting a lot of experience. It's not so much about how you wrote it as it is about what you write about.

STEP THREE

Q: I don't understand how bad writing can help anyone write better. Can you explain it to me?

A: What you have to say is just as important as how you write it. Writing is a way of thinking, sort of like thinking out loud—a way of thinking through things and reflecting more deeply on things. It feels awesome to write with reckless abandon and show no concern for punctuation or grammar. It helps you think unhindered, to find out how you truly think and feel. Thoughts and feelings have little concern for these things. Looking back at your thoughts that you have written you can see your thoughts. Then you can look at how you have written. Being observant and introspective of your own writing will help you develop better writing skills.

Q: Okay, but is it an idea that makes sense to you?

A: Definitely, I prefer to write badly. I believe that it's a better expression of my actual thoughts, flaws and all. When I write on my computer my spellcheck goes crazy with "fragment sentences." But who cares? That's what I want to say and that is how it comes out and how it sounds in its natural state. I don't change it. Give me all your green squiggly underlinings, Windows Vista. It has been driven into so many students that we have to write perfectly—use correct punctuation, no vague pronouns, correct verb tense, good sentence syntax, and structure. I think that writing should be more than that. I think that it should be more of a form of expression.

Q: What exactly (i.e., quotation) does Ballenger say that makes you feel that way?

A: "Many of my students come to me similarly voiceless, because they mistakenly believe that how they say it matters more than discovering what they have to say."

I have never actually used the "double-entry" journal method before. I think it gave me a more articulate and clear idea of what I thought and how I came to think that. It became a map of my thought process. I usually have trouble pulling my thoughts in my writing together, but this gave me my thoughts more concisely. I also liked that

I had a record of my thoughts and that regardless of the quality of writing, it was an accurate record because we all know that memory is not all that reliable. I think that method would be good when you have to opine on a subject at length. I liked the explore, explain, evaluate, and reflect structure because when you are writing off the top of your head it is easy to lose focus. So this helps keep you on track.

Read to Write and Write to Read

In this chapter I'm making a case for an approach to reading that is probably unfamiliar to you. It includes the following:

1. **When you read to write, do it with certain goals in mind**. For many of us this isn't new—we often do read with purpose—but these goals are often limited to two things: comprehending and cherry-picking. The lesson of the SAT is that comprehension is what reading is all about since that is what you get tested on. Similarly, the five-paragraph theme and other formulaic forms of writing, which are so popular in school, teach us that reading to write is no more than plucking information from sources to plug into paragraphs to support topic sentences. But reading can also be a kind of conversation in which we talk with others with an open mind.

2. **Questions shift your perspective on what you read**. When we read to write we may have only one question in mind: What do I understand this to be saying? That's a good question, of course, but it's not the only one that can guide your thinking. Photographers consciously change lenses, angles, and distances on their subjects to see them in new ways. Questions have the same effect when you read—especially those that *explore, explain, evaluate,* and *reflect.*

3. **When you read to write you can write *and* read**. Some of us underline, highlight, and even make marginal notes when we read to write. But I'm encouraging you to do much more writing than that as you read, and after you read. If writing about your personal experiences can be a process of discovery, as I claimed in Chapter 1, then you can use the same method to explore anything else you want to think about. In other words, if you're trying to figure out what you think about what you're reading, then you can *write* your way to new understandings.

4. **Good readers develop *rhetorical knowledge***. You already have more of this kind of knowledge than you think. You know, for example, to read a text message differently than a textbook. But the best readers pay a lot of attention to learning explicitly about this. They remember what different reading situations demand from them. For example, they learn to distinguish goals for reading to write about a short story from goals for reading to write about marketing. They also develop knowledge about genre. Good readers, for instance, know that Web pages are often designed to put the most important information across the top and down the left side.

THE WRITING PROCESS

INQUIRY PROJECT: THE READING LITERACY MEMOIR

In Chapter 1 you wrote a memoir on your writing life. This chapter will end the same way, but this time your three- to five-page essay will focus on your experiences as a reader. You've already started writing and thinking about this in Exercises 2.1 and 2.2. If you can, draw on some of that material and draft a personal essay that does two things:

- Tells stories about some of your reading experiences, in school and out
- Reflects on what you understand about those experiences now, as you look back on them

For your reflection, exploit, if you can, some of the information in this chapter, particularly ideas about what the differences might be between a "good" reader and a novice reader and where you see yourself as a reader now, what you think you need to learn, and why it matters.

Unfortunately, schooling can brand us and give us ideas about ourselves that are hard to change. I was told in subtle and unsubtle ways that I was not good at English. When it comes to reading—the major focus of language arts classes—one moment stands out that affected the way I thought about myself as a reader for a long time. My memoir, for example, might start like this:

In 1965, I moved from green to orange in the SRA reading packet but never moved again. In those days, orangeness was a sign of mediocrity. The shame of never busting through orange to blue, the color Jeff Brickman, Mark Levy, and Betsy Cochran seemed to achieve with such ease quite naturally made it easy to convince me that reading was just not my thing. From then on I hated English (a feeling I freely shared on the inside covers of my class yearbooks), except the time we studied the lyrics of Simon and Garfunkel's "The Sounds of Silence." I was a high school sophomore, and while I would sometimes, in my own way, think deeply on things, I was attached more to *the idea* of thinking deeply on things, usually expressed in the ponderous and self-consciously deep lyrics of early Simon and Garfunkel's. To *feel* deep, I thought, was to *be* deep.

■ STUDENT ESSAY

Reading Literacy Memoir
Briana Duquette-Shackley

I was born into a very blue-collar family, almost anti-intellectual. You read recipes, you read car repair manuals, you read the TV guide or on occasion you read those novels that they sell on the shelf at the checkout aisle. There was very little emphasis on learning or intellect. Instead you were told to be who you are and do what you like best. There was never anyone pushing me to be a doctor and when I said I wanted to be one, my parents said "OK." I said I wanted to be a racecar driver and they said "if that's what you want to do." I said that I wanted to be a fashion designer and they said "that's a fine idea."

Under this intellectual neutrality I just went with what interested me and I blossomed in the reading and language department. I could speak and read at an early age and was reading at a college freshman level in the fifth grade. If I wanted a book, my parents bought it; so when I asked for *The Scarlet Letter* at an early age, they didn't seem concerned about the content or the level of reading. I read it. There were some things that I had to reread, but I read it. I was a good student and consistently on the honor roll.

It was not that my parents didn't praise me for my academics, but they just didn't push me in any one direction. I found a love of reading, and once I started to read I didn't want to stop. I would read anything that I could get my hands on, and I continue to be like that to this day. I read *People*, *Us Weekly*, and *Good Housekeeping*, not because they are what I love to read but because it's the only thing to read at work. I could spend days in Barnes and Noble and not buy anything. And all the librarians at my local library know me by name.

In kindergarten I remember reading the books that they have that teach you how to read, the same "decodable" books I read to my own daughter, and I loved them. I would read aloud at the kitchen counter as my mom cooked dinner. I now find myself with a compulsion to read anything that is in front of me no matter how lame: cereal boxes, random pamphlets, those weird quips in the phonebook. I love the communication and the nuances between words, their meanings, and their usage. It's like how I look at fashion magazines for ideas on how to dress, I look to literature to show me examples of how to speak and write, and even to try out who I might want to be.

I have gone through phases where I want to explore an area of myself or life and I will turn to literature for information about it. During my punk rock phase in high school, I read books and periodicals about revolution and anarchy and became very politically savvy. I went through an artistic phase where I wanted to learn about the great artists and how to revolutionize the art world. I went to the library and checked out art book after art book. I went through an indie rock, intellectual phase and read exclusively books by the beat writers. Then I went through a Che Guevara phase and read *The Motorcycle Diaries* and his lengthy autobiography. I noticed toward the end of the bio that I didn't even want to read it; I really couldn't

(continued)

(continued)

care less about the flawed bureaucracy of the new Cuban government. I was mostly in love with the romantic ideal of the revolutionist, no matter how misguided. But I read it all, to have the sense of accomplishment and for fear that I might miss out on something.

6   Reading is something less that I do because I want to; it seems more like a compulsion. It's part pleasure and part practicality. I read for information, but I only read about things that I want to know about. I always have at least one book by my bed that I am reading. When I was a child, my parents read to me every night before bed. Even when I could read they would still read to me. But this wasn't about learning; it was about enjoyment. It was something that they shared with me; they liked doing it and I like being read to. So through the two—information and enjoyment—this compulsion arose.

7   Unfortunately, this passion for reading did not always help me in school. In elementary school, I struggled with reading comprehension. I guess I equated reading really fast with being a good reader. I didn't think about what the words were saying. When we would have a test I would read the piece and then not be able to answer any of the questions about what I had just read. When I would get my test back I would have A's in everything but reading comprehension. Working with my teacher after school, I learned to slow down to understand the words instead of merely repeating them.

8   Even now I will find myself "just trying to make it through" texts that I am not really all that into. And then I will look back and think that I have gotten absolutely nothing out of what I have just read and then have to reread it. I read extremely slowly when I am really trying to read and comprehend something that I don't really want to read. Yet when I am reading something that I really like, the same slow reading makes all else in my environment fade. When I read what I want and what I enjoy, comprehension is totally effortless. I have to give the piece value, and then I can enjoy it; I have to try to find one thing that I can derive pleasure from, and then I can get into it.

9   I think that my love of reading comes from the fact that I come from a blue-collar background. And herein lies the irony. Blue-collar people, from my observations, tend to be more rebellious. I guess reading and becoming more literate was my way of rebelling, too. And maybe that was what asking for *The Scarlet Letter* was all about. Reading a book that was considered a "great" or a "classic" was my equivalent to getting a facial piercing or a tattoo. Also, it is just in my nature to be curious and want to know about things. Since I always hated to ask anyone, for whatever reason, going and reading a book seemed like a much better and more direct route. I have a friend who told me that there is this Jewish philosophy that says that the only thing that you can take with you when you die is knowledge. Now I don't necessarily agree with this, but I think that knowledge can and will make the life that you are currently living much more rich and fulfilling. And the best place to get information is to read it. There are countless books and other sources of text, literature, prose, and everything in between. Thanks to the Internet you can read about anything at the touch of your fingertips, and you don't even have to get up. Reading to get information just makes good sense in my world.

10   At the moment, I am going through an, as of yet, unnamed phase, but I am reading Aleister Crowley. Someday, I hope to look back and see the story of myself in what I was reading and hope that what I was reading made my life better in some way.

INQUIRING INTO THE DETAILS

The Double-Entry Journal

A double-entry journal is essentially a written dialog between a reader and a text. As a reader you ask questions, make connections, and note memories and associations.

Here's how it works: You can either draw a line down the middle of a page to make two columns, or you can use the spine of your notebook for the line and use two opposing pages.

What the Text Says	What I Think
In the left column, write out the passages from the reading that confuse you, surprise you, make you think of other ideas, seem key to your understanding of what it says, and so on.	In the right column, write out your response to those passages. Sometimes you'll do a fastwrite; other times you may simply jot down quick thoughts.

- Jot down direct quotes, paraphrases, summaries, facts, claims.

- Note page numbers next to each passage or summary/paraphrase. Put them in the far right margin next to the borrowed material or ideas.

Play the doubting game, questioning the source; play the believing game, trying to find its virtues, even if you disagree.

- Shift to other reading perspectives.

- Tell the story of your thinking about what you're reading: *My initial reaction to this is… but now I think… and now I think…*

- List questions you have about the source's ideas, your emotional responses, other ideas or readings it connects to.

Continue this process for the entire reading, moving back and forth across the columns. Remember that you want to explore your response to a text, make connections to other works and your own writing, and analyze the writer's choices in terms of language, style, detail, and so forth. *Be sure to note all the bibliographic information from the source at the top of the page.*

INQUIRING INTO THE DETAILS

Encountering Unfamiliar Genres

The only time most of us ever really pay attention to genre is when we encounter one that defies our expectations. When the low-budget film *Memento* was released several years ago, its puzzling narrative structure (beginning at the end of the story and proceeding to the beginning), its use of an unreliable narrator, and its alternation between black-and-white and color took audiences by surprise and generated lots of print by movie critics. Ultimately, the film became a phenomenal success, partly because its approach was so unexpected. *Memento* got people talking about a completely different way to think about filmmaking.

An ad for the film *Memento*

The response to the movie was so significant because we are a nation of moviegoers who are quite familiar with the genre, and *Memento* made us wonder how much we really know about film. These kinds of *Memento* movements happen to readers all the time, especially when we're in an academic setting and aren't familiar with the genres we're asked to read—a poem, a lab report, an academic argument, a minimalist painting. Our first response might be to question how well we can read, even though we've all been reading for a very long time.

One way of dealing with this is to simply apply reading strategies that we've used successfully in other genres. For example, because your verbal score on the reading comprehension portion of the SAT was so high, why not approach reading the essay on the need for a new immigration policy the same way, and try to decode exactly what the writer must have meant and leave it at that? Well, your instructor will likely say, "Fine, but I want to know what you think about his argument."

A better approach when you encounter types of readings that are new to you is to let the reading situation be your guide.

- Ask yourself, *Why am I reading this? How is it relevant to my inquiry question?* or *What exactly is my instructor asking me to do with this text?*

- Are there clues in the text about how it might be efficiently read? For instance, do subheadings provide guidance? Is there a preface that reviews the argument? Does the concluding section have the most weight?

■ Who is the intended audience for this text and what clues does that provide about the writer's purpose? Might that explain not only how she composed the text—its language, organization, and so on—but also what she hoped to accomplish with it?

■ Whenever possible, "frontload" before you read something challenging; that is, learn as much as you can about the subject and even the writer's relationship to the subject. This knowledge will make a big difference in how much you understand.

USING WHAT YOU HAVE LEARNED

Inquiry-based writing and reading begins with an open-eyed sense of wonder. Instead of initially asking, *What should I say?* you ask, *What do I think?* You begin by trying to find questions that interest you, knowing that there isn't necessarily a single right answer. At the same time, you know that just as you open up possible meanings, at some point you need to narrow them. You are both creative *and* critical, moving back and forth between collecting and focusing, exploring and evaluating, narrating and reflecting.

As you continue in *The Curious Writer*, I'll encourage you to apply this process to nearly every assignment. Before long, it will become second nature to you; you'll find yourself naturally shifting back and forth between the creative and the critical, whether you're exploring a topic for an assignment, reading an essay that you'll discuss in class, or analyzing an advertisement. Techniques that you've already practiced such as fastwriting and listing, the double-entry journal, and generating questions will help this along.

INQUIRY PROJECTS

Writing a personal essay is like seeing an old picture of yourself. This publicity photograph of my mother, my brother, and me in the 1950s returns me to that world—a time when fathers were often missing from the picture.

WRITING A PERSONAL ESSAY 3

WRITING ABOUT EXPERIENCE

Most us were taught and still believe that we need to know what we are going to write before we actually pick up the pen or sit in front of the computer. My student Lynn was typical.

"I think I'll write about my experience organizing the street fair," she told me the other day. "That would be a good topic for a personal essay, right?"

"Do you think so?" I said.

"Well, yes, because I already know a lot about it. I'll have a lot to write about."

"Okay, but is there anything about this experience that you want to understand better?" I said. "Anything about it that makes you curious?"

"Curious? It was just a street fair," she said.

"Sure, but is there something about what happened that makes you want to look at the experience again? Is there a chance that you might learn something about yourself, or about street fairs, or about the community, or about people, or...?"

Lynn was clearly sorry she asked. What I should have said was much more to the point: The best essay topics are those that are an itch you need to scratch. These tend not to be topics you have already figured out. While the topics can be familiar to you, the results of your inquiry are usually much better if you don't yet know what you think about your topics and you're interested to learn more about them.

> ## What You'll Learn in This Chapter
>
> - How personal essays can help you with academic writing.
> - What distinguishes a personal essay from other forms.
> - How to write a sketch.
> - Why a confusing topic may be better than one you have all figured out.
> - Questions for revising personal essays.

The best topics ask to be written about because they make you wonder *Why did I do that? What does that mean? Why did that happen? How did I really feel? What do I really think*?

Unlike most other forms of inquiry, the personal essay invites an initial display of confusion or uncertainty from writers regarding their subjects. In other words, writers do not have to have their subjects figured out when starting a personal essay. This form of inquiry is a vehicle for writers to work through their thinking and feeling on a subject directly in front of their readers.

> The personal essay is a vehicle for writers to work through their thinking and feeling on a subject directly in front of their readers.

As a form, the *personal* essay places the writer at center stage. This doesn't mean that once she's there, her responsibility is to pour out her secrets, share her pain, or confess her sins. Some essays do have these confessional qualities, but more often they do not. Yet a personal essayist, no matter the subject of the essay, is still *exposed*. There is no hiding behind the pronoun "one," as in "one might think" or "one often feels," no lurking in the shadows of the passive voice: "An argument will be made that...." The personal essay is first-person territory.

In this sense, the personal essay is much like a photographic self-portrait. Like a picture, a good personal essay tells the truth, or it tells *a* truth about the writer/subject, and it often captures the writer at a particular moment of time. Therefore, the experience of taking a self-portrait, or confronting an old picture of oneself taken by someone else, can create the feeling of exposure that writing a personal essay often does.

But it does more. When we gaze at ourselves in a photograph we often see it as yanked from a larger story about ourselves, a story that threads its way through our lives and gives us ideas about who we were and who we are. This is what the personal essay demands of us: We must somehow present ourselves truthfully and measure our past against the present. In other words, when we hold a photograph of ourselves we know more than the person we see there knew, and as writers of the personal essay, we must share that knowledge and understanding with readers.

MOTIVES FOR WRITING A PERSONAL ESSAY

Essai was a term first coined by the sixteenth-century French nobleman Michel de Montaigne, a man who had lived through occurrences of the plague, the bloody civil war between French Catholics and Protestants, and his own ill health. These were tumultuous and uncertain times when old social orders and intellectual traditions were under assault, and it proved to be ideal ferment for the essay. The French verb *essaier* means "to attempt" or "to try," and the essay became an opportunity for Montaigne to work out his thoughts about war, the education of children, the evils of doctors, and the importance of pleasure. The personal essay tradition inspired by Montaigne is probably unlike the essays you are familiar with in school. The school essay is often formulaic—a five-paragraph theme, or thesis-example paper—while the personal essay is an open-ended form that allows for uncertainty and inconclusiveness. It is more about the process of coming to know than presenting *what* you know. The personal essay attempts *to find out* rather than *to prove*.

It is an ideal form of inquiry if your purpose is exploratory rather than argumentative, and if you're particularly interested in working out the possible relationships between your subject and yourself. Because the personal essay is openly subjective, the writer can't hide. The intruding *I* confronts the writer with the same questions over and over again: *Why does this matter to me? What do I make of it? How does this change the way I think of myself and the way I see the world?* Because of this, one of the principal dangers of the personal essay is that it can become narcissistic; it can go on and on about what the writer thinks and feels, and the reader can be left with that nagging question—*So what?* The personal essayist must always find some way to hitch the particulars of his or her experience to something larger—an idea, a theme, or even a feeling that readers might share.

On the other hand, one of the prime rhetorical advantages of the personal essay is its subjectivity. Because it is written with openness and honesty, the essay is often a very intimate form, inviting the reader to share in the writer's often concealed world. In the personal essay, we often get to see the face sweating under the mask. Honesty is one of the essay's primary virtues, and because the form allows for uncertainty and confusion, the writer doesn't need to pretend that he has *the* answer, or that he knows more than he lets on about his subject.

THE PERSONAL ESSAY AND ACADEMIC WRITING

In some ways, the personal essay might seem like a dramatic departure from the kind of academic writing you've done in other classes. Openly subjective and sometimes tentative in its conclusions, the personal essay is a relatively open form that is not predictably structured, like much academic writing. Additionally, the tone of the personal essay is conversational, even intimate, rather than impersonal and removed. If your sociology or economics professor will never ask for a personal essay, why bother to write one in your composition class?

It's a fair question. While the pleasures of personal essay writing can be significant, and reason alone to write essays, there are other important reasons to practice the form. The most obvious is that the essay, more than any other form, gives you an opportunity to use exploration as a method of inquiry, and to practice those habits of mind that are so important to academic inquiry: suspending judgment, tolerating ambiguity, and using questions to challenge easy assumptions.

> The essay, more than any other form, gives you an opportunity to use exploration as a method of inquiry.

But the purpose of writing personal essays in your composition class goes beyond this. For one thing, the essay emphasizes the *process* of coming to know about yourself and your subject, exposing your reasoning and the ways you use knowledge to get at the truth of things. Reflecting on these things in a personal essay can tell you a lot about how you think. The *dialectical thinking* required by the personal essay—the movement back and forth between critical and creative thinking—is a useful mental exercise for a range of academic situations. Finally, much of what you are asked to write in college depends on your willingness to step forward and express a belief, make an assertion, or pose a relevant question. The personal essay is a form that puts the writer in the spotlight. You can't hide in the wings, concealed in the shadow of other people's opinions or someone else's findings. What *you* think is what the essay is all about.

FEATURES OF THE FORM

There are many different kinds of personal essays, of course, but certain conventions are present in most of them. Keep these in mind as you read the professional essays that follow. Which of the conventions listed here seem to be present? Can you detect any others?

- *Personal essays are usually written in the first person.* There is no pretense of scientific objectivity in personal essays.

- *The subject of the essay is often commonplace.* Although essayists sometimes write about dramatic things, they most often are interested in the drama of everyday life.

- *Narrative is often the primary method of development.* Personal essays often tell two kinds of stories—they relate narratives of the writer's experiences and observations, and they tell the story of the writer's thinking about what those experiences and observations might mean.

- *The thesis can be implicit, and it frequently emerges late, rather than at the beginning, of the essay.*

- *Of the four sources of information, the personal essay relies on memory and observation most of all.* Because of the subjectivity of the essay, the writer often reports *what has happened* to her as a means to account for *what happens.*

- *The essay often mimics the dialectical process that helped the writer compose it, shifting back and forth from the then and now, what happened to what happens, and showing and telling.*

READINGS

■ PERSONAL ESSAY 1

The essayist Scott Russell Sanders once observed that an essay "scatters a bunch of rabbits that go bounding in all directions.…If you refuse to chase any of them, and keep plodding along in a straight line, you and your reader will have a dull outing. If you chase too many, you will soon wind up lost in a thicket of confusion…." In "Buckeye," Sanders flushes a few rabbits of his own, chasing down ideas about coping with grief, the life in a piece of wood, and learning to love land that doesn't yield easily to such affection. In this sense, it's a complicated essay; in another, it's as simple as an Ohio buckeye, rubbed shiny from handling. The essay that follows exemplifies one of the most appealing features of the personal essay: Its subject is often ordinary, familiar. In "Buckeye," Sanders is doing no more than telling stories about his father, a handmade wooden box, and a November afternoon. Yet the piece is anything but ordinary in its language, and especially in what it comes to say about how to "dwell in our place with a full heart."

BUCKEYE

Scott Russell Sanders

Years after my father's heart quit, I keep in a wooden box on my desk the two buck- 1
eyes that were in his pocket when he died. Once the size of plums, the brown seeds are shriveled now, hollow, hard as pebbles, yet they still gleam from the polish of his hands. He used to reach for them in his overalls or suit pants and click them together, or he would draw them out, cupped in his palm, and twirl them with his blunt carpenter's fingers, all the while humming snatches of old tunes.

"Do you really believe buckeyes keep off arthritis?" I asked him more than once. 2

He would flex his hands and say, "I do so far." 3

My father never paid much heed to pain. Near the end, when his worn knee of- 4
ten slipped out of joint, he would pound it back in place with a rubber mallet. If a splinter worked into his flesh beyond the reach of tweezers, he would heat the blade of his knife over a cigarette lighter and slice through the skin. He sought to ward off arthritis not because he feared pain but because he lived through his hands, and he dreaded the swelling of knuckles, the stiffening of fingers. What use would he be if he could no longer hold a hammer or guide a plow? When he was a boy he had known farmers not yet forty years old whose hands had curled into claws, men so crippled up they could not tie their own shoes, could not sign their names.

"I mean to tickle my grandchildren when they come along," he told me, "and I 5
mean to build doll houses and turn spindles for tiny chairs on my lathe."

(continued)

(continued)

6   So he fondled those buckeyes as if they were charms, carrying them with him when our family moved from Ohio at the end of my childhood, bearing them to new homes in Louisiana, then Oklahoma, Ontario, and Mississippi, carrying them still on his final day when pain a thousand times fiercer than arthritis gripped his heart.

7   The box where I keep the buckeyes also comes from Ohio, made by father from a walnut plank he bought at a farm auction. I remember the auction, remember the sagging face of the widow whose home was being sold, remember my father telling her he would prize that walnut as if he had watched the tree grow from a sapling on his own land. He did not care for pewter of silver or gold, but he cherished wood. On the rare occasions when my mother coaxed him into a museum, he ignored the paintings or porcelain and studied the exhibit cases, the banisters, the moldings, the parquet floors.

8   I remember him planing that walnut board, sawing it, sanding it, joining piece to piece to make foot stools, picture frames, jewelry boxes. My own box, a bit larger than a soap dish, lined with red corduroy, was meant to hold earrings and pins, not buckeyes. The top is inlaid with pieces fitted so as to bring out the grain, four diagonal joints converging from the corners toward the center. If I stare long enough at those converging lines, they float free of the box and point to a center deeper than wood.

9   I learned to recognize buckeyes and beeches, sugar maples and shagbark hickories, wild cherries, walnuts, and dozens of other trees while tramping through the Ohio woods with my father. To his eyes, their leaves, their bark, their winter buds were as distinctive as the set of a friend's shoulders. As with friends, he was partial to some, craving their company, so he would go out of his way to visit particular trees, walking in a circle around the splayed roots of a sycamore, laying his hand against the trunk of a white oak, ruffling the feathery green boughs of a cedar.

10   "Trees breathe," he told me. "Listen."

11   I listened, and heard the stir of breath.

12   He was no botanist; the names and uses he taught me were those he had learned from country folks, not from books. Latin never crossed his lips. Only much later would I discover that the tree he called ironwood, its branches like muscular arms, good for axe handles, is known in the books as hophombeam; what he called tuliptree or canoewood, ideal for log cabins, is officially the yellow poplar; what he called hoop ash, good for barrels and fence posts, appears in books as hackberry.

13   When he introduced me to the buckeye, he broke off a chunk of the gray bark and held it to my nose. I gagged.

14   "That's why the old-timers called it stinking buckeye," he told me. "They used it for cradles and feed troughs and peg legs."

15   "Why for peg legs?" I asked.

16   "Because it's light and hard to split, so it won't shatter when you're clumping around."

He showed me this tree in late summer, when the fruits had fallen and the   17
ground was littered with prickly brown pods. He picked up one, as fat as a lemon,
and peeled away the husk to reveal the shiny seed. He laid it in my palm and closed
my fist around it so the seed peeped out from the circle formed by my index finger
and thumb. "You see where it got the name?" he asked.

I saw: what gleamed in my hand was the eye of a deer, bright with life, "It's   18
beautiful," I said.

"It's beautiful," my father agreed, "but also poisonous. Nobody eats buckeyes,   19
except maybe a fool squirrel."

I knew the gaze of deer from living in the Ravenna Arsenal, in Portage County,   20
up in the northeastern corner of Ohio. After supper we often drove the Arsenal's
gravel roads, past the munitions bunkers, past acres of rusting tanks and wrecked
bombers, into the far fields where we counted deer. One June evening, while mist
rose from the ponds, we counted three hundred and eleven, our family record. We
found the deer in herds, in bunches, in amorous pairs. We came upon lone bucks,
their antlers lifted against the sky like the bare branches of dogwood. If you were
quiet, if your hands were empty, if you moved slowly, you could leave the car and
steal to within a few paces of a grazing deer, close enough to see the delicate lips, the
twitching nostrils, the glossy fathomless eyes.

The wooden box on my desk holds these grazing deer, as it holds the buckeyes   21
and the walnut plank and the farm auction and the munitions bunkers and the
breathing forests and my father's hands. I could lose the box, I could lose the
polished seeds, but if I were to lose the memories I would become a bush
without roots, and every new breeze would toss me about. All those memories
lead back to the northeastern corner of Ohio, the place where I came to consciousness, where I learned to connect feelings with words, where I fell in love
with the earth.

It was a troubled love, for much of the land I knew as a child had been ravaged.   22
The ponds in the Arsenal teemed with bluegill and beaver, but they were also laced
with TNT from the making of bombs. Because the wolves and coyotes had long since
been killed, some of the deer, so plump in the June grass, collapsed on the January
snow, whittled by hunger to racks of bones. Outside the Arsenal's high barbed
fences, many of the farms had failed, their barns carving in, their topsoil gone.
Ravines were choked with swollen couches and junked washing machines and cars.
Crossing fields, you had to be careful not to slice your feet on tin cans or shards of
glass. Most of the rivers had been dammed, turning fertile valleys into scummy play-
grounds for boats.

One free-flowing river, the Mahoning, ran past the small farm near the Arsenal   23
where our family lived during my later years in Ohio. We owned just enough land to
pasture three ponies and to grow vegetables for our table, but those few acres
opened onto miles of woods and creeks and secret meadows. I walked that land in

(continued)

(continued)

every season, every weather, following animal trails. But then the Mahoning, too, was doomed by a government decision; we were forced to sell our land, and a dam began to rise across the river.

24   If enough people had spoken for the river, we might have saved it. If enough people had believed that our scarred country was worth defending, we might have dug in our heels and fought. Our attachments to the land were all private. We had no shared lore, no literature, no art to root us there, to give us courage, to help us stand our ground. The only maps we had were those issued by the state, showing a maze of numbered lines stretched over emptiness. The Ohio landscape never showed up on postcards or posters, never unfurled like tapestry in films, rarely filled even a paragraph in books. There were no mountains in that place, no waterfalls, no rocky gorges, no vistas. It was a country of low hills, cut over woods, scoured fields, villages that had lost their purpose, roads that had lost their way.

25   "Let us love the country of here below," Simone Weil urged. "It is real; it offers resistance to love. It is this country that God has given us to love. He has willed that it should be difficult yet possible to love it." Which is the deeper truth about buckeyes, their poison or their beauty? I hold with the beauty; or rather, I am held by the beauty, without forgetting the poison. In my corner of Ohio the gullies were choked with trash, yet cedars flickered up like green flames from cracks in stone; in the evening bombs exploded at the ammunition dump, yet from the darkness came the mating cries of owls. I was saved from despair by knowing a few men and women who cared enough about the land to clean up trash, who planted walnuts and oaks that would long outlive them, who imagined a world that would have no call for bombs.

26   How could our hearts be large enough for heaven if they are not large enough for earth? The only country I am certain of is the one here below. The only country I am certain of is the one here below. The only paradise I know is the one lit by our everyday sun, this land of difficult love, shot through with shadow. The place where we learn this love, if we learn it at all, shimmers behind every new place we inhabit.

27   A family move carried me away from Ohio thirty years ago; my schooling and marriage and job have kept me away ever since, except for visits in memory and in flesh. I returned to the site of our farm one cold November day, when the trees were skeletons and the ground shone with the yellow of fallen leaves. From a previous trip I knew that our house had been bulldozed, our yard and pasture had grown up in thickets, and the reservoir had flooded the woods. On my earlier visit I had merely gazed from the car, too numb with loss to climb out. But on this November day, I parked the car, drew on my hat and gloves, opened the door, and walked.

28   I was looking for some sign that we had lived there, some token of our affection for the place. All that I recognized, aside from the contours of the land, were two weeping willows that my father and I had planted near the road. They had been slips the length of my forearm when we set them out, and now their crowns rose higher

than the telephone poles. When I touched them last, their trunks had been smooth and supple, as thin as my wrist, and now they were furrowed and stout. I took off my gloves and laid my hands against the rough bark. Immediately I felt the wince of tears. Without knowing why, I said hello to my father, quietly at first, then louder, as if only shouts could reach him through the bark miles and years.

Surprised by sobs, I turned from the willows and stumbled away toward the drowned woods, calling to my father. I sensed that he was nearby. Even as I called, I was wary of grief's deceptions. I had never seen his body after he died. By the time I reached the place of his death, a furnace had reduced him to ashes. The need to see him, to let go of this land and time, was powerful enough to summon mirages; I knew that. But I also knew, stumbling toward the woods, that my father was here.   29

At the bottom of a slope where the creek used to run, I came to an expanse of gray stumps and withered grass. It was a bay of the reservoir from which the water had retreated, the level drawn down by engineers or drought. I stood at the edge of this desolate ground, willing it back to life, trying to recall the woods where my father had taught me the names of trees. No green shoots rose. I walked out among the stumps. The grass crackled under my boots, breath rasped in my throat, but other- wise the world was silent.   30

Then a cry broke overhead and I looked up to see a red-tailed hawk launching out from the top of an oak. I recognized the bird from its band of dark feathers across the creamy breast and the tail splayed like rosy fingers against the sun. It was a red-tailed hawk for sure; and it was also my father. Not a symbol of my father, not a reminder, not a ghost, but the man himself, right there, circling in the air above me. I knew this as clearly as I knew the sun burned in the sky. A calm poured through me. My chest quit heaving. My eyes dried.   31

Hawk and father wheeled above me, circle upon circle, wings barely moving, head still. My own head was still, looking up, knowing and being known. Time scat- tered like fog. At length, father and hawk stroked the air with those powerful wings, three beats, then vanished over a ridge.   32

The voice of my education told me then and tells me now that I did not meet my father, that I merely projected my longing onto a bird. My education I've read, no les- son reached by logic has ever convinced me as utterly or stirred me as deeply as did that red-tailed hawk. Nothing in my education prepared me to love a piece of the earth, least of all a humble, battered country like northeastern Ohio; I learned from the land itself.   33

Before leaving the drowned woods, I looked around at the ashen stumps, the wilted grass, and for the first time since moving from this place I was able to let it go. This ground was lost; the flood would reclaim it. But other ground could be saved, must be saved, in every watershed, every neighborhood. For each home ground we need new maps, living maps, stories and poems, photographs and paintings, essays and songs. We need to know where we are, so that we may dwell in our place with a full heart.   34

Inquiring into the Essay

Throughout *The Curious Writer*, I'll invite you to respond to readings such as "Buckeye," using questions based on the four methods of inquiry discussed in Chapter 2. The following questions, therefore, encourage you to explore, explain, evaluate, and reflect to discover and shape what you think about the reading. If you're using a double-entry journal, use these questions to prompt writing on the right page of your notebook. Use the opposing left page to collect passages, details, and quotations from the reading that you think might be important.

1. Sanders handles a pair of buckeyes that once belonged to his father, and this triggers stories that allow him to look into ideas about grief and love of the land. It's a powerful thing, this recognition that the same ordinary objects hold a "deeper center," a meaning we don't often recognize unless we stop to look. In your journal, brainstorm a list of objects that hold significance for you. Choose one, and spend seven full minutes fastwriting in your journal about the stories it inspires. If the writing stalls, choose another. Keep your pen moving. Finally, skip a line and finish this sentence: *What surprised me most about what I just wrote is...*

2. Personal essays often tell two stories: the story of what happened, and the story of what the writer came to understand about the meaning of what happened. Explain your understanding of that second story in "Buckeye."

3. Though we rarely link the personal narrative and the argument, personal essays often make at least implicit arguments. "Buckeye" does. For example, Sanders writes that the steady destruction of the Ohio landscape has to do with the absence of a "shared lore" or art or literature that celebrates the land in the Midwest. "The Ohio landscape never showed up on postcards or posters," writes Sanders, "never unfurled like tapestry in films, rarely filled even a paragraph in books." What does Sanders assume to be true for this claim to be believable? Do you agree?

4. While "Buckeye" is not a confessional essay, it is quite personal. Reflect on how comfortable you are writing, as Sanders did, about the details of your life.

■ PERSONAL ESSAY 2

Try this exercise: Think about things, ordinary objects, that you have held onto all these years because you simply can't throw them away. They *mean* something to you. They are reminders of another time, or a turning point in your life, or a particular moment of joy, or sadness, or perhaps fear. Consider a few of mine: a green plaster Buddha, handmade; a glow-in-the-dark crucifix; an old pair of 7 × 50 Nikon binoculars; a 1969 Martin D 28 guitar; a brown-handled flathead screwdriver with a touch of red nail polish on the handle; a homemade lamp made from a wooden wallpaper roller; a red dog's collar. While they are meaning-less to you, naturally, to me each of these objects carry a charge; they remind me of a story, a moment, a feeling. The personal essay makes space for writers to explore the meanings of such ordinary things.

Taking Things Seriously: 75 Objects with Unexpected Meanings, the book from which the following short essay was taken, is a gallery of objects—a bottle of dirt, a Velveeta Cheese box, a bear lamp, a pair of shells, and more—that are displayed along with the meditations on their significance by the writers who have carefully kept them as reminders on a shelf, in a closet, by their beside. Laura Zazulak's short essay focuses on a doll that she snatched from a neighbor's trash can. Just telling a story about what happened is not enough in an essay. The essay must have something to say to someone else. As you read Zazulak's brief piece, consider what that might be.

Every Morning for Five Years
Laura Zazulak

1   Every morning for five years, I was not so welcomingly greeted by my middle-aged, developmentally disabled neighbor across the street. Scotty never smiled and seemed to hate everyone. He never left the perimeter of his mother's lawn and apparently didn't know how to do anything but rake, shovel, take out the trash, and yell in a high pitched voice. I'd pull out of my driveway and see him there, wearing a neon orange hunting cap, raking absolutely nothing at the same spot that he'd raked the day before. I'd think to myself, "Don't make eye contact!" But I always did. He'd stare at me and neither of us would blink.

2   Near the end of my fifth year on the street, Scotty stopped coming out of his house. At first, I was thankful. But as time passed, I began to worry. Then one Saturday morning in the middle of January I noticed that his window was wide open. Later that day, a police car showed up. Maybe Scotty and his mother got into one of their screaming matches again? Then a funeral-home van pulled up and they brought out Scotty's body. Although it came as a surprise to me to discover that he knew how miserable his life was, he had killed himself.

3   The next day Scotty's uncle came over and began furiously carting things off to the dump. He left behind a garbage can in the driveway piled with all of Scotty's earthly possessions. I noticed two little pink feet sticking up into the air.

4   After dark, I crept across the street to the garbage can, armed with a travel-sized bottle of hand sanitizer. I looked left, then right. I dashed forward, tugged at the feet, and then ran as fast as I could back into my own backyard with my prize. Only then did I look at what I'd rescued. I would like you to meet Mabel.

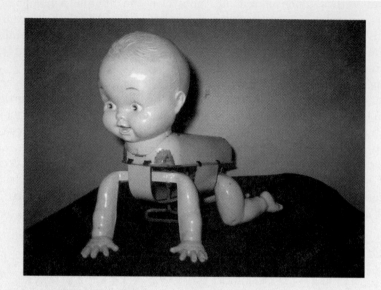

Inquiring into the Essay

Use the four methods of seeing what you've read—exploring, explaining, evaluating, and reflecting—to find out what you think about "Every Morning for Five Years."

1. All of the essays in the book *Taking Things Seriously*, from which the piece you just read was taken, have this to say: It is remarkable how much meaning we can invest in the ordinary when we take the time to notice. This is an idea you can explore. Brainstorm a list of objects that might have "unexpected significance" for you. Choose one and fastwrite about it for four minutes. Then skip a line, choose another, and write for another four minutes. If this is interesting to you, repeat this over a few days and create a collage of brief stories that four or five objects inspired. Are there any themes that seem to run through all of them? Do they speak to each other in any way?

2. Read together, explain how the photograph and the essay work together to create meanings that might not be apparent if read separately.

3. Evaluate the effectiveness of the last line, which is arguably one of the most important in any essay.

4. Okay, so you have this object that means something to you—say a bobby pin with a hand-stitched white daisy attached to it. How do you make it mean something to someone else? And, especially, what is the process you might use for figuring that out?

■ PERSONAL ESSAY 3

America is a nation of immigrants, and their stories often haunt their children. Judith Ortiz Cofer moved from Puerto Rico as a child with her family in the mid-1950s to a barrio in Paterson, New Jersey. There she became both part of and witness to a familiar narrative, that of the outsider who finds herself wedged between two worlds, two cultures, and two longings: the desire to return "home" and the desire to feel at home in the new place. While this is a story most immigrants know well, it is also a deeply personal one, shaded by particular places, prejudices, and patterns.

In "One More Lesson," Cofer describes both the places that competed for her sense of self—the Puerto Rico of her childhood, where she spent time as a child while her Navy father was away at sea, and an apartment in New Jersey where she would go when he returned.

One More Lesson

Judith Ortiz Cofer

I remember Christmas on the Island by the way it felt on my skin. The temperature dropped into the ideal seventies and even lower after midnight when some of the more devout Catholics—mostly older women—got up to go to church, *misa del gallo* they called it; mass at the hour when the rooster crowed for Christ. They would drape shawls over their heads and shoulders and move slowly toward town. The birth of Our Savior was a serious affair in our *pueblo*.   1

At Mamá's house, food was the focal point of *Navidad*. There were banana leaves brought in bunches by the boys, spread on the table, where the women would pour coconut candy steaming hot, and the leaves would wilt around the sticky lumps, adding an extra tang of flavor to the already irresistible treat. Someone had to watch the candy while it cooled, or it would begin to disappear as the children risked life and limb for a stolen piece of heaven. The banana leaves were also used to wrap the traditional food of holidays in Puerto Rico: *pasteles*, the meat pies made from grated yucca and plantain and stuffed with spiced meats.   2

Every afternoon during the week before Christmas Day, we would come home from school to find the women sitting around in the parlor with bowls on their laps, grating pieces of coconut, yuccas, plantains, cheeses—all the ingredients that would make up our Christmas Eve feast. The smells that filled Mamá's house at that time have come to mean anticipation and a sensual joy during a time in my life, the last days of my early childhood, when I could still absorb joy through my pores—*when I had not yet learned that light is followed by darkness, that all*   3

(continued)

(continued)

of creation is based on that simple concept, and maturity is a discovery of that natural law.

4   It was in those days that the Americans sent baskets of fruit to our barrio—apples, oranges, grapes flown in from the States. And at night, if you dared to walk up to the hill where the mango tree stood in the dark, you could see a wonderful sight: a Christmas tree, a real pine, decorated with lights of many colors. It was the blurry outline of this tree you saw, for it was inside a screened-in-porch, but we had heard a thorough description of it from the boy who delivered the fruit, a nephew of Mamá's, as it had turned out. Only, I was not impressed, since just the previous year we had put up a tree ourselves in our apartment in Paterson.

5   Packages arrived for us in the mail from our father. I got dolls dressed in the national costumes of Spain, Italy, and Greece (at first we could not decide which of the Greek dolls was the male, since they both wore skirts); my brother got picture books; and my mother, jewelry that she would not wear, because it was too much like showing off and might attract the Evil Eye.

6   Evil Eye or not, the three of us were the envy of the pueblo. Everything about us set us apart, and I put away my dolls quickly when I discovered that my playmates would not be getting any gifts until *Los Reyes*—the Day of the Three Kings, when Christ received His gifts—and that even then it was more likely that the gifts they found under their beds would be practical things like clothes. Still, it was fun to find fresh grass for the camels the night the Kings were expected, tie it in bundles with string, and put it under our beds along with a bowl of fresh water.

7   The year went by fast after Christmas, and in the spring we received a telegram from Father. His ship had arrived in Brooklyn Yard. He gave us a date for our trip back to the States. I remember Mother's frantic packing, and the trips to Mayagüez for new clothes; the inspections of my brother's and my bodies for cuts, scrapes, mosquito bites, and other "damage" she would have to explain to Father. And I remember begging Mamá to tell me stories in the afternoons, although it was not summer yet and the trips to the mango tree had not begun. In looking back I realize that Mamá's stories were what I packed—my winter store.

8   Father had succeeded in finding an apartment outside Paterson's "vertical barrio," the tenement Puerto Ricans called *El Building*. He had talked a Jewish candy store owner into renting us the apartment above his establishment, which he and his wife had just vacated after buying a house in West Paterson, an affluent suburb. Mr. Schultz was a nice man whose melancholy face I was familiar with from trips I had made often with my father to his store for cigarettes. Apparently, my father had convinced him and his brother, a look-alike of Mr. Schultz who helped in the store, that we were not the usual Puerto Rican family. My father's fair skin, his ultra-correct English, and his Navy uniform were a good argument. Later it occurred to me that my father had been displaying me as a model child when he took me to that store with him. I was always dressed as if for church and held firmly by the hand. I imagine he did the same with my brother. As for my mother,

her Latin beauty, her thick black hair that hung to her waist, her voluptuous body which even the winter clothes could not disguise, would have been nothing but a hindrance to my father's plans. But everyone knew that a Puerto Rican woman is her husband's satellite; she reflects both his light and his dark sides. If my father was respectable, then his family would be respectable. We got the apartment on Park Avenue.

Unlike El Building, where we had lived on our first trip to Paterson, our new home was truly in exile. There were Puerto Ricans by the hundreds only one block away, but we heard no Spanish, no loud music, no mothers yelling at children, nor the familiar *¡Ay Bendito!*, that catch-all phrase of our people. Mother lapsed into silence herself, suffering from *La Tristeza*, the sadness that only place induces and only place cures. But Father relished silence, and we were taught that silence was something to be cultivated and practiced.   9

Since our apartment was situated directly above where the Schultzes worked all day, our father instructed us to remove our shoes at the door and walk in our socks. We were going to prove how respectable we were by being the opposite of what our ethnic group was known to be—we would be quiet and inconspicuous.   10

I was escorted each day to school by my nervous mother. It was a long walk in the cooling air of fall in Paterson and we had to pass by El Building where the children poured out of the front door of the dilapidated tenement still answering their mothers in a mixture of Spanish and English: "Sí, Mami, I'll come straight home from school." At the corner we were halted by the crossing guard, a strict woman who only gestured her instructions, never spoke directly to the children, and only ordered us to "halt" or "cross" while holding her white-gloved hand up at face level or swinging her arm sharply across her chest if the light was green.   11

The school building was not a welcoming sight for someone used to the bright colors and airiness of tropical architecture. The building looked functional. It could have been a prison, an asylum, or just what it was: an urban school for the children of immigrants, built to withstand waves of change, generation by generation. Its red brick sides rose to four solid stories. The black steel fire escapes snaked up its back like an exposed vertebra. A chain-link fence surrounded its concrete playground. Members of the elite safety patrol, older kids, sixth graders mainly, stood at each of its entrances, wearing their fluorescent white belts that criss-crossed their chests and their metal badges. No one was allowed in the building until the bell rang, not even on rainy or bitter-cold days. Only the safety-patrol stayed warm.   12

My mother stood in front of the main entrance with me and a growing crowd of noisy children. She looked like one of us, being no taller than the sixth-grade girls. She held my hand so tightly that my fingers cramped. When the bell rang, she walked me into the building and kissed my cheek. Apparently my father had done all the paperwork for my enrollment, because the next thing I remember was being led to my third-grade classroom by a black girl who had emerged from the principal's office.   13

Though I had learned some English at home during my first years in Paterson, I had let it recede deep into my memory while learning Spanish in Puerto Rico. Once again I   14

(continued)

(continued)

was the child in the cloud of silence, the one who had to be spoken to in sign language as if she were a deaf-mute. Some of the children even raised their voices when they spoke to me, as if I had trouble hearing. Since it was a large troublesome class composed mainly of black and Puerto Rican children, with a few working-class Italian children interspersed, the teacher paid little attention to me. I re-learned the language quickly by the immersion method. I remember one day, soon after I joined the rowdy class when our regular teacher was absent and Mrs. D., the sixth-grade teacher from across the hall, attempted to monitor both classes. She scribbled something on the chalkboard and went to her own room. I felt a pressing need to use the bathroom and asked Julio, the Puerto Rican boy who sat behind me, what I had to do to be excused. He said that Mrs. D. had written on the board that we could be excused by simply writing our names under the sign. I got up from my desk and started for the front of the room when I was struck on the head hard with a book. Startled and hurt, I turned around expecting to find one of the bad boys in my class, but it was Mrs. D. I faced. I remember her angry face, her fingers on my arms pulling me back to my desk, and her voice saying incomprehensible things to me in a hissing tone. Someone finally explained to her that I was new, that I did not speak English. I also remember how suddenly her face changed from anger to anxiety. But I did not forgive her for hitting me with that hard-cover spelling book. Yes, I would recognize that book even now. It was not until years later that I stopped hating that teacher for not understanding that I had been betrayed by a classmate, and by my inability to read her warning on the board. *I instinctively understood then that language is the only weapon a child has against the absolute power of adults.*

15   I quickly built up my arsenal of words by becoming an insatiable reader of books.

Inquiring into the Essay

Explore, explain, evaluate, and reflect on Cofer's "One More Lesson."

1. In the 1950s and 1960s, many saw America as a "melting pot." The idea then was that although we may have many different immigrant backgrounds, we should strive toward some common "Americanism." For some, this is still a powerful idea, but for others the melting pot is a metaphor for cultural hegemony or even racial prejudice, a demand that differences be ignored and erased rather than celebrated. In your journal, write about your own feelings on this controversy. Tell the story of a friend, a relative, a neighbor who was an outsider. Tell about your own experience. What did it mean to assimilate, and at what cost?

2. Personal essays, like short fiction, rely heavily on narrative. But unlike fiction, essays both *show* and *tell*; that is, they use story to reveal meaning (*show*) and they also explain that meaning to the reader (*tell*). Identify

several places in the essay where Cofer "tells." What do you notice about the placement of these moments of reflection?

3. Does this essay make an evaluation, and, if so, what is it asserting about cultural assimilation in America during the 1950s and 1960s? Is Cofer's evaluation still relevant?

4. One of the most common reasons students cite for liking a story is that "they could relate to it." Does that criterion apply here? Reflect on whether it's a standard you often use as a reader to judge the value of something. What exactly does it mean to "relate to" a text?

SEEING THE FORM

Nautilus Shell

We think of most forms of writing as linear—beginning to end, thesis to supporting evidence, claims to reasons—in a steady march to a conclusion. And yes, much writing is like that. The essay is not. Or at least that's true of the essay inspired by the first essayist Montaigne, a sixteenth-century French nobleman who coined the term "essai," which in its verb form means to attempt, to try. A better analogy for the essay is the spiral rather than the line. It is the uncoiling of thought. The essay begins, much like a nautilus shell, when writers make tight spirals around a particular moment, object, observation, or fact that

(continued)

Seeing the Form (*continued*)

makes them wonder. The personal essay is an inductive form, working from the small things to larger ideas about them, with larger turns of thought. The work challenges writers to move outward from small, private chambers of experience to finally emerge into the more open spaces that others can share, meanings that others can understand even though they don't share exactly the same experience.

WRITING IN THE DISCIPLINES

The Personal Academic Essay

"You can't use 'I' in an academic essay," one of my students insisted. "It's just not done."

This is always the beginning of a great discussion about academic conventions, objectivity, and personal writing. Many of us accept, without question, the "rules" that we've learned about writing, especially school writing. Here are the things my fifteen-year-old daughter reports that she "can't do" in an essay:

1. Use first person.

2. Put a thesis anywhere but the first paragraph.

3. Write a paragraph without a topic sentence.

Anything that violates these rules is something called "creative" writing. Where do these ideas come from? The injunction against using "I" in academic writing, probably the most common assumption, isn't without support. After all, a great deal of academic writing avoids any reference to the author, or if it must, uses the more neutral pronoun "one." The question that is rarely asked is, Why is this so?

One reason is that scholars believe that "objectivity"—or at least the appearance of objectivity—gives their research more authority. In addition, in some disciplines, especially the sciences, the attention needs to be on the data and not the author. For these reasons, among others, avoiding first person in academic writing became a tacit tradition.

And yet, there are a surprising number of academic articles published in the first person, and not just in the humanities where you might expect authors to be more likely to acknowledge bias. While "autobiographical criticism" has been around for some time in literature, there is personal scholarship in many disciplines, including business, anthropology, education, nursing, and even geology. This first-person writing often tells a story, sometimes through a case study, a narrative of the writer's experiences, or an account of his or her intellectual journey.

WRITING IN YOUR LIFE

Essaying "This I Believe"

The essay genre, which has been around for about 500 years, is a vibrant and increasingly common form of writing on the radio and online audio. Why? One reason might be that the intimacy of the essay—the sense of a writer speaking directly to a reader without the masks we often wear when we write—seems particularly powerful when we *hear* the voice of writing embodied in speech. Certainly, the ease with which we can "publish" essays as podcasts accounts for the explosion of online essayists.

"This I Believe," a program on National Public Radio, is typical of the radio programs (which are then subsequently published as podcasts) that actively seek student writing. The program began in the 1950s by famed journalist Edward R. Murrow, who invited radio listeners and public figures to submit very brief (350–500 word) essays that stated some core belief that guides the writers' "daily lives." The program, which was revived several years ago, is enormously popular on NPR and features work from people from all walks of life, including college students who may have written a "This I Believe" essay in their writing courses.

The program's Web site offers this advice to essayists:

1. Find a way to succinctly and clearly state your belief.

2. If possible, anchor it to stories.

3. Write in your own voice.

4. "Be positive," and avoid lecturing the listener.

THE WRITING PROCESS

> ## INQUIRY PROJECT: WRITING A PERSONAL ESSAY
>
> Write a 1,000-word personal essay that explores some aspect of your experience. Your instructor may provide additional details. Choose your topic carefully. Because of the essay's exploratory methods, the best topics are those that you want to write about *not* because you know what you think, but because you want to *discover* what you think. The essay should have the following qualities:
>
> - It must do more than tell a story; there must be a *purpose* behind telling the story that speaks in some way to someone else.
> - It should, ultimately, answer the *So what?* question.
> - Your essay should include some reflection to explain or speculate about what you understand *now* about something that you didn't understand *then*.
> - It should be richly detailed. Seize opportunities to *show* what you mean, rather than simply explain it.

Thinking About Subjects

When you are assigned a personal essay, it's essential to embrace uncertainty and be willing to suspend judgment. This is risky. Obviously, one of the risks when you start out with uncertainty is that you also might end up that way; your draft may just seem to go nowhere. The key to writing strong personal essays is accepting that first drafts might be real stinkers. But there's a payoff to this risk—the personal essay frequently yields surprise and discovery.

Generating Ideas

Begin exploring possible subjects by generating material in your notebook. This should be an open-ended process, a chance to use your creative side, not worrying too much about making sense or trying to prejudge the value of the writing or the subjects you generate. In a sense, this is an invitation to play around.

ONE STUDENT'S RESPONSE

Margaret's Journal: Listing Questions

Is my cat extremely unusual or can any cat be taught to walk and be as needy and attached as her?

Does testosterone really make one more confident? Is there a correlation between high T and aggressiveness?

How did I once find Dr. Laura so compelling?

Why are women seldom loyal to each other? How are female friendships different from male ones? Can women and men be friends without an underlying sexual tension?

Listing Prompts. Lists can be rich sources of triggering topics. Let them grow freely, and when you're ready, use an item as the focus of another list or an episode of fastwriting. The following prompts should get you started.

1. Make a fast list of experiences you've had that you can't forget. Reach into all parts and times of your life.

2. Make a list of questions that have always nagged you about some of the following: school, men or women, fast food, hair, television, public restrooms, shoes, and sports.

Fastwriting Prompts. In the early stages of generating possible topics for an essay, fastwriting can be invaluable, *if* you allow yourself to write "badly." Once you've tentatively settled on something, use a more focused fastwrite, trying to generate information and ideas within the loose boundaries of your chosen topic.

1. Choose an item from any one of the preceding lists as a prompt. Just start fastwriting about the item; perhaps start with a story, a scene, a situation, a description. Follow the writing to see where it leads.

2. Most of us quietly harbor dreams—we hope to be a professional dancer, a good father, an activist, an Olympic luger, or a novelist. Begin a fastwrite in which you explore your dreams. When the writing stalls, ask yourself questions: *Where did this dream come from? Do I still believe in it? In what moments did it seem within reach? In what moments did it fade?* Plunge into those moments.

3. What was the most confusing time in your life? Choose a moment or scene that stands out in your memory from that time, and, writing in the present tense, describe what you see, hear, and do. After five

minutes, skip a line and choose another moment. Then another. Make a collage.

4. What do you consider "turning points" in your life, times when you could see the end of one thing and the beginning of something else? Fastwrite about one of these for seven minutes.

Visual Prompts. Sometimes the best way to generate material is to see what we think in something other than sentences. Boxes, lines, arrows, charts, and even sketches can help us see more of the landscape of a subject, especially connections between fragments of information that aren't as obvious in prose. The clustering or mapping method is useful to many writers early in the writing process as they try to discover a topic. (See the "Inquiring into the Details" box on page 101 for more details on how to create a cluster.) Figure 3.1 shows my cluster from the first prompt listed here.

1. What objects would you most regret losing in a house fire? Choose a most-treasured object as the core for a cluster. Build a web of associations from

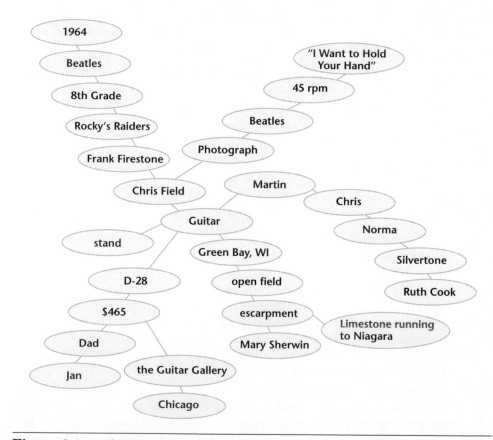

Figure 3.1   A cluster built around the one object I would most regret losing in a house fire: my Martin guitar

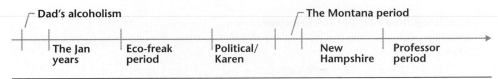

Figure 3.2   A sample timeline from my own life

it, returning to the detail in the core whenever a strand dies out. One of the wonderful complexities of being human is that we are sometimes deeply conflicted (I'm not suggesting this is always fun). Pair two opposed attributes that you consider typical of yourself. For example, *ambivalence/commitment, fear/risk taking, lonely/sociable, beautiful/ugly, composed/flaky,* and so on. Use these paired words as a core for a cluster.

2. Draw a long line on a piece of paper in your journal. This is your life. Divide the line into segments that seem to describe what feels like distinct times in your life. These may not necessarily correspond to familiar age categories like adolescence or childhood. More likely, the periods in your life will be associated with a place, a relationship, a dilemma, a job, a personal challenge, and so on, but because this is a timeline, these periods will be chronological. Examine your timeline and, as a fastwrite prompt, put two of these periods in your life together. Explore what they had in common, particularly how the earlier period might have shaped the later one. See Figure 3.2 for a sample timeline.

Research Prompts. Things we hear, see, or read can be powerful prompts for personal essays. It's tempting to believe that personal essays are always about the past, but just as often essayists are firmly rooted in the present, commenting and pondering on the confusions of contemporary life. In that sense, personal

INQUIRING INTO THE DETAILS

Clustering or Mapping

One of the virtues of clustering as a method of generating information is that it defies the more linear nature of writing, putting one sentence after another in a chain of thought. When you make a cluster, there are multiple chains, each growing from a core word, phrase, or idea. In Figure 3.1, I clustered the word *guitar*. I'm not just thinking of any guitar, of course, but my 1969 Martin D-28 with

(continued)

Inquiring into the Details (*continued*)

Brazilian rosewood and the ding on the front. This is the one object I'd rescue from a fire.

Clusters are in code; each item in the web says more than it says, at least to me, because I'm familiar with its meaning. You don't have that kind of knowledge, obviously, so my cluster wouldn't say much to you. Each strand suggests a story, an idea, or a feeling that I might explore.

Typically, clustering is most useful at the beginning of the writing process as you test a possible subject and want to see its landscape of possibilities. I can see, for example, possible essays about not only the significance of this guitar, but essays on the eighth grade, my old friend Chris Field, and the natural history of limestone. The best clusters are richly suggestive that way, but they're only starting places for more writing. How do you cluster?

1. Begin with a blank page in your journal. Choose a core word, phrase, name, idea, detail, or question; write it in the middle of the page and circle it.

2. Relax and focus on the core word or phrase, and when you feel moved to do so, build a strand of associations from the core, circling and connecting each item. Write other details, names, dates, place names, phrases, and so on—whatever comes to mind.

3. When a strand dies out, return to the core and begin another. Keep clustering until the page looks like a web of associations. Doodle, darkening lines and circles, if that helps you relax and focus.

4. When you feel the urge to write, stop clustering and use one of the strands as a prompt for journal work.

---

essayists are researchers, always on the lookout for material. Train your eye with one or more of the following prompts.

1. Return to the list of questions you made in the "Listing Prompts" section. Choose one nagging question about any of the subjects you were asked to consider and set aside time to explore it by carefully *observing* them. Write down exactly what you see…and what you think about it. (The double-entry notebook method is particularly useful for this.)

2. Newspaper "filler"—short stories, often about odd or unusual things—can be a wonderful source of inspiration for personal essays. Read your local paper for a few days, clipping these brief articles. Paste them in your journal and use them as prompts for fastwriting.

3. Although the Internet offers infinite opportunities for procrastination, with some focus it can also be a great source for jump-starting ideas. What happened to your best friend from kindergarten? Type her name into the Google search engine and find out. Think about your favorite vacation—a search for "Grand Canyon" might help jog your memory.

Judging What You Have

Generating may produce messy, incoherent writing that would earn you bad grades in most classes. If this material is going to go anywhere, it must be judged, shaped, and evaluated; the writer must emerge from particulars of his/her experience and find a vantage point to see what, if anything, those particulars add up to.

The initial challenge in producing a first draft is clarifying your topic: What are you really writing about? Suspend judgment for a bit and work through the following questions as you scrutinize the material you've collected so far in your journal.

What's Promising Material and What Isn't?   A good topic for a personal essay need not be dramatic or profound; in fact, some of the most compelling essays are about quite ordinary things. But as you examine your journal writing so far, consider the following:

- **Abundance.** What subject generated the most writing? Do you sense that there is much more to write about?
- **Surprise.** What material did you find most confusing in interesting ways?
- **Confusion.** What subject raises questions you're not sure you can answer easily?
- **Honesty.** What subjects are you willing to write honestly about?

Questions About Purpose and Audience.   Obviously, why you're writing and for whom will profoundly influence your approach. That's a fundamental principle of rhetoric, one that you applied when you jotted that note to your teacher explaining the late assignment or texted your friend about your new bicycle. With many types of writing, it's wise to consider your purpose and audience very early on—like, say, for an essay exam or an e-mail requesting information about a job. Sometimes, however, thinking too soon about purpose and audience will squeeze off your writing.

To begin with, then, embrace the open-ended process of "trying out" possible subjects. Initially, don't rule out anything because you think other people might find the topic boring. For now, you're the most important audience, and what you want to know from your writing is this:

- What topics raise questions about your experiences that you find puzzling or intriguing?
- What did you say that you didn't expect to say?

Choose a topic for your essay not because you know what you think but because you want to find out what you think.

Questions for Reflection.   After you've generated enough material on your topic, seize opportunities to reflect. Remember that this move to reflect is an essential part of the dialectical thinking that helps writers make sense of things, going back and forth between *what happened* and *what happens*, between *showing* and *telling*, and *observations of* and *ideas about*. If you need help finding reflective distance, questions are the best way to do it. Use one or more of the following questions as prompts for thinking or writing in your journal.

- What do you understand now about this topic that you didn't fully understand when you began writing about it?
- What has surprised you most? Why?
- What seems to be the most important thing you're trying to say so far?
- Focus on how your thinking has changed about your topic. Finish this seed sentence as many times as you can in your notebook: Once I thought _____, and now I think _____.
- Quickly write a narrative of thought about your topic: When I began writing about my father's alcoholism, I thought I felt relieved when he died. Then I decided that when he died some part of me died with him, and then I realized that the real truth is...
- Finish this sentence in your journal: As I look back on this, I realize that...Follow that sentence with another, and another, until you feel there's nothing more to say.

Writing the Sketch

It's hard to say when it's time to begin composing the draft, particularly with open-ended forms such as the personal essay. But bear in mind that working from abundance is particularly important when you're using writing to discover, the essayist's main motive.

Before you write a full draft, you'll compose a *sketch* or two of what seems to be the most promising material. A sketch is a brief treatment—probably no more than 300 words—that is composed with a sense of audience but not necessarily a clear sense of a thesis, theme, or controlling idea (see Chapter 1). Later, you'll revise a sketch into a draft personal essay.

Your instructor may ask you to write several sketches using the most promising material you've developed from the prompts. *The following guidelines apply to all sketches.*

- *The sketch should have a tentative title.* This is crucial because a title can hint at a possible focus for the revision.
- *The sketch should be approximately 300 to 500 words.* The sketch is a brief look at a topic that may later be developed into a longer essay.
- *The sketch should be a relatively fast draft.* Avoid the temptation to spend a lot of time crafting your sketch. Fast drafts are easier to revise.

- *The sketch may not have a clear purpose or theme.* That's what you hope to discover by writing the sketch.

- *The sketch should have a sense of audience.* You're writing your sketch to be read by someone other than you. That means you need to explain what may not be apparent to someone who doesn't know you or hasn't had your experiences.

- *The sketch should be richly detailed.* Personal essays, especially, rely on detail to help the writer and, later, the reader see the possible meanings of events or observations. Essayists are inductive, working from particulars to ideas. In early drafts especially, it's important to get down the details by drawing on all your senses: What exactly was the color of the wallpaper? How exactly did the beach smell at low tide? How exactly did the old man's hand feel in yours? What exactly did the immigration officer say?

■ STUDENT SKETCH

Amanda Stewart's sketch, "Earning a Sense of Place," faintly bears the outlines of what might be a great personal essay. When they succeed, sketches are suggestive; it is what they're not quite saying that yields promise. On the surface, "Earning a Sense of Place" is simply a piece about Amanda Stewart's passion for skiing. So what? And yet, there are lines here that point to larger ideas and unanswered questions. For example, Amanda writes that the "mental reel" of her swishing down a mountain on skis is "the image that sustains me when things are hard, and when I want to stop doing what is right and start doing what is easy." Why is it that such a mental image can be sustaining in hard times? How well does this work? The end of the sketch is even more suggestive. This really might be a piece about trying to find a "sense of place" that doesn't rely on such images; in a sense, the sketch seems to be trying to say that joy on the mountain isn't enough.

The pleasure of writing and reading a sketch is looking for what it might teach you, learning what you didn't know you knew.

Earning a Sense of Place
Amanda Stewart

The strings to my earflaps stream behind me, mixing with my hair as a rooster-tail flowing behind my neck. Little ice crystals cling to the bottom of my braid and sparkle in the sunlight. The pompom on top of my hat bobs up and down as I arc out, turning cleanly across the snow. I suck in the air, biting with cold as it hits my hot lungs, and breathe deep as I push down the run.

1

(continued)

(continued)

2   This is what I see when I picture who I want to be. It's the image that sustains me when things are hard, and when I want to stop doing what is right and start doing what is easy. I have made so many terrible decisions in the past that I know how far astray they lead me; I don't want that. I want the girl in the mental reel in her quilted magenta jacket and huge smile. She's what I grasp at when I need help getting through the day.

3   She's an amalgam of moments from the past mixed with my hopes for the future. I love to ski, and have since my parents strapped little plastic skis onto my galoshes when I was a year and a half old. From that day I flopped around our snow-covered yard, I've been in love with skiing. It's the only time I feel truly comfortable. Day to day I often feel so awkward. I wonder if my hair is right, or if my clothes fit. Last night, my roommate had a boy over, and as he sat on the couch talking to me, all I felt was discomfort and awkwardness. I didn't know what to say, felt judged, felt out of place. I never feel that way on skis. Even floundering in heavy, deep snow, or after a fall that has packed my goggles with snow and ripped the mittens off my hands I know exactly what to do. I'm a snow mermaid, only comfortable in my medium. I often wish I could trade in my walking legs for something like a tail that is more truly me.

4   My dad's coffee cup at home says, "I only work so I can ski," and for him, it's true. Sometimes I feel like I only push through my daily life so I can get to the next mountain and zip up my pants and go. I don't want to live like that though: it's too much time looking forward to something, and not enough looking at what I'm living in. I need to appreciate my life as it is, snowy cold or sunny warm. That sense of place I have on skis can probably be earned here on the flat expanses of campus just as easily as I got it pushing myself down the bunny slopes so long ago. I just have to earn it.

Moving from Sketch to Draft

A sketch is often sketchy. It's generally underdeveloped, sometimes giving the writer just the barest outline of his or her subject. But as an early draft, a sketch can be invaluable. A sketch might suggest a focus for the next draft, or simply a better lead. Learning to read your sketches for such clues takes practice.

Evaluating Your Own Sketch. Initially, you're the most important reader of your own sketches. It's likely that you're in the best position to sense the material's promise because you understand the context from which it sprang better than any reader can. What are the clues you should look for in a sketch?

1. What surprised you? Might this discovery be the focus of the draft? Chances are, if it surprised you, it will surprise your readers.

2. What is the most important line in the sketch? What makes it important? Might this line be a beginning for more fastwriting? Might it be the theme or controlling idea of the draft?

3. What scene, moment, or situation is key to the story you're telling? Could this be the lead in the draft?

4. What's your favorite part of the sketch? What would happen if you cut it?

Questions for Peer Review. If you'll be sharing your sketch with one or more of your classmates, you'll likely need the most help with clarifying your purpose and focus for a draft. Here are some useful questions that might guide peer responses to your personal essay sketches.

■ What does the writer seem to want to say but doesn't quite say in the sketch?

■ What line appears most important to the meaning of the sketch, as you understand it?

■ What was most surprising about what the writer said or showed?

■ What part of the story seems most important? What part might need to be told and isn't?

Reflecting on What You've Learned. Before you begin working on the draft of your personal essay, take a few minutes in your journal to think about your thinking. Finish the following sentence, and follow it in a fastwrite for at least five minutes. The thing that struck me most about writing and sharing my sketch on _____ was.... When you finish, quickly complete the following sentences:

1. The *real* story I seem to be trying to tell is _____.

2. So what? I'd answer that question by saying _____.

3. The main thing I'm planning to do in the draft is _____.

Research and Other Strategies: Gathering More Information

METHODS FOR PEER REVIEW OF SKETCHES

1. Choose a partner, exchange sketches, read, and comment both in writing and through conversation.

2. Create a pile of sketches in the middle of the classroom. Everyone takes one (not his or her own, obviously), provides written comments, returns it to the pile, and takes another. Repeat this until everyone has read and commented on at least four sketches.

3. Share sketches online on the class Web site.

If everything has gone well so far, then your sketch has already given you a sense of direction and some ideas about how to develop your topic. But remember the importance of that dialectical movement between sea and mountain, or collecting and composing. Now that you have a topic and a tentative sense of purpose for your personal essay, journal work can be even more valuable because it can be *more focused*. Before you begin composing the draft—or during that process—consider using the following prompts to generate more information in your notebook:

- *Explode a moment.* Choose a scene or moment in the story or stories you're telling that seems particularly important to the meaning of the essay. Re-enter that moment and fastwrite for a full seven minutes, using all your senses and as much detail as you can muster.

- *Make lists.* Brainstorm a list of details, facts, or specifics about a moment, scene, or observation. List other experiences that seem connected to this one (see the *"Cluster"* point below).

- *Research.* Do some quick-and-dirty research that might bring in other voices or more information that will deepen your consideration of the topic.

- *Cluster.* In your journal, try to move beyond narrating a single experience and discover other experiences, moments, or scenes that might help you see important patterns. Use the preceding list of related experiences or observations and fastwrite about those, or develop a cluster that uses a key word, phrase, or theme as its core, and build a web of associations. For example, let's say your sketch is about your experience working with the poor in Chile. Have you had other encounters with extreme wealth or extreme poverty? Can you describe them? What do they reveal about your feelings or attitudes about poverty or your reactions to what happened in Chile? See Figure 3.3.

Composing the Draft

Some of my students get annoyed at all the "stuff" I encourage them to do before they begin a first draft of a personal essay. In some cases, all the journal work isn't necessary; the writer very quickly gets a strong sense of direction and feels

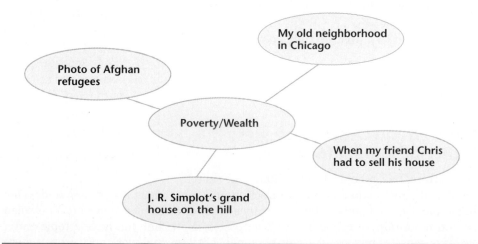

Figure 3.3   The start of a cluster built around poverty/wealth

ready to begin composing. But from the beginning I've encouraged you to gravitate toward topics that you find confusing, and with that kind of material exploratory writing is time well spent. Remember, too, that journal writing counts as writing. It not only offers the pleasures of surprise, but it can ultimately make the drafting process more efficient by generating material that you won't have to conjure up during those long, painful periods of staring at the computer screen wondering what to say next. This front-end work may also help abbreviate the end of the writing process—essentially, all this work in your journal and sketches is revision (see Chapter 13 for more on prewriting as a method of revision).

As you begin drafting, keep in mind what you've learned from your writing so far. For example:

- What is the question(s) behind your exploration of this topic?
- What do you understand now that you didn't understand fully when you started writing about it?
- How can you show *and* explain how you came to this understanding?
- Have you already written a strong first line for the draft? Can you find it somewhere in all your journal writing?

INQUIRING INTO THE DETAILS

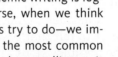

More Than One Way to Tell a Story

This is my daughter Julia telling a story:
"And she was like…"
"And then I was like…"
"And then she was like…"

Generally there are two structures for organizing information: reason and experience. Sometimes writing will combine both, but much academic writing is logically organized rather than experientially organized. Of course, when we think about organizing experiences—something that personal essays try to do—we immediately think of narrative, and then, naturally, we consider the most common narrative structure of all: chronology. This is Julia's method of oral storytelling, as it is for most of us.

Yet in essay writing, strict chronology—this happened and then this and then this—may not be the best way to tell a story. Once locked into a strictly chronological narrative, you may feel compelled to tell the *whole* story. It's a misconception that because it "happened that way" you have to tell the whole story in a personal essay. What you need to do is to tell those *parts* of the story (or stories) that are relevant to the question you're exploring or the thing you're trying to say.

(continued)

Inquiring into the Details (*continued*)

While chronological storytelling might be a good way to remember what happened as you explore your experiences in your journal or in early drafts, it isn't the only choice for structuring your essay. Structure in the personal essay, as in all writing, must be a servant to purpose. Simply put, purpose is how you might answer a potential reader who wants to know this: *So what? Why should I read this?*

Organize a narrative essay with the *So what?* question in mind. That means, first and foremost, that you start a narrative essay in that part of the story that illuminates the dilemma you're trying to solve, the question you're exploring, or the idea you're trying to understand. Typically, the beginning of the story ("The alarm clock went off at 6 AM, and I was groggy from sleep") isn't the best place to emphasize your dilemma, question, or idea. Sometimes, the middle or even the end is better for that.

Notice, for example, that Scott Sanders's essay "Buckeye" (see page 83) begins in the present, not the past, and in doing so he not only sidesteps the problem of telling his story from beginning to end, but he begins the essay reflectively. The most important part of organizing a personal narrative is not how you tell what happened. It is what you *now* think about the significance of what happened. It is this shift from past to present, from what you remember and what you understand about it now that you didn't then, that is the most important structure of all.

Methods of Development. How might you use some of the typical forms of development to develop your subject?

Narrative. The backbone of the personal essay is often, but not always, narrative. Remember, however, that narrative can work in an essay in at least three ways: (1) you tell an extended story of what happened, (2) you tell one or more anecdotes or brief stories, or (3) you tell the story of your thinking as you've come to understand something you didn't understand before. Often a single essay uses all three types of narrative.

Consider beginning your draft with an anecdote or the part of the story you want to tell that best establishes your purpose in the essay (see "Inquiring into the Details: More Than One Way to Tell a Story"). If you're writing about the needless destruction of a childhood haunt by developers, then consider opening with the way the place looked *after* the bulldozers were done with it.

A personal essay can stitch together not just one narrative but several stories, all of which are connected by the essay's theme or question. Time in writing is nothing like real time. You can write pages about something that happened in seven minutes or cover twenty years in a paragraph. You can ignore chronology, if it serves your purpose, too. The key is to tell your story or stories in ways that emphasize what's important. Ask yourself, *What does the reader most need to know to understand my thinking and feelings about this topic? What should I show about what happened that gives the reader a clear sense of what happened?*

Using Evidence. How do you make your essay convincing, and even moving, to an audience? It's in the details. This form thrives, like most literary genres, on particularity: What exactly did it look like? What exactly did she say? What exactly did it sound and smell like at that moment? Evidence that gives a personal essay authority are details that make a reader believe the writer can be trusted to observe keenly and to remember accurately. All of the professional essays in this chapter are rich in detail. There are the buckeyes, "as fat as a lemon," in Scott Russell Sanders' essay, and Laura Zazulak's neighbor with the "neon orange hunting cap" who rakes the same spot every day, and wilting banana leaves that curl around the coconut candy in Judith Ortiz Cofer's "One More Lesson." This focus on the particular—what it *exactly* looked like, smelled like, felt like, sounded like—makes an essay come alive for both writer and reader.

As you draft your essay, remember the subtle power of details. Tell, but always show, too.

Workshopping the Draft

If your draft is subject to peer review (see Chapter 14 for details on how to organize workshop groups), think carefully about the kind of responses you need from readers at this point in the process. In general, you should encourage comments that make you want to write again.

Reflecting on the Draft. To prepare for the workshop, make an entry in your journal that explores your feelings about the draft:

- What do you think worked?
- What do you think needs work?

Following the workshop session, do a follow-up entry in your notebook that summarizes what you heard, what made sense and what didn't, and how you plan to approach the next draft. Your instructor may ask you to share this information in a cover letter submitted with the revision.

Questions for Readers. A writer can structure responses to a draft in many ways. Some of them are discussed in detail in Chapter 14, "The Writer's Workshop." The key is to find a way to get what you need *at this stage in the writing process* that will be most helpful as you revise.

There are a few questions, however, that you might pose to your group that are particularly relevant to the personal essay:

1. Is there a story I'm telling that I need to develop more? Is there a story I'm not telling that I should?

2. What do you think is the *real* story? In other words, what idea or theme lurks beneath the accounts of my experiences and observations?

3. What seems the most important detail, the one that seems to say more than it says, that *reveals* some important feeling, attitude, or idea? What detail seems less important, less revealing?

4. Do my reflective observations seem obvious or overly abstract and general? If so, what questions do you have about what I say that might direct back into the essay's details, where I'm more likely to have better insights?

5. Do I explain things that are unnecessary to explain, that are better told through *showing* rather than *telling*?

Revising the Draft

Revision is a continual process—not a last step. You've been revising—literally "re-seeing" your subject—from the first messy fastwriting in your journal. But the things that get your attention during revision vary depending on where you are in the writing process. You've generated material, chosen a topic, done some research, and written both a sketch and a draft. Most students think that the only thing left to do is "fix things." Check for misspellings. Correct an awkward sentence or two. Come up with a better title. This is editing, not revision, and while editing is important, to focus solely on smaller "fixes" after writing a first draft squanders an opportunity to really *learn* from what the draft is telling you, or perhaps not quite telling you.

Chapter 13 can help guide these discoveries. The questions you can ask a draft fall into five categories: purpose, idea, information, development, and editing. Use the following chart to find the revision strategies in Chapter 13 that might help you re-see what you've written so far.

GUIDE TO REVISION STRATEGIES	
Problems in the Draft (Chapter 13)	**Page Number**
Unclear purpose ■ Not sure what the essay is about? Fails to answer the *So what?* question?	551
Unclear thesis, theme, or main idea ■ Not sure what you're trying to say?	557
Lack of information or development ■ Needs more details; more showing and less telling?	564
Disorganized ■ Doesn't move logically or smoothly from paragraph to paragraph?	568
Unclear or awkward at the level of sentences and paragraphs ■ Seems choppy or hard to follow at the level of sentences or paragraphs?	577

Personal essay drafts typically have some of the following problems:

- They don't answer the *So what?* question. Are you telling a story but don't help your readers understand *why* you're telling it?
- There is too much showing and not enough telling. In other words, do you *reflect* sufficiently in the draft, contributing your new understandings of what happened?
- There isn't enough detail. Because personal essays often rely heavily on narrative, they should show as well as tell. That is, help readers not only understand the significance of your experiences but in some small way experience those significant moments themselves.

Polishing the Draft

After you've dealt with the big issues in your draft—is it sufficiently focused, does it answer the *So what?* question, is it organized, and so on—you must deal with the smaller problems. You've carved the stone into an appealing figure but now you need to polish it. Are your paragraphs coherent? How do you manage transitions? Are your sentences fluent and concise? Are there any errors in spelling or syntax? Section 5 of Chapter 13 can help you focus on these issues.

Before you finish your draft, work through the following checklist:

✓ Every paragraph is about one thing.

✓ The transitions between paragraphs aren't abrupt.

✓ The length of sentences varies in each paragraph.

✓ Each sentence is concise. There are no unnecessary words or phrases.

✓ You've checked grammar, particularly for verb agreement, run-on sentences, unclear pronouns, and misused words (*there / their, where / were,* and so on). (See the handbook at the end of the book for help with these grammar issues.)

✓ You've run your spellchecker and proofed your paper for misspelled words.

■ STUDENT ESSAY

In my part of the country, the seasonal migration of field workers occurs quietly; most of us rarely notice the cars parked on the country roads and the children sitting in the shade waiting near them. We don't notice the bent backs in the fields, moving methodically from row to row. We are dimly aware, of course, that seasonal workers are key to the beet and potato harvests, but these men and women are largely invisible to us.

Julia Arredondo's essay, "Beet Field Dreams," provides a glimpse of this life. She migrated from Texas to Idaho with her family for nearly fourteen years, where they worked the fields from May to October. For many years, when assigned the ubiquitous topic "What I Did on My Summer Vacation" in school, Julia made up stories about another Julia, one with a "normal" life of picnics, barbecues, and days spent at amusement parks. In this personal essay, the Julia who migrated "like a goose" comes to terms with the truth of those summers, and what they have come to mean.

Beet Field Dreams
Julia C. Arredondo

1   I was born in Welsaco, Texas, and for my entire childhood I considered myself Tejana—a Texan. It was true that I didn't live my entire life—or even my childhood—in the Rio Grande Valley of Southern Texas, but El Valle was my home, where my family and I lived on our own, where I went to school, where we celebrated the major holidays— Thanksgiving, Christmas, New Year's, and everyone's birthdays. Yet the Mini-Cassia, Magic Valley, area of Southern Idaho was also my home—and in a way, not my home—as a child. My father's parents—and their parents before them—were all migrant, seasonal farm workers. This was more than a kind of tradition; it was a way of life, a way of survival, and after a time, it began to feel that it was what my family was meant to do in this world.

2   Every year from late May to August my parents worked alongside my extended family hoeing sugar beets in the fields of Burley, Rupert, Heyburn, Paul, Oakley, and Twin Falls, Idaho. It was either thinning and chopping down beets to make room for more or searching for weeds to eliminate and protect the beets. From September to late October they worked in the spud harvest. Twelve to fourteen hour days picking clots out of the clusters of potatoes that flashed before their eyes, and they worked on combines, as if that's what God had put them here to do. And so we migrated. And migrated. And migrated.

* * *

3   School usually started in early September, but by the time we returned to Texas, Alamo public schools had been running for at least a couple of months. I hated being the new kid in school every year and I especially hated it when people started asking where I'd been, why I was coming into the semester late.

4   It was the infamous "How I spent my summer vacation" essay assignment that would always make me lie like Pinocchio. When the essay topic was assigned, I would panic and begin to feel my heart beat faster. I couldn't tell them what I had really been doing all five months of summer. I could not help it; I'd write about a stranger's summer: picnics, vacations, amusement parks, barbecues. A family trip to Fiesta Texas was the biggest, fictional vacation my elementary mind could conjure up and I think I believed the trip myself. I raved in my essay about how we'd spent an entire week in the

San Antonio amusement park, how the rides were awesome and how much fun I had had—all the while hoping, praying that no one would uncover the lies, and wishing that the teacher would never really read it. After all, they were only dreams that would never come true. I never told about the car. About the fields. Instead, I continued with the grand fabrications.

* * *

We slept in the car, of course. No hotels. Abandoned parking lots. Grocery store parking lots. My Dad liked to park the car somewhere where there was always a lot of light shining. One year in Moab, Utah, we had a really hard time finding a resting spot. First we stopped at a store on the main road that ran through the small town; but then a police officer came around and asked us to keep on moving. He said it was illegal for people driving through to just park anywhere to sleep and pointed us toward a rest area just on the edge of Moab. We went there. Dad parked the car under the only light post in the middle of the dirt parking lot. Then, he got off the car and walked to the pay phone just out of reach of the glowing light. Only a few minutes later, a large truck roared into the empty parking lot. Men's voices shouted and hollered from within as they circled our car, picking up speed, raising up dust clouds, tying a knot in my throat. And then just like that, they were gone. My dad came back to the car, got in, and we drove off.

After that, we mostly slept in truck stops. They were always lit, always alive. They were twenty-four-hour oases for travelers on the go. We had bathrooms available— no matter what time my bladder decided I needed to pee. We had hot food within reach. Hot coffee. So whenever Pa wanted to wake up and drive his family on, he could have a cup. It was almost as convenient as a hotel except that we slept amongst the trucks, their thunderous vibrations never really let me sleep. We'd put towels up as curtains, to block out some of the light—noise. But sometimes when I woke up in the middle of the night, and everyone in the car was asleep, I would look out and wonder where these monsters were going and whether they were as driven as we were to move.

* * *

As a kid I'd wake up on most summer mornings to the sound of doors slamming shut and cool breezes of fresh morning wind sweeping into the car, making me shiver. I could feel the weight of the car shift as the grown-ups pulled their hoes from the trunk. Their voices lingered outside the vehicle for minutes as they prepared for the day's work, waiting for the first light of day to guide their strokes. I'd lay still and listen as their voices became distant, then I would slowly drift back to my dreams.

Some mornings, when the sun wasn't quite strong enough to warm us up, my sister Debra and I would stay inside the car. I'd lounge around in the front seat—a place I hardly ever got to ride in—and impatiently wait for the adults to return to the *caheceras*. From the car they looked miniature as they moved at a hurried pace along the mile long rows. Debra and I would guess which one was Ma and which one was Pa. Sometimes we

(continued)

5

6

7

8

(continued)

were right. Sometimes I'd drift back to sleep and miss them reaching our end of the field. I'd awake to find they were already halfway back across the field and feel my heart weigh down.

9   I was always looking for a reason to join them in their hard labor; years later when I would have to really start working I knew exactly how hard it was. Still, I'd mention to my parents how I could work too, how we'd make more money that way. I'd ask them to break a hoe in half and let me have it. They only laughed and said when the time came for me to work I wasn't going to want to, so for me to just enjoy this time.

10   Sometimes near the field there would be a farmhouse from which laughter floated down towards us. Sometimes we could spot kids that looked our age jumping on their trampoline, swimming in their pool and I'd find myself longing to be them. Normal. Playing on a lawn, instead of a field. Waking in a bed, instead of a car's backseat. Eating lunch at a table, instead of from tin foil while I sat in the dirt on the shady side of the car to avoid the hot sun.

* * *

11   When I was fourteen we finally stopped moving. Field work continued being our main source of income, but we made Idaho our permanent home. And as the years passed, returning to Texas became preposterous; we were always too afraid to fall back into the old migrating lifestyle. Yet, even today I am a migrant. And it's not merely the fact that I've spent more than half my life migrating—like a goose—according to the seasons, but because it was a lifestyle that penetrates and becomes part of who I am for the rest of my life. As I grew older, I began to slowly acknowledge to others the kind of lifestyle my family lived during my childhood. Though no longer on the move, I will always be a migrant and sugar beet dreams will always haunt my sleep.

Evaluating the Essay

Discuss or write about your response to Julia Arredondo's essay using some or all of the following questions.

1. What is the essay's greatest strength? Is this something you've noticed in your own work, or the drafts of classmates?

2. Is the balance between exposition and narration, showing and telling, handled well in "Beet Field Dreams"? Does it read fairly quickly or does it drag at points?

3. The essay uses line breaks between sections. What do you think of this technique? What are its advantages and disadvantages?

4. What would you recommend to Arredondo if she were to revise "Beet Field Dreams"?

USING WHAT YOU HAVE LEARNED

My students often love writing personal essays. At its best, the genre is a rare opportunity to reexamine our lives and better understand our experiences. The insights we earn are often reward enough, but what have you learned in this assignment that you might apply in other writing situations?

1. The personal essay you wrote relies heavily on narrative and personal experience. How might an ability to tell a good story, using your experiences or the experiences of others, be a useful academic skill? How might you use it to write a paper for another class?

2. The personal essay is a deeply subjective form, seeming to put it at odds with formal academic writing, which strives for "objectivity." Are they at odds?

3. Based on your experience writing a personal essay, what do you think are its most important qualities? If you were to write more personal essays, what would you strive to do next time?

"If you want to write about mankind, write about a man," advises author E. B. White. The profile is a form that accomplishes this by giving an idea, a feeling, or an issue a human face.

WRITING A PROFILE

WRITING ABOUT PEOPLE

Some years ago, when I was writing a book on the culture of the New England lobster fishing industry, I wandered into the lighthouse keeper's house in Pemaquid Point, Maine. The lighthouse, built in 1827, was automated—like all but one lighthouse on the East Coast—but the empty keeper's house had been turned into a tiny fishing museum. I found my way there one late spring day, stepped inside, and was greeted by Abby Boynton, sitting on a folding chair working on needlepoint. I had come to look at historical objects related to lobster fishing, but instead I encountered Abby, an elderly widow whose husband, a local lobsterman, had died of cancer several years before.

We struck up a conversation, and within minutes she was leading me to the back of the museum to show me a picture book, now out of print, that documented a few days of her husband's work at the traps offshore from New Harbor, Maine. She told me the story of the New York photographer who asked her husband if he wouldn't mind company fishing that day. "He was always taking people out," she said, "so my husband said 'sure.'" That trip with the photographer led to other trips and the book that followed, *Fred Boynton, Lobsterman*. The museum copy was well thumbed and the binding was broken, but Mrs. Boynton assured me that there were still a few copies around. "I've got two copies at home," she said, "but I can't part with those. They'll be nice for the kids and the grandchildren."

What You'll Learn in This Chapter

- How the profile and the academic case study are related.
- What distinguishes the profile from other forms.
- The importance of close observation.
- Interview techniques.
- Ways to find a profile subject who is representative of a certain group of people.
- Questions for revising a profile.

Abby Boynton showed me a picture of the New Harbor house she had lived in with Fred all the years they were married. She moved three years ago because it was "too much house." As I was leaving she directed me to a model of her husband's boat, the *Dwayne B*, in a back room of the museum. It was named after their youngest son. A brass plaque on the boat model said, "In memory by his friends and fellow fishermen."

What was it like being a lobster man's wife? I asked, heading toward the sunshine. "Spent most of my time trying to keep his dinner warm," said Mrs. Boynton, resuming her post in the folding chair by the door. I glanced at the needlepoint in her lap, but couldn't read the stitched letters, which had not yet formed a word. After my fifteen minutes with Abby Boynton that seemed fitting; what didn't need a plaque or a label in this museum was the most powerful thing I found there. It occurred to me later that Abby Boynton was as bound to her husband's memory as she was to life. Only now she keeps more than his dinner warm as she waits.

This accidental interview with the lobsterman's wife reveals much more than I could explain about one aspect of community in Maine's fishing villages—the partnership between spouses who have chosen such a hard life. I can't imagine a better way to dramatize the level of devotion these marriages can demand than Abby Boynton's shrine to the memory of her husband—a worn book, a dusty model of his boat, and a picture of the New Harbor home they shared. You can hear it in her voice, too, and how quickly she directs a stranger to these relics. But all of this probably doesn't need explaining; you can sense it from the vignette.

> There may be no better way of dramatizing the impact of a problem or the significance of an idea than showing how it presents itself in the life of one person.

This piece could have easily continued, perhaps including information from the book *Fred Boynton, Lobsterman* or interviews about Abby and Fred from others in New Harbor who knew them. It might have included statistics about the divorce rate among Maine fishing families, or information about the economic pressures on families during a bad fishing season—all the factors that might easily make it hard for a marriage to survive. Most of all, I might have spent more time with Abby Boynton. The result would have been a profile, not a vignette, that would put a face on the idea that lobster fishing is difficult, but for many, a good life.

MOTIVES FOR WRITING A PROFILE

E. B. White, author of the children's classics *Charlotte's Web* and *Stuart Little* and many essays for the *The New Yorker* magazine, once offered this advice: "If you want to write about mankind, write about a man." The profile is a form that accomplishes this by giving a general idea or feeling a face. Through Abby Boynton we presumably can see something about other lobster-men's wives and families. In that sense, the profile is like the personal essay—the experiences and particulars about a living subject create, as Scott Russell Sanders once said, "a door through which [readers] might have passed." In a profile, however, the obvious subject is usually not the writer but the person he writes about.

The profile is a familiar form in the popular magazine. We can't seem to know enough about other peoples' lives. The celebrity profile is ubiquitous, but some of the best profiles are of ordinary people like Abby Boynton who are typical in some way of the people touched by the subject a writer is interested in. There may be no better way of dramatizing the impact of a problem, the importance of a question, or the significance of an idea than showing how it presents itself in the life of one person.

THE PROFILE AND ACADEMIC WRITING

While the profile may not be a common academic form, the case study is, and in a sense a profile is a form of extended case study. Almost any topic affects people's lives (if it doesn't, is it really that significant or interesting?). The profile or case study attempts to document these impacts. For example, suppose you're interested in examining the success of your university's commitment to ethnic and racial diversity—a principle the administration has publicly embraced. One way to approach the topic is to profile one international student. What has been her experience on campus? Which campus programs have proved useful? What programs are needed? The voice of your profile subject and the details of her experience would help dramatize an otherwise abstract policy debate, and the story she tells could offer a foundation from which to explore the issue.

You can write a profile in the service of an argument or as a way to explore the personal impact of an event. The profile may be part of a larger project that examines some aspect of a local culture, cultural trend, or place (see Chapter 9, "Writing an Ethnographic Essay"). It can, like good fiction, provide insight into the complexities of the human mind and soul.

> The profile relies on interviews and observation, particularly those revealing details that say something about the character or feelings of the person profiled.

More than any other form of inquiry, the profile relies on interviews for information—the voice of the writer's subject should come through—as well as observation, particularly those revealing details that say something about the character or feelings of the person profiled. In some cases, these details are merely descriptive—what the subject looks like, for instance. However, telling details can often be indirect evidence of a person's character, things like the way one man stands with his feet apart and arms folded on his chest to emphasize his biceps (arrogant), how a woman carefully knots the scarf around her neck (fastidious), and so on. Writers who want to practice interview skills—a key method of collecting information in communications and the social sciences—will find the profile a useful challenge.

FEATURES OF THE FORM

Some typical characteristics of the form include the following:

- *A profile usually provides a detailed look at one person.* The key is to decide who that person should be.

- *Alone, a profile may not provide enough substantiation for an argument.* While the writer may choose a profile to dramatize a problem or support a claim, it's always dangerous to generalize from a single case, particularly if the typicality of the subject is in doubt.

- *A profile uses narrative as a method of organization.* As in the personal essay, storytelling is frequently the backbone of the profile. This may take the form of a series of anecdotes about the writer's subject, or the subject's account of an experience.

- *The profile is usually written from one of two points of view—either the writer narrates in the first person or the subject is portrayed in the third person, and the writer stays out of the way.* A profile told in the first person can give an added dimension of the writer's own feelings and reactions, but risks distracting the reader from the real subject, the person being profiled. Portraying the subject in the third person loses the drama of the interaction between the writer and the person profiled, but keeps the focus on the subject.

- *Profiles go beyond mere description of subjects and reveal information about character much as a short story does, through telling details and the subject's own voice.* Letting the subject speak for herself is particularly important, but to do this well makes special demands on the writer. (See "Inquiring into the Details: Recording Interviews" later in the chapter.)

- *A strong beginning is essential, particularly when the subject of a profile isn't famous.* We read a celebrity profile because of the fame of its subject. But when writing about ordinary people, we need to quickly give readers a reason to be interested.

- *Scene and setting often provide useful information in a profile.* We know characters not just by what they say but what they do and where they do it.

- *The more time writers can spend with their subjects, the more revealing the profile.* The more information you have about your subject, the easier it is to focus the piece, and the more likely you are to get to the truth of things about your subject.

READINGS

■ PROFILE 1

In "Thumb-Sucking Girl," a brief essay that appeared recently in the journal *Brevity*, Sonja Livingston gives us a snapshot profile. It works because the vignette is familiar—who hasn't seen a thumb-sucking child?—but Livingston's close observation makes the scene fresh and new. Among other things, profiles often require careful attention to what we see, and this isn't easy because we must actively search for particulars that are revealing, and then find the words to describe them.

While barely more than a paragraph long, "Thumb-Sucking Girl" succeeds in creating a meaningful portrait of an unnamed girl in a difficult situation. As you read it, speculate about how Livingston might have composed the piece. Other than observing carefully, what other sources of information might she have used?

Thumb-Sucking Girl
Sonja Livingston

Look at me.   1

  At me, over here.   2

  Look and shake your head all you want. At my uneven bangs, these broken-down   3
shoes, my momma, all us kids and all our belongings shoved into just one car. Whisper and
sigh all you want, because I have something better than good clothes and a permanent
address. I've got my thumb. My right thumb, to be precise—and the soft pink underside of
its arch. Forget that the nail on that thumb grows as smooth and flat as the inside of a seashell
on account of all that sucking. Forget that my mother has tried everything (except hot pepper and mustard on my thumb, like my cousin Judith suggests, because my mother, though
determined to rid me of my disgusting habit, thinks pepper and mustard too cruel for a
child). Forget that I once deprived myself of the luxury of my thumb for a whole month just
to show I could. Forget that my teeth have begun to split down the front, that the space will
stretch wide eventually, that it will ruin my permanent teeth, according to my mother. Forget
all that and understand that the plug of it in my mouth is what brings me sleep, and until
you've plopped a thumb into your mouth and sucked on it while using the index finger of
that same hand to cradle the line of bone under your eye, to rub up and down the fleshy
valley of your nose—until you have done such a thing, you know nothing of comfort.

Inquiring into the Essay

Use the four ways of inquiring to investigate your ideas about "Thumb-Sucking Girl."

1. In your notebook, play with close observation. Go somewhere—the campus
    library or student union, a coffee shop, a bowling alley, the hallways outside

your classroom—and watch. Choose people to discreetly observe, making fast lists of details.

2. An interesting aspect of "Thumb-Sucking Girl" is its unusual point of view. This is a profile from the girl's vantage point. Explain how Livingston—or any writer who wants to write a profile this way—would need to write and research the piece.

3. When it sometimes seems that you have to write pages and pages to get a point across, a brief essay like this one can be inspiring. Evaluate the effectiveness of "Thumb-Sucking Girl" as a *meaningful* essay, despite its brevity. What evidence would you offer from the essay about how this meaningfulness is achieved in so few words?

4. Scientific investigations, among others, require close observation. Watching carefully is an underrated skill. Assess your own observation skills. Based on Livingston's essay, what does looking closely demand?

■ PROFILE 2

One of the most memorable segments on the TV show *Seinfeld* was about the "Soup Nazi," a character inspired by the following profile. Published in *The New Yorker* by one of the staff writers, "Soup" profiles soup chef Albert Yeganeh, the tough-talking, impatient, demanding owner of a small restaurant on West Fifty-fifth Street. The force of Yeganeh's personality comes through brilliantly in this piece especially because the writer steps aside and lets the man speak for himself through extensive—and sometimes lengthy—quotations. It's hard to overstate how important it is to allow readers to hear the voices of profile subjects.

But this essay is also a great example of how important close and careful observation is to a profile. We can know people by the contexts in which they live and work, something that we could simply explain—"Yeganeh owns a soup restaurant on West Fifty-fifth Street in New York"—or describe—"The first thing you notice about it is the awning, which proclaims 'Homemade Hot, Cold, Diet Soups.'" These more specific observations bring the man's tiny world to life around him and contribute powerfully to our understanding of who he is.

Soup

Anonymous, The New Yorker

1   When Albert Yeganeh says "Soup is my lifeblood," he means it. And when he says "I am extremely hard to please," he means that, too. Working like a demon alchemist in a tiny storefront kitchen at 259-A West Fifty-fifth Street, Mr. Yeganeh creates anywhere from eight to seventeen soups every weekday. His concoctions are so popular

that a wait of half an hour at the lunchtime peak is not uncommon, although there are strict rules for conduct in line. But more on that later.

"I am psychologically kind of a health freak," Mr. Yeganeh said the other day, in a lisping staccato of Armenian origin. "And I know that soup is the greatest meal in the world. It's very good for your digestive system. And I use only the best, the freshest ingredients. I am a perfectionist. When I make a clam soup, I use three different kinds of clams. Every other place uses canned clams. I'm called crazy. I am not crazy. People don't realize why I get so upset. It's because if the soup is not perfect and I'm still selling it, it's a torture. It's *my* soup, and that's why I'm so upset. First you clean and then you cook. I don't believe that ninety-nine percent of the restaurants in New York know how to clean a tomato. I tell my crew to wash the parsley *eight* times. If they wash it five or six times, I scare them. I tell them they'll go to jail if there is sand in the parsley. One time, I found a mushroom on the floor, and I fired that guy who left it there." He spread his arms, and added, "This place is the only one like it in…in…the whole earth! One day, I hope to learn something from the other places, but so far I haven't. For example, the other day I went to a very fancy restaurant and had borscht. I had to send it back. It was *junk*. I could see all the chemicals in it. I never use chemicals. Last weekend, I had lobster bisque in Brooklyn, a very well-known place. It was *junk*. When I make a lobster bisque, I use a whole lobster. You know, I never advertise. I don't have to. All the big-shot chefs and the kings of the hotels come here to see what *I'm* doing."

As you approach Mr. Yeganeh's Soup Kitchen International from a distance, the first thing you notice about it is the awning, which proclaims "Homemade Hot, Cold, Diet Soups." The second thing you notice is an aroma so delicious that it makes you want to take a bite out of the air. The third thing you notice, in front of the kitchen, is an electric signboard that flashes, saying, "Today's Soups…Chicken Vegetable… Mexican Beef Chili…Cream of Watercress…Italian Sausage…Clam Bisque…Beef Barley…Due to Cold Weather…For Most Efficient and Fastest Service the Line Must… Be Kept Moving…Please…Have Your Money…Ready…Pick the Soup of Your Choice…Move to Your Extreme…Left After Ordering."

"I am not prejudiced against color or religion," Mr. Yeganeh told us, and he jabbed an index finger at the flashing sign. "Whoever follows that I treat very well. My regular customers don't say anything. They are very intelligent and well educated. They know I'm just trying to move the line. The New York cop is very smart—he sees everything but says nothing. But the young girl who wants to stop and tell you how nice you look and hold everyone up—*yah!*" He made a guillotining motion with his hand. "I tell you, I hate to work with the public. They treat me like a slave. My philosophy is: The customer is always wrong and I'm always right. I raised my prices to try to get rid of some of these people, but it didn't work."

The other day, Mr. Yeganeh was dressed in chef's whites with orange smears across his chest, which may have been some of the carrot soup cooking in a huge pot on a little stove in one corner. A three-foot-long handheld mixer from France sat on the sink, looking like an overgrown gardening tool. Mr. Yeganeh spoke to two young helpers in

(continued)

(continued)

a twisted Armenian-Spanish barrage, then said to us, "I have no overhead, no trained wait-resses, and I have the cashier here." He pointed to himself theatrically. Beside the door-way, a glass case with fresh green celery, red and yellow peppers, and purple eggplant was topped by five big gray soup urns. According to a piece of cardboard taped to the door, you can buy Mr. Yeganeh's soups in three sizes, costing from four to fifteen dollars. The order of any well-behaved customer is accompanied by little waxpaper packets of bread, fresh vegetables (such as scallions and radishes), fresh fruit (such as cherries or an orange), a chocolate mint, and a plastic spoon. No coffee, tea, or other drinks are served.

6   "I get my recipes from books and theories and my own taste," Mr. Yeganeh said. "At home, I have several hundreds of books. When I do research, I find that I don't know anything. Like cabbage is a cancer fighter, and some fish is good for your heart but some is bad. Every day, I should have one sweet, one spicy, one cream, one vegetable soup—and they *must* change, they should always taste a little different." He added that he wasn't sure how extensive his repertoire was, but that it probably includes at least eighty soups, among them African peanut butter, Greek moussaka, hamburger, Reuben, B.L.T., asparagus and caviar, Japanese shrimp miso, chicken chili, Irish corned beef and cabbage, Swiss chocolate, French calf's brain, Korean beef ball, Italian shrimp and eggplant Parmesan, buffalo, ham and egg, short rib, Russian beef Stroganoff, turkey cacciatore, and Indian mulligatawny. "The chicken and the seafood are an addiction, and when I have French garlic soup I let people have only one small container each," he said. "The doctors and nurses love that one."

7   A lunch line of thirty people stretched down the block from Mr. Yeganeh's doorway. Behind a construction worker was a man in expensive leather, who was in front of a woman in a fur hat. Few people spoke. Most had their money out and their orders ready.

8   At the front of the line, a woman in a brown coat couldn't decide which soup to get and started to complain about the prices.

9   "You talk too much, dear," Mr. Yeganeh said, and motioned her to move to the left. "Next!"

10   "Just don't talk. Do what he says," a man huddled in a blue parka warned.

11   "He's downright rude," said a blond woman in a blue coat. "Even abusive. But you can't deny it, his soup is the best."

Inquiring into the Essay

Use the four methods of inquiry—exploring, explaining, evaluating, and reflecting—to generate a response to "Soup."

1. Use a "narrative of thought" response to explore your initial reactions to "Soup." Immediately after reading the piece, open your notebook and begin a five-minute fastwrite, starting with the following phrase: The first thing that comes to mind after reading this essay is _____. And then...And then...Whenever the writing stalls, seize on the phrase *and then* to get you going. Feel free, however, to digress on some aspect of the profile you

want to think about through writing. After five minutes, stop and finish the following sentence: Now that I look back on what I've said about "Soup," the thing that strikes me the most is...

2. If you're profiling someone famous, you really don't have to worry much about reader interest; fame alone gives you a rhetorical advantage. But when you write about someone, like Yeganeh, who is relatively unknown, you have to "hook" your readers within the first paragraph or two, giving them a reason to read on. Explain how the writer of "Soup" attempted to do this in the first paragraph of the essay.

3. Review the essay and any writing you've done on the essay. Make a quick list of words that best describe Yeganeh. Choose one of them and, using evidence from the essay, find specific information that supports the choice. What is the strongest evidence you found that best explains the aptness of the word you chose to describe him? Evaluate the qualities of good evidence in a profile essay.

4. Go ahead and admit it. You like reading *People* occasionally (or maybe often). Now consider how you felt about reading "Soup." Were your motives and responses the same? How would you distinguish between a *People* piece on Nicole Kidman and the *New Yorker* profile of Albert Yeganeh?

■ PROFILE 3

It's possible to profile the dead. The growth of archives that include interview transcripts, photographs, audio recordings, and video clips—much of it online (see "Writing in the Disciplines," page 151)—makes it easier than ever before to create a portrait of both famous and ordinary people who died decades ago. This is the work of historians, of course, but novices like the rest of us, especially with the accessibility of archives, can do it too.

William Henry David Murray (nicknamed "Alfalfa Bill") was elected governor of Oklahoma in 1930. He was a man "who could talk for hours without interruption, fueled by caffeine and nicotine," writes Timothy Egan. "He drank two pots of black coffee a day and was never without a cigar." Murray was also a hopeless bigot who presided—ineffectively—over the Dust Bowl in Oklahoma, America's worst environmental tragedy. "Alfalfa Bill" is one of many compelling profiles in Egan's stunning history of the drought and destruction that overtook parts of Texas, Kansas, Colorado, and Oklahoma in the 1930s. The excerpt that follows, from Egan's book *The Worst Hard Time*, is a wonderful example of a different kind of profile that relies on archival information. It is possible, after all, to bring the dead to life.

Alfalfa Bill
Timothy Egan

1   The new governor of Oklahoma gave people hope, but he also tried to get them to hate. William Henry David Murray had been elected in 1930 after scandal drove the last two governors from office, both of them impeached. With a campaign slogan that railed against what he called "The Three C's—Corporations, Carpetbaggers, and Coons," Murray won by a huge margin, 301,921 votes to 208,575. He was known as "Alfalfa Bill" for his ceaseless advocacy of agriculture as the cornerstone of society. Alfalfa Bill said anything could grow in Oklahoma. His daddy, David, had made wine not long after grabbing a piece of dirt in the 1889 Sooner land rush; his Murray Mosel was so well-known that President Teddy Roosevelt had declared it "the bulliest wine of the land." Alfalfa Bill was himself a bully, but these times needed such a man, he said. Born in Toadsuck, Texas, in 1869, Murray ran away from home at the age of twelve, worked on a series of farms, and then got involved in populist politics. He bought a newspaper, educated himself so well he passed the bar, and made a name as president of the Oklahoma statehood convention in 1906. Oklahoma, he said at the time, could be a great state only if blacks were separated from whites and kept in the proper jobs—in the fields or factories. Next door, in Texas, lawmakers had institutionalized that sentiment forty years earlier with Reconstruction laws that said blacks could work only as field hands. Blacks were inferior to whites in all ways, Murray said, and must be fenced from society like quarantined hogs. At the start of the twentieth century, many people felt otherwise, but Alfalfa Bill tried to set his view into the proposed constitution. At the same time, he welcomed even black support, if done properly.

2   "I appreciate the old darkie who comes to me talking softly in that humble spirit which should characterize their actions and dealings with the white man," he said to wide applause at the constitutional convention. Murray hated Jews as well. Blacks had some virtues, but Jews had none, in his view. Nor did he like the handful of Italians who had come to the High Plains. The "low grade races" of southern Europe, he said, were a threat to civilization. Oklahoma became the forty-sixth state only after President Theodore Roosevelt forced Murray to remove the segregationist planks of the constitution. Murray was furious; he never let go of his grudge against the Roosevelt family.

3   At the start of the Depression, Alfalfa Bill was a mustachioed, haunt-eyed, big-eared man of sixty who could talk for hours without interruption, fueled by caffeine and nicotine. He drank two pots of black coffee a day and was never without a

cigar—his method of ingesting "the great civilizer," as he called tobacco. Storming around Oklahoma in 1931, he said he could not make the sun less oppressive, but he promised to use muscle to fix the broken land. His muscle was the National Guard. As governor, Murray ruled by martial law, calling out the guard twenty-seven times in his first two years in office. When oil prices fell to a new low in 1931, the governor sent his troops to the oil fields to force a shutdown of three thousand wells as a way to drive up prices. When Texas backed a toll bridge across the Red River on the border with Oklahoma, Murray sent the guard to the bridge, nearly provoking a shooting war between the two states. In the midst of the standoff he showed up with an antique revolver, waving it in the faces of Texas Rangers. And when blacks tried to hold an Emancipation Day parade in a park in Oklahoma City, the governor imposed martial law on the city and ordered his guard troops to shut them down. Blacks were supposed to be invisible in his state, quietly working the land or manning a factory station. All told, the governor issued thirty-four declarations of martial law during his four years in office.

The land dried up in the spring of 1932. Month after month, going into the height of the growing season, there was no rain. The sky was white and hot, and it took until well after midnight for the heat to dissipate. Alfalfa Bill urged people to fight nature with force. The unemployment rate in his state was 29 percent. To show them what could be done, he plowed up the grass on the grounds of the capitol and let people plant vegetable gardens. And to demonstrate how water could be taken from the ground, Murray went on a building binge, trying to create lakes and ponds in places that had neither. The ground could be mined at the deepest levels for water, using new and powerful centrifugal pumps, to create the garden state of Oklahoma. They could grab onto that underground lake, the Ogallala Aquifer, like the Sooners had grabbed the old Cherokee lands, and so what if the water was nearly seven hundred feet deep and had taken at least a hundred centuries to build up—it was there to be grubstaked.

In Boise City, Alfalfa Bill's plans sounded like a tonic. God knows they needed water. It wasn't trickling out of the distant Rockies. The Cimarron, once a roaring river, was now a tear trail. And it wasn't coming from overhead. It rained barely ten inches in all of 1932. The sun glared down at nesters in No Man's Land, every dawn a new punishment. It was time for man to stand up to the puckered face of the elements.

"Human progress has now reached the stage where it can master these mighty forces of nature," wrote the *Boise City News*, in support of a proposed dam in No Man's Land.

In the spring of 1932, Alfalfa Bill decided to run for president. He would follow the model that got him elected governor. In running for the statehouse, he had campaigned on the Three C's. Now he ran on a platform of promising people the "Four B's: Bread, Butter, Bacon, and Beans." That a governor could run for the highest office of the land with a campaign that offered people calories said something about 1932.

Inquiring into the Essay

1. According to Timothy Egan, "Alfalfa Bill" was a racist and an anti-Semite. Is it possible for you to get past these two serious character flaws and find anything redeeming in someone like Governor Murray? Does the historical context in which he lived matter at all? Explore these two questions in your journal in a four-minute fastwrite.

2. Choose a single word that you would use to describe your dominant impression of William Murray (other than "racist" and "anti-Semite"). Go back to the profile and find specific evidence that seems to support that dominant impression. Then, if you can, find some evidence that does not support it.

3. *The Worst Hard Times*, the book from which this character sketch of "Alfalfa Bill" was taken, is an environmental history. It makes the argument that there are aspects of the Dust Bowl that will help us understand all environmental disasters. Though you have to read the book to really appreciate that argument, speculate about how this profile might contribute to the idea that the Dust Bowl is a cautionary tale. What do you infer from the profile of William Murray about how his response to Oklahoma's environmental disaster is relevant, even today?

4. Reflect on what archival sources Timothy Egan could have used to write this piece.

■ PROFILE 4

Joe Cool, aka Lonnie Beasley, worked in the produce department at Kroger, and he was the emcee of overstock. "Hey folks," he said on the store PA, "this is Joe Cool and my manager's jumpin' all over me 'cause I done stacked too many beans out there. . . . So, please—come on over and buy some of these beans so I can get my manager off my back." The following profile of Beasley was originally published in the *Journal of Management Inquiry*. It is a work of academic scholarship, even if it doesn't read like one.

The discipline of business and economics, like many academic fields, is finding that this kind of alternative scholarship offers knowledge that traditional forms of research lack. For example, one business scholar who reviewed "Learning About Work from Joe Cool" wrote that "this story represents a more holistic view of work . . . than is usually the case in studies of organizational behavior." Another wrote that this profile is "powerful in reminding us that the analysis of work is ultimately etched in the life experiences of workers." The chance to look into the life of someone like Beasley, these scholars argue, provides knowledge that traditional quantitative research does not.

Learning About Work from Joe Cool
Gib Akin

The announcement over the supermarket PA system cut through the anonymous burble
of shopping talk: "Hey folks, this is Joe Cool and my manager's jumpin' all over me
'cause I done stacked too many beans out here. Old Joe won't be COOOOL no more if
he don't get these things movin'. So, please—come on over and buy some of these
beans so I can get my manager off my back. And while you're here we've got a great
buy on California navel oranges."

Here's Joe Cool himself: slim, angular, small turned-up nose on a face that is
slightly dished, older than what you would expect from the name. But that's part of
what makes him cool, acting so youthful, even at 55, and sporting an intensely
white beard. The hair is striking in its contrasting black, and is parted in the middle, with a wing-like sweep back over each temple, plastered flat. It gives him an
old fashioned look, like your jolly barkeep from the 1890s. A name tag on his
denim apron makes it official that he really is Joe Cool. He's constant motion and
constant talk, moving produce, keeping the customers, especially women customers, happy.

Lonnie Beasley became Joe Cool in the Kroger produce department, first only
behind the scenes and then out front with the customers. He started produce
work in 1971 and by 1975 his coworkers had begun to corroborate the
Joe Cool persona. They gave him a pair of sunglasses to emulate the Peanuts
cartoon showing Snoopy as Joe Cool. Stickers of the cartoon character began
appearing on his locker, as well as near the water fountain and the time clock. The
back room was becoming Joe Cool's domain. The work there was physically
demanding, and all were amazed at Lonnie's youthful strength and endurance—
lifting, unloading trucks, and stacking and moving large four-wheeled carts of
produce.

But the idea that Lonnie was cool came mainly from his constant joking, talking,
and relentlessly youthful attitude. "He would say anything." The mostly younger
coworkers liked it that someone older could be like them, always fooling around, not
serious, "a nut." But he also retained his seniority, and was paternal as well. He helped
everybody. Susan Marsh remembers that "he always made me feel like a daughter he
hadn't seen in quite a while." (She didn't know the circumstances that give her simile
its keenness.)

And, he rode a motorcycle to work, the crash helmet worn for protection
also creating his nineteenth-century hairdo. He didn't ride a mean machine as
an aging outlaw biker, but a friendly, playful one as the fresh-air kid. That was
really cool. He had a sly affection for the slightly wild image of a motorcyclist,
even though he claimed he started riding motorcylces because of the good gas
mileage.

(continued)

(continued)

6   When the store moved to a new location, a system of weighing and pricing produce in the section rather than at the register was started, and Lonnie was given the "out front" job as scale man. That's when grocery shoppers got to meet Joe Cool. Donald Linke, who also worked in produce and like Lonnie had come from the other store, now made an "official" name tag that read JOE COOL.

7   From his new job out front, Lonnie also became the idol of the airwaves. When he got on the PA system to announce some special promotion, people in the store would be quiet so they could hear what Joe Cool was going to say. On one Fourth of July holiday, the store manager, in response to running out the year before, had over-stocked hamburger and hot dog rolls. As the day wore on and there were mountains of unsold buns remaining, Lonnie gave the play-by-play: "Folks, the manager has gone crazy, flipped his lid, gone bananas. He's giving away rolls, two for the price of one." And ten minutes later, "He's getting worse, now the poor fool has gone completely over the edge. He's giving four for the price of one. Y'all better get over here and stop this before we have to carry him off." As people arrived, Lonnie would load their baskets and whisk them off. What to do with all the buns? Nobody worried; it was Joe Cool.

8   Someone said to the manager, "Do you hear what that guy is saying about you?"

9   "Don't bother me none. Them rolls are moving aren't they?"

10   Lonnie was especially attentive to the ladies. He claimed that his beard had turned white as a result of all the smooching he had done (wink, touch your shoulder). Women shoppers always knew that both they and their vegetables were beautiful. Having been raised on a farm and always having his own garden even when living in town, Lonnie knew about produce and would help women pick the best vegetables and then advise on preparation.

11   Attention to women was also about kids. Kids loved Joe Cool and would have their mothers take them to see him.

12   The grocery store job was a second one, even though for most of the time it was a 40-hour-a-week commitment, a full-time job in its own right. Lonnie had always been a two-job man. "I guess working is just my thing." He had worked as a salesman at Sears and drove a Yellow cab as a second job. He sold life insurance as a first job and sold tires at the B. F. Goodrich store as a second. In 1971, he joined the University of Virginia police department working the graveyard shift and soon after began working days at the supermarket.

13   The police job had a lot of the same opportunities to help people. Lonnie claimed only 30 percent was crime fighting, and 70 percent was helping people and doing PR. And especially with University police, you got to deal with better people. Still, the people in produce were an antidote to some of the unfixable unhappiness he saw as a police officer.

Coworkers at the store would wonder how, and why, he would do it. "How much   14
sleep you get?"

"Three or four hours."   15

"You call that living?"   16

"Depends on your aim."   17

Lonnie had two aims in work. One was simple, conventional, economic, and easy   18
to talk about. Lonnie described himself as a depression baby, born in 1931.
His parents separated when he was five, and his mother carried him back to the
country where her people were. They never had anything but always worked to
pay their way. You didn't want to owe anything or anybody. And what you did
was work.

He had always wanted to go back to the country, and the work earnings   19
eventually allowed the purchase of a house and seven acres—not really a farm,
but a place that could be lived on farm-like. In an open, ramshackle barn,
is stored his second motorcycle, a blue 500cc Yamaha that replaced the Honda
350 he started with in 1976. They look faded and scrawny next to his current ride,
a huge Honda Gold Wing with a sidecar. There's also a little-used RV. Three
old cars live on the acreage, only three of many projects in various states of
completion.

Depression babies, who never had anything, don't throw things away. Lonnie and   20
Nancy's house was full of things collected deliberately or just impossible to part with.
And they all had stories connected with them. Lonnie told the stories while Nancy listened. She sometimes interjected to show physical traces of the story, a photo, a card,
a toy, a piece of clothing. (There was quite a collection of icons of the Snoopy Joe
Cool character, modeled in banks, T-shirts, soap, a radio.) In retrieving one thing,
something else always surfaced, and that kicked off another story. It wasn't having the
things themselves, it was that they provided a kind of archaeology, the shards in
which their life was encoded, an aid to the remembering and telling that make things
real.

The accumulation has now attained some sort of critical mass so that there is not   21
the same need to work so much. (Nancy, who Lonnie always calls "Mamma" or "doll,"
has never worked.) Part of the fullness has been achieved by inheriting some money,
primarily from Nancy's side of the family. The farmers who were her kin may have
lived poorly, but in the end their land had substantial cash value, which helped
Lonnie and Nancy finally have something.

The other aim of Lonnie's work was less conventional and harder to tell.   22

Lonnie and Nancy referred to their son, James Irvin, as the achievement of their   23
life. He was born in 1954, two years after they were married. At the age of two, James
Irvin was taken sick with encephalitis and spent the rest of his life in need of special
care. He died in a hospital in Lynchburg, 60 miles away from his family, in 1976.

(continued)

(continued)

While he was alive, Lonnie, always devoted to helping people, couldn't really help as he would have liked.

24   During the time when James Irvin was alive and after his death, work was a form of therapy. "Cheaper than a psychiatrist," Lonnie claimed. It was a way to keep busy, a way to keep from worrying himself into the hospital.

25   Nancy quietly did most of the direct care giving, while Lonnie, feeling more and more distressed, took a second job and spent more time working. A friend admonished Nancy that Lonnie was running away and not helping. But Nancy, uncharacteristically, stood up strong, defending that Lonnie was doing his part by working to pay the bills, doing what he could do in his own way for James Irvin.

26   When his son died, Lonnie cried, but he kept on working.

27   Lonnie also couldn't help his daughter as he would have liked. Born seven years after James Irvin and named Nancy like her mother, she always knew her dad was cool. What was really cool was being delivered to school by taxi, a regular treat when Lonnie worked a second job as a driver for Yellow Cab. She recalled motorcycle trips to visit relatives in the Tidewater and that her dad would do anything to help someone in need, including her and her stricken brother.

28   The younger Nancy was married before finishing high school. Her dad didn't exactly approve ("I may be Joe Cool, but I'm a square"). He remained supportive of her, nevertheless. Nancy and her husband had a daughter, but soon separated, and Nancy went to California—a place that for Lonnie was mysterious and dangerous, a place that changed people and made his daughter into someone he didn't know. He worried that she was drawn to men who were bad for her. But he was still there for her, even helping her move back to California after some time back at home. When she left with "her fellah" (Lonnie still can't say the name of the man he so disliked), Nancy's daughter Amber stayed with her grandparents.

29   Later, Lonnie and Nancy sued for custody of Amber, who was living with them. At the time, the younger Nancy was angry that her parents were trying to take her daughter away. She now sees it differently, that Lonnie had to make this arrangement to be able to get Amber into school and to be able to provide medical care. Her reframing keeps alive the father she knows as helping people, as being supportive of her even if not approving.

30   When the younger Nancy's "fellah" was killed in an accident, Lonnie paid for the funeral and helped Nancy get resettled. And Nancy, exactly as her father would have done, managed the pain and confusion by going to work. Employed as a receptionist at a psychiatric hospital, she was back at her job the next day. When a fellow employee, surprised that she was working so soon after the loss, asked what she was doing there, she replied, "To keep from going crazy. And if I do go crazy here you

can just put me in one of the rooms down the hall." Work as therapy seemed to be an idea with genetic connections.

Lonnie doesn't like to talk about these times. It's as if he doesn't know how, that there is no understandable face to put on it, no way to make anyone happy. It's not like what he could do at work. 31

There is less pain now, and there are fewer bills to pay. Lonnie wants to spend time with Amber. And with the two Nancys. Be at home more. Lonnie is so social at work you might expect him in retirement to want to be around other people. He's a self-declared "people person," but that doesn't mean just being social: it means being personal. Sociability covers much of the pain that comes from not being able to help, to make someone else happy. There's less of that now, so there isn't as much need for work as therapy. 32

When an early leave plan was offered by the grocery company in late 1986, Joe Cool could retire. He still worked the graveyard shift as a university police officer, but spent more time at home with Amber and Nancy, his wife of 41 years and a "right cute chick" he still likes to do things for. 33

On a recent Sunday, as Lonnie, Amber, and the two Nancys were strolling the local shopping mall, they were approached by a young mother. "Aren't you Joe Cool? I want you to say hello to my son." 34

Inquiring into the Essay

Once again, use the four methods of inquiry to investigate your thoughts and feelings about Akin's profile, "Learning About Work from Joe Cool."

1. Academic reviews of this essay suggest that this kind of scholarship offers us knowledge of subjects that traditional academic research does not. In your notebook, explore that idea. Take three minutes to make a fast list in response to this question: *What does knowing Joe Cool through this profile tell me about the nature of some workers and workplaces?*

2. Choose one or more of the segments in this essay—the sections separated by white space—and explain its purpose. What particular knowledge about workers or workplaces does the segment seem to offer? Why was it included?

3. Evaluate the effectiveness of "Joe Cool" as research. Do you agree that this kind of research—informal case studies that read like stories—make a valuable contribution to our knowledge of a subject? What are their strengths and weaknesses?

4. Reflect on what you would do if you were Gib Akin, the author of this story, charged with writing a profile of Joe Cool. What parts of the process would you enjoy? What parts would you find hard? As you consider writing your own profile of somebody, do you anticipate any personal challenges?

SEEING THE FORM

Roy Takeno Reading Paper in Front of Office by Ansel Adams

The photographer and the painter who are after a truthful portrait of someone confront the same problem as the writer: How can you possibly capture the complexity of a human being in a single image or on a few pages? The answer, of course, is that you can't. The best you can do is find, in the moment when you press the shutter release, a picture that says something more. A good photographic portrait, like a good written profile, reveals some aspect of who the subjects are, creates some particular impression, or, as in this photograph by Ansel Adams, uses the portrait to comment not just on the subject but a larger problem.

Ansel Adams, *Roy Takeno Reading Paper in Front of Office*, 1943 (Library of Congress Prints and Photographs Division).

In 1943, Adams, best known for his landscape photographs, took more than 200 photographs at the Manzanar War Relocation Center in California, one of a number of internment camps created by the U.S. government to detain Japanese Americans during World War II. Look closely at Adams's picture of Roy Takeno. If this were a written profile about the man, what would be an idea around which the profile is organized?

THE WRITING PROCESS

INQUIRY PROJECT: REPRESENTATIVE PROFILE

Write a 1,000- to 1,200-word profile of someone who strikes you as representative, in some ways, of a larger group. For example, write a profile of your neighbor, the Harley Davidson aficionado, because he seems typical, in some ways, of bikers. Profile a nurse because that's a profession you're interested in. Write about an African American student on your predominantly white campus to discover what of his or her experience might represent the experience of other minority students there. Your instructor may give you additional instructions.

   Work toward a profile that has the following qualities:

- It is ultimately organized around ways your profile seems representative or typical of the larger group to which your subject belongs.
- The profile includes at least three anecdotes, or little stories, that help reveal this theme.
- You bring in the voice of your subject through selective quotations.
- The end of the essay circles back to the beginning.

For additional reading, writing, and research resources, go to **www.mycomplab.com**

Thinking About Subjects

Sometimes you don't choose the subject; he or she chooses you. That was frequently my experience when I researched my book on lobsters—as I traveled and talked to people about the subject I was researching, I found fascinating people whose experience, like Abby Boynton's, would powerfully reveal some aspect of lobstering that seemed important. One way to find suitable profile subjects, therefore, is simply to look for them in the course of doing your research. Who have you read or heard about or perhaps met who might provide a useful focus for a subject in which you're interested?

   On the other hand, you might have an idea of who you'd like to profile now, someone you know or would like to know. But if you'd like to play around with some ideas, the following prompts should help. As always, keep generating ideas until you feel you have some potentially promising material.

Generating Ideas

Play with possible subjects, withholding judgment for the moment about what might be a good one. Again, as in the previous chapter, don't let your critical side stifle your creative side. At this point in the process, you can let yourself explore freely.

Listing Prompts. To select a topic within which you'd like to find someone to profile, try the following:

1. Make these lists in your journal, quickly generating each one in thirty seconds. Consider doing a profile of someone in one of the categories you generate.

   - List types of people—categories like "musicians" or "car mechanics"—that either interest you or with whom you have had contact.
   - Make a list of local issues, controversies, or problems that you feel something about.
   - Make a list of jobs that interest you.

2. Develop a "snapshot profile." Go to a public place—a café, the campus library, a fast-food restaurant—and observe people. Choose someone whom you can discreetly observe for at least ten minutes. Generate a list of observations of that person, double-entry style, in your notebook, using the left-facing page. Concentrate on particulars.

ONE STUDENT'S RESPONSE

Jennifer's Journal

LIST OF OBSERVATIONS:
CELL PHONE SALESWOMAN

blonde and brown streaked hair	silver watch
straight to shoulders	"hey you" to girlfriend passing by
black cotton sweater	black nametag
low-cut green patterned blouse	Kimberly
long fingernails, painted white	eyebrows rise when smiles
pecks at computer keys carefully	"Get the only RAZR that's got it all"
cell phone to ear	looks into eyes of customer when talking
performs one-handed: writing form, pecking at computer, opening boxes	takes long strides when walking
	black pants
	black shoes, low heels

SNAPSHOT PROFILE
CELL PHONE SALESWOMAN

Kimberly does her job one-handed because the other hand is always holding a cell phone to her ear. Selling cell phones obviously means using cell phones while you sell them. She is young, perhaps 22, and has long nails that are carefully enameled in white. These present problems when she types on the computer, slowing down her hunting and pecking considerably, a process that is performed, as always, with her right hand, since the left holds the cell phone to her ear. Kimberly works at a Verizon wireless counter that is a kind of island in the middle of the mall, and she moves effortlessly in the small square area behind the counter that she shares with two other salespeople. They share a private joke, and she smiles, and when she does one of her eyebrows lifts. This is not a freak accident. It happens again and again, and makes her seem skeptical. She unfolds a large brochure showing the company's national service area—accomplished once more single handedly—and points with a long white fingernail at something. The customer nods. Kimberly smiles, and the eyebrow lifts once again.

Fastwriting Prompts. Fastwriting is a great way to loosen up your creative side and at the same time generate raw material. Here are a few prompts to get you writing:

1. Choose the name of someone you know who you might want to profile. Use the "seed sentences" below to launch two separate fastwrites on your subject, each lasting at least three minutes (unless you can't stop writing).

   - When I first think of _____, I think of _____.
   - The one word I would use to describe _____ would be _____.
   - _____ had a strange habit.
   - Typically, _____ would _____.
   - _____ is best known for _____.
   - The one thing that most people fail to notice about _____ is _____.
   - When I first met _____, I noticed _____.
   - _____ said, "_____."

2. Review the data you collected for your "snapshot profile" under Listing Prompt 2, especially noting those that are suggestive in some way about your subject and how exactly you see her. On the right-facing page of your notebook, compose a fast paragraph that uses the best evidence you collected, all working toward some dominant impression or idea about your subject that you'd like to communicate to a reader. Use this material as the basis for a short vignette like "Thumb-Sucking Girl."

Visual Prompts. Maps, clusters, lines and arrows, charts, and even sketches can help us piece together subjects in ways that writing sometimes cannot. Consider the following options:

1. Put the name of a possible profile subject in the center of a cluster. Build a web of associations for five minutes, and then begin fastwriting when you feel the urge.

2. Go through old photographs for ideas about profile subjects; this might be especially useful for reminding yourself of family and friends who might be good subjects.

Research Prompts. It is impossible to write a profile without conducting research of some sort, if not in the library or online, then in the field with one's subject. Doing some research up front, then, can be a useful way to find a subject to write about.

1. Return to the list you generated earlier in the "Listing Prompts" section. Choose a controversy in the community or on campus as the focus for your profile. Check the community and campus newspapers to discover who has been active as an advocate on the issue, or who has been impacted by it. Is any one person suitable for a profile?

2. Discuss your topic with your friends or people in your class. Who do they know who would be good as a profile subject?

3. On the Internet, search the archives of the local newspaper to find the names of potential profile subjects on an issue or controversy in which you're interested.

4. If you have a career interest, a profile of a working member of the profession can be compelling. Call the state professional association for suggestions about how to find an interview subject, or ask friends and family for suggestions.

ONE STUDENT'S RESPONSE

Bruce's Journal

RESEARCH ON LIST OF ISSUES

Issue	Interview Subjects
Recall	Margaret the storekeeper, Mayor Coles
Owyhee's wilderness	Congressperson, Simpson, Pat Ford
Migrant workers	Miguel Gomez, Rep. Bieter
Foothills preservation	Jack Coulter, Mayor, Nancy Maynard

Judging What You Have

You should have a considerable body of material to work with. It may not be coherent at this point, but again it's always better to work from abundance than from scarcity.

What's Promising Material and What Isn't? Let's look critically at the material you've generated. How will you choose the best profile subject? Consider the following criteria:

- *Accessibility.* The greatest subject in the world is no good to you if he or she is inaccessible.

- *Background.* Lacking time to spend with an interview subject, writers often look for information that may already exist: perhaps an article or two, a diary, a cigar box full of old pictures. Might you have access to such information on a possible subject?

- *Typicality.* Is the subject representative in some way of an aspect of a topic you'd like to investigate?

- *Extremity.* On the other hand, you may look for a subject who represents not the norm in a category of experience but an extreme.

- *Spontaneity.* Less experienced subjects, the kind you are most likely to profile, often have appeal because they *aren't* practiced at talking about themselves. There's freshness and even naiveté sometimes about what they say and how they say it that makes profiles particularly compelling.

- *Quotability.* Sometimes you simply can't know how quotable a subject might be until the interview. But if you do know beforehand that someone speaks in an interesting way, you may have a great profile subject.

- *Willingness.* I put this last for a reason. Most of us assume that people resist the kind of interviews a profile demands. A few profile subjects may, at first, resist the *idea* of being interviewed, but in reality people simply love to talk about themselves. An interview gives a subject a willing listener; how often do we enjoy the undivided attention of someone who is vitally interested in what we have to say about ourselves?

Questions About Audience and Purpose. As always, profile writing begins with a personal motivation. Is there something you think you can learn from your subject, perhaps something about an aspect of the world you are interested in, or something about the human spirit? By interviewing someone else is it possible to even learn something about yourself? You might also begin with a simpler, less grand, but no less important motive: Is there something this subject knows or feels that should be documented and preserved?

> The profile can, like good fiction, provide insight into the complexities of the human mind and soul.

As you evaluate the material you've generated, consider some of the following purposes that transcend your personal ones.

- *Which possible profile subject best fits the details of the assignment?* Your instructor may have provided guidance on how to approach the profile, including suggestions about choices of a profile subject or things to consider about audience. Which subject seems to best fit these guidelines?

- *Does this profile subject help illuminate an idea, issue, or controversy that might interest some of your readers?* The historical profile earlier in this chapter of "Alfalfa Bill," governor of Oklahoma during the Dust Bowl, is a small window through which readers can see the causes of environmental devastation. When given a face, a larger issue has a focus.

- *Does a profile subject represent a "type" of person that might interest readers?* Perhaps you're interested in the culture of sorority life on your campus and you have a willing subject who has belonged to Kappa Kappa Gamma for the last three years. Or perhaps you want to become a registered labor and delivery nurse. A profile of a working obstetric nurse will not only teach you something about your career choice but convince others that such a job is interesting, demanding, or not for them.

- *Is the profile subject an interesting character?* What often makes profile subjects interesting is that they shatter our assumptions about people and how they are in the world—a ninety-year-old man who still hikes fourteen-thousand-foot peaks, a fourteen-year-old college student, a therapist with marital problems, a lesbian activist in rural Mississippi, the president of an antifraternity fraternity. We are all composed of contradictions like these, but some are more surprising than others.

- *Who is your audience?* A key factor in any writing situation is audience. Who are you writing for in this assignment and which possible profile subjects would that audience find most compelling?

Interviewing

His interview subjects sometimes see John McPhee, one of the great profile writers, as "thick-witted." At times McPhee seems to ask the same questions over and over, and he frequently seems to possess only the most basic information about his subjects. According to William Howarth, when McPhee "conducts an interview he tries to be as blank as his notebook pages, totally devoid of preconceptions." His theory is that unless his interview subjects "feel superior or equal to their interviewer" they won't talk as freely or at length. McPhee never uses a tape recorder, but jots down spare notes in a notebook—these are the telling details and facts that reveal his subject's character.

McPhee is what some have called an *immersion journalist,* someone who spends substantial time with his subjects, getting to know them more intimately. This is the best basis for writing a profile because it generates enough information to get closer to the truth about the subject.

You can find more information about interviewing techniques in Chapter 11, "Research Techniques," but the following tips should help you start developing a plan for your interviews.

Making Contact. I'm a fairly shy guy. In fact, when I began writing nonfiction articles many years ago, the worst part of the work was calling people to ask

WRITING IN YOUR LIFE

Digital Profiles

Susan is a graduate student of mine who is working on a memoir about growing up on a farm in the desolate desert country of southern Idaho. Though her plan is to publish her book, Susan's project is typical of the kind of family history projects that have inspired millions to unravel genealogies, interview aging grandparents, and revisit the places where family roots run deep.

Interviews with living family members can become compelling profiles; they are characters in a longer story we can discover about ourselves. For example, Susan's Uncle Al, her father's brother, was not only an invaluable source of information; he became a memorable presence in her story and a richer portrait than any photograph or painting could be.

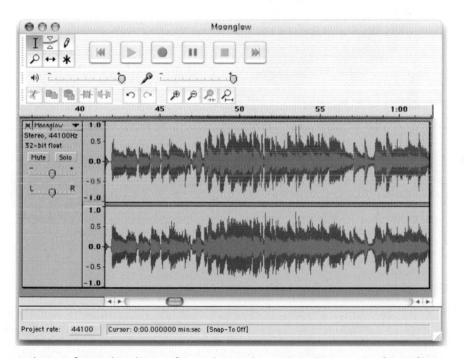

Audacity is free audio editing software that can be used to edit interviews for profiles.

There are many genealogical resources online (just try Googling "researching family history") but the audio recordings you make of your living family members create profiles that likely wouldn't exist unless you took the time to do them. It's

(continued)

Writing in Your Life (*continued*)

easier than ever. Digital recording, which has largely replaced tape, is easily edited on your computer using free audio editing software like Audacity. You can trim and move audio clips from your interview into a more coherent profile, and even add voice-overs or music. Your audio files can be easily converted to MP3 format, which can be played on MP3 players and computers and sent to your relatives in Kansas. These family profiles can also be combined with visuals using a program like Microsoft's Photo Story, another free download, and you can tell an even more powerful story about someone who matters in your family.

Microsoft Photo Story, a free download, can be used to tell a story with photos.

for their time to do an interview. These conversations almost always ended well for a simple reason—people love to talk about themselves. That's hardly surprising.

Asking a family member or friend to be an interview subject is easy, but how do you ask a stranger? You start by introducing yourself and straightforwardly describing the profile assignment, including your feeling that the subject would be a great focus for your piece. You must be prepared to answer the almost inevitable follow-up question: "Well, gee, I'm flattered. But what is it about me that you find interesting?" Here's where McPhee's elementary knowledge is crucial: Although you need to know only a very little about your interview subject, you must know enough to say, for instance, that you're aware of his role in a bit of history or his involvement in a local issue, or recognize him as being knowledgeable about a topic you find of interest.

What you want from this initial contact is time. The conventional interview—when you sit across from your informant asking questions and writing down answers—can be very useful, but it may be more productive if you can spend time *doing* something with your profile subject that relates to the reason you've chosen him. For example, if you are profiling a conservative activist, spend an hour watching him work the telephone, lining up people for the meeting at city hall. Your interview with a homeless woman could take place during lunch at the local shelter. *Seeing* your subject in a meaningful situation can generate far more information than the conventional interview. Imagine what those situations might be.

What do you do if your subject doesn't want to be interviewed? In that unlikely event, you're permitted to ask why. If your reassurances aren't sufficient to change the person's mind, then you need to find another subject.

Conducting the Interview. Should you prepare questions? Sure, but be prepared to ignore them. Interviews rarely go as planned, and if they do, they are often disappointing. An interview is a *conversation,* and these are best when they head in unexpected directions.

Certain generic questions can reveal things about a subject's character. These are *open-ended questions* that often lead in surprising and interesting directions. Some of these open-ended questions include the following:

- In all your experience with _____, what has most surprised you?
- What has been the most difficult aspect of your work?
- If you had the chance to change something about how you approached _____, what would it be?
- Can you remember a significant moment in your work on _____? Is there an experience with _____ that stands out in your mind?
- What do you think is the most common misconception about _____? Why?
- What are significant trends in _____?
- Who or what has most influenced you? Who are your heroes?
- If you had to summarize the most important thing you've learned about _____, what would you say? What is the most important thing that people should know or understand?

Notetaking during an interview is a challenge. A popular method is to use a tape or digital recorder (see "Inquiring into the Details: Recording Interviews"), but even if you do it's essential to take handwritten notes as well. Jot down any facts, details, phrases, mannerisms, or even personal reactions you have during the interview.

INQUIRING INTO THE DETAILS

Recording Interviews

Digital recorders have made tape recorders obsolete. This is good. For one thing, it's much easier to manage and edit digital files, and "running out of tape" in the middle of an interview is not a problem. The hard drives on digital recorders hold a lot of interviews.

Here are some tips on recording your interviews digitally:

- *You can use your MP3 player.* If you have the music player—and don't have a digital recorder—then you can buy an adapter that turns your MP3 player into a digital recorder. It's cheap, too. One manufacturer sells the adapter for less than $20.

- *You can record phone conversations.* A $20 adapter will also allow you to record phone conversations, but legally you must ask your subject's permission to do so. Covert recordings are very uncool. You can also use Skype to record phone conversations.

- *You can use software to transcribe recordings.* Several free programs (e.g., www.transana.org and www.trans.sourceforge.net) available online, for example, will help you control the playback speed so you can more easily type what you're hearing and will allow you to label and reorganize interview clips.

- *Take notes.* A combination of old (well, really old) technology, like handwritten notes, with the new technology, like digital recording, makes it more likely that your interview will yield the best material. Your notes—even if sketchy—provide an outline of what you've recorded and help you to find that great quote or essential piece of information more easily.

While my students have used the double-entry journal effectively as a note-taking format for profiles, putting the observed information and quotations on the left page and personal responses on the right, I'm keen on those pocket-sized memo books. They're incredibly unobtrusive and easy to carry, and they force you to be spare. I especially like the ease with which I can take the memo book out and put it away, at times using it to signal to my subject that I'm more—or less—interested in something he's saying.

Listening and Watching. The art of interviewing relies, more than anything else, on the craft of listening. Few of us are good listeners, which is why profile writing can be so hard. First you must control your anxiety about getting things down, asking the next question, and making your subject relaxed.

What makes a good conversation? When it generates the kind of information that will help you write the profile, including the following:

- *Stories.* Interesting stories and anecdotes help you build a narrative backbone to your essay.

- *Memorable quotations.* A typical interview produces only a handful of these, so don't desperately write down everything a subject says. Wait until you hear something that is nicely put or distinctive, particularly quotes that reveal something about your subject's character.

- *Background information.* This can be in the form of stories, but might also be basic but essential information such as your subject's age, place of birth, and history of involvement in relevant jobs or issues.

- *Feeling.* A good conversation is an honest one in which the subject is willing to let the mask slip to reveal the face sweating underneath. Be alert to those moments of feeling when your subject seems to be revealing herself— what *really* matters to her, what might be hard, where she finds joy.

■ INTERVIEW NOTES

Below are interview notes that Margaret Parker took in preparation for writing the powerful profile "Medical Student," which appears at the end of this chapter. As you read her notes, imagine the kinds of questions she had to ask to produce this kind of specific information about her subject, JD. Note the care Parker takes to get the facts straight, as well as her work to create a story through scenes and characterizations.

Your interview notes are the main source of information for your profile. If they're skimpy—brief or vague—you can't possibly write a profile that brings your subject to life.

Selected Interview Notes: "Medical Student"

Margaret Parker

"Oh my God JD you look so...together!"

Day begins at 3:30 a.m and ends at 8:30. Every fifth day "On-Call," goes to bed around nine in the student call room, divided by a sheet, sleeps in scrubs and sweatshirt and thick socks because it's freezing, around midnight a trauma comes in and have to do surgery. Then back to work the next day at 5:00 a.m, start with rounds and quizzed at 6:30 by residents.

Notice how careful the writer is to collect specific details— exact times, descriptions, and so on.

(continued)

(continued)

110 hr/week is average...120 hrs one week because she had call three times.

Operating Room (OR) environment—everything is sterile, only see eyes of people, must keep hands between waist and shoulders at all times, if not, the OR nurses scream at you and you have go leave and rescrub, shames, OR nurses like Nazis, her first week she was screamed at constantly, you just don't realize how hard it is to keep hands in place and the terror of getting yelled at. Just trying to please and doing really menial tasks like holding retractors or skin and muscle back so that the surgeon can do his thing, back spasms, very exhausting for five or eight hours, terrified to move. Med students are everybody's peon, the OR nurses are the worst...

The Worst Day

> In her notes, the writer integrates quotations within the overall narrative. She organizes her notes by roughly following the story she wants to tell. This often isn't possible because you don't yet know the story when you interview.

Supposed to be there at 5:00 for rounds, and meet with residents at 6:30 for the residents, her alarms didn't go off and the clock read 5:45. It takes forty-five minutes to drive from her apartment to Olympia Fields hospital, arrives at 6:27, "peeing my pants," Kelley—a short mall rat junior high looking girl, starts screaming at all of them, she asks JD a question and she doesn't know it, she walks away and the team is angry with JD. She scrubs in for the surgery, a cholecystectomy of a 16 yr. old girl, expected to last two hours, hands drop below the waist slightly and the OR nurse screams "I don't believe this crap, Student, you better go rescrub," the attending with open contempt in his eyes, the resident satisfied smirk barely detectable below the mask, holds the camera in the stomach for hours, the surgery starts to go badly, it is apparent it will take much longer than two hours, drags into its fourth hour, struggle to keep still, back spasms, "Wrong Goddamn direction!", everybody in shock, the camera is still in the girl's stomach, nobody moves to do anything, then he gets a hold of himself and resumes, it goes on, terrified, trying not to shake, part of her wants to walk out, screw him, she didn't sign up for this, paying 30 grand a year to be shaken and terrorized by psychopaths, but she stays, five hours the surgery is over, "God walks out," Kelly comes up and says, "Oh my God JD, don't worry about it, he's a jerk," and for a second these words are gratefully received, felt like an abused woman wanted to get in a car wreck so she wouldn't have to go, cried the whole way home, calculating the hours till she has to go back.

The Team

> Here the writer breaks with the narrative to get down descriptions of other characters.

Ryan—top of his class, wanted to do surgery but after the first week decided on Family UP practice or ER, counseled each other every day, go and hid and bitch

Keith "Special K"—disorder, you name it he's got it, OCD, super book smart but no social skills, disappears for hours, she tried to follow him but he lost her, then her friend Bernie called and swore that he saw him on campus, a good 45 minutes away, "Where the f—k is Keith," SD had to take over his surgeries because certain nurses wouldn't work with him, he touched his head and was generally unresponsive to their abuse, yet they wouldn't tell him, "SD tell him to put on his scrubs, tell him to go away," every night nightmares

Kelly—"so bipolar," seems like your chatty mall rat friend but then she turns into a demon

Trauma was better, the people were nicer, she was more valued, did useful things like chest compressions, took patient histories so they read her notes, Wendy Marshall the head honcho—British, teacher in every aspect, 'Pump-firing away of questions...'

"I have always wanted to be a doctor, and I couldn't really explain why. It was kind of a joke during my medical school interviews, because they always ask you, why do you want to be a doctor? And I'd reply with the generic, I wanna help people. But I guess now I think that I really like talking to people, and maybe in medicine I can help them. I think talking is the most important way to help sick people, not the real medicine that they teach you in school. People have such absolute faith in their doctor, and I love that feeling, that people confide in me."

> An extended quotation. These help the reader really hear your subject's voice, and they can be quite revealing. They're also hard to get without a tape recorder or excellent notetaking skills.

Writing the Sketch

When you think you've collected enough information about your profile subject from interviews, observations, and background research, compose a 500-word typewritten sketch. The sketch is a brief treatment of a promising subject that may lack a clear sense of purpose but does not lack specific information. For your profile sketch, your instructor will tell you which of the following elements you should incorporate:

- At least two potentially revealing anecdotes or brief stories about your profile subject.
- At least two strong quotations from your subject.
- A title.
- A paragraph of background information, including your informant's age, a physical description, and perhaps relevant job or personal history.
- A strong lead (perhaps one of the anecdotes) and an ending that somehow returns to the beginning.

Moving from Sketch to Draft

A sketch is generally underdeveloped, sometimes giving the writer just the barest outline of his subject. But as an early draft, a sketch can be invaluable. It might hint at what the "real" subject is, or what questions seem to be behind your inquiry into the subject. A sketch might suggest a focus for the next draft, or simply a better lead. Here are some tips for finding clues in your sketch about directions you might go in the next draft.

Evaluating Your Own Sketch. You must begin evaluating your sketch with more reasonable ambitions. It *is* impossible to capture the whole person, but what you are working toward in your profile is to capture an *aspect* of that person, some particular quality that stands out. Read your sketch, paying attention to one or both of those purposes:

1. *Dominant impression.* What feeling or personality trait do I want to communicate about my profile subject? Can I name it? Is there evidence in the sketch that points to this?
2. *Role.* What exactly am I trying to show—or might I show in the next draft—about my subject's participation in an idea, an issue, or an event?

Questions for Peer Review. Peer review of sketches can help writers clarify purpose. You've already done some thinking about that; now ask readers for help. You might pose the following questions:

■ If you were to use one word to describe your main impression of the person I profiled, what would it be?

■ What evidence would you point to in the sketch that contributes to that impression?

■ Did you find my portrait sympathetic or critical?

■ In a sentence, what seems to be my subject's main point of view, attitude, or belief?

■ What one detail—a fact, observation, description, or quotation—struck you as most revealing? What did it reveal?

■ What would you like to know more about in the next draft?

■ After reading the draft, what did you come to understand about the type of person profiled that you didn't know when you began the draft?

Reflecting on What You've Learned. Before you begin composing the next draft, make a journal entry that explores your thinking about the sketch and everything you heard. Begin an entry with the prompt, Based on what I've learned so far about my profile subject, the main thing I seem to be trying to show is _____.

Follow this prompt, continuing to reflect on what your intentions might be in the next draft. When the writing stalls, skip a line and make a quick list: The three things I heard during peer review that I want to remember are: (1) _____; (2) _____; and (3) _____.

Research and Other Strategies: Gathering More Information

If you emerged from the experience of writing and sharing your sketch with a stronger sense of purpose, then you're close to being ready to draft. If you didn't, return to your notes or share your sketch with a few more readers. In either case, you'll probably need to collect more information before you begin the draft. Most important, plan another interview with your subject. This one will likely be quite different; now that you have a clearer purpose for your profile, your questions will be directed at getting the information you need to more fully develop your piece.

You might consider other sources of information as well:

- Interview people who know your profile subject.
- If your subject is a public figure, do library or Web research for background.
- Do background research on your profile subject. Find out more about what she does or where she does it. Find out how she fits into a larger context. If you're writing about a **nurse-midwife, find out how** many are working in the state and what their licensing requirements might be.

The quotes and information you gather can be used in your profile, usually with attribution. Research the idea, issue, or event, if any, that provides the context for your profile.

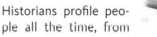

WRITING IN THE DISCIPLINES

Giving History a Face and a Voice

Historians profile people all the time, from vignettes of individuals in larger narratives (see "Alfalfa Dill" on page 120) to book-length biographies. Much of this work relies on so-called "primary sources"—original materials from sources who were first-hand witnesses or that come from a profile subject's own mouth and hand. Examples include letters, newspaper accounts, journals, transcripts, and oral histories. Libraries often archive this material. The Library of Congress (loc.gov) may be one of the richest sources of primary documents on a wide range of topics, and increasingly these are available online. You can find digital copies of historic photographs, letters written by famous (and ordinary) people, recorded interviews, oral histories, and original documents. This is interesting stuff. For example, you can hear the voices of individuals who suffered through the depression, endured slavery, fought in World War I, witnessed the 9/11 attacks, or pioneered the blues. These materials can bring any historical research project to life by providing profiles of the people who were there when it happened.

Composing the Draft

If you haven't collected enough information, you'll run aground pretty quickly in the draft.

If you're confident that you're working from abundance, consider beginning the drafting process by writing multiple leads. For example, work toward three one-paragraph beginnings—perhaps each focused on a different anecdote—and decide which one seems to point the draft in the direction you want it to go and is most likely to capture your readers. Once you've chosen a lead, follow it. You'll likely find that the leads you didn't use find a place for themselves somewhere else in the draft.

Methods of Development. You can pursue various strategies to develop your profile.

Narrative. The profile form often relies on narrative. It can do this in several ways; perhaps the most familiar is that the piece tells the story of the writer's encounter with her subject. For example, the profile of Albert Yeganeh (see p. 124), the "soup Nazi," is organized around the writer's visit one day to Yeganeh's Soup restaurant. The account includes the writer's reactions to what he was saying and doing. Profile writers are often drawn to the first-person account—my day with my subject—which is obviously a convenient structure if that matches the experience of the interviewer. However, consider whether a first-person point of view interrupts the narrative too much and interferes with the reader's view of the profile subject. After all, the writer isn't the subject of the profile.

Known to Unknown. If your profile subject is a public figure and your motive is to reveal a less well-known aspect of your subject's life or work, beginning the essay with information that first seems to confirm public perceptions but then promises to challenge them—in other words, moving from what's known to what's less known—can be an effective way to structure the profile. This method of development is quite common for celebrity profiles.

Using Evidence. The most authoritative information in a profile is the voice of your subject. It is also the information that will be most heavily scrutinized by the subject herself: "Did I really say that?" Readers of the profile often believe that the subject's voice is the most authentic information because it is less mediated by the writer, an assumption that isn't always accurate. After all, unless quotations come directly from the tape recorder, interviewers must rely on their notetaking skill. Even with a recorded transcription, writers commonly tidy up bad grammar and remove irrelevant utterances such as "uh" and "um."

A profile writer must also establish his authority by giving readers a sense that he is a keen and careful observer; he does so by carefully using not just quotation but detail, description, and research. Consider how the author of "Soup" did this when profiling restaurant owner Albert Yeganeh.

Workshopping the Draft

If your draft is subject to peer review (see Chapter 14 for details on how to organize workshop groups), think carefully about the kind of responses you need from readers at this point in the process. The following questions might help you prepare.

Reflecting on the Draft. As you prepare your draft for peer review, think about what you most need in a response. Are you reasonably confident that the purpose and focus of your profile is clear? Or are you feeling anxious about how well you managed to pull it all together? Your initial feelings about the draft will be a factor in the kind of response you request from your group.

- Make a journal entry in which you reflect in a five-minute fastwrite about how you feel about the draft. What worked? What needs work?

- If the writing stalls, consider this question: *If I could change the process of writing this draft, from initially generating a subject to write about to this first draft, what would I change?* Follow this with a fastwrite until you have nothing more to say.

Questions for Readers. As you prepare for peer review, certain questions are also particularly useful to consider when drafting profiles. Pose to your group any of these questions that seem relevant to your draft or possible plans for revision.

1. What dominant impression did the draft create of its subject? What words would you use to describe that impression?

2. In a sentence or two, what does the draft seem to be *saying* about its subject?

3. Does the end strain to return to the beginning, or does it give the profile a sense of wholeness or unity?

4. What is the strongest/weakest quote? What is the strongest/weakest anecdote?

5. What do you want to know about the profile subject that the draft doesn't say?

6. Did you find this person interesting? Why or why not?

7. Did you learn anything about this type of person?

Revising the Draft

Revision is a continual process, not a last step. You've been revising—literally "re-seeing" your subject—from the first messy fastwriting in your journal. But the things that get your attention during revision vary depending on where you are in the writing process. You've generated material, chosen a topic, done some research, and written both a sketch and draft. Most students think that the only thing left to do is "fix things." Check for misspellings. Correct an awkward sentence or two. Come up with a better title. This is editing, not revision, and while editing is important, to focus solely on smaller "fixes" after writing a first draft squanders an opportunity to really *learn* from what the draft is telling you, or perhaps not quite telling you.

Chapter 13 can help guide these discoveries. The questions you can ask about a draft fall into five categories: purpose, idea, information, development, and editing. Use the following chart to find the revision strategies in Chapter 13 that might help you re-see what you've written so far.

GUIDE TO REVISION STRATEGIES

Problems in the Draft (Chapter 13)	Page Number
Unclear purpose ■ Not sure what the essay is about? Fails to answer the *So what?* question?	551
Unclear thesis, theme, or main idea ■ Not sure what you're trying to say?	557
Lack of information or development ■ Needs more details; more showing and less telling?	564
Disorganized ■ Doesn't move logically or smoothly from paragraph to paragraph?	568
Unclear or awkward at the level of sentences and paragraphs ■ Seems choppy or hard to follow at the level of sentences or paragraphs?	577

Profiles typically have some of the following problems, most of which can be addressed by selecting appropriate revision strategies, or by repeating some of the earlier steps in this chapter.

- The draft lacks a single coherent theme, or dominant impression. Is your profile organized from beginning to end around one main thing you're trying to say about your subject?

- The theme or dominant impression is obvious but isn't developed with enough specific information. Do you need to do another interview?

- You find your subject interesting, but you haven't given your readers enough reason to agree. Does your lead make a strong enough case? Is there another story you should tell?

Polishing the Draft. After you've dealt with the big issues in your draft—is it sufficiently focused, does it answer the *So what?* question, is it organized, and so on—you must deal with the smaller problems. You've carved the stone into an appealing figure, but now you need to polish it. Are your paragraphs coherent? How do you manage transitions? Are your sentences fluent and concise? Are there any errors in spelling or syntax? Section 5 of Chapter 13 can help you focus on these issues.

Before you finish your draft, work through the following checklist:

✓ Every paragraph is about one thing.

✓ The transitions between paragraphs aren't abrupt.

✓ The length of sentences varies in each paragraph.

✓ Each sentence is concise. There are no unnecessary words or phrases.

✓ You've checked grammar, particularly verb agreement, run-on sentences, unclear pronouns, and misused words (*there / their, where / were,* and so on). (See the handbook at the end of the book for help with these grammar issues.)

✓ You've run your spellchecker and proofed your paper for misspelled words.

■ STUDENT ESSAY

What impresses me most about the following profile is the way that Margaret Parker managed to write in a style that captures the intensity of her subject's experience during a single day as a medical student. The piece has a breathless, panicked quality that wonderfully matches the writer's purpose in the profile. The essay is also richly detailed, keeping our attention riveted on the subject throughout. An amazing thing about this is that Parker didn't actually witness the story she writes about; all of the material was gathered from her interviews (see "Selected Interview Notes: 'Medical Student,'" earlier in the chapter). Can you imagine what questions she must have asked to be able to write these scenes?

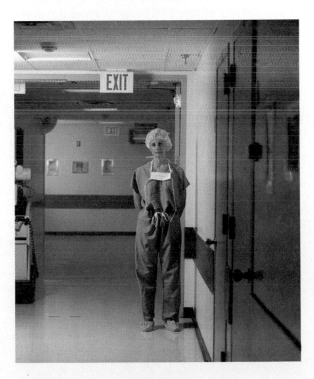

Medical Student

Margaret Parker

The Worst Day

1   Something is terribly wrong. For starters, she feels almost rested. The deep black pitch of the room has begun to soften into the gray light of dawn. JD's stomach plummets as she sees the glaring red numbers on her alarm clock.

2   *5:45 a.m. Ohmygodohmygodohmygod . . .*

3   She swears she set the alarm for 3:30 the night before, but it didn't go off. Rounds start at 6:30, but she's supposed to arrive at Olympia Fields Hospital by 5:00 a.m. to examine all her patients and prepare for the resident's inquisition at 6:30. There's no time to brush her teeth, eat, drink, think; she throws on some clothes, dives into her car and screams obscenities in the air throughout the frantic forty-five-minute drive. By some miracle she makes it to the hospital by 6:27. Ryan and Keith, the other third-year medical students on her surgery rotation team, cast disapproving glances tinged with terror in her direction.

4   Chief Resident Kelly saunters up to the students; even at this ungodly hour she is bright-eyed and menacing, ready for the kill. She assesses each of them with a consciously intimidating drawn-out glare, and once again displaying an uncanny instinct for sensing weakness in her prey, zones her attention on JD.

5   "Hey Student, tell me about Mrs. Gomez's labs."

6   The collective fear of the group is palpable. JD bites the bullet and replies the unthinkable, "I don't know."

7   Rage and disgust wash over Kelly's face. "You're all so pathetic," she says, and then turns and walks away. Rounds end early this morning; they have all failed.

8   Ryan won't even look at her he's so furious and even Keith snorts angrily and stomps off. If Keith thinks you're a loser, you know it must be true. The residents call him "Special K" because he suffers from obsessive-compulsive disorder and just about every other mental ill-ness you can imagine. He hasn't been able to adapt to the turbo-intense lifestyle of the gen-eral surgery rotation. He'll show up to his scheduled surgery without his scrubs, ask the same question repeatedly, or simply disappear for hours at a time. On any other day the "team screw-up" award would invariably go to him, but on this hellish morning, JD has emerged the winner.

9   But there's no time to dwell. She has to go to the pre-op room and scrub in for surgery. This morning she will assist Dr. Donnelly, Chief Attending Surgeon, Kelly, and an OR nurse in the cholecystectomy of a sixteen-year-old girl. Donnelly isn't too worried about it; he told the girl's parents it would take two hours, max.

10   All scrubbed in and donning a surgical mask, cap, and scrubs, JD marches into the OR room where the others are already waiting for her. For just a split second, her hands fall below her waist, and she immediately corrects her stance and looks around to make sure no one has seen her slip. The OR nurse is fuming in her direction. It amazes JD how much emo-tion a person can express when half of her face is covered with a mask.

"Student get the hell outta here and rescrub! Jesus!" she booms throughout the room. Donnelly and Kelly roll their eyes and share a moment of mutual disgust.   11

JD can't believe she did this again, and on this morning of all mornings. Her first week of surgery was pure torture as she was constantly being thrown out of the OR for allowing her hands to drift out of the sacred "waist to shoulders" zone, but she's a sharp girl, and their scare tactics had effectively beat it into her. But her tardiness this morning has frazzled her nerves, and she's not herself.   12

She sucks in a deep breath, closes her eyes, and reenters the OR to begin the surgery. Donnelly has her position a long probe with a tiny camera attached to it into the patient's stomach so he can view what he is doing on a TV monitor. She must hold this position in complete stillness for the entire surgery.   13

The two-hour mark passes, and it becomes clear to all that the procedure is not going well. Donnelly starts swearing and muttering under his mask, and the tension in the room rises. Three and a half hours. Donnelly is seething; he just can't seem to get it right. He snaps at JD to turn the camera at a different angle; she does this. He barks at her to turn it again, just slightly to the right, and she complies.   14

Then he snaps.   15

"Student you've got it the wrong goddamn way!" he snarls at her, grabbing her arm and painfully bearing his fingers into her. He loses it, starts shaking her violently in spite of the instrument she is still holding inside the patient's stomach. Kelly and the nurse stare dumbly at them both.   16

Donnelly stops shaking her, composes himself and turns his focus back on the patient. The others emerge from their stupor and do the same. JD is dumbfounded. Should she leave, walk out? If she had an ounce of self respect left she would. Who does this guy think he is? But she knows if she leaves, he'll fail her, and she's worked way too hard to fail now.   17

After five hours, the surgery is a success. Donnelly closes the patient up, and with the air of a god, swaggers out of the OR. Once he's outside and well out of earshot, Kelly whispers to JD conspiratorially: "Oh my God JD, don't worry about it...he's such a jerk."   18

For a split second, JD's eyes water over and she is touched by this rare display of kindness from the girl she calls "the demon." But it doesn't last. It dawns on her that Kelly hadn't said a word to Donnelly; she'd let him take it all out on the medical student to save her own ass.   19

Thank God for Ryan. He doesn't hold a grudge from this morning; he can't afford to. JD and Ryan barely knew each other before this rotation began, but war has a way of bonding soldiers together. They spend the hours between surgery and rounds seeking out hiding places in the hospital where they spew out all the crap they've had to deal with that day. As they whisper in a janitor's closet, a voice sounds over the hospital intercom: "Surgery extern report to OR-3, surgery extern, report to OR-3."   20

"Why do they call us 'externs'? That makes it sound like we get to go home," she laughs.   21

"Doesn't 'Special K' have surgery in 3 today?" Ryan asks.   22

"Oh crap," JD says. She knows what this means. There's a certain OR nurse who refuses to work with Keith. He simply lacks the Pavlovian response mechanism that allows creatures to   23

(continued)

(continued)

learn from negative feedback; no matter how much she screams at him, he continues to touch his head in the OR and let his arms droop to his sides. But no one will tell Keith that he's been banned. Instead they page JD to fill in for him and leave Keith clueless.

24   JD jogs over to OR-3 where Keith is purposefully scrubbing in. As usual, no one has told him. The OR nurse approaches JD. "Student, tell him he can't scrub in."

25   "Uh, Keith," she says, "why don't you go check on your patients' labs or something."

26   Keith looks crushed as the situation sinks in. He knows he is failing, and every day he seems more and more unstable. He mutters some obscenity and storms off. JD scrubs in for another five-hour procedure.

27   It's 8:00, almost time to go home. She's had nothing to eat or drink all day. Surgeons severely limit their intake of liquids because they cannot under any circumstances leave the OR to use the bathroom. Her urine is bloody from dehydration. After evening rounds are over, she slugs into the locker room to change back into her normal clothes. Keith is standing there, perfectly still, wearing ridiculously skin-tight scrubs.

28   "JD," he says in a faraway voice without looking at her, "do you have any trauma scissors?"

29   "Sure," she says. "Why?"

30   "These scrubs are so tight," he says. "I don't know how I ever got into them. Could you cut them off of me?"

31   JD ponders this for a moment, wondering if he has finally lost it completely.

32   "Sure, Keith." She starts at his feet and cuts a sliver all the way up to his neckline. He peels them off like skin and stands before her in his boxers. An eerie, uncomfortable silence lingers between them. She gathers her things and leaves.

33   JD climbs into her car and starts the drive home. She starts crying, and soon her whole body is heaving with sobs. As she drives on the busy Chicago streets, the thought that's been pestering her mind like a virus since she began the surgery rotation returns to her. She fantasizes about swerving off the road—oh, not to die, really, just to be injured enough to not have to go back to that hellhole tomorrow. She doesn't want to be a doctor anymore, not if this is what it is really like. If she weren't $75,000 in debt, she would drop out right now and never look back. It's almost 9:00. In six and a half hours it will all begin again.

Evaluating the Essay

1. How does Margaret Parker craft the essay to give it the panicked, breathless feeling that contributes so much to her overall profile of JD? What does she do at the sentence and paragraph level that gives it those qualities?

2. "Medical Student" focuses on a single day. In what other ways might you use time to help you organize and focus a profile?

3. Like many profiles, "Medical Student" focuses on a single person as part of an effort to give the reader a glimpse at a category of people (med

students) or experiences (internships at hospitals). Is there a danger of overgeneralizing from a specific case? How do writers avoid that?

4. If the essay were to continue, what else would you want to know or see about JD and the life she leads?

USING WHAT YOU HAVE LEARNED

You've read published profiles and one written by a student. You've also had the chance to write your own. What have you learned about the profile genre of writing and how might you use this in other writing situations?

1. What are the ethical obligations of writers to their profile subjects? For example, do you think it should be standard practice for subjects to approve profiles before they're published? What is reasonable for a profile subject to expect from a writer?

2. While a profile isn't an academic form, can you imagine how you might use some of the methods and approaches you tried here in papers for other classes?

3. A profile of one person who is representative of a larger social group is decidedly unscientific. It just isn't possible to make scientifically reliable generalizations about the group from a single case. Then what good is a profile?

Reviewer Mark Kermode describes Johnny Depp as a "brilliantly physical performer" capable of "finely honed movements," yet regards his work as Captain Jack Sparrow in *Pirates of the Caribbean: Dead Man's Chest* as some of his "very worst work to date."

WRITING A REVIEW

WRITING THAT EVALUATES

One of the occasions when I feel fairly stupid is after watching a movie with my wife, Karen. She always wants to know what I think. I don't have much of a problem arriving at a gut reaction—I loved the movie *Amelie,* for example, but I have a hard time saying why. Beyond statements such as, "It was pretty good," or "It was pure Hollywood," a comment I mean to be critical, the conversation scares me a little because Karen is wonderfully analytical and articulate when describing her feelings about a film. In comparison, I stutter and stammer and do my best to go beyond a simple judgment.

Essentially, Karen is asking me to evaluate a film, to make a judgment about its quality. This is something we do all the time. Buying a pair of jeans involves evaluating the reputation of the manufacturer, the quality of the denim and its particular design, and especially aesthetic judgments about how the jeans look on us when we wear them. I think most of us like to think these decisions are quite rational. On the contrary, many of our evaluations are more emotional than logical. We *really do* buy that pair of jeans because an ad suggests that we'll look sexy or attractive in them. Or consider this: How would you evaluate the quality of your mother's or father's parenting? Will this be a rational judgment? It's unlikely. Even though we're qualified to make such a judgment—after all, who is a better authority on the parenting skills of parents than their children—our views toward our parents are always awash in feelings.

You know, then, that part of the challenge of evaluating something is keeping an open mind, sometimes *despite* our initial feelings about it. Because all evaluation stems from what are essentially subjective value judgments, a tension

What You'll Learn in This Chapter

- The role of evaluation in a review.
- How feelings and reason can form the basis of evaluation.
- How to develop criteria for making judgments.
- Questions that will help you revise a review.

always exists between our *desire* to prove our point and our *need* or *willingness* to learn more about the subject.

That emotion figures into our judgments of things isn't a bad thing. It's a human thing. But one of the reasons it's useful to consciously consider *how* we make such judgments is that we're more likely to introduce logical considerations in mostly emotional evaluations, or emotional considerations in mostly logical ones. This awareness also helps us suspend judgment long enough to get a more balanced look at something.

Evaluation involves three things:

1. *Judgment.* Something is good or bad, useful or not useful, relevant or not relevant, convincing or not convincing, worth doing or not worth doing, or perhaps shades in between.

2. *Criteria.* These form the basis by which we judge whether something is good or bad, useful or not useful, and so on. Often our criteria are implicit; that is, we aren't even consciously aware of the criteria that inform judgments. The more familiar we are with the thing—say, cars, movies, or mystery novels—the more elaborate and sophisticated the criteria become.

3. *Evidence.* Criteria provide the principles for making a judgment, but evidence—specific details, observations, or facts about the thing itself—is what makes an evaluation persuasive.

If this sounds a lot like making an argument, you're right, because evaluation is the basis of argument. But I suspect that emotion, at least initially, figures more in our judgments of things than our reasoned arguments about them. In fact, evaluation can be a way of seeding the field of argument because it helps you identify the things about which you have strong opinions.

MOTIVES FOR WRITING A REVIEW

Evaluative writing is one of the most common kinds of writing I do, from commenting on student papers, to writing reference letters for former students, to writing a memo to my colleagues about a proposed departmental policy. Evaluative writing is an enormously practical form, relevant in all sorts of situations in and out of school. Quite simply, we turn to it when we are asked to make a judgment of value, and then develop that judgment into something that goes beyond a gut reaction and unstated assumptions.

I once had a professor, Peter Sandman, who had a theory of behavior that was inspired, in part, by advertising research. Sandman argued that while we want to believe that our actions are based on reasoned judgments, frequently we decide to do something based on an "irrational motivator." We buy toothpaste, for example, not because of the evidence of its effectiveness but on the promise of sex appeal. It's only *after* we behave irrationally that we actively seek out information that makes our choice seem sensible. That's one reason why, after you purchase a car, you start noticing that make and model everywhere and feel pleased with yourself that others endorse your choice.

A motive for turning to evaluative writing like reviews is to work against emotion as a sole reason for doing or thinking something. When the worth of our judgments must be measured against particular criteria and evidence, sex appeal isn't enough to justify buying Crest toothpaste. We need to really know what we're talking about.

> Evaluative writing is an enormously practical form, relevant in all sorts of situations in and out of school.

Evaluative writing helps you work from that feeling outward into reason, which will make your judgment persuasive to others *and* help shape your future judgments about other similar things. That's why my conversations with Karen about movies, once I stop feeling stupid, can be so helpful: because she challenges me to find reasons for what I feel, reasons that I am slowly learning to apply to my judgments of other films.

If you feel strongly about something, turn to evaluative writing and thinking as a way to help yourself and others understand why.

THE REVIEW AND ACADEMIC WRITING

We don't usually think of the review as an academic form, although you may be asked to review a film you're shown in an English class or perhaps a performance in a theater class. But evaluative writing, a process you'll practice when writing a review, is among the most common types of writing in all kinds of college classrooms.

Once you start thinking about evaluative writing, you'll find it everywhere— the book reviews in the Sunday *Times,* the music reviews in *Spin,* the analysis of Web sites on WebSitesThatSuck.com. It's probably the most common form of

---

WRITING IN THE DISCIPLINES

Evaluation Across the Disciplines

Evaluation is an important part of academic writing in many disciplines. Here are a few examples of the different types of evaluative writing you may be asked to compose in your college courses.

- In a science class, you may need to evaluate the methodology of an experiment.
- Business writing may require evaluation of a marketing strategy, a product, or a business plan.
- Philosophy frequently involves the evaluation of arguments.
- In a literature class, you may be asked to evaluate the effectiveness of a story or a character.
- In a theater class, you may write a review of a dramatic performance.
- In a composition class, you're often asked to evaluate the writing of peers.

workplace writing, too, from assessing the performance of an employee to evaluating a plan to preserve historic buildings.

FEATURES OF THE FORM

Like all forms of writing, evaluation genres vary widely. Perhaps the least likely form is one in which the writer formally announces a judgment, lists criteria, and then offers evidence using the criteria. That is, at least, an approach that you'll have a hard time finding outside school. Much evaluative writing is more subtle than that—and much more interesting—because the writer blends judgments, criteria, and evidence seamlessly throughout. If you've ever read a review of a band, a computer, or a book, you probably never noticed its structure because if the review is well written the structure isn't noticeable. But most reviews share some features, and many of them are a part of all kinds of evaluative writing.

- *A review is usually clear about categories.* Of course, the effectiveness of all writing depends on responding to a certain situation, but evaluative writing is particularly sensitive to the *category* of thing you're writing about. For example, the inverted pyramid in Figure 5.1 shows the narrowing of categories of film, working toward a more limited category—say, feature films about space travel. It's easier to come up with convincing criteria to judge a narrower category than a broad, general one.

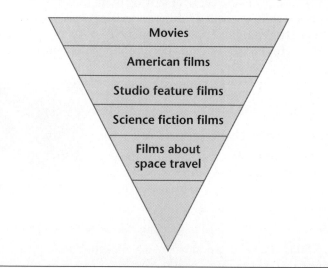

Figure 5.1   Narrowing the category of evaluation. One of the keys for developing useful and relevant criteria for judging something is making sure that you're focusing on the neighborhood, not the globe. In this example, it's much more helpful to talk about what makes a good Hollywood science fiction film about space travel than attempt to describe the qualities of the much broader category—all movies. After all, what makes a foreign art film effective is probably different from what makes a romantic comedy effective.

- *Reviews usually describe the thing they evaluate.* How much you describe depends on your readers' knowledge of what you're evaluating. If they haven't seen the performance, don't know the actor, haven't read the book, or don't know the type of product you're reviewing, then readers need the necessary background to understand what exactly you're talking about. Summaries can be vital.

- *Evaluation criteria are matched to purpose, category, and audience.* Obviously, a writer has reasons for making a judgment about something. Always in the back of the writer's mind is the purpose of the evaluation. what exactly he or she is writing about (and *not* writing about). If your aim is to help businesses understand which Web sites are likely to sell the most T-shirts, your criteria will be different from those used to evaluate the Web sites nonprofit groups might use to educate people about world hunger. Like all persuasive writing, the review is shaped by its audience.

- *In reviews, feelings often lead judgment but they are never enough.* Although evaluation is a form of argument, reason doesn't always lead judgment. Frequently, we first *feel* something—the Web site turns us off, or the new music video is captivating, or the reading assignment puts us to sleep. These feelings often lead us to an initial judgment—something we might acknowledge to readers—but they are never enough. The challenge of persuasive evaluation is to introduce reason into the process.

- *Judgments range from an overall assessment (it was good or bad, helpful or useless, and so on) to more specific commentary on particular evidence or aspects of the thing.* These judgments don't reside in one place in some kind of grand thesis, but are scattered throughout a review essay, working toward a more complicated assessment of the movie, book, or performance you're evaluating.

> The challenge of persuasive evaluation is to introduce reason into the process.

- *Reviews frequently attempt to offer a balanced assessment.* Hey, it can't be *all* bad. (Okay, sometimes it is.) The most persuasive negative evaluations tend to include some positive judgments, and positive evaluations frequently make some concessions about a thing's flaws.

- *Criteria may be stated or unstated.* You'll rarely find a piece of evaluative writing that neatly lists all the criteria used to judge the thing; in fact, some criteria may be implicit. Why? A common reason is that the writer and audience *share* certain assumptions about how to judge the value of a thing.

- *Relevant comparisons may form the backbone of a review.* Our fascination with winners and losers is reflected in one of the most ubiquitous evaluations in American culture: rankings. We rank cars, movies, music videos, celebrities' tastes in fashion, colleges, cameras, diets, and Web sites. The key, of course, is making sure that the things you're comparing do indeed belong in the same class, that you're comparing apples to apples and not apples to oranges.

READINGS

■ REVIEW 1

Mark Kermode is a British film critic who recently called the 2006 film *Little Man* "genuinely evil," and added "if you go and see it, shame on you." While I don't think I've heard him be that unequivocal about the faults of a film, Kermode's dislike of the *Pirates of the Caribbean* series, which stars the actor Johnny Depp, is well known to the fans who listen to his reviews on the BBC. In the review that follows, Kermode takes the second film in the trilogy, *Pirates of the Caribbean: Dead Man's Chest*, to task for its absence of narrative, its "pout performances," and most of all, its "interminable length."

Popular film criticism relies heavily on what Aristotle called *ethos,* or the character of the speaker. As readers, we want to appreciate the wit and intelligence of a reviewer, even when we disagree with him or her. A mindless rant or vacant praise simply won't engage readers. As you read Kermode's movie review, consider why you find him persuasive or why you don't.

Pirates of the Caribbean: Dead Man's Chest
Mark Kermode

1   Given my contempt for the first *Pirates of the Caribbean* movie, a triumph of turgid theme-park hackery over the art of cinema, it was assumed that I would have nothing positive to say about this sequel. On the contrary: the digitally enhanced squid-face of villain Davy Jones (he of the locker) is very well rendered, demonstrating the wonders of CGI and motion-capture technology. Reliable British actor Bill Nigh performs the human duties behind the high-tech make-up, lending an air of rancid fun to this slimy sea beast, who yo-ho-hos around the ocean accompanied by a crew of rum-sodden crustaceans.

2   There are a few moments of zany slapstick too, such as a fruit-throwing chase scene in which a skewered Captain Jack Sparrow becomes a human kebab, harking back to the days when the film's director, Gore Verbinski, made such innocuous fare as the slapstick farce *MouseHunt*. And I did laugh at one verbal gag about 'making the pleasure of your carbuncle'. So that's a thumbs up for the squid, the kebab and the carbuncle. Which is three more things than I liked about the last one.

Other than that, it's boring business as usual for this second instalment in what is now a trilogy in the manner of all things post-*Lord of the Rings*. The plot (and I use the word loosely) is episodic to the point of incoherence, constantly reminding us that this is a film franchise based upon a fairground ride. Every five minutes a new quest is announced, sending us rattling off on another tack, each more fatuously inconsequential than the last. Go get Jack Sparrow's magic compass! Go seek out this magic key! Go track down the Flying Dutchman! Go dig up Davy Jones's locker! Go and harvest 99 souls in three days! An early line about 'setting sail without knowing his own heading' seems to apply to the screenwriters as much as the pirates, and it's a full 40 minutes before any sense of direction is established at all.

The romping tone may aspire to the nostalgic swashbuckle of Steven Spielberg's *Raiders of the Lost Ark* series (replete with John Williams-lite 'ta-ran-ta raaa' score by Hans Zimmer), but it is the rambling blather of Lucas's *Star Wars* prequels which is most pungently evoked. So muddled is the narrative that the characters have to keep stopping and explaining the story to each other ('You mean, if I find the chest, I will find Will Turner...'). By the time the closing credits roll the story hasn't actually gone anywhere, and there's still a whole other movie to come.

In the absence of narrative we are left with a string of 'spectacular' set pieces to hold our attention. Verbinski may be a witless hack, but he understands the laws of supply and demand and doesn't skimp on the money-shots. Thus we get giant-tentacled Kraken attacks, ghost ships rising from the dead, and multiple storm-riven battle scenes. When it comes to directing performances, however, Verbinski is completely at sea, leaving his rudderless cast to indulge themselves to their heart's content.

The fact that Johnny Depp received an Oscar nomination for his boggle-eyed, drawl-mouthed Keith Richards' impression doesn't change my opinion that the role of Jack Sparrow has produced some of the actor's very worst work to date. Depp is a brilliantly physical performer whose finely honed movements have breathed eerie life into characters as diverse as Ed Wood and Edward Scissorhands, and whose expressive voice lent an air of melancholy magic to the animated gem Corpse Bride.

Yet Verbinski is no Tim Burton, and under his slack direction Depp defaults to an untrammelled showiness not seen since the sub-Buster Keaton antics of Benny and Joon. In *Dead Man's Chest,* every moment is a symphony of eye-rolling, hair-tossing, lip-pouting, finger-fiddling narcissism. It's like being trapped in a room with a drunk karaoke singer who's having much more fun than his audience.

As for poor old Orlando Bloom, where does one start to document the tidal wave of wetness which he brings to these proceedings? No matter how much sea water Verbinski throws at the set, nothing gets as damp as Mr. Bland, whose expressions run the gamut from perky to peeved with occasional interludes of petulance.

(continued)

(continued)

9   An early scene finds an imprisoned Keira Knightley saucily telling her fiancé: 'If it weren't for these bars, I'd have you already.' The idea of anyone 'having' this doe-eyed waif is hilarious, and a frightened looking Orlando promptly runs away to sea, leaving a trail of froth in his wake. Knightley, meanwhile, puts her best teeth forward and does her haughty Head Girl act, stopping only to lock lips with Depp in a red herring subplot which will presumably spark some dreary love triangle misunderstanding in Part Three. How on earth will Orlando react? I'm betting on 'prissy'.

10   Lumpen direction, lousy writing and pouting performances aside, the worst thing about *Dead Man's Chest* is its interminable length. The entire *Pirates of the Caribbean* franchise may be a horrible indicator of the decline of narrative cinema (and probably Western civilization), but the rank consumerist decrepitude of it all would be tolerable if the film wasn't quite so boring. At a bum-numbing two-and-a-half hours, this is what weak-bladdered studio boss Jack Warner used to refer to as 'a three-piss picture'—in every sense. Thank heavens for the squid.

Inquiring into the Essay

Explore, explain, evaluate, and reflect on "Pirates" by Mark Kermode.

1. Initiate a conversation in your journal with Kermode about his review. Imagine that you're engaged in an instant-message conversation with Kermode. He's just sent you a message that observes that "it's boring business as usual for this second installment" of *The Pirates of the Caribbean,* adding that in *Dead Man's Chest* "every moment [watching Depp] is a symphony of eye-rolling, hair tossing, lip-pouting, finger-fiddling narcissism." Write back. Try to play the believing and doubting games in your response. How do you agree? How do you disagree? What has Kermode failed to consider?

2. Analyze the ways that "Pirates" reflects the "Features of the Form" listed earlier in the chapter. Explain exactly where in Kermode's review he seems to incorporate those features.

3. All reviews make an argument, but it often can't be reduced easily to a single thesis or central claim. Reread Kermode's review, and try to list the claims he's making about the film. Which do you find most persuasive? Which are least persuasive? Why?

4. One way to get better as a writer who persuades readers is to pay attention to how *you* respond to written arguments. Tell the story of your thoughts and feelings as you read Kermode's review. Reread the review, pausing after the first paragraph to write for two minutes in

your journal about what you're feeling about Kermode, what he's saying, and how he's saying it. What story do these three episodes of writing tell about your experience of the review? What do they suggest about effective argument?

■ REVIEW 2

Criterion for a great car: You turn the key and it starts. Okay, so I don't have sophisticated taste in automobiles. For better or for worse, we are a car-loving culture, and, for some, every detail of an automobile like the Lotus Exige S 240, from the size of the intercooler to the automated launch-control system, is a source of fascination. It isn't the $70,000 price tag that inspires such devoted interest. Some people just love cars at any price. Though with diminishing oil reserves and global warming, many of us are now devoted to our bicycles, the vast majority of us still drive cars, and even if you're not a fan it makes sense to pay attention to judgments about quality.

We're not talking about Fords here, though. *New York Times* writer Ezra Dyer's review of the 2008 Lotus that follows is clearly written for automobile aficionados. It's interesting, however, even for readers who are not—particularly if they notice those moments when the piece seems to work for them and moments when it does not. These are moments that say a lot about how a piece of writing is crafted with a particular rhetorical situation in mind.

The 2008 Lotus Exige S 240.

A Ton (Just Barely) of Fun

Ezra Dyer

1   Colin Chapman, the racecar builder and founder of Lotus, followed a straightforward path to high performance: ignore the horsepower wars and focus on keeping weight low.

2   In 1990, a Lotus Esprit SE driven by Richard Gere made a memorable cameo in *Pretty Woman*. That car was powered by a small turbocharged 4-cylinder engine, yet with a weight of less than 3,000 pounds it was able to reach 60 miles an hour in less than five seconds.

3   Since then, the industry trend has been toward vehicles that are bigger, heavier and more powerful. Not at Lotus, the British sports car maker: the 2008 Exige S 240 is smaller, lighter and less powerful than that 1990 Esprit. It's also faster.

4   In another couple of decades, you might expect the Lotus flagship to be an electron with a steering wheel. Even then, they'll be trying to get it down to a quark.

5   Building a car with an emphasis on austerity and light weight starts a happy chain reaction of performance-enhancing consequences. For instance, because the Exige is light—just 2,077 pounds, Lotus says—it can generate ferocious road grip with relatively skinny tires. Each of the 195-width front tires on the Exige is actually a bit narrower than the rear tire of a 2009 Yamaha Vmax motorcycle.

6   As a result, the Exige gets by without power steering, trimming away a few more pounds. (Fearless assertion: the Exige has the most delicious steering feel of any current production car.) And you might even sweat off a few pounds wrestling that nonassisted steering at parking-lot speeds. Who needs Jenny Craig when you've got Colin Chapman?

7   The Exige is more comfortable than it looks. The seats are wafer-thin and barely adjustable. (The driver's seat moves fore and aft; the passenger seat is bolted to the floor.) But once you've limboed your way inside, it's not a bad place to be.

8   There is plenty of legroom and those severe-looking seats actually prove surprisingly accommodating. Need to adjust the passenger-side door mirror? It's not motorized, but you can reach it from the driver's seat. As for amenities, there's air-conditioning, power windows, power locks and even a strikingly minimalist cup holder consisting of little more than a small ring of aluminum that suspends a leather strap. Lotus should trademark this design and call it the Coffee Thong.

9   The S 240 is powered by a 1.8-liter Toyota 4-cylinder, supercharged to an output of 240 horsepower, that drives the rear wheels. The mid-mounted engine has a huge intercooler perched on top, so rearward visibility could charitably be described as compromised. You learn to back into parking-lot spaces, because reversing into traffic would be an invitation to catastrophe.

10   Lotus says the Exige S 240 is the quickest car it has ever made ever, with a zero-to-60 time of 4.1 seconds. (The S 240's "quickest Lotus" honors will probably cede next month to the Exige S 260, which has 17 more horsepower and, through generous use of carbon fiber, is 50 pounds lighter.)

The supercharger, besides cranking up the horsepower, smoothes out the power delivery. With the naturally aspirated version of the little engine—originally developed with Yamaha for the Toyota Celica GT-S—output was tepid until the variable valve timing shifted into its high-r.p.m. mode, unleashing an abrupt surge of power.

With the S 240, you don't have to work that hard. There's still a manic rush to the rev limiter (which, for brief moments, can allow up to 8,500 r.p.m.), but the Exige also feels tractable around town. You can shoot the gaps in traffic without crossing your fingers and hoping the power will arrive in time. Which is important when you're driving a car so small it has you looking up from the driver's seat to see the tailpipe of a Camry.

The Exige isn't shy about proclaiming its racecar intentions. Its Yokohama Advan Neova tires have a treadwear rating of 60, the lowest (and hence stickiest) number I have ever seen on a street tire. (A Porsche GT3 comes in at 80.) On a skid pad, this thing grips so hard that *you feel like an astronaut in a centrifuge.*

The Exige is so good at convincing you it's a racecar that you'll pull into gas stations and scream, "Gimme new tires on the right side and set the wing for more downforce at the rear!"

Speaking of gas stations, two fill-ups of the 10.6-gallon tank cost $18 and $19, respectively, even with the required premium fuel. The E.P.A. mileage rating is 20 m.p.g. in town and 26 on the highway, reasonable numbers for a vehicle with this level of performance.

Say what you will about the economy, but premium gas for less than $2 a gallon makes it really cheap to run your Lotus. Which is nice, because the rather heady base price of $65,815 ($70,650 as tested) puts the Exige S 240 in the territory of a Corvette Z06 or a Nissan GT-R.

Either of those cars is generally more agreeable on public roads. With the Lotus, you'll occasionally find yourself driving with a shoeless right foot: the pedals are so close you'll be mashing the brake when trying to accelerate.

The quirks don't end there. The headlights and instruments are always lighted, but at night you must remember to click the light switch to activate the taillights—an electrical idiosyncrasy (for a 2008 car, anyway) that I learned about thanks to a helpful local constable. And you'll inadvertently honk the horn at inopportune moments because the buttons are right where your thumbs tend to land on the steering wheel spokes.

In the era of ultra-refined, focus-grouped transport modules, the Exige still gives the impression that it was designed by an autocrat with a penchant for speed and a belief that ergonomics are an urban legend.

From that, you might conclude that the Exige is a throwback, a relic of simpler days. On the contrary, I see it as a harbinger of the future. *It's simple, light and fun. Its mileage is good. It shows how much performance can be wrung from modest engines.* If volatile oil prices and the faltering economy conspire to push sports cars toward a more spartan ideal, that might not be a bad thing.

The Exige has its warts, but once you've felt the tingle of electricity coming through that little Momo steering wheel, once you've clicked off a perfect motorcycle-quick upshift just as the motor reaches its snarling peak, even the most jaded proponent of V-8-powered excess will admit that Lotus is onto something.

Inquiring into the Essay

1. Explore your own experience with a car. Tell the story of a first car, a worst car, a car that got you through a particular time in your life, or one that helped you to define that time. Fastwrite about this for six minutes. It should be fun. Skip a line and write for two more minutes about how the review of the Lotus connects—or does not connect—in some way to the experience you wrote about.

2. Explain who you think was the audience for the Lotus review. Describe the demographics of that audience, and identify passages from the review that seem particularly geared toward those readers.

3. Evaluate the effectiveness of "A Ton (Just Barely) of Fun" for a reader like you. How could it be revised to be more interesting to another audience? Be specific.

4. Reading in college often involves an experience like the one you may have had reading this review. Did you feel like an insider or an outsider as a reader of the piece? When did you first feel that and how did it influence your response to the piece?

▪ REVIEW 3

The video gaming industry hauls in something like $10 billion a year, so it's no surprise that more writers are penning reviews of the latest releases. These reviews, if they're any good, have to balance technical information about the game with attention to the experience of playing it. It is a well-described gaming experience, not arcane detail, that will appeal to most readers. That's why Seth Schiesel's review of "Grand Theft Auto IV," a hugely popular video game released in 2008, is such a great example of how to write a review that might make even non-video game players interested in giving it a try.

Like many reviews, the criteria Schiesel uses to determine the qualities of a good game are largely implicit. But it isn't hard to find them. One criterion he clearly uses is what we often look for in film and literature: "fully realized characters." When you think about it, this is a pretty extraordinary accomplishment in a video game. After all, characters in a game like "Grand Theft Auto IV" must consistently service the action, making things (usually violent things) happen, and this wouldn't seem to provide the time or the situations to develop character. But according to Schiesel, the protagonist of the fourth version of the game, Niko Bellic, is "one of the most fully realized characters that video games have yet produced."

Seth Schiesel sidesteps the ethics of producing games like "Grand Theft Auto IV," which makes efficient killing a key to advancement. But this is a review, not a public argument on the virtues of gaming, and his readers likely

Niko Bellic (top center) is the main character of the video game "Grand Theft Auto IV," a game that Seth Schiesel calls "violent, intelligent, profane, endearing, obnoxious, sly, richly textured and throughly compelling."

aren't interested in such ethical and moral questions. They just want to know whether the game is any good. As you read "Grand Theft Auto Takes on New York," consider what exactly Schiesel means by that. On what other criteria does he base his judgment?

Grand Theft Auto Takes on New York

Seth Schiesel

I was rolling through the neon deluge of a place very like Times Square the other night in my Landstalker sport utility vehicle, listening to David Bowie's "Fascination" on the radio. The glittery urban landscape was almost enough to make me forget about the warehouse of cocaine dealers I was headed uptown to rip off. 1

Soon I would get bored, though, and carjack a luxury sedan. I'd meet my Rasta buddy Little Jacob, then check out a late show by Ricky Gervais at a comedy club around the corner. Afterward I'd head north to confront the dealers, at least if I 2

(continued)

(continued)

could elude the cops. I heard their sirens before I saw them and peeled out, tires squealing.

3   It was just another night on the streets of Liberty City, the exhilarating, lusciously dystopian rendition of New York City in 2008 that propels Grand Theft Auto IV, the ambitious new video game to be released on Tuesday for the Xbox 360 and PlayStation 3 systems.

4   Published by Rockstar Games, Grand Theft Auto IV is a violent, intelligent, pro-fane, endearing, obnoxious, sly, richly textured and thoroughly compelling work of cultural satire disguised as fun. It calls to mind a rollicking R-rated version of Mad magazine featuring Dave Chappelle and Quentin Tarantino, and sets a new standard for what is possible in interactive arts. It is by far the best game of the series, which made its debut in 1997 and has since sold more than 70 million copies. Grand Theft Auto IV will retail for $60.

5   Niko Bellic is the player-controlled protagonist this time, and he is one of the most fully realized characters video games have yet produced. A veteran of the Balkan wars and a former human trafficker in the Adriatic, he arrives in Liberty City's rendition of Brighton Beach at the start of the game to move in with his affable if naïve cousin Roman. Niko expects to find fortune and, just maybe, track down some-one who betrayed him long ago. Over the course of the story line he discovers that revenge is not always what one expects.

6   Besides the nuanced Niko the game is populated by a winsome procession of grifters, hustlers, drug peddlers and other gloriously unrepentant lowlifes, each a car-icature less politically correct than the last.

7   Hardly a demographic escapes skewering. In addition to various Italian and Irish crime families, there are venal Russian gangsters, black crack slingers, argyle-sporting Jamaican potheads, Puerto Rican hoodlums, a corrupt police commis-sioner, a steroid-addled Brooklyn knucklehead named Brucie Kibbutz and a former Eastern European soldier who has become a twee Upper West Side metrosexual.

8   Breathing life into Niko and the other characters is a pungent script by Dan Houser and Rupert Humphries that reveals a mastery of street patois to rival Elmore Leonard's. The point of the main plot is to guide Niko through the city's criminal un-derworld. Gang leaders and thugs set missions for him to complete, and his success moves the story along toward a conclusion that seems as dark as its beginning. But the real star of the game is the city itself. It looks like New York. It sounds like New York. It feels like New York. Liberty City has been so meticulously created it almost even smells like New York. From Brooklyn (called Broker), through Queens (Dukes), the Bronx (Bohan), Manhattan (Algonquin) and an urban slice of New Jersey (Alderney), the game's streets and alleys ooze a stylized yet unmistakable authenticity. (Staten Island is left out however.)

9   The game does not try to represent anything close to every street in the city, but the overall proportions, textures, geography, sights and sounds are spot-on. The

major landmarks are present, often rendered in surprising detail, from the Cyclone at Coney Island to the Domino Sugar factory and Grand Army Plaza in Brooklyn and on up through the detritus of the 1964–65 World's Fair in Queens. Central Park, the Empire State Building, various museums, the Statue of Liberty and Times Square are all present and accounted for. There is no Yankee Stadium, but there is a professional baseball team known, with the deliciousness typical of the game's winks and nods, as the Swingers.

At least as impressive as the city's virtual topography is the range of the game's audio and music production, delivered through an entire dial's worth of radio stations available in almost any of the dozens of different cars, trucks and motorcycles a player can steal. From the jazz channel (billed as "music from when America was cool") through the salsa, alt-rock, jazz, metal and multiple reggae and hip-hop stations, Lazlow Jones, Ivan Pavlovich and the rest of Rockstar's audio team demonstrate a musical erudition beyond anything heard before in a video game. The biggest problem with the game's extensive subway system is that there's no music underground. (Too bad there are no iPods to nab.)   10

The game's roster of radio hosts runs from Karl Lagerfeld to Iggy Pop and DJ Green Lantern. It is not faint praise to point out that at times, simply driving around the city listening to the radio—seguing from "Moanin'" by Art Blakey and the Jazz Messengers to the Isley Brothers' "Footsteps in the Dark" to "The Crack House" by Fat Joe featuring Lil Wayne—can be as enjoyable as anything the game has to offer.   11

Grand Theft Auto IV is such a simultaneously adoring and insightful take on modern America that it almost had to come from somewhere else. The game's main production studio is in Edinburgh, and Rockstar's leaders, the brothers Dan and Sam Houser, are British expatriates who moved to New York to indulge their fascination with urban American culture. Their success places them firmly among the distinguished cast of Britons from Mick Jagger and Keith Richards through Tina Brown who have flourished by identifying key elements of American culture, repackaging them for mass consumption and selling them back at a markup.   12

It all adds up to a new level of depth for an interactive entertainment experience. I've spent almost 60 hours practically sequestered in a (real world) Manhattan hotel room in recent weeks playing through Grand Theft Auto IV's main story line and the game still says I have found only 64 percent of its content. I won't ever reach 100 percent, not least because I won't hunt down all 200 of the target pigeons (known as flying rats here) that the designers have hidden around the city.   13

But like millions of other players I will happily spend untold hours cruising Liberty City's bridges and byways, hitting the clubs, grooving to the radio and running from the cops. Even when the real New York City is right outside.   14

Inquiring into the Essay

Explore, explain, evaluate, and reflect on the review, "Grand Theft Auto Takes on New York" using the following questions:

1. This review doesn't address the moral and ethical questions raised by a game that celebrates "gloriously unrepentant lowlifes" including potheads, gangsters, and "crack slingers." "Grand Theft Auto IV" may be no worse than other violent video games, and unless you've played it, criticism or praise of this particular game is unfair. But in a four-minute fastwrite, explore your own feelings about violent video games. In his review, Schiesel argues that "Grand Theft Auto IV" is cultural satire. Can games like this serve a larger, even useful purpose?

2. Define, in your own words, what Seth Schiesel seems to believe are the qualities of a good video game.

3. Evaluate the rhetorical effectiveness of this review. Imagine what parts of the piece would work—or wouldn't—for the following categories of readers:

    a. People who have never played a video game in their lives but might consider it.

    b. People who are avid and experienced gamers.

    c. People who, when asked, usually consider playing video games a "waste of time."

4. Video game reviews are but one of a growing number of review genres, including movies, books, blogs, Web sites, best and worst dressed, and so on. Consider the reviews you read or might read. What exactly would you be looking for in a "good" review on that subject?

SEEING THE FORM

Choosing the Best Picture

When documentary photographer Dorothea Lange encountered Florence Thompson and her family camped by a frozen pea field, she came away with one of the most indelible images of the Depression, a picture that was later titled *Migrant Mother*. But Lange took multiple pictures that day, and only one of them became famous. Why? If you were charged with evaluating all six shots that Lange took of Thompson and her family that you see here, on what basis would you choose the best shot? What criteria would you use for making such a judgment?

Six photographs Dorothea Lange took of Florence Thompson.

THE WRITING PROCESS

INQUIRY PROJECT: WRITING A REVIEW

Write a 1,000- to 1,200-word review. You choose the subject—a performance, a book, a Web site, a consumer product, a film, whatever. Just make sure your review has the following qualities:

- You're able to put your subject in a manageable category for more useful comparisons; for example, rather than evaluating a Web site against all others, you're going to focus on Web sites for classroom use.
- The essay has all three elements of evaluation: judgment, criteria, and evidence.
- The criteria are reasonable and appropriate for what you're evaluating; they aren't overly idealistic or general.
- The evaluation seems balanced and fair.

Thinking About Subjects

Possible subjects for a review abound. What will you choose? Perhaps you're a sports fan who regularly seeks information on the Web. Which sites strike you as the most informative? Which would you recommend? Or maybe you are interested in photography, but really don't have any idea how to evaluate the landscape shots you took during a recent trip to Maine. Are they any good? The best inquiry projects begin with a question, not an answer, so try to choose a topic because you want to discover what you think instead of one about which you already have a strong opinion. You'll learn more and probably write a stronger, more balanced, more interesting essay.

> The best inquiry projects begin with a question, so choose a topic because you want to discover what you think instead of one about which you already have a strong opinion.

Generating Ideas

Play around with some ideas first by using some of the following triggers for thinking-through-writing in your journal. Suspend judgment. Don't reject anything. Explore.

Listing Prompts. Lists can be rich sources of triggering topics. Let them grow freely, and when you're ready, use an item as the focus of another list or an episode of fastwriting. The following prompts should get you started.

1. Fold a piece a paper into four equal columns. You'll be making four different brainstormed lists. In the first column, write "Things I Want." Spend two minutes making a quick list of everything you wish you had but don't—a new computer, a classical guitar, a decent boyfriend, and so on.

2. In the next column, write "The Jury Is Still Out." In this column, make a fast list of things in your life that so far are hard to judge—the quality of the school you attend, this textbook, your opinion about the films you saw last month, how well Susie cuts your hair, and so on.

3. In the third column, write "My Media." Devote a fast list to particular films, TV shows, books, Web sites, or musicians you like or dislike—jot down whatever you watch, listen to, or read regularly.

4. Finally, make a list of "Things of Questionable Quality." Try to be specific.

Fastwriting Prompts. Remember, fastwriting is a great way to stimulate creative thinking. Turn off your critical side and let yourself write "badly."

1. Choose an item from any of the four preceding lists as a prompt for a seven-minute fastwrite. Explore your experience with the subject, or how your opinions about it have evolved.

2. Begin with the following prompt, and follow it for five minutes in a fastwrite: Among the things I have a hard time judging is _____.... If the writing stalls, shift subjects by writing, And another thing I can't judge is _____....

Visual Prompts. Sometimes the best way to generate material is to see what we think represented in something other than sentences. Boxes, lines, webs, clusters, arrows, charts, and even sketches can help us see more of the landscape of a subject, especially connections between fragments of information that aren't as obvious in prose.

1. On a blank page in your journal, cluster the name of an artist, musician, film, book, author, performance, band, building, academic course or major, restaurant, university bookstore, PDA, computer, food store, or pizza joint. Cluster the name of anything about which you have some sort of feeling, positive or negative. Build a web of associations: feelings, details, observations, names, moments, facts, opinions, and so on. Look for a single strand in your essay that might be the beginning of a review.

2. Draw a sketch of what you think is an *ideal version* of something you need or use often: a computer, a classroom, a telephone, a wallet or handbag, and so on. If you could design such a thing, what would it look like? Use this as a way of evaluating what is currently available and how it might be improved.

Research Prompts. The depth of a review depends on the writer's knowledge of the criteria and evidence through which she judges her subject. Unless she is already an expert on her subject, research of some form will be a necessity. At this stage in the writing process, a little advance research can help you find a subject.

1. Do an Internet or library search for reviews on one of your favorite films, books, sports teams, artists, and so on. Do you agree with the evaluations? If not, consider writing a review of your own that challenges the critics.

2. Take a walk. Look for things to evaluate that you see as you wander on and off campus—downtown architecture, the quality of local parks, paintings in the art museum, neighborhoods, coffee shops. You'll be amazed at how much is begging for a thoughtful judgment.

3. Here's an entertaining generating activity: Plan a weekend of movie watching with a few friends. Ask each of them to contribute two or three titles of their favorite films, then rent a slew of them, and when you're thoroughly spent watching movies, discuss which might be most interesting to review.

Judging What You Have

Generating may produce the messy, incoherent writing that would earn you bad grades in most classes. Its virtue, however, should be obvious by now: "Bad" writing gives a writer material to work with. Remember that it's always better to work from abundance than scarcity. But if this material is going to go anywhere, it must be judged, shaped, and evaluated.

WRITING IN YOUR LIFE

Online Product Reviews

Amazon, the biggest bookseller in the world, publishes thousands of customer book reviews, and these have a big enough impact on sales that authors and publishers monitor them closely. One study suggests, in fact, that nearly a quarter of Americans who buy products online first consult customer reviews. British online consumers are apparently even more dedicated to reading reviews. Seventy percent report that they first read customer reviews of a product before they buy it. Few pieces of self-published writing wield that kind of influence.

It's possible to get paid for online reviews. Epinions.com is probably the best known site that pays contributors for product reviews, a sum that's calculated on how often your review is seen. But the best motive for writing product reviews is the satisfaction of influencing how people think about something you love (or don't). Like any persuasive writing, an online product review must be readable and convincing. It's a genre that requires honesty and directness. The relative brevity of these reviews makes it especially important that your point is clear. Since you aren't necessarily an authority on the thing you review, establishing a convincing ethos or persona is key. You want to come across as someone who is thoughtful and fair, and yet feels strongly.

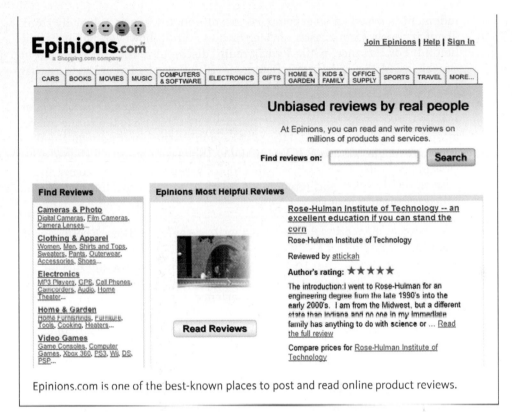

Epinions.com is one of the best-known places to post and read online product reviews.

What's Promising Material and What Isn't? My favorite coffee shop in my hometown of Boise, Idaho, is a place called the Flying M. It's a funky place with an odd assortment of furniture, overstuffed couches, worn armchairs, and wobbly tables. On the walls, there's work from local artists, mostly unknowns with talent and unusual taste. There are other coffee places in town, including the ubiquitous Starbucks and another more local chain called Moxie Java. I don't find much difference in the coffee at any of these places, and they're all rather pleasant. What makes me prefer the Flying M?

I've never really thought about it. That's one of the reasons I liked the idea of reviewing my favorite local coffeehouse when the Flying M appeared on one of my lists. The best inquiry-based projects begin when you're not quite sure what you think and want to explore a topic to find out.

- *Is there anything in your lists and fastwrites that you might have an initial judgment about but really haven't considered fully?* For example, you really dislike the sixties architecture that dominates your campus, but you're not quite sure what it is about it that leaves you cold.

- *As you consider possible subjects for your review, do some clearly offer the possibility of comparison with other similar things in that category?* Often judgment is based on such comparisons, although we may not really think about it much. Comparison isn't always essential, however, but it can be helpful. For instance, while I can't really distinguish the coffee served at Starbucks, Moxie Java, or the Flying M—it's all good—I'm pretty sure that my preferences have more to do with the atmosphere.

- *Do any of your possible subjects offer the possibility of primary research, or research that might involve direct observation?* Can you listen to the music, attend the performance, read the novel, examine the building, visit the Web site, look at the painting? If I were doing this assignment, I'd choose a review of local cafés over other possible topics because it would give me an excuse to drink coffee and hang out in some of my favorite haunts. This is called research. Seriously.

Questions About Audience and Purpose. If I write a review of Boise's coffeehouse scene, I can immediately think of where I could publish it. *The Boise Weekly* is a local alternative magazine that frequently features food reviews and has an audience that certainly includes a high percentage of gourmet coffee drinkers. Many readers of the *Weekly* have direct experience with the coffeehouses I'd review and may even have judgments of their own about which are best. I'm reasonably confident that they might care about what I have to say on the topic.

The Internet is the easiest and fastest way to find an audience for a review. Sites like Epinions.com (see the feature "Writing in your Life" on page 180) invite, and sometimes pay for, reviews of a wide range of products. If you're devoted to a certain kind of product—books, movies, video games, or whatever—then consider blogging your review. It's easy to set up a blog (try www.blogger.com), and if your work is well-written and informative, you'll find an audience.

EXERCISE 5.1

From Jury to Judgment

Writing an evaluation of a thing requires that you become something of an expert about it. As you complete the following steps of the exercise, you'll generate material to work with that will make writing the draft much easier.

STEP ONE: Begin with a focused fastwrite that explores your initial feelings and experiences, if any, about your subject. In your notebook, use one of the following prompts to launch an exploration of your personal experiences with your topic. If the writing stalls, try another prompt to keep you going for five to seven minutes.

- *Write about your first experience with your subject.* This might be, for example, the first time you remember visiting the restaurant, or hearing the performer, or seeing the photographs. Focus on scenes, moments, situations, and people.

- *Write about what you think might be important qualities of your subject.* Ideally, this would be what the thing should be able to do well or what effects it should have on people who use it or see it. Say you're evaluating laptop computers for college students. Under which conditions would a laptop be most useful? What have you noticed about the way you use one? In which common situations do student laptops prove vulnerable to damage? What have you heard other people say they like or dislike about their machines?

- *Write about how the thing makes you feel.* So much of our evaluation of a thing begins with our emotional responses to it. You love the photography of Edward Weston, or the music of Ani DiFranco, or you really dislike Hitchcock movies. Explore not just your initial good, bad, or mixed feelings about your subject but the place from where those feelings arise.

- *Compare the thing you're evaluating with something else that's similar.* I appreciate the Flying M café largely because it's so different from Starbucks. Focus your fastwrite on a relevant comparison, teasing out the differences and similarities and thinking about how you feel about them.

STEP TWO: Research your subject on the Web, gathering as much relevant background information as you can.

- *Search for information on product Web sites or Web pages devoted specifically to your subject.* If your review is on Ford's new electric car, visit the company's Web site to find out what you can about the vehicle. Find Green Day's home page or fan site for your review of the band's new CD.

- *Search for existing reviews or other evaluations on your subject.* One way to do this is to Google using the keyword "review" or "reviews" (or "how to evaluate") along with your subject. For example, "laptop reviews" will produce dozens of sites that rank and evaluate the machines. Similarly, there are countless reviews on the Web of specific performers, performances, CDs, consumer products, and so on.

STEP THREE: If possible, interview people about what they think. You may do this formally by developing a survey, or informally by simply asking people what they like or dislike about the thing you're evaluating. Also consider whether you might interview someone who's an expert on your subject. For example, if you're evaluating a Web site, ask people in the technical communications program what they think about it, or what criteria they might use if they were reviewing something similar.

STEP FOUR: This may be the most important step of all: *Experience* your subject. Visit the coffeehouses, examine the Web site, listen to the music, attend the performance, read the book, view the painting, visit the building, look at the architecture, watch the movie. As you do this, gather your impressions and collect information. The best way to do this methodically is to collect field notes, and

ONE STUDENT'S RESPONSE

Sam's Journal

EXERCISE 5.1
STEP ONE: FROM JURY TO JUDGMENT

Reviewing River Birch Golf Course

I picked up the phone two weeks early to make my reservation. I was determined to be one of the first people to set foot on the new golf course to play. A friend of mine answered the phone at the golf course; she put me down for one of the earliest tee times available on opening morning. When opening day came my dad and I raced down to the course to warm up. As we pulled into the parking lot, though, our enthusiasm died. The club house was still under construction and the entire operation was being run out of a Coca-Cola stand. It was exactly like those at the fairgrounds. It even sold the same stuff, except for the addition of golf. Still slightly depressed, my dad and I paid for our rounds and wandered over to the first tee box. The head professional was waiting for us; she was sending people out with a friendly warning. Like we needed a warning after finding out the course was run out of a Coke stand! Our expectations were low enough. She said, "Winter rules today boys. Lift clean and place." This only meant one thing; the course was in bad shape, so bad that the head pro gave the players permission to cheat.

the double-entry journal is a good note-taking system for this purpose. Put your observations on the left page and explore your impressions and ideas on the opposing right page of your notebook.

By now, you have some background information on your subject and have gathered observations and impressions that should shape your judgment about it. Maybe you've decided the film is a stinker, the CD is the best one you've heard, or the student union isn't meeting students' needs. After comparing Starbucks and the Flying M—and visiting both places—I'm even more convinced about which one I prefer. But why? This is a key stage in the process of evaluation: On what basis do you make the judgment? In other words, what *criteria* are you using?

Thinking About Criteria

Professional reviewers—say, consultants who evaluate marketing plans or people who write film reviews—may not sit down and make a list of their criteria. They're so familiar with their subjects that they've often internalized the criteria they're using, and their clients and readers may not insist on knowing on what they base their judgments. But it can be enormously helpful at this stage in the process to try to articulate your criteria, at least as a way of thinking more thoroughly about your subject.

Criteria might be quite personal. There are certain things that *you* think are important about a coffeehouse, student union, modern dance performance, fusion jazz CD, and so on. These opinions are what make the review yours, and not somebody else's. But they should be reasonable to others. Your criteria for judgment shouldn't set an unrealistic standard or seem nitpicky or irrelevant.

I asked my daughter Rebecca, a dancer, what criteria she would use to judge a modern performance (see the accompanying box). I don't completely understand all of the criteria she listed because I know little about dance, but her list seems sensible and I can imagine how it might guide her in evaluating the next performance of the Balance Dance Company. What I don't understand, she can explain to me.

As you write your sketch, keep your criteria in mind. You may not mention all of them, or even any of them in your draft, but they'll help direct you to the evidence you need to make your judgment seem persuasive to others.

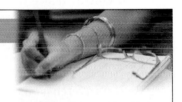

INQUIRING INTO THE DETAILS

Collaborating on Criteria

Need help determining the criteria for your evaluation? Asking others for their opinions can help. Consider the following strategy:

1. Write the category of the thing you're reviewing—a modern dance performance, coffeehouses, a hip-hop CD, a science fiction novel, and so on—on the top of a piece of newsprint.

2. Post your newsprint on the wall of your classroom.

3. For twenty minutes, everyone in class rotates around the room to each newsprint, trying to answer the following question about the category listed there: *In your judgment, what makes a particularly good _____?* (rap song, science fiction story, coffeehouse, and so on).

4. Briefly list your criteria for judging each category on the newsprint, or elaborate on a criteria that is already there. In other words, in your mind, what makes a good _____?

5. If you don't know that much about the category, make a reasonable guess about a basis for judging it.

BECCA'S CRITERIA

A good modern dance performance has...

1. Interesting features—props, comedy, or music?
2. Something improvised
3. Visible expressions of the dancers' enjoyment
4. Interesting variation
5. Good balance in choreography between repetition and randomness
6. Beginning, middle, and end, seamlessly joined

Writing the Sketch

As with the other inquiry projects, begin with a sketch of your review. This should be about 500 to 600 words (two to three double-spaced pages) and include the following:

- A tentative title.
- An effort to help readers understand why they might have a stake in the thing you're evaluating. What's significant about this particular CD, book, performance, place, or product?
- Specific evidence from the thing itself to help explain and support your judgment of it.

■ STUDENT SKETCH

Sam Battey's sketch is like a lot of early drafts. He's found his topic—a review of a relatively new golf course in his hometown—but he's still trying to get some purchase on what he wants to say about it. It's only at the end of the sketch that we get a sense of where he might want to go in the next draft (see it at the end of this chapter). Sam likes River Birch Golf Course despite its shortcomings, which include an "evil" groundskeeper named John who is a grass "savant." But what, exactly, does Sam like about the golf course? It has "matured," he writes. What does this mean? And can the next draft be more specific about that?

River Birch: A Diamond in the Rough

Sam Battey

1   As I pulled into the parking lot of River Birch Golf Course my attitude quickly changed from excitement to depression. I had seen a lot of golf courses in my time, but

none that had been run out of a fairground-type Coca-Cola stand. Regardless of its initial appearance, I was there to play golf, so I gritted my teeth and tried to look past the obvious shortcomings of a brand new golf course. Patiently, I waited to be called to play, my eyes already examining the course, my mind planning the game. I was shaken from my daze by the grating voice of the head professional. She seemed nice, but her shrill voice kept my partners and me at a safe distance. We anxiously looked out across the first fairway but had no idea where to go. The fairway snaked over a hill, hiding the hole. The head professional tried to explain, but we were utterly lost with her directions, so she ended her speech with, "Winter rules boys. Lift clean and place." A sense of uneasiness swept over my group; we were experienced enough to know what that phrase meant. It was the nice way to tell people, "The course is in such bad condition that it's ok to cheat." Our expectations severely lowered, we teed off and set out down the first fairway.

That was five years ago, but the public has had a hard time forgetting the past. The course has come a long way since. Now as people enter the parking lot, they don't see a Coca-Cola stand ushering players onto a muddy and beaten first tee box. Instead, they see employees hustling about trying to earn a few dollars in tips, a completed clubhouse, and players being ushered onto a much less muddy and beaten first tee box. Unless you're about to host the U.S. Open, parts of the golf course will always be beaten and muddy. Every day, dozens of people will stampede over the same tracts of land. These tracts suffer constant abuse from the spikes on a golfer's shoes, the tires of a golf cart, and the merciless hacking of a poor golfer trying to make contact with the ball, but only abusing the dirt behind it. It's no wonder how parts of the course can look so damaged. River Birch's clientele isn't sympathetic to the groundskeepers and blindly goes about destroying the course, yet the course stays in such excellent condition. This is all due to the genius of the course's superintendant, John.

John is pure evil, but he's a savant when it comes to growing grass. There isn't a man in existence who knows more random, useless facts about grass than John. He spends nearly twelve hours a day, seven days a week, patrolling the golf course, tirelessly repairing its damage and making it look pristine. His people skills leave a little to be desired, because if he sees any players make the smallest infraction against his course, he'll make sure to scream in their faces until they either break down and cry or leave to go home. What John lacks in people skills, the clubhouse employees make up for.

The clubhouse is the perfect place to escape from the superintendant when he gets into a bad mood, and the employees capitalize on this. When John goes on a tirade, golfers stream into the clubhouse seeking refuge, and the employees are there to comfort. The staff knows firsthand how evil John can seem, so their first goal seems to be to make you laugh or, at the very least, make you smile. Golf can be stressful, and after a bad round sometimes all it takes is a good joke to turn your mood around and make you come back a second time, although not all rounds are salvageable with a smile and a wave. Sometimes you'll blunder into the clubhouse after shooting some outlandishly high number and your only comfort can come from the grill.

(continued)

(continued)

5   This is where River Birch falls short. The diversity of food is limited. It's not like a country club, where waiters come to your table and obey your every command. Also, the food is absolutely terrible for you. That doesn't stop anyone, because it tastes so good. The scent of hot dogs always looms over the heads of the players who are just stopping to get a drink, but it eventually consumes them. It's almost a hypnotic scent that forces players to get a hot dog. Much like the food, the merchandise is sparse, but again, the quality is largely overlooked. None of the merchandise is cheaply made, and it is priced fairly for the type of player that frequents the course; there just isn't much diversity.

6   Five years ago, there were mounds of dirt strewn about the practice grounds, not all of the grass had fully grown or matured, and the clubhouse wasn't even finished. Time changes everything, and with time River Birch has matured into a respectable course. The public dwells too much on the past. They can't see past the Coke stand that used to take their money or the evil old man who yells at them for putting their golf bag down on the green. Five years is a long time when you stop and look back; plenty has changed at River Birch.

Moving from Sketch to Draft

A sketch usually gives the writer just the barest outline of his or her subject. But as an early draft, a sketch can be invaluable. It might hint at what the real subject is, or what questions seem to be behind your inquiry into the subject. A sketch might suggest a focus for the next draft, or simply a better lead. Learning to read your sketches for such clues takes practice. The following suggestions should help.

Evaluating Your Own Sketch. A sketch is an early draft; it should help expose gaps that you can fill in revision. Begin evaluating your sketch by looking for the following possible omissions:

1. Do you provide enough background about what you're reviewing so that readers unfamiliar with the subject know enough to believe and understand your claims?

2. Do you feel that your treatment of the topic was balanced? For example, did you include perspectives that differ from yours? Did you consider some positive qualities of your topic in an unflattering review or negatives in a positive review?

3. Do you use any helpful comparisons?

4. Are your judgments supported by specific evidence? Is there enough of it?

5. Having written the sketch, has your judgment changed at all? Should you strengthen, qualify, or elaborate on it? Do you feel as if it would be more honest to change it altogether?

Questions for Peer Review. Because a review is a form of persuasive writing, comments from other readers are crucial. In your workshop session, get your peers to comment on how persuasive they find your sketch by asking some of the following questions:

- After reading the sketch, what one thing do you remember most?

- Do you agree with my review of _____? If so, what did you find *least* convincing? If you disagreed, what did you find *most* convincing?

- What criterion seemed key to my judgment? Are there others that you thought I might mention but didn't?

- How do I come across in the sketch? Do I seem to know what I'm talking about? Or does it seem like a rant?

Reflecting on What You've Learned. Following your workshop session, write for five to seven minutes in your journal, beginning with a fastwrite in which you try to remember everything that you heard. Do this double-entry style, on the left page of your notebook. It will help you remember if you tell the story of your workshop session: The workshop began when...And then,...And then,.... When you're done trying to recall everything you can about what group members said to you, shift to the opposing right page and fastwrite about your reactions to what they said. What made sense? What didn't? How might you try one or more of the suggestions you like in the next draft?

Research and Other Strategies: Gathering More Information

If your workshop went well, you might feel ready to start the next draft. But remember this: It is always best to work from an abundance of information. It almost always pays off to resist the temptation to rush the draft and spend a little more time collecting information that will help you write it. Consider the following:

Re-Experience. Probably the single most useful thing you can do to prepare for the next draft is to collect more observations of your subject. Why? You're much more focused now on what you think, what criteria most influence that judgment, and what particular evidence you were lacking in the sketch that will make your review more convincing.

Interview. If you opted not to spend much time talking to people, you should strongly consider collecting the comments, opinions, and observations of others about the subject of your review. If you reviewed a concert or other event, find others who attended to interview. If you reviewed a film, get a small group of friends to watch the movie with you and jot down their reactions afterward. If it would be helpful to collect data on how people feel, consider designing a brief survey.

Also consider interviewing someone who is an expert on the thing you're reviewing.

Read. Go to the library and search for information about your subject. That will make you more of an expert. Look for books and articles in the following categories:

- *Information about how it's made or designed.* You love Martin's newest classical guitar but you really don't know much about the rosewood used in it. Search for books and articles on the qualities of wood that guitar makers value most.

- *Other reviews.* Search the Web and the library for other reviews of your subject. If you're reviewing a consumer product or some aspect of popular culture, check a database of general-interest periodicals such as *The General Reference Center* or *Reader's Guide Abstracts.* Also check newspaper databases. Has anyone else written about your topic?

- *Background information on relevant people, companies, traditions, local developments, and so on.* For example, if you're reviewing Bob Dylan's new CD, it would be helpful to know more about the evolution of his music. Check the electronic book index for a Dylan biography. Reviewing a modern dance performance? Find out more about the American tradition in the genre by checking the *Encyclopedia of Dance and Ballet* in the library's reference room.

Composing the Draft

Seth Schiesel's review of the fourth version of the video game "Grand Theft Auto" (see page 173) begins this way:

> I was rolling through the neon deluge of a place very like Times Square the other night in my Landstalker sport utility vehicle, listening to David Bowie's "Fascination" on the radio. The glittery urban landscape was almost enough to make me forget the warehouse of cocaine dealers I was headed uptown to rip off.

It isn't simply the punchy language that makes this lead paragraph compelling (e.g., "neon deluge" and "rip off"). It does three things that good beginnings should do:

1. Raises questions the reader might want to learn the answers to.
2. Creates a relationship between reader and writer.
3. Gets right to the subject without unnecessary scaffolding.

While we know from the title of the piece that this is about a video game, Schiesel's opening makes us wonder about what exactly is going on here, who this guy is, and what he is talking about. And the lead does what reviews of video games should do: get right to the *experience* of playing the game. He doesn't squander his beginning on providing background information, or talking about himself, or unnecessary pronouncements ("This paper will blah, blah, blah.").

Here are some other approaches to a strong lead for a review:

- Begin with a common misconception about your subject and promise to challenge it.
- Begin with an anecdote that reveals what you like or dislike.

- Help readers realize the relevance of your subject by showing how it's used, what it says, or why it's needed in a familiar situation.
- Provide interesting background that your readers may not know.

Methods of Development. What are some ways to organize your review?

Narrative. If you're reviewing a performance or any other kind of experience that has a discrete beginning and end, then telling a story about what you saw, felt, and thought is a natural move. Another way to use narrative is to tell the story of your thinking about your subject, an approach that lends itself to a delayed thesis essay where your judgment of final claim comes late rather than early.

Comparison/Contrast. You already know that comparison of other items in the same category you're evaluating—say, other science fiction films, or other electric cars, or laptops—can be a useful approach to writing an evaluation. If comparison is an important element, you might structure your essay around it, looking first at a comparable item and then contrasting it with another.

Question to Answer. One of the most straightforward methods of structuring a review is to simply begin by raising the question we explored earlier: *What makes _____ good?* This way, you make your criteria for evaluation explicit. From there, the next move is obvious—how well does the thing you're evaluating measure up?

Using Evidence. The most important evidence in an evaluation is your observations of the thing itself. These should be specific. Who was the best performer, or who was the worst? When did that become obvious during the show? What did he or she say or do? You will most likely obtain this evidence through *primary research*. You'll attend the concert, listen to the CD, or visit the coffeehouse. You may also use evidence from secondary sources; for example, what did another critic say or observe? But in general, the most authoritative evidence in an evaluation comes from direct observation.

Workshopping the Draft

If your draft is subject to peer review, see Chapter 14 for details on how to organize workshop groups and decide on how your group can help you, something that depends on how you feel about the work so far and the quality of your draft. The following journal activities and questions should help you make the most of your opportunity to get peer feedback on your work in progress.

Reflecting on the Draft. Prepare for peer review of your draft by spending three minutes fastwriting in your journal from the following prompt: The thing that I liked most about this draft was... Now fastwrite for three more minutes beginning with the following prompt: The thing that bothered me most about this draft was...

Finally, choose one part of your draft that you are *least* sure of; perhaps you think it's unconvincing or cheesy or unclear. Present this passage to your workshop group and ask what they think without initially voicing your concerns about it.

ONE STUDENT'S RESPONSE

Christy's Journal

REFLECTING ON THE DRAFT

The thing I liked most about this draft is the introduction. However, it does need some work structurally. But I feel I came in strong. The next paragraph gives the reader some clue as to what my criteria are, which gives me a foundation and a slant for the rest of the paper.

The thing I liked least about the paper is the ending. The conclusion needs to be bulked up a bit, and I think I need to say a little more about Ilsa's character. I need to look at thoughts that might be a little too condensed, and try to elaborate on them.

Questions for Readers. Because evaluative writing is meant to be persuasive, pose some questions for your workshop group that help you gauge how convincing your draft is.

1. At what point in the draft did you think my argument was most effective?

2. When was it least effective?

3. Did you care about what I was evaluating? If not, how might I make you care more?

4. How do I come across as a speaker in this essay? What descriptive words would you use to describe me (*fair, critical, serious, nitpicky,* and so on)?

5. Is there a relevant comparison I might have made here but didn't?

OPTION FOR REVIEW ESSAY WORKSHOP

1. Divide each workshop group into two teams—believers and doubters.

2. Believers are responsible for presenting to doubters why the writer's review is convincing and fair.

3. Doubters challenge the writer's judgments and respond to the believers' claims.

4. The writer observes this conversation without participating.

5. After five minutes, believers and doubters drop their roles and discuss suggestions for revision with the writer.

Revising the Draft

Revision is a continual process, not a last step. You've been revising—literally "reseeing" your subject—from the first messy fastwriting in your journal. But the things that get your attention during revision vary depending on where you are in the writing process. You've generated material, chosen a topic, done some research, and written both a sketch and draft. Most students think that the only thing left to do is "fix things": Check for misspellings. Correct an awkward sentence or two. Come up with a better title. This is editing, not revision, and while editing is important, to focus solely on smaller "fixes" after writing a first draft squanders an opportunity to really *learn* from what the draft is telling you, or perhaps not quite telling you.

Chapter 13 can help guide these discoveries. The questions you can ask a draft fall into five categories: purpose, idea, information, development, and editing. Use the chart on page 194 to find the revision strategies in Chapter 13 that might help you resee what you've written so far.

Review drafts also have some fairly typical problems, most of which can be addressed by repeating some of the steps in this chapter or selecting appropriate revision strategies in Chapter 13.

- Do you provide enough background on your subject for readers who aren't as familiar with it as you?

- Is the draft's *ethos* effective? In other words, does the writer come across as judgmental yet fair, authoritative yet cautious? Is the tone or voice of the draft persuasive to its audience?

- Is there enough evidence? Does the draft offer enough specific information about its subject so that the reader can understand exactly why the writer makes a particular judgment about it?

- Does the writer go beyond a simple assessment of the subject—"it was good or bad because..." and offer a range of commentary on the subject's strengths and weaknesses?

Polishing the Draft

After you've dealt with the big issues in your draft—is it sufficiently focused, does it answer the *So what?* question, is it well organized, and so on—you must deal with the smaller problems. You've carved the stone into an appealing figure, but now you need to polish it. Are your paragraphs coherent? How do you manage transitions? Are your sentences fluent and concise? Are there any errors in spelling or syntax? Section 5 of Chapter 13 can help you focus on these issues.

Before you finish your draft, work through the following checklist:

- ✓ Every paragraph is about one thing.
- ✓ The transitions between paragraphs aren't abrupt.
- ✓ The length of sentences varies in each paragraph.

GUIDE TO REVISION STRATEGIES

Problems in the Draft (Chapter 13)	Page Number
Unclear purpose ■ Not sure what the essay is about? Fails to answer the *So what?* question?	551
Unclear thesis, theme, or main idea ■ Not sure what you're trying to say? Judgment isn't clear?	557
Lack of information or development ■ Needs more details; more evidence from the review subject? ■ Criteria need work?	564
Disorganized ■ Doesn't move logically or smoothly from paragraph to paragraph?	568
Unclear or awkward at the level of sentences and paragraphs ■ Seems choppy or hard to follow at the level of sentences or paragraphs?	577

✓ Each sentence is concise. There are no unnecessary words or phrases.

✓ You've checked grammar, particularly verb agreement, run-on sentences, unclear pronouns, and misused words (*there/their, where/were,* and so on). (See the handbook at the end of the book for help with these grammar issues.)

✓ You've run your spellchecker and proofed your paper for misspelled words.

■ STUDENT ESSAY

How do you judge a golf course? I have no idea. I'm not a golfer. When I read Sam Battey's sketch (see page 186), which reviewed his local golf club, River Birch, I still wasn't sure what criteria might apply. Sam's revision solved that problem. (There's the clubhouse, though that might not be the best gauge of course quality, and there's the mastery of the groundskeeper, who puts his heart and soul into the fate of grass.) But Sam's rewrite did something else that any essay needs to do: It organizes the piece around the one main thing the writer wants to say. This is something you should know *before* you start with some kinds of writing—the essay exam, for instance, or some kinds of proposals. But inquiry is about discovery, and we enlist the writing process to help that along. Set side by side, Sam's sketch and final essay on River Birch tell the story of how a writer can discover what he didn't know he knew.

River Birch: A Diamond in the Rough

Sam Battey

Golf is a game created by drunk, loud Scotsmen who decided it would be fun to make a new drinking game. The idea was to take a bent piece of wood and metal and hack away at a feather-filled leather sack until the sack arrived at an agreed-upon spot in a certain number of strokes. Once a Scotsman had reached said goal, he would take a shot of alcohol and move on to the next location, even louder and drunker than before. This informal system was eventually transformed by wealthier golfers who made much more lavish courses, and golf became dubbed "a gentleman's game." Drunken Scots and their ilk weren't welcome. Lately, especially in Star, Idaho, golf has fallen back to its origins. The gentlemen have been replaced by the commoners who like to use golf as an excuse to be drunk and loud. Star's River Birch Golf Course doesn't hold the standards of the expensive country clubs, and it adheres to what normal people want out of a golf course.

It wasn't always that way. Once River Birch was below the standards of normal people, almost enough so to drive them away. Five years ago, when the course first opened, my friends and I pulled into the parking lot and saw what looked like a fairground with a Coca-Cola stand. Regardless of its initial appearance, we were there to play golf, so we gritted our teeth and tried to look past the obvious shortcomings of a brand new golf course. Patiently, I waited to be called to play, my eyes already examining the course, my mind planning the game. I was shaken from my daze by the grating voice of the head professional. She seemed nice, but her shrill voice kept my partners and me at least arm's distance away. We anxiously looked out across the first fairway but had no idea where to go. The fairway snaked over a hill, hiding the hole. The head professional tried to provide directions, but we were utterly confused, so she ended her speech with, "Winter rules boys. Lift clean and place." It was the nice way to say, "The course is in such bad condition that it's ok to cheat." Our expectations severely lowered, we teed off and set out down the first fairway.

That was five years ago. The Coca-Cola stand has since been sold and replaced by an actual clubhouse, and the course itself has had plenty of time to mature. Winter rules don't apply anymore. Unfortunately, River Birch's reputation hasn't improved among those who haven't played there recently. Most will say that the course is unplayable because the ground is so hard, or the rough is so thin that your ball always sinks through the grass to the dirt. All golf courses start out hard as concrete with extraordinarily thin grass. It takes years for this maturing process to happen at a normal course, unless your head groundskeeper is John.

John is an old curmudgeon, in the purest sense. He mostly keeps to himself, unless he needs to yell at you for being lazy or doing something wrong. He never stops working and looking after his course. John averages twelve hours a day, seven days a week, and nothing sends him home for long. One day, while working on an air compressor, one of the interior belts snapped while John's hands were near it. The shock made his hands spasm into the gear system, cutting off the end of his index finger. He winced, picked up the end of his finger, wrapped a towel around his hand, and drove himself to the emergency room to have it

(continued)

(continued)

reattached. Three hours later, and against the doctor's will, John was back at work mowing the tenth green. This kind of devotion makes a great golf course. Unless the course has been vandalized, it's always in pristine condition, and John is always right behind the stampeding masses, fixing what they've hurt. John may slave endlessly keeping it green and pretty, but he can't change the course's geography.

5 River Birch was built on a shoestring budget, so the design is simple. Most holes are straight and wide. Some holes have more than ten acres of fairway. The contour of the course is gradual and forgiving. The more experienced player may be discouraged hearing this, but River Birch was designed for casual, less-experienced golfers who are out for a good time. The gentle contour makes for an easy walk for those who are so inclined; and for those who aren't and choose to take a golf cart, it makes for a gentle drive. From this gentle contour also comes an easy, forgiving golf course. Golf can get very expensive if you spend most of the day hitting three-dollar golf balls out onto the road or into the lake, so River Birch was designed to be easy on the golfer's wallet. There is still trouble to be had—just not so much that you'll be sent home after nine holes because you ran out of supplies. After you've spent enough time wandering the course, you'll want somewhere to sit down with your buddies and reminisce about the round. What better place than the nineteenth green and the clubhouse?

6 The clubhouse is the hub of all pre-and post-game activities. It's a bustle of players and employees trying to get organized or relax. Most courses are immediately judged by the clubhouse. Sure, it's nice to get out and play, but what most golfers crave is to get back inside, sit down with their partners and a cold beer, and brag about how they just had the best game of their lives. The River Birch clubhouse is off-putting to some who are too impatient to really see the quality. Most golfers complain about the lack of food choices. There isn't a grill, so most of the food is served cold or heated made in a microwave or a cooking rack. This dissuades people who haven't tried the food; but when they are hungry enough, they'll eat it and realize that although it may not have been slow roasted over a wood fire, it still tastes great. On the other side of the clubhouse from the dining area is the golf shop. People pay for their rounds and buy equipment in the golf shop, but, as is the case with the food, the selection is limited. Items are, however, always brand name and good quality. Occasionally, people stroll in and ask for merchandise that only major franchises have, but that doesn't mean River Birch can't get it.

7 The head professional, Mike, is the king pin of the golf course. He resides in the golf shop, looking over his domain, making sure everything runs smoothly. His staff is a loyal crew who does his bidding without hesitation because they trust his judgment. Having been the head professional at a busy southern California golf course, Mike's experience is second to none in Idaho. He is the type of man who looks after those who are loyal to him, especially his customers. He makes everyone feel welcome, whether that means telling a joke or just listening to a drunk golfer boast; he has made it his mission to make sure every golfer leaves the course in a better mood than when he or she came in.

8 Five years ago, mounds of dirt littered the practice areas, the grass hadn't fully grown in, and a Coca-Cola stand was trying to pass for a clubhouse. John made the first major change—he brought the aesthetic pleasure to the course. By slaving for hours every day, the course matured rapidly into one that is great for all players, especially those who are new to the game. Mike

took charge of getting people to notice. He knew that word of mouth was the best way to attract business, so he made sure that whenever someone set foot on the golf course, his or her experience would be one to praise and tell others about. So, through word of mouth, people will hopefully overlook what River Birch golf course once was and see an establishment that has taken a gentleman's game and made it fun for everyone. While the game will never return to that of a bunch of drunken Scots chasing a feather-filled ball, this is one golf course that even they might sense brings golf back—at least a little—to its humbler and simpler roots.

Evaluating the Essay

1. The argument in this review is suggested in the last sentence of the lead paragraph—River Birch Golf Course isn't elegant but promises to meet the expectations of "normal" golfers. This claim is revived and extended in the last paragraph. River Birch brings the game back to its "humbler and simpler roots." In between the lead and the final paragraph there should be meaty evidence that makes the claim convincing. Is there? What evidence seems strongest? What evidence seems less relevant?

2. Reviews often thrive on the persona—and the voice—of the reviewer. They can just as easily falter if readers aren't convinced that the reviewer has the authority to make a judgment. Do you think Sam effectively establishes that authority in the River Birch review? How?

3. Suppose Sam wanted to publish this review. Can you imagine the contexts in which he might find an interested audience?

4. If "River Birch: A Diamond in the Rough" was going to be revised, how might Sam incorporate more research beyond his anecdote about the "drunken Scots" who discovered golf? Who might he interview? What might he read?

USING WHAT YOU HAVE LEARNED

1. A review is a form of argument. Spend sixty seconds making a focused list of everything you learned about how to write persuasively from this assignment.

2. Judgments aren't always rational; in fact, we often have gut reactions that guide our evaluations of people and things. What have you learned in this chapter about how you might approach judgments in ways that combine both feelings and reason?

3. Suppose you had to evaluate the methodology of a biology experiment, or the effectiveness of a business plan. What are the first three things you would do?

A global problem like world hunger does not yield readily to simple solutions. A proposal focused on a local problem—how to educate students about sustainable food initiatives on campus, for example—can powerfully reveal important aspects of a larger problem.

WRITING A PROPOSAL

WRITING ABOUT PROBLEMS AND SOLUTIONS

A small group of students sits around the round table in my office. Two are college sophomores, one is a junior, and the other is about to graduate. We're talking about problems each of us would love to solve. "I've got a short story due at three this afternoon and I've only written three pages," says Lana. Everyone nods sympathetically. "I'd really like to feel better about work," confides Amy, who works as a chef at a local restaurant. "Most days I just don't want to go." Margaret, who sits across the table from me, is a history major, familiar with the making and unmaking of nations and other grand narratives of colonialism, war, and social change. Her problem, however, is a bit more local. "I can't get my boyfriend to clean up the apartment," she says.

What about you, they ask me?

"The problem I most want to solve today is how to avoid getting scalded in the shower when someone in my house flushes the toilet," I say, getting into the spirit of things.

This conversation had not gone quite the way I expected. I know these students are socially engaged, politically aware, and academically gifted people. When I asked about problems that need solutions I expected that they might mention local issues such as housing developments that threaten the local foothills, or perhaps the difficulty of nontraditional students adjusting to the university, or possibly budget cuts that threaten the availability of courses next semester. If they had been thinking on a larger scale, say nationally or even internationally, perhaps the conversation would have turned to the spiraling federal deficit, the

What You'll Learn in This Chapter

- How to define a problem so that your readers have a stake in the solution.
- How to write a research proposal.
- What makes a proposal persuasive.
- Questions that will help you revise a proposal.

conflict in Darfur, or even some of the little-known problems associated with the use of cotton in the garment industry. Of course, I hadn't asked them to suggest social or economic problems. I had simply asked them what problems most vexed them at the moment.

I should not have been surprised that these would be boredom with work, too little time, and a messy boyfriend. These problems are quite real, and they demand attention, *now*. One was easy to solve. Lana would carve out extra time in the afternoon to finish her story—"I already know what I need to do," she said. But the other two problems—disenchantment with work and a boyfriend who's a slob—well, both Amy and Margaret saw these not so much as problems but realities they had to live with. In fact, all the students admitted that they rarely look at the world from the perspective of problem solving.

"What if you did?" I asked.

"Then I guess I'd ask myself if there was an opportunity to learn something," said Amy.

Problems of Consequence

While not all problems are equally solvable, the process of seeking and proposing solutions can be rewarding if you see, as Amy did, the opportunity to learn. There's another motivation, too: If the problem is shared by others, whatever you discover may interest them. Part of the challenge is recognizing problems *of consequence*. What makes a problem consequential?

1. It potentially affects a number of people.
2. The solution may not be simple.
3. There may be multiple solutions and people disagree about which is best.

My problem with getting scalded in the shower if somebody flushes a toilet is certainly a problem of consequence for me. It's painful. And I know that more than a few people have this problem. But the solution isn't complicated; all I need to do is go to Ace Hardware and buy a device for the shower head that senses dramatic temperature change. Problem solved. But what about Margaret's problem with her boyfriend? Is that a problem of consequence? Undoubtedly there are lots of people with messy mates, the solution is not at all obvious (just ask Margaret), and there are likely multiple ways of dealing with the problem. But has anyone else said anything about the topic? Like many other forms of inquiry, problem solving usually requires some research. After all, if we already knew the solution, we wouldn't have the problem. A final consideration, then, is whether anyone else has said something about the problem that might help you think about the best ways to solve it.

> While not all problems are equally solvable, the process of seeking and proposing solutions can be rewarding if you see the opportunity to learn.

A quick search of the Web and several of the university library's databases of articles produced an article on the psychological need of some women for tidiness, a Web page with advice on "Living with a Messy Man," and several scholarly articles on orderliness in the workplace and perceptions of messiness. That's not a bad beginning for background on an essay that looks at the problem and proposes some possible solutions. While Margaret may not succeed in her effort to get her boyfriend to pick up his socks, she will probably learn a few things about how to deal with the problem.

Problems of Scale

While our personal problems are very real, and they can be problems of consequence, the challenges of world hunger, war, environmental destruction, economic development, and human rights matter to far more people on the planet. These are also among the most complex problems to solve. I'm always delighted when writers in my classes are passionate about these issues, and they certainly can be great topics for writing. But as always, narrowing the topic to something manageable—with a limited focus that allows you to decide what *not* to consider—is a crucial first step. Obviously, you're not going to have anything meaningful to say about solving the world's hunger problems in a five-page essay (see Figure 6.1). But it might be possible to write a focused essay about the troubles

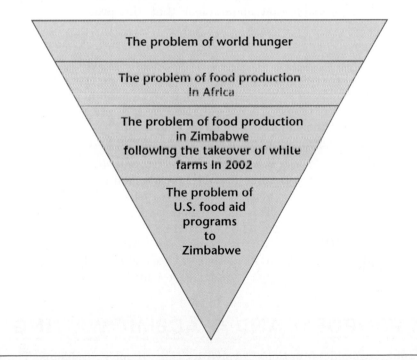

Figure 6.1 Narrowing the focus of the problem. Most of us want to find solutions to the big problems of the world, but big problems such as world hunger are complicated and do not readily yield to simple solutions. Unless you are writing a book-length proposal, it is better to narrow the focus of the problem to which you will propose solutions.

over food production in Zimbabwe, once one of Africa's most productive agricultural nations. Even better, narrow the topic further and investigate the particular U.S. aid policies that are failing to help feed hungry Zimbabwe children. Your interest in hunger can also easily lead to topics with a local angle—say, the reluctance of some hungry families in your community to use food stamps because of a local supermarket's policies. By focusing on the narrower problem, you can often reveal aspects of the larger problem much more powerfully.

The *scale* of the problems that you choose to explore, and their potential consequences, are two initial considerations when writing to solve problems. But why would you want to write about a problem in the first place?

MOTIVES FOR WRITING A PROPOSAL

Motives for writing a proposal include the following:

- *You* care *about the problem.* Whether it's something in your personal life—avoiding procrastination, having a more obedient dog, or finding a way to use less water in the garden—or a public issue—protecting bicyclists from traffic, increasing neighborhood police protection, or battling adolescent obesity—you should feel that the problem deserves your attention.

- *You hope to change something.* Writing a proposal is a way of overcoming powerlessness. Maybe you feel helpless about the daily deluge of scammers and junk messages in your e-mail. You can just complain about it. I do. But you can also research a proposal that might help you—and in turn the many others who are affected by the problem—better protect yourself from the Nigerian scammers who want to "give" you $8.5 million if you just send them a copy of your passport and $1,750.

- *You hope to learn something.* Does this go without saying? I don't think so. A proposal is like all other inquiry projects: You choose a topic because you're motivated to discover things you don't know. This motive alone isn't sufficient, of course. Others must be affected by the problem and have a stake in considering your solution. But if the problem is sufficiently complex and the solutions varied, then you stand to learn a lot.

> Writing a proposal is a way of overcoming powerlessness.

THE PROPOSAL AND ACADEMIC WRITING

Numerous academic situations involve writing to solve problems. The case-study approach, popular in business, medicine, and some social sciences, is essentially the presentation of a real-world problem for you to solve. Related to this is the growing popularity of problem-based learning, particularly in the sciences. Problem-based learning is an approach to inquiry that begins with a messy problem, rather than a question, and involves learners in coming up with tentative solutions. In these cases, writers' intentions may be less to persuade readers that certain solutions are best than to suggest a range of possibilities to consider.

In some classes, you'll be asked to write proposals. For example, political science courses may include an assignment to write a policy proposal, or an essay that looks at a specific public policy problem—say, the organization of the city government, or the state's role in wolf management (a big issue here in Idaho)—and suggest some possible solutions. In a marketing class, you might be asked to draft a proposal for dealing with a particular management problem. How do you motivate workers in a period when wages and benefits are flat? Research proposals are very common in the natural and physical sciences. These identify a particular problem—air pollution inversions in the valley, energy inefficiencies in buildings, declining populations of bull trout—and then propose a certain research program to study it. All of these forms of the proposal differ in the details but share many features and certainly an overall purpose: to get people to do something differently.

FEATURES OF THE FORM

The proposal is an academic form but it's even more common in everyday settings and situations. You can find writing that solves problems in the brochure at your doctor's office that suggests ways to deal with depression; you'll find it in your local newspaper in editorials that back a tax to create more parks; you'll find it in the case studies on marketing a new toy in your business textbook; you'll find it in the countless magazine articles and books that focus on "how to" and "self-help," on topics from anorexia to removing water marks on antique furniture.

The proposal is one of the most common forms of writing about problems and solutions. Here are some of its features:

- *Proposals usually deal with* both *problems and solutions.* What's interesting is seeing how the emphasis on each varies (see the next two points).
- *Proposals that emphasize solutions usually work from the premise that there is agreement on the problem.* That brochure in the doctor's office on depression may devote a single panel to describing the various ways the illness presents itself, and the rest of the brochure to what those who suffer from depression can do about it. Everybody agrees that depression is a problem, so it isn't necessary to persuade readers of the fact; therefore the emphasis is on solutions.
- *Proposals that emphasize the problem usually work from the premise that the problem isn't well known or well understood.* I recently read an

article in the *New York Times* that described, at length, the problem that teen stars like Britney Spears have in holding their audience as they get older. Apparently, it's a problem shared by virtually all people who become celebrities as children, and "the majority don't get to the next level." Much of the article explored the nature of this problem because it isn't widely understood. The discussion of solutions was relatively brief, and of course featured an analysis of Madonna's many successful transformations.

■ *The writer usually includes outside perspectives on the problem or its solutions.* If you're writing about a problem of consequence, then other people have said something about it or will have something to say if you ask them. Occasionally, the writer might be an expert on the topic and won't think it's necessary to do much research. But more often, we learn about the problem as we seek to solve it and actively seek outside perspectives and ideas.

■ *Proposals that advocate certain solutions often use visual rhetoric.* If a main motive is to persuade people to buy something, support something, fund something, vote for something, or otherwise change their behavior, then writers may focus on the many visual ways they might get their point across. Some proposals use graphic devices such as bulleted lists or boldfaced headlines and other techniques for emphasis, drawing readers' attention to elements of the proposal that make it easier to read or more convincing, or give the impression that the writer is professional.

■ *Proposals justify their solutions.* You know, of course, that any claim is more convincing with supporting evidence, and solutions are a kind of argumentative claim. Typically proposals that offer certain solutions over others offer evidence—or justifications—for why. A proposal that calls for erecting a memorial statue that pays tribute to Vietnam veterans rather than creating a rose garden in their name might feature evidence from interviews with local vets or information about the success of similar monuments in other communities. Successful grant proposals depend on a convincing justification that would persuade a foundation or agency to fund one solution over competing ones.

READINGS

■ PROPOSAL 1

David Johnston has a problem and it's personal. But it's also a problem for others like him—military service members who find themselves stuck with homes they can't sell and debt they can't handle because they were called for duty in some other state or country. The economy these days is bad news for nearly everybody, but Johnston argues in "Housing and Our Military" that service people who often have no choice about when and where they'll be posted may be forced to sell their homes at a major loss. Worse, some banks may hold the sellers responsible for paying off the debt on the lost equity. Johnston finds himself paying a mortgage on a home he doesn't even own anymore. There's an appealing simplicity to Johnston's proposal. The problem-solution structure of the essay is obvious and it's concise and to-the-point. But like any argument (and proposals are a form of argument), "Housing and Our Military" works from premises or "warrants" that may or may not be obvious. In other words, what do you have to believe is true to find Johnston's solutions persuasive?

A few pages ago, I noted that an important motive for writing a proposal is that you hope to change something. Soon after David Johnston's essay was published in *USA Today,* several members of Congress read the piece and adopted most of Johnston's recommendations, in some cases word for word. Forty days later, the reforms he advocated became law as part of the American Recovery and Reinvestment Act of 2009. "I think forty days from argument essay to law of the land must be some kind of record," Johnston noted. "Words have power but timing is indispensible."

Housing and Our Military
David S. Johnston

The collapsing housing market has prompted many political and financial leaders to make urgent pleas to aid those owners who are facing the loss of their homes. But there is one group that gets little attention in that regard: the military family.   1

When change-in-duty-station orders arrive, these families do not have the option of waiting out the market for a return to pre-slump prices. Many military homeowners have lost equity in their houses and now owe more for their homes than they are worth.   2

I know this firsthand. Like many other servicemembers, I purchased a home near a military installation before the 2006 real estate decline. My family was too large to be given on-post housing in the Washington, D.C., market in 2004. But at the time,   3

(continued)

(continued)

we thought, "No problem," since we had just received a small inheritance that we could use for a down payment. If we got orders to move, we planned to rent or sell the house because we had equity and the market was climbing.

Change of Duty Station

4   I got orders sooner than I expected in the spring of 2006. So my wife and I put our house on the market for rent or sale and moved away. Then it happened: That same summer, the housing market began to crumble.

5   For the next two years, we were unable to sell the house. We lost our inheritance, all of our equity, and sold it for 40 percent less than its market high. Worse, the lenders levied the difference against us after the house was sold. We are now making payments on a house we no longer own.

6   If I declare bankruptcy, that jeopardizes my security clearances, so I am stuck. And I have heard similar stories from other soldiers. Although changes of duty stations are a part of military life, there should be a safety net in the travel regulations not unlike the rules for base closure/reduction-in-force regulations.

7   In response to the rise in home foreclosures, the Defense Department has heightened awareness of its family assistance programs that focus on financial counseling and education. But this does little to forestall the pressure of foreclosure or bankruptcy caused by the economic downturn.

Necessary Changes

8   Here's what I think should be done: First, the Pentagon should set up a program, perhaps in conjunction with the Veterans Benefits Administration (VBA), to refinance homes of struggling military members at 95 percent of the current market value while subsidizing the difference.

9   For those members who have lost their homes in foreclosure or by "short sell," and whose banks did not forgive any of the loss in the home's value, the government should provide incentives for the banks to forgive them or, potentially, assume the remainder of the unsecured loan.

10   Furthermore, the VBA should reconsider its loan program qualifications so that it would still allow good loans to families with poor credit if and only if that poor credit was a result of the housing market collapse and not of personal financial mismanagement.

11   Second, if the military relocates a servicemember who is a homeowner and the local housing market drops, a relocation assistance program ought to be available similar to Pentagon civilian programs that provide funds to cover a relocation.

12   When all options have been exhausted and the home will not sell, the servicemember should have the option to sell the property to the government at the amount owed. If the government acts soon, it can help many military families overcome these financial problems.

13   Nobody saw this coming, but military families really are hurting as never before.

Inquiring into the Essay

Use the four categories of inquiry questions—exploring, explaining, evaluating, and reflecting—to examine your ideas about David Johnston's "Housing and Our Military."

1. Explore your reaction to the premises behind Johnston's argument that the government should provide incentives and subsidies to service people who lose big on real estate because they were forced to sell when posted elsewhere. One premise, for example, is that while most enter the service knowing they may move around a lot, people who serve should be protected from big real estate losses when the market turns sour. Write fast for three minutes about what you think about this.

2. Explain other premises or (as logician Toulmin noted) "warrants" that you have to buy to find Johnston's solutions convincing.

3. Remember Aristotle's rhetorical triangle? (See page 10.) Evaluate how effectively this essay uses ethos, pathos, and logos. Which of these does it emphasize most? How might that reflect how Johnston imagines his audience?

4. Not every personal problem will be useful as a focus for a public proposal like this one. Here's a list of what's bugging me today: The dog won't stop barking, my income tax materials are all over the place, my daughter Julia keeps borrowing my favorite guitar, my Windows computer boots up sloooowly, and the gray February weather is depressing. Which of these might be problems that others share and have solutions in which others might have some stake? In other words, what makes a personal problem worthy of a proposal like the ones we're discussing in this chapter?

▪ PROPOSAL 2

A lot of people can't imagine a proposal without PowerPoint (or Keynote for Mac users). It's a remarkably versatile program that exploits the potential of visual rhetoric. You can combine images with text, animation, and even audio. Presentation slides challenge the user to think about what ideas to emphasize and which visual arrangements might dramatize them to an audience. Depending on how you order the slides, you can tell a different story. Maybe because of all these possibilities, PowerPoint presentations can be boring. There may be too much text, the animation can be obnoxious, or the images might be distracting. Worse still, the presenter uses presentation slides like a script rather than a technique for focusing emphasis on key points. Watching someone's back while he or she reads a PowerPoint text is an invitation to nod off.

The following PowerPoint proposal, "Green Dining," describes how the dining services at University of California–Santa Cruz are trying to solve the problem of energy inefficiency in the kitchen. This proposal doesn't dramatize the problem. It doesn't really need to since most everyone agrees that wasting energy in dining halls (or any other campus building, for that matter) is a problem. This slide presentation focuses on some solutions, and it works well because the proposal has modest ambitions. It addresses one very specific aspect of the campus dining operation: dishwashing. Even better, there is concrete evidence that one solution is already making a difference in energy use. After documenting this success, "Green Dining" goes on to present other measures that should have a similar impact.

Notice how much can be accomplished with simple images, minimal text, and logical arrangement.

Benefits

- Saves water
- Saves energy
- Saves money
- Cleans faster
- Less splash back
- Covers larger surface area

Success at UC Santa Cruz

5 "low-flow" nozzles were installed in various locations: • Crown/Merrill Dining • College 8/9 Dining • Owl's Nest Café • Terra Fresca Cafe	Nozzles were supplied and installed FOR FREE through the "Smart Rinse Program," a program of Ecology Action, a local Santa Cruz non-profit

Quantifiable Savings

Energy Saving Estimates

Total # of Nozzles	Hours used per day	Gallons saved per day	Therms saved per day	Annual Dollar Savings
5	.00	0020	16.00	$9,175

Current Dining Projects

T8 Lighting retrofit

- 5 major dining halls
- Upgrade 32 watts → 28 Watts
- 1248 Lamps counted
- Roughly 5 KW saved

Future Dining Project

Variable control exhaust hoods

- Controls for commercial kitchen ventilation exhaust hoods
- Reduce energy costs by up to 70% during slow cooking periods

Project Benefits

- Massive energy savings
- Improved indoor air quality
- Optimum kitchen comfort
- Improved fire safety
- 1–4 year payback
- $1,500–$10,00 in annual savings

Questions?

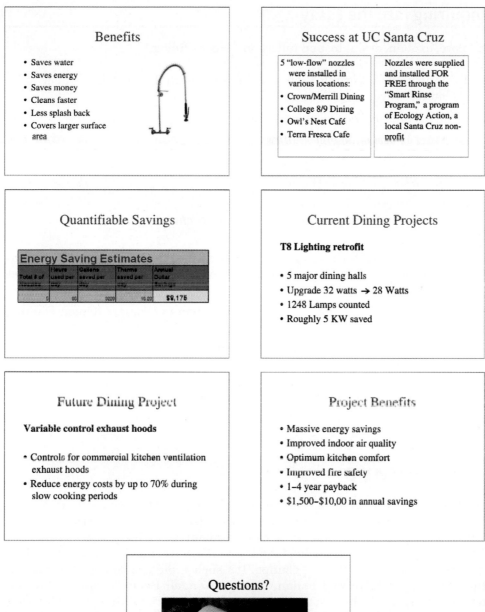

Inquiring into the Essay

Explore, explain, evaluate, and reflect on "Green Dining."

1. Finish the following sentences in your journal, and follow them for a minute if you can. Write quickly.

   a. *As far as I'm concerned, PowerPoint is* _____.

   b. *The best slide presentations* _____.

   c. *The worst slide presentations* _____.

   d. *When I do PowerPoint (or Keynote), the main thing I think about is* _____.

   e. *A lot of times, people do PowerPoint when they should* _____.

2. Using some of the ideas you generated in the first question, craft a definition of an effective PowerPoint proposal, identifying specifically what qualities it should have.

3. Use your definition in the previous question to evaluate "Green Dining." Is it persuasive?

4. The preceding series of questions, if used consecutively, constitutes a method for thinking through writing about what you've read, working toward a more thoughtful evaluation. Reflect on how that process worked for you. Did you end up getting better ideas about what you think because you took time to do the prewriting?

■ PROPOSAL 3

Psychologists talk about people who have learned helplessness. Like Eeyore in *Winnie the Pooh,* they are people who feel like their world basically stinks and there is nothing they can do about it. "Why bother?" they say. "What difference will it make?" And yet, it's hard not to feel a little like Eeyore in the face of climate change. It's such a big problem, and what can the little guy do? Michael Pollan, quoting Wendell Berry, argues in the following essay that this is the "cheap-energy mind" talking, the one that encourages us to believe that we're hopelessly dependent on other people and their grand technologies to get what we need. The climate problem *is* huge, but in "Why Bother?" Pollan has a simple solution: Grow a vegetable garden, even a tiny one. What is so intriguing about his essay is not just the simplicity of the solution it offers but that Pollan manages to make it persuasive. See if you agree.

Why Bother?

Michael Pollan

Why bother? That really is the big question facing us as individuals hoping to do   1
something about climate change, and it's not an easy one to answer. I don't know
about you, but for me the most upsetting moment in *An Inconvenient Truth* came
long after Al Gore scared the hell out of me, constructing an utterly convincing case
that the very survival of life on earth as we know it is threatened by climate change.
No, the really dark moment came during the closing credits, when we are asked
to…change our light bulbs. That's when it got really depressing. The immense dis-
proportion between the magnitude of the problem Gore had described and the puni-
ness of what he was asking us to do about it was enough to sink your heart.

But the drop-in-the-bucket issue is not the only problem lurking behind the "why   2
bother" question. Let's say I do bother, big time. I turn my life upside-down, start bik-
ing to work, plant a big garden, turn down the thermostat so low I need the Jimmy
Carter signature cardigan, forsake the clothes dryer for a laundry line across the yard,
trade in the station wagon for a hybrid, get off the beef, go completely local. I could
theoretically do all that, but what would be the point when I know full well that
halfway around the world there lives my evil twin, some carbon-footprint
doppelgänger in Shanghai or Chongqing who has just bought his first car (Chinese car
ownership is where ours was back in 1918), is eager to swallow every bite of meat I
forswear and who's positively itching to replace every last pound of CO_2 I'm struggling no longer to emit. So what exactly would I have to show for all my trouble?

A sense of personal virtue, you might suggest, somewhat sheepishly. But what good   3
is that when virtue itself is quickly becoming a term of derision? And not just on the
editorial pages of the *Wall Street Journal* or on the lips of the (former) vice president,
who famously dismissed energy conservation as a "sign of personal virtue." No, even in
the pages of the *New York Times* and the *New Yorker*, it seems the epithet "virtuous,"
when applied to an act of personal environmental responsibility, may be used only
ironically. Tell me: How did it come to pass that virtue—a quality that for most of history
has generally been deemed, well, a virtue—became a mark of liberal softheadedness?
How peculiar, that doing the right thing by the environment—buying the hybrid, eating
like a locavore—should now set you up for the Ed Begley Jr. treatment.

And even if in the face of this derision I decide I am going to bother, there arises   4
the whole vexed question of getting it right. Is eating local or walking to work really
going to reduce my carbon footprint? According to one analysis, if walking to work
increases your appetite and you consume more meat or milk as a result, walking
might actually emit more carbon than driving. A handful of studies have recently suggested that in certain cases under certain conditions, produce from places as far away
as New Zealand might account for less carbon than comparable domestic products.

(continued)

(continued)

True, at least one of these studies was co-written by a representative of agribusiness interests in (surprise!) New Zealand, but even so, they make you wonder. If determining the carbon footprint of food is really this complicated, and I've got to consider not only "food miles" but also whether the food came by ship or truck and how lushly the grass grows in New Zealand, then maybe on second thought I'll just buy the imported chops at Costco, at least until the experts get their footprints sorted out.

5   There are so many stories we can tell ourselves to justify doing nothing, but perhaps the most insidious is that, whatever we do manage to do, it will be too little too late. Climate change is upon us, and it has arrived well ahead of schedule. Scientists' projections that seemed dire a decade ago turn out to have been unduly optimistic: the warming and the melting is occurring much faster than the models predicted. Now truly terrifying feedback loops threaten to boost the rate of change exponentially, as the shift from white ice to blue water in the Arctic absorbs more sunlight and warming soils everywhere become more biologically active, causing them to release their vast stores of carbon into the air. Have you looked into the eyes of a climate scientist recently? They look really scared.

6   So do you still want to talk about planting gardens?

7   I do. . . .

8   For us to wait for legislation or technology to solve the problem of how we're living our lives suggests we're not really serious about changing—something our politicians cannot fail to notice. They will not move until we do. Indeed, to look to leaders and experts, to laws and money and grand schemes, to save us from our predicament represents precisely the sort of thinking—passive, delegated, dependent for solutions on specialists—that helped get us into this mess in the first place. It's hard to believe that the same sort of thinking could now get us out of it.

9   Thirty years ago, Wendell Berry, the Kentucky farmer and writer, put forward a blunt analysis of precisely this mentality. He argued that the environmental crisis of the 1970s—an era innocent of climate change; what we would give to have back *that* environmental crisis!—was at its heart a crisis of character and would have to be addressed first at that level: at home, as it were. He was impatient with people who wrote checks to environmental organizations while thoughtlessly squandering fossil fuel in their everyday lives—the 1970s equivalent of people buying carbon offsets to atone for their Tahoes and Durangos. Nothing was likely to change until we healed the "split between what we think and what we do." For Berry, the "why bother" question came down to a moral imperative: "Once our personal connection to what is wrong becomes clear, then we have to choose: we can go on as before, recognizing our dishonesty and living with it the best we can, or we can begin the effort to change the way we think and live."

10   For Berry, the deep problem standing behind all the other problems of industrial civilization is "specialization," which he regards as the "disease of the modern character." Our society assigns us a tiny number of roles: we're producers (of one thing) at work, consumers of a great many other things the rest of the time,

and then once a year or so we vote as citizens. Virtually all of our needs and desires we delegate to specialists of one kind or another—our meals to agribusiness, health to the doctor, education to the teacher, entertainment to the media, care for the environment to the environmentalist, political action to the politician. . . .

Here's the point: Cheap energy, which gives us climate change, fosters precisely the mentality that makes dealing with climate change in our own lives seem impossibly difficult. Specialists ourselves, we can no longer imagine anyone but an expert, or anything but a new technology or law, solving our problems. Al Gore asks us to change the light bulbs because he probably can't imagine us doing anything much more challenging, like, say, growing some portion of our own food. We can't imagine it, either, which is probably why we prefer to cross our fingers and talk about the promise of ethanol and nuclear power—new liquids and electrons to power the same old cars and houses and lives.

The "cheap-energy mind," as Wendell Berry called it, is the mind that asks, "Why bother?" because it is helpless to imagine—much less attempt—a different sort of life, one less divided, less reliant. Since the cheap-energy mind translates everything into money, its proxy, it prefers to put its faith in market-based solutions—carbon taxes and pollution-trading schemes. If we could just get the incentives right, it believes, the economy will properly value everything that matters and nudge our self-interest down the proper channels. The best we can hope for is a greener version of the old invisible hand. Visible hands it has no use for.

But while some such grand scheme may well be necessary, it's doubtful that it will be sufficient or that it will be politically sustainable before we've demonstrated to ourselves that change is possible. Merely to give, to spend, even to vote, is not to do, and there is so much that needs to be done—without further delay. In the judgment of James Hansen, the NASA climate scientist who began sounding the alarm on global warming 20 years ago, we have only 10 years left to start cutting—not just slowing—the amount of carbon we're emitting or face a "different planet." Hansen said this more than two years ago, however; two years have gone by, and nothing of consequence has been done. So: eight years left to go and a great deal left to do.

Which brings us back to the "why bother" question and how we might better answer it. The reasons not to bother are many and compelling, at least to the cheap-energy mind. But let me offer a few admittedly tentative reasons that we might put on the other side of the scale:

If you do bother, you will set an example for other people. If enough other people bother, each one influencing yet another in a chain reaction of behavioral change, markets for all manner of green products and alternative technologies will prosper and expand. (Just look at the market for hybrid cars.) Consciousness will be raised, perhaps even changed: new moral imperatives and new taboos might take root in the culture. Driving an SUV or eating a 24-ounce steak or illuminating your McMansion like an airport runway at night might come to be regarded as

(continued)

11

12

13

14

15

(continued)

outrages to human conscience. Not having things might become cooler than having them. And those who did change the way they live would acquire the moral standing to demand changes in behavior from others—from other people, other corporations, even other countries.

16   All of this could, theoretically, happen. What I'm describing (imagining would probably be more accurate) is a process of viral social change, and change of this kind, which is nonlinear, is never something anyone can plan or predict or count on. Who knows, maybe the virus will reach all the way to Chongqing and infect my Chinese evil twin. Or not. Maybe going green will prove a passing fad and will lose steam after a few years, just as it did in the 1980s, when Ronald Reagan took down Jimmy Carter's solar panels from the roof of the White House.

17   Going personally green is a bet, nothing more or less, though it's one we probably all should make, even if the odds of it paying off aren't great. Sometimes you have to act as if acting will make a difference, even when you can't prove that it will. That, after all, was precisely what happened in Communist Czechoslovakia and Poland, when a handful of individuals like Vaclav Havel and Adam Michnik resolved that they would simply conduct their lives "as if" they lived in a free society. That improbable bet created a tiny space of liberty that, in time, expanded to take in, and then help take down, the whole of the Eastern bloc.

18   So what would be a comparable bet that the individual might make in the case of the environmental crisis? Havel himself has suggested that people begin to "conduct themselves as if they were to live on this earth forever and be answerable for its condition one day." Fair enough, but let me propose a slightly less abstract and daunting wager. The idea is to find one thing to do in your life that doesn't involve spending or voting, that may or may not virally rock the world but is real and particular (as well as symbolic) and that, come what may, will offer its own rewards. Maybe you decide to give up meat, an act that would reduce your carbon footprint by as much as a quarter. Or you could try this: determine to observe the Sabbath. For one day a week, abstain completely from economic activity: no shopping, no driving, no electronics.

19   But the act I want to talk about is growing some—even just a little—of your own food. Rip out your lawn, if you have one, and if you don't—if you live in a high-rise, or have a yard shrouded in shade—look into getting a plot in a community garden. Measured against the Problem We Face, planting a garden sounds pretty benign, I know, but in fact it's one of the most powerful things an individual can do—to reduce your carbon footprint, sure, but more important, to reduce your sense of dependence and dividedness: to change the cheap-energy mind.

20   A great many things happen when you plant a vegetable garden, some of them directly related to climate change, others indirect but related nevertheless.

Growing food, we forget, comprises the original solar technology: calories produced by means of photosynthesis. Years ago the cheap-energy mind discovered that more food could be produced with less effort by replacing sunlight with fossil-fuel fertilizers and pesticides, with a result that the typical calorie of food energy in your diet now requires about 10 calories of fossil-fuel energy to produce. It's estimated that the way we feed ourselves (or rather, allow ourselves to be fed) accounts for about a fifth of the greenhouse gas for which each of us is responsible.

21

Yet the sun still shines down on your yard, and photosynthesis still works so abundantly that in a thoughtfully organized vegetable garden (one planted from seed, nourished by compost from the kitchen and involving not too many drives to the garden center), you can grow the proverbial free lunch—CO_2-free and dollar-free. This is the most-local food you can possibly eat (not to mention the freshest, tastiest and most nutritious), with a carbon footprint so faint that even the New Zealand lamb council dares not challenge it. And while we're counting carbon, consider too your compost pile, which shrinks the heap of garbage your household needs trucked away even as it feeds your vegetables and sequesters carbon in your soil. What else? Well, you will probably notice that you're getting a pretty good workout there in your garden, burning calories without having to get into the car to drive to the gym. (It is one of the absurdities of the modern division of labor that, having replaced physical labor with fossil fuel, we now have to burn even more fossil fuel to keep our unemployed bodies in shape.) Also, by engaging both body and mind, time spent in the garden is time (and energy) subtracted from electronic forms of entertainment.

22

You begin to see that growing even a little of your own food is, as Wendell Berry pointed out 30 years ago, one of those solutions that, instead of begetting a new set of problems—the way "solutions" like ethanol or nuclear power inevitably do—actually beget other solutions, and not only of the kind that save carbon. Still more valuable are the habits of mind that growing a little of your own food can yield. You quickly learn that you need not be dependent on specialists to provide for yourself—that your body is still good for something and may actually be enlisted in its own support. If the experts are right, if both oil and time are running out, these are skills and habits of mind we're all very soon going to need. We may also need the food. Could gardens provide it? Well, during World War II, victory gardens supplied as much as 40 percent of the produce Americans ate.

23

But there are sweeter reasons to plant that garden, to bother. At least in this one corner of your yard and life, you will have begun to heal the split between what you think and what you do, to commingle your identities as consumer and producer and citizen. Chances are, your garden will re-engage you with your neighbors, for you will have produce to give away and the need to borrow their tools. You will have

(continued)

(continued)

reduced the power of the cheap-energy mind by personally overcoming its most debilitating weakness: its helplessness and the fact that it can't do much of anything that doesn't involve division or subtraction. The garden's season-long transit from seed to ripe fruit—*will you get a load of that zucchini?!*—suggests that the operations of addition and multiplication still obtain, that the abundance of nature is not exhausted. The single greatest lesson the garden teaches is that our relationship to the planet need not be zero-sum, and that as long as the sun still shines and people still can plan and plant, think and do, we can, if we bother to try, find ways to provide for ourselves without diminishing the world.

Inquiring into the Essay

Explore, explain, evaluate, and reflect on Michael Pollan's "Why Bother?"

1. Fastwrite in your journal for five minutes without stopping and explore how your life might operate from a "cheap-energy mind." You might tell yourself the story of what you did, say, yesterday that shows how that mindset operates. Be specific.

2. Test your understanding of Pollan's argument. After reading "Why Bother?" compose a fast paragraph that summarize how Pollan answers his own question: Why bother? Do this on the left page of your journal.

3. So are you convinced? On the right journal page, answer this question: Will you be digging up the lawn to plant zucchini?

4. Proposals like this, which advocate lifestyle change, seek to do something that is enormously difficult—to get people to change not just their behavior but their habits. Reflect on what you think are the best ways to accomplish this. What *kinds* of persuasion does changing behavior demand?

WRITING IN THE DISCIPLINES

Writing a Research Proposal

A research proposal is a kind of action plan that explains your research question, what you expect might be the answer, how your investigation contributes to what has already been said on the topic, and how you will proceed.

While the format varies, most research proposals aim to persuade readers that (1) the project is reasonable given the investigator's time and resources, (2) the research question or problem is significant, and (3) the researcher has a good plan for getting the job done.

The following elements are typically included in a research proposal:

- **Title:** Short and descriptive.
- **Abstract:** A brief statement of what you intend to do, including your research question and hypothesis, if you've got one.
- **Background or context:** Why is the project worth doing? What problem does it solve, or how does it advance our understanding of the subject? This key section establishes where your question fits into the ongoing conversation about your topic, in your class, in the academic literature, or both. You also want to demonstrate that you've done your homework—you've got a handle on the relevant literature on your topic and understand how you might build on it.
- **Methodology or research design:** How will you try to answer your research question? How will you limit your focus? What information will you need to gather, and how will you do it?
- **Results:** This isn't a common section for proposals in the humanities, but it certainly is in the sciences. How will you analyze the data you collect?
- **References or works cited:** Almost all research proposals, because they review relevant literature, include a bibliography. Sometimes you may be asked to annotate it (see Appendix C, "The Annotated Bibliography").

Because the research proposal is a persuasive document, craft it to keep your reader engaged; find a good balance between generalities and detail, avoid jargon, and demonstrate your curiosity and eagerness to pursue your question.

SEEING THE FORM

A Problem in Pictures

When members of the San Francisco Bicycle Coalition (SFBC) wanted to dramatize the problem of insufficient space for bikes on a city commuter train, they did it with pictures. It was a powerfully simple idea. They took shots of three morning trains, each overloaded with bicycles and nearly empty of passengers. The contrast is obvious. And so is the solution to the problem: Add more space for bicycles on trains. A few months later, transit authorities did just that.

(continued)

Seeing the Form (*continued*)

No Space for Bikes:
A photo study of trains bumping cyclists out of SF.

1: Train 134: Sept 22 9:07 AM

2: Train 134: Sept 22 9:07 AM

3: Train 230: Sept 24 8:53 AM

4: Train 230: Sept 24 8:53 AM

5: Train 332: Sept 30 8:56 AM

6: Train 332: Sept 30 8:56 AM

Submitted to JBP Oct 2
by Benjamin Damm

THE WRITING PROCESS

INQUIRY PROJECT: WRITING A PROPOSAL

A problem needs to be solved and you have an idea how to do it. Developing your idea and presenting it is the general purpose of this assignment. Ultimately, you'll write a 1,000- to 1,500-word draft that has the following features:

- It addresses a problem of consequence and is written to an audience that might be interested in solutions.
- It is a problem of local concern. In other words, the scale of the problem is limited to the details that in some way affect your community.
- You justify the solutions you propose.
- The form of your proposal is linked to your purpose and audience.

PEARSON
mycomplab

For additional reading, writing, and research resources, go to
www.mycomplab.com

Thinking About Subjects

Amy, Lana, and Margaret, the three students with whom I talked about problems at the start of this chapter, didn't have much trouble coming up with them: Amy hates her work, Lana procrastinates, and Margaret has a messy boyfriend. Initially, each problem seemed a relatively private matter, hardly a suitable topic for a proposal. But it became apparent later that at least one of them—Margaret's problem with her boyfriend—was actually something that was both shared by other women and a topic about which something had been said.

> The explosion of "how to" and "self help" books and articles is evidence of the popularity of writing that attempts to solve problems.

Perhaps you already have a topic in mind for your proposal. But if you don't, or you want to explore some other possibilities, begin by generating a list of problems you'd like to solve without worrying about whether they're problems of consequence. Also don't worry too much yet about whether you have solutions to the problems you're generating. You can come up with those later. Try some of the generating exercises that follow.

Generating Ideas

Play with some ideas about subjects for the proposal assignment. Remember not to judge the material at this stage.

Listing Prompts. Lists can be rich sources of triggering topics. Let them grow freely, and when you're ready, use an item as the focus of another list or an episode of fastwriting. The following prompts should get you started.

ONE STUDENT'S RESPONSE

Caesar's Journal

LISTING PROMPTS

Problems in my life

Procrastination
Can't stick to a budget
Credit card debt
Hate the winter
Failing calculus
Girlfriend prefers Hector
Balancing studying and social life
Can't afford to travel
Work too much

Problems on campus

No sense of community
Drying up of work-study funds
Not enough diversity
Lines at the registrar
Recent tuition hike

Legislature underfunds higher
    education
Lousy food at the SUB
Textbooks are too expensive
Waiting list for child-care center

Problems in community

Overdevelopment of foothills
Litter and degradation of Boise River
Too few child-care options
Hate crimes
Concert venues inadequate
Traffic
Air pollution in Valley
Smell from sugar beet factory
Range fires

1. In your journal, spend three minutes brainstorming a list of problems in your personal life that you'd like to solve. Let the ideas come in waves.

2. Spend three minutes brainstorming a list of problems *on your campus, at your workplace*, or *in the local community* that affect you in some way, or that you feel something about. Don't worry about repeating items from the list you made in Listing Prompt 1.

3. Explore some possible causes of the problem by finishing the following sentence as many times as you can: This is a problem because _____.

Fastwriting Prompts. In the early stages of generating possible topics for an essay, fastwriting can be invaluable, *if* you allow yourself to write badly. Initially, don't worry about staying focused; sometimes you find the best triggering topics by ranging freely. Once you've tentatively settled on something, use a more focused fastwrite to try to generate information and ideas within the loose boundaries of your chosen topic.

1. Pick any of the items from the preceding lists as a launching place for a five-minute fastwrite. Explore some of the following questions:

    ■ When did I first notice this was a problem?

    ■ What's the worst part about it?

- What might be some of its causes?
- What moment, situation, or scene is most typical of this problem? Describe it as if you're experiencing it by writing in the present tense.
- How does this problem make me feel?
- What people do I associate with it?

2. Depending on how familiar you are with a problem that interests you, do a five-minute focused fastwrite that explores solutions, beginning with the sentence I think one of the ways to deal with _____ is _____. Follow that sentence as long as you can. When the writing stalls, use the following prompt: Another possible solution to the problem of _____ might be _____. Repeat these prompts as often as you can for ten minutes.

ONE STUDENT'S RESPONSE

Gina's Journal: Fastwrite

I first became aware of how wasteful the modern lifestyle is about three years ago, when I first started dating Vinnie. What's bad is that most people aren't aware of the destruction they cause the environment, believe there is no other way, or are too lazy to think progressively. It's unfortunate when people choose to follow old habits instead of making daily active choices. This problem makes me feel dread, helplessness, and anger. I feel angry because I know that people can make a difference; I believe change is possible in the smallest and easiest of actions. I think the cause of this problem is the example the government leads, some of the media, and the influence parents have on their children. One specific example of this problem and how one small decision could greatly impact the Earth is with the restaurant chain, Subway. Right now, Subway wraps every sandwich it makes for customers in paper and then places it in a plastic bag. The plastic bags create an enormous amount of waste. If Subway merely made the decision to ask people if they wanted a bag, then less plastic would pollute the Earth. I believe many people wouldn't want a bag because they are immediately going to eat their sandwich and throw the bag away anyway.

One solution to this problem is being open to change and new modes of thinking. People would need to question everything and think through the logistics completely. Some people may not know how to start, in which case I recommend reading literature and magazines that propose solutions such as *Ode, Back Home,* and *Mother Jones.* They could also attend renewable energy festivals and take workshops if they want to increase their awareness even further. I think one of the ways to deal with modern thinking and living styles is providing a good example for others. Make your choices wisely and don't give in to the "easy" decision.

Visual Prompts. Cluster a problem that concerns you. Build associations that help you think about people you associate with the problem, situations when it's most obvious, how it makes you feel, things that might cause the problem, and even possible solutions.

INQUIRING INTO THE DETAILS

Causation

One of my favorite clichés is, "This is a solution in search of a problem." Obviously, there's no point in proposing a solution if you can't win agreement that there's a problem in the first place. But once you do establish that there is a problem, the next thing is to examine what *causes* the problem. Controlling some of the causes may be the beginning of finding the solution. This exercise might help you discover those possibilities in the problem you've chosen to explore.

Begin with some journal work to flesh out your initial understandings and feelings about the problem.

1. At the top of a journal page, write *Causes*. Brainstorm a quick list of things that you believe contribute to or cause the problem. These might be composed as "because" statements. For example, if the problem is the lack of diversity on your campus, make a fast list of possible reasons by beginning with There is a lack of diversity on the Boise State campus because...

   - Idaho is sometimes perceived as a state with racial problems.
   - too few scholarships are targeted to minorities.
   - the history of African Americans and Latinos in Idaho isn't widely known among whites.
   - campus organizations don't do enough to promote diversity.
   - too few courses in the curriculum would appeal to minority students.
   - and so on.

   Remember that at this point you're brainstorming a fast list of *possible* causes. You may or may not know enough about the causes of the problem to be very certain about what you're saying here.

2. Choose *one* of the causes on your list that seems most plausible to you as contributing significantly to the problem, *or* that you find most interesting. Use this as a prompt for a five-minute fastwrite. Explore some of the following questions:

   - Do you have any personal experience with this particular cause?
   - In what ways, exactly, might it contribute to the problem?

> ■ Does this possible cause of the problem suggest anything about a possible solution?
>
> ■ When you compare it with other possible causes, what makes this one unique or significant?
>
> If the writing stalls, choose another cause from your list in Step 1, and explore it through writing using the preceding questions, if they're helpful.
>
> One of the things this exercise might do is help you to use cause/effect as a mode of inquiry that exposes relationships, and not just the connections between the problem and some of the reasons it exists, but also the problem and its possible solutions. Remember, your goal is to write a proposal; it's not enough to simply dramatize the problem.

Research Prompts. Research—reading, observing, and talking to people—can be enormously generative at any stage in the inquiry process, including the beginning. It's one of the best ways to discover a topic, and it almost always generates information you can use later in your essay once you've chosen a topic. Try some of the following research prompts to help you along.

1. Interview your classmates about what they think are the biggest problems facing them as students. Interview student or faculty leaders or administrators about what they think are the biggest problems facing the university community. Do the same with community leaders.

2. Design an informal survey targeted to a particular group that you're interested in—students, student-athletes, local businesspeople, sports fans, migrant workers, and so on. This group may or may not be one to which you belong. Discover what they believe are the most serious problems they face.

3. Become a student of a local newspaper. In particular, pay attention to the letters to the editor and the local community pages. What seems to be a recurrent problem that gets people's attention? Clip articles, letters, or editorials that address the problem.

Judging What You Have

Feeling a little overwhelmed? See problems everywhere? It can be wearing to focus on what's wrong with your life, your university, and your community. But remember that your ultimate goal is to write a proposal that suggests ways these problems might be resolved. You may have already explored some of these solutions, but if you haven't, don't worry; you'll get the chance later. Begin by scrutinizing the material you generated for possible topics.

What's Promising Material and What Isn't? We've talked about some initial judgments you can make. Now look at the material you generated in the fastwrites, lists, research, or clusters and ask yourself which of the problems listed *do you* *care about the most*, or which *are you most interested in*? Once you've selected some tentative topics for your proposal, narrow them down using the following questions:

- *Does someone aside from you have a stake in finding a solution?* Remember that you want to develop a proposal that addresses a problem that isn't merely a private matter but one that others care about, too.

- *Is there an identifiable audience for proposals about how to solve the problem?* A key part of the assignment is writing your proposal with a particular audience in mind. Can you readily identify who that audience might be?

- *Have other people said something somewhere about the problem or solutions?* Are you aware, through your initial research, whether there are experts, articles, reports, studies, Web pages, and other sources that explore your topic?

- *Which subject offers you the most opportunity for learning?* Amy saw problem solving as an opportunity to learn. This is most likely to occur if you choose to write about something that you may not fully understand. These are almost always the best topics for an inquiry-based project.

Questions About Audience and Purpose. This assignment asks you to identify an audience for your proposal. When you do, consider what exactly might be your purpose with respect to that audience. Do you want to:

- *Inform* them about the problem and explore possible solutions?

- *Advocate* certain solutions as the best ways to solve the problem?

- *Inform and advocate*, dramatizing the problem because your audience may not fully appreciate and understand it, and then persuade them to support the solutions you favor?

These purposes will shape your approach. But also consider how your audience might already think and feel about both the problem you're tackling and the solutions you offer. Use the chart in Figure 6.2.

Questions of Form. Although it might be premature to decide the *form* your proposal will take, sometimes an awareness of purpose and audience will suggest an approach. For example, if Cheryl's purpose is to advocate for a new nontraditional student center on campus, and her audience is school administrators, then she'll need to consider how best to get her message across. She might, for example, write her proposal in the form of a letter to the university's president. Gerald's proposal on how to deal with Internet plagiarism on campus might be written as a Web page that could be used as a link on the writing program or writing center's site.

Research Considerations. Research provides crucial support for most proposals and it is not too soon to do a little even at this early stage in the process. While

Awareness of the problem	If low, increase emphasis on dramatizing the problem.	If high, emphasize proposed solutions.
Initial disposition toward proposed solution	If favorably disposed, emphasize action that needs to be taken to implement solution. Emphasize pathos over logos.	If unfavorably disposed, offer balanced treatment of possible solutions before stating yours. Emphasize logos over pathos.
Attitude toward speaker	If positive, emphasize stronger action to solve the problem.	If negative, emphasize the views or experience speaker *does* share with audience.

Figure 6.2   Audience analysis chart

it's useful to do some quick and dirty research on your topic (for which the Web is ideal), avoid the temptation to while away the hours doing it. Collect just enough information to get you thinking and to give you relevant material you might incorporate into the sketch.

Writing the Sketch

Begin by drafting a sketch of your proposal. It should:

- be at least 500 to 600 words
- have a tentative title
- be written with the appropriate audience in mind
- not only dramatize the problem, but advocate or explore solution(s)

You might also develop this sketch in a form that you think might be particularly effective given your purpose and audience. Perhaps your sketch will be a letter, for example, or the text of a brochure, or an ad, or an essay.

■ STUDENT SKETCH

Gina's journal work kept pointing her to a potential problem—the wastefulness of American consumerism. Initially, we often circle subjects like birds lifted high on thermals, seeing an entire landscape below us. This is especially true when we focus on problems we think need to be solved. Gina had the good sense to know that consumerism was too large to work with, so she descended quickly and in her sketch landed on something far more focused: clothing. Later, in her draft, notice how she narrows this topic even further.

Clothing Optional
Gina Sinisi

1   Should you wear your green T-shirt and corduroys today or your leather jacket and combat pants? Perhaps you feel like wearing your good old trustworthy blue jeans instead. No matter what you choose, you must choose something because in American society getting dressed is not an option. While you are not allowed to roam freely in your birthday suit, whatever suit you do wear is your decision, as is where you get your clothes and what they are made of. It's easy to drive to the mall and consume to your heart's desire, but what about these traditional American clothing stores? Are they the best shopping option? What if I told you your blue jeans are deadly? Literally. Are they worth the life of another person? Would you trade them for your mom? It's important to know what you're wearing, who made it, and where it came from. It's also important to know you have choices.

2   Blue jeans are the favorite pants of Americans, but because of the toxic dyeing processes used to make them and the unfortunate chemical-laden cotton growing practices, they put their creators in dangerous situations. I believe in the good old "Do unto others as you would have done to yourself" mantra, and like I mentioned earlier, would you trade your mom for your jeans? No? Then why ask someone else to do the same?

3   If you are attached to wearing jeans, and your old ones are too worn out for your liking, then it is still possible to find some new ones. One great alternative to buying new clothes is buying secondhand, used, or vintage clothing. This option is the most environmentally friendly one because it's reusing what already exists and doesn't add to material waste. Secondhand shopping is also a great bargain and usually incredibly cheap. Garage sales are a great means for selling or buying new clothes and it's usually possible to bargain over the price. If you really get excited about clothes and know people who have enviable wardrobes, organizing a clothing swap is another option. This way, you can always borrow something back if you miss it too much, and you also know your clothes can be found on friendly bodies.

4   If you have a fair budget and you feel that secondhand shopping doesn't always suit your needs, then buying clothing made out of organic cotton or hemp is another agriculturally responsible decision. Typical cotton production is toxic and dangerous. "Because the cotton plant is susceptible to disease and pests, it's usually doused with a potent mix of agricultural chemicals. Some of these poisons are carcinogenic; others have been linked to headaches, dizziness, lung infections, asthma, depression and birth defects" (Visscher 22). While hemp is a much more sustainable plant than cotton and grows easily almost anywhere, the government unfortunately doesn't allow farmers to grow it in the States, so if you buy a product made of hemp, understand that you are not buying locally or nationally, but instead supporting a different country and contributing to major transportation costs.

5   While searching through the racks at secondhand stores and reading labels takes more time than bouncing from store to store at the mall, it is kind of like a treasure hunt and the harder you work at searching for the treasure the better the treasure is. You have to get

dressed. You don't have an option. You do, however, have the option of deciding what to wear and what role you want to play in the American clothing industry.

Works Cited

Visscher, Marco. "Imps & Elfs: Fashion Sense." *Ode* Apr. 2006: 22–24. Print.

Moving from Sketch to Draft

Prepare to revise your sketch by assessing it yourself and inviting comments from peers in workshop.

Evaluating Your Own Sketch. Before your proposal is subject to peer review, answer the following questions. Your instructor may ask you to hand in your responses with your sketch or simply make an entry in your notebook.

1. Assume that you're a reader who might be critical of your proposals. What do you say in the sketch that such a reader might disagree with? What might those objections be? Have you adequately responded to them or addressed them in the sketch?

2. Are there parts of the problem you're addressing here that you don't understand yet? Are there things about the solutions you propose that you need to know more about? What are they?

3. Have you changed your mind about anything on this topic after writing the sketch? If so, what?

ONE STUDENT'S RESPONSE

Gina's Journal

1. A reader might disagree with my idea that the current American clothing industry is harmful to the environment and human health. I did not support my claims with enough factual evidence to be believable and get the reader's attention. It seems that I devoted more time to proposing solutions than exploring the problem.

2. There is one part of the problem that I don't quite understand which is the dyeing process of blue jeans. I'm not sure where current factories are located and what methods they use. I have only heard negative rumors regarding current practices. I have also heard opposing information regarding synthetic dyes versus natural indigo. I'm not sure which is worse or better. I would also like to know more about hemp, which is one of the solutions I propose.

(continued)

> **One Student's Response** (*continued*)
> 3. I have slightly changed my mind regarding this topic and that is because I'm not sure about natural and synthetic dyes. I used to think synthetic ones were more harmful, but now I'm not sure.

Questions for Peer Review. Because the assignment asks you to draft your proposal with a particular audience in mind, your workshop discussions may require a bit more imagination than usual. As when you evaluated your own sketch, you may have to ask your peer reviewers to imagine themselves as the readers you want them to be.

Begin your peer review session by clarifying your audience. Then the group might discuss the following questions about your sketch.

- After reading the sketch, repeat the problem you believe the sketch is addressing and why this solution is the best one?
- Is the solution offered sufficiently justified?
- Can you imagine other solutions the writer might consider?
- What part of the proposal did you find most interesting?
- Given the purpose and audience of the proposal, is there another form it might take?

Reflecting on What You Learned. While your proposal sketch is being peer reviewed, record the comments. Draw a line down the middle of a journal page, and on the left side jot down every suggestion or comment about the sketch that you hear—everything, even if you don't agree with it. Following the workshop, fastwrite on the right side about all of the comments you received. Explore how you might follow those suggestions and how they might change your approach to the next draft.

Research and Other Strategies: Gathering More Information

Unless you're an expert on the problem you're writing about, you're going to need to do more research. While the quick and dirty research you did earlier might have given you enough information to draft the sketch, at the very least you'll likely need to fill gaps in your explanation of the problem or more fully justify or explore alternatives to the solutions you propose. Where should you look?

- *Exploit local publications*. Because the assignment asks you to choose a topic of local interest, then sources such as the local daily newspaper, government reports, and university policies may be important sources for your proposal. Some of these, such as local newspapers and government documents, may be available in your campus library.

WRITING IN YOUR LIFE

Grant Proposals and Group Ethos

If your career takes you into the sciences, engineering, or nonprofit work, then you'll be writing grant proposals. Expert grant writers say that finding a potential funder for your project isn't the hardest part. Proposals often fail because they aren't persuasive or don't follow the application guidelines. The effectiveness of a grant proposal depends on some of the same things that you're trying in this chapter, but they are also a specialized genre.

Imagine that you will often be competing with hundreds—and in some cases, thousands—of others who are chasing the same dollars from government and foundation grant programs. And unlike a proposal from an individual, grant proposals often come from institutions and organizations. Consequently, when you propose a solution that you think should be funded, you're selling two things: the proposed solution *and* your organization.

This is one of the ways that workplace writing is distinct from academic writing. Remember Aristotle's rhetorical triangle? One of the three elements of persuasion was ethos, or the credibility of the speaker. Usually we think of ethos as merely reflecting the writer's persona, but frequently writers are speaking for an institution and not for themselves. Suppose you are writing a foundation grant proposal for a local library to seek funds for a new reading program that will boost outreach into low-income neighborhoods. If you were the proposal writer, how would you want the library to come across, and how would you manage that presentation? When you're writing for a group and not for yourself, how does that change things like voice, tone, the information you might emphasize, or your methods of persuasion? How does the writing you do on behalf of a group differ from the writing you do for you?

Fortunately, if you want to write a grant, there is an industry waiting to help you: countless books, training seminars, and services to locate funders. Here are two helpful places to start online:

- *The Foundation Center* (http://foundationcenter.org/), a site that focuses on funding opportunities from private foundations.

- *Grants.gov,* a one-stop shop for all grant opportunities from the federal government.

- *Interview experts*. In Chapter 4, you practiced interview skills. Here's a chance to put them to use again. One of the most efficient ways to collect information for your revision is to talk to people who have knowledge about the problem. These may be experts who have researched the problem or people affected by it.

- *Search for experience with similar solutions elsewhere.* If your proposal calls for an education program on binge drinking, what other universities might have tried it? What was their experience? Search for information using keywords that describe the problem you're writing about ("binge drinking"), and try adding a phrase that describes the solution ("binge drinking education programs"). Also check library databases that might lead you to articles in newspapers, magazines, and journals on the problem and its solutions.

Composing the Draft

Establishing the problem your proposal addresses and possibly even dramatizing the problem is a very common way to begin the form. As you begin your draft, consider how much you need to say in the beginning about the problem. If your readers aren't aware of the problem, should you dramatize it in some way, perhaps telling a story of someone who is a victim of the problem, or forcefully describing its effects?

Alternatively, you might want to begin the next draft by establishing your solution, a particularly strong beginning if your motive is advocacy and your audience already recognizes the problem. For example, everyone agrees that 9/11 is a national tragedy. There's no need to make that argument in a proposal for a memorial, so the architects' proposal began simply:

This memorial proposes a space that resonates with the feelings of loss and absence that were generated by the destruction of the World Trade Center and the taking of thousands of lives on September 11, 2001, and February 26, 1993.

Here are some possible approaches to beginning your next draft:

1. Consider opening with an anecdote, image, description, or profile that dramatizes the problem you're writing about.
2. Lead with an explicit explanation of your proposal, simply stating the problem and advocating your solution.
3. Sometimes the form will influence your method of beginning. For example, if you're writing a brochure, the front panel—the first part readers will see—might include very little text and perhaps a graphic. A Web page might have similar constraints. A grant proposal might begin with an abstract. Choose a beginning that is appropriate to the form or genre of your proposal.
4. Frame the question or pose the problem. What is the question that you're trying to answer, or what part of the problem most needs a solution?

Methods of Development. What are some ways you might organize your proposal?

Problem to Solution. This is the most straightforward way to structure the draft, one that you'll commonly find in proposals of all kinds. In its simplest form, a proposal that works from problem to solution will devote varying emphasis to each, depending on how aware the intended audience is of the problem the proposal addresses. Obviously, more emphasis will be placed on establishing the problem or helping readers understand it if they lack awareness.

The problem–solution structure need not be a simple two-step performance—first problem, then solution—but rather a two-part harmony in which the writer moves back and forth between discussion of an aspect of the problem and a solution that addresses it.

Cause and Effect. It's only natural when presented with a problem to ask, *What causes it?* This can be an essential part of explaining the problem, and also a way to introduce solutions; after all, most proposals address in some way the causes of the problem. If one of the causes of procrastination is perfectionism, then a solution will be to have more realistic expectations, perhaps by lowering your standards.

Conventions of the Form. Because this assignment encourages you to consider writing a proposal that might depart from the usual essay form, the method of development might be determined, in part, by the conventions that govern that genre. For example, a proposal for a new course, say, on Chicano literature, written for the English department's curriculum committee, might have to follow a certain format, beginning with the course description followed by a justification. Sometimes these conventions might be more subtle or flexible. Web pages have no strict format, but Web designers do work from some general principles that you'd do well to learn before you design one. This can be one aspect of your research for this assignment. Sometimes merely looking closely at examples of a genre helps you infer some of the basic techniques of writing in that form.

Combining Approaches. As always, the methods of development often involve combining these and other approaches to structuring your draft. The sample proposals in this chapter are a mix of problem to solution, cause and effect, and genre-specific ways of organizing the material.

Using Evidence. What kind of evidence and how much of it you provide to justify the solutions you propose depends, as it often does, on your audience. *How much* evidence you need to provide depends on whether your intended audience is likely to be predisposed to agree or disagree with the solutions you propose. Obviously, if readers need convincing, you need to offer more justification. The "Inquiring into the Details: Evidence—A Case Study" box illustrates how the *type* of evidence you provide is a function of audience, too. As you compose your draft, consider who your readers will be and the kinds of evidence they will find most persuasive.

INQUIRING INTO THE DETAILS

Evidence—A Case Study

Suppose a proposal argues that the university needs an alternative or independent film series. The proposal, in the form of a memo, is written to the Student Activities Board, a group of students who decide how to spend student fee money collected at registration. Which of the following types of evidence used to justify such a film series would be *most* persuasive to that audience?

1. The writer's personal enjoyment of foreign films.

2. A petition signed by 100 people that supports the idea.

3. A quotation from Woody Allen about the educational and cultural virtues of independent films.

4. Information about the success of the independent film theater in town.

5. A quote from an English professor supporting the idea.

6. An estimate that shows that the cost of renting five independent films is half the cost of renting the same number of Hollywood films.

7. A survey of 200 students that indicates that 60 percent support the idea.

8. Data on good attendance at a similar series at another larger university.

Choosing the strongest evidence in a proposal is an exercise in audience analysis. Is your audience likely to favor your idea, oppose it, or have no opinion? If they're neutral or opposed, then you'd better be sure you not only have *appropriate* evidence but a lot of it. What makes evidence appropriate for a particular audience? *It is evidence the audience members are most likely to believe.*

Workshopping the Draft

If your draft is subject to peer review, see Chapter 14 for details on how to organize workshop groups and decide on how your group can help you. The following journal activities and questions should help you make the most of your opportunity to get peer feedback on your work in progress.

Reflecting on the Draft. After you've finished the draft, make an entry in your journal that follows these prompts:

- If I were going to write this over again, the one thing I think I'd do would be...

- The most important thing I learned about writing a proposal so far is...

- The most difficult part of the process for me was...
- The biggest question I have about the draft is...

Your instructor may ask you to hand in your responses to these prompts with your draft.

Following the workshop session, repeat the method of reflection you used following peer review of your sketch, drawing a line down the middle of a notebook page and recording your group's comments and suggestions on the left side and, later, your reactions on the right.

Questions for Readers. Again remind your workshop group about the particular audience you had in mind for your proposal. The group might then consider the following questions as they discuss the draft.

1. On a scale from 1 to 5, with 5 being "extremely serious" and 1 being "not serious at all," how would you describe your feelings about the severity of the problem addressed in this draft? Discuss the reasons for your ranking. Remember to imagine that you're the audience for whom the proposal was intended.

2. On the same scale, rank how convinced you were that the solutions proposed in the draft were the best ones. A 5 would indicate that you were totally convinced and a 1 would indicate that you weren't convinced at all. Discuss what was convincing and/or how the solutions offered could be more convincing. Be specific.

3. What questions did you have that weren't adequately answered in the draft?

Revising the Draft

Revision is a continual process—not a last step. You've been revising—literally "re-seeing" your subject—from the first messy fastwriting in your journal. But the things that get your attention during revision varies depending on where you are in the writing process. You've generated material, chosen a topic, done some research, and written both a sketch and draft. Most students think that the only thing left to do is "fix things." Check for misspellings. Correct an awkward sentence or two. Come up with a better title. This is editing, not revision, and while editing is important, to focus solely on smaller "fixes" after writing a first draft squanders an opportunity to really *learn* from what the draft is telling you, or perhaps not quite telling you.

Chapter 13 can help guide these discoveries. The questions you can ask a draft fall into five categories: purpose, idea, information, development, and editing. Use the following Guide to Revision Strategies chart to find the revision strategies in Chapter 13 that might help you re-see what you've written so far.

GUIDE TO REVISION STRATEGIES

Problems in the Draft (Chapter 13)	Page Number
Unclear purpose ■ Not sure what the essay is about? Fails to answer the *So what?* question?	551
Unclear thesis, theme, or main idea ■ Not sure what you're trying to say? Proposal isn't clear?	557
Lack of information or development ■ Needs more information to justify proposed solution? ■ Evidence offered isn't persuasive enough?	564
Disorganized ■ Doesn't move logically or smoothly from paragraph to paragraph?	568
Unclear or awkward at the level of sentences and paragraphs ■ Seems choppy or hard to follow at the level of sentences or paragraphs?	577

Proposals also have some fairly typical problems at this stage in the process, most of which can be addressed by repeating some of the steps in this chapter or selecting appropriate revision strategies in Chapter 13. Here are some questions to consider as you decide which of these strategies might be most helpful.

✓ Have you done enough to dramatize the problem if you're writing for an audience that may not recognize the problem? Should you do more to establish how your readers have a stake in solving the problem?

✓ How well have you justified your solution? Is there enough evidence? Is it appropriate evidence for your audience?

✓ Have you overemphasized one solution at the expense of others? Would your proposal be more balanced and persuasive if you considered alternatives, even if you ultimately reject them?

When you refer to Chapter 13, "Revision Strategies," for ideas on how to revise your draft following your workshop, use the preceding table as a guide. Remember that a draft may present problems in more than one category.

Polishing the Draft

After you've dealt with the big issues in your draft—is it sufficiently focused, does it answer the *So what?* question, is it well organized, and so on—you must deal with the smaller problems. You've carved the stone into an appealing figure, but now you need to polish it. Are your paragraphs coherent? How do you manage transitions? Are your sentences fluent and concise? Are there any errors in spelling or syntax? Section 5 of Chapter 13 can help you focus on these issues.

Before you finish your draft, work through the following checklist:

- ✓ Every paragraph is about one thing.
- ✓ The transitions between paragraphs aren't abrupt.
- ✓ The length of sentences varies in each paragraph.
- ✓ Each sentence is concise. There are no unnecessary words or phrases.
- ✓ You've checked grammar, particularly verb agreement, run-on sentences, unclear pronouns, and misused words (*there/their, where/were*, and so on). (See the handbook at the end of the book for help with these grammar issues.)
- ✓ You've run your spellchecker and proofed your paper for misspelled words.

▪ STUDENT ESSAY

It's August in Boise and cotton is king. I'm sitting here clothed from head to toe in 100 percent cotton, but until I read Gina Sinisi's essay on the problems of cotton production, I never imagined that these shorts, manufactured in Sri Lanka, might have contributed to obscenely low wages in foreign manufacturing plants and health problems among American workers who harvest the crop. But Gina's essay, like all good proposals, doesn't leave it at that. There are things we can do, beginning with being aware that our consumer choices echo into other people's lives, some of whom live on the other side of the world.

Clothing Optional
Gina Sinisi

Should you wear your green T-shirt and corduroys today or your leather jacket and combat pants? Perhaps you feel the urge to strut in your trustworthy blue jeans instead. While you are not allowed to roam freely in your birthday suit, whatever suit you do

(continued)

1

(continued)

choose is up to you, along with where you get it and what it is made of. It is easy to drive to the mall and consume to your wardrobe's content, but what about these traditional North American clothing stores? Are they the best shopping option? What if I told you your blue jeans are deadly? Literally. Are they worth the life of another person? Would you trade them for your mom? Your dad? It's important to know what you're wearing, who made it, and where it came from. It's also imperative to know you have choices. The impact of your political and social ideals on the clothing industry begins with your underwear.

2   The United States yields to the high demand of cotton by closely following China as the number two producer of cotton in the world, growing enough to manufacture about 9 billion T-shirts ("Clothes for a Change"). The good news is that North Americans can support local farmers by purchasing cotton grown in the United States; the downside is that North American citizens are also the ones directly affected by the chemicals sprayed on the cotton. According to the World Health Organization, pesticide poisoning annually afflicts three million people, killing between 20,000 and 40,000 of them ("Clothes for a Change"). While this statistic doesn't single out cotton as a cause of human health problems, the crop does require unusually high applications of pesticides. While as an agricultural product, cotton only takes up 3% of the world's farmland, it demands a quarter of the globe's pesticides and fertilizers ("Cotton and the Environment"). According to Visscher, "Because the cotton plant is susceptible to disease and pests, it's usually doused with a potent mix of agricultural chemicals. Some of these poisons are carcinogenic; others have been linked to headaches, dizziness, lung infections, asthma, depression and birth defects" (22).

3   I believe in the familiar credo, "Do unto others as you would have done to yourself," and to repeat my earlier question, would you trade your mom for your jeans? No? Then why ask someone else to do the same?

4   Cotton contributes not only to poor environmental and health standards, but also to poor working conditions. Because the majority of consumers are not willing to pay higher prices for well-made clothing, and instead prefer cheap clothing that changes with the seasons, most manufacturers have "outsourced" their production to countries like Viet Nam and China, where workers are paid extremely low wages, "as low as 13 cents an hour" ("Clothes for a Change"). If you buy these products you are condoning unacceptable work ethics. You can choose otherwise.

5   If you feel that common cotton growing and production practices are unnecessary and hazardous but can't detach yourself from cotton clothing and blue jeans, there is an agriculturally responsible decision you can make. Organic cotton is being grown in more than 18 countries worldwide, including the United States ("Clothes for a Change"), and worldwide sales are increasing by about 25% annually (Eshelby). If you can't find clothing made from organic cotton in your city, there are hundreds of clothing stores available online that support humane and environmentally conscious clothing practices.

6   A second alternative to traditional cotton clothing is buying hemp clothing products. Before the industrial revolution, hemp was a popular fiber in the United States because it

is strong and grows quickly and easily in a variety of soil types. The first paper was made from hemp, and, ironically some say, the Declaration of Independence was written on hemp paper.

Growing hemp in the United States is currently illegal because it is frequently confused with marijuana. While pot and hemp are the same plant species, hemp contains "virtually no" THC, the ingredient in marijuana that makes users "high." Most likely, hemp is illegal because it would dramatically drown the cotton industry and because of the ignorance that surrounds its false connection with marijuana.   7

While it is currently illegal to grow hemp in the United States, it is legal to sell hemp clothing products. A few clothing stores do exist throughout the country, but once again, it is always possible to easily find these products online. Unlike some rumors that declare hemp is itchy and rough on your skin, it is actually softer, more absorbent, extremely breathable and significantly longer lasting than clothing made from cotton.   8

One dilemma you must face when deciding to buy hemp products is whether or not you want to support a nonlocal product and all of the energy it takes to get the product from its point of origination to your body. Hemp has a high rate of "embodied energy," which is a term used to define all of the energy a product uses to be created and then transported to its final destination.   9

If you have a hard time choosing between the damage caused by cotton practices, the embodied energy included in hemp, and the petroleum base in many synthetic fabrics, and don't like ordering organic cotton clothing online without being able to try it on first, there is one final solution: A great alternative to buying new clothes is buying secondhand or vintage clothing. This option is the most environmentally friendly one because it's reusing what already exists and doesn't add to material waste. Secondhand shopping is usually incredibly cheap and a great means for selling or buying new clothes. It's usually possible to haggle for a lower price, too.   10

Vintage clothing is often more sturdy and durable than recently produced clothing; you also don't need to worry about anyone else showing up to a party wearing the same outfit as you. If you are a fashion fox and know people who have enviable wardrobes, organizing a clothing swap is another option. This way, you can always borrow something back if you miss it too much, and you also know your clothes can be found on friendly bodies. A final reason why it is better to buy used clothing is because old clothes no longer off-gas their chemicals into your skin and the air you breathe. They are safer, cheaper, and readily available.   11

While searching through the racks at secondhand stores and reading labels takes more time than bouncing from store to store at the mall, it is time well spent. When you know your clothes come from a righteous source, you can flaunt them with pride and revel in your own good health. You have to get dressed. You don't have an option. You do, however, have the option of deciding what to wear and what role you want to play in the clothing industry. Does the day call for an organic cotton T-shirt with hemp shorts, or a vintage tunic with Salvation Army jeans? You decide.   12

(continued)

(continued)

Works Cited

"Clothes for a Change." *Organic Consumers Association*. Web. 1 Aug. 2006.
"Cotton and the Environment." *Organic Trade Association*. Web. 1 Aug. 2006.
Eshelby, Kate. "Organic Cotton." *Ecologist* 36.1 (2006): 34–39. *Academic Search Premier*.
      Web. 7 Aug. 2006.
Visscher, Marco. "Imps & Elfs: Fashion Sense." *Ode* Apr. 2006: 22–24. Print.

Evaluating the Essay

1. The authority of a proposal depends on the evidence. Assess the evidence Gina provides to make her case that nonorganic cotton production is a serious problem. Do you find it convincing?

2. Is the solution she offers—use of organic cottons, hemp, or "vintage" clothing—a viable one? How could she strengthen the case for her proposal?

3. Can you imagine how this essay might have incorporated visuals—pictures, graphs, tables, and so on—that would have enhanced the argument?

USING WHAT YOU HAVE LEARNED

1. Think about the proposal draft you've written, and all those that you've read, both in this chapter and in your workshop group. Spend one minute answering, in writing, the following question: *What do you need to know to write an effective proposal?*

2. Draw a line down the middle of the page of your journal. Compare the proposal with another genre of writing you've tried in this book, looking specifically at the following:

   - degree of difficulty (which was harder, and why?)

   - audience awareness (when and how much did you consider who you were writing for?)

   - level of discovery (how much did you learn about your subject, or about yourself?)

■ application to other situations (how much and what might you use
   from this form of writing and apply in other writing situations?)

3. What approaches or ideas will you borrow from proposal writing that you
    can apply to other forms of writing and other writing situations? Can you
    imagine revising an essay you've already written in another genre using
    what you've learned here?

United States, newspapers and magazines publish the opinion pieces of ordinary citizens, and these essays are among our liveliest forums for public debate.

While we often think of persuasive writing as stiff and formal, the op-ed essay is usually lively and engaging. Here's a sample of some opening lines from published op-ed pieces:

> Many of the hundreds of thousands of Hispanic demonstrators who poured out into the streets on Monday may not know much English, but they've learned the language of American politics: Flags. Tons of flags. And make them American.
>
> —"Immigrants Must Choose," Charles Krauthammer

> Maybe it was at the moment I found myself on my knees in my bathrobe, carefully prying tiny shards of paper out of the immobilized teeth of the shredder, that it finally hit me: The shredder had a paper jam. I had an info jam.
>
> —"C'mon, America, Fire Up Those Shredders," Lisa Johnston

> On the premise that spring is too beautiful for a depressing topic like Iraq, I thought I'd take up a fun subject—global warming.
>
> —"Global Warming: What, Me Worry?" Molly Ivins

> Persuasive essays like the op-ed are a great way to participate in public debates that affect your campus and community, and even your nation.

While these essays are often informal, they are still persuasive forms, and as you'll see later, they often employ the same methods of more formal arguments. However, unlike formal arguments—the kind you might write in a logic or philosophy course—persuasive essays of this kind have a much larger audience, and they are a great way to participate in public debates that affect your campus and community, and even your nation. In this chapter, you'll learn how to use some principles of argument to write persuasive essays like the op-ed that will give voice to things you care about, and that will increase the likelihood that voice will be heard.

What Is Argument?

Argument is not war.

When I was growing up, argument meant only one thing: indigestion. My father loved to argue at the dinner table, hotly pursuing any stray comment that would give him the chance to demonstrate his superior knowledge and logic. What I remember about these "arguments" was the hot-faced humiliation and anger I felt back then, and later, the feeling that I would prefer to avoid an argument at any cost. When I mention argumentative writing to my students, I think I recognize in the slumped shoulders and distant looks of some of them that they might have similar feelings.

Some of us think argument is impolite. It means uncomfortable conflict. It is the verbal equivalent of war.

And yet, we engage in argument every day when we attempt to persuade an instructor to extend the deadline on a paper, try to convince our spouse to help more around the apartment, or seek a loan from a bank.

Arguments *can* involve conflict, but they are rarely combat—despite the war metaphors like "finding ammunition" or "attacking a position." Far more often, the motives for arguing are more benign. We want others to consider seeing the world the way we see it. Or we want to encourage them to *do* something we believe is in their interests as well as ours. These are the motives behind the attempts at persuasion of several of the assignments you may have completed earlier in *The Curious Writer:* the review, the proposal, and the critical essay.

In a sense, all writing is persuasive. *See the world my way*, we ask of readers, *at least for a moment*.

> **There aren't just two sides.**

Two Sides to Every Argument?

TV talk shows stage "discussions" between proponents of diametrically opposed positions. Academic debating teams pit those for and those against. We are nurtured on language like *win* or *lose, right* and *wrong,* and *either/or*. It's tempting to see the world this way, as neatly divided into truth and falsehood, light and dark. Reducing issues to two sides simplifies the choices. But one of the things that literature—and all art—teaches us is the delightful and nagging complexity of things. By inclination and upbringing, Huck Finn is a racist, and there's plenty of evidence in *Huckleberry Finn* that his treatment of Jim confirms it. Yet there are moments in the novel when we see a transcendent humanity in Huck, and we can see that he may be a racist, *but.* . . . It is this qualification—this modest word *but*—that trips us up in the steady march toward certainty. Rather than *either/or,* can it be *both/and?* Instead of two sides to every issue, might there be thirteen?

Here's an example:

One side: General education requirements are a waste of time because they are often irrelevant to students' major goal in getting a college education—getting a good job.

The other side: General education requirements are invaluable because they prepare students to be enlightened citizens, more fully prepared to participate in democratic culture.

It's easy to imagine a debate between people who hold these positions, and it wouldn't be uninteresting. But it *would* be misleading to think that these are the only two possible positions on general education requirements in American universities. One of the reasons why people are drawn to arguing is that it can be a method of discovery, and one of the most useful discoveries is some side to the story that doesn't fall neatly into the usual opposed positions. The route to these discoveries is twofold: *initially withholding judgment* and *asking questions*.

For instance, what might be goals of a university education other than helping students get a good job and making them enlightened citizens? Is it possible that a university can do both? Are general education courses the only route to enlightenment? Are there certain situations in which the vocational motives of students are inappropriate? Are there certain contexts—say, certain students at particular schools at a particular point in their education—when general education requirements might be waived or modified?

All of these questions, and more, tend to unravel the two sides of the argument and expose them for what they often are: *starting points* for an inquiry into the question, *What good are general education requirements?*

Premises are what hold up claims.

I actually asked my first-year students recently what they thought of general education or "core" classes at our university. It provoked a lively debate. Here's what one of them said:

> "I am all for the rant about higher education costing a fortune. The core classes are a joke, to be quite honest. Who hasn't had math, science, and history in high school?"

What interests me here is not the claim that "core classes are a joke" but a key assumption behind the claim that the writer assumes her readers agree with. Are high school math, science, and history classes equivalent to university core classes in the same subjects? It's a premise that isn't addressed, yet her argument fundamentally depends on our consent that it is true. In logical persuasion, not all premises need explanation because the audience may grant their truth without it—racism is bad, depression is a treatable condition, citizens in a democracy have a right to vote. But when writers ignore controversial premises, the argument is a house of cards, vulnerable to the slightest push back.

In argument, premises or assumptions are reasons that we believe something is true, and one way to find the path back from a claim to a reason is to use the word "because." *Core classes are a joke <u>because</u> their content is similar to what most students learn in high school.*

Arguments prove claims with appropriate evidence.

"I have a headache" is a statement, not a claim, because no one is likely to disagree with it. "Headaches can be caused by secondhand smoke" is a statement that is a claim because reasonable people might agree or disagree with it. Claims are at the heart of argument, and if you think about it, you already know this. Every time you make a judgment, interpretation, or evaluation, you make a claim. We do this daily: "Macs are better than PCs." "The food in this place sucks." "This town needs more buses."

However, unlike these often-offhand comments, argumentative writing is organized around convincing someone else that the claim is true. This means not only establishing the reasons behind why we think so, but providing evidence that seems convincing. For example, a comparison between the syllabi for my high school history course and my college core course in history shows that 60 percent of the time they cover the same material. Hmmm. Maybe core classes can be a "joke."

Not just any evidence will do, of course. It depends on the situation (see "Writing in the Disciplines," page 282). For example, statistical data are appropriate evidence in a environmental health paper on the effect of inversions and

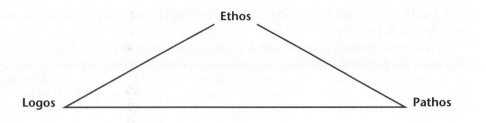

Figure 7.1   Aristotle's rhetorical triangle

not personal experience. An opinion essay on the need to act on air inversions might use statistics but is just as likely to use the writer's personal experience.

There is an artful balance between persona, emotion, and logic.

Persuasion, as Aristotle reminded us a few thousand yeas ago, depends not just on good reasoning (*logos*), but on moving an audience (*pathos*) and making it believe the speaker is someone worth listening to on the subject (*ethos*). Figure 7.1 shows Aristotle's famous rhetorical triangle, a visual presentation of this idea.

What may be a little misleading about Aristotle's graphic is the idea that the recipe for good argument is equal measures of ethos, pathos, and logos. Not at all. These are blended in varying amounts depending on the situation. One factor, for example, is the disposition of an audience toward your claim.

Figure 7.2 broadly describes the balance between Aristotle's three categories of appeals in the three most common rhetorical situations: when an audience is resistant to what you're trying to say, neutral about it, or receptive. For instance, direct-mail marketers, particularly those trying to raise money for nonprofit groups and political causes, make a living buying and cultivating lists of people who might be receptive to their messages. Direct-mail letters, therefore, are strong on emotional appeals (*pathos*): The humane society will include photographs of a sad-looking abandoned puppy, a conservative political action group will raise fears about threats to "family values," and so on. There's no need to spend a great deal reasoning (*logos*) with an audience that already agrees with your message. Move them with emotion!

In contrast, resistant audiences immediately suspect the credibility of speakers or writers (*ethos*), and so their challenge is to establish some common

Disposition of Audience	*Ethos*	*Pathos*	*Logos*
Resistant	Most important	Least important	Most important
Neutral	Important	Important	Important
Receptive	Least important	Most important	Least important

Figure 7.2   Audience and the balance of ethos, logos, and pathos

ground with their audiences. Emotional appeals will be unlikely to move this audience, at least initially.

Neutral audiences may be difficult to gauge. Sometimes an emotional appeal will spark its members' interest. Sometimes a well-reasoned argument (*logos*) will move them, and sometimes a neutral audience will be persuaded by the credibility of the speaker. Frequently, a careful combination of all three of Aristotle's appeals transforms a neutral audience into one that is receptive to what you have to say.

For many of us, then, argument in civic and private discourse is bound by our *feelings* about argument—how comfortable we are with conflict, how confident we are in our ability to say what we think, and how strongly we feel about our opinions. These feelings are complicated by our beliefs about the purpose of argument. Sorting through these beliefs can help us discover new, perhaps more productive ways of approaching argument. Does argument make you uncomfortable? What do you consider a "good" argument? What is a "bad" argument?

Argument and Inquiry

Like all inquiry projects, the process of writing an argument involves both suspending judgment and making judgments (see Figures 7.3 and 7.4). Directly or indirectly, arguments address some kind of problem that needs to be solved—global warming, lack of funding for local preschool education, online music piracy, or whatever issue is complex and interesting.

Suspending Judgment. When you suspend judgment you openly explore a problem, including your own initial assumptions about it, if you have any. This is your chance to discover what you think by looking at the evidence and arguments others have already put forward. One of the things this might inspire is clarifying what the problem really is that most needs a solution.

Making Judgments. Since all arguments are organized around a claim, clarifying the problem will help you determine what that might be. This is the most important judgment you'll make. From there, the process is a more familiar one of establishing the reasons behind your claim and then finding and organizing the relevant evidence that will make them convincing to someone else.

Inquiry arguments work best under the following conditions:

1. You choose a topic that you find confusing in interesting ways, which may not yield easily to obvious solutions.

2. You may have tentative ideas about what you think, but you're willing to change your mind.

3. You're willing to wrestle with viewpoints other than your own, even after you've decided on the claim you want to prove.

Suspending Judgment

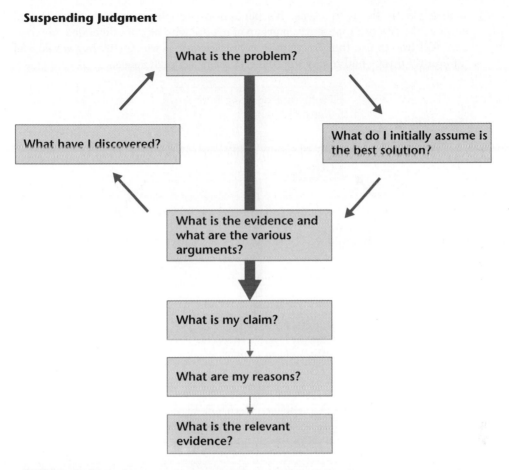

Making Judgments

Figure 7.3 An inquiry argument. Rather than rushing to judgment, inquiry-based arguments begin with an open exploration of the problem. The aim, as always, is discovery. These discoveries are the basis for clarifying the problem and then making a claim about what should be done about it. (See Figure 7.4 for an example of how this might work.)

Analyzing Argument

How might you analyze this letter writer's argument?

Dear editor,

As part of my required humanities class, I was forced to see the art exhibit "Home of the Brave" at the university gallery. As a combat veteran, what I saw there deeply offended me. I saw so-called "art" that showed great American military leaders like General Petraeus with skulls superimposed on their faces, and a photo of a man with an American flag wrapped around his head and lashed with a plastic tie at his neck. It's popular to say these days that we should support the troops. Apparently, a group of artists who haven't defended our freedom feel free to use that freedom to be unpatriotic. I wonder if they would feel differently if they had to pay the real cost for freedom of speech.

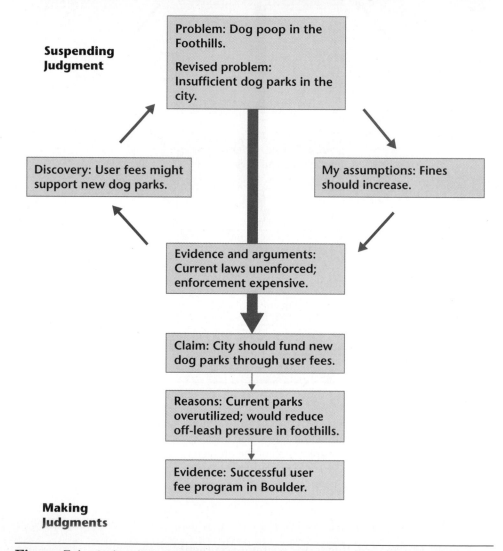

Suspending Judgment

Problem: Dog poop in the Foothills.

Revised problem: Insufficient dog parks in the city.

Discovery: User fees might support new dog parks.

My assumptions: Fines should increase.

Evidence and arguments: Current laws unenforced; enforcement expensive.

Claim: City should fund new dog parks through user fees.

Reasons: Current parks overutilized; would reduce off-leash pressure in foothills.

Evidence: Successful user fee program in Boulder.

Making Judgments

Figure 7.4   An inquiry argument: Example. Here's how you might apply the inquiry process to discovering an argument. In Boise, Idaho, where I live, there are more dogs per capita than nearly every other city in the U.S. That's a lot of dog poop, particularly on trails in the surrounding foothills. When you don't rush the claim and suspend judgment for a bit you're more likely to find a more insightful—and more focused—argument. For instance, instead of simply declaring, "There are too many dog piles on hiking paths!" you might discover a more interesting and useful claim: "Boise needs more off-leash dog parks."

Most arguments like this don't provoke an analytical response at first. We react emotionally: "This guy is so full of it!" or perhaps, "It's about time someone spoke up about the cost of freedom!" This letter, like many that raise controversial issues, triggers a whole set of deeply held beliefs about things like patriotism, freedom of speech, and the purpose of art. These are things that *should* provoke discussion—and inevitably trigger feelings. But without involving the head as well as the heart, it's impossible to have a civil discussion—one that will lead to new understanding. We need to understand not only what we ourselves believe but also what the other guy believes.

Using Toulmin. Fortunately, there are tools to help with this analysis. For example, Stephen Toulmin, an English philosopher, argued that arguments about any subject have features that include:

- claims
- evidence (grounds)
- warrants (reasons)
- backing

The most penetrating aspect of Toulmin's approach is the idea that *warrants*—or assumptions about the way things are—are key to the logical relationship between evidence and claims. For example, my colleague Dr. Michelle Payne does an exercise with her students in which she empties her purse and asks, "What claim might you make about what kind of person I am based on the evidence before you?" Michelle's students once inferred, for example, that the fact she carries three credit cards meant that she had a lot of money (she doesn't). Others claimed that the cards suggested she carried a lot of debt (actually, no). How might these opposing claims be evaluated? That's where warrants come in. "What do you need to believe is true," Michelle asked, "if your claims from the evidence are valid?" The backers of the high-debt claim agreed they would have to believe that there is a relationship between the number of credit cards one has and the amount of debt one carries. That's the warrant, and there actually is some factual backing for it. The success of any argument, Toulmin believed, depends on the validity of its warrants.

Earlier in the chapter, we talked about warrants as assumptions or premises, and they're pretty much the same things, except that Toulmin's model highlights a more formal relationship between evidence, claims, warrants, and backing. Figure 7.5 shows how we might use Toulmin to chart the claim Michelle's students made about the contents of her purse.

As you can see, arguing well isn't simply a matter of lining up ducks. The task isn't to make a claim and then hunt up evidence to support it. Toulmin reminds us that wedged between evidence and claims are warrants—things the writers assume must be true for their claims to be believable. These warrants may be implicit or explicit, and one of the best ways to analyze an argument is to figure out what the warrants are and to decide if they have enough backing to be believable.

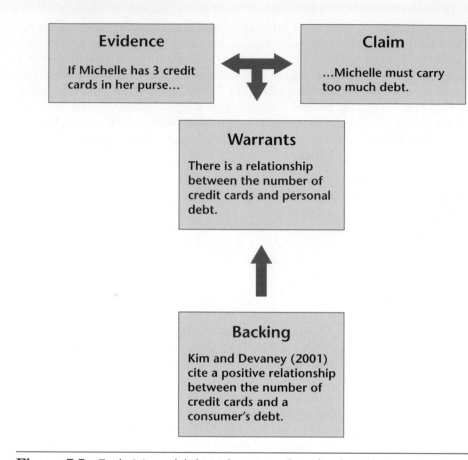

Figure 7.5   Toulmin's model shows how to analyze the claim that carrying three credit cards means that one is also carrying too much debt.

Let's apply Toulmin's approach to the letter to the editor that began this section. What's the claim? What are its warrants? Here's one take:

Evidence and Claim: If artists subject "great American military figures" to ridicule in a time of war, they are being unpatriotic.

Warrant #1: During wartime, Americans should temper their criticism of the military.

Warrant #2: Those who haven't seen military service don't fully appreciate the costs associated with protecting freedom.

Warrant #3: Art can be unpatriotic.

These are not the only warrants implied by the letter writer's claim, and it's certainly debatable if I've actually got the claim right. But if someone asked me to go beyond an emotional reaction to the letter and offer a reasoned response, then these warrants might be the ideas I would start with. Do I agree with them? Why or why not? What backing might support or refute a particular warrant?

Using Logical Fallacies. Toulmin's method is just one of many ways to analyze the arguments that we encounter in our reading.

INQUIRING INTO THE DETAILS

Common Logical Fallacies

An important way to evaluate the soundness of an argument is to examine its logic and, in particular, look for so-called logical fallacies that may lead writers' reasoning astray. Aristotle was one of the first to point out many of these, and a quick search on the Web using the term "logical fallacies" will reveal dozens and dozens of them that plague public argument. Many of them have indecipherable Latin names, testifying to their ancient origins.

Here are ten of the most common logical fallacies. I think they cover about 90 percent of the ways in which writers stumble when making an argument.

1. *Hasty generalization:* We're naturally judgmental creatures. For example, we frequently make a judgment about someone after just meeting him or her. Or we conclude that a class is useless after attending a single session. These are generalizations based on insufficient evidence. Hasty generalizations *might* be true— the class might turn out to be useless—but you should always be wary of them.

2. *Ad hominem:* When arguments turn into shouting matches, they almost inevitably get personal. Shifting away from the substance of an argument to attack the person making it, either subtly or explicitly, is another common logical fallacy. It's also, at times, hard to resist.

3. *Appeal to authority:* We all know that finding support for a claim from an expert is a smart move in many arguments. But sometimes it's a faulty move because the authority we cite isn't really an expert on the subject. A more common fallacy, however, is when we cite an expert to support a claim without acknowledging that many experts disagree on the point.

4. *Straw man:* One of the sneakiest ways to sidetrack reason in an argument is to misrepresent or ignore the actual position of an opponent. Unfortunately, the "straw-man" fallacy thrives in many political debates: "I can't support this proposal for universal health care," says politician A. "It's clear that politician A doesn't really take the problem in American health care seriously," says politician B. Huh?

5. *False analogy:* Analogies can be powerful comparisons in argument. But they can also lead us astray when the analogy simply doesn't hold. Are A and B *really* similar situations? For example, when a critic of higher education argues that a public university is like a business and should be run like one, are the two really analogous? Fundamentally, one is nonprofit and the other is designed to make money. Is this really a useful comparison?

(continued)

Inquiring into the Details (*continued*)

6. *Post hoc or false cause:* Just because one thing follows another doesn't necessarily mean one *causes* the other. It might be coincidence, or the cause might be something else entirely. For example, if you're really keen on arguing that losing the football coach was the cause of the team's losing record, you might link the two. And it's possible that you're right, but it's also just as possible that the injury to the quarterback was one of the real reasons.

7. *Appeal to popularity:* In a country obsessed by polls and rankings, it's not hard to understand the appeal of reasoning that argues that because it's popular it must be good or true. Advertisers are particularly fond of this fallacy, arguing that because their brand is most popular it must be the best. In fact, this might not be the case at all. The majority can be wrong.

8. *Slippery slope:* I love the name of this one because it so aptly describes what can happen when reasoning loses its footing. You might start out reasonably enough, arguing, for example, that a gun control law restricts the rights of some citizens to have access to certain weapons, but pretty soon you start sliding toward conclusions that simply don't follow, such as that a gun control law is the beginning of the end of gun ownership in the country. Now you might really believe this, but logic isn't the route to get there.

9. *Either/or fallacy:* In a black-and-white world, something is right or wrong, true or false, good or bad. But ours is a colorful world with many shades. For instance, while it might be emotionally satisfying to say that opponents of the war in Iraq must not support the troops there, it is also possible that the war's opponents are against the war *because* they're concerned about the lives of American service people. Rather than *either/or* it might be *both/and*. We see this fallacy often in arguments that suggest that there are only two choices and each are opposites.

10. *Begging the question:* This one is also called circular reasoning because it assumes the truth of the arguer's conclusion without bothering to prove it. An obvious example of this would be to say that a law protecting people from Internet spam is good because it's a law, and laws should be obeyed. But *why* is it a good law?

MOTIVES FOR WRITING AN ARGUMENT

Argument, obviously, is a part of everyday life, though as I noted before, it doesn't always go well. I'm constantly trying to persuade my wife Karen that it would be a good thing if I added another guitar to my acoustic collection. I was thinking a new Martin with mahogany back and sides and onboard Fishman electronics would be good.

"You've already got seven guitars," she said. "How many more do you need?"

We argue to get something we want but these are often the least interesting arguments to make.

Classical rhetoricians like Plato, Aristotle, and Cicero had a great deal to say about how to argue well, and while their focus was largely on public speaking, their ideas are foundational for a modern understanding of argument. For

Aristotle, there were three arenas for persuasion—before the courts, before legislators and others who make public policy, and at social occasions.

Of course, there are plenty of other reasons to argue. In academic writing, the purpose of argument is usually to establish the truth of something. Modern advertising, the most common medium of modern persuasion, attempts to influence people's behaviors. Generally speaking, you can distinguish between these two purposes—to establish the validity of a certain way of seeing things and the desire to move people to action—but because the persuasive essay you will be writing in this chapter can do both, we won't make much of the distinction between these two purposes here.

Arguing is a civic duty. In fact, it is an essential activity in any democratic culture, and it's certainly a major element of academic discourse; academic argument is one of the key means of making new knowledge.

Knowing how to argue well has practical value, even if you don't become a lawyer. It might help you make the best case to a local legislator to support the bill providing tuition relief to students, or even bargaining with the used-car dealer for a better price on that black convertible Mazda Miata. Understanding argument helps you find the flaws in *other people's* arguments as well. Knowing how to analyze an argument gives me a language to talk about the flawed arguments in the letters to the editor in *The Idaho Statesman,* and it also helps me thoughtfully and critically read articles and essays that make claims.

Finally, the most important motive behind writing and studying argument is that you care about something. Throughout this book, I've argued that the personal motive for writing is the most powerful one of all; in this case, you're passionate about a question or an issue, and building a written argument channels that passion into prose that can make a difference.

THE ARGUMENT AND ACADEMIC WRITING

Argumentative writing is one of the most common of all academic forms. One reason for this is that the ability to argue well requires some command of subject matter. There is another motive for mastering argument in academic settings, however, and it has less to do with proving that you know your stuff. Argument is really about trying to get at the truth.

> Argument is one of the key means of making new knowledge.

In college, the audiences for your arguments are often your instructors. As experts in a particular discipline, professors argue all the time. They're not simply trying to be contrary but trying to get at the truth. Arguing is the main way that the academic community makes knowledge.

Notice I used the word *make*. While it often seems that the facts we take for granted are immutable truths—as enduring as the granite peaks I can see through my office window—things aren't often that way at all. Our knowledge of things—how the planet was formed, the best ways to save endangered species, the meaning of a classic novel, how to avoid athletic injuries—is entirely made up of ideas that are *contested*. They are less mountains than the glaciers that carved them, and in some cases the sudden earthquakes that bring them down. The primary tool for shaping and even changing what we know is argument.

FEATURES OF THE FORM

Generally speaking, persuasive writing can take many forms. Indeed, reviews and proposals, two essays addressed earlier in this book, both represent different types of persuasive writing. The argument essay we are covering in this chapter, however, more obviously embodies persuasive writing than either of these two other forms. This essay typically makes explicit claims and backs them up with hard evidence. It also employs the well-established rhetorical devices and the reasoning of formal argumentation in the effort to sway readers to its point of view. However, unlike more formal academic papers, the argument you'll be writing in this chapter is intended for a more general audience. It's what we might call a *public argument*. It's the kind of piece you might see in your local newspaper, or in a magazine. *Newsweek*'s "My Turn" column is an excellent example. (See Figure 7.6 for a comparison of argument essays.)

Here are some of the features of the public argument essay:

- *Public arguments are often relatively brief treatments of a topic.* Readers of newspapers and many magazines read fast. They want to quickly get the gist

Rhetorical Context	Academic Argument Essay	Public Argument Essay
Audience	Academic discourse community	Publication's readers
Speaker	You as a member of above	You as an authority on subject
Purpose	To demonstrate your authority	To make something happen
Subject	Of academic interest	Of community interest
Voice	Conventional, academic	Personal, informed
Research	Always	Usually
Citations	Yes	No
Length	Varies, usually 8–25 pages	Varies, usually 500–1,000 words
How to read	Slowly, thoughtfully	Rapidly, mining for meaning

Figure 7.6 A comparison of academic and informal argument (Devan Cook, Boise State University)

of an essay or article and move on to the next story. In addition, space is often limited, particularly in newspapers. As a result, the op-ed or opinion piece rarely exceeds 1,000 words, or about four double-spaced manuscript pages.

- *Subject matter often focuses on issues of public concern.* The magazines and newspapers that publish argument essays typically report on news, events, or issues that might affect a lot of people. Not surprisingly, then, writers of these essays are keen observers of public debates and controversies.

- *A public argument has a central claim or proposition.* Sometimes we also call this a *thesis*, a term that's a holdover from the scientific terminology that dominated American scholarship from the end of the nineteenth century. Classical arguments, the kind many of us wrote in high school, usually state this central claim or thesis in the introduction. But many arguments, particularly essays that rely on narrative structure or explore the answer to a question or problem, may feature the thesis in the middle or at the end of the essay.

- *The central claim is based on one or more premises or assumptions.* You already know something about this from the discussion earlier in the chapter. Basically, a premise suggests that something is true *because* of something else; it expresses the relationship between *what* you claim and *why* you believe that claim to be true. This is discussed at greater length later in the chapter.

- *The public argument relies on evidence that a general audience will believe.* All arguments should use evidence appropriate for a particular audience. Academic writers in marine biology, for example, rely on data collected in the field and analyzed statistically because this kind of evidence is most persuasive to other marine biologists. Anecdotes or personal observation alone simply won't cut it in the *Journal of Marine Biology*. But the persuasive essay's more general audience finds a greater range of evidence convincing, including personal experience and observation. Writers of persuasive essays are likely to do the kind of research you use to write research papers—digging up statistics, facts, and quotations on a topic.

- *They sometimes invite or encourage a response.* Earlier I noted a broad distinction between the purposes of argument: (1) to establish the validity of a writer's way of seeing what's true and (2) to move or persuade an audience to act a certain way. The second purpose is most obvious in the advertisement, which is a visual argument that asks viewers to *do* something—buy a Jeep or change toilet bowl cleaners. But public arguments sometimes ask for or imply a course of action readers should take. An op-ed piece might attempt to change the views and behaviors of political leaders, or influence how people vote for them. It might urge support for a school bond issue, or encourage fellow students to protest against the elimination of an academic program.

- *Readers won't respond unless they know what's at stake.* An essential element of argument is establishing why a certain action, policy, or idea *matters*. How will opposition to the administration's strip-mining policies in West Virginia and Kentucky make a difference in the quality of life in those states, but even more important, why should someone in Boise, Idaho, care? The best arguments are built to carefully establish, sometimes in quite practical terms, how a certain action, belief, or idea might make a difference in the lives of those who are the argument's audience.

WRITING IN YOUR LIFE

Public Argument in a Digital Age

Winning an argument with Northwest Airlines over whether they owe you a lunch voucher after your flight was cancelled is typical of the way persuasion is an everyday concern. But in a larger sense—and probably more important one—arguing well and arguing ethically is a civic duty in a democratic society. A few thousand years ago, the Greeks and Romans created schools of rhetoric where people could learn the art of speaking persuasively in public settings.

These days, probably more than ever, argument is a vibrant part of civic life in the United States, particularly on the Internet. Here are a few of the many genres of public argument available to you for moving people to think or do something you consider important:

- *Op-ed essays:* These are possibly the most common brief argumentative essays for a general audience. The term "op-ed" refers to the editorial essays that are published opposite of the editorial page, a ubiquitous feature in most American newspapers.

- *Editorials:* Brief statements of opinion, often 500 words or less, represent the institutional judgment about a policy issue of a newspaper, radio or TV station, online publication, and so on.

- *Blogs:* One of the newest forms of public argument is the blog. Hosted by on-line sites like Google's "Blogger," the so-called blogosphere is sixty times larger than it was three years ago.

- *Photo essay:* Over 100 years ago, Jacob Riis used photographs of immigrants' squalid conditions in New York City tenements to incite a public outcry—and policy change—on how we treat the poor.

- *Letters to the editor:* These appear in print or online and, unlike editorials, people read them.

- *YouTube:* It's not just a forum for published videos on weird cat tricks.

- *PowerPoint:* Former Vice President Al Gore's slide presentation, "An Inconvenient Truth," made the point that there really is power in PowerPoint. Of course, more often these presentations are really awful.

READINGS

■ ARGUMENT 1

It's hard to imagine that one of the chief planners of the September 11, 2001, attacks on New York and Washington, D.C., might invoke George Washington as his hero. In the excerpt that follows, Kahlid Sheikh Mohammed, a commander for al Queda, who has been in custody since 2003, argues that Islamic extremists, like Washington, are just fighting for their independence. The language of war, says Mohammed, is universal, and that language is killing.

This partial transcript of Mohammed discussing his role in the 9/11 attacks, the murder of journalist Daniel Pearl, and the hotel bombings in Bali, was released by the U.S. Department of Defense and later appeared in *Harper's Magazine*.

The Language of War Is Killing
Khalid Sheikh Mohammed

I'm not making myself a hero when I said I was responsible for this or that. You   1
know very well there is a language for any war. If America wants to invade Iraq, they will not send Saddam roses or kisses. They send bombardment. I admit I'm America's enemy. For sure, I'm America's enemy. So when we make war against America, we are like jackals fighting in the night. We consider George Washington a hero. Muslims, many of them, believe Osama bin Laden is doing the same thing. He is just fighting. He needs his independence. Many Muslims think that, not only me. They have been oppressed by America. So when we say we are enemy combatants, that's right, we are. But I'm asking you to be fair with many detainees who are not enemy combatants. Because many of them have been unjustly arrested. You know very well, for any country waging war against their enemy, the language of the war is killing. If man and woman are together as a marriage, the others are kids, children. But if you and me, two nations, are together in war, the others are victims. This is the way of the language. You know forty million people were killed in World War I. Many people are oppressed. Because there is war, for sure, there will be victims. I'm not happy that three thousand have been killed in America. I feel sorry even. Islam never gives me the green light to kill people. Killing, in Christianity, Judaism, and Islam, is prohibited. But there are exceptions to the rule. When you are killing people in Iraq, you say, We have to do it. We don't like Saddam. But this is the way to deal with Saddam. Same language you use I use. When you are invading two thirds of Mexico, you call your war "manifest destiny."

(continued)

(continued)

It's up to you to call it what you want. But the other side is calling you oppressors. If now we were living in the Revolutionary War, George Washington would be arrested by Britain. For sure, they would consider him an enemy combatant. But in America they consider him a hero. In any revolutionary war one side will be either George Washington or Britain. So we considered American Army bases in Saudi Arabia, Kuwait, Qatar, and Bahrain. This is a kind of invasion, but I'm not here to convince you. I don't have to say that I'm not your enemy. This is why the language of any war in the world is killing. The language of war is victims. I don't like to kill people. I feel very sorry kids were killed in 9/11. What will I do? I want to make a great awakening in America to stop foreign policy in our land. I know Americans have been torturing us since the seventies. I know they are talking about human rights. And I know it is against the American Constitution, against American laws. But they said, Every law has exceptions. This is your bad luck—you've been part of the exception to our laws. So, for me, I have patience. The Americans have human rights, but enemy combatant is a flexible word. What is an enemy combatant in my language? The Ten Commandments are shared between all of us. We are all serving one God. But we also share the language of War. War started when Cain killed Abel. It's never gonna stop killing people. America starts the Revolutionary War, and then the Mexican, then the Spanish, then World War I, World War II. You read the history. This is life. You have to kill.

Inquiring into the Essay

Explore, explain, evaluate, and reflect on "The Language of War."

1. Does Mohammed have a point when he compares Islamic extremists who fight for "freedom" to American revolutionaries like George Washington who fought for independence? Fastwrite on this question in your journal for five minutes, exploring what you think. When you're done, skip a line and compose a one-sentence answer to this question: *What surprised you most about what you said in your fastwrite?*

2. Summarize in your own words what you think is Mohammed's main claim.

3. Make a list of reasons that he states in (or you infer from) the transcript that are meant to support Mohammed's main claim. Remember that reasons are ideas that can be attached to a claim using the word "because." For example, "Because most professors are liberals (reason), an open and balanced political discussion in the college classroom is unlikely (claim)." Choose one or more of these reasons, and evaluate whether they are convincing. If not, why not?

4. The September 11 attacks have, understandably, made many Americans very emotional about terrorism and terrorists. What did you notice about

your emotional reaction to Mohammed's argument in "The Language of War"? Did you find it difficult to read the transcript analytically, as the previous questions asked you to do? If so, is this a problem?

INQUIRING INTO THE DETAILS

Some Basic Argument Strategies

- **Argument from generalization:** What I've seen or observed of a particular group is true of the group as a whole. *Risk: Are you sure that what you've observed is typical of the larger population?*

- **Argument from analogy:** If it is true in one situation, it's likely true in another similar situation. *Risk: Are the situations really similar?*

- **Argument from cause:** If one thing always seems present with something else, then one probably causes the other. *Risk: Is cause and effect really the relationship between the two things?*

- **Argument from authority:** If an expert said it, it's true. *Risk: Is the expertise of the authority really relevant to the question at issue?*

- **Argument from principle:** This general principle (which most of us agree with) applies in this case. *Risk: Is there really agreement on the rightness of the principle, and does it actually apply in this specific context?*

Adapted from Richard Fulkerson, *Teaching the Argument in Writing.* Urbana, IL: National Council of Teachers of English, 1996.

ARGUMENT 2

Faith and reason don't have to clash. In his encyclical on the subject, Pope John Paul II wrote that "faith and reason are like two wings on which the human spirit rises to the contemplation of truth." Before the modern era of science, any conflict between the two could be easily resolved by simply accepting that any proposition can, at the same time, be true by reason and false by faith. But these days, such a contradiction is hard to swallow. Take evolution. Darwin's scientific argument intensified the clash between faith and reason, and it still produces pitched battles between school boards and teachers, preachers and scientists, and believers and nonbelievers of all types.

One answer to the conflict is simple. Choose one or the other:

1. When science and scripture collide, scripture wins.

2. When science and scripture collide, science wins.

In the op-ed essay that follows, *Boston Globe* columnist Jeff Jacoby seems to offer another alternative. Using the intellectual success—and deep religious commitment—of one great figure, Jacoby argues that faith and reason aren't necessarily incompatible.

A Teacher with Faith and Reason
Jeff Jacoby

1   Did you hear about the religious fundamentalist who wanted to teach physics at Cambridge University? This would-be instructor wasn't simply a Christian; he was so preoccupied with biblical prophecy that he wrote a book titled *Observations on the Prophecies of Daniel and the Apocalypse of St. John*. Based on his reading of Daniel, in fact, he forecast the date of the Apocalypse: no earlier than 2060. He also calculated the year the world was created. When Genesis 1:1 says "In the beginning," he determined, it means 3988 BC.

2   Not many modern universities are prepared to employ a science professor who espouses not merely "intelligent design" but out-and-out divine creation. This applicant's writings on astronomy, for example, include these thoughts on the solar system: "This most beautiful system of sun, planets, and comets could only proceed from the counsel and domination of an intelligent and powerful Being...He governs all things, and knows all things that are or can be done."

3   Hire somebody with such views to teach physics? At a Baptist junior college deep in the Bible Belt, maybe, but the faculty would erupt if you tried it just about anywhere else. Many of them would echo Oxford's Richard Dawkins, the prominent evolutionary biologist, who writes in "The God Delusion" that he is "hostile to fundamentalist religion because it actively debauches the scientific enterprise....It subverts science and saps the intellect."

4   Equally blunt is Sam Harris, a PhD candidate in neuroscience and another unsparing foe of religion. "The conflict between religion and science is inherent and (very nearly) zero-sum," he has written. "The success of science often comes at the expense of religious dogma; the maintenance of religious dogma always comes at the expense of science." Less elegant but more influential, the National Science Education Standards issued by the National Academy of Sciences in 1995 classified religion with "myths," "mystical inspiration," and "superstition"—all of them quite incompatible with scientific study. Michael Dini, a biologist at Texas Tech University in Lubbock, made headlines in 2003 over his policy of denying letters of recommendation for any graduate student who could not "truthfully and forthrightly affirm a scientific answer" to the question of mankind's origin. Science and religion, he said in an interview at the time, "shouldn't overlap."

5   But such considerations didn't keep Cambridge from hiring the theology- and Bible-drenched individual described above. Indeed, it named him to the prestigious

Lucasian Chair of Mathematics—in 1668. A good thing too, since Isaac Newton—notwithstanding his religious fervor and intense interest in Biblical interpretation—went on to become the most renowned scientist of his age, and arguably the most influential in history.

Newton's consuming interest in theology, eschatology, and the secrets of the   6
Bible is the subject of a new exhibit at Hebrew University in Jerusalem (online at jnul.huji.ac.il/dl/mss/Newton). His vast religious output—an estimated 3 million words—ranged from the dimensions of Solomon's Temple to a method of reckoning the date of Easter to the elucidation of Biblical symbols. "Newton was one of the last great Renaissance men," the curators observe, "a thinker who worked in mathematics, physics, optics, alchemy, history, theology, and the interpretation of prophecy and saw connections between them all." The 21st-century prejudice that religion invariably "subverts science" is refuted by the extraordinary figure who managed to discover the composition of light, deduce the laws of motion, invent calculus, compute the speed of sound, and define universal gravitation, all while believing deeply in the "domination of an intelligent and powerful Being." Far from subverting his scientific integrity, the exhibition notes, "Newton's piety served as one of his inspirations to study nature and what we today call science."

For Newton, it was axiomatic that religious inquiry and scientific investigation   7
complemented each other. There were truths to be found in both of the "books" authored by God, the Book of Scripture and the Book of Nature—or as Francis Bacon called them, the "book of God's word" and the "book of God's works." To study the world empirically did not mean abandoning religious faith. On the contrary: The more deeply the workings of Creation were understood, the closer one might come to the Creator. In the language of the 19th Psalm, "The heavens declare the glory of God, and the sky above proclaims his handiwork."

To be sure, religious dogma can be a blindfold, blocking truths from those who   8
refuse to see them. Scientific dogma can have the same effect. Neither faith nor reason can answer every question. As Newton knew, the surer path to wisdom is the one that has room for both.

Inquiring into the Essay

Explore, explain, evaluate, and reflect on "A Teacher with Faith and Reason."

1. Perhaps the central claim of this essay appears, as it often does in an op-ed essay, two thirds of the way into the piece, when Jacoby writes,

    > The 21st-century prejudice that religion invariably "subverts science" is refuted by the extraordinary figure who managed to discover the composition of light, deduce the laws of motion, invent calculus, compute the speed of

sound, and define universal gravitation, all while believing deeply in the "domination of an intelligent and powerful Being."

When you analyze an argument, it's often helpful to first explore—in a relatively open-ended way—what you think about the central claim. Do that now in a four-minute fastwrite in your journal. Do you agree or disagree that Isaac Newton's legacy "refutes" the current "prejudice" that religion undercuts scientific inquiry? Try writing a narrative of thought, beginning with "The first thing I think about this is...And then I think...And then..." Allow yourself to digress if that's where your writing takes you.

2. Define the two key terms in this debate—reason and faith—in your own words.

3. An argument about potential conflicts between faith and reason can easily become too abstract to evaluate well. So consider the case Jacoby mentions in his essay: A Texas Tech biology professor routinely refused to write recommendations for any graduate student who didn't provide a "scientific answer" to explain the beginnings of humankind. Do you find Jacoby's argument helpful in developing your own response to that particular situation?

4. This is one of those social issues that trigger strong feeling which, at times, can cloud reasoning. Reflect on your own response to issues like this one. When you have an emotional response to a public argument, how do you get past it?

■ ARGUMENT 3

During the fall semester, 2008, Laredo businessman Loye Young agreed to teach a business management class at nearby Texas A&M International University (TAMIU). Like many instructors, he toiled over his syllabus, trying to make sure his course policies were clear, especially a section on the consequences of plagiarism in his class. Young warned that plagiarists would not only flunk the course, they would be reported to university officials. That's fairly standard punishment at most universities. What got critics' attention was Young's warning that he would publicly humiliate any student caught cheating.

True to his word, when he caught six students plagiarizing a paper, Young published their names on his blog, and soon after, TAMIU officials fired him, arguing that he violated the Family Educational and Privacy Act, a policy designed to protect the confidentiality of certain student information. Young, a former attorney, strongly disagreed.

The firing ignited a national controversy and a wild debate in the blogosphere over whether Loye Young's decision to out students he suspected of academic dishonesty was effective, ethical, and fair. In response to one of his critics, Loye posted the following defense of his approach on his blog.

Is Humiliation an Ethically Appropriate Response to Plagiarism?

Loye Young

I'm a business owner in Laredo, Texas. I had never taught a college course before, and I never asked to teach. The department asked me to teach this course. I accepted because of my commitment to Laredo's future.

I worked hard on the syllabus, and everything in the syllabus was deliberate. Specifically, the language about dishonesty was based on moral and pedagogical principles. The department chairman, Dr. Balaji Janamanchi, reviewed the syllabus with me line-by-line, and I made a few changes in response to his comments.

I was surprised by how common and blatant plagiarism turned out to be. Six students in one class is an extraordinarily high number. I thought and prayed about what to do for about a week before following through on my promise. I decided I had only one moral choice. I am certain it was right.

My decision was guided by two factors: What is good for the students themselves? and What is good for other students?

What is good for the students themselves?

I am cognizant of the extraordinary moral difficulty involved when deciding what is in another's best interests. Nonetheless, I am convinced that public disclosure, including the concomitant humiliation, is in the interests of the student because it is the best way to teach the student about the consequences of dishonesty and discourage the student from plagiarizing again. Humiliation is inextricably part of a well-formed conscience.

The Vice President-elect, Senator Joseph Biden, is perhaps the most well-known plagiarizer in recent history. Biden was caught plagiarizing while at Syracuse Law School. The school gave him an F, required him to retake the course, and subsequently treated the incident as confidential.

Unfortunately, Biden didn't learn his lesson at law school. He continued to plagiarize for another 20 years. During the 1988 presidential campaign, Senator Biden's career of plagiarizing came to light, and he was forced to end his presidential bid.

It is my belief that the Syracuse incident left a subtle and subliminal message in Biden's mind: plagiarism is not a deal breaker. Consequently, he continued to plagiarize. Unfortunately for the Senator, the facts came to public light at the worst possible time: when he was running for President.

I believe that had the Syracuse incident been available publicly, Mr. Biden would have actually learned his lesson and would not have plagiarized later. Twenty years later, if the incident had come up at all, the Senator would have plausibly and convincingly maintained that the incident was a youthful mistake.

There is yet another reason for publicity in such cases: unjustly accused students are protected, for two reasons. One, a professor will be more careful before blowing

(continued)

(continued)

the whistle. I myself knew that posting the students' names would be appropriately subject to intense public scrutiny. Therefore, I construed every ambiguity in the students' favor. Two, public disclosure ensures that subsequent determinations by the university are founded on evidence and dispensed fairly.

12   What is good for other students?

13   On the second question, four reasons convince me: deterrents, fairness, predictability, and preparedness for life.

14   Deterrents—Only if everyone knows that violations of plagiarism will be exposed and punished will the penalties for plagiarism be an effective deterrent. (As a lawyer once told me after hearing of another lawyer's disbarment, "I'm damn sure not going to do THAT again!") In fact, one of the six students had not plagiarized (to my knowledge) until the week before I announced my findings. Had I announced the plagiarism earlier, it is possible that student would not have plagiarized at all.

15   Fairness—Honest students should have, in fairness, the knowledge that their legitimate work is valued more than a plagiarizer's illegitimate work. In my course, the students were required to post their essays on a public website for all to see. Thus, anyone in the world could have detected the plagiarism. Had another student noticed the plagiarism but saw no action, the honest student would reasonably believe that the process is unfair.

16   Predictability—By failing publicly to follow through on ubiquitous warnings about plagiarism, universities have convinced students that the purported indignation against deceit is itself deceitful and that the entire process is capricious. TAMIU's actions in this case have confirmed my suspicions that such a perception is entirely justified.

17   Preparedness for life—In the real world, deceitful actions have consequences, and those consequences are often public. Borrowers lose credit ratings, employees get fired, spouses divorce, businesses fail, political careers end, and professionals go to jail. Acts of moral turpitude rightly carry public and humiliating consequences in real life, and students need to be prepared.

18   In closing, I submit that education died when educators came to believe that greater self-esteem leads to greater learning. In fact, the causality is backwards: self-esteem is the result of learning, not the cause.

Inquiring into the Essay

Explore, explain, evaluate, and reflect on "Is Humiliation an Ethically Appropriate Response to Plagiarism?"

1. If you accept that plagiarism is a problem, then what should an instructor do about it? What would you consider not just an ethical policy but one that you think might be an effective deterrent? Fastwrite about this question in your journal for four minutes, exploring what you think.

2. How would *you* define plagiarism? Is it possible that some students might be understandably confused about what it means?

3. Loye Young writes, "Humiliation is inextricably part of a well-formed conscience." How would you evaluate that claim? Can you imagine the *reasons* that Young believes it's true? (Try filling in the blank in this sentence: *Because _____, humiliation is inextricably part of a well-formed conscience.*) Do you agree with them?

4. Reflect on the blog as a genre of public argument. How would you distinguish it from, say, an op-ed essay or a letter to the editor?

SEEING THE FORM

The "Imagetext" as Argument

While model Kate Moss is likely disturbed by the appropriation of her image by advocates in the pro-anorexia ("pro-ana") movement, Moss's picture along with those of other celebrities such as Calista Flockhart, Mary-Kate Olsen, and Keira Knightley appear as "thinspiration" on Web sites that argue that eating disorders are a "lifestyle choice," not a disease. Some of these images (though not this one) are digitally altered to make the models seem even thinner than they really are. In a recent article on the "imagetexts" used by these controversial Web sites, Robin Jensen observes that images rarely argue in isolation, a phenomenon that is particularly relevant to the Web, which often combines pictures and verbal texts. Jensen notes that when pictures like this one of Kate Moss are given a new "visual frame," quite different from the one originally intended, the meaning of the picture can be manipulated. Imagine, for instance, that the Kate Moss photograph appeared in a "thinspiration" gallery of celebrity photographs on a "pro-ana" Web site, and included the following caption: "Maintaining a weight that is 15 percent below your expected body weight fits the criteria for anorexia, so most models, according to medical standards, fit into the categeory of being anorexic." Analyze this "imagetext" rhetorically. How does this picture of Moss combined with the caption serve the purpose of the "pro-ana" movement? What message is it meant to convey and is it persuasive to its intended audience?

Kate Moss in ultra-thin pose.

THE WRITING PROCESS

INQUIRY PROJECT: WRITING A PUBLIC ARGUMENT

Now that you've explored various approaches to persuasion and argument, try your hand at writing an argument essay. Remember that these are brief (700- to 1,000-word) essays meant for a general audience. Imagine, for example, that you're writing an op-ed piece for the campus newspaper, the local daily, or the *New York Times*. Your essay should be lively and logical, with a strong personal voice, and also have the following features:

- It focuses implicitly or explicitly on a question. This is always the starting point for inquiry in any genre. In an argumentative essay, you are providing evidence to support a particular answer to this question.

- The essay makes clear premises and claims, including one central claim around which the draft is organized. In other words, *the essay should be clear about what it is asking its readers to do or to believe.*

- It provides specific and appropriate evidence in support of the claims, including research when relevant.

- The essay should address one or more of the counterarguments offered by those who take a different position from yours.

Thinking About Subjects

Gun control, abortion rights, and other hot-button public controversies often make the list of banned topics for student essays. This is not because they aren't important public debates. Instead, the problem is much more that the writer has likely already made up his mind and sees the chance to ascend a soapbox.

> The best argument essays make a clear claim, but they do it by bowing respectfully to the complexity of the subject, examining it from a variety of perspectives, not just two opposing poles.

Now, I have my own favorite soapboxes; people with strong convictions do. But as you think about subjects for your essay, consider that the soapbox may not be the best vantage point for practicing inquiry. If you've already made up your mind, will you be open to discovery? If you just want to line up ducks—assembling evidence to support an unwavering belief—will you be encouraged to think deeply or differently? Will you be inclined to filter the voices you hear rather than consider a range of points of view?

The best persuasive essays often emerge from the kind of open-ended inquiry that you might have used writing the personal essay. What do you want to understand better? What issue or question makes you wonder? What controversies are you and your friends talking about? Be alert to possible subjects that you might write about *not* because you already know what you think, but because you want to find out. Or consider a subject that you might have feelings about but feel uninformed, lacking the knowledge to know exactly what you think.

Generating Ideas

Play around with some ideas first by using some of the following triggers for thinking-through-writing in your journal. Suspend judgment. Don't reject anything. Explore.

Listing Prompts. Lists can be rich sources of triggering topics. Let them grow freely, and when you're ready, use an item as the focus of another list or an episode of fastwriting. The following prompts should get you started.

1. In your journal, make a quick list of issues that have provoked disagreements between groups of people in your hometown or local community.

2. Make a quick list of issues that have provoked disagreements on your college's campus.

3. Make another list of issues that have created controversy between groups of people in your state.

4. Think about issues—local, statewide, regional, national, or even international—that have touched your life, or could affect you in some way in the following areas: environmental, health care, civil rights, business, education, crime, or sports. Make a quick list of questions within these areas you wonder about. For example, *Will there be enough drinking water in my well if the valley continues to develop at this rate?* Or *Will I be able to afford to send my children to the state college in twelve years?* Or *Do new domestic antiterrorism rules threaten my privacy when I'm online?* Or *Will I benefit from affirmative action laws when I apply to law school?*

5. Jot down a list of the classes you're taking this semester. Then make a quick list of topics that prompt disagreements among people in the field that you're studying. For example, in your political science class, did you learn that there are debates about the usefulness of the electoral college? In your biology class, have you discussed global warming? In your women's studies class, did you read about Title 9 and how it affects female athletes?

Fastwriting Prompts. Remember, fastwriting is a great way to stimulate creative thinking. Turn off your critical side and let yourself write "badly." Don't worry too much about what you're going to say before you say it. Write fast, letting language lead for a change.

1. Write for five minutes beginning with one of the questions you raised in Question 4 in the "Listing Prompts" section. Think through writing about when you first began to be concerned about the question, how you think it might affect you, and what you currently understand are the key questions this issue raises. Do you have tentative feelings or beliefs about it?

2. In a seven-minute fastwrite, explore the differences between your beliefs and the beliefs of your parents. Tell yourself the story of how your own beliefs about some question evolved, perhaps moving away from your parents' positions. Can you imagine the argument you might make to help them understand your point of view?

3. Choose an item from any of the lists you generated in the "Listing Prompts" section as a starting place for a fastwrite. Explore what you understand about the issue, what the key questions are, and how you feel about the issue at the moment.

Visual Prompts. In your journal, cluster one or more of the following phrases:

"Things that seem unfair"

"Things that bug me the most"

"There oughta be a law about…"

"Problems that must be solved"

"The worst thing about living here"

Let your cluster grow as many branches as possible; when one dies out start another. Focus on ideas, people, places, facts, observations, questions, experiences,

---

ONE STUDENT'S RESPONSE

Ben's Journal

FASTWRITE
WHY DO STUDENTS SEEM SO APATHETIC ABOUT POLITICS?

We're in the midst of presidential elections and I can't seem to get anyone interested in talking about it. I wonder why that is? Are college students more cynical about politics and politicians than other groups? It seems like it to me. I can think of a few reasons right off the bat. First, college students are mostly young (though certainly not all at this school) so they don't have the habit of going to the polls. Whenever a generation loses the habit of voting, I'll bet the next generation is even more likely to be apathetic. I also think my generation has seen so few effective politicians. My dad talks about being inspired by the likes of JFK but I can't think of too many national politicians who have inspired me as much as JFK inspired him. I also wonder if there is that basic sense of powerlessness. We just don't feel like much of anything makes a difference. I wonder if that is also reflected in volunteerism. Do students volunteer less than they used to? Have to check on that. I guess I just find politics kind of interesting. I wonder why? Hmmm…I think it had something to do with my Dad. But I guess I also have this basic belief in voting as an important part of being a citizen. Seems like one of the best ways to be patriotic…

and details that pop into your mind when you focus on the pair of words at the center of your cluster. Look for interesting argument topics when you're done. See Figure 7.7 for an example.

Research Prompts. By definition, argument essays deal with subjects in which people beyond the writer have a stake. And one of the best ways to collect ideas about such issues is to do a little quick and dirty research. Try some of the following research prompts:

1. Spend a few days reading the letters to the editor in your local paper. What issue has people riled up locally? Is there one that you find particularly interesting?

2. Do a Web search to find op-ed essays written by one or more of the following national columnists: Ellen Goodman, Cal Thomas, George Will, David Broder, Nat Hentoff, Mary McGrory, Molly Ivins, Bob Herbert, or Clarence Page. Read their work with an eye toward topics that interest you.

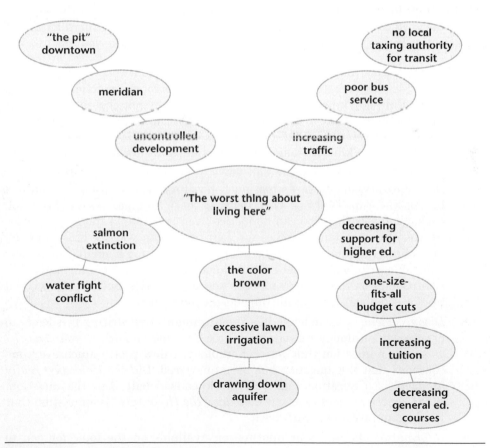

Figure 7.7   Sample cluster

3. Do a Google search for terms or phrases on an issue that interests you, such as "global warming Greenland glaciers" or "pro-anorexia Web sites." Did you produce any results that make you curious or make you feel something about the issue, one way or another?

4. Interview people you know—on or off campus—about the public issues that they care about most.

Judging What You Have

Shift back to your more critical mind and sift through the material you generated. Did you discover a topic that might be interesting for your argument essay? Did you stumble over some interesting questions you'd like to explore further? Did anything you wrote or read make you *feel* something? Evaluate the raw material in your journal and keep the following things in mind as you zero in on a topic for your argument essay.

What's Promising Material and What Isn't?   Let's take a critical look at the subjects you've generated so far. What promising topics might be lurking there for an argumentative essay? Consider some of the following as you make your choice.

- *Interest.* This almost goes without saying. But you were warned earlier about seizing on a topic if you already have strong convictions about it. Do you already know what you think? If so, why not choose a topic that initially invites more open-ended inquiry? On the other hand, it matters a lot whether you *care*. What topic might touch your life in some way? Do you have some kind of stake in how the questions are answered?

- *Focus.* One of the most common flaws of student drafts in all genres is that they attempt to cover too much territory. A more *limited* look at a larger landscape is always best. Because these argument essays are brief, consider topics that you can do justice to in less than a thousand words. As you review potential topics for your essay, can you see how some aspect of a larger question can be addressed by asking a smaller question? You can't write a short piece about the negative impact of affirmative action policies on the nation's colleges and universities, but you can write a brief op-ed about the specific impacts on your school.

- *Disagreement.* A topic lends itself to argumentative writing if it leads to disagreement among reasonable people. *Is smoking bad for your health?* was once a question that was debatable, but now pretty much everyone concedes that this question has been answered. *Did the Holocaust really happen?* is a question that only blockheads debate. But the question, *What are the motives of people who deny the Holocaust?* is a question that would generate a range of views.

- *Information.* Is sufficient information available on the topic for you to make a reasonable judgment about what is true? Is it accessible? One great advantage of choosing a local question as the focus for an argumentative essay is that often the people are close by and the relevant information can easily be had. It's also essential that you can obtain information from more than just a single viewpoint on the question.

■ *Question.* What makes a topic arguable is that it raises questions to which there are multiple answers. Which of them makes the most sense is at issue. But some questions are merely informational. For example, *How do greenhouse gases contribute to global warming?* is a question that will likely lead to explanations rather than argument. On the other hand, *Is the U.S. rejection of the Kyoto accords on global warming a responsible policy?* is an arguable, rather than informational, question.

Questions About Audience and Purpose. Persuasive writing is a very audience-oriented form. *To whom* you make your case in an argument matters a lot in *how* you make it, but audience also matters in *whether* one topic is a better choice for an essay than another topic. The public argument is written for a more general audience. Your readers are unlikely to be experts on your topic, and they are likely to read your essay quickly rather than slowly and thoughtfully. What does this imply about the best subjects?

■ *Do your readers have a stake in the question you're answering?* The word *stake* can be broadly considered. For example, a topic may directly affect the readers of your essay; say you're writing for fellow college students on your campus, all of whom pay tuition, and your topic addresses whether a 12 percent hike in fees is justified. Sometimes, however, you choose a topic because readers need to know that they *do* have a stake in how a question is answered. For instance, the argument that new antiterrorist rules threaten online privacy is something you believe your readers, most of whom surf the Web, should consider.

■ *Can you identify what your readers might already believe?* One of the key strategies of persuasion is to find ways to link the values and attitudes of your audience with the position you're encouraging them to believe. Does your potential topic lend itself to this kind of analysis?

■ *Is your purpose not only to inform readers but also to encourage them to believe or do something?* As you know by now, one of the things that distinguishes argument essays such as the op-ed piece from other forms of writing is the writer's intention to change his or her audience.

Research Considerations. While writing this argument essay does involve some research, it isn't exactly a research paper. A research paper is a much more extended treatment of a topic that relies on more detailed and scholarly information than is usually needed for an argument essay. In Chapter 11, you'll find information on research strategies that will help you with this project, especially how to conduct effective Internet searches and how to evaluate the sources you find. The section on library research, particularly key references, may also be valuable.

To develop a working knowledge of the topic for your public argument essay, focus your research on the following:

1. *The back-story:* What is the history of the controversy? When did it begin, who was involved, how was the issue addressed, what were the problems?
2. *Popular assumptions:* What do most people currently believe is true about the issue?
3. *The evidence:* Who has said what that seems to support your claim or provide backing for your assumptions?
4. *Opposing arguments:* Who offers a counterargument that you might need to consider?

Consider working through some of the following research strategies to find this information.

Researching on the Web

- Google (for relevant Web sites, online periodicals, and some newspapers)
- Google Scholar (if your topic is discussed by scholars)
- Google Blog Search (to get the gist of the public discussion of your topic)
- GPO Access (go to http://www.gpoaccess.gov/ to search for relevant federal documents)
- Online version of local newspaper (if your topic has a local angle)
- State and Local Government on the Net (go to http://www.statelocalgov.net/ if your topic is an issue of policy)

Researching in the Library

- General subject databases (these cover a wide range of subjects, and many include nonacademic publications as well)
- Newspaper databases (for example National Newspaper Index or Newspaper Source)
- Newspapers on microfilm (your university library might archive copies of the local paper on microfilm, going back for many years)

While both the Web and the university library are great sources of information on your topic, often the best way to learn about it—and get some good quotes for your essay—is to find someone to talk to. Your reading will probably give you the best clues about who to contact. Who is often quoted in news stories? Who has been writing or blogging about the issue? You might also be able to find someone on your own campus. If you're writing, say, about measures that attempt to protect students from date rape on your campus, someone in the Criminal Justice department or in Student Affairs can tell you more about the issue in a few minutes than you might learn in a couple hours online.

Narrowing the Question. I've been vaguely aware of the crisis in Medicaid funding—federal health care support for the poor—but the issue really came home when officials told Dorothy Misner, a ninety-two-year-old woman in nearby Nampa, that she would have to gum her food because the state refused to pay for dentures. Probably the best way to make a larger controversy a manageable writing topic is to find a local angle. In this case, for example, the larger question—*Should the national Medicaid program do more to support the poor without health insurance?*—becomes a much narrower question: *Is the state's Medicaid program failing people like Dorothy Misner?* Whenever possible, make big issues smaller by finding some connection to the local.

That isn't always possible, however. Unless you live in Alaska, for instance, the debate over development of the Arctic National Wildlife Refuge is hard to cut as a local issue. Then it becomes important to find a narrower question, something that may not be possible until after you've done a little research. For example, the question, *Should the Arctic National Wildlife Refuge be open to oil development?* could be narrowed by asking, *Are oil company claims about the potential of recoverable oil in the refuge reasonable?*

Another way to narrow the focus of an argument is to find a useful case study, anecdote, or example that somehow typifies some aspect of the issue you want to examine. Finally, do what journalists do: Peg your essay to a recent event related to the issue you're writing about. George Will's approach to many of his op-ed essays is to use a newly released study, report, academic article, or interview with an expert as the anchor for his piece. He then takes off on his own from there. Other events might include a relevant hearing, a protest, a court decision, a crime, an accident, and so on.

Writing the Sketch

Now draft a sketch of roughly 500 to 600 words with the following elements:

- It has a tentative title.
- It makes at least one claim and offers several reasons that support the claim.
- It presents and analyzes at least one contrasting point of view.
- The sketch includes specific evidence to support (or possibly complicate) the reasons offered in support of the claim, including *at least* several of the following: an anecdote or story, a personal observation, data, an analogy, a case study, expert testimony, other relevant quotations from people involved, or a precedent.

■ STUDENT SKETCH

Inspiring young voters isn't easy. In my own classes, I almost never hear younger students talk casually about elections. On the rare occasions that I actually see a button on a backpack for one candidate or another, I'm always a little surprised. Are young voters apathetic? And if they are, what should be done about it? Those were Ben Bloom's questions, both of which arose from a fastwrite. Here is his sketch on the topic. Where should he go from here? What should he research before the next draft? What should he consider that he doesn't consider here?

How to Really Rock the Vote

Ben Bloom

1   MTV sponsors "Rock the Vote." Presidential candidates swing through college campuses wearing blue jeans and going tieless. There's even an organization called "Kid's Vote" that tries to get high school students involved in the political process. It's pretty clear that student vote matters but are these efforts paying off?

2   It doesn't seem so. On my own campus, fewer than a few hundred students vote in the annual elections for the Student Senate. I can't even get my roommate to talk about the Presidential election, much less who's running for student body president.

3   What seems typical is the following comment from a college-age columnist: "On the issue of voter apathy, I look at myself first. I'm not even registered to vote, which is as apathetic as it gets. I do, however, educate myself about presidential candidates and their proposed policies—I just never have thought my one, lonesome vote could matter. I've neglected registering because it has never seemed logical to inconvenience myself, through the registration process, only to give another drop of water to an ocean (to add one vote to millions)."

4   "Never seemed logical to inconvenience" yourself to participate in the most basic part of the democratic process? Has it gotten this bad?

5   The student journalist above was responding to a survey that came out two years ago from a group called Project Vote Smart. It found what I suspected from my own experiences: young voters are staying away from the polls.

6   According to the study, there has been a decline in the numbers of 18- to 25-year-olds voting by 13% over the last twenty-five years. Actually, I think the situation is worse than that. The main reason they cite is that young people don't think their votes make a difference.

7   What should be done about this? How can we convince young voters to believe in the power of their vote? Are organizations like "Rock the Vote" or "Project Vote Smart" going to convince students like the guy who finds voting "inconvenient" that it's worth the effort?

8   In my opinion, celebrities and rock stars won't make a difference. The key is for political candidates to find a way to talk about issues so that young voters overcome their apathy and actually *feel* something. In the sixties, it was the draft. I'm not sure what the issues with emotional impact are these days. But the people who want students to vote have got to find them.

Moving from Sketch to Draft

A sketch is often sketchy. It's generally underdeveloped, sometimes giving the writer just the barest outline of his subject. But as an early draft, a sketch can be invaluable. It might hint at what the real subject is, or what questions seem to be behind your inquiry into the subject. A sketch might suggest a focus for the next draft, or simply a better lead. Here are some tips for finding clues in your sketch about directions you might go in the next draft.

Evaluating Your Own Sketch. You've read and written about an issue you care about. Now for the really hard part: getting out of your own head and into the heads of your potential readers, who may not care as much as you do. At least not yet. Successful persuasion fundamentally depends on giving an audience the right reasons to agree with you, and these are likely both logical and emotional, involving both *logos* and *pathos,* as you learned earlier in this chapter.

Another element of argument is the way the writer comes across to readers—his or her *ethos*. What's the ethos of your sketch? How might you be perceived by a stranger reading the sketch? Is your tone appealing, or might it be slightly off-putting? Do you successfully establish your authority to speak on this issue, or do you sense that the persona you project in the sketch is unconvincing, perhaps too emotional or not appearing fair?

As we develop convictions about an issue, one of the hardest things to manage in early argument drafts is creating a persuasive persona (*ethos*). Another is finding ways to establish connections with our audience; this does not merely involve connecting writers and readers but includes creating some common ground between readers and *the topic*. There are many ways to do this, including the following:

1. Connecting your readers' prior beliefs or values with your position on the topic.

2. Establishing that readers have a *stake,* perhaps even a personal one, in how the question you've raised is answered; this may be self-interest, but it may also be emotional (remember the advertiser's strategy).

3. Highlighting the common experiences readers may have had with the topic and offering your claim as a useful way of understanding that experience.

As you look over your sketch, evaluate how well you create this common ground between your topic and your intended audience. Might you revise it by exploiting one or more of the strategies listed here?

Finally, is there enough evidence to support the reasons you've provided to support your claims? Initial drafts commonly lack enough specifics. Do you see places in the sketch that could be developed with specific information in the next draft?

Questions for Peer Review. Because the argument essay is such an audience-oriented form, these initial peer reviews of your sketch are invaluable in helping you get your bearings. Much of what you might have felt about how you managed the ethos and connections with readers can be confirmed or challenged by this first public reading. Ask your workshop group some of the following questions:

- How is the *ethos* of the sketch? Do I come across in the sketch as an advocate for my position? For example, am I *passionate, preachy, reasonable, one-sided, sympathetic, overbearing, intimate, detached, objective, subjective, uncaring, empathetic, humorous, serious, angry, mellow, contemptuous, approachable, patronizing, respectful, thoughtful, presumptuous, fair,* or *judgmental?*

- In your own words, what do you think was my central claim?

- Which reasons did you find most convincing? Which were least convincing?

- What do you think was the best evidence I offered in support of my reasons? Where exactly did you feel that you needed more evidence?

- What were the stated or unstated "warrants" or assumptions behind the claims? What do you need to assume is true to believe in their validity?

Reflecting on What You've Learned. Spend a few minutes following your peer review workshop to generate a list of everything you heard, and then begin a five-minute fastwrite that explores your reaction to these suggestions and your tentative plan for revision. In particular, what will you change? What will you add, and what will you cut in the next draft? What problems were raised that you don't yet know how to solve? What problems *weren't* raised that you expected might be? Do you still need to worry about them? End your fastwrite by writing about what you understand now about your topic, and your initial beliefs about it, that you didn't fully understand when you began writing about it.

Research and Other Strategies: Gathering More Information

Here's a mortifying thought: You've completely changed your mind about what you think about your topic and what you want to say in your argument. That's unsettling, but it's also a sign that you're willing to allow things to get a bit messy before they get sorted out. This is good because it's much more likely to result in an essay that gets at the truth of what you feel than if you doggedly stick to a particular point of view, come what may. If you *have* changed your mind, you have a lot of collecting to do. Return to the Web sites of current publications and search for information that might be relevant to your emerging idea.

Another research strategy can be helpful whether you change your mind or not: the interview. People who are somehow involved in your topic are among the best sources of new information and lively material. An interview can provide ideas about what else you should read or who else you might talk to, and it can be a source of quotations, anecdotes, and even case studies that will make the next draft of your argument essay much more interesting. After all, what makes an issue matter is how it affects people. Have you sufficiently dramatized those effects?

When appropriate, you can also add images to dramatize your claims or your evidence. They're easier than ever to find on nearly any subject using online services like Google Image Search. But they must be relevant. Figure 7.8, for example, is an ad by the National Eating Disorders Association that focuses on the relationship between our genetic disposition to be a certain body size.

Figure 7.8   Sometimes your research for a public argument will include visual sources. This poster for National Eating Disorders Awareness Week reads, "Be comfortable in your genes. Your genes play a role in determining your body size and shape. So be kind to your body. Stop trying to turn it into something it's not. Wear jeans that fit the REAL you."
Source: http://www.gurze.com/productdetails.cfm?PC=1588 National Eating Disorders Association, http://www.nationaleatingdisorders.org/index.php

Imagine if the image was dropped into an argument essay—or a PowerPoint presentation—that argued for the strong influence of an "obesity gene."

For more information on face-to-face interviewing, see Chapter 4, "Writing a Profile," as well as Chapter 11, "Research Techniques." The Internet can also be a source for interview material. Look for e-mail links to the authors of useful documents you find on the Web and write to them with a few questions. Interest groups, newsgroups, or electronic mailing lists on the Web can also provide the voices and perspectives of people with something to say on your topic. Remember to ask permission to quote them if you decide to use something in your draft. For leads on finding Web discussion groups on your topic, visit the following sites:

- **Google Groups,** http://groups.google.com, allows you to search for online discussion groups on virtually any topic.
- **Yahoo Groups** offers a similar service, allowing you to search for groups by keyword. Find it at http://groups.yahoo.com.
- **Catalist,** the official catalog of electronic mailing lists, http://www.lsoft.com/lists/listref.html, has a database of about 15,000 discussion groups.

One of the most useful things you can do to prepare for the draft is to spend forty-five minutes at the campus library searching for new information on your topic. Consider expanding your search from current newspapers and periodicals to books or government publications (see Chapter 11 for more information about searching for government documents). In addition, you can refer to almanacs such as *Infoplease* (http://www.infoplease.com) and the *CIA World Factbook* (http://www.odci.gov/cia/publications/factbook/) as well as statistical information available from sources such as the U.S. Census Bureau's *American Fact Finder* (http://factfinder.census.gov/home/saff/main.html?_lang=en), which is a wonderful resource that draws on the agency's massive database of information on U.S. trends.

Composing the Draft

As always, it's best to work from abundance rather than scarcity. If you don't have enough evidence to support your argument, find more. But if you're feeling reasonably well prepared to develop your argument essay from a sketch (or proposal) to a longer draft, then begin by crafting a strong lead. There are so many ways to begin an essay like this one; which is best? As always, think of a beginning that might not only interest your readers in your topic but also hints at or states your purpose in writing about it. Through tone, your beginning also establishes your relationship with your readers. Here's instructor Andrew Merton's lead in "The Guys Are Dumbing Down," a piece that argues that students' baseball caps in class indicate something other than studiousness.

Here is the big social note from the campus of the University of New Hampshire, where I teach: Dumbing down is in. For guys.

Merton's tone is a strong element of this lead. He begins casually—"Here is the big social note…"—suggesting some friendly, almost chatty relationship with his readers. This lead also does what many argument essay beginnings do: It states the writer's main claim. You may assume it is always required to state your thesis in your introduction, but this isn't true at all. Some argument essays, especially op-ed pieces, have a delayed thesis, in which the writer works methodically toward his or her point. Which approach should you use in your draft? In part, that depends on your method of development.

Methods of Development. What are some of the ways you might organize the next draft?

Narrative. Telling a story is an underrated way of developing an argument. Can you imagine a way to turn your topic into an extended story, perhaps by focusing on the experience of a particular person or group of people, in a particular place, at a particular time? Somehow the story must be logically linked to your claim; obviously, just any old story won't do.

There are other ways to use narrative, too. Anecdotes, or brief stories used to illustrate an idea or a problem, are frequently used in argument essays. One effective way to begin your essay might be to tell a story that highlights the problem you're writing about or the question you're posing.

Question to Answer. Almost all writing is an attempt to answer a question. In the personal essay and other open forms of inquiry, the writer may never arrive at a definite answer, but an argument essay usually offers an answer. An obvious method of development, therefore, is to begin your essay by raising the question and end it by offering your answer.

Are there several key questions around which you might organize your draft, leading to your central claim at the end?

Problem to Solution. This is a variation on the question-to-answer structure. But it might be a particularly useful organization strategy if you're writing about a topic readers may know very little about. In that case, you might need to spend as much time establishing what exactly the problem is—explaining what makes it a problem and why the reader should care about it—as you do offering your particular solution.

Effect to Cause or Cause to Effect. At the heart of some arguments is the *relationship* between two things, and often what is at issue is pinpointing the real causes for certain undesirable effects. Once these causes are identified, then the best solutions can be offered. Sadly, we know the effects of terrorism, but what are its causes? If you argue, as some do, that Islamic radicalism arose in response to U.S. policies toward Israel and the Palestinians, then the solution offered might be a shift in foreign policy. The international debate over global warming, for some participants, is really an argument about causes and effects. If you don't believe, for example, that U.S. contributions to atmospheric carbon dioxide in the next ten years will match contributions from the developing world, then the U.S. refusal to sign the Kyoto treaty—one proposed solution—may not matter that much. Some arguments like these can be organized simply around an examination of causes and effects.

Combining Approaches. As you think about how you might organize your first draft, you don't necessarily have to choose between narrative, problem-to-solution, or cause-to-effect structures. In fact, most often they work well together.

Using Evidence. All writing relies on evidence, usually some specific information in relationships with general ideas (see the "Inquiring into the Details: What Evidence Can Do" box). Evidence in an argumentative essay often has a *particular* relationship to ideas; most often it is offered to support ideas the writer wants the reader to believe. What *kind* of evidence to include is a rhetorical question. To whom are you writing, and what kind of evidence will they be more likely to believe? Generally speaking, the narrower and more specialized the audience, the more particular they will be about the types of evidence they'll find convincing.

For example, as you write more academic papers in your chosen major, the types of evidence that will help you make a persuasive argument will be more and more prescribed by the field. In the natural sciences, the results of quantitative studies count more than case studies; in the humanities, primary texts count more than secondary ones. The important thing for this argument essay, which you're writing for a more general audience, is that you attempt to *vary* your evidence. Rather than relying exclusively on anecdotes, include some quotes from an expert as well.

INQUIRING INTO THE DETAILS

What Evidence Can Do

Usually we think of using evidence only to support an idea or claim we're making. But evidence can be used in other ways, too. For example, it can do the following:

- *support* an idea, observation, or assertion
- *refute* or challenge a claim with which you disagree
- *show* that a seemingly simple assertion, problem, or idea is really more complex
- *complicate* or even contradict an earlier point you've made
- *contrast* two or more ways of seeing the same thing
- *test* an idea, hypothesis, or theory

Workshopping the Draft

If your draft is subject to peer review, see Chapter 14 for details on how to organize workshop groups and decide on how your group can help you. The following journal activities and questions should help you make the most of your opportunity to get peer feedback on your work in progress.

Reflecting on the Draft. After you've finished the draft, prepare for peer review by making a journal entry that explores your experience writing the essay.

- What proved hardest?
- What most surprised you about the process?
- What did you find particularly gratifying? What was especially frustrating?
- How did your process for writing this type of essay differ from writing the personal essay or some other form?
- If you were going to start all over again, what would you do differently?

Discuss the insights that might have emerged from this open-ended writing in class or in your workshop group. After your draft has been discussed, make some notes in your journal in response to the following questions:

- What most surprised you about your group's response to your essay?
- What did you hear that most made you want to write again?
- What specifically do you think you need to do in the next draft?

Questions for Readers. Here are some questions that might prompt members of your workshop group to offer helpful advice on your argument draft.

1. What was the most interesting part of the draft? What was the least interesting?
2. What did you believe about my topic before you read the draft? What did you believe after you read it?
3. What reason most strongly supported my main point? What reason seemed the weakest?
4. What was the most convincing evidence I offered? What was the least convincing?

Revising the Draft

Revision is a continual process—not a last step. You've been revising—literally "re-seeing" your subject—from the first messy fastwriting in your journal. But the things that get your attention during revision vary depending on where you are in the writing process. You've generated material, chosen a topic, done some research, and written both a sketch and draft. Most students think that the only thing left to do is "fix things." Check for misspellings. Correct an awkward

WRITING IN THE DISCIPLINES

Argument in Academic Disciplines

Arguing is the main way that academic communities make knowledge. While the process for developing and making an argument can be applied in any discipline, the types of evidence and the forms of arguments can vary widely from one discipline to another. Knowing what kind of knowledge is valued in a particular discipline can help you to shape effective academic arguments as you move from subject to subject throughout your college career.

Discipline	Common Types of Argument	Valued Evidence
humanities	interpretive essays textual analyses reviews formal arguments	textual details personal observations and experience historical background personal insights biographical evidence about authors and creators ethnographic (small-scale) studies
social sciences	causal analyses historical trends projections about effects of policies	demographics and statistics research data large-scale studies interviews
natural sciences	lab reports experimental studies	experimental data quantitative data visual information
applied sciences	feasibility reports recommendations and proposals	quantitative data research data field research findings firsthand observations
business	proposals	case studies survey data

sentence or two. Come up with a better title. This is editing, not revision, and while editing is important, to focus solely on smaller "fixes" after writing a first draft squanders an opportunity to really *learn* from what the draft is telling you, or perhaps not quite telling you.

GUIDE TO REVISION STRATEGIES

Problems in the Draft (Chapter 13)	Page Number
Unclear purpose ■ Not sure what the paper is about?	551
Unclear thesis, theme, or main idea ■ Not sure what you're trying to say?	557
Lack of information or development ■ Need more convincing evidence? Need to check for logical fallacies?	564
Disorganized ■ Doesn't move logically or smoothly from paragraph to paragraph?	568
Unclear or awkward at the level of sentences and paragraphs ■ Seems choppy or hard to follow at the level of sentences or paragraphs?	577

Chapter 13 can help guide these discoveries. The questions you can ask about a draft fall into five categories: purpose, idea, information, development, and editing. Use the Guide to Revision Strategies chart above to find the revision strategies in Chapter 13 that might help you re-see what you've written so far.

Draft argument essays have some typical problems at this stage in the process. Do any of these apply to yours?

- Is your central claim or thesis stated clearly?
- Do you employ any logical fallacies? See "Inquiring into the Details: Common Logical Fallacies."
- Do you have sufficient evidence or information to make your assertions convincing? Do you need to gather more facts?
- Have you considered any counterarguments in your essay? This is especially important if you think the audience for your essay might not be inclined to initially agree with your position.
- Have you clearly established what stake your readers have in the issue you're writing about?
- Does the draft use *pathos, logos*, and *ethos* effectively? (See Figure 7.1.)

Polishing the Draft

After you've dealt with the big issues in your draft—is it sufficiently focused, does it answer the *So what?* question, is it well organized, and so on—you must deal with the smaller problems. You've carved the stone into an appealing figure, but now you need to polish it. Are your paragraphs coherent? How do you manage transitions? Are your sentences fluent and concise? Are there any errors in spelling or syntax? Part 5 of Chapter 13 can help you focus on these issues.

Before you finish your draft, work through the following checklist:

✓ Every paragraph is about one thing.

✓ The transitions between paragraphs aren't abrupt.

✓ The length of sentences varies in each paragraph.

✓ Each sentence is concise. There are no unnecessary words or phrases.

✓ You've checked grammar, particularly verb agreement, run-on sentences, unclear pronouns, and misused words (*there/their, where/were*, and so on). (See the handbook at the back of the book for help with these grammar issues.)

✓ You've run your spellchecker and proofed your paper for misspelled words.

■ STUDENT ESSAY

Many Americans are fond of talking about our country's native people in the past tense. We admire the tribal cultures as they existed a century or two ago, and borrow freely from them, engaging in "vision quests" and drumming circles. We feel the tug of nostalgia for these lost tribes, and yes, guilt for the sad history of relations between the mostly white immigrants who dispossessed the tribes and the Indian people who were confined to reservations. It's convenient to assume that the problems were in the past because contemporary Native Americans are largely invisible to us—except if you happen to drive through a reservation as Kelly Sundberg would on her way to visit friends at a nearby university.

Confronting Native Americans in the present tense forced Kelly to examine her own prejudices, and in the essay that follows she argues that the route to understanding begins at school.

I Am Not a Savage

Kelly Sundberg

1   Salmon, Idaho, is named after the river that runs through it, a river that is filled with turbulent whitewater punctuated by deep and calm pools and shallow riffles. In the spring, I have looked into these riffles and seen waves of silver and red moving gently just underneath the surface of the water.

2   We call them "reds"—spawning salmon. Nowadays, they are diminished in numbers, but at one time the river was full of them, and full of abundance as well for the

Lemhi Indians who once lived on the banks. For the Lemhi, the salmon was not solely for sustenance, but also an integral part of their culture and spirituality.

Today there are few "reds" and almost no Lemhi left in the valley.   3

The initial influx of Mormon settlers followed by migrations of Californians and Midwesterners forced Native Americans out of the valley. Still, upon entering the Salmon city limits from Highway 28, a large sign proclaims, "Welcome to Salmon, Idaho. Birthplace of Sacagawea!" In a time when anything related to Lewis and Clark means profit, the city of Salmon, my hometown, has now chosen to capitalize on this marketable heritage, even though they once ignored it or treated it derisively.   4

My high school mascot is the "Salmon Savage." The marquee in front of the school has   5
a picture with an Indian warrior on it, and when the football team scores a touchdown a white girl wearing war paint and a "made in China" headdress will ride a horse around the track in celebration.

I never questioned the integrity or intent of these symbols until I was a sophomore at   6
the school. For Civil Rights Day, the school invited Rosa Abrahamson, a Lemhi Indian, to speak to the students. She cried as she spoke about the injustice of the name "savage." "My people are not savages," she said. "We are peaceful and do not take pride in that name." When she finished speaking the applause was polite but subdued.

The next speaker was a rancher named Bud, who lit into a tirade about the govern-   7
ment subsidizing "lazy Indians." As he finished with fists raised into the air, he was greeted by a standing ovation. For the first time in my life, I felt ashamed to be a part of the community.

It wasn't that those of us in the gym had consciously made the decision to be racist. It   8
was simply ignorance. Despite the history of the Lemhi in the valley, our ideas of their culture are shaped from drives through the reservation on the way to campus visits at the University of Idaho. Our perceptions were safely gleaned from inside of an automobile and never involved real interaction with Native Americans.

Once, when asked to write our opinions about reservations in a U.S. government class,   9
I wrote that I thought the government was making it "too easy on the Native Americans and they had become apathetic and unmotivated because of subsidies."

I got a better glimpse at my Lemhi neighbors recently reading Sherman Alexie's   10
novel *The Lone Ranger and Tonto Fistfight in Heaven*. Alexie, a member of the Spokane/ Coeur d'Alene tribes, conveys the opposition between contemporary and traditional Native American culture. His characters are torn and struggle to reconcile the two: "At the halfway point of any drunken night, there is a moment when an Indian realizes he cannot turn back toward tradition and that he has no map to guide him toward the future."

My own community struggles to reconcile two conflicting ideas as well—we embrace   11
the symbols of savagery to inspire the football team, yet in order to make a profit we proudly claim Sacagawea as one of our own. Still, when the Lemhi wanted to build a school near Sacagawea's birthplace, the county refused to sell them the land, claiming it would become a "mini-reservation."

(continued)

(continued)

12   Ironically, Salmon shares more than it cares to admit with its neighbors on the reservation. Poverty, alcoholism, and depression are a way of life for many Salmon residents. Yet the perception in the community is that an alcoholic white man is somehow superior to a "drunk Indian."

13   In Salmon, all students are required to take an Idaho history class, yet this class makes almost no mention of Native American history in the valley. None of the readings in Advanced Placement English classes are by Native American authors, and government classes don't address Native American issues at all.

14   Is it any wonder that racism persists?

15   The local school system needs to lead. English teachers should require readings by authors like Alexie, they should provide field trips to local and national archeological sites, and they should bring in Native American interpreters to speak about local history. By letting go of negative and outdated ideas, the city of Salmon and the Lemhi can take the first step toward healing.

Evaluating the Essay

Discuss or write about your response to Kelly Sundberg's essay using some or all of the following questions:

1. What is the thesis of the essay? Where in the piece is it most clearly stated?

2. Refer to the box that lists ten common logical fallacies and reread Sundberg's essay. Do you suspect there are any logical fallacies in "I Am Not a Savage"?

3. Consider the *ethos* of this essay. How does the writer come across? Is her persona effective?

4. What do you think is the most effective paragraph in the essay? Why? What is the least effective?

USING WHAT YOU HAVE LEARNED

You've read published op-ed essays and a student draft. You've also worked on your own argument essay, a genre that may be new to you. Take a moment to consider how you might use what you've learned.

1. Reflect on how your thinking about argument and argumentative writing may have changed because of the reading and writing in this chapter by finishing the following sentence in your journal at least four times: Before I began this chapter I thought _____, but now I think _____.

2. The personal essay (discussed in Chapter 3) and the argument essay might seem at first to be fundamentally different kinds of writing. Do you see any connections between the two genres now?

3. Examine the letters to the editor or the editorials in your local newspaper. How do you read these pages differently after studying and writing an argument? Clip a letter or editorial that might best demonstrate what you've learned.

stories, and poems can help us slowly unroll the tightly bound threads of feeling—our fears, joys, desires, or sorrows—and help us follow them back to the heart and out into the world. Literature helps us understand ourselves, and in attending to the experiences of others as they are represented in strings of words, we can see how we're delicately tethered to others. Peggy Jordan can see in Butcher's poems that there is a way to grow older that she hadn't yet imagined. But would she have seen this as clearly if she hadn't written about it? I don't think so.

MOTIVES FOR WRITING A CRITICAL ESSAY

By now you understand that writing is a means of thinking and learning, so when your writing comes in contact with the writing of others, the conversation illuminates them both. Sometimes, this dialogue has very personal dimensions. It did for Peggy Jordan because she reread Grace Butcher's poem with an open heart and mind, and because Jordan chose a form of the critical essay—autobiographical criticism—that actively encourages such personal connections. But even more formal critical essays, those that don't involve self-disclosure or first-person writing, can offer personal revelation. After all, what draws you to a certain author, essay, story, or poem is often a feeling, a response that is initially closer to the heart than the head. From there you sustain an intimate encounter with the material, reading closely and reflecting on what it might mean.

It isn't necessary that the story you're writing about be an experience you can relate to, or even about a person anything like you. Reading about different lives, strangely, can help us understand ourselves in unexpected ways. Like a carnival mirror, stories, essays, and poems about others can cause us to reflect on ourselves in ways that make us seem strange, sometimes almost unrecognizable, to ourselves. We see ourselves as others see us. Suddenly, the familiar seems strange.

These are personal reasons for writing about literature, but there are other motives as well. One is that the writing can, simply, help us *understand* what we read and appreciate it much more. You've already practiced methods such as the double-entry journal, in which you create conversations with all kinds of texts—essays, excerpts, and even photographs. When it works, this process helps you figure out what you think and what you might want to say about the thing you're looking at. This is also true when that thing is a literary text, and it becomes even more important to structure these written conversations because what makes texts literary is their complexity.

Most of us are pretty literal, which is why one response to reading, say, a short story is to simply declare, "It's *just a story*! Why do we have to squeeze some deep meaning out of it?" It's a pretty common view that English teachers have created an industry out of squeezing water from stones, of demanding that readers look more deeply at the things they read and consider what might be implied rather than what is explicit. This can be annoying at times, but the intentions are good. To fully appreciate what authors are saying or what effects they're trying to create in an essay, poem, or story, you often need to look closely, and in doing so, you see beyond the obvious. When you make this reading an act of imagination, you consider possible meanings that weren't necessarily immediately apparent. In the conversation between what a text says and what it *might* be saying, you discover fresh understandings of what you read. You share these discoveries by writing about them.

> To fully appreciate what authors are saying or what effects they're trying to create in an essay, poem, or story, you often need to look closely, and in doing so, you see beyond the obvious.

This is not really impersonal, even if you never mention yourself in your essay, because to do this well you need to bring yourself to the encounter. Whatever interpretations or ideas you discover about a poem, story, or essay are shaped by who you are—the personal experiences, the feelings, the dreams, and the ideas—that lead you to notice some things but not others in a text. You imagine in your own particular ways. How productive this is, however, depends on *how* you read and how you use writing to help you understand and interpret texts. The *process* of reading and writing about literary texts, the subject of this chapter, involves a range of choices, something that you can individualize, too.

THE CRITICAL ESSAY AND ACADEMIC WRITING

Summarizing a work, something that made *CliffsNotes* (and now *SparkNotes*) an industry, is a useful activity, and often is a step in the process, but rarely is it the purpose of a critical essay. (One exception to this is the annotated bibliography; see Appendix C for more information about this form.) Most forms of critical essays are organized around *the writer's ideas* about a text.

In that sense, a critical essay is like most of the other inquiry projects we've discussed so far, with one important difference: The main source of information for the writing is a text, usually a work of literature. Yet the process of thinking and writing is much the same with critical essays as it is in a personal essay, an argument, and a review: You begin with questions, explore possible answers, make judgments and interpretations, and offer evidence that supports, qualifies, or complicates your judgments. You apply all the habits of mind we've discussed throughout the book: dialectical thinking, suspending judgment, and so on. In that sense, writing critical essays prepares you for many other kinds of academic writing, especially if it involves working with published texts.

You will encounter various forms of the critical essay mostly in English classes. They might include the following:

- *Short response papers*. As an initial response to reading, you may be asked to write fairly brief analytical, exploratory, or personal responses. These, by our definition, are essentially sketches that may or may not lead to longer essays. Sometimes a response paper focuses on explication of a certain aspect of the essay, poem, or story, like explaining or analyzing use of metaphor or character.

- *Autobiographical criticism.* Personal and sometimes fairly open-ended responses to literary works, such as Peggy Jordan's essay mentioned at the beginning of the chapter, are sometimes encouraged by English instructors. This type of personal criticism makes the critic's emotional relationship to texts explicit, but seeks to illuminate both the writer and the text.

- *Formal critical analysis.* Among the most common forms is the critical essay that makes an argument about the text. Like all other forms, these essays begin with questions: Does Ken Kesey's *One Flew over the Cuckoo's Nest* use Big Nurse as a misogynistic symbol? Does E. B. White's essay "Once More to the Lake" comment on mortality and identity? These critical essays generally offer a central claim or thesis, and then, using the literary text as evidence, try to make that claim or thesis convincing.

FEATURES OF THE FORM

Although the critical essay can exhibit considerable variation, there are some common conventions. These include the following:

- *The text is the most important source of information.* Usually everything must be anchored firmly to the text you're writing about or things (letters, interviews, and so on) the writer has said about it.

- *Most critical essays make an argument.* Critical essays are built around a main idea, claim, or interpretation you are making about a text. The arguments you make frequently focus on a problem or pattern in the work (e.g., you notice a relationship between references in a story to wilderness and images of evil). What doesn't quite fit or is puzzling? What elements are repeated?

- *What has already been said often forms the context for the writer's question.* Typically a critical essay initially establishes what other critics have claimed about the aspect of the essay, poem, or story on which the writer is focusing. These other sources provide the context for putting forward your own take on the question, and establish the ongoing conversation (if any) about the writer or the work.

> Critical essays are built around a main idea, claim, or interpretation you are making about a text.

- *Most critical essays assume readers are not familiar with the text.* Unless the literary work is extremely well known, critics generally assume that an audience needs to have its memory refreshed. That means that there may be some background information on the essay, story, or poem, and possibly on the author and his or her other similar works. Frequently this means adding a summary of the story or background on the poem or novel.

READINGS

■ SHORT STORY 1

This is an unusual and troubling story. It's not troubling in the usual way, though. There isn't a character with whom we sympathize who must endure some sadness. There isn't an unexpected accident or death. On the contrary, the story seems to be about happiness. Ursula Le Guin's "The Ones Who Walk Away from Omelas" is also unusual because it reads like a fable that the narrator seems desperate for the reader to believe.

You will also notice reading Le Guin's story that it is, in some ways, structured like a nonfiction essay, moving back and forth from the main narrative and reflection on how that narrative might be understood. But like much fiction, themes in "The Ones Who Walk Away from Omelas" are ambiguous. What could this story be saying about "the terms" that we must accept to be happy?

The Ones Who Walk Away from Omelas
Ursula Le Guin

With a clamor of bells that set the swallows soaring, the Festival of Summer came to the city Omelas, bright-towered by the sea. The rigging of the boats in harbor sparkled with flags. In the streets between houses with red roofs and painted walls, between old moss-grown gardens and under avenues of trees, past great parks and public buildings, processions moved. Some were decorous: old people in long stiff robes of mauve and grey, grave master workmen, quiet, merry women carrying their babies and chatting as they walked. In other streets the music beat faster, a shimmering of gong and tambourine, and the people went dancing, the procession was a dance. Children dodged in and out, their high calls rising like the swallows crossing flights over the music and the singing. All the processions wound towards the north side of the city, where on the great water-meadow called the Green Fields boys and girls, naked in the bright air, with mud-stained feet and ankles and long, lithe arms, exercised their restive horses before the race. The horses wore no gear at all but a halter without bit. Their manes were braided with streamers of silver, gold, and green. They flared their nostrils and pranced and boasted to one another; they were vastly excited, the horse being the only animal who has adopted our ceremonies as his own. Far off to the north and west the mountains stood up half encircling Omelas on her bay. The air of morning was so clear that the snow still crowning the Eighteen Peaks burned with white-gold fire across the miles of sunlit

(continued)

(continued)

air, under the dark blue of the sky. There was just enough wind to make the banners that marked the racecourse snap and flutter now and then. In the silence of the broad green meadows one could hear the music winding through the city streets, farther and nearer and ever approaching, a cheerful faint sweetness of the air that from time to time trembled and gathered together and broke out into the great joyous clanging of the bells.

2   Joyous! How is one to tell about joy? How describe the citizens of Omelas?

3   They were not simple folk, you see, though they were happy. But we do not say the words of cheer much any more. All smiles have become archaic. Given a description such as this one tends to make certain assumptions. Given a description such as this one tends to look next for the King, mounted on a splendid stallion and surrounded by his noble knights, or perhaps in a golden litter borne by great-muscled slaves. But there was no king. They did not use swords, or keep slaves. They were not barbarians. I do not know the rules and laws of their society, but I suspect that they were singularly few. As they did without monarchy and slavery, so they also got on without the stock exchange, the advertisement, the secret police, and the bomb. Yet I repeat that these were not simple folk, not dulcet shepherds, noble savages, bland utopians. They were not less complex than us. The trouble is that we have a bad habit, encouraged by pedants and sophisticates, of considering happiness as something rather stupid. Only pain is intellectual, only evil interesting. This is the treason of the artist: a refusal to admit the banality of evil and the terrible boredom of pain. If you can't lick 'em, join 'em. If it hurts, repeat it. But to praise despair is to condemn delight, to embrace violence is to lose hold of everything else. We have almost lost hold; we can no longer describe a happy man, nor make any celebration of joy. How can I tell you about the people of Omelas? They were not naive and happy children—though their children were, in fact, happy. They were mature, intelligent, passionate adults whose lives were not wretched. O miracle! but I wish I could describe it better. I wish I could convince you. Omelas sounds in my words like a city in a fairy tale, long ago and far away, once upon a time. Perhaps it would be best if you imagined it as your own fancy bids, assuming it will rise to the occasion, for certainly I cannot suit you all. For instance, how about technology? I think that there would be no cars or helicopters in and above the streets; this follows from the fact that the people of Omelas are happy people. Happiness is based on a just discrimination of what is necessary, what is neither necessary nor destructive, and what is destructive. In the middle category, however—that of the unnecessary but undestructive, that of comfort, luxury, exuberance, etc.—they could perfectly well have central heating, subway trains, washing machines, and all kinds of marvelous devices not yet invented here, floating light-sources, fuelless power, a cure for the common cold. Or they could have none of that; it doesn't matter. As you like it. I incline to think that people from towns up and down the coast have been coming in to Omelas during the last days before the Festival on very fast little trains and double-decked trams, and

that the train station of Omelas is actually the handsomest building in town, though plainer than the magnificent Farmers Market. But even granted trains, I fear that Omelas so far strikes some of you as goody-goody. Smiles, bells, parades, horses, bleh. If so, please add an orgy. If an orgy would help, don't hesitate. Let us not, however, have temples from which issue beautiful nude priests and priestesses already half in ecstasy and ready to copulate with any man or woman, lover or stranger, who desires union with the deep godhead of the blood, although that was my first idea. But really it would be better not to have any temples in Omelas—at least, not manned temples. Religion yes, clergy no. Surely the beautiful nudes can just wander about, offering themselves like divine soufflés to the hunger of the needy and the rapture of the flesh. Let them join the processions. Let tambourines be struck above the copulations, and the glory of desire be proclaimed upon the gongs, and (a not unimportant point) let the offspring of these delightful rituals be beloved and looked after by all. One thing I know there is none of in Omelas is guilt. But what else should there be? I thought at first there were not drugs, but that is puritanical. For those who like it, the faint insistent sweetness of *drooz* may perfume the ways of the city, *drooz* which first brings a great lightness and brilliance to the mind and limbs, and then after some hours a dreamy languor, and wonderful visions at last of the very arcana and inmost secrets of the Universe, as well as exciting the pleasure of sex beyond belief; and it is not habit-forming. For more modest tastes I think there ought to be beer. What else, what else belongs in the joyous city? The sense of victory, surely, the celebration of courage. But as we did without clergy, let us do without soldiers. The joy built upon successful slaughter is not the right kind of joy; it will not do; it is fearful and it is trivial. A boundless and generous contentment, a magnanimous triumph felt not against some outer enemy but in communion with the finest and fairest in the souls of all men everywhere and the splendor of the world's summer: this is what swells the hearts of the people of Omelas, and the victory they celebrate is that of life. I really don't think many of them need to take *drooz*.

Most of the procession have reached the Green Fields by now. A marvelous smell   4
of cooking goes forth from the red and blue tents of the provisioners. The faces of small children are amiably sticky; in the benign grey beard of a man a couple of crumbs of rich pastry are entangled. The youths and girls have mounted their horses and are beginning to group around the starting line of the course. An old women, small, fat, and laughing, is passing out flowers from a basket, and tall young men wear her flowers in their shining hair. A child of nine or ten sits at the edge of the crowd, alone, playing on a wooden flute. People pause to listen, and they smile, but they do not speak to him, for he never ceases playing and never sees them, his dark eyes wholly rapt in the sweet, thin magic of the tune.

He finishes, and slowly lowers his hands holding the wooden flute.   5

As if that little private silence were the signal, all at once a trumpet sounds from the   6
pavilion near the starting line: imperious, melancholy, piercing. The horses rear on their
(continued)

(continued)

slender legs, and some of them neigh in answer. Sober-faced, the young riders stroke the horses' necks and soothe them, whispering, "Quiet, quiet, there my beauty, my hope...." They begin to form in rank along the starting line. The crowds along the racecourse are like a field of grass and flowers in the wind. The Festival of Summer has begun.

7   Do you believe? Do you accept the festival, the city, the joy? No? Then let me describe one more thing.

8   In a basement under one of the beautiful public buildings of Omelas, or perhaps in the cellar of one of its spacious private homes, there is a room. It has one locked door, and no window. A little light seeps in dustily between cracks in the boards, secondhand from a cobwebbed window somewhere across the cellar. In one corner of the little room a couple of mops, with stiff, clotted, foul-smelling heads stand near a rusty bucket. The floor is dirt, a little damp to the touch, as cellar dirt usually is. The room is about three paces long and two wide: a mere broom closet or disused tool room. In the room a child is sitting. It could be a boy or a girl. It looks about six, but actually is nearly ten. It is feeble-minded. Perhaps it was born defective, or perhaps it has become imbecile through fear, malnutrition, and neglect. It picks its nose and occasionally fumbles vaguely with its toes or genitals, as it sits hunched in the corner farthest from the bucket and the two mops. It is afraid of the mops. It finds them horrible. It shuts its eyes, but it knows the mops are still standing there; and the door is locked; and nobody will come. The door is always locked; and nobody ever comes, except that sometimes—the child has no understanding of time or interval—sometimes the door rattles terribly and opens, and a person, or several people, are there. One of them may come in and kick the child to make it stand up. The others never come close, but peer in at it with frightened, disgusted eyes. The food bowl and the water jug are hastily filled, the door is locked, the eyes disappear. The people at the door never say anything, but the child, who has not always lived in the tool room, and can remember sunlight and its mother's voice, sometimes speaks. "I will be good," it says. "Please let me out. I will be good!" They never answer. The child used to scream for help at night, and cry a good deal, but now it only makes a kind of whining, "eh-haa, eh-haa," and it speaks less and less often. It is so thin there are no calves to its legs; its belly protrudes; it lives on a half-bowl of corn meal and grease a day. It is naked. Its buttocks and thighs are a mass of festered sores, as it sits in its own excrement continually.

9   They all know it is there, all the people of Omelas. Some of them have come to see it, others are content merely to know it is there. They all know that it has to be there. Some of them understand why, and some do not, but they all understand that their happiness, the beauty of their city, the tenderness of their friendship, the health of their children, the wisdom of their scholars, the skill of their makers, even the abundance of their harvest and the kindly weathers of their skies, depend wholly on this child's abominable misery.

10   This is usually explained to children when they are between eight and twelve, whenever they seem capable of understanding; and most of those who come to see the child are young people, though often enough an adult comes, or comes back, to see the child. No matter how well the matter has been explained to them, these young spectators are

always shocked and sickened at the sight. They feel disgust, which they had thought themselves superior to. They feel anger, outrage, impotence, despite all the explanations. They would like to do something for the child. But there is nothing they can do. If the child were brought up into the sunlight out of that vile place, if it were cleaned and fed and comforted, that would be a good thing indeed; but if it were done, in that day and hour all the prosperity and beauty and delight of Omelas would wither and be destroyed. Those are the terms. To exchange all the goodness and grace of every life in Omelas for that single, small improvement: to throw away the happiness of thousands for the chance of the happiness of one: that would be to let guilt within the walls indeed.

The terms are strict and absolute; there may not even be a kind word spoken to   11
the child.

Often the young people go home in tears, or in a tearless rage, when they have   12
seen the child and faced this terrible paradox. They may brood over it for weeks or years. But as time goes on they begin to realize that even if the child could be released, it would not get much good of its freedom: a little vague pleasure of warmth and food, no doubt, but little more. It is too degraded and imbecile to know any real joy. It has been afraid too long ever to be free of fear. Its habits are too uncouth for it to respond to humane treatment. Indeed, after so long it would probably be wretched without walls about it to protect it, and darkness for its eyes, and its own excrement to sit in. Their tears at the bitter injustice dry when they begin to perceive the terrible justice of reality, and to accept it. Yet it is their tears and anger, the trying of their generosity and the acceptance of their helplessness, which are perhaps the true source of the splendor of their lives. Theirs is no vapid, irresponsible happiness. They know that they, like the child, are not free. They know compassion. It is the existence of the child, and their knowledge of its existence, that makes possible the nobility of their architecture, the poignancy of their music, the profundity of their science. It is because of the child that they are so gentle with children. They know that if the wretched one were not there sniveling in the dark, the other one, the flute-player, could make no joyful music as the young riders line up in their beauty for the race in the sunlight of the first morning of summer.

Now do you believe in them? Are they not more credible? But there is one more   13
thing to tell, and this is quite incredible.

At times one of the adolescent girls or boys who go to see the child does not go   14
home to weep or rage, does not, in fact, go home at all. Sometimes also a man or woman much older falls silent for a day or two, and then leaves home. These people go out into the street, and walk down the street alone. They keep walking, and walk straight out of the city of Omelas, through the beautiful gates. They keep walking across the farmlands of Omelas. Each one goes alone, youth or girl, man or woman. Night falls; the traveler must pass down village streets, between the houses with yellow-lit windows, and on out into the darkness of the fields. Each alone, they go west or north, towards the mountains. They go on. They leave Omelas, they walk ahead into the darkness, and they do not come back. The place they go towards is a place even less imaginable to most of us than the city of happiness. I cannot describe it at all. It is possible that it does not exist. But they seem to know where they are going, the ones who walk away from Omelas.

Inquiring into the Story

Explore, explain, evaluate, and reflect on Le Guin's "The Ones Who Walk Away from Omelas."

1. Works of fiction are often implicit. Some stories don't tell you what to think or what the author is trying to say. There are many possibilities. That's one reason why, at least initially, exploring is an important method of inquiry in a critical response. This exploration is most productive if it doesn't stray from the evidence—specific scenes, characters, images, and lines in the story itself. The double-entry journal is invaluable for this kind of work. Reread the story and, when you do, copy key passages on the left page of your notebook. These are passages that seem important as you grope to understand the story. On the right-facing page, fastwrite in an open-ended way about what you collected and what it might mean.

2. Omelas is a happy place, or so it seems. But there is a "wretched" child, condemned to a dirt cellar, whose suffering "makes possible the nobility of [Omelas's] architecture, the poignancy of their music, the profundity of their science." Based on your understanding of the story, explain how this can be.

3. Working with ideas you generated in your journal from the previous questions, develop an interpretation of Le Guin's story using the following sentence as a template for your inquiry question: What is the relationship between _____ and _____ in Ursula Le Guin's "The Ones Who Walk Away from Omelas"? Use this question to work toward a thesis.

4. When you're reading fiction, do you mark up the text? If so, how? Is there some kind of code you use to signal the significance of what you mark? Do you mark up fiction the way you mark up nonfiction?

ONE STUDENT'S RESPONSE

Bernice's Double-Entry Journal

"There was just enough wind to make the banners that marked the race-course snap and flutter now and then. In the silence of the broad green meadows one could hear the music winding through the city streets, farther and nearer and ever approaching, a cheerful faint sweetness of the air that from time to time trembled and gathered together and broke out into the great joyous clanging of the bells."

The setting of this immediately brings to mind castles and old English. I wonder why Le Guin builds this setting, with "broad green meadows" and "joyous clanging of bells" only to tell us in the next few lines that this place isn't what it seems? Is she trying to break down our preconceived notions, dispel our assumption right off the bat?

"They were not barbarians. I do not know the rules and laws of their society, but I suspect that they were singularly few. As they did without monarchy and slavery, so they also got on without the stock exchange, the advertisement, the secret police, and the bomb. Yet I repeat that these were not simple folk, not dulcet shepherds, noble savages, bland utopians. They were not less complex than us."

"One thing I know there is none of in Omelas is guilt. But what else should there be? I thought at first there were not drugs, but that is puritanical. For those who like it, the faint insistent sweetness of *drooz* may perfume the ways of the city, *drooz* which first brings a great lightness and brilliance to the mind and limbs, and then after some hours a dreamy languor, and wonderful visions"

"Do you believe? Do you accept the festival, the city, the joy? No? Then let me describe one more thing."

"In the room a child is sitting. It could be a boy or a girl. It looks about six, but actually is nearly ten. It is feeble-minded. Perhaps it was born defective, or perhaps it has become imbecile through fear, malnutrition, and neglect. It picks its nose and occasionally fumbles vaguely with its toes or genitals, as it sits hunched in the corner farthest from the bucket and the two mops. It is afraid of the mops. It finds them horrible. It shuts its eyes, but it knows the mops are still standing there; and the door is locked; and nobody will come."

I like this idea of these people being "like us" yet not like us. Being happy but not simple, joyous but not childlike. It's intriguing since so often we assume that happiness can only come at the price of Knowledge. After all Adam and Eve were happy until they ate the fruit of the tree of knowledge, and mankind was content until Prometheus lit the fire. It's a common thread in human mythology that knowledge brings pain.

It's interesting that it's guilt and not sin that Le Guin removes from her society. Why guilt? Why not hate, or lust, or murder, or fear? What does the lack of guilt have to do with contentment and joy?

No I don't, I don't trust human nature enough to believe this place of warm joy and contentment. Something is missing, that lizard brain bit of humanity that bites and claws and kills for pleasure seems to be missing in this place.

And now I believe it. Perhaps it's my lack of faith (something Le Guin is driving at?) in humanity. I can believe this place exists, and that people allow it to exist for the price of a single human, a child, an innocent with no voice or choice. I can believe that.

(continued)

> **One Student's Response** (*continued*)
>
> "Each alone, they go west or north, towards the mountains. They go on. They leave Omelas, they walk ahead into the darkness, and they do not come back. The place they go towards is a place even less imaginable to most of us than the city of happiness. I cannot describe it at all. It is possible that it does not exist. But they seem to know where they are going, the ones who walk away from Omelas."
>
> I guess that sometimes comfort and contentment just isn't enough to combat the realities of a child being an entire society's whipping boy. There are always those who simply will not accept that type of exchange. But is there any place to go?

■ SHORT STORY 2

Leslie Marmon Silko was raised on the Laguna Pueblo reservation in New Mexico, a place she came to understand more fully through stories that were told to her by her father, her aunt, and her grandmother. The storytelling tradition, much of it oral rather than written, is often a powerful element in Native American tribes, preserving certain ways of knowing and helping members recognize their connection to the community. But these stories are living things, adapting and changing to reflect tribal members' struggles to adjust to an often hostile world. They can even be a source of healing, as in the short story "Lullaby," which you're about to read here.

Silko is widely recognized as one of the finest living Native American writers, and her novel *Ceremony*, published in 1977, received critical acclaim. She's also a talented poet and essayist. Above all, Leslie Marmon Silko is a storyteller in the Laguna tradition, using a kind of narrative that in many ways will be familiar to nonnative readers. There are characters and scenes and a significant event, but also notice how landscape figures into the telling of this story, and in particular what the narrator's relationship is with the natural world. One of the motives for telling a story like this is to deal with loss by seeking recovery through balance or harmony. This may not be at all obvious when you read this story, which on the surface is an unrelentingly sad tale. Do you see redemption or perhaps resistance here?

Lullaby

Leslie Marmon Silko

1   The sun had gone down but the snow in the wind gave off its own light. It came in thick tufts like new wool—washed before the weaver spins it. Ayah reached out for it like her own babies had, and she smiled when she remembered how she had

laughed at them. She was an old woman now, and her life had become memories. She sat down with her back against the wide cottonwood tree, feeling the rough bark on her back bones; she faced east and listened to the wind and snow sing a high-pitched Yeibechei song. Out of the wind she felt warmer, and she could watch the wide fluffy snow fill in her tracks, steadily, until the direction she had come from was gone. By the light of the snow she could see the dark outline of the big arroyo a few feet away. She was sitting on the edge of Cebolleta Creek, where in the springtime the thin cows would graze on a grass already chewed flat to the ground. In the wide deep creek bed where only a trickle of water flowed in the summer, the skinny cows would wander, looking for new grass along winding paths splashed with manure.

Ayah pulled the old Army blanket over her head like a shawl. Jimmie's   2
blanket—the one he had sent to her. That was a long time ago and the green wool was faded, and it was unraveling on the edges. She did not want to think about Jimmie. So she thought about the weaving and the way her mother had done it. On the tall wooden loom set into the sand under a tamarack tree for shade. She could see it clearly. She had been only a little girl when her grandma gave her the wooden combs to pull the twigs and burrs from the raw, freshly washed wool. And while she combed the wool, her grandma sat beside her, spinning a silvery strand of yarn around the smooth cedar spindle. Her mother worked at the loom with yarns dyed bright yellow and red and gold. She watched them dye the yarn in boiling black pots full of beeweed petals, juniper berries, and sage. The blankets her mother made were soft and woven so tight that rain rolled off them like birds' feathers. Ayah remembered sleeping warm on cold windy nights, wrapped in her mother's blankets on the hogan's sandy floor.

The snow drifted now, with the northwest wind hurling it in gusts. It drifted up   3
around her black overshoes—old ones with little metal buckles. She smiled at the snow which was trying to cover her little by little. She could remember when they had no black rubber overshoes; only the high buckskin leggings that they wrapped over their elkhide moccasins. If the snow was dry or frozen, a person could walk all day and not get wet; and in the evenings the beams of the ceiling would hang with lengths of pale buckskin leggings, drying out slowly.

She felt peaceful remembering. She didn't feel cold any more. Jimmie's blanket   4
seemed warmer than it had ever been. And she could remember the morning he was born. She could remember whispering to her mother, who was sleeping on the other side of the hogan, to tell her it was time now. She did not want to wake the others. The second time she called to her, her mother stood up and pulled on her shoes; she knew. They walked to the old stone hogan together, Ayah walking a step behind her mother. She waited alone, learning the rhythms of the pains while her mother went to call the old woman to help them. The morning was already warm even before dawn and Ayah smelled the bee flowers blooming and the young willow growing at the springs. She could remember that so clearly, but his birth merged into the births of the other children and to her it became all the same birth. They named him for the summer morning and in English they called him Jimmie.

(continued)

(continued)

5   It wasn't like Jimmie died. He just never came back, and one day a dark blue sedan with white writing on its doors pulled up in front of the boxcar shack where the rancher let the Indians live. A man in a khaki uniform trimmed in gold gave them a yellow piece of paper and told them that Jimmie was dead. He said the Army would try to get the body back and then it would be shipped to them; but it wasn't likely because the helicopter had burned after it crashed. All of this was told to Chato because he could understand English. She stood inside the doorway holding the baby while Chato listened. Chato spoke English like a white man and he spoke Spanish too. He was taller than the white man and he stood straighter too. Chato didn't explain why; he just told the military man they could keep the body if they found it. The white man looked bewildered; he nodded his head and he left. Then Chato looked at her and shook his head, and then he told her, "Jimmie isn't coming home anymore," and when he spoke, he used the words to speak of the dead. She didn't cry then, but she hurt inside with anger. And she mourned him as the years passed, when a horse fell with Chato and broke his leg, and the white rancher told them he wouldn't pay Chato until he could work again. She mourned Jimmie because he would have worked for his father then; he would have saddled the big bay horse and ridden the fence lines each day, with wire cutters and heavy gloves, fixing the breaks in the barbed wire and putting the stray cattle back inside again.

6   She mourned him after the white doctors came to take Danny and Ella away. She was at the shack alone that day they came. It was back in the days before they hired Navajo women to go with them as interpreters. She recognized one of the doctors. She had seen him at the children's clinic at Cañoncito about a month ago. They were wearing khaki uniforms and they waved papers at her and a black ball-point pen, trying to make her understand their English words. She was frightened by the way they looked at the children, like the lizard watches the fly. Danny was swinging on the tire swing on the elm tree behind the rancher's house, and Ella was toddling around the front door, dragging the broomstick horse Chato made for her. Ayah could see they wanted her to sign the papers, and Chato had taught her to sign her name. It was something she was proud of. She only wanted them to go, and to take their eyes away from her children.

7   She took the pen from the man without looking at his face and she signed the papers in three different places he pointed to. She stared at the ground by their feet and waited for them to leave. But they stood there and began to point and gesture at the children. Danny stopped swinging. Ayah could see his fear. She moved suddenly and grabbed Ella into her arms; the child squirmed, trying to get back to her toys. Ayah ran with the baby toward Danny; she screamed for him to run and then she grabbed him around his chest and carried him too. She ran south into the foothills of juniper trees and black lava rock. Behind her she heard the doctors running, but they had been taken by surprise, and as the hills became stepper and the cholla cactus were thicker, they stopped. When she reached the top of the hill, she stopped to listen in case they were circling around her. But in a few minutes she heard a car

engine start and they drove away. The children had been too surprised to cry while she ran with them. Danny was shaking and Ella's little fingers were gripping Ayah's blouse.

She stayed up in the hills for the rest of the day, sitting on a black lava boulder in the sunshine where she could see for miles all around her. The sky was light blue and cloudless, and it was warm for late April. The sun warmth relaxed her and took the fear and anger away. She lay back on the rock and watched the sky. It seemed to her that she could walk into the sky, stepping through clouds endlessly. Danny played with little pebbles and stones, pretending they were birds eggs and then little rabbits. Ella sat at her feet and dropped fistfuls of dirt into the breeze, watching the dust and particles of sand intently. Ayah watched a hawk soar high above them, dark wings gliding; hunting or only watching, she did not know. The hawk was patient and he circled all afternoon before he disappeared around the high volcanic peak the Mexicans called Guadalupe.

Late in the afternoon, Ayah looked down at the gray boxcar shack with the paint all peeled from the wood; the stove pipe on the roof was rusted and crooked. The fire she had built that morning in the oil drum stove had burned out. Ella was asleep in her lap now and Danny sat close to her, complaining that he was hungry; he asked when they would go to the house. "We will stay up here until your father comes," she told him, "because those white men were chasing us." The boy remembered then and he nodded at her silently.

If Jimmie had been there he could have read those papers and explained to her what they said. Ayah would have known then, never to sign them. The doctors came back the next day and they brought a BIA policeman with them. They told Chato they had her signature and that was all they needed. Except for the kids. She listened to Chato sullenly; she hated him when he told her it was the old woman who died in the winter, spitting blood; it was her old grandma who had given the children this disease. "They don't spit blood," she said coldly. "The whites lie." She held Ella and Danny close to her, ready to run to the hills again. "I want a medicine man first," she said to Chato, not looking at him. He shook his head. "It's too late now. The policeman is with them. You signed the paper." His voice was gentle.

It was worse than if they had died: to lose the children and to know that somewhere, in a place called Colorado, in a place full of sick and dying strangers, her children were without her. There had been babies that died soon after they were born, and one that died before he could walk. She had carried them herself, up to the boulders and great pieces of the cliff that long ago crashed down from Long Mesa; she laid them in the crevices of sandstone and buried them in fine brown sand with round quartz pebbles that washed down the hills in the rain. She had endured it because they had been with her. But she could not bear this pain. She did not sleep for a long time after they took her children. She stayed on the hill where they had fled the first time, and she slept rolled up in the blanket Jimmie had sent her. She carried the pain in her belly and it was fed by everything she saw: the blue sky of their last

(continued)

(continued)

day together and the dust and pebbles they played with; the swing in the elm tree and broom stick horse choked life from her. The pain filled her stomach and there was no room for food or for her lungs to fill with air. The air and the food would have been theirs.

12   She hated Chato, not because he let the policeman and doctors put the screaming children in the government car, but because he had taught her to sign her name. Because it was like the old ones always told her about learning their language or any of their ways: it endangered you. She slept alone on the hill until the middle of November when the first snows came. Then she made a bed for herself where the children had slept. She did not lie down beside Chato again until many years later, when he was sick and shivering and only her body could keep him warm. The illness came after the white rancher told Chato he was too old to work for him anymore, and Chato and his old woman should be out of the shack by the next afternoon because the rancher had hired new people to work there. That had satisfied her. To see how the white man repaid Chato's years of loyalty and work. All of Chato's fine-sounding English talk didn't change things.

13   It snowed steadily and the luminous light from the snow gradually diminished into the darkness. Somewhere in Cebolleta a dog barked and other village dogs joined with it. Ayah looked in the direction she had come, from the bar where Chato was buying the wine. Sometimes he told her to go on ahead and wait; and then he never came. And when she finally went back looking for him, she would find him passed out at the bottom of the wooden steps at Azzie's Bar. All the wine would be gone and most of the money too, from the pale blue check that came to them once a month in a government envelope. It was then that she would look at his face and his hands, scarred by ropes and the barbed wire of all those years, and she would think, this man is a stranger; for forty years she had smiled at him and cooked his food, but he remained a stranger. She stood up again, with the snow almost to her knees, and she walked back to find Chato.

14   It was hard to walk in the deep snow and she felt the air burn in her lungs. She stopped a short distance from the bar to rest and readjust the blanket. But this time he wasn't waiting for her on the bottom step with his old Stetson hat pulled down and his shoulders hunched up in his long wool overcoat.

15   She was careful not to slip on the wooden steps. When she pushed the door open, warm air and cigarette smoke hit her face. She looked around slowly and deliberately, in every corner, in every dark place that the old man might find to sleep. The bar owner didn't like Indians in there, especially Navajos, but he let Chato come in because he could talk Spanish like he was one of them. The men at the bar stared at her, and the bartender saw that she left the door open wide. Snowflakes were flying inside like moths and melting into a puddle on the oiled wood floor. He motioned to her to close the door, but she did not see him. She held herself straight and walked across the room slowly, searching the room with every step. The snow in her hair melted and she could feel it on her forehead. At the far corner of the room, she

saw red flames at the mica window of the old stove door; she looked behind the stove just to make sure. The bar got quiet except for the Spanish polka music playing on the jukebox. She stood by the stove and shook the snow from her blanket and held it near the stove to dry. The wet wool smell reminded her of new-born goats in early March, brought inside to warm near the fire. She felt calm.

In past years they would have told her to get out. But her hair was white now   16
and her face was wrinkled. They looked at her like she was a spider crawling slowly across the room. They were afraid; she could feel the fear. She looked at their faces steadily. They reminded her of the first time the white people brought her children back to her that winter. Danny had been shy and hid behind the thin white woman who brought them. And the baby had not known her until Ayah took her into her arms, and then Ella had nuzzled close to her as she had when she was nursing. The blonde woman was nervous and kept looking at a dainty gold watch on her wrist. She sat on the bench near the small window and watched the dark snow clouds gather around the mountains; she was worrying about the unpaved road. She was frightened by what she saw inside too: the strips of venison drying on a rope across the ceiling and the children jabbering excitedly in a language she did not know. So they stayed for only a few hours. Ayah watched the government car disappear down the road and she knew they were already being weaned from these lava hills and from this sky. The last time they came was in early June, and Ella stared at her the way the men in the bar were now staring. Ayah did not try to pick her up; she smiled at her instead and spoke cheerfully to Danny. When he tried to answer her, he could not seem to remember and he spoke English words with the Navajo. But he gave her a scrap of paper that he had found somewhere and carried in his pocket; it was folded in half, and he shyly looked up at her and said it was a bird. She asked Chato if they were home for good this time. He spoke to the white woman and she shook her head. "How much longer?" he asked, and she said she didn't know; but Chato saw how she stared at the boxcar shack. Ayah turned away then. She did not say good-bye.

She felt satisfied that the men in the bar feared her. Maybe it was her face and the   17
way she held her mouth with teeth clenched tight, like there was nothing anyone could do to her now. She walked north down the road, searching for the old man. She did this because she had the blanket, and there would be no place for him except with her and the blanket in the old abode barn near the arroyo. They always slept there when they came to Cebolleta. If the money and the wine were gone, she would be relieved because then they could go home again; back to the old hogan with a dirt roof and rock walls where she herself had been born. And the next day the old man could go back to the few sheep they still had, to follow along behind them, guiding them, into dry sandy arroyos where sparse grass grew. She knew he did not like walking behind old ewes when for so many years he rode big quarter horses and worked with cattle. But she wasn't sorry for him; he should have known all along what would happen.

(continued)

(continued)

18   There had not been enough rain for their garden in five years; and that was when Chato finally hitched a ride into the town and brought back brown boxes of rice and sugar and big tin cans of welfare peaches. After that, at the first of the month they went to Cebolleta to ask the postmaster for the check; and then Chato would go to the bar and cash it. They did this as they planted the garden every May, not because anything would survive the summer dust, but because it was time to do this. The journey passed the days that smelled silent and dry like the caves above the canyon with yellow painted buffaloes on their walls.

19   He was walking along the pavement when she found him. He did not stop or turn around when he heard her behind him. She walked beside him and she noticed how slowly he moved now. He smelled strong of woodsmoke and urine. Lately he had been forgetting. Sometimes he called her by his sister's name and she had been gone for a long time. Once she had found him wandering on the road to the white man's ranch, and she asked him why he was going that way; he laughed at her and said, "You know they can't run that ranch without me," and he walked on determined, limping on the leg that had been crushed many years before. Now he looked at her curiously, as if for the first time, but he kept shuffling along, moving slowly along the side of the highway. His gray hair had grown long and spread out on the shoulders of the long overcoat. He wore the old felt hat pulled down over his ears. His boots were worn out at the toes and he had stuffed pieces of an old red shirt in the holes. The rags made his feet look like little animals up to their ears in snow. She laughed at his feet; the snow muffled the sound of her laugh. He stopped and looked at her again. The wind had quit blowing and the snow was falling straight down; the southeast sky was beginning to clear and Ayah could see a star.

20   "Let's rest awhile," she said to him. They walked away from the road and up the slope to the giant boulders that had tumbled down from the red sand-rock mesa throughout the centuries of rainstorms and earth tremors. In a place where the boulders shut out the wind, they sat down with their backs against the rock. She offered half of the blanket to him and they sat wrapped together.

21   The storm passed swiftly. The clouds moved east. They were massive and full, crowding together across the sky. She watched them with the feeling of horses—steely blue-gray horses startled across the sky. The powerful haunches pushed into the distances and the tail hairs streamed white mist behind them. The sky cleared. Ayah saw that there was nothing between her and the stars. The light was crystalline. There was no shimmer, no distortion through earth haze. She breathed the clarity of the night sky; she smelled the purity of the half moon and the stars. He was lying on his side with his knees pulled up near his belly for warmth. His eyes were closed now, and in the light from the stars and the moon, he looked young again.

22   She could see it descend out of the night sky: an icy stillness from the edge of the thin moon. She recognized the freezing. It came gradually, sinking snowflake by snowflake until the crust was heavy and deep. It had the strength of the stars in Orion, and its journey was endless. Ayah knew that with the wine he would sleep.

He would not feel it. She tucked the blanket around him, remembering how it was when Ella had been with her; and she felt the rush so big inside her heart for the babies. And she sang the only song she knew to sing for babies. She could not remember if she had ever sung it to her children, but she knew that her grandmother had sung it and her mother had sung it:

> The earth is your mother,
> she holds you.
> The sky is your father,
> he protects you.
> Sleep,
> sleep.
> Rainbow is your sister,
> she loves you.
> The winds are your brothers,
> they sing to you.
> Sleep,
> sleep.
> We are together always
> We are together always
> There never was a time
> when this
> was not so.

Inquiring into the Story

Use the methods of inquiry—exploring, explaining, evaluating, and reflecting—to discover what you think about Silko's short story, and move toward your own interpretations. The following questions might serve as journal prompts and triggers for class discussion.

1. On the left page of your notebook, jot down at least five lines or passages that you believe were key to your understanding of the story. These may include details that seem important, moments that signify turning points, or feelings or ideas suggested by the narrator or another character. On the opposing right page, openly fastwrite about the passages you collected. What do they seem to suggest about possible themes for the story? What do you notice about Ayah, the main character and narrator? What do you consider the significant events that affect all the characters, and how do these events change them?

2. Explain the significance of the poem that ends "Lullaby."

3. A recurring detail in the story is the blanket that Ayah received from her son, Jimmie. Trace every mention of the blanket in the story. What accumulated meaning does this detail acquire in the story?

4. Some critics have argued that "Lullaby" is a story of healing and recovery. Do you agree or disagree? What evidence in the story would you point to that either supports or contradicts that contention?

5. One of the most common responses we have to stories we enjoy is to say that we "could relate to it." Did you feel that way about "Lullaby" even though you might not be Native American? Certainly the story helps those of us who are not Native American understand an aspect of the Indian experience in America, but does it also help us understand ourselves?

ONE STUDENT'S RESPONSE

Noel's Journal

DOUBLE-ENTRY JOURNAL RESPONSE TO "LULLABY"

"It was worse than if they had died: to lose the children and to know that somewhere, in a place called Colorado, in a place full of sick and dying strangers, her children were without her."

"She stayed on the hill where they had fled the first time, and she slept rolled up in the blanket Jimmie had sent her."

I think this sets the tone of the whole story. She loses one son to the war and the other two were taken from her. Knowing that one son had died and wouldn't ever come home again. The other two were alive and well but they would not grow up with their mother and were kept from their own culture by the government.

After she lost all her children she finds comfort in the blanket her older son had sent her. She sleeps in the place where she spent the last moments with her other two children.

She carries the blanket with her wherever she goes. This is how she spent her time mourning her loss and memories.

WRITING IN THE DISCIPLINES

Why Literary Theory Is Not a Sleep Aid

The discipline of literary studies is interested in theories, or coherent ideas about how we interpret essays, poems, short stories, drama, and novels. Yawn, you say? I can understand that reaction, even if you're an English major. A mention of theory might seem to be an invitation to nod off.

But here's a way to understand the relevance of theory in any discipline, including literary studies. Good theories help you understand and explain what you see. Here's an example of what I mean. A group of scholars has always been interested in how we tell stories, and one of these scholars, Joseph Campbell, was a mythologist who developed ideas about how most of the stories we tell are variations on the same story that has been told forever: the hero's journey. This journey has identifiable stages, Campbell argued, including (1) first we see the hero in his or her ordinary world, (2) then the hero is presented with a challenge, (3) he or she resists the challenge, (4) the hero gets encouraged by a wise mentor, (5) and the hero embarks, encountering the first test, and so on until the journey is completed and the hero returns to the ordinary world again, but transformed and possessing something that makes that world better. Think *Star Wars*.

Campbell's theory that stories conform to the outlines of this basic journey can be used to analyze a novel, film, short story, or even personal essay. His ideas provide a framework—better yet, an optic instrument like a microscope that helps to reveal in a text what you wouldn't ordinarily see.

There are many literary theories that you can turn to when you want to direct your gaze in a certain way at a particular work.

- **New criticism:** It isn't really new anymore but still influential. These theories encourage readers to look at a poem or story as an object that can be analyzed independently from the author's intentions or historical contexts.

- **Reader response criticism:** You can't understand a work independently of a reader's response to it, say reader response theorists. Whatever meaning exists is necessarily a transaction between, say, the short story and the reader's experience of the short story, an experience informed by the reader's personal history and other texts he or she has read.

- **Feminist criticism:** This diverse body of theory argues, among other things, that gender figures prominently in writing and reading literature. A critic might notice, for example, how male authors have historically depicted female characters in their work, or find in often-neglected women writers an alternative view of female characters and even methods of storytelling.

- **New historicism:** We're used to interpreting a poem or story by seeing it in historical context. If you want to understand *Huck Finn*, for instance, consider the history of racial conflict in the American South. New historicism proposes that this way of using history to interpret literature is way too simplistic. New historicists believe that while history is a useful way to interpret literature, it's only one of many interrelated "discourses" a critic should consider.

If you want to apply a literary theory to your analysis of a work, you don't have to read a score of books about it. You can find excellent summaries of each theory's methods online, including some examples of how to apply them.

■ ESSAY

The essayist Vivian Gornick once wrote that there are two essential parts to a memoir or personal essay: the *situation* and the *story*. The situation is the easy part. It describes what happens—the narrator is arrested for dealing drugs, the parents divorce, the beloved pet dog dies, and so on. These need not be extraordinary occurrences; on the contrary, the situation is often quite undramatic. The story, on the other hand, is what the writer (or narrator) *makes* of what happens, why it is significant, what it says about being a parent, a child, a teenager, a politician, a student, or whatever. In Chapter 1, we talked about this very thing when we distinguished between our observations of things and our ideas about them, or between evidence and theories, or what happened and what *happens*. The back and forth between these two kinds of thinking is a method of inquiry at the heart of *The Curious Writer*.

But this movement can also help us as *readers* of nonfiction because it is a pattern that is also evident in the work itself. Take Sarah Vowell's essay, "Shooting Dad." The situation is that Vowell and her father have always seemed profoundly different from each other, and that often got on Vowell's nerves. One loves guns, the other doesn't. One is a Republican, the other a Democrat. But what is the *story*? What ultimately is Vowell trying to say to the rest of us about the parent–child divide?

Sarah Vowell's work, including this essay, is often written for radio, and is frequently featured on the NPR program *This American Life*.

Shooting Dad

Sarah Vowell

1   If you were passing by the house where I grew up during my teenage years and it happened to be before Election Day, you wouldn't have needed to come inside to see that it was a house divided. You could have looked at the Democratic campaign poster in the upstairs window and the Republican one in the downstairs window and seen our home for the Civil War battleground it was. I'm not saying who was the Democrat or who was the Republican—my father or I—but I will tell you that I have never subscribed to *Guns & Ammo*, that I did not plaster the family vehicle with National Rifle Association stickers, and that hunter's orange was never my color.

2   About the only thing my father and I agree on is the Constitution, though I'm partial to the First Amendment, while he's always favored the Second.

3   I am a gunsmith's daughter. I like to call my parents' house, located on a quiet residential street in Bozeman, Montana, the United States of Firearms. Guns were everywhere: the so-called pretty ones like the circa 1850 walnut muzzleloader hanging on the wall, Dad's clients' fixer-uppers leaning into corners, an entire rack right

next to the TV. I had to move revolvers out of my way to make room for a bowl of Rice Krispies on the kitchen table.

I was elevan when we moved into that Bozeman house. We had never lived in town before, and this was a college town at that. We came from Oklahoma—a dusty little Muskogee County nowhere called Braggs. My parents' property there included an orchard, a horse pasture, and a couple of acres of woods. I knew our lives had changed one morning not long after we moved to Montana when, during breakfast, my father heard a noise and jumped out of his chair. Grabbing a BB gun, he rushed out the front door. Standing in the yard, he started shooting at crows. My mother sprinted after him screaming, "Pat, you might ought to check, but I don't think they do that up here!" From the look on his face, she might as well have told him that his American citizenship had been revoked. He shook his head, mumbling, "Why, shooting crows is a national pastime, like baseball and apple pie." Personally, I preferred baseball and apple pie. I looked up at those crows flying away and thought. I'm going to like it here.

Dad and I started bickering in earnest when I was fourteen, after the 1984 Democratic National Convention. I was so excited when Walter Mondale chose Geraldine Ferraro as his running mate that I taped the front page of the newspaper with her picture on it to the refrigerator door. But there was some sort of mysterious gravity surge in the kitchen. Somehow, that picture ended up in the trash all the way across the room.

Nowadays, I giggle when Dad calls me on Election Day to cheerfully inform me that he has once again canceled out my vote, but I was not always so mature. There were times when I found the fact that he was a gunsmith horrifying. And just *weird*. All he ever cared about were guns. All I ever cared about was art. There were years and years when he hid out by himself in the garage making rifle barrels and I holed up in my room reading Allen Ginsberg poems, and we were incapable of having a conversation that didn't end in an argument.

Our house was partitioned off into territories. While the kitchen and the living room were well within the DMZ, the respective work spaces governed by my father and me were jealously guarded totalitarian states in which each of us declared ourselves dictator. Dad's shop was a messy disaster area, a labyrinth of lathes. Its walls were hung with the mounted antlers of deer he'd bagged, forming a makeshift museum of death. The available flat surfaces were buried under a million scraps of paper on which he sketched his mechanical inventions in blue ball-point pen. And the floor, carpeted with spiky metal shavings, was a tetanus shot waiting to happen. My domain was the cramped, cold space known as the music room. It was also a messy disaster area, an obstacle course of musical instruments—piano, trumpet, baritone horn, valve trombone, various percussion doodads (bells!), and recorders. A framed portrait of the French composer Claude Debussy was nailed to the wall. The available flat surfaces were buried under piles of staff paper, on which I penciled in the pompous orchestra music given titles like "Prelude to the Green Door" (named after an O. Henry

(continued)

4

5

6

7

(continued)

short story by the way, not the watershed porn flick *Behind the Green Door*) I started writing in junior high.

8   It has been my experience that in order to impress potential suitors, skip the teen Debussy anecdotes and stick with the always attention-getting line "My dad makes guns." Though it won't cause the guy to like me any better, it will make him handle the inevitable breakup with diplomacy—just in case I happen to have any loaded family heirlooms lying around the house.

9   But the fact is, I have only shot a gun once and once was plenty. My twin sister, Amy, and I were six years old—six—when Dad decided that it was high time we learned how to shoot. Amy remembers the day he handed us the gun for the first time differently. She liked it.

10   Amy shared our father's enthusiasm for firearms and the quick-draw cowboy mythology surrounding them. I tended to daydream through Dad's activities—the car trip to Dodge City's Boot Hill, his beloved John Wayne Westerns on TV. My sister, on the other hand, turned into Rooster Gogburn Jr., devouring Duke movies with Dad. In fact, she named her teddy bear Duke, hung a colossal John Wayne portrait next to her bed, and took to wearing one of those John Wayne shirts that button on the side. So when Dad led us out to the backyard when we were six and, to Amy's delight, put the gun in her hand, she says she felt it meant that Daddy trusted us and that he thought of us as "big girls."

11   But I remember holding the pistol only made me feel small. It was so heavy in my hand. I stretched out my arm and pointed it away and winced. It was a very long time before I had the nerve to pull the trigger and I was so scared I had to close my eyes. It felt like it just went off by itself, as if I had no say in the matter, as if the gun just had this *need*. The sound it made was as big as God. It kicked little me back to the ground like a bully, like a foe. It hurt. I don't know if I dropped it or just handed it back over to my dad, but I do know that I never wanted to touch another one again. And, because I believed in the devil, I did what my mother told me to do every time I felt an evil presence. I looked at the smoke and whispered under my breath, "Satan, I rebuke thee."

12   It's not like I'm saying I was traumatized. It's more like I was decided. Guns: Not For Me. Luckily, both my parents grew up in exasperating households where children were considered puppets and/or slaves. My mom and dad were hell-bent on letting my sister and me make our own choices. So if I decided that I didn't want my father's little death sticks to kick me to the ground again, that was fine with him. He would go hunting with my sister, who started calling herself "the loneliest twin in history" because of my reluctance to engage in family activities.

13   Of course, the fact that I was allowed to voice my opinions did not mean that my father would silence his own. Some things were said during the Reagan administration that cannot be taken back. Let's just say that I blamed Dad for nuclear proliferation and Contra aid. He believed that if I had my way, all the guns would be confiscated and it would take the commies about fifteen minutes to parachute in and assume control.

We're older now, my dad and I. The older I get, the more I'm interested in becoming a better daughter. First on my list. Figure out the whole gun thing.   14

Not long ago, my dad finished his most elaborate tool of death yet. A cannon. He built a nineteenth-century cannon. From scratch. It took two years.   15

My father's cannon is a smaller replica of a cannon called the Big Horn Gun in front of Bozeman's Pioneer Museum. The barrel of the original has been filled with concrete ever since some high school kids in the '50s pointed it at the school across the street and shot out its windows one night as a prank. According to Dad's historical source, a man known to scholars as A Guy at the Museum, the cannon was brought to Bozeman around 1870, and was used by local white merchants to fire at the Sioux and Cheyenne Indians who blocked their trade access to the East in 1874.   16

"Bozeman was founded on greed," Dad says. The courthouse cannon, he continues, "definitely killed Indians. The merchants filled it full of nuts, bolts, and chopped-up horseshoes. Sitting Bull could have been part of these engagements. They definitely ticked off the Indians, because a couple of years later. Custer wanders into them at Little Bighorn. The Bozeman merchants were out to cause trouble. They left fresh baked bread with cyanide in it on the trail to poison a few Indians."   17

Because my father's sarcastic American history yarns rarely go on for long before he trots out some nefarious ancestor of ours—I come from a long line of moonshiners, Confederate soldiers, murderers, even Democrats—he cracks that the merchants hired some "community-minded Southern soldiers from North Texas." These soldiers had, like my great-great-grandfather John Vowell, fought under pro-slavery guerrilla William C. Quantrill. Quantrill is most famous for riding into Lawrence, Kansas, in 1863 flying a black flag and commanding his men pharaohlike to "kill every male and burn down every house."   18

"John Vowell," Dad says, "had a little rep for killing people." And since he abandoned my great-grandfather Charles, whose mother died giving birth to him in 1870, and wasn't seen again until 1912. Dad doesn't rule out the possibility that John Vowell could have been one of the hired guns on the Bozeman Trail. So the cannon isn't just another gun to my dad. It's a map of all his obsessions—firearms, certainly, but also American history and family history, subjects he's never bothered separating from each other.   19

After tooling a million guns, after inventing and building a rifle barrel boring machine, after setting up that complicated shop filled with lathes and blueing tanks and outmoded blacksmithing tools, the cannon is his most ambitious project ever. I thought that if I was ever going to understand the ballistic bee in his bonnet, this was my chance. It was the biggest gun he ever made and I could experience it and spend time with it with the added bonus of not having to actually pull a trigger myself.   20

I called Dad and said that I wanted to come to Montana and watch him shoot off the cannon. He was immediately suspicious. But I had never taken much interest in his work before and he would take what he could get. He loaded the cannon into the back of his truck and we drove up into the Bridger Mountains. I was a little worried that the National   21

(continued)

(continued)

Forest Service would object to us lobbing fiery balls of metal onto its property. Dad laughed, assuring me that "you cannot shoot fireworks, but this is considered a fire*arm*."

22   It is a small cannon, about as long as a baseball bat and as wide as a coffee can. But it's heavy—110 pounds. We park near the side of the hill. Dad takes his gunpowder and other tools out of this adorable wooden box on which he has stenciled "PAT G. VOWELL GANNON-WORKS," Cannonworks: So that's what NRA members call a metal-strewn garage.

23   Dad plunges his homemade bullets into the barrel, points it at an embankment just to be safe, and lights the fuse. When the fuse is lit, it resembles a cartoon. So does the sound, which warrants Ben Day dot words along the lines of *ker-pow!* There's so much Fourth of July smoke everywhere I feel compelled to sing the national anthem.

24   I've given this a lot of thought—how to convey the giddiness I felt when the cannon shot off. But there isn't a sophisticated way to say this. It's just really, really cool. My dad thought so, too.

25   Sometimes, I put together stories about the more eccentric corners of the American experience for public radio. So I happen to have my tape recorder with me, and I've never seen levels like these. Every time the cannon goes off, the delicate needles which keep track of the sound quality lurch into the bad, red zone so fast and so hard I'm surprised they don't break.

26   The cannon was so loud and so painful, I had to touch my head to make sure my skull hadn't cracked open. One thing that my dad and I share is that we're both a little hard of hearing—me from Aerosmith, him from gunsmith.

27   He lights the fuse again. The bullet knocks over the log he was aiming at. I instantly utter a sentence I never in my entire life thought I would say. I tell him, "Good shot, Dad."

28   Just as I'm wondering what's coming over me, two hikers walk by. Apparently, they have never seen a man set off a homemade cannon in the middle of the wilderness while his daughter holds a foot-long microphone up into the air recording its terrorist boom. One hiker gives me a puzzled look and asks, "So you work for the radio and that's your dad?"

29   Dad shoots the cannon again so that they can see how it works. The other hiker says. "That's quite the machine you got there." But he isn't talking about the cannon. He's talking about my tape recorder and my microphone—which is called a *shotgun* mike. I stare back at him, then I look over at my father's cannon, then down at my microphone, and I think, Oh. My. God. My dad and I are the same person. We're both smart-alecky loners with goofy projects and weird equipment. And since this whole target practice outing was my idea, I was no longer his adversary. I was his accomplice. What's worse, I was liking it.

30   I haven't changed my mind about guns. I can get behind the cannon because it is a completely ceremonial object. It's unwieldy and impractical, just like everything else I care about. Try to rob a convenience store with this 110-pound Saturday night special, you'd still be dragging it in the door Sunday afternoon.

I love noise. As a music fan, I'm always waiting for that moment in a song when something just flies out of it and explodes in the air. My dad is a one-man garage band, the kind of rock 'n' roller who slaves away at his art for no reason other than to make his own sound. My dad is an artist—a pretty driven, idiosyncratic one, too. He's got his last *Gesamtkunstwerk* all planned out. It's a performance piece. We're all in it—my mom, the loneliest twin in history, and me.

31

When my father dies, take a wild guess what he wants done with his ashes. Here's a hint: It requires a cannon.

32

"You guys are going to love this," he smirks, eyeballing the cannon. "You get to drag this thing up on top of the Gravellies on opening day of hunting season. And looking off at Sphinx Mountain, you get to put me in little paper bags. I can take my last hunting trip on opening morning."

33

I'll do it, too. I will have my father's body burned into ashes. I will pack these ashes into paper bags. I will go to the mountains with my mother, my sister, and the cannon. I will plunge his remains into the barrel and point it into a hill so that he doesn't take anyone with him. I will light the fuse. But I will not cover my ears. Because when I blow what used to be my dad into the earth, I want it to hurt.

34

INQUIRING INTO THE DETAILS

How to Read Nonfiction

While nonfiction essays often seem a lot like short stories, there are some significant differences. For one, we assume that the stories they tell *actually happened*. We also assume that the narrator and author are the same person. This means we read essays a little differently from fiction. Here are some additional frameworks for reading nonfiction essays.

- **Truthfulness:** In nonfiction, there's an implicit contract between reader and writer. We expect everything in an essay to be true, to have actually happened. What happens if you suspect this isn't the case?

- **Ethos:** How do authors of essays come across? Do we believe what they are saying? Do we trust their authority to speak on the subject they're writing about?

- **Questions:** The essay is an exploratory form, and sometimes we can understand writers' purposes best by identifying the question they're trying to answer. This may also mean that it isn't always easy to reduce a literary essay to a thesis or theme. Insights are often "earned"—arrived at through much thought

(continued)

> **Inquiring into the Details** (*continued*)
> and questioning—and tentative. Essay writers are less concerned with proving a point.
>
> ■ ***The "reflective turn":*** Because essays both show *and* tell, it's important to be alert for moments when essayists say what they mean. Cumulatively, these moments of reflection help establish the themes of essays.

Inquiring into the Essay

Explore, explain, evaluate, and reflect on "Shooting Dad."

1. It's pretty common for there to be some kind of ideological divide between a parent and a child, and these differences aren't just political. To see your own way into this topic, try this: *Describe yourself from the point of view of your father, your mother, or someone else in your family.* Devote at least five minutes to drafting this material. Skip a line, and then describe that person from your point of view. What do you make of the differences? The similarities?

2. Vowell writes; "We're older now, my dad and I. The older I get, the more I'm interested in becoming a better daughter." Define what you think she means by "better daughter."

3. You know the situation, what is the story here? What does Vowell seem to say about finding ways to bridge the gap between parent and child when both have such different passions?

4. Consider that this essay was read on the radio, to be heard once without a written text to follow. Explain some of the ways that might change the way Vowell wrote the piece.

SEEING THE FORM

Christina's World by Andrew Wyeth

If a photograph can be thought of as a form of nonfiction, then a painting compares well with fiction or poetry. The painting certainly has a strong relationship to the real; after all, the painter sees the world we all live in and expresses that vision in the work. That expression may be realistic, impressionistic, or abstract, but it is firmly rooted in things that can be seen, smelled, heard, and touched. Yet unlike photographers who work with the visual materials presented to them through the viewfinder, the painter can transform these materials through invention. If it works better that the woman's dress is pink rather than blue, then pink it shall be. Similarly, fiction writers' primary obligation is to the story, not reality, and they invent characters and make them do things that contribute tension and meaning to the narrative.

Andrew Wyeth, *Christina's World*, 1948. Tempera on gessoed panel, $32\frac{1}{4}'' \times 47\frac{3}{4}''$. The Museum of Modern Art, New York. Purchase. (16. 1949), © Andrew Wyeth.

Interpreting a painting, then, like Andrew Wyeth's famous work *Christina's World*, is much like interpreting fiction. The painting acts as a text that, like a short story, is a complete invention and whose meaning is implicit rather than explicit. Therefore "reading" Wyeth's painting should involve the kind of interpretive moves you might employ in reading any literature.

In analyzing *Christina's World* and other paintings, it can be helpful to consider the following basic terms and concepts:

- **Line:** In artistic composition, the line is the direction the viewer's gaze travels when looking at the painting, something that is managed by the placement of forms and their relative size. In a good painting, the viewer's eye is directed to the main focal point of the picture, and away from unimportant elements. Some questions to ask about line include whether the painting succeeds in encouraging your gaze to move smoothly to the main objects of interest, or whether the line is confusing, making you feel as if you're not quite sure where to look. Do things flow visually?

- **Hierarchy:** Do you sense that some visual elements are more important than others? In a well-composed painting, you should. Artists can manage this in a number of ways, including the size and location of various objects in the painting, and in doing so they are communicating something important about the overall theme of the work. What, for example, might the emphasis on certain objects in the painting imply about its meaning? What is the relationship among these things, and what does that imply?

(continued)

Seeing the Form (*continued*)

- *Color:* The arrangement of color in a painting influences its mood. Certain colors are cool—blues, greens, purples, and their many combinations—and these tend to recede in a painting. Other colors—yellows, oranges, and reds—are warm and can be perceived as coming forward. Color is obviously enormously expressive when handled well. How do the colors the artist chose affect the mood of the work? How might that mood contribute to its overall theme or idea?

- *Value:* To create the sense of dimension, artists use light and dark tones. In a black-and-white drawing, these tones are white to black and all the shades of gray in between. In a color painting, value is often managed by using various shades of a color. Without value, a painting looks flat, one-dimensional. With it, the subjects look more realistic. How much emphasis is there on value in the painting? How realistic is the image?

- *Composition:* All of these qualities—line, color, value, hierarchy—and more contribute to a painting's composition. One of the key qualities of composition is balance, and this can be achieved in a number of ways, including arranging visual elements symmetrically or asymmetrically, or using something called the "golden mean," an ancient mathematical concept that has historically influenced art and architecture, and which represents proportions often seen in nature, including the spiral of a sea shell, and the proportions of the human body (see Figure 8.1). What do you notice about the composition of the painting? How is it arranged to influence your feelings, and how does it seem to contribute to the overall theme or idea?

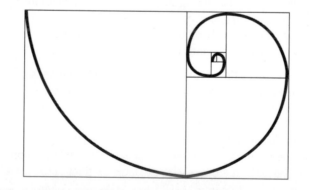

Figure 8.1   The golden mean is a mathematical formula that when applied to a rectangle creates spatial relationships that are particularly pleasing to the eye. This is the so-called golden rectangle. For centuries, artists have exploited this principle, creating proportions in paintings and buildings based on these calculations. Can you see how Wyeth's painting is visually organized to adhere to the golden rectangle?

THE WRITING PROCESS

INQUIRY PROJECT: WRITING A CRITICAL ESSAY

Look at a story, essay, or poem, possibly one of the works in this chapter. Interpret it as you did Wyeth's painting, looking closely at what the literary work says and how it says it, and, using some of the elements of literary analysis, offer readers a way of understanding the work that they would find convincing. The full draft should be about 1,000 to 1,500 words. You should do the following:

- Organize the essay around a question you're trying to answer about the text and its possible meanings. (For example: *Is Silko's "Lullaby" a story that highlights the power of women in Navajo culture?*)

- Use your question as a guide for reading the story selectively.

- As you shape your answer to the question, rely mostly on passages and other information from the primary work—the story or essay—as a source of evidence.

- If possible, use research with secondary sources (articles about the author, published criticism about the work, and so on) to help you revise your paper.

For additional reading, writing, and research resources, go to
www.mycomplab.com

Thinking About Subjects

It's likely that your instructor will ask you to write a critical essay on one or more of the readings in this chapter, or perhaps an assigned reading from another book. If you can choose among the three readings here, consider which work you found most moving. Although analysis often demands a level of detachment and cool logic, literary works are usually intended to make us *feel*. This is a wonderful starting place for a closer look at the story because it's sensible to wonder what it was that made you feel something. The answer will be found in the text, of course, by looking at how the author tells the story and what he says. But it will also be found in what you bring to the text—your own experiences, associations, and values.

The writer Joan Didion once wrote that writing is an "act of aggression," an implicit demand that readers see things the way the writer sees them. We react to stories sometimes because they are asking us to believe something we don't believe, or don't want to believe, or they are imagining us as readers we don't want to be. A good starting point, then, for choosing to write about a work is to

> In the conversation between what a text says and what it *might* be saying, you discover fresh understandings of what you read.

choose it because you find yourself resisting it in some way, rather than "re-lating to it."

Generating Ideas

Spend some time in your notebook generating material for possible essays. The following prompts will invite you to first play around, and even write "badly." Approach this material initially in an open-ended way. When you can, let the writing lead thought. The following prompts will be general enough to apply to any text, even if it isn't one of the three in this chapter.

Listing Prompts. Lists can be rich sources for triggering topics. Let them grow freely, and when you're ready, use an item as the focus of another list or an episode of fastwriting. The following prompts should get you started:

1. Brainstorm a list of questions about the work that you find puzzling.

2. List the names of every important character or person in the story or es-say. Choose one or two that seem most important. Under each name, make two new headings: Dreams and Problems. Under Dreams, list the things that character seems to desire most, even if he or she isn't fully aware of it. Under Problems, list everything that seems to be an obstacle to that character's achieving those desires.

3. List details or particulars from the story that seem to say more than they say. In other words, do any details recur? Do any objects have particular significance to one or more characters? Do any descriptions suggest the feelings, dispositions, or values of a particular character?

Fastwriting Prompts. Remember, fastwriting is a great way to stimulate creative thinking. Turn off your critical side and let yourself write "badly."

1. Write a narrative of thought. Begin with *When I first read this story or es-say I thought...And then I thought...And then...And then...*

2. Choose three lines or passages that are key to your current understand-ing of the themes or ideas behind the story or essay. Write these down on the left page of your notebook. On the opposing right page, fastwrite about each, beginning with *The first thing I notice about this passage is...And then...And then...And then...* When the writing stalls, write about the next line or passage until you've written about all three.

3. Use one of the following "seed sentences" as a prompt for fastwriting:
   - What is the relationship between _____ and _____?
   - The most important scene in the story is _____ because _____.

- The title of the work might be significant because _____.
- If I was going to divide the poem, story, or essay into parts, the first part would be _____.
- The narrator in the work seems to want _____.

Visual Prompts. Sometimes the best way to generate material is to see what we think represented in something other than sentences. Boxes, lines, webs, clusters, arrows, charts, and even sketches can help us see more of the landscape of a subject, especially connections between fragments of information that aren't as obvious in prose.

1. Create a cluster using the name of the main character as the core word. Reread the story and then build as many associations as you can from that character. Think about feelings and ideas you associate with that person as well as any particulars you remember from the story.

2. Make a visual map of the story. Begin by placing a brief description of what you believe is the most significant moment in the story at the center of a blank page. This might be a turning point, or the point of highest tension, or perhaps the moment when the main character achieves his or her desires and dreams. Consider that moment the destination of the story. Now map out events or details in the narrative that threaten to lead the protagonist away from that destination, and those that appear to lead the protagonist toward it.

Research Prompts. When writing a critical essay, the most important research you do is carefully reading and rereading the primary text, or the poem, story, or essay you're writing about. But secondary sources can be a great help, too. A background article on the writer might help you understand his or her motives in writing the piece. A little historical research can give you a deeper understanding of the setting.

1. Put the story or essay in a biographical context. First, search the Web for anything you can find about the author. Begin by searching with the term "authors" in Google. You'll find a listing of a range of Web pages with biographical information about authors; one or more might feature yours. Several library databases are also useful, including The Literary Index.

2. Put the story or essay in a historical context. Search the Web for background information about the period, place, or events relevant to the story. For example, if you were writing about "Lullaby," search for information about life among the Navajo in the late 1940s.

INQUIRING INTO THE DETAILS

Common Literary Devices

Many key concepts provide useful frameworks for analyzing literature. The key is to see the following ideas as an angle for seeing an essay, story, or poem, much as you might move around a subject with a camera. Each provides a different way of seeing the same thing. In addition, each becomes a platform from which to pose a question about a text.

- *Plot and significant event:* This is what happens in a story that moves it forward. One way of thinking about plot is to consider this: What are the key moments that propel the story forward? Why do you consider them key? How do they add tension to the story? In an essay, these moments often give rise to the question the writer is exploring. In short stories, there is often a significant event that may happen in or outside of the story, but the entire narrative and its characters act or think in response to that event.

- *Characters:* Imagine a still pond upon which small paper boats float. Someone throws a rock in the pond—big or small—and the ripples extend outward, moving the boats this way and that. Depending on the size of the ripples, some of the boats may list or capsize, sinking slowly. Characters in a short story are like those boats, responding in some way to something that happened, some significant event that is revealed or implied. They move almost imperceptibly, or quite noticeably, or even violently. Is there logic to their response? How exactly are they changed? How do they relate to each other?

- *Setting:* Where a story takes place can matter a lot or a little, but it always matters. Why? Because where a story takes place signals things about characters and who they are. A story set in rural Wyoming suggests a certain austere, ranching culture in which the characters operate. Even if they're not ranchers, they must somehow deal with that culture. Similarly, a story set in Chicago's predominantly black South Side introduces another set of constraints within which characters must operate. In some cases, setting even might become a kind of character.

- *Point of view:* In nonfiction essays, point of view is usually straightforward—we assume the narrator is the author. But in fiction, it's much more complicated; in fact, *how* a story is told—from what perspective—is a crucial aesthetic decision. Stories told from the first-person point of view in the present tense give the story a sense of immediacy—this feels like it's happening *now*—but at the same time limit our understanding of other characters because we can't get into their heads. So-called omniscient narrators can introduce a feeling of distance from the action, but they are also gratifyingly godlike because they can see everything, hovering above all the action and even entering characters' minds at will. Why might an author have chosen a particular point of view? Is the narrator trustworthy? What might be his or her biases and how might they affect the telling?

- **Theme:** One way to understand a story or essay is to consider that everything—character, point of view, and setting—all contribute to a central meaning. In a good story, everything is there for a purpose—to say something to the reader about what it means to be human. In essays, this theme may be explicit because essays both show *and* tell. Short stories and especially poems are often short on explanation of theme, operating with more ambiguity. The writer hopes the reader can *infer* certain ideas or feelings by paying close attention to what he *shows* the reader. To get at the theme, begin with the simple question: *So what?* Why is the author telling this story or sharing this experience? What significance are we supposed to attach to it?

- **Image:** Stories and poems ask us to see. When I read them, I imagine that writers take my face in their hands and gently—or sometimes brutally—direct my gaze. What are they insisting that I look at and how do they want me to see it? Images that recur may also be significant.

Judging What You Have

Now it's time to look more critically at what you've generated. Do you see some possible directions you could follow in a sketch? Are there tentative ideas and interpretations you might develop? Are there potential beginnings you could follow? The following suggestions use material generated by the prompts in the preceding section.

What's Promising Material and What Isn't? If your assignment is to write about one of the stories in this chapter, by now you should have a sense of which one interests you most. That initial sense usually starts with a gut reaction—the story makes you *feel* something. That's a good starting point, but the generating prompts should give you a fuller sense of *why* you feel something. As you examine the material you generated, consider the following:

- *What's your question?* A good opening question is specific enough to guide your rereading of the work, encouraging you to look at certain parts rather than the whole thing.

- *What surprised you?* In your fastwrites, do you find that the writing led you from an initial impression or interpretation of the story but then took you toward ideas you didn't expect? Did you find a lot to say about the significance of certain passages?

- *Does a character in the story seem to emerge as a focus?* A helpful way to write about a story is to focus on the actions and motivations of a particular character. *How* the character attempts to overcome obstacles in the way of his desires can say a lot about the meaning of the story.

- *Is there a recognizable significant event in the story and how do the important characters respond to it?* Was there a scene or moment that seemed to alter the course of the narrative or its characters?

- *Does the story's context help explain the author's purpose?* Literature isn't created in a vacuum. Like all art, it is often a response to things that are going on within and around the artist. Do these contexts help you to read the story differently? What questions do they raise about its meanings?

- *Do you feel ready to answer the* So what? *question?* Stories aren't merely entertainment. Authors always have certain purposes—ideas they're exploring, comments they want to make, or questions they're trying to answer. After generating material, you may be ready to finish this sentence: *What I think this story or essay is* really *saying is…* If you like what you come up with, turn it into a question that will help organize your rereading of the story.

Questions About Audience and Purpose. Why analyze a work of literature? For the same reason that some of us want to talk about anything complicated, whether it's a relationship gone south or a wrenching movie about war: We simply want to understand. It's fundamentally human to try to make sense of things, and it's reassuring when we can. The best stories offer a glimpse at the human spirit—at what makes people tick, at their longings and fears and possibilities. Ultimately, we learn about ourselves and our own humanity.

Critical analysis of literature is simply a method of discovering these things. You can use these tools for several purposes. The most basic is to simply write a summary of what happens to whom in a story. Often called a plot summary, this is useful as a way of initially understanding the work, but it isn't often a college assignment. In general, however, critical essays offer some *interpretation* of what the story or essay seems to be saying, a move that often begins with a question.

In the broadest sense the opening question is simple: *What might this story mean?* But to be really useful, the question needs to be more specific. For example, a slightly more specific question might be, *What are the racial themes in Silko's story "Lullaby"?* Will such a question allow you to read Silko's story selectively? Probably not. What about this: *What is the significance of the recurring image of the blanket in "Lullaby"?* Is this too specific? Possibly. But it's not a bad starting point for your inquiry into the story because the question gives you direction about where to look to find the answers.

Critical essays don't simply ask questions; they attempt to answer them. There is a range of methods for doing that, including the following:

1. You can focus on a particular element such as character, setting, or plot development, analyzing how it contributes to one or more of the story's themes.

2. You can put the story in relevant contexts—perhaps the biography of the author, background about the story's time and place, or certain kinds of

theories or ideas about literature—and exploit these as a way of unraveling the story's themes and ambiguities.

3. You can argue for an interpretation of a story's meaning, and use *both* particular elements, such as character and setting, and relevant contexts to help you make your interpretation convincing to others.

Each approach implies a different emphasis on certain kinds of information in the essay. *But no matter what angle you use, the text of the story—the words, phrases, passages, and ideas that make up the story—will always be the most important source of evidence.* I want to emphasize this because one of the most common weaknesses of writing about a reading is the failure to mine material from the text itself.

The audience for a critical essay, as for any form of writing, will make a big difference in what you say and how you say it. For the assignment that follows, assume you're writing for an audience of peers. Ask your instructor whether you should assume that your audience is familiar with the work you're writing about (which might be the case if you're all writing about the same story or essay) or assume that your readers are unfamiliar with the work. If the latter is the case, then you'll obviously have to do some summarizing about the plot and characters that wouldn't be necessary if your readers knew your story or essay.

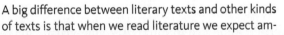

INQUIRING INTO THE DETAILS

What Is a "Strong Reading"?

A big difference between literary texts and other kinds of texts is that when we read literature we expect ambiguity. When I was reading the instructions for how to set the alarm on my daughter's iPod clock radio the other day, I would not have tolerated ambiguity. I'm interested in only one meaning for the word *plug*. But if I were reading the same word in a poem, I might imagine something other than the thing with two flat metal prongs that fit into a wall socket.

If a literary work can have multiple meanings, isn't the author's intended meaning the "right" way to interpret it? While discerning the author's intention, particularly in nonfiction, is a factor in interpreting a work's meaning, it is hardly the only one. What the reader *brings* to the text—his or her experiences, cultural biases, reading habits, and so on—is probably even more important.

That must mean that *any* interpretation of a literary text is fair game, right? Of course not. It has to be a *plausible* interpretation, one that the reader can explain convincingly using evidence from the text, the work of other critics, historical context, or the author's body of work. Readers must make arguments for their interpretations of literature, and the best arguments not only use strong evidence but account for as much of the work as possible.

(continued)

Inquiring into the Details (*continued*)

A "strong reading" of a literary work should be your goal.* This is a reading that goes "against the grain." A story, poem, or essay may seem to beg to be read and interpreted a particular way. If you want to know which way that is, simply take a quick look at the literary essays for sale on the Internet on any popular work. These kinds of readings—which are usually the most obvious interpretations—are often reflections of stories about ourselves we like to believe or that feel familiar. They might be what we often call "universal themes." A "strong reading" is one that recognizes this reflex and offers alternative, often less obvious interpretations. A strong reading is one that begins to notice the ways a work *breaks* with our usual understandings of things: "At first, this story seemed to reflect what I felt about growing up, but in these ways it helped me to understand that differently."

*Flower Linda, Kathleen McCormick, and Gary Waller. *Reading Texts: Reading, Responding, Writing.* Lexington, MA: Heath, 1987. Print.

Writing the Sketch

We'll begin again with an early draft, a sketch that represents an initial attempt to discover what you want to focus on and what you might have to say about the literary work you've chosen.

Develop your sketch with the following things in mind:

- It should have a tentative title. This time, the title should be the question about the work you're trying to answer. (For example, *What is the significance of Ayah's relationship to nature in Silko's "Lullaby"?*)

- It should be at least 500 to 600 words.

- Write it with the appropriate audience in mind. Are you writing for readers who are familiar with the text?

- Explore your question by paying close attention to what the story you're writing about says.

■ STUDENT SKETCH

You've met Bernice Olivas before, in the first chapter, where she writes a memoir of herself as a writer. Here Bernice tackles a sketch for a critical essay on Ursula Le Guin's story, "The Ones Who Walk Away from Omelas," which appears earlier in this chapter. While Bernice confesses that she hasn't had much experience with the critical essay, she knows a great deal about writing to inquire, and it shows here as she drafts a sketch that circles high above Le Guin's story until she spots what most interests her and the questions that raises.

Who Are "The Ones Who Walk Away from Omelas"?

Bernice Olivas

In the short story "The Ones Who Walk Away from Omelas," Ursula Le Guin creates three distinct, yet abstract, characters. First is the city itself, which she describes as "joyous" and "green." Bells ring and a child plays a haunting tune on a flute. The people are content and know nothing of guilt. The city is a metaphor for a society that is as complex and complicated as ours but where the people have learned to accept contentment. They are happy.

Then there is the child, locked in a cellar, sitting in its own filth that bears the burden of all this joy and contentment. A metaphor, perhaps, for the sweat shop kid in Korea churning out cheap plastic toys to put in our happy meals—meals with more meat in each one than this kid will see in a month, or maybe more. The city knows the child and accepts the existence of the child as the price of all that happiness. They comfort themselves by paying homage to the child's sacrifice. Le Guin writes, "It is the existence of the child, and their knowledge of its existence, that makes possible the nobility of their architecture, the poignancy of their music, the profundity of their science."

The final character in this strange cast is "the ones who walk away." These are the few who cannot bear the knowledge of the child.

It's tempting to read into this story a certain type of martyr mythology—get caught up in images of Jesus or Prometheus or evoke the picture of Sioux Indians hanging from the Sun Pole in supplication to the Great Spirit. After all, mythology is full of martyrs, those who take on the burden of the sins of man. Western society believes wholeheartedly in martyrs.

Or on the flipside, this story could be read as a dark fable speaking to the awfulness of man, condemning those who would sacrifice an innocent and then justify that sacrifice. After all, humanity can never be better than it is, right? All yin must have a yang, and all coins have two sides? Of course neither of these ways of reading the story touches on the third character, "those who walk away."

It's "those who walk away" that intrigue me most, those few who were headed to a place the author could not describe. I want to read them as noble, see them as the few who would not accept the price of contentment—but I can't. What I see are cowards. Those who stay behind are making a choice to accept the existence of the child in the basement. Maybe it's the right choice, maybe it's the wrong choice, or maybe it's the only choice—but it is a choice. "Those who walk away" are making a choice too. After they see the child, and they know it to be a terrible thing, and they realize they can't live with the reality of the child in the basement, they choose to leave, and they choose to leave the child behind. There is no nobility is simply seeing a problem and walking away from it.

To me the theme, the driving point of this story, is the idea that the child continues to exist in our basement, not just because the majority of us are only too willing to accept its existence and to accept that a child needs to be sacrificed, but because even those who aren't willing to live with the burden of that child refuse to ask why the child needs to be there in

(continued)

(continued)

the first place. Nobody says our happiness and contentment lie in our own making; let's take the child out of the basement and if the city falls around us we'll come together and rebuild. Nobody questions the perceived status quo. Walking away isn't enough; walking away isn't noble because in the end no matter how many leave nothing has really changed.

Moving from Sketch to Draft

Prepare to revise your sketch by first evaluating it yourself and then sharing it in a small group workshop.

Evaluating Your Own Sketch. Among the key concerns in evaluating this early draft of your critical essay is whether you've discovered a workable focus and whether you're beginning to get some clear idea of what you're trying to say. In your journal or on a separate sheet you can provide to your instructor when you hand in the sketch, try to answer the following questions:

1. Did the question you were asking about the text help you focus on certain parts of the story? What were they? Was the question too broad or too specific? What might be a more refined question as a focus for the next draft, or are you happy with the original question you posed?

2. Can you summarize in a sentence or two how you might now answer the question you posed in your sketch? Can you summarize an answer to another question that emerged that interests you more?

3. Based on what you tentatively seem to be saying in the sketch about the text you're writing about, what do you think you might do in the rewrite?

Questions for Peer Review. Workshop groups that are discussing the sketches should consider the following questions:

- If you're unfamiliar with the text the writer is analyzing, do you have enough information about the story or essay to understand what the writer is saying about it? What else would you like to know?

- Does the sketch seem to answer the question it's asking? In your own words, what do you think the writer seems to be saying?

- Where is the sketch most convincing? Where is it least convincing?

- Are there any questions or approaches that seem like good alternatives to the one the writer chose?

Reflecting on What You've Learned. To make the best use of the workshop, try to listen without commenting on the discussion of your sketch. Use the double-entry journal approach of taking notes during the discussion. On the left page of your notebook, record all the comments and suggestions you hear, whether you agree with them or not. Later, on the right page, fastwrite your reactions and thoughts about the comments you recorded on the opposing page.

Research and Other Strategies: Gathering More Information

Before you wrote your sketch, you did some initial research that may have helped provide a *context* for the work you're writing about. Now it's time to dig a little deeper. How deep you dig depends on the scope of your project and the details of the assignment.

This time, your campus library, rather than the Web, will be the focus of your investigations, although many of the following sources and databases are probably accessible through your library's Web pages.

- *Researching the author.* Check the online book index to find biographies of your author. You can also gather biographical information on the author you're writing about by consulting the following references at your university library:
  - *Author's Biographies Index.* A key source on 300,000 writers of every period.
  - *Biography Index: A Cumulative Index to Biographical Material in Books and Magazines.* Remarkably extensive coverage, which includes biographies, as well as autobiographies, articles, letters, and obituaries.
  - *Contemporary Authors.* Up-to-date information on authors from around the world.
- *Researching the critics.* What do other people say about your author or the work you're writing about? Check these references or databases:
  - *MLA International Bibliography.* The most important database in which to find articles by others on the work or author you're writing about.
  - *Literary Index.* A database of author biographies.
  - *Literature Index Online.* Browse by author, work, or topic.
  - *Magill's Bibliography of Literary Criticism.* Citations, not excerpts, of criticism on more than 2,500 works.
  - *Book Review Index.* Citations for tens of thousands of book reviews on even fairly obscure works.
- *Researching the genre or tradition.* Investigate the type of writing or the literary tradition that critics associate with the work. A number of useful reference works are online, including the *Oxford Encyclopedia of American Literature,* the *Cambridge History of English and American Literature,* and *The Literary Encyclopedia.* You can also find reference works (or books) at the library that focus specifically on cultural and ethnic traditions, like African American or Native American literature, or literature from a particular region.

Composing the Draft

Before you begin writing the draft, make sure that you have a workable focusing question that will drive the draft. It needs to be specific enough to allow you to

INQUIRING INTO THE DETAILS

Literature on the Web

You can access a host of useful literature resources on the Internet. A small sampling of what is available includes the following:

- **Bartleby.com** (http://bartleby.com): Offers a range of poetry, fiction, and nonfiction and access to the *Columbia Encyclopedia, The American Heritage Dictionary, Roget's Thesaurus, Bartlett's Familiar Quotations,* and many resources for writers, all for free.

- **Bibliomania** (http://www.bibliomania.com): Offers 2,000 classic texts for free, author biographies, book summaries, bibliographies, and more.

- **The Electronic Text Center** (http://etext.lib.virginia.edu): Contains 70,000 texts in thirteen languages, many of them available for free.

- **Literary Resources on the Web** (http://andromeda.rutgers.edu/jlynch/Lit/): Broken into a range of categories, including British and American, periods, and traditions.

- **Literature Webliography** (http://www.lib.lsu.edu/hum/lit/lit.html): A rich harvest of links to references, guides, authors, and bibliographies.

- **The Online Books Page** (http://digital.library.upenn.edu/books/archives.html): This online archive contains lists to countless Web sites devoted to literature in English and in foreign languages.

- **The Oxford English Dictionary** (http://dictionary.oed.com/entrance.dtl): The online version of the world's most definitive English dictionary details the shifting meaning and usage of words from their first use in writing to present. Access available only on a subscription basis.

- **Voice of the Shuttle** (http://vos.ucsb.edu): A general humanities research site with great links to literary sites.

reread the story or essay you're writing about selectively, focusing on certain parts rather than the whole thing. But it also needs to be general enough to allow you to develop the answer in 1,000 to 1,500 words.

This type of question—one that focuses on a particular detail or aspect of plot development—can work extremely well as a focus for a short critical essay. But unless that detail or development seems attached to other details, developments, and themes in the story, it probably won't do.

Here's a good focusing question for a literary analysis, one that strikes a nice balance between specificity and generality: *Why does Silko end "Lullaby" with the poem, and how does it figure into Ayah's efforts to confront her losses?* It seems as if there might be a lot to say about this without resorting to generalities. The question focuses on a particular part of the Silko story, yet also expands outward into other aspects of the work, particularly those relevant to the theme of recovery.

Methods of Development. What are some of the ways you might organize your critical essay?

Narrative. An entirely different approach is to use your question as the starting point for a story you tell about how you arrived at an answer. This approach is more essayistic in the sense that it provides the story of *how* you came to know rather than reporting *what* you think. A narrative essay might also involve relevant auto-biographical details that influenced your reading of the literary work, explaining your interest in certain aspects of the story or the question you're asking about it.

Question to Answer. Because the assignment is designed around a question you're trying to answer about a literary work, the question-to-answer design is an obvious choice. Consider spending the first part of your essay highlighting the question you're interested in. Alternatively, establish the importance of the question by highlighting your understanding of the story's meaning or the author's intentions, or perhaps even how the question arises out of your own personal experiences with the events or subjects in the work. The key is to convince readers that yours is a question worth asking, and that the answer might be interesting to discover.

Compare and Contrast. Critical essays often benefit from this method of development. The approach might be to compare and contrast certain elements within the story or essay—perhaps several characters, symbols or metaphors, plot developments, and so on—or you might compare the work to others by the same or even different authors. These comparisons have to be relevant to the question you're asking.

Combining Approaches. Frequently a critical essay uses several or even all of the methods of development mentioned here—question to answer, comparison and contrast, and narrative. Consider how you might put them all to work, especially in certain sections of your draft.

Using Evidence. You need to consider two main kinds of evidence in a critical essay: evidence that comes from so-called *primary* sources, especially the work itself, but also letters or memoirs by the author; and evidence that comes from *secondary* sources, or books, articles, and essays by critics who are also writing about the work or author. Primary sources are generally most important. In more personal literary responses, however, your personal associations, anecdotes, stories, or feelings may be used as evidence, if they're relevant to the question you're posing.

Workshopping the Draft

When you finish revising your sketch, you should have a more developed draft with a clearer purpose and focus. After all this work, you may feel pretty good about it. Before you submit your draft for further peer review, explore your own feelings and tentative ideas about what you need to do in the next, and probably final, revision.

WRITING IN YOUR LIFE

Book Groups

Here's an obscure writer's dream: She wrote a novel; let's call it *The Snowstorm in August,* which is published by an equally obscure publisher. Sales of the book are miniscule. But in this dream, Oprah appears, looking saintly, striding through a small bookstore, where she sees *The Snowstorm in August* on a remainder table. Oprah picks it up. She buys it. She makes it a selection for Oprah's Book Club. Our obscure writer is obscure no more.

While Oprah's Book Club is the largest and most influential of its kind, lovers of literature have plenty of other options for sharing their passion. Online book clubs are all over the Internet. Some focus on particular genres like science fiction or biography, while others have more general interests. Members not only get ideas for good reads but share their reviews and analyses of favorite books. Alternatively, there are book clubs meeting face-to-face in homes across America, including mine. Advice about how to organize these abound (just Google "book clubs"). Major publishers also provide discussion guides for popular books in their lists designed for these gatherings of friends.

Another variation of the book club is community-wide "read one book" programs, often sponsored by local libraries, which get everyone in town reading the same thing and gathering to discuss it. The Library of Congress's "Center for the Book" (http://www.loc.gov/loc/cfbook) has a state-by-state search engine for these programs.

Reflecting on the Draft. Take a look at the draft before you and circle the passage you think is the best in the essay so far. Now circle the passage that you think is weakest.

In your notebook, fastwrite for five minutes about both passages. What seems to be working in the better passage? What problems do you notice about the weaker one? Does either one address the question you're writing about? If so, how? If not, how might it? When you compare the two passages, what do you notice about the differences? How might you make the weaker passage more like the stronger one? How might you make the rest of the essay stronger?

Questions for Readers. Share your essay in small groups before you begin the final revision. Group members might consider the following questions about each draft they discuss:

1. If you're unfamiliar with the story or essay the writer is writing about, do you have enough background information about it to understand the draft?

2. Does the draft stay focused, from beginning to end, on the focusing question? If not, where exactly does it seem to stray?

3. Do you find the interpretation of the literary work convincing? Where is the draft most convincing? Where is it least convincing?

4. Where exactly could the writer use more evidence?

5. What part of the draft was most interesting? What part was least interesting?

Revising the Draft

Revision is a continual process—not a last step. You've been revising—literally "re-seeing" your subject—from the first messy fastwriting in your journal. But the things that get your attention during revision vary depending on where you are in the writing process. You've generated material, chosen a topic, done some research, and written both a sketch and draft. Most students think that the only thing left to do is "fix things." Check for misspellings. Correct an awkward sentence or two. Come up with a better title. This is editing, not revision, and while editing is important, to focus solely on smaller "fixes" after writing a first draft squanders an opportunity to really *learn* from what the draft is telling you, or perhaps not quite telling you.

Chapter 13 can help guide these discoveries. The questions you can ask about a draft fall into five categories: purpose, idea, information, development, and editing. Use the chart on the following page to find the revision strategies in Chapter 13 that might help you re-see what you've written so far.

Critical essays typically have some of the following problems to solve. Do any of these apply to your draft?

- When you make an assertion about the significance or importance of something in the work, is it supported by specific evidence from the work itself?

- Are you clear about your audience? Do you assume that readers are familiar or unfamiliar with the story, and have you written the draft with that assumption in mind?

- When you quote a passage from the work, do you analyze it with your own commentary? In particular, are you clear about the relevance of the passage to the argument you're making about the work?

- Is your thesis clear? By the end of your essay, could a reader state without much confusion the main thing you're trying to say about the poem, story, or essay?

For help addressing some of these questions and others, refer to Chapter 13, "Revision Strategies." Use the following table as a guide to the appropriate revision strategies. Remember that a draft may present problems in more than one category.

Polishing the Draft

After you've dealt with the big issues in your draft—is it sufficiently focused, does it answer the *So what?* question, is it well organized, and so on—you must deal with the smaller problems. You've carved the stone into an appealing figure, but now you need to polish it. Are your paragraphs coherent? How do you manage

GUIDE TO REVISION STRATEGIES

Problems in the Draft (Chapter 13)	Page Number
Unclear purpose ■ Not sure what the paper is about? ■ Not focused enough?	551
Unclear thesis, theme, or main idea ■ Not sure what you're trying to say?	557
Lack of information or development ■ Need more convincing evidence?	564
Disorganized ■ Doesn't move logically or smoothly from paragraph to paragraph?	568
Unclear or awkward at the level of sentences and paragraphs ■ Seems choppy or hard to follow at the level of sentences or paragraphs?	577

transitions? Are your sentences fluent and concise? Are there any errors in spelling or syntax? Chapter 13 can help you focus on these issues.

Before you finish your draft, work through the following checklist:

✓ Every paragraph is about one thing.

✓ The transitions between paragraphs aren't abrupt.

✓ The length of sentences varies in each paragraph.

✓ Each sentence is concise. There are no unnecessary words or phrases.

✓ You've checked grammar, particularly verb agreement, run-on sentences, unclear pronouns, and misused words (*there/their, where/were,* and so on). (See the handbook at the back of this book for help with these grammar issues.)

✓ You've run your spellchecker and proofed your paper for misspelled words.

■ STUDENT ESSAY

When I asked Bernice to write a critical essay on Ursula Le Guin's short story "The Ones Who Walk Away from Omelas," she confessed that she hadn't written a response to a literary work in some time. "I'm not sure I'll do a good enough job," she said, "but I'll do my best." If you've followed Bernice's journey throughout this chapter as she worked on the essay, then you know her lack of experience with the critical essay didn't really matter. What did matter was that, through the writing, she found a handful of questions that gave her the leverage to pry open a few puzzling aspects of Le Guin's story. Bernice then discovered what she had to say about them. The title of her essay, "Can You Really Walk Away?" is also the opening question of her inquiry, and this leads inevitably to more questions she must explore. One of the things I really admire about Bernice's essay is how effectively she uses questions as guides for her analysis. She makes an argument, ultimately, but she arrives at the thesis at the end of her investigation and we follow the narrative of thought that got her there.

Can You Really Walk Away?

Bernice Olivas

"Joyous!
How is one to tell about joy?
How to describe the Citizens Of Omelas?
Ursula Le Guin

In "The Ones Who Walk Away from Omelas" Ursula Le Guin creates a complex moral dilemma with a deceptively simple story. The author gives us Omelas, described as "joyous" and "green," where bells ring and a child plays a haunting tune on a flute. The people in Omelas are unique in that they are "mature, intelligent, passionate people." They have learned to discriminate between what is "necessary, what is neither necessary nor destructive and what is destructive." Le Guin makes it clear that these people are as sophisticated as we are and perhaps even more civilized: "As they did without monarchy and slavery, so they also got on without the stock exchange, the advertisement, the secret police, and the bomb. Yet I repeat that these were not simple folk, not dulcet shepherds, noble savages, bland utopians. They were not less complex than us." And yet, somehow the people of Omelas seemed to possess something extraordinarily simple, something readers of the tale envy: "One thing I know there is none of in Omelas is guilt." Why, then, would anyone "walk away" from this presumed utopia? That is the question at the heart of the tale.   1

The story does offer one compelling reason for guilt and a reason to leave. There is a child locked in a cellar, sitting in its own filth, a disturbing fact that never seems to bother any but a few. Somehow, and Le Guin doesn't explain how, the misery of this single child ensures the happiness and health of the entire city. It is kept on the edge of starvation; it's not allowed a single kind word. The child locked in the basement is simply part of city life. It is the unwitting martyr, the sacrificial lamb, rotting away with no voice beneath a city where, "all know it is there, all the people of Omelas.... [T]hey all understand that their happiness, the beauty of their city,...the health of their children...even the abundance of their harvest...depend wholly on this child's abominable misery."   2

The city accepts the child's misery as the price of happiness. Le Guin writes, "It is the existence of the child, and their knowledge of its existence, that makes possible the nobility of their   3

(continued)

(continued)

architecture, the poignancy of their music, the profundity of their science." It's easy to believe that the people of the city find ways to justify its existence. It's harder to believe they do it without guilt. It's tempting to read into this story a certain type of martyr mythology, get caught up in images of Jesus on the cross, Prometheus chained to the rock, or Atlas with the world on his shoulders. But the child is not a martyr since the child didn't choose its fate.

4   It's also tempting to read it as a dark fable speaking to the awfulness of man, condemning those who would sacrifice an innocent and then justify that sacrifice. After all, humanity can never be better than it is, right? All yin must have a yang, and all coins have two sides? Of course neither of these ways of reading the story touches on "those who walk away," the Omelians who have seen the child and can't bear to live with the knowledge.

5   It's the ones who walk away who raise the most interesting questions because they would seem to tread on firmer moral ground. Le Guin writes, "At times one of the adolescent girls or boys who go to see the child does not go home to weep or rage, does not, in fact, go home at all. Sometimes also a man or woman much older falls silent for a day or two, and then leaves home. These people go out into the street, and walk down the street alone. They keep walking, and walk straight out of the city of Omelas, through the beautiful gates."

6   Why do they walk away? Is it a noble act of conscience? Where do they go? And do they find a kind of happiness that can coexist with guilt? Are they the heroes of the story, or the villains? What is the reader supposed to learn, or understand about the ones who walk away?

7   At first glance those who walk away are the heroes of this tale. I want to read them as noble. I want to believe that they truly see the evil beneath their city, which they refuse to live with; and they are compelled to walk away, unable to accommodate the child's neglect as the cost of happiness. This makes them better than the rest of the citizens, doesn't it? They leave the city in search of a place with no hidden child. I want to believe they feel guilt.

8   Yet there is no honor or heroism in walking away. To walk away is an act of cowardice. It is a reminder that all it takes for evil to prosper is for the rest of us to do nothing. The mere recognition of suffering and then searching elsewhere for a place where it might not exist does nothing for those who suffer. Those who walk away refuse to ask why the child needs to be there in the first place. Nobody steps up and demands that we take responsibility for our own happiness. Nobody demands we take the child out of the basement and let the city fall so we can rebuild it, however imperfectly, on something other than the misery of the Other.

9   Omelas is more like the real world than we like to think and at the same time less than we realize. Like the citizens of Omelas some of us ignore the reality of the evil we live with. We stop seeing the homeless in the street; we don't think of the sweat shop kids, the sex slaves, the poor, the hungry, the lost. We go on, day in and day out, living our lives within evil's presence and oblivious to it. Others walk away and spend their lives searching for a place without evil.

10   The big difference between us is that we feel guilt and shame. And we ache for those we cannot help, and we are better for it. We know we are obligated by our humanity to step into the dark, take the child by the hand, and bring it into the light. We should strive to be heroes even in the face of overwhelming odds and certain failure, even in the face of pain and despair—even at the cost of the city.

We should never stop pushing ourselves to work harder, to love deeper, and to be better people. Life in Omelas is beautiful, but shallow. The absence of pain is not joy. Being content with the status quo is not enough. We need to bring down the city built on misery, stand together in the rubble, and work together to rebuild a city with no hidden basements. That way at the end of the day, when we try to sleep at night, we can sleep without hearing the child crying in the dark.   11

Evaluating the Essay

1. In some ways, Bernice Olivas's critical analysis of the Ursula Le Guin story departs from the more conventional approach to writing papers on literature. Typically, you make an argument that begins—often in the introduction—with a statement of your thesis: "In this paper, I will argue that the 'people who walk away are....'" Instead, Bernice begins by stating what she thinks is the most important question the short story raises for her, and then goes on to explore it. What are the strengths and weaknesses of each approach? Which are you more interested in reading? Why?

2. Does "Can You Really Walk Away?" ultimately have a thesis or main point? If so, what is it?

3. Is this essay persuasive?

USING WHAT YOU HAVE LEARNED

Although literary texts are quite different from the kinds of texts you usually read in school for other classes, practice with writing the critical essay can be useful even if you're not an English major. But how?

1. Think about your experience with this assignment. Can you point to something about *the process* that you could apply to another writing situation? What did you do here that you've done for other assignments in *The Curious Writer?*

2. Compare one of the short stories in this chapter with one of the research essays in Chapter 11. What are the differences between these two kinds of texts: literary fiction and expository writing, or a short story and a research essay? What are the similarities? Do you read them differently? Do you read them in similar ways?

3. In sixty seconds, generate a focused list that describes the most important things you've learned about writing a critical essay. How many of these things apply to writing other kinds of papers?

Writing an ethnographic essay will test your research skills by bringing them out of academia and into the field. That might be to a park where skateboarders gather, a hall where World War II veterans meet, a mall where fifteen-year-olds congregate, or the fields where migrant workers toil.

WRITING AN ETHNOGRAPHIC ESSAY

WRITING ABOUT CULTURE

My daughter hates spiders. In fact, she's so repulsed by spiders she refuses to utter the word, calling them "s-words" whenever she spots one of the bugs. In sadistic moments, I want to explain to her that there are invisible webs everywhere and that we walk into them all the time. In fact, we may spin a few threads ourselves occasionally. Like the spiders in our basement, subcultures abound right under our very noses. We just have to learn to see the webs they weave.

The "web of culture" is a good metaphor because, like spider webs, the many cultures and subcultures we encounter in our everyday lives are often difficult to detect. These webs are also something in which we are all enmeshed, whether we know it or not. To some extent they limit our movements, shape our beliefs, and determine our traditions.

Ethnography is a method of inquiry into culture that exposes the web in which members of a group are enmeshed, much the way the morning dew exposes the intricacies of a spider web in your backyard. In this chapter, you'll practice this approach to research and learn some ways that you can apply ethnographic techniques to all kinds of research projects. The real value of trying ethnography isn't that you'll be writing lots of ethnographies in other classes—you probably won't. Instead, writing an ethnographic essay will test your research skills by bringing them out of academia and into the field. That might be to the park where skateboarders gather, a hall where World War II veterans meet, a mall where fifteen-year-olds congregate, or

What You'll Learn in This Chapter

- How to sharpen your observation skills.
- The many ways that culture disciplines our behavior.
- Techniques for field research.
- Awareness of more subjective methods of research.

the fields where migrant workers toil. You might even wander online, where electronic subcultures abound. You'll learn to be a more careful observer. And ethnography will also raise interesting questions about whether all research can be objective.

> Ethnography is a method of inquiry into culture that exposes the web in which members of a group are enmeshed.

MOTIVES FOR WRITING ETHNOGRAPHY

Ethnography may be new to you, but you've almost certainly enjoyed its nonacademic versions. Magazine articles on other cultures in *National Geographic* and *Discover* have some elements of ethnography, and arguably so do some of the reality TV shows. These popular versions of ethnography invite readers and viewers to briefly enter unfamiliar worlds and learn a little about other people's ways of seeing and knowing. Essentially, the goal of such articles and programs is to show how things work in particular social contexts—a Los Angeles police department, a poor village in South Africa, or the neighborhood bowling alley. While the study of a culture can take the researcher overseas, it can just as easily take him or her down the street or across town.

Why might fieldwork like this make sense? If the inquiry questions that interest you involve how certain people behave in social settings, then you can learn more by actually *watching* them operate in their own worlds. Sure, you can read published accounts, relying on the observations of others. And you should. But actually observing for yourself how labor and delivery nurses on the night shift interact with patients at your local hospital is a much richer source of data. Seeing for yourself is almost always better.

Of course, the world is not a laboratory. You can't control the many variables that influence what people say and what they do. But that's the point. From the outset, ethnography concedes that social communities are complicated. Fieldwork will never be able to completely untangle them. But it can unknot a few strands. Ethnographers try to do this while acknowledging their own bias. Like much "qualitative" research, ethnography is subjective, but in many ways this adds to the richness of the results. We get a truer look at the chemistry between the observer and the observed, something that is always present in research with human subjects but frequently hidden behind the veil of "objectivity."

ETHNOGRAPHY AND ACADEMIC WRITING

Interest in academic ethnography has boomed in recent years, something you'll probably discover if you take an anthropology course. But you may also encounter ethnographic ways of seeing—or interest in the ways social groups behave and believe—in sociology, English, and even the visual arts, where something called "visual ethnography" might be practiced in formal or informal ways. Some researchers are using both film and still photography to capture a subculture in action, something you might consider as you work on your own ethnographic project.

But even if you never are asked to write a formal ethnography for a college class, the skills and habits of mind you practice while writing one here will help you in several ways. Writing ethnographically requires that you expand your repertoire of research to include interview and fieldwork, two methods of collecting that can help you with all kinds of research projects. In addition, the ethnographic essay is closely related to the case study, a method of research frequently used in the social sciences and especially in business. Finally, the project you're about to tackle calls on something you've practiced already—the willingness to suspend judgment while you collect information and then interpret the possible significance of what you've found. Once again, you enact the dialectical thinking that's been a part of every inquiry project in *The Curious Writer:* your observations of and your ideas about something, your record of what happened, and your sense of what *happens.*

FEATURES OF THE FORM

Like other inquiry projects in this book, ethnography is a form with many variations. However, most ethnographic essays share some features:

- *They focus on groups of people who identify themselves as group members.* We all belong to subcultures that we don't recognize we belong to—or perhaps refuse to acknowledge. But ethnography tends to focus on people who, at least when pressed, freely identify with a specific group.

- *Ethnography depends on close observation over time.* More than in other forms of inquiry, ethnographers must spend time in the field simply watching and taking notes. Particularly if you're an outsider to the culture you're studying, you can't possibly discover its artifacts, rituals, and insider language unless you hang out long enough with group members.

- *The bulk of the research takes place in the natural settings where group members gather.* You want to research interstate truck drivers? Go to a truck stop on I-84. You're interested in the culture of college women's basketball? Go to the locker room and spend time at practice. The goal of ethnography is to observe a culture as it behaves normally in typical situations. The hard part, sometimes, is inserting yourself into these situations without disrupting the way things usually are, which is another reason why spending enough time in the field is important; it helps your study subjects get used to you.

- *Ethnography looks closely at the few to get hints about the many.* By carefully describing a very small subset of the larger group—a group of five teenage skateboarders, or one women's basketball team—they hope to be able to infer something about the big picture.

> More than in other forms of inquiry, ethnographers must spend time in the field simply watching and taking notes.

- *Ethnography is often openly subjective.* Since the writer/researcher is the instrument for collecting data as well as interpreting its significance, the subjectivity of the method is inescapable. Consequently, ethnographers frequently have a strong presence in their studies, acknowledging their particular angles of vision. But the aim of the ethnographer, ultimately, is to overcome the potential screen of subjectivity and *see the world the way their study subjects see it.*

READINGS

■ ETHNOGRAPHIC ESSAY 1

Identity, as any fifteen-year-old knows, is a transaction. You give a little and you get a little from the social groups you like, and you don't do business with those you don't, except maybe to make sure you don't look or act like "one of them." This is not, however, free enterprise. Certain identities carry more social power. In my high school, those were not just the varsity football and basketball players but the well-to-do kids whose homes had huge "rec rooms" in the basement where they held parties for a select few.

You don't have a choice, however, about belonging to some groups. For example, you may be African American, Latina, or Native American. Perhaps you are disabled. While there's more tolerance of difference these days, Judith Ortiz Cofer observes in "The Myth of the Latin Woman" that it is nearly impossible, as someone who is different, to escape the assumptions others have about who you are. Sometimes these perceptions have serious consequences—you aren't hired or you can't rent the house. What can you do about this? Understandably, you might get angry. In her essay, Cofer suggests another response: Sometimes it is "custom,...not chromosomes," that helps explain difference. Cofer's essay, like the others in this chapter, is not a formal ethnography, but it is a great introduction to ethnography as a form of inquiry. "The Myth of the Latin Woman" helps us to see how the people we observe look back at us. Since we are visitors in their world, doing ethnography means working hard to understand that world in *their* terms, not ours.

The Myth of the Latin Woman: I Just Met a Girl Named Maria

Judith Ortiz Cofer

1   On a bus trip to London from Oxford University where I was earning some graduate credits one summer, a young man, obviously fresh from a pub, spotted me and as if struck by inspiration went down on his knees in the aisle. With both hands over his heart he broke into an Irish tenor's rendition of "Maria" from *West Side Story*. My politely amused fellow passengers gave his lovely voice the round of gentle applause it deserved. Though I was not quite as amused, I managed my version of an English smile: no show of teeth, no extreme contortions of the facial muscles—I was at this time of my life practicing reserve and cool. Oh, that British control, how I coveted it. But María had followed me to London, reminding me of a prime fact of my life: you can leave the Island, master the English language, and travel as far as you can, but if you are a Latina, especially one like me who so obviously belongs to Rita Moreno's gene pool, the Island travels with you.

2   This is sometimes a very good thing—it may win you that extra minute of someone's attention. But with some people, the same things can make *you* an island—not so much a tropical paradise as an Alcatraz, a place nobody wants to visit. As a Puerto Rican girl growing up in the United States and wanting like most children to "belong," I resented the stereotype that my Hispanic appearance called forth from many people I met.

3   Our family lived in a large urban center in New Jersey during the sixties, where life was designed as a microcosm of my parents' casas on the island. We spoke in Spanish, we ate Puerto Rican food bought at the bodega, and we practiced strict Catholicism complete with Saturday confession and Sunday mass at a church where our parents were accommodated into a one-hour Spanish mass slot, performed by a Chinese priest trained as a missionary for Latin America.

4   As a girl I was kept under strict surveillance, since virtue and modesty were, by cultural equation, the same as family honor. As a teenager I was instructed on how to behave as a proper señorita. But it was a conflicting message girls got, since the Puerto Rican mothers also encouraged their daughters to look and act like women and to dress in clothes our Anglo friends and their mothers found too "mature" for our age. It was, and is, cultural, yet I often felt humiliated when I appeared at an American friend's party wearing a dress more suitable to a semiformal than to a

playroom birthday celebration. At Puerto Rican festivities, neither the music nor the colors we wore could be too loud. I still experience a vague sense of letdown when I'm invited to a "party" and it turns out to be a marathon conversation in hushed tones rather than a fiesta with salsa, laughter, and dancing—the kind of celebration I remember from my childhood.

I remember Career Day in our high school, when teachers told us to come dressed as if for a job interview. It quickly became obvious that to the barrio girls, "dressing up" sometimes meant wearing ornate jewelry and clothing that would be more appropriate (by mainstream standards) for the company Christmas party than as daily office attire. That morning I had agonized in front of my closet, trying to figure out what a "career girl" would wear because, essentially, except for Marlo Thomas on TV, I had no models on which to base my decision. I knew how to dress for school: at the Catholic school I attended we all wore uniforms; I knew how to dress for Sunday mass, and I knew what dresses to wear for parties at my relatives' homes. Though I do not recall the precise details of my Career Day outfit, it must have been a composite of the above choices. But I remember a comment my friend (an Italian American) made in later years that coalesced my impressions of that day. She said that at the business school she was attending the Puerto Rican girls always stood out for wearing "everything at once." She meant, of course, too much jewelry, too many accessories. On that day at school, we were simply made the negative models by the nuns who were themselves not credible fashion experts to any of us. But it was painfully obvious to me that to the others, in their tailored skirts and silk blouses, we must have seemed "hopeless" and "vulgar." Though I now know that most adolescents feel out of step much of the time, I also know that for the Puerto Rican girls of my generation that sense was intensified. The way our teachers and classmates looked at us that day in school was just a taste of the culture clash that awaited us in the real world, where prospective employers and men on the street would often misinterpret our tight skirts and jingling bracelets as a come-on.

Mixed cultural signals have perpetuated certain stereotypes—for example, that of the Hispanic woman as the "Hot Tamale" or sexual firebrand. It is a one-dimensional view that the media have found easy to promote. In their special vocabulary, advertisers have designated "sizzling" and "smoldering" as the adjectives of choice for describing not only the foods but also the women of Latin America. From conversations in my house I recall hearing about the harassment that Puerto Rican women endured in factories where the "boss men" talked to them as if sexual innuendo was all they understood and, worse, often gave them the choice of submitting to advances or being fired.

It is custom, however, not chromosomes, that leads us to choose scarlet over pale pink. As young girls, we were influenced in our decisions about clothes and colors by the women—older sisters and mothers who had grown up on a tropical island where the natural environment was a riot of primary colors, where showing your skin was one way to keep cool as well as to look sexy. Most important of all, on the island,

(continued)

5

6

7

(continued)

women perhaps felt freer to dress and move more provocatively, since, in most cases, they were protected by the traditions, mores, and laws of a Spanish/Catholic system of morality and machismo whose main rule was: *You may look at my sister, but if you touch her I will kill you.* The extended family and church structure could provide a young woman with a circle of safety in her small pueblo on the island; if a man "wronged" a girl, everyone would close in to save her family honor.

8   This is what I have gleaned from my discussions as an adult with older Puerto Rican women. They have told me about dressing in their best party clothes on Saturday nights and going to the town's plaza to promenade with their girlfriends in front of the boys they liked. The males were thus given an opportunity to admire the women and to express their admiration in the form of *piropos:* erotically charged street poems they composed on the spot. I have been subjected to a few piropos while visiting the Island, and they can be outrageous, although custom dictates that they must never cross into obscenity. This ritual, as I understand it, also entails a show of studied indifference on the woman's part; if she is "decent," she must not acknowledge the man's impassioned words. So I do understand how things can be lost in translation. When a Puerto Rican girl dressed in her idea of what is attractive meets a man from the mainstream culture who has been trained to react to certain types of clothing as a sexual signal, a clash is likely to take place. The line I first heard based on this aspect of the myth happened when the boy who took me to my first formal dance leaned over to plant a sloppy overeager kiss painfully on my mouth, and when I didn't respond with sufficient passion said in a resentful tone: "I thought you Latin girls were supposed to mature early"—my first instance of being thought of as a fruit or vegetable—I was supposed to *ripen,* not just grow into womanhood like other girls.

9   It is surprising to some of my professional friends that some people, including those who should know better, still put others "in their place." Though rarer, these incidents are still commonplace in my life. It happened to me most recently during a stay at a very classy metropolitan hotel favored by young professional couples for their weddings. Late one evening after the theater, as I walked toward my room with my new colleague (a woman with whom I was coordinating an arts program), a middle-aged man in a tuxedo, a young girl in satin and lace on his arm, stepped directly into our path. With his champagne glass extended toward me, he exclaimed, "Evita!"

10   Our way blocked, my companion and I listened as the man half-recited, half-bellowed "Don't Cry for Me, Argentina." When he finished, the young girl said: "How about a round of applause for my daddy?" We complied, hoping this would bring the silly spectacle to a close. I was becoming aware that our little group was attracting the attention of the other guests. "Daddy" must have perceived this too, and he once more barred the way as we tried to walk past him. He began to shout-sing a ditty to the tune of "La Bamba"—except the lyrics were about a girl named María whose exploits all rhymed with her name and gonorrhea. The girl kept saying "Oh, Daddy" and looking at me with pleading eyes. She wanted me to laugh along with the others.

My companion and I stood silently waiting for the man to end his offensive song. When he finished, I looked not at him but at his daughter. I advised her calmly never to ask her father what he had done in the army. Then I walked between them and to my room. My friend complimented me on my cool handling of the situation. I confessed to her that I really had wanted to push the jerk into the swimming pool. I knew that this same man—probably a corporate executive, well educated, even worldly by most standards—would not have been likely to regale a white woman with a dirty song in public. He would perhaps have checked his impulse by assuming that she could be somebody's wife or mother, or at least *somebody* who might take offense. But to him, I was just an Evita or a María: merely a character in his cartoon-populated universe.

Because of my education and my proficiency with the English language, I have   11
acquired many mechanisms for dealing with the anger I experience. This was not true for my parents, nor is it true for the many Latin women working at menial jobs who must put up with stereotypes about our ethnic group such as: "They make good domestics." This is another facet of the myth of the Latin woman in the United States. Its origin is simple to deduce. Work as domestics, waitressing, and factory jobs are all that's available to women with little English and few skills. The myth of the Hispanic menial has been sustained by the same media phenomenon that made "Mammy" from *Gone with the Wind* America's idea of the black woman for generations; María, the housemaid or counter girl, is now indelibly etched into the national psyche. The big and the little screens have presented us with the picture of the funny Hispanic maid, mispronouncing words and cooking up a spicy storm in a shiny California kitchen.

This media-engendered image of the Latina in the United States has been docu-   12
mented by feminist Hispanic scholars, who claim that such portrayals are partially responsible for the denial of opportunities for upward mobility among Latinas in the professions. I have a Chicana friend working on a Ph.D. in philosophy at a major university. She says her doctor still shakes his head in puzzled amazement at all the "big words" she uses. Since I do not wear my diplomas around my neck for all to see, I too have on occasion been sent to that "kitchen," where some think I obviously belong.

One such incident that has stayed with me, though I recognize it as a minor of-   13
fense, happened on the day of my first public poetry reading. It took place in Miami in a boat-restaurant where we were having lunch before the event. I was nervous and excited as I walked in with my notebook in my hand. An older woman motioned me to her table. Thinking (foolish me) that she wanted me to autograph a copy of my brand new slender volume of verse, I went over. She ordered a cup of coffee from me, assuming that I was the waitress. Easy enough to mistake my poems for menus, I suppose. I know that it wasn't an intentional act of cruelty, yet of all the good things that happened that day, I remember that scene most clearly, because it reminded me of what I had to overcome before anyone would take me seriously. In retrospect I understand that my anger gave my reading fire, that I have almost always taken

(continued)

(continued)

doubts in my abilities as a challenge—and that the result is, most times, a feeling of satisfaction at having won a convert when I see the cold, appraising eyes warm to my words, the body language change, the smile that indicates that I have opened some avenue for communication. That day I read to that woman and her lowered eyes told me that she was embarrassed at her little faux pas, and when I willed her to look up at me, it was my victory, and she graciously allowed me to punish her with my full attention. We shook hands at the end of the reading, and I never saw her again. She has probably forgotten the whole thing but maybe not.

14   Yet I am one of the lucky ones. My parents made it possible for me to acquire a stronger footing in the mainstream culture by giving me the chance at an education. And books and art have saved me from the harsher forms of ethnic and racial prejudice that many of my Hispanic *compañeras* have had to endure. I travel a lot around the United States, reading from my books of poetry and my novel, and the reception I most often receive is one of positive interest by people who want to know more about my culture. There are, however, thousands of Latinas without the privilege of an education or the entrée into society that I have. For them life is a struggle against the misconceptions perpetuated by the myth of the Latina as whore, domestic or criminal. We cannot change this by legislating the way people look at us. The transformation, as I see it, has to occur at a much more individual level. My personal goal in my public life is to try to replace the old pervasive stereotypes and myths about Latinas with a much more interesting set of realities. Every time I give a reading, I hope the stories I tell, the dreams and fears I examine in my work, can achieve some universal truth which will get my audience past the particulars of my skin color, my accent, or my clothes.

15   I once wrote a poem in which I called us Latinas "God's brown daughters." This poem is really a prayer of sorts, offered upward, but also, through the human-to-human channel of art, outward. It is a prayer for communication, and for respect. In it, Latin women pray "in Spanish to an Anglo God / with a Jewish heritage," and they are "fervently hoping / that if not omnipotent, / at least He be bilingual."

Inquiring into the Essay

Explore, explain, and evaluate Cofer's "The Myth of the Latin Woman."

1. Being different and being born different are two quite different things. But different from what? Who gets to decide what is "normal" or "conventional"? And is there anything we can do about it? Fastwrite about these questions for four minutes without stopping.

2. Imagine that Cofer's essay is "data" for an ethnographic project on Latina culture, specifically first-generation Puerto Rican girls who attend an urban high school. In your own words, summarize what this "subject" (Cofer) contributes to your effort to understand those girls' world.

3. One thing that makes this essay interesting to read is Cofer's reliance on anecdote, and especially scenes, as a way of making her argument. This essay both shows and tells. Choose one of these moments (e.g., the London bus trip, high school Career Day, the hotel encounter, the poetry reading) and explain why you found it particularly persuasive.

4. Reflect on this problem: Ethnography doesn't pretend to be "objective." The writer/observer is intimately involved in collecting and interpreting the data. And yet, like all "qualitative" research, ethnographers hope to produce accurate insights. How can the ethnographer attempt to minimize bias?

ETHNOGRAPHIC ESSAY 2

In a multicultural nation like the United States, ethnic differences are among the most obvious webs in which we are enmeshed. I grew up in an Italian American family, and as a boy that meant that meals were social events and the quantity of food consumed was a measure of gratitude to the cook. Still, I was two generations away from the Italian immigrants in my family, and these rituals were fairly self-conscious expressions of my heritage. Most of the time, I didn't really feel that Italian.

Many among us, however, are recent immigrants, and ethnic ties bind these Americans more tightly to another place and culture. Among the challenges this group faces is how much to retain the rituals and traditions of the place from which they came, and how much to adopt and adapt to traditionally American ways. This dilemma is particularly hard for the children of immigrants. For those of us several generations away from this, it's hard to imagine how profound this dilemma can be.

For California teenage girls who are Muslim, one way these cultural tensions can be explored is by looking at a rite of passage that for many Americans symbolizes adolescence—the prom. How do the Muslim daughters of Pakistani-American parents celebrate the prom—one of high school's most important coming-of-age rituals—when their faith does not permit them to dress in a manner perceived as immodest around boys or allow boys to touch girls? The article that follows, "For the Muslim Prom Queen, There Are No Kings Allowed," is a fascinating look at the cultural adaptation of a new generation of sons and daughters of immigrants. Their solution to the dilemma of negotiating old and new cultures is to reshape the new culture to fit the old, rather than the other way around. Muslim teenagers can have a prom, but it won't look much like the one I attended.

Like most of the essays in this chapter, the piece that follows isn't a formal ethnography. But notice how much you can learn about culture by focusing on how people participate in a single ritual. In this case, it's the high school prom, but it could just as easily be an initiation rite of a fraternity, a funeral, or a birthday. Consider such an approach when you write your own ethnographic essay. Is there a ritual event that could be the focus of your essay?

For the Muslim Prom Queen, There Are No Kings Allowed

Patricia Leigh Brown

1   The trappings of a typical high school prom were all there: the strobe lights, the garlands, the crepe pineapple centerpieces and even a tiara for the queen. In fact, Fatima Haque's prom tonight had practically everything one might expect on one of a teenage girl's most important nights. Except boys.

2   Ms. Haque and her friends may have helped initiate a new American ritual: the all-girl Muslim prom. It is a spirited response to religious and cultural beliefs that forbid dating, dancing with or touching boys or appearing without a hijab, the Islamic head scarf. While Ms. Haque and her Muslim friends do most things other teenagers do—shopping for shoes at Macy's, watching "The Matrix Reloaded" at the mall or ordering Jumbo Jack burgers and curly fries at Jack in the Box—an essential ingredient of the American prom, boys, is off limits. So they decided to do something about it.

3   "A lot of Muslim girls don't go to prom," said Ms. Haque, 18, who removed her hijab and shawl at the prom to reveal an ethereal silvery gown. "So while the other girls are getting ready for their prom, the Muslim girls are getting ready for our prom, so we won't feel left out."

4   The rented room at a community center here was filled with the sounds of the rapper 50 Cent, Arabic pop music, Britney Spears and about two dozen girls, including some non-Muslim friends. But when the sun went down, the music stopped temporarily, the silken gowns disappeared beneath full-length robes, and the Muslims in the room faced toward Mecca to pray. Then it was time for spaghetti and lasagna.

5   It is perhaps a new version of having it all: embracing the American prom culture of high heels, mascara and adrenaline while being true to a Muslim identity.

6   "These young women are being very creative, finding a way to continue being Muslim in the American context," said Jane I. Smith, a professor of Islamic studies at the Hartford Seminary in Connecticut. "Before, young Muslims may have stuck with the traditions of their parents or rejected them totally to become completely Americanized. Now, they're blending them."

7   Non-Muslim students at San Jose High Academy, where Ms. Haque is president of the student body, went to the school's coed prom last month—renting cars or limousines, dining at the Sheraton, going to breakfast at Denny's and, for some, drinking. Ms. Haque, meanwhile, was on her turquoise cellphone with the smiley faces organizing the prom. She posted an announcement on Bay Area Muslim Youth, a Yahoo news group scanned by young people throughout the San Francisco Bay area, home to one of the country's largest and most active Muslim communities.

8   "We got so close, we wanted to hang," said Fatin Alhadi, 17, a friend, explaining the farewell-to-high-school celebration, which involved cooking, shopping and

decorating the room, rented with a loan from Ms. Haque's parents. "It's an excuse to dress and put makeup on. Everyone has so much fun at the prom."

The sense of anticipation was palpable at Ms. Haque's house this afternoon, including an occasional "Relax, mom!" For Ms. Haque and her friends, the Muslim prom—like any prom—meant getting your eyebrows shaped at the last minute and ransacking mother's jewelry box. It was a time to forget about the clock, to look in the mirror and see a glamorous woman instead of a teenager. To be radiant.   9

Ms. Haque and her Muslim girlfriends dwell in a world of exquisite subtlety in which modesty is the underlying principle. Though she wears a hijab, Ms. Alhadi recently dyed her black hair auburn. "Everyone asks me why, because nobody sees it," she said. "But I like to look at myself."   10

Ms. Haque, who will attend the University of California at Berkeley in the fall, is one of a growing number of young Muslim women who have adopted the covering their mothers rejected. Islamic dress, worn after puberty, often accompanies a commitment not to date or to engage in activities where genders intermingle.   11

Her parents immigrated from Pakistan, and her mother, Shazia, who has a master's degree in economics, does not wear the hijab.   12

Ms. Haque's decision to cover herself, which she made in her freshman year, was nuanced and thoughtful.   13

"I noticed a big difference in the way guys talked," she said. "They were afraid. I guess they had more respect. You walked down the street and you didn't feel guys staring at you. You felt a lot more confident." Her parents were surprised but said it was her decision.   14

Ms. Haque faced some taunting after the terror attacks on Sept. 11, 2001. "They call you terrorist, or raghead because high school students are immature," she said.   15

But she and her friends say Muslim boys, who are not distinguished by their dress, may have a tougher time in American society.   16

"The scarf draws the line," said Ms. Alhadi, the daughter of a Singaporean mother and Indonesian father. "It's already a shield. Without it everything comes to you and you have to fight it yourself."   17

Ms. Haque is enrolled in the academically elite International Baccalaureate program at San Jose High Academy, a public school where, as her friend Morgan Parker, 17, put it, "the jocks are the nerds."   18

But the social pressures on Muslims, especially in less-cloistered settings, can be intense.   19

"I felt left out, big time," said Saira Lara, 17, a senior at Gunn High School in Palo Alto, of her school's prom. But she gets a vicarious taste of dating by talking with her non-Muslim friends.   20

"The drama that goes on!" Ms. Lara said, looking dazzling at the Muslim prom in a flowing maroon gown. "The Valentine's Day without a phone call or a box of chocolates!"   21

Imran Khan, 17, a senior at Los Altos High School, admitted that his school's prom was not easy.   22

(continued)

(continued)

23   "When I told my friends I wasn't going, they all said, 'Are you crazy?'" he said in a telephone interview. "Prom is a you-have-to-go kind of thing. Obviously if all your friends are going and you're not, you're going to feel something. That day I was, 'Oh man, my friends are having fun and I'm not.' But I don't regret not going."

24   Most of Mr. Khan's school friends are not Muslim, and his Muslim friends are scattered across the Bay area.

25   "A lot of times it's difficult," he said. "We guys blend in so you can't tell we're Muslim. We're not supposed to touch the opposite gender. My friends who are girls understand, but when other girls want to hug you or shake your hand, it's hard. I don't want them to think I'm a jerk or something."

26   Adeel Iqbal, 18, a senior at Bellarmine College Preparatory, a boys' Catholic school in San Jose, went stag to his coed senior prom. Mr. Iqbal decided to go in his official capacity as student body president as well as a representative of his Muslim beliefs.

27   "Every day we're bombarded with images of sex and partying and getting drunk, in music and on TV, so of course there's a curiosity," he said. "When you see your own peers engaging in these activities, it's kind of weird. It takes a lot of strength to not participate. But that's how I've been raised. When your peers see you're different in a positive way, they respect it."

28   Nearly all parents of adolescents worry about the pressures of sex, drugs and alcohol, but the anxiety is especially acute in Muslim families who strictly adhere to traditional Islamic dress and gender separation. Many Muslim parents disapprove of what they see as an excessively secularized and liberalized American culture, and are deeply concerned that young Muslims, especially girls, not be put in compromising situations.

29   Ms. Haque's father, Faisal, a design engineer at Cisco Systems, said that the pressure to conform was "very significant." It is the subject of frequent family discussions.

30   "It's difficult at best," Mr. Haque said. "It takes a lot of self-control. I have a lot of respect for these kids."

31   The Haques supported their daughter's decision to organize the Muslim prom. "You have to live in this country," Mr. Haque said. "In order to function, the children have to adapt. Prom is a rite of passage. You don't want them to feel like they don't belong."

32   Ms. Haque would like the Muslim prom to become an annual event. "My goal is an elegant ballroom with a three-course dinner—no paper plates—women waiters and a hundred girls," she said.

33   Tonight, the prom room was filled with promise as the young women whirled around the dance floor, strobe lights blinking. "Show off whatever you've got!" Ms. Lara exhorted the throng, sounding like a D.J. "Come on, guys. This is the most magical night of your life!"

Inquiring into the Essay

Use the four ways of inquiring to think about your response to Patricia Leigh Brown's article.

1. If you went to an American high school, then you had to decide whether to attend the prom. Was this much of a decision for you? Fastwrite for five minutes in your journal about your social status then. Were you an insider or outsider? How was the prom at your school symbolic of the ways in which social status was expressed at your high school? In what ways was this reflected in how people dressed, what they did, who they hung out with, and how they behaved? Write about your own observations of this and your feelings about it back then.

2. Based on what you may have written in your journal in response to the first question, explain the markers of social status in your high school. How could you tell an insider from an outsider, the popular from the less popular, the socially mainstream from the less so? Be as specific as you can.

3. How would the students of your school respond to Fatima Haque, the girl who organized the Muslim prom described in the article, if she came to the prom in her hijab (head covering) and shawl? What does this suggest about the culture of your high school?

4. Critics of multiculturalism might read this article and argue that recent immigrants should work harder to assimilate and adopt conventional American traditions and rituals. In other words, perhaps what these girls needed to do was to find a way to bend their own beliefs to accommodate the typical prom, rather than appropriate the prom to conform to their own beliefs. How would you evaluate that claim?

5. Empathy is essential if we're going to understand the lives of people with different cultural, racial, or social backgrounds. When you read and write about people who are fundamentally different from you, how do you attempt to get outside of your own biases and the limitations of your own experience?

■ ETHNOGRAPHIC ESSAY 3

A few years ago, an anthropology professor in her fifties decided to move into the freshman dorm at her university. She registered as a freshman with an undeclared major and spent an academic year doing exactly what other freshmen did: attending parties, going to classes, making new friends. But she was also quietly collecting data on her experience for an ethnography about student life that was then published as a book, *My Freshman Year.*

The professor, Cathy Small, assumed a pseudonym for her project, Rebekah Nathan, and managed to conduct her research without arousing the suspicion of fellow freshmen at the school, Northern Arizona University. Her research was based not only on extensive observations, but also on a number of interviews with fellow students, including international students who attended the school. In the excerpt that follows, Small reports on how students from England, Germany, Japan, Mexico, India, China, and the United Arab Emirates (UAE) viewed an American college and its students. It isn't often that we can see ourselves as these students see us, and the portrait is revealing.

My Freshman Year: Worldliness and Worldview

Rebekah Nathan

1   The single biggest complaint international students lodged about U.S. students was, to put it bluntly, our ignorance. As informants described it, by "ignorance" they meant the misinformation and lack of information that Americans have both about other countries and about themselves. Although most international students noted how little other students asked them about their countries, almost all students had received questions that they found startling: "Is Japan in China?" "Do you have a hole for a bathroom?" "Is it North Korea or South Korea that has a dictator?" "Where exactly is India?" "Do you still ride elephants?" "Do they dub American TV programs into British?"

2   These are just a few of the questions American students actually asked of international students. While they no doubt came from the less sophisticated among their classmates, it was clear that international students across the board felt that most Americans—even their own friends—are woefully ignorant of the world scene. It is instructive to hear how students from diverse countries discuss their perceptions of American students' views of themselves and the world.

JAPAN: Really, they don't know very much about other countries, but maybe it's just because a country like Japan is so far away. Japanese probably don't know about the Middle East. Sometimes, students keep asking about ninjas.

UAE: American students are nice, but they need to stop being so ignorant about other countries and other cultures. Americans need to look at the world around them, and even the cultures around them in their own country.

MEXICO: The U.S. is not the center of the world. [Americans] don't know anything about other countries. Many of them don't have an interest in learning about other cultures. The only things students ever ask me about in my culture is food.

CHINA: Americans know very little about China or its culture. Most people think China is still very poor and very communist-controlled, with no freedom. There is a very anticommunist feeling, and people know little about today's China, which is quite changing and different. New Zealanders know much more about China—perhaps it's their proximity. I think that older people here have more of a sense of history, and that history, about the wars, about the cold war, makes them understand more about the world. Younger people seem to have no sense of history.

ENGLAND: People here know surprisingly little about England, and they assume a lot of things, some true, some not. People's impressions of me when I say I'm from England is that I might drink tea off a silver tray, and maybe live in a castle, and use a red telephone box. That's the honest truth. The questions that I've been asked are unbelievable.

MALAYSIA: I tell people that I am Muslim, and they take for granted that I'm an Arab. How can they not realize that not all Muslims are Arabs when they have many Muslims here who are American?

GERMANY: American students are much more ignorant of other countries and cultures. I suppose it's because it's so big, and knowing about California for you is like us knowing about France. It's a neighbor. The U.S. is less dependent on other cultures, and maybe that's why they need to know less. Still, Americans come across as not interested in other cultures, like they don't really care about other countries. So they think things like Swedish people are only blonds.

INDIA: Somebody asked me if we still ride on elephants. That really bothered me. If I say I'm Indian, they ask which reservation? I say I'm from Bombay. "Where is Bombay?" Some people don't even know where India is. A friend of mine and I tried to make these Americans see what it was like and we asked them where they're from. They said California. And we said, Where was that?

FRANCE: People here don't know where anything is. For World War II, the teacher had to bring in a map to show where Germany and England are—it was incredible! I read somewhere a little research that said only 15 to 20 percent of Americans between the ages eighteen to twenty-five could point out Iraq on a map. The country will go to war, but it doesn't know where the country is!

Despite the critical consensus in these comments, it would be unfair of me to represent international student perspectives as roundly negative. In general, students from outside the United States warmly appreciated the American educational system as well as the spirit of the American college student. The criticisms that they did have, though, were pointed and focused. Taken together, they amounted to nothing less than a theory of the relationship among ignorance, intolerance, and ethnocentrism in this country, one that international eyes saw bordering on profound self-delusion. When I asked the linked questions, "What would you want American students to see about themselves?" and "What advice would you give them?" one German student stated succinctly what many students communicated to me at greater length: "Americans seem to think they have the perfect place to live, the best country, the best city. I hear that all the time. I used to think you just got that from politicians, but now I see it's from regular people too. The patriotism thing here really bothers me." 3

It is sobering to hear these words from a German student, whose country's historical experience in the 1930s and 1940s taught him the dangers of hypernationalism. To his fellow U.S. students he offered this recommendation: "I'd give them advice to live elsewhere. They should recognize that the way of living in the U.S. is fine, but it 4

(continued)

(continued)

isn't necessarily the best way for everyone. I don't like to evaluate, and I'd like that applied to me. Be more informed. Information leads to tolerance."

5   It bothered a Chinese student who read in an article that American students don't want to study a foreign language because they believe that the world language will be English. "I think they need to learn about the world, to learn a foreign language," he urged. It bothered a British student, who lamented how much of world music American students seem to miss. "Everything here [on his corridor] is either black gangster rap or punk rock, and that's basically it. They don't want to hear other music—contemporary music from around the world."

6   The connection between lack of information and intolerance translated occasionally into personal stories of frustration, hitting home in the lives of some students. "I wish they [his hall mates] were accepting of more different music," said an Indian student. "I play my own music. I play it loud just like they do—Arabic and Punjabi and other stuff—and they complain to the RAs. But it's my right to play that too. Why don't they understand that?"

7   "They don't accept other cultures," speculated one Japanese student.

> Once I was eating the food I had made—Japanese noodles—and we Japanese eat noodles with a noise. Somebody else in the kitchen area looked at me funny. She asked, "Why are you making so much noise?" I told her that's the way Japanese eat their noodles, and I can see by her face that she is disapproving. It hurt me to see that. Some Americans don't care about other worlds.

8   One key toward creating a more positive cycle of information, self-awareness, and tolerance was for many the university and university education itself. Learn a foreign language and study overseas, many recommended for individual students. Use your education to expand your purview beyond your own country. For the university, other students recommended a greater emphasis on self-awareness, including a more critical eye directed to our own institutions and history.

9   For one Chinese student, the need to be more reflective about the media representation of news and issues was critical: "Media coverage has a very great influence here. In China, it has less influence because everyone knows it's propaganda. Here it is not seen that way because there is a free press. But it's curious." In American newspaper articles and TV news, "the individual facts are true often, but the whole is not sometimes. I can see how Americans need to question the way stories are being represented to them."

10   A French student beseeched us to examine our own educational system:

> Americans teach like the only important thing is America. There is no required history course in college. The history course I took on Western civ. at AnyU was middle-school level, and it was very biased. I mean they taught how, in World War II, America saved France and saved the world, how they were so great. The courses don't consider what Americans have done wrong. All the current events here is news about America and what America is doing. If it's about another country, it's about what America is doing there. There's nothing about other countries

and their histories and problems. [In France] we had lots of history and geography courses, starting very young. I learned about France, but then we had to take a course in U.S. industrialization, in China, Russia, Japan, too. We got the history and geography of the world, so we could see how France now fits into the bigger picture.

For the international students I interviewed, American college culture is a world   11 of engagement, choice, individualism, and independence, but it is also one of cross-cultural ignorance and self-delusion that cries out for remediation. It was a Somali student who summed up all of their hopes for "America": "You have so much here, and so many opportunities. I wish America would ask more what this country can do to make the world a better place."

Inquiring into the Essay

Explore, explain, evaluate, and reflect to discover what you think about the excerpt from *My Freshman Year.*

1. International students, according to Nathan's research, feel that many American college students are "ignorant" about the world, even ethnocentric, often feeling as if the United States is the only place worth living. This sometimes translates into a kind of supernationalism or patriotism that further feeds Americans' isolation from other cultures. This is a strong assertion. Fastwrite for seven minutes about whether you believe this is true, turning your writing whenever you can to your own personal experiences with other cultures on and off campus.

2. Would-be members of a culture learn what it is they need to do to join, and later, how they should behave to maintain their status. These international students are obviously confused about what it takes to belong to American student culture. Explain how they've got it wrong, and how they've got it right.

3. Ethnography and most other qualitative research attempts to infer from the few what might be true of the many. Evaluate the generalizability of the data about international students and how they view us reported here. Do you find Nathan's findings plausible? Why or why not?

4. Reflect on the methodology of this ethnography. Imagine, for example, that you were one of the students who lived on the same dorm floor as Rebekah Nathan. How would you have responded to her presence? How reliable do you think were the data she collected?

SEEING THE FORM

Mrs. Smith's Kitchen Table and Vanity the Day After She Died

My brother Buzz's neighbor, Mrs. Smith, lived in her small bungalow in Santa Cruz, California, for nearly all of her life. The day after she died, Buzz, a professional photographer, was in Mrs. Smith's house and took the pictures below. One of the many reasons I love these shots is how much can be revealed about a life by the things we choose to surround ourselves with. In these two pictures, I get a sense of a life

that was suddenly interrupted; we are confronted with the frozen image of a coffee cup and saucer, an open phone book, a crumpled tissue, bottles of medicine, and a picture of a fair-haired boy. An ethnographic "reading" of these pictures would place particular emphasis on what these things imply about Mrs. Smith's social status or as markers and artifacts of a culture to which she belonged.

Reading pictures like these, simply to speculate about the kind of person Mrs. Smith was, is a great exercise in ethnographic seeing. Spend a few minutes looking very closely at the pictures. Inventory as many details in the images as you can, perhaps cataloging them in your journal. As you consider these particulars, speculate about Mrs. Smith. What kind of person do you imagine she was? What kinds of things did she seem to care about? What does this brief moment in time suggest about the kind of life she was leading the day she died?

THE WRITING PROCESS

INQUIRY PROJECT: WRITING AN ETHNOGRAPHIC ESSAY

This assignment will take you into the field to observe a subculture in the community. You'll write a 2,500- to 3,000-word essay that uses field research and reading as the basis for an interpretation of how the subculture sees things. This necessarily will be a limited picture, so it should focus on some aspect of the culture that emerges from your observations.

The essay should also have the following qualities:

- Have a limited focus.

- Be organized around some thesis or interpretation of how this culture sees things. For example, how does the culture view authority figures, or what constitutes a leader in the group? (See the "Inquiring into the Details: Questions Ethnographers Ask" box, page 365.)

- Offer a rationale for why this group constitutes a distinct culture.

- Provide enough evidence from your field observations to make your interpretations and commentary convincing.

PEARSON
mycomplab
For additional reading, writing, and research resources, go to
www.mycomplab.com

Thinking About Subjects

Like any of the inquiry projects described in *The Curious Writer*, success depends on what motivates you. What might make you curious about studying a certain local culture? Do you have a family member you've always wanted to know better who just happens to be a truck driver, a farmer, an emergency room nurse, a migrant worker? Maybe your best friend is a member of a social group you'd like to study—a Baptist youth group, rock climbers, or Deadheads—and can offer access. If you're an older student, perhaps you have a niece or a nephew or possibly one of your own children who is a member of the local girls' tennis team, the youth ballet company, or the bowhunters club.

Might your professional interests be relevant to this project? Say you want to be a police officer; might it be enlightening to hang out with a few officers to find out what the life is like? If you have an interest in writing, then the ethnography assignment promises to be a great learning experience, no matter what culture you choose to study. You'll get practice in observation, note taking, interviewing, and profiling—skills that are invaluable for writers of any kind.

Possible subjects for your ethnography are all around you. We are all enmeshed within intricate webs of cultures. But what should you choose to write about? If you're a student at an urban campus, then the possibilities are nearly

WRITING IN YOUR LIFE

Commercial Ethnography

Ethnography isn't just for academics. Increasingly, businesses are using the method to analyze consumer behavior, and they are finding that ethnography is often better than the usual surveys, questionnaires, and focus groups. Why? Because the information researchers get from observing people where they work and live is a more accurate measure of what they think. Even more important, since ethnographers are interested in watching how people behave, not just in surveying their attitudes, researchers get a much more realistic picture about what people are willing to actually *do*. Using video, photographs, audio, interviews, and observation, commercial application of ethnography gives designers and marketers a glimpse into cultural norms or can reveal some of the ways a product may—or may not—fit into our ordinary lives.

limitless, but even if you attend a rural university you can still find a culture to study on your own campus.

Generating Ideas

Begin exploring possible subjects for a review by generating material in your notebook. This should be an open-ended process, a chance to use your creative side without worrying too much about making sense or trying to prejudge the value of the writing or the subjects you generate. In a sense, this is an invitation to play around.

Listing Prompts. Lists can be rich sources of triggering topics. Let them grow freely, and when you're ready, use an item as the focus of another list or an episode of fastwriting. The following prompts should get you started.

1. In class or in your journal, create a four-column table, labeling the first column Trends, the second Hobbies, the third Community Groups, and the fourth Campus Groups (see the following example). Brainstorm a list of *cultural trends* that are a visible part of American culture in the new millennium. For example, snowboarding is a sport that has boomed in recent years, nearly eclipsing skiing. Write the name of each trend under the first column in the table. Create a similar list for popular hobbies (note that trends and hobbies often overlap—snowboarding can also be a hobby) and write the name of each hobby in the second column. Finally, brainstorm a list of identifiable social groups in the community and on campus—fraternities, truck drivers, goths, and so on. Write these, respectively, in the third and fourth columns of your table.

Trends	Hobbies	Community Groups	Campus Groups
Snowboarding	Fly fishing	Kiwanis	Fraternities
Blogging (participating in Web logs)	Ballroom dancing	Pentecostal church	Black student alliance
	Computer games	Gospel singers	Graduate students
Atkins/South Beach/low-carb diet craze	Autograph collecting	Truck drivers	
Reality TV programming			

2. Create a new three-column table, labeling the first column Artifacts, the second Language, and the third Rituals. Now choose one of the trends, hobbies, community groups, or campus groups from your first table and under the first column of the new table list all of the artifacts—tools, equipment, devices, clothing—that you can think of that people typically use when they participate in the activity/group you have selected. In the second column, list the language—special terms, jargon, and other words or phrases—that group members regularly use. In the third column, list the rituals—habits, patterns of behavior, or traditions—that are typical of the activity/group. Creating the new table will help you expose some of the threads of a particular activity's or group's culture. Objects that group members typically use, their ways of speaking, and the traditions and rituals that govern their behavior are three key elements you need to consider when writing an ethnographic essay. The accompanying table identifies some of the artifacts, language, and rituals of fly fishing.

FLY FISHING

Artifacts	Language	Rituals
Fly rod (not "pole")	"Working water"	Keeping physical distance from other fly fishers
Artificial fly	"Skunked"	Catch and release of fish
Vest	"Meat fisherman"	Winter fly tying

Fastwriting Prompts. Choose an item from one of your lists as a fastwrite prompt. Write quickly, exploring each of the following questions:

1. What are your own experiences and observations with this trend, hobby, or group?

2. What are your presuppositions, biases, or assumptions about this trend, hobby, or group? What do you assume about the kind of people who participate in it, for example, and what might their motives be for belonging?

3. Based on what you know now, what things—or artifacts—seem particularly important to participants?

4. What questions do you have about why this trend exists, or why people participate in the group or hobby?

Visual Prompts. Sometimes the best way to generate material is to see what we think represented in something other than sentences. Boxes, lines, webs, clusters, arrows, charts, and even sketches can help us see more of the landscape of a subject, especially connections between fragments of information that aren't as obvious in prose.

1. If you like to take photographs, go through your collection looking for suggestive pictures of subcultures you've captured. Perhaps you took pictures of an on-campus or community event, or you have some shots of people back home that represent certain social groups.

2. Take a word or phrase from the table you created from the first question in the "Listing Prompts" section and use it as a nucleus word for a cluster on a blank page of your journal. When you cluster a hobby, cultural trend, or community or campus group, build associations using the five W's: *what, when, where, who,* and *why. Where* do participants of this hobby, group, or trend gather, and *when? Who* are the kind of people who belong? *What* are their activities and rituals? *Why* do people belong?

Research Prompts. Research can be helpful even this early in the process. New or more detailed information might trigger ideas about possible topics for your paper that you otherwise would never have considered. At this stage, your research will be open-ended and not particularly methodical. Just enjoy poking around.

1. In the United States, there's a magazine for nearly every subculture. Go to a bookstore and survey the hobby and special-interest magazines. The Web also has useful sites with links to resources on American subcultures or information on cultural trends (see "Inquiring into the Details: Researching Trends and Subcultures on the Web"). Do any of these interest you?

2. One quick way to gain entry to a culture you don't belong to is to find someone in your class who is a member. Stay alert to what others in the class say about their own identification with certain social groups and interview any who belong to a culture that interests you.

INQUIRING INTO THE DETAILS

Researching Trends and Subcultures on the Web

If you're browsing for ideas about a topic, or researching the cultural group you've chosen to investigate, a number of sites on the Internet can help.

- *The Pew Internet and American Life Project* features up-to-date information on trends in Internet use. http://www.pewinternet.org

- *The Statistical Abstract of the United States* is an annual Census Bureau publication that is a gold mine of data on all kinds of trends. http://www.census.gov/compendia/statab

- *The Gallup Poll* Web site features recent survey results on social trends. http://poll.gallup.com

- *The Open Directory Project,* a subject catalog of Web information, includes a useful directory on subcultures as varied as geeks and polygamists. http://dmoz.org/Society/Subcultures/

- *The Google Directory* also lists subcultures with links to resources on the Web. http://www.google.com/Top/Society/Subcultures/

- *Wikipedia,* the "free encyclopedia," isn't necessarily a good source for academic writing, but it is the "largest reference site on the Web." The list of subcultures is impressive. http://en.wikipedia.org/wiki/Category:Subcultures

Judging What You Have

Generating may produce the messy, incoherent writing that would earn you bad grades in most classes. Its virtue, however, should be obvious by now: "bad" writing gives a writer material to work with. And while it's always better to work from abundance rather than scarcity, this material still must be judged, shaped, and evaluated.

What's Promising Material and What Isn't? In deciding what to write about, keep in mind that you should choose a local culture that meets the following qualifications:

1. The culture is accessible to you.
2. The culture's members gather at places that you can visit.
3. The culture interests you in some way.
4. The culture might lend itself to library or online research.
5. You are not a member of this culture.

The last criterion—that you shouldn't be a member of the group you're studying—isn't a hard and fast rule, especially if you have just a few weeks to complete the assignment, but it is preferred. As an outsider, it takes a bit more time to gain access to the group and earn the members' trust, but this is a particularly useful vantage point for observing the culture because first impressions are enormously valuable. Also, as an outsider you'll be more open to what you see and more likely to see more.

How can you know whether a study subject will meet the definition of a culture? If the answer to the following questions is *yes*, then your subject probably will qualify:

- Does the group you want to study feel, at least implicitly, a sense of identification with each other as members? (This doesn't necessarily mean that they all like each other or always get along.)
- Do group members share certain behaviors, outlooks, beliefs, or motivations for belonging?
- Do they share a common language? Do they tend to describe things in similar ways, or use words or phrases that have special significance to the group?
- Do they share an interest in certain objects or artifacts? Do they invest these things with similar significance?

This list of questions might seem limiting, but because we are all immersed in social groups that have these kinds of cultural affinities you should find it easy to discover a culture to study from the ideas you generated. Cultures are everywhere, including your campus.

Questions About Audience and Purpose. No matter how fascinated you are by the people who do medieval battle reenactments at the park, you still have to have something *to say* about the subculture to readers who may not share your fascination. Most academic ethnographies are written to fellow experts. Researchers, to some extent, assume prior knowledge and interest in their subjects. However, you're writing an ethnographic *essay,* a much shorter, less extensively researched, and more general reader-friendly work. Imagine an audience that may know something about your subject—after all, most of us are aware of many social groups—but your essay should help readers to see what perhaps they've seen before in a way they haven't seen it. Good essays make the familiar strange.

How do you do this?

1. *Look hard and look closely.* If you're going to see anything new, you have to have as much data as you can. That means doing as much fieldwork as you can.

2. *Focus on what is less obvious.* If you're going to surprise your audience you need to surprise yourself. What are you noticing about those battle reenactors that you never noticed before?

3. *Find the question.* What aspect of your culture are you most interested in exploring?

4. *Discover one main thing you're trying to say.* You can't know what this is until you've done a lot of fieldwork and some reading. But in the final draft the main idea you're trying to get across about the group you observed should be clear.

5. *Tell stories, provide profiles, use dialogue, incorporate heavy description.* To bring the culture you studied to life for readers, try to employ some of the literary techniques you know from good storytelling.

Research Considerations. Prepare to do fieldwork by confirming the best places to conduct observations of the culture in which you're interested. Sometimes that's easy to figure out: Snowboarders hang out at the lodge, surfers at the beach, fraternity brothers at the fraternity house, homeless men at the shelter. But there will also be less obvious gathering places, locations you may only learn of through interviews with group members. Are there other locations where group members gather to socialize, plan activities, celebrate successes, or learn from each other?

> Writing ethnographically requires that you expand your repertoire of research to include interviews and fieldwork.

INQUIRING INTO THE DETAILS

Questions Ethnographers Ask

When you study a social group, whether it's skateboarders or opera singers, there are certain basic things you want to find out about how that group operates. For example,

- How do group members view outsiders?
- What motivates members to belong?
- What artifacts are present, how are they typically used, and what significance is attached to them?
- What is the nature of gender relations in the group?
- Where does the group gather and why?
- What is the group's social hierarchy, and how is it organized and maintained?
- What's the relationship between this local culture and the larger culture with which it identifies?
- Does this group seem to define itself *in opposition to* other groups, and if so, why?
- What are the culture's most symbolic or significant rituals? Why is meaning assigned to them?
- Is there an initiation of some kind?

If the sites you want to visit aren't public, you may need permission to conduct your observation. In addition, make sure you plan for your own safety. While it's unlikely that you'll study a city gang or a gun-toting right-wing militia or some similar group that can be dangerous to outsiders, make sure that you will be safe wherever you go. Bring a friend with you; tell others where you'll be and for how long.

Taking Notes. The most important source of information for your essay will be the observation notes you take in the field. You've practiced notetaking during the profile assignment, but the notes for the ethnography project will involve more observation. In the initial stages, focus on your first impressions of the group you're studying. Jot down everything.

Photographs. Visual ethnography uses photographs, film, or video to document local culture. These can be enormously rich records because pictures extend our perception and preserve information for later study and analysis. In addition, sharing the photographs we take with our study subjects can yield valuable insight about the meanings of the things in the images. A twelve-year-old skateboarder, for example, might look at the picture of someone attempting a trick and offer a commentary about the rider's motives and techniques, and the meanings of his moves. Digital photography has made it possible to instantaneously share this material.

INQUIRING INTO THE DETAILS

Ethnography and Ethics

Unlike most other undergraduate research projects, an ethnography involves work with human subjects. As you might imagine, this raises some ethical issues. How open should you be with your research subjects about your project? Do you need their permission? What responsibility do you have to protect your subjects' identities?

For faculty who do research with people, a university review board charged with protecting human subjects must approve the project. That probably won't be necessary for your ethnographic essay, but there are still ethical guidelines you should follow:

1. Let your research subjects know what you're doing and why you're doing it.

2. Obtain their permission to be included in your research. While a written "informed consent" may not be necessary, there should at least be a clear verbal understanding between you and the people you're studying.

3. Protect their anonymity. You have an obligation to make certain that your subjects' identities are protected. It's often a wise practice to use pseudonyms in your research.

For the American Anthropological Association's ethical guidelines, visit http://www.aaanet.org/committees/ethics/ethcode.htm.

Bring your camera along on your site visits and record what you see. When you print the pictures, attempt to place them in a meaningful order. Try to establish relationships among the pictures. Do they fall into certain categories of activity or significance? In addition, study the photographs for information that you might have missed in your field notes. What do you notice about artifacts, clothing, or the context in which the action is taking place?

Interviews. There is only so much we can see. Simply observing people won't tell us what they think or feel; we have to ask. Your earlier practice with interviews will have prepared you for this method of collecting information; see Chapter 4 and Chapter 11 for more information on interview methods and techniques.

Artifacts. If you can, collect or describe things from the site or that people in this culture routinely make, talk about, or use. For example, if you're studying a truck stop, collect menus, placemats, and so on. If you're studying people in a bowling league, describe the differences among bowling balls or collect score sheets. Photographs can also be helpful in identifying artifacts that you can't haul away. Collecting such things can help you to determine what meaning, if any, is assigned to them by group members. For example, do members of a male bowling league see the weight of a bowling ball as a measure of not only a bowler's strength but also his manhood?

Maps. One way to analyze a group's social relationships and the context in which activities take place is to observe where and how members occupy space. Imagine, for example, your own family dinner table as you were growing up. Did everyone sit in the same chair every night? Was there any logic to that arrangement? Does it say anything about the social roles of each family member? If you were to draw a map of your family's seating arrangement, and then add arrows that follow the movement of each member of your family during a typical meal, what would that suggest about social roles and relationships? In my family, my mother's chair was always nearest the kitchen, and she moved far more than the rest of us, mostly back and forth, to and from the oven, table, and sink. Consider making similar maps of your study site, noting the arrangement of things and people, as well as their movements.

Reading Research. Because you have weeks rather than months to write your ethnographic essay, you will probably need to rely somewhat on the work of others who have formally or informally studied the culture in which you're interested. This may include reading the hobby or specialty magazines that group members read; visiting Web sites, newsgroups, chat rooms, and electronic mailing lists that group members frequent online; and searching the library databases for any academic research that scholars may have published on the culture you're studying (see the "Inquiring into the Details: Useful Library Databases for Ethnography," page 372). You'd be surprised at how much work has been done on local culture in the United States.

■ FIELD NOTES

Rita Guerra hasn't bowled often in the past twenty years, but she has fond memories of holding birthday parties at the local bowling alley when she was a girl, and now her own children clamor from time to time to do some ten-pin bowling. Guerra remembers her hometown bowling alley as a social and cultural center for her small town. Wouldn't such a place be a great site to do some fieldwork for her ethnographic essay?

What follows are Guerra's field notes following her first visit to Emerald Lanes—"The Best Alley in the Valley." At this stage, she is focused on collecting data—transcribing conversations she hears, carefully describing what she sees, jotting down text from signs and notices, mapping the space, and simply watching to see what happens when. She uses double-entry field notes. On the left are her observations, and on the right are her impressions or ideas about what she sees, hears, smells, or feels. Notice that she gets a dialogue going between the two columns—speculating, interpreting, and raising questions on the right in response to specific information she collected on the left.

The success of your ethnographic essay depends on the success of your field notes. Always collect more information than you can use—which probably means multiple visits to your field sites—and push yourself to reflect on what you've found as you collect the information. Rita Guerra's field notes are a good model.

Field Notes on Friday Afternoon at Emerald Lanes

Rita Guerra

OBSERVATIONS OF	IDEAS ABOUT
4/9/04	
4:32 Sounds of balls hitting maple lanes, thundering toward pins. There is a constant hum of noise—rolling balls, lane chatter, country music, clanking of pins. Smells like cigarettes and beer. Smoking is allowed throughout the alley.	A Friday afternoon at Emerald Lanes appear to be more family oriented, no league play. But I was impressed by how many strong bowlers, mostly young couples played. Emerald Lanes seems a family-friendly place though I was surprised that the entire place allowed smoking. This might be indicative of the bowling culture—smoking is still okay.

"That will be a triple," says a woman in shorts and green tank top. She is bowling with two other young couples and they all bowl well, alternating between strikes and spares. Successful frame usually produces a kind of dance, clenched fists, "yessss!" Poor frame—silence, stone faced.

Scores are tallied electronically on monitors above each lane. Large number of families on Friday afternoon, including birthday party in far lanes.

"Got it right where I wanted to," says young player with girlfriend. He cups the ball underneath before his swing and when releasing it give it a spin. Ball breaks from left to right. Wears own bowling shoes, no rentals, and black wrist band. Spends very little time preparing but picks up his ball, sights the pins, and goes into motion within 15 seconds.

"The Best Alley in the Valley"
"The Bowling Guy's Pro Shop" Ball polisher
Tropical theme—three plastic palm trees between lanes.
Budweiser sign: Welcome to Emerald Lanes. Good Family Fun?
Movement

Need to check for "bowling lingo" on the Internet. What is a "triple"? Three strikes in a row? I was really interested in watching the preparation and releases of bowlers. Seems like you could tell the experienced bowlers from inexperienced ones by the smoothness of their release and especially the velocity of the ball. But maybe more than anything, I began to interpret their reactions to a good frame and bad frame. Strike produces a "yesss!" and clenched fist but not extended celebration. Bad frame a stony face. No anger, no laughter. Seemed to be no difference in this between men and women. Less experienced bowlers would react with more exaggeration.

I need to learn more about the theories behind introducing spin in releasing the ball. The ability to do this seems to distinguish the more skilled from the less skilled bowlers. This player consistently produced a left-to-right break by cupping the ball and obviously spinning it right before he releases it.

Might be interesting to actually time how long it takes for bowlers to prepare to bowl when it is their turn. My impression is that more experienced bowlers waste very little time; novices diddle and dawdle.

Like a lot of bowling alleys I've seen this one seems a bit tacky from the outside, and inside seems friendly but with an atmosphere of Budweiser beer and smoke. On a Friday afternoon, though, it seemed family friendly. Need to plan next visit for a Saturday night during league play. I have a sense that it's an entirely different culture.

Writing the Sketch

Write a sketch that provides a verbal snapshot of the culture you're studying. Using the ethnographer's questions (posed earlier) as guides for your field observation, go to a place where you can observe your culture in action. Collect observations and interviews that will allow you to create a snapshot of your group in action. For example, if you're interested in gender relations among young skateboarders, go to the skateboard park and carefully observe how the boys and girls interact. If possible, talk to some of them. Take lots of notes, and consider taking photographs as visual records, too.

Try working through the following three steps in your journal in preparation for drafting your sketch.

1. **Narrative of thought.** In your notebook, tell the story of how your thinking has evolved. When you first chose your subject, what did you think about that culture? What assumptions did you make and what did you expect to find? And then? And then? And then? And how about now?

2. **Look at strands in the web.** Which of the following features of a culture apply to the one you're studying?

    ■ *Shared language* (for instance, are there insider phrases and words that have significance to group members?)

    ■ *Shared artifacts* (for instance, are there objects that have particular significance to group members?)

    ■ *Common rituals and traditions* (for instance, are there patterns of behavior that surround certain activities, or are there historical understandings of how something must be done?)

    ■ *Shared beliefs and attitudes* (for instance, are there common attitudes toward other insiders, toward outsiders, toward new initiates; do group members share beliefs in the significance of the group and its activities?)

    ■ *Common motivations* (for instance, do members participate for some of the same reasons?)

3. **Examine one strand.** Choose *one* of the preceding features. In your notebook/journal, generate specific evidence from your research or fieldwork that supports your finding.

After you complete the above steps, write a 500- to 600-word sketch that describes what you saw and heard during one or more of your field experiences. The key is not to simply *explain* what you noticed but to *show* it, too. In addition:

■ Choose a title for your sketch.

■ Whenever possible, *show* what you observed or heard using description, scene, dialogue, and similar literary devices.

■ Offer a tentative theory about a belief or attitude that group members seem to share based on your initial field observations and interviews.

Moving from Sketch to Draft

If it was successful, your sketch provided an initial snapshot of the group you're studying. The draft, of course, will provide a fuller picture. But what should that picture focus on? What kind of information should you try to gather now? Your sketch can provide some useful clues.

Evaluating Your Own Sketch. You have a significant advantage over the people in your workshop group who will read and discuss your sketch: you witnessed what you're writing about. You spent time in the field gathering impressions and information, but quite a bit of that probably didn't end up in your sketch. Use that extra knowledge to guide your revision. But before you workshop your sketch, reread it, and in your notebook fastwrite responses to the following questions:

1. *What is my strongest impression of the group so far? What kinds of things did I see, hear, or read that gave me that impression?*

2. *What is another impression I have?*

3. *Which one of these two impressions might be a focus for the next draft?*

4. *What do I most want to know now about the culture I'm observing? What questions do I have?*

Questions for Peer Review. Everyone in your workshop group is working on a similar ethnography project, so you can help each other out by identifying the typical problems that these early drafts present: too little information, lack of focus, and insufficient interpretation of the information. Questions for the group to consider about each ethnography sketch include the following:

- What information or observations in the sketch seemed most striking?
- Which of the questions listed in the "Inquiring into the Details: Questions Ethnographers Ask" box seem to be addressed in the sketch? If the next draft focused on one or two of these, what might they be?
- Based on what you've read so far about this group, what theory would you propose about how its members see things?

Reflecting on What You've Learned. Follow up your workshop by making a schedule that describes your plan for additional research and field observations over the next few weeks. For example:

Sunday	Monday	Tuesday	Wednesday	Thursday	Friday	Saturday
2–4 Field observations at the park		3 PM Pick up photos		7 PM Library research		10–12 Field observations, interview w/Karen

Research and Other Strategies: Gathering More Information

The most important thing you can do to improve the next draft of your ethnography is return to the field for more observations and interviews. This project doesn't permit the kind of immersion in a culture that most ethnographic researchers enjoy, so it's essential that you focus on gathering as much data as you can in the time you have. This will take careful planning and scheduling and your schedule will help. (In fact, your instructor may ask you to hand in your schedule.)

If photography is part of your data gathering, spend some time analyzing the pictures you've taken. Begin by arranging them in some kind of logical order, and note that chronology isn't the only arrangement that makes sense. Do you see the pictures grouping around certain typical activities? Do they seem relevant to any of your particular research questions? Does a sequence suggest something about how group members interact with each other or occupy space? Do certain arrangements of photographs tell a story that seems significant?

Study individual photographs as well. Because the camera's eye misses little, a single picture can be a rich source of detailed information about the context or setting in which important group activities take place. A picture can also capture data about artifacts and even the relationships among group members. All of this information can help you write a more informative, interesting draft and make your interpretations of what you've seen more convincing.

Finally, don't forget to continue library and Internet research. Consult specialized indexes and databases you might have skipped earlier (see "Inquiring into the Details: Useful Library Databases for Ethnography" below). What can you learn from what others have observed and said about the culture you're studying?

INQUIRING INTO THE DETAILS

Useful Library Databases for Ethnography

Don't forget to research existing ethnographies that may be published on the culture you're studying. If your library has them, the following specialized databases are worth checking:

- Anthropological Index Online
- EHRAF Collection of Ethnography
- Sociological Abstracts
- Ethnographic Bibliography of North America
- Abstracts in Anthropology
- Abstracts of Folklore Studies
- International Bibliography of the Social Sciences

Composing the Draft

Here's a checklist to consider before you start drafting:

✓ *Do you have enough information?* Have you gathered sufficient field notes and done enough research?

✓ *Do you have a focus?* If you want your ethnographic essay to be interesting and informative, you must focus on an aspect of the culture you're studying.

✓ *Do you have a theory?* By now, you've hopefully got an idea or two about some significant patterns you've observed in the relationships, artifacts, rituals, and behaviors of the culture you're studying. What are they?

Methods of Development. As an extended form of inquiry, the ethnographic essay will probably combine some of the methods of development described here.

Narrative Structures. Because ethnography often involves scene or setting, character, dialogue, and action, it's a form that naturally accommodates storytelling. Try one or more of these narrative techniques.

1. *A typical day.* One way to capture your culture is to describe, in some detail, what happened on a single day that seems representative. This focus on a particular time, place, and people gives your ethnographic essay a dramatic and limited focus.

WRITING IN THE DISCIPLINES

Digital Ethnography

In 2007, Kansas State anthropology professor Michael Wesch, pondering the potential of digital texts compared with print, posted a video on YouTube, "The Machine is Us/ing Us." Within days the spot got millions of viewings. Along with with his students, Wesch is now working on an ethnography of YouTube. Wesch's work dramatizes how easily and quickly information can be distributed on what is now called "Web 2.0." But he also argues that this new media isn't just an exciting new form of communication; it is fundamentally changing "human relationships," something that ethnographers should study. "We know the value of participant observation in understanding social worlds," he wrote recently. "Now we need to understand the new forms of sociality emerging in this quickly changing mediated world." The field is responding. Increasingly, ethnographies are published digitally, incorporating text with videos, photographs, and audio. Consider those possibilities with your own ethnographic essay. Can you imagine ways to present your findings using some combination of digital media?

2. *Collage.* Sometimes it's effective to generate a series of significant snapshots of your subjects in their natural setting. For example, an ethnography of eighth-grade cheerleaders might feature a collage of scenes with titles like "Making the Team" or "The Squad's Social Hierarchy."

3. *Narrative of thought.* Tell the story of your initial presumptions about the culture and how your observations and research influenced those. Or state an initial theory and then tell the story of whether the evidence supported it.

Question to Answer. Inquiry projects are motivated by questions and you can use them to structure your draft.

Begin by establishing your focusing question (e.g., "What is the social hierarchy of dog handlers and how is it maintained?"). Then consider including some or all of the following:

- Provide some background from research about other studies (if any) that have directly or indirectly addressed the question.

- Explain the writer's interest in the question. What observations, interviews, or readings suggest that the social hierarchy of dog handlers might be interesting or significant to look at?

- Explain the methods the writer used to focus on the question.

- Offer a theory, a possible answer to the question. For example, Based on my initial impressions, handlers and trainers who have established reputations as successful breeders tend to get the most respect.

Compare and Contrast. When I teach graduate workshops in creative nonfiction, I often wonder how gender shapes my students' responses to each other and the work being discussed. If I conducted a study that focused on such a question, I probably would find a range of ways in which men and women interact with each other. One useful way of exploring these would be to look for similarities and differences, to compare and contrast. In fact, it's hard to imagine any ethnography not exploiting this method of development in at least a small way, and it's easy to imagine that comparisons might form the backbone of some essays.

Using Evidence. Ethnographic research is distinctive because it studies social groups in their own environments. It follows, then, that the most important evidence in this kind of essay will be the investigator's detailed field observations. In addition, because the purpose of an ethnography is to attempt to see the world the way your study subjects see it, interviews that bring the voices of group members into the essay provide valuable evidence. After all, who can better articulate a group's beliefs and perspectives than its members? Ethnography mostly relies on *primary* research like this, but secondary sources—articles and essays about the group you're studying—can be useful, too, particularly if they come from academic sources. But it's time in the field that is the most important element in the success or failure of this kind of writing.

Workshopping the Draft

If your draft is subject to peer review, see Chapter 14 for details on how to organize workshop groups and decide on how your group can help you. The following journal activities and questions should help you make the most of your opportunity to get peer feedback on your work in progress. But first, are you happy with the way the first draft turned out? Here is a check to determine the strengths and weaknesses of your draft:

- Is your purpose clear? Do you think readers will understand the question that interests you or what your particular motives were when writing about this culture?

- Have you taken a landscape picture when you needed a close-up? Does the draft try to cover too much territory, include too much information, or say too much?

- Is there enough specific information—observations, scenes, facts, dialogue, and so on? Do you show as well as tell in the draft?

- Is it clear what you're trying to say about this group? Do you propose a certain theory about how it operates or sees things? Do you make a central claim or have a main point? Are you working toward a dominant impression or interpretation of the group?

Reflecting on the Draft. Review the preceding list, and fastwrite for seven minutes in your journal exploring your answers to some of the questions. End the fastwrite by generating a quick list of ideas in response to this question. *What things might I do to improve this draft when I revise it?*

Questions for Readers. Make the most of your peer review session by asking readers of your draft to answer one or more of the following questions:

1. If you had to summarize in a sentence or two your main impression of the group I studied, what would it be?

2. If you were to imagine the draft as a kind of documentary film that allows you to get a good look at a culture, where in the draft were the camera shots most vivid? Where in the draft did you wish there were close-ups, or long shots?

3. What questions did the draft seem to try to answer about the culture? Which of these seem most important or interesting?

Revising the Draft

Revision is a continual process—not a last step. You've been revising—literally "re-seeing" your subject—from the first messy fastwriting in your journal. But the things that get your attention during revision vary depending on where you are in the writing process. You've generated material, chosen a topic, done some research, and written both a sketch and draft. Most students think that the only thing left to do is "fix things." Check for misspellings. Correct an awkward sentence or two. Come up with a better title. This is editing, not revision, and while editing is important, to focus solely on smaller "fixes" after writing a first draft squanders an opportunity to really *learn* from what the draft is telling you, or perhaps not quite telling you.

Chapter 13 can help guide these discoveries. The questions you can ask of a draft fall into five categories: purpose, idea, information, development, and editing. Use the following chart to find the revision strategies in Chapter 13 that might help you re-see what you've written so far. Ethnographic essays typically have some of the following problems that should be addressed in revision:

- Does your draft fail to give clear enough pictures to readers about the group you studied? The problem is usually that there simply isn't enough information from field observations of the group. The solution? Get back out into the field.

- Do your self-references in the draft—how you felt at a particular moment, what you were thinking, and so on—serve a purpose? Do they contribute in some way to an effort to clarify your biases or methodology, or do they help readers understand how your study subjects see things? If not, cut those self-referential passages to keep the focus on your subjects.

- Does the draft try to say things about the group rather than focus on a single main thesis, interpretation, or question?

GUIDE TO REVISION STRATEGIES

Problems in the Draft (Chapter 13)	Page Number
Unclear purpose ■ Not sure what the paper is about?	551
Unclear thesis, theme, or main idea ■ Not sure what you're trying to say?	557
Lack of information or development ■ Need more convincing evidence?	564
Disorganized ■ Doesn't move logically or smoothly from paragraph to paragraph?	568
Unclear or awkward at the level of sentences and paragraphs ■ Seems choppy or hard to follow at the level of sentences or paragraphs?	577

- If your time for fieldwork was limited, did you make up for it by finding some useful research about the culture you studied in the library or on the Web?

Refer to Chapter 13, "Revision Strategies," for ideas about how to address these and many other problems. Use the following table to find other appropriate revision strategies. Remember that a draft may present problems in more than one category.

Polishing the Draft

After you've dealt with the big issues in your draft—is it sufficiently focused, does it answer the *So what?* question, is it well organized, and so on—you must deal with the smaller problems. You've carved the stone into an appealing figure but now you need to polish it. Are your paragraphs coherent? How do you manage transitions? Are your sentences fluent and concise? Are there any errors in spelling or syntax? Section 5 of Chapter 13 can help you focus on these issues.

Before you finish your draft, work through the following checklist:

✓ Every paragraph is about one thing.

✓ The transitions between paragraphs aren't abrupt.

✓ The length of sentences varies in each paragraph.

✓ Each sentence is concise. There are no unnecessary words or phrases.

✓ You've checked grammar, particularly verb agreement, run-on sentences, unclear pronouns, and misused words (*there/their, where/were,* and so on). (See the handbook at the back of the book for help with these grammar issues.)

✓ You've run your spellchecker and proofed your paper for misspelled words.

■ STUDENT ESSAY

The term *gaydar* entered the American lexicon in the past decade or two, though few thought the idea that gay men and women can intuitively distinguish gay from straight was much more than urban legend. Recent research, however, seems to confirm that there just might be something to it. The ethnographic essay that follows asks whether gay men use means other than intuition to make judgments about the sexual orientation of strangers.

This study of four Boise gays is a fascinating look at gay culture. But it's a limited one, too. Like all qualitative research, "Beyond Gaydar" hopes to find useful insight into the many by looking at the few. This project, like most ethnographies conducted in a composition class, is based on only several weeks of fieldwork, rather than the years that most ethnographies require. Still, the essay offers a useful glimpse at the world of young gay men, and it seems to amplify some of the published research. Kersti Harter's essay is cited using APA guidelines.

Running head: BEYOND GAYDAR   1

Kersti Harter

Beyond "Gaydar": How Gay Males Identify Other Gay Males

A Study with Four Boise, Idaho Men

Introduction

1   While people who do not fit into the codified norms of behavior in contemporary urban life are often marginalized by the mainstream, this very fact
often serves to empower and reinforce the behavior of its members in marginalized groups. This is the case within gay male culture in United States urban
society. Because gay males remain heavily stigmatized, they have formed a
large "outside" group with subtle yet unmistakably designated patterns and
categories of behavior, action, clothing, and taste. These patterns and behaviors may not be identifiable to the larger society, but they are well-known
among gay men. One of these social rituals is the patterns through which gay
men attempt to identify other gay males. I had very little prior knowledge that
this pattern existed, but through interviews and observations of several gay
men in Boise, Idaho, aged 18–25, I discovered how some gay males identify
others who are gay.

I was able to model this pattern and the categories of behavior that exist
within it.

Background

2   Several studies suggest that so-called "gaydar," the use of intuition to determine the sexual orientation of someone without asking the person outright
whether he or she is gay, might have a basis in fact. A recent study (Lawson,
2005) demonstrated that when provided with "neck-up" photographs of
strangers who weren't wearing jewelry or makeup, homosexuals were better
than heterosexuals in making the correct identification of the stranger's sexual

BEYOND GAYDAR   2

orientation, making this judgment in 2 seconds or less (p. 30). Martins et al. (2005) also reported that "gay men were found to be particularly good at detecting the scent of other gay men" (p. 694). In addition, another study argued that "eye gaze," with distinct variations, is "crucial to forces that either trigger or reinforce one gay's perception of another gay's identity during social encounters" (Nicholas, 2004).

Identifying Other Gay Males: Place

There are, however, other methods of gay identification used by male homosexuals that don't rely on "gaydar" or intuition. One such method, depicted in Figure 1, relies on contextual cues or markers. The number one identifier among the four contextual cues is place: if he's in the gay bar, he's likely gay. But this does not mean for sure that any man in a gay club is gay.

3

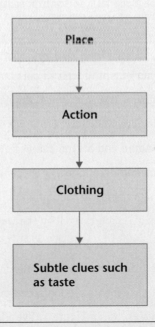

Figure 1   The sequence of judgments used by gay men to identify other gay men

BEYOND GAYDAR   3

Julian recounted a story in which he accidentally "hit on" a straight male who was in a gay club:

> It was at a gay club, so I'm not entirely at fault. This guy was just sitting there, kind of like, I don't know, just sitting there at the bar, looking kind of, well, sitting there sulking I guess. And I thought he was pretty good looking, so I thought I'd go talk to him, I wasn't going to pick him up or anything. And so I went up and was talking to him, and he would answer me in one-syllable replies. And I just walked off and I found out that he was actually the bouncer that worked there and he had the night off.

4   Julian's story suggests that "gaydar" isn't always reliable. Sexual orientation signaling is based on more than intuition. It also means that place is not the only identifier of gay males, although it is often accurate. So what happens when the identifier of place fails to confirm sexual orientation?

Action

5   Then we must move onto appearance. I use "appearance" here because my participants claimed that movement as well as personal style played into identifying whether a man is gay. I have subdivided appearance into action, or movements and other behaviors, and clothing, which I discuss below. During my group interview, both Aaron and Steven claimed that movement is the more important part of appearance in determining a man's orientation:

> Me: Does clothing or movement clue you in more to whether or not a person is gay? Aaron: Movement...You can tell by the way a person gesticulates, by how they walk. I can tell how I walk...I'm like God, everyone knows I'm a homo [laughs]! Like I like it, but yeah, it's definitely how they move.

6   It seems that certain movements are ingrained qualities that help gay males identify other gay males. So, in Figure 1, I've identified the next step my

BEYOND GAYDAR   4

subjects might use to identify another gay male as "Action." Some of these
movements are evident even to straight observers, and occasionally the actions
have to do with associations with other gay men. For example, another participant, Jeff, pointed out, "Well, if they are with a guy, then yeah, they're gay."

If action is not enough to identify the man's orientation, an observer   7
might move on to more subtle parts of clothing style or even personal tastes.
But this would probably not happen in such a situation, and actions are likely
telling enough.

Clothing and Personal Style

There are times, however, when gay men are in places less exclusively   8
gay, or in places not defined as gay at all. Then one must skip to the latter
steps, identifying the less obvious markers of sexual orientation such as personal style.

When I began my research, I sat with my friend Steven in a popular   9
downtown Boise coffee shop, The Flying M. While being widely known as the
"gay" coffee shop, it is not exclusively so. Wednesday, according to Steven, has
become known to some in the gay community as "Gay Night." This Wednesday
was the first time that I met his friend Aaron, who later helped me in the
group interview. I would ask Steven, "Is that guy over there gay?" and so on,
and he would answer yes, because the man was simply at this coffee shop on
Gay Night, or because he acted a certain way, or dressed a certain way.

When he would identify them as gay because of the way they looked,   10
David would often cite things like button-down Abercrombie and Fitch shirts or
spiky hair. There was a definite gay look that he was able to identify. Steven
was able to identify gay males, even though we were in a setting that was not
necessarily exclusively gay. Clothing, though it is used less than place and

action, still can provide clues about sexual orientation. There are also categories of gay male dress style that the men that I interviewed identified.

Stylistic Stereotypes Among Gay Males

11   To outsiders, clothing and personal style would be one of the easiest
identifiers of gay males. But it is actually, according to my subjects, a less obvious marker than place or action. Personal style also comes in many shapes
and forms in the gay community. It's as if there is a set of emic values (distinc-
tions that members of a group recognize that may not be apparent to outsiders) that are stereotypical of the gay male. This is an instance where the
pattern of behavior in the group is broken down into diverse categories.

12   For example, Green and Ashmore, in "Taking and Developing Pictures in
the Head: Assessing the Physical Stereotypes of Eight Gender Types" (1998),
asked college students to picture various stereotypes in their heads and
describe what they saw. They asked them to picture both "nerd" and "homosexual," and they found that:

> Perceivers have similar pictures of the homosexual and the nerd in their
> heads. Both were frequently described as being slender and of average
> height, wearing glasses, and wearing the "uniform" of the male college
> student (e.g., button-down shirt, pants or jeans, sneakers or casual
> shoes). (p. 1627)

13   Though these college students pictured "the nerd" and "the homosexual"
together, the men I talked with identified a picture of the homosexual that
was quite different from the one these college students identified. The men
also emphasized that there were many different types of gay male style, not
just one. They all identified several emic stereotypes, and disagreed with the
"nerd" and "homosexual" being lumped together in similar stylistic categories.

BEYOND GAYDAR   6

  When I mentioned this article to Julian, he explained to me why people   14
might lump the "nerd" with the "homosexual":

> In Europe they used to associate Jews and homosexuals, they were kind
> of lumped together. And so maybe whoever's on the outside is kind of la-
> beled together...I don't think that's a look that gay guys go for as far as
> trying to look like that...there's sort of that geek chic that a lot of peo-
> ple do, pretty much if you see that you know they're straight.

  According to Julian, though the outside sees homosexuals and   15
nerds having similar styles because of their roles as the "outsiders," homosexuals have a different view of their styles, one that is much more rich
and varied.

  In the essay "Gay Masculinity in the Gay Disco," Cheseboro and Klenk   16
(1981) identify several categories of symbol-using in the gay disco. Though
written more than twenty-five years ago, it gives insight into some incipient
analyses of stylistic categories that gay men employ. Cheseboro and Klenk describe "The Virility Component":

> One concept asserted in the gay disco is an exaggerated, if not flagrant,
> form of masculinity in appearance...an extreme case of this composite
> image includes an explicitly displayed, muscularly developed body, a flan-
> nel shirt, a leather vest, denim or leather pants, construction or cowboy
> boots. (p. 95)

  Though perhaps less in vogue now, the hyper-masculine male look is still 17
a symbolic type that some gay males employ. At first, I described these men as
"bears," a more masculine type of gay male, but Julian corrected me and said
that perhaps I was referring to something more like a butch. Julian thought
that perhaps butch gay males care about their appearance and attempt to look

BEYOND GAYDAR 7

masculine while bears don't really care about their appearance at all, and are more like the general straight male.

18   Julian's uncertainty about what exactly the hyper-masculine gay man would be called perhaps reflects current fashion. With the rise of more males in high fashion, the advent of television programs such as *Queer Eye for the Straight Guy,* and the heterosexual adaptation of the homosexual stereotype, or the "metrosexual," it seems that the bear style has fallen out of favor. It seems that now, instead of taking its fashion cues from the heterosexual world, homosexuals are creating styles that are being used by the world of high fashion and by straight people, who dress more in the mainstream. Julian expressed this concern:

> Me and some of my friends were talking and we were mad because we feel that straight people are stealing our stuff, like have you noticed the guys wearing pink shirts? Yeah, I just don't think they have a right to do that. Like my friends and I were joking that we might go up to one of these guys and be like, "You better have put that in the laundry with something red," you know like it was white before.

19   There is a feeling of resentment within the gay community that symbols are being appropriated by the larger population. In *Gays, Lesbians, and Consumer Behavior* (1996), Wardlow explains the cause of this resentment:

> When the symbolism of the community becomes framed as the basis for a target market from an "outside" perspective, the styles become divorced of the meanings they once held...and the style takes on new or more vague meanings. Based on the perspectives expressed in our interviews, the issue is not so much that meaning has become diluted or that a symbol has been stolen, as it is that manufacturers are selling the product as "cool" or "hip" without reference to its meaning. (pp. 99–100)

BEYOND GAYDAR   8

The manufacturing world is taking symbols highly popularized in the gay   20
community and making them available for the mainstream, for example, the
pink shirts that Julian cited which are becoming increasingly popular with
heterosexual males.

Appealing to both a homosexual and a heterosexual (or perhaps metrosex-   21
ual) audience is a good strategy for a clothing manufacturer; it can target two
highly valuable markets at once. Based on my research, it's obvious that no other
company does this better than Abercrombie and Fitch, as every interviewee cited
the popular clothing company and its ubiquity among gay males. This leads me
to the associated stereotypes of "flamer" and "Abercrombie bitch." Both of these
types would wear Abercrombie and Fitch clothing, but the flamer would not wear
it exclusively. These two types would perhaps, if we could put all the different
gay styles on a spectrum, fall closer to femininity than butch or bear would.

What happens when place, action, and personal style all fail to disclose a   22
man's sexual orientation, or when one of these categories is missing or frag-
mentary? Then clues can be found in personal taste, or habitus.

Subtle Clues in Personal Taste

Among the gay men I interviewed, I found that there is a distinct musical   23
taste that gay males recognize is characteristically gay. I focused on musical
taste because my interviewees discussed it the most when I brought up gay
preferences in things other than clothing. During the group interview, I asked
them to comment on gay musical taste. Jeff mentioned that "they all listened
to techno" and expressed his exasperation over it. They cited Barbara Streisand
as gay music. Steven stressed that, "You can't be gay and not have Cher."

So how could musical taste signal sexual orientation? It's difficult to imag-   24
ine such a situation when place, action, and personal style would fail to show

BEYOND GAYDAR   9

sexual orientation. Personal taste might be a more cultivated part of the gay habitus, one which would be formed later after the other qualifications were met, and therefore would not be present without the other gay qualities. In other words, musical taste cannot be seen as only a signal to other gay men of a man's orientation. For example, a man who contradicted the other gay qualities regarding place, action, and personal style would probably not be viewed by the others as gay, if he simply expressed an affection for alternative music.

Conclusions

25   In interviewing four gay males in Boise, Idaho, over a period of a month, I saw some general patterns emerge. I discovered that the most importance in discovering sexual orientation was placed on the actual location where a man was seen. Behaviors and movements were also highly important, though being in a gay location might outweigh any straight symbolism that a certain man would possess, e.g., Julian's experience of assuming a man in a gay bar was gay, when in reality he was straight. Clothing can also be a signal to other males of sexual orientation, but it is not as telling as place and action. Personal tastes in things like music are less of a signal of sexual orientation and more of a cultivated gay taste.

26   In concluding my research, I also should point out that these things I have observed have merely scratched the surface of gay male identification. I do not even attempt to explain verbal behavior and its relation to nonverbal clues. I did not consider hearsay among the gay community or when gay males have simply identified themselves verbally. I do not assume that these are the only ways that gay males identify each other or that they are the most commonly used. I also do not want to trivialize intuition or conclude that there is absolutely nothing to "gaydar."

BEYOND GAYDAR   10

References

Cheseboro, J. W., and Klenk, K. L. (1981). Gay masculinity and the gay disco. In J. W. Cheseboro (Ed.), *Gayspeak: Gay male and lesbian communication* (pp. 87–103). New York: Pilgrim Press.

Green, R. J., and Ashmore, R. D. (1998). Taking and developing pictures in the head: Assessing the physical stereotypes of eight gender types. *Journal of Applied Social Psychology, 28*(17), 1609–1636.

Lawson, W. (November–December 2005). Gay men really do find it easier to spot other gays. *Psychology Today*, 30.

Martins, Y., Crabtree, C. R., Runyan, Vainius, A. A., and Wysocki, C. J. Preference for human body odors is influenced by gender and sexual orientation. *Psychological Science*, 16 (2005), 694–701.

Nicholas, C. L. (2004). Gaydar: Eye-gaze as identity recognition among gay men and lesbians. *Sexuality and Culture*, 8 (Winter), 60–86.

Wardlow, D. L. (1996). *Gays, lesbians, and consumer behavior: Theory, practice, and research issues in marketing.* New York: Harrington Park Press.

(All references to "Julian," Steven, Jeff, or Aaron come from either participant observation or interviews collected between November 3, 2004, and November 29, 2004.)

However, the research essay does present a few differences: First, the research essay may be the most thoroughly documented of the essays you've written so far, and it may be the one that is most likely to require scholarly sources such as journal articles and academic books. It's also likely to be a project that takes more time to do, and may be the longest essay you're assigned, ranging from eight to twenty pages. A writing project with such an extended process of inquiry is more complicated to manage—it has more steps, you have more information to organize, and it's often harder to figure out what you want to say. For all of these reasons, the research essay is a form of inquiry that deserves special attention.

> Research is something writers naturally do whenever they have questions they can't answer on their own.

Still, research is hardly something alien to you. You've written research essays before, and although you probably don't consider yourself a researcher, for most of us research is a daily affair, whether looking up the details on new laptop computers in order to buy the right one or hunting for a new apartment in a highly competitive real estate market. Finally, research need not be boring at all. On the contrary, reading, observing, and interviewing can crack open worlds of study you never imagined.

RESEARCH ESSAYS, RESEARCH PAPERS, AND RESEARCH REPORTS

While any piece of writing can be researched—including things like short stories, blogs, and personal essays—academic research assignments typically fall into one of three categories: research reports, research papers, and research essays (see Figure 10.1). The least common of these in college is the research

	Research Report	Research Paper	Research Essay
Purpose	To explain	To prove	To discover
Thesis	None	Up front	Delayed
Documentation	Yes	Yes	Usually
Organization	Summary-explanation	Thesis-support	Question-answer
Use of "I"	No	Sometimes	Usually
Inquiry	Low	High	Highest

Figure 10.1   Three genres of academic research

report. This is the familiar paper many of us wrote in high school that simply explains—Wikipedia-like—what is known about some topic. The writer of a research report isn't trying to *use* the information to make a point or investigate a question.

A far more common (and useful) college writing assignment is the research paper, a term that is loosely used to describe an essay that is an extended argument on some topic. It's like the essay you might have tackled in Chapter 8—the public argument—except that the research paper leans much more heavily on outside sources and is intended for a more academic audience. Its goal is to prove a thesis using the evidence the writer gathers.

The research essay is the most inquiry-based of the three genres. While the research paper certainly can involve an open-ended investigation, the paper itself usually reports conclusions rather than the questions that gave rise to them. Both the research paper and research essay have a thesis, but in the essay it might appear late in the work, as the writer works through questions and evidence to arrive at an understanding of the topic. While it may be a less common assignment than the argumentative research paper, the research essay is much more likely to encourage the habits of mind that encourage genuine inquiry. It invites writers to begin with questions rather than answers, to suspend judgment, and accept that ambiguity—even confusion—is a natural part of the research process.

> The research essay is likely to encourage the habits of mind that encourage genuine inquiry and accepting ambiguity as a natural part of the process.

In the three professional readings that follow in this chapter, you'll get a chance to see the range of approaches to research writing, from the informal and undocumented researched essay to the formal research paper. Most of these readings focus on a single subject—courtship and sexuality on the American college campus—which will help you appreciate how the different forms of research writing offer different ways of examining a subject.

MOTIVES FOR WRITING A RESEARCH ESSAY

I was in the market for a new guitar, and for several weeks I'd been studying back issues of an acoustic guitar magazine, searching the Web for guitar makers, and talking to people who play. My process was driven by particular questions I had: What are the best tone woods for a classical guitar? *What are the various models and how much do they cost? What are the sound qualities to consider when selecting an instrument?* While I probably would never write an essay using my research, the stakes were rather high. I was likely to spend a lot of money on a guitar and I didn't want to make a mistake.

Although everyday research may not be as methodical as academic research, both approaches employ many of the same skills and share the same motive: curiosity. Sometimes this curiosity is intellectual interest—What are the origins of radical Islam?—and sometimes it's in response to a need for information: What is the best-quality acoustic guitar? Either way, the process begins as all inquiry projects do, with a question.

Not just any question will do. It has to be one that will drive the process for the few weeks it takes for you to learn about your topic and know enough to discover your own ideas about it. For example, the question, "Is Elvis dead?" will take about a second to answer: Yes, the King is dead. Why people keep asking that particular question is much more interesting and a more researchable question that just might work for an extended investigation. But whatever question you ask, it must be interesting to *you*.

Academic researchers *always* ask questions that interest them; curiosity is the most important motive. It should be for you, too. The essential thing you must learn about research writing is how to craft a good question that makes you wonder enough to live with the question long enough for you to write on it. This takes more skill than you might imagine, but once you know how to ask researchable questions, you'll be much more likely to see research writing the way your professors do—an opportunity for discovery.

THE RESEARCH ESSAY AND ACADEMIC WRITING

The research paper is a fixture in high school courses, usually lodged in the junior or senior English class and advertised as preparation for The College Research Paper. (Even my nine-year-old daughter wrote research papers.) Research-based writing assignments are probably among the most common in college, across the curriculum. In fact, at my own university almost three-quarters of the faculty surveyed said they assign an "academic paper that requires research." That's one reason you're writing a research essay in your composition class—to help prepare you to write papers in other courses.

These writing assignments can take a number of forms, including term papers, proposals, literature reviews, abstracts, and reports. But they all demand facility with finding information in the library, on the Web, or in the field; the skills to evaluate the information you have uncovered; and the ability to *use* that information appropriately and purposefully. Because research writing involves dealing with all of these things—something like a novice juggler trying to keep five balls in the air—even talented writers can see their prose fall apart when trying to communicate their findings. Additionally, the writers' beliefs and assumptions may make it harder to get the work done, and their beliefs and assumptions may even be misleading, if not downright wrong.

Some years ago, I surveyed about 250 first-year writing students about the research paper assignment, and at least 60 percent of them shared the following beliefs:

- "I have to be objective."
- "I have to know my thesis before I start."
- "I need to follow a formal structure."
- "I can't use 'I'."

There is an element of truth to each of these, but each of these beliefs *works against* a genuine understanding of what it means to do academic research. Then what *is* the nature of academic research and the research essay?

FEATURES OF THE FORM

There's quite a range of research-based writing. Nearly every assignment you've done so far in *The Curious Writer* might be considered research based; reading, interviewing, and observing could be elements of any of the inquiry projects you've attempted while using this book. But the research essay has a few distinctive features:

- *Academic research is driven by questions, not answers.* Most scholarship begins with a question about something: What is the impact of congressional redistricting on representation of minorities? What are the various ways the river might be understood symbolically in *Huckleberry Finn*? What is the distribution of bracken fern in a mature upland forest? What are the rhetorical strategies of pro-anorexia groups on the Web? Researchers begin with a question, not an answer, and although they may hypothesize, researchers are always prepared to be proved wrong. Framing the question is a crucial and often difficult part of the process.

- *The question is put in the context of what has already been said.* You're interested in whether so-called relational aggression between girls might be present in your niece's second-grade classroom. That's a great research question. What have others already said about it? How might the answers to your question contribute to the ongoing conversation about how young girls treat each other? This often means that you will need to become familiar with the published conversation about your topic, a step in the research process called a literature review (see Appendix B for details about literature reviews).

- *Source material is used in the service of what writers are trying to say about their topics.* Research essays are not like encyclopedia entries or the research reports you may have written in high school. They do not merely present information gathered from source material. Instead, they actively *use* the information to explore or answer questions or to test the truth of an idea or thesis. In this sense, the research essay is very much like the other kinds of essays you have written so far.

■ *Sources that contributed to a writer's thinking are formally given credit.* The larger purpose of academic inquiry is to make new knowledge, to contribute in some way to what people understand about how the world works. This always involves standing on the shoulders of others who have already said something about your topic, and this is something that you acknowledge explicitly through citation. While citation has all sorts of conventions, and yes, it can be a pain, the acknowledgment of your sources is both a gracious gesture and a source of authority for you—it indicates that you're party to the ongoing conversation about your topic. Accurately acknowledging your sources is also an ethical obligation that all good researchers take seriously.

■ *Most research essays have a clearly stated thesis.* Like a long train, research essays carry a lot of freight and they must stay on track. One way to do this is to clearly organize the information you gather around an explicit focusing question. This question should lead readers to some answers, particularly one main idea, claim, or thesis that seems most persuasive to the writer. While some formal research papers state this thesis in the introduction, research essays typically have a "delayed" thesis that may be stated somewhere near the end.

■ *Research essays typically use four sources of information.* Nonfiction writing draws on four sources of information: memory or experience, observation, interviews, and reading. It's not unusual to read a personal essay that relies solely on the writer's memory of an experience as a source of information. A profile might use two or three sources, including observation and interview. But a research essay may draw information from *all four* sources. Writers cast as wide a net as possible to discover the answers to their questions.

READINGS

■ UNDOCUMENTED RESEARCH ESSAY

You will read Brian Doyle's essay "Joyas Voladoras" and will think, "Surely, this is not a research paper," and you would be partly right. The reading that follows was not written for specialists, and does not have the ambition of much academic writing to contribute to an ongoing conversation in a discipline. For this reason, it doesn't have citations. But "Joyas Voladoras" is an essay that relies on research, and a lot of it. The great wonder is how such a lovely, moving essay isn't ruined by facts, as we might expect. Consider that as you read Doyle's essay.

Whenever we write about a subject as large as the human capacity for love—what Doyle calls the "house of the heart"—it's easy to lose our footing in the specific and the concrete and drift, like people in a hot air balloon, up into the thin air of abstraction or generalization. This is particularly easy to do in research writing. There is so much terrain, so much to cover, and so much to know! Doyle's essay demonstrates how to avoid this. He finds a focus in the particulars of a hummingbird's "racecar heart," which becomes the tiniest window into his meditation on love and connection. Doyle helps us to see big things *through* small ones. This is the goal of much research as well, whether it's sampling invertebrates to make a judgment on the health of a creek or sorting through information and claims about how Facebook might affect friendship.

Mostly, though, it's inspiring to encounter researched writing like "Joyas Voladoras" that reminds us that what we learn from others can help us discover more about ourselves.

Joyas Voladoras
Brian Doyle

Consider the hummingbird for a long moment. A hummingbird's heart beats ten times a second. A hummingbird's heart is the size of the pencil eraser. A hummingbird's heart is a lot of the hummingbird. *Joyas voladoras,* flying jewels, the first white explorers in the Americas called them, and the white men had never seen such creatures, for hummingbirds came into the world only in the Americas, nowhere else in the universe, more than three hundred species of them whirring and zooming and nectaring in hummer time zones nine times removed from ours, their hearts hammering faster than we could clearly hear if we pressed our elephantine ears to their infinitesimal chests.

Each one visits a thousand flowers a day. They can dive at sixty miles an hour. They can fly backward. They can fly more than five hundred miles without pausing to

(continued)

1

2

(continued)

rest. But when they rest they come close to death: on frigid nights, or when they are starving, they retreat into torpor, their metabolic rate slowing to a fifteenth of their normal sleep rate, their hearts sludging nearly to a halt, barely beating, and if they are not soon warmed, if they do not soon find that which is sweet, their hearts grow cold, and they cease to be. Consider for a moment those hummingbirds who did not open their eyes again today, this very day, in the Americas: bearded helmeterests and booted racket-tails, voilet-tailed sylphs and violet-capped woodnymphs, crimson topazes and purple-crowned fairies, red-tailed comets and amethyst woodstars, rainbow-bearded thornbills and glittering-bellied emeralds, velvet-purple coronets and golden-bellied star-frontlets, fiery-tailed awlbills and Andean hillstars, spatuletails and pufflegs, each the most amazing thing you have never seen, each thundcrous wild heart the size of an infant's fingernail, each mad heart silent, a brilliant music stilled.

3   Hummingbirds, like all flying birds but more so, have incredible enormous immense ferocious metabolisms. To drive those metabolisms they have racecar hearts that eat oxygen at an eye-popping rate. Their hearts are built of thinner, leaner fibers than ours. Their arteries are stiffer and more taut. They have more mitochondria in their heart muscles—anything to gulp more oxygen. Their hearts are stripped to the skin for the war against gravity and inertia, the mad search for food, the insane idea of flight. The price of their ambition is a life closer to death; they suffer more heart attacks and aneurysms and ruptures than any other living creature. It's expensive to fly. You burn out. You fry the machine. You melt the engine. Every creature on earth has approximately two billion heartbeats to spend in a lifetime. You can spend them slowly, like a tortoise, and live to be two hundred years old, or you can spend them fast, like a hummingbird, and live to be two years old.

4   The biggest heart in the word is inside the blue whale. It weighs more than seven tons. It's as big as a room. It *is* a room, with four chambers. A child could walk around in it, head high, bending only to step through the valves. The valves are as big as the swinging doors in a saloon. This house of a heart drives a creature a hundred feet long. When this creature is born it is twenty feet long and weighs four tons. It is waaaaay bigger than your car. It drinks a hundred gallons of milk from its mama every day and gains two hundred pounds a day, and when it is seven or eight years old it endures an unimaginable puberty and then it essentially disappears from human ken, for next to nothing is known of the mating habits, travel patterns, diet, social life, language, social structure, diseases, spirituality, wars, stories, despairs, and arts of the blue whale. There are perhaps ten thousand blue whales in the world, living in every ocean on earth, and of the largest mammal who ever lived we know nearly nothing. But we know this: the animals with the largest hearts in the world generally travel in pairs, and their penetrating moaning cries, their piercing yearning tongue, can be heard underwater for miles and miles.

5   Mammals and birds have hearts with four chambers. Reptiles and turtles have hearts with three chambers. Fish have hearts with two chambers. Insects and mollusks have hearts with one chamber. Worms have hearts with one chamber, although they

may have as many as eleven single-chambered hearts. Unicellular bacteria have no hearts at all; but even they have fluid eternally in motion, washing from one side of the cell to the other, swirling and whirling. No living being is without interior liquid motion. *We all churn inside.*

So much held in a heart in a lifetime. So much held in a heart in a day, an hour, a moment. We are utterly open with no one, in the end—not mother and father, not wife or husband, not lover, not child, not friend. *We open windows to each but we live alone in the house of the* heart. Perhaps we must. Perhaps we could not bear to be so naked, for fear of a constantly harrowed heart. When young we think there will come one person who will savor and sustain us always; when we are older we know this is the dream of a child, that all hearts finally are bruised and scarred, scored and torn, repaired by time and will, patched by force of character, yet fragile and rickety forevermore, no matter how ferocious the defense and how many bricks you bring to the wall. You can brick up your heart as stout and tight and hard and cold and im-pregnable as you possibly can and down it comes in an instant, felled by a woman's second glance, a child's apple breath, the shatter of glass in the road, the words "I have something to tell you," a cat with a broken spine dragging itself into the forest to die, the brush of your mother's papery ancient hand in the thicket of your hair, the memory of your father's voice early in the morning echoing from the kitchen where he is making pancakes for his children.

Inquiring into the Essay

Explore, explain, evaluate, and reflect on "Joyas Voladoras."

1. At the end of his essay, Doyle writes, "We open windows to each but we live alone in the house of the heart." Does this ring true for you? In your journal, tell yourself a story about a time when you tried to do more than open windows and invited someone into the "house of your heart." Write fast for five full minutes. Now skip a line, and write a text message to Doyle that responds to his sentence based on what you've learned from your own fastwriting.

2. Make a list of at least four methods or techniques that Doyle uses to keep the many facts in "Joyas Voladoras" from making it dull reading. Or if you think it *is* dull, explain why using two relevant passages from the essay.

3. What is the implicit argument in this essay? Do you agree with it?

4. Like many research essays, the thesis in "Joyas Voladoras" comes toward the end of the piece rather than at the beginning. Reflect on other ways in which you might distinguish this piece from more conventional research papers. What can you learn from Doyle's essay that might apply to academic research writing?

■ DOCUMENTED RESEARCH ESSAY

When I went to college in the seventies, dating was dead but "hooking up," at least in its current meaning, was not all that common. Though the "sexual revolution" of the sixties still resonated on campuses thirty years ago, people generally were still interested in commitment when they sought intimacy. However, I dated in high school, as did most of my friends. There were dances, dinners, movies, and concerts, all occasions that demanded dates. I imagine that it's hard for my younger students today to picture the dating scene, which is why the following academic essay, excerpted from the book *From Front Porch to Back Seat: Courtship in the Twentieth Century,* is so illuminating.

Using the popular magazines of the day as sources, Beth Bailey describes the rise of dating as a social ritual in the 1940s and 1950s. This historical context is useful when considering the argument in the preceding reading, "Courting Confusion," that we need new rituals like dating that stop way short of "hooking up."

While "The Worth of a Date," unlike some research essays, makes an argument from the outset, it is a less formal treatment of its subject and taps largely popular sources rather than academic ones. Notice, however, that it is a scholarly essay that includes citations and references. Unlike the preceding essay, "The Worth of a Date" is intended for other academics, but it's written to be accessible to nonspecialists, too.

The Worth of a Date
Beth Bailey

1   Before the sexual revolution of the 1960s provided juicier material, *Esquire* was fond of running cartoons featuring a short, elderly, and paunchy millionaire escorting a tall, enormous-breasted young showgirl through opulent settings. The captions didn't really matter. The cartoons worked best subtextually, and all contained variations on the same theme: money and sex; the coupling of wallet and bosom.

2   It is easy, today, to center on the objectification of woman represented by the showgirl, a caricature stripped to her essentials: legs, breasts, and greed. She is clearly a commodity, purchased by man's wealth. But the man, too, is objectified. His value to her lies only in what he can buy. He is interchangeable with any other well-stuffed wallet. Their relationship is obviously mutually exploitative: the man is as much a commodity to the woman as she is a commodity to him.

3   The millionaire and the showgirl are a long way from our image of young love, but this mass-produced image can illustrate some of the values inherent in the American dating system. In courtship, no less than in the culture at large, we find America's "culture of consumption"—a way of seeing that encourages the paired acts of consumption and commodification.

The culture of consumption, as Jackson Lears and Richard Wrightman Fox de- 4
scribe it in a book of that title, is not simply the system of values underlying a consumer economy or a society "saturated by mass-produced and mass-marketed
goods." It is also "an ethic, a standard of living, and a power structure" that centers
on consumption, in which "individuals have been invited to seek commodities as
keys to personal welfare...even to conceive of their own selves as commodities"
(Wrightman and Lears ix–xvii). And, I might add, to transform personal relationships
into commodities.

In dating, American young people sought their "personal welfare" through dates 5
(and later through steadies), as commodities that afforded public validation of popularity, of belonging, of success. Whether or not one liked the date (person), the date
(event) was valuable, a necessary commodity in youth culture. As commodities, dates
(events) were valued differentially by the level of consumption they entailed—in
short, by their cost. The date (person) could also become a commodity. In this system, men and women often defined themselves and each other as commodities, the
woman valued by the level of consumption she could demand (how much she was
"worth"), and the man by the level of consumption he could provide.

The particular form the American dating system took as it emerged in the early 6
twentieth century was determined, in large part, by the new centrality of money in
the act of courtship. As "going somewhere" became the thing to do, the man had to
spend money to provide entertainment, refreshments, and transportation for the couple. Gradually, as dating became the dominant form of courtship, participants and observers recognized how important money had become. In general, dates had come to
be defined by the fact that they cost money. Over and over in the national media,
women and men, girls and boys, advisers and experts insisted on this definition of
dating. Money was central: a date took place when a couple "went out" and spent
money.

All the polls and columns and books on dating in the second third of the twenti- 7
eth century made abundantly clear that American youth did not consider spending
time with a member of the opposite sex the same as dating. In almost all instances, a
date centered around an act of consumption: going out for dinner or a Coke, seeing a
movie, buying access to some form of entertainment. Of course, the emphasis was
not on unbridled consumption. The act had to take place within certain limits and according to many conventions, one of the most important being that the man pay the
woman's way.

The "sub-deb" adviser for the *Ladies' Home Journal* shows the extent of these im- 8
plicit definitions of a date in a 1944 column. She tells the story of a young girl—about
fourteen—who is "fed up" because she can't get a date. The girl, as the author describes her, has a good social life—lots of friends, including boys who like her well
enough to meet her and sit beside her at the movies. The adviser does not give the
obvious moral. Instead of pointing out that this sub-deb should concentrate on enjoying the movie and the boy's company, she approvingly recounts the girl's "plan": she

(continued)

(continued)

will concentrate on "Pete," the "likeliest one" (note that she does not say "the one she likes best"). "When he sits by me in the movies," the girl says, "I'm going to pretend he paid my way in. I'm going to play-act it's a real date" (Woodward 8). The only thing lacking, evidently, is knowledge that the boy *paid* for her.

9   A real girl, Margaret Graves of St. Louis, had a similar opinion on the subject. Writing to *Senior Scholastic* in 1951, she said, "If a girl has to pay her own way [on a date], she might as well go alone or with girl friends" (Head 24). To her, the date was not the event, was not the companionship, was not even being *seen* with the boy. A date meant being paid for. And boys agreed. A *Senior Scholastic* poll on dating found that while 90 percent of the girls questioned would agree to "occasionally," if reluctantly, share expenses, 50 percent of the boys strenuously objected to the idea. "If a boy is financially embarrassed," one boy wrote, "he shouldn't date" (Head 24). . . .

10   This concern with being seen is crucial, for it relates to the role of the date in youth culture. . .[D]ates often functioned in youth culture as tools for acquiring popularity—much as did clothes, cars, and other consumer goods. But a date that had no independent content, that was only a marker for popularity, had no meaning if no one knew about it. The date had to be public.

11   The boy who longed for a date, as Margaret Mead noted in the 1940s, was not longing for a girl, much less for a relationship with a particular girl (Mead 145). He desired to be in the public situation that defined a date: he desired to *have* a date, and he desired for others to see that he had a date. This sort of date, "had" and displayed, is itself a commodity. . . .

12   Of course, some dates were prized more than others. Teen advice books warned girls to be understanding and hospitable to the boy who was occasionally low on funds, but not to let him get in the habit of hanging around their living rooms with no "real" dates in exchange. And real dates, the public culture of dating constantly emphasized, were expensive and flamboyant. While most polls discovered that teens' usual dates were for a movie and a snack, the magazines that conducted these polls frequently described the unusual dates—the "ideal" dates—in loving detail. . . .

13   The high school prom, the biggest social event of the year, represented the "ideal" date to most students. Proms were, of course, something more than special dates. They were a kind of rite of passage that transformed boys and girls into young men and women; they were occasions for magical extravagance. They required elegant evening attire and transportation, and included postprom entertainment at the fanciest night spot the area offered. . . .

14   Proms offered high school students not only a taste of the "ideal" extravagant dates otherwise largely denied them (at least until they were older) but also a forum for social competition. The first level of competition was simply rating a bid or getting a date; the next was getting the "right" date. Beyond these basics, proms stressed competition through material goods. With all (who qualified) brought

together, it was easy to compare dresses, to see who rated an orchid and who just a gardenia, to rank postprom destinations and modes of transportation. The pressure could be intense, and during the Depression years of the 1930s, Chicago high school principals frequently cancelled school proms because they feared the many students who couldn't afford them would be "psychologically wounded" by that failure (Gutowski 256)....

In college, the pressure was more consistent. College students didn't have to contend with only one prom or ideal date a year, but with a whole succession of extravagant events. College football weekends were glamorized by a wide range of national magazines as one dizzy succession of brunches and lunches and dances and dinners—at a cost to men, *Good Housekeeping* estimated in 1953, of about $83 a weekend (Frey 225). *Mademoiselle*, in its 1954 college issue, showed the pressure for expensive dates by defining "Quiet Evening" as "Any nocturnal date that results in a heightened feeling of well being and costs less than $5" (Frey 309). The previous year *Good Housekeeping* had published results of an informal survey of the cost of college "big" dates. Average outlays for one date ranged from a low of $25 in Boston and Dallas to a high of $35 in St. Louis. Paducah, Kentucky, with a population of 35,000, came in just about average at $30 (Frey 224)....   15

Flowers, both in college and outside, exemplify the dating system's emphasis on competing through consumption. Almost every description of a "big date," from the 1920s through the 1950s, features the kind of corsage the girl or woman wears, and sample budgets for major dates allot anywhere from $2 to $10 for corsages (Frey 225). These flowers were not private gifts—cut flowers for the woman's dressing table—but public symbols. They said, for the man, "See what I can afford," and for the woman, "See how much I'm worth." The girl who said she could buy her own Cokes understood that in the dating competition the companionship of a Coke date couldn't match the symbolic importance of flowers on a big date.   16

In quite literal terms, women gauged their own value in dating by how much money men spent on them....In this system, that the man pay for the date was crucial. Beyond that, the more he spent—publicly—the better.   17

Works Cited

Frey, Richard L. "The High Cost of Dating." *Good Housekeeping* Aug. 1953: 224–309. Print.

Gutowski, Thomas. "The High School as Adolescent-Raising Institution: An Inner History of Chicago Public Secondary Education, 1856–1940." Diss. of Chicago, 1978. Print.

Head, Gay. "Boy Dates Girl Jam Session." Senior Scholastic 11 Apr. 1951: 24. Print.

Mead, Margaret. "The Male and Female." *Ladies' Home Journal* Sept. 1949: 145. Print.

Woodward, Elizabeth. "The Sub-Deb: I'm Fed Up." *Ladies' Home Journal* Jan. 1944: 2. Print.

Wrightman, Richard Fox, and T. J. Jackson Lears, eds. *The Culture of Consumption*. New York: Pantheon, 1983. Print.

Inquiring into the Essay

Use the ways of inquiring—exploring, explaining, evaluating, and reflecting—to discover what you think about "The Worth of a Date."

1. Historical research such as "The Worth of a Date" is a frame through which we can see the present, in this case specifically the ways that social rituals such as dating have changed. As soon as you finish the essay, try to use the frame that Bailey provides as a way to look at your own experience. In your journal, write for five full minutes, using the reading as a prompt. Begin by exploring what struck you most by this description of dating in the 1930s through the 1950s, especially when compared with your own experiences in the present.

2. Using the window into fifties dating that "The Worth of a Date" provides, how would you contrast the social rituals then and now? Could you make an argument that they haven't really changed much despite the current era of texting, Twitter, and Facebook?

3. The argument in "The Worth of a Date" is implied by its title. Do you find the idea that dating was "commodified" persuasive? Even more important, is such a claim relevant?

4. Some years ago, a writer used the term *presentism* to describe how modern readers often unfairly apply contemporary moral standards and values to historical events. It wouldn't be hard to do the same thing here. Reflect on how a modern researcher can avoid being blinded by presentism.

INQUIRING INTO THE DETAILS

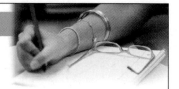

Reading Academic Research Essays

Just as reading a poem demands some different reading strategies than reading an essay, making sense of academic writing presents its own peculiar challenges. Here are some tips for picking your way through an academic journal article.

- Pay particular attention to the *justification* for why this research question is worthy of study. Do you understand how it extends existing scholarship on the topic?

- Imagine an artichoke. You have to work your way through the leaves to get to the heart, the best part. In a journal article, this is the main argument, thesis, finding, or claim. You will find this in a range of locations—sometimes it's stated in an "abstract" (if there is one), at the end of an introduction or literature review, or even at the very end of the article.

- You don't have to understand all the jargon, just enough that you understand the research question and the conclusions.

- You're probably not in a position to evaluate the methods used, but make an effort to identify and understand them.

- When doing your own research, pay attention to names of people who are cited often. These are often people who have said the most in the ongoing conversation about the topic.

- Carefully consider how the author qualifies his or her conclusions. This often mutes the significance of the findings and helps you understand how seriously to take them.

■ DOCUMENTED RESEARCH PAPER

Though the following academic paper, published in the *Journal of Sex Research,* was originally written as an undergraduate honors thesis, chances are that, unless you're going on to graduate school, you won't write a paper that will end up in a scholarly journal. But depending on the field you choose, you will be expected to think and write like the author of this essay. That means that you must learn to ask researchable questions that somehow extend or challenge what has already been said by others on your topic. It also means that you will collect and analyze evidence of some kind to test your hunches. And above all, being an academic researcher means you explore topics that genuinely interest you and might make a difference to others.

"Pluralistic Ignorance and Hooking Up" does all of these things. Tracy Lambert and her coauthors take an idea that has been around for a while and wonder whether it might apply to hooking up behaviors on her college campus. She suspects that something called "pluralistic ignorance," or the sense that what makes you feel uncomfortable probably doesn't bother other people nearly as much, strongly operates among men and women who hook up. With the help of her professors, Tracy designs a study to test the hypothesis.

Like most social-science research, this paper follows a prescribed format: introduction (literature review and purpose of the study), methods, results, and discussion. At first, these conventions might seem alien to you (see "Inquiring into the Details: Reading Academic Research Essays"), but once you get used to navigating academic discourse, a whole new world of information opens.

Pluralistic Ignorance and Hooking Up
Tracy Lambert, Arnold Kahn, and Kevin Apple

"Hooking up"—when two people agree to engage in sexual behavior for which there is no future commitment—has become popular on college campuses. In this study we examined the extent to which pluralistic ignorance affects hooking up. One hundred

(continued)

(continued)

thirty-six female and 128 male college students answered questions regarding their own comfort and their perceived peers' comfort in engaging in a variety of sexual behaviors while hooking up. We hypothesized and found that both women and men rated their peers as being more comfortable engaging in these behaviors than they rated themselves. Men expressed more comfort than did women in engaging in these behaviors, and both sexes overestimated the other gender's comfort with hooking up behaviors. Pluralistic ignorance appears to apply to hooking up on college campuses, and we explore some potential consequences of pluralistic ignorance in this context.

1   Although one-night stands and uncommitted sexual behaviors are not a recent phenomenon, past research has focused on personality traits, attitudes, and individual differences in willingness to engage in such behaviors (e.g., Gerrard, 1980; Gerrard & Gibbons, 1982; Simpson & Gangestad, 1991; Snyder, Simpson, & Gangestad, 1986). The tacit assumption in this past research was that sexual behaviors within a committed and loving relationship were unproblematic, but that unloving, uncommitted sexual relations had to be explained. However, today on college campuses across the United States what was once viewed as problematic has now become normative, and students refer to this process as "hooking up."

2   Hooking up occurs when two people who are casual acquaintances or who have just met that evening at a bar or party agree to engage in some forms of sexual behavior for which there will likely be no future commitment (Boswell & Spade, 1996; Kahn et al., 2000; Paul, McManus, & Hayes, 2000). The couple typically does not communicate what sexual behaviors they will or will not engage in, and frequently both parties have been drinking alcohol (Kahn et al., 2000; Paul et al., 2000). Paul et al. (2000) found that 78% of women and men on the campus being studied had engaged in hooking up at least once. In the Kahn et al. (2000) sample of college students, 86% of the women and 88% of the men indicated they had hooked up. Almost one half (47%) of the men and one third of the women in the Paul et al. sample engaged in sexual intercourse during the hookup, and Kahn et al. found that their sample believed petting below the waist, oral sex, and sexual intercourse occurred with some regularity in the process of hooking up.

3   *Pluralistic ignorance,* a concept first coined by Floyd Allport (1924, 1933), exists when, within a group of individuals, each person believes his or her private attitudes, beliefs, or judgments are discrepant from the norm displayed by the public behavior of others. Therefore, each group member, wishing to be seen as a desirable member of the group, publicly conforms to the norm, each believing he or she is the only one in the group experiencing conflict between his or her private attitude and his or her public behavior. Group members believe that most others in their group, especially those who are popular and opinion leaders (Katz & Lazarsfeld, 1955), actually endorse the norm and want to behave that way, while they themselves privately feel they are going along with the norm because of a desire to fit in with the group and exemplify the norm (Prentice & Miller, 1993, 1996). In this study we examined the extent to which pluralistic ignorance might be related to U.S. college students' comfort

levels with sexual behaviors involved in hooking up. Consistent with the premise of pluralistic ignorance, we hypothesized that college students would perceive others as having a greater comfort level engaging in a variety of sexual behaviors than they themselves would have.

Prentice and Miller (1993) demonstrated pluralistic ignorance among college students in the area of alcohol consumption. On a campus where heavy alcohol use was the perceived norm, Prentice and Miller found that students estimated both the average student and their friends to have less discomfort with the level of alcohol consumption on campus than they reported for themselves. Furthermore, for male but not female students, they found greater consistency between respondents' comfort levels with alcohol consumption and the perceived norm and between respondents' reported drinking levels and the perceived norm at the end of the semester than at the beginning of the semester. Although correlational in nature, these results suggest that over time, male students may have changed their attitudes and behaviors to bring them more in line with the perceived norm. Perkins and Berkowitz (1986) reported similar findings with regard to the discrepancy between college students' own comfort with the amount of drinking at the university and what they estimated to be the general campus attitude.

Although pluralistic ignorance was originally conceptualized as a discrepancy between public behavior and private beliefs (Miller & McFarland, 1987), others have used the concept to refer to situations in which there is not direct evidence of behavioral similarity (e.g., Fields & Schuman, 1976; O'Gorman & Garry, 1976). More recently, Cohen and Shotland (1996) invoked the concept of pluralistic ignorance in a variety of dating situations for which public scrutiny was absent. They found that both men and women believed that the average other person of their sex had more liberal sexual expectations than they set for themselves, both sexes believing the average other person of their sex would expect sexual intercourse much sooner in a relationship than they themselves would expect it. When asked whether a same-sex peer would expect to have sexual intercourse with a person with whom they were emotionally involved but for whom they felt no physical attraction, both men and women believed the average man and woman would expect sexual intercourse, while only approximately 50% of the participants would expect sex themselves in such a relationship, and an even smaller percentage reported having had sex in such a relationship. Finally, when there was neither emotional nor physical attraction to a partner, few women or men expected that they would have sexual intercourse with the partner, but believed the average man and woman would indeed expect sexual intercourse.

Pluralistic ignorance might have consequences when beliefs about the norm condone intimate sexual behaviors. In the process of hooking up, pluralistic ignorance may lead one or both sexual partners to act according to the perceived norm rather than to their own convictions. There is a large literature showing that men have more liberal attitudes towards sexual behaviors and expect sexual intercourse sooner in a

(continued)

4

5

6

(continued)

relationship than do women (Cohen & Shotland, 1996; Knox & Wilson, 1981; Oliver & Hyde, 1993) and that men are much more receptive than are women to offers of sexual intercourse (Clark & Hatfield, 1989). Byers and Lewis (1988) found that disagreements among dating partners on the desired level of sexual behavior was almost always in the direction of the male partner wanting a higher level of sexual intimacy than that desired by the female partner. Thus, it is possible that many men go into hooking-up situations hoping to engage in more intimate sexual behaviors than are desired by their female partners. Because men are expected to initiate sexual activity (DeLamater, 1987; Peplau & Gordon, 1985), it is possible that in the process of hooking up, some women will experience unwanted sexual advances and possibly even sexual assault or rape.

7   In their research on hooking up, Kahn et al. (2000) asked 92 female and 50 male college students if they had ever had a "really terrible hooking up experience." Nearly one half of the women (42%) and the men (46%) indicated they had had such an experience. A "terrible experience" for the men was usually due to the women wanting a relationship or to the use of too much alcohol or drugs; none mentioned pressure to go further than they desired. However, nearly one half of the women (48.3%) who reported having a terrible hooking-up experience indicated that they were pressured to go further than they had wanted to go. They gave responses such as "I hooked up with a guy who didn't understand the meaning of 'no'" and "I didn't want to—he did—he wouldn't back off." These women may have experienced sexual assault during a hook up but did not label their experiences as such because they believed the behaviors to be normative. In addition, 10.3% of the women and 11.1% of the men in this sample said the hook up was terrible because they had gone too far without mentioning pressure from their partner. Going too far might have been the consequence of pluralistic ignorance, conforming to a presumed norm.

8   The present study sought to extend the findings of Cohen and Shotland (1996), which were restricted to expectations of sexual intercourse in dating situations, to the area of hooking up. Further, we wanted to examine whether pluralistic ignorance occurred with other sexual behaviors besides sexual intercourse. Based on the research on pluralistic ignorance and gender differences in expected sexual behaviors, we hypothesized that both male and female students would see other students as more comfortable with various hooking-up behaviors than they were themselves. Although we expected individuals would vary in their own comfort levels with various hooking-up behaviors, we expected they would believe other students to be uniformly more comfortable engaging in those behaviors than they were themselves. Furthermore, consistent with previous literature, we hypothesized that men would be significantly more comfortable than women with engaging in all hooking-up behaviors. Finally, we hypothesized that due to pluralistic ignorance, both women and men would overestimate the other gender's comfort with all hooking-up behaviors.

Method

Participants

One hundred seventy-five female and 152 male undergraduate students from a mid-sized residential southeastern public university that has few nontraditional students served as participants for the study. The convenience sample represented a moderately even distribution of years in school: for first years, $n = 79$ (41 females, 38 males); for sophomores, $n = 70$ (37 females, 33 males); for juniors, $n = 84$ (45 females, 39 males); and for seniors, n = 93 (52 females, 41 males). A female experimenter approached students as they entered the university library and asked them to volunteer to answer some questions about hooking up and sexual behaviors as part of her senior honors project. She approached other students in their residence halls. No differences appeared between these two samples for any of the dependent measures. Analyses concerning pluralistic ignorance and comfort with hooking up are based on the data from 136 women (77.7%) and 128 men (84.2%) who indicated that they had hooked up.

Materials and Procedure

The questionnaire consisted of questions developed by the authors to examine student attitudes toward hooking up. On the first page, students read that the investigator was interested in "students' attitudes and behaviors with regard to dating and 'hooking up,'" and hooking up was defined as "a sexual encounter between two people who may or may not know each other well, but who usually are *not* seriously dating." Participants also signed an informed consent form, which indicated all information would be anonymous and confidential. To insure anonymity and encourage honest responding, the only demographic information obtained was the participants' year in school. We made no attempt to determine sexual orientation or marital status: however, on this residential campus the overwhelming majority of students come to the university directly from high school, identify themselves as heterosexual, and have never been married (James Madison University Office of Institutional Research, 2001–2002). Participants were told they were not required to complete the survey if they became uncomfortable.

Students who said they had hooked up were instructed to continue to the next page. We constructed 11-point scales modeled after those used by Prentice and Miller (1993) on which 3 points were labeled: 1 = not at all comfortable, 6 = *neutral,* and 11 = *very comfortable*. Participants responded to the question "How comfortable are you with the amount of hooking up that goes on at [school name]?" They then responded to the question "How comfortable are you with engaging in the following activities during a hook up?" with regard to "petting above the waist," "petting below the waist," "oral sex," and "sexual intercourse." Participants used the same scales in response to the questions "How comfortable do you think the *average female* student is with the amount of hooking up that goes on at [school name]?" and "How comfortable do you think the *average female* student is with engaging in the following activities during a hook up?" Finally, they responded to the questions "How comfortable do you think the *average male* student is

(continued)

9

10

11

(continued)

with the amount of hooking up that goes on at [school name]?" and "How comfortable do you think the *average male* student is with engaging in the following activities during a hook up?"

12   Students who indicated that they had never hooked up were asked to skip to a different page of the survey, which contained questions regarding why they did not hook up and whether or not they believed that there was a relationship between hooking up and sexual assault. This part of the questionnaire was included so that all participants would work on the survey for approximately the same amount of time without knowing who had or had not hooked up.

13   Participants completed the questionnaire privately, usually within a short distance of the researcher. Those participating at the library placed their completed questionnaires in a large box, and those participating in their residence hall placed completed questionaires in a large envelope. When they were finished, participants were encouraged to ask questions and discuss the questionnaire with the researcher, who provided them with a debriefing statement and a list of campus resources for sexual assault.

Results

14   We tested the hypothesis that students would experience pluralistic ignorance regarding hooking up with a 2 (Gender) X 2 (Target: self or other) ANOVA, with target as a within-subjects variable. As hypothesized, participants demonstrated pluralistic ignorance by evaluating their own comfort level with the amount of hooking up. $M = 7.08$, $SD = 2.31$, significantly lower than their estimate of a same-sex peer's comfort level, $M = 7.75$, $SD = 2.08$, $F (1.262) = 24.24$, $p < .0001$, partial $\eta^2 = .085$. Participants believed that other college students were more comfortable with the amount of hooking up than were they. This main effect of target was qualified by a significant gender by target interaction, $F (1. 262) = 7.55$, partial $\eta^2 = .028$, $p < .01$. Both men and women showed the same pattern of overestimating their peers' comfort levels: however, the pattern was more pronounced among the male students (9.01_{peer} vs. 7.95_{self}), $t(127) = 4.68$, $p < .0001$, $d = .502$, than among the female students (6.57_{peer} vs. 6.26_{self}), $t(135) = 1.85$, $p < .05$, one-tailed, $d = .185$. Table 1 presents these means and standard deviations.

15   A dependent t test for equality of variances revealed that participants showed significantly less variability in their ratings of peer comfort level in hooking up than in their

Table 1   Ratings of Own and Average Same-Sex Student's Comfort with Hooking Up

Measure	Self: *M* (*SD*)	Average student: *M* (*SD*)
Women	6.26 (1.79)	6.57 (1.63)
Men	7.95 (2.48)	9.01 (1.74)

Note. Ratings were made on 11-point scales (1 = *not at all comfortable* and 11 = *very comfortable*).

Table 2 Ratings of Men's and Women's Own Comfort with Hooking-Up Behaviors

	Men: *M (SD)*	Women: *M (SD)*
Petting above the waist	9.12 (2.47)	7.29 (2.68)
Petting below the waist	8.42 (2.60)	5.13 (2.73)
Oral sex	7.56 (3.05)	3.49 (2.63)
Sexual intercourse	5.65 (3.57)	2.15 (2.31)

self-ratings: $t(262) = 1.96$, $p < .05$, one-tailed. When rating their own comfort levels, the standard deviation in participants' responses was 2.31. However, the standard deviation significantly decreased to 2.08 when participants estimated their peers' comfort with hooking up. This decrease in variability when estimating others' comfort provides some evidence for an illusion of universality. That is, participants showed greater uniformity in their beliefs about others' comfort levels compared to their own actual comfort levels.

We used multivariate analysis of variance (MANOVA) to examine the hypothesis regarding men's and women's own comfort levels with various sexual behaviors, with participant gender as the between-subjects variable. Men reported significantly greater comfort with these behaviors than did women. $F(4.259) = 35.17$, $p < .0001$, partial $\eta^2 = .352$. Table 2 shows that men's greater comfort occurred with all four hooking-up behaviors. [16]

We tested the hypothesis that both men and women would overestimate the other gender's comfort with hooking-up behaviors using two separate MANOVAS. The first examined the men's estimates of the average woman's comfort, and the second examined the women's estimates of the average man's comfort. To evaluate the accuracy of these estimates, the comfort estimates were compared with the means of the actual comfort ratings of these hooking up behaviors. Both the men, $F(4, 259) - 7.82$, $p < .0001$, partial $\eta^2 = .108$, and the women, $F(4, 259) = 16.25$, $p < .0001$, partial $\eta^2 = .201$, significantly overestimated the other gender's actual comfort levels with various hooking-up behaviors. As shown in Table 3, this overestimation occurred for both sexes on each of the four hooking-up behaviors. [17]

Discussion

Cohen and Shotland (1996) found evidence of pluralistic ignorance regarding expectations of sexual intercourse on a date. The current research extended these findings to other sexual behaviors, and did so in the context of hooking up. We found that both women and men reported less comfort with their perceived norm of hooking up than they believed was experienced by their same-sex peers, with men showing a greater difference between self- and peer-ratings than women. In addition, both men and women believed members of the other gender experienced greater comfort with hooking-up behaviors than members of the other gender actually reported. Men were less comfortable with engaging in hooking-up behaviors than women believed them to be, and women [18]

(continued)

(continued)

Table 3   Differences Between Each Gender's Own Comfort Level with Hooking-Up Behaviors and Estimates of the Other Gender's Comfort Levels

	Women's estimate of men: *M* (*SD*)	Men's actual comfort level: *M* (*SD*)	Men's estimate of women: *M* (*SD*)	Women's actual comfort level: *M* (*SD*)
Petting above the waist	9.80 (1.45)	9.12 (2.47)	7.73 (1.92)	7.29 (2.68)
Petting below the waist	9.30 (1.67)	8.42 (2.60)	6.38 (2.07)	5.13 (2.73)
Oral sex	8.61 (1.93)	7.56 (3.04)	5.49 (2.19)	3.49 (2.62)
Sexual intercourse	7.62 (2.24)	5.65 (3.57)	4.28 (2.36)	2.15 (2.31)

were less comfortable with engaging in hooking-up behaviors than men believed them to be. These findings appear to be due to pluralistic ignorance: Hooking up has become the norm for heterosexual sexual relationships on this campus, and since the great majority of students do in fact hook up, it appears that most students believe that others are comfortable—more comfortable than they are themselves—with engaging in a variety of uncommitted sexual behaviors. It is likely that most students believe others engage in these hooking-up behaviors primarily because they enjoy doing so, while they see themselves engaging in these behaviors primarily due to peer pressure.

19   Consistent with other pluralistic ignorance research (e.g., Prentice & Miller, 1993), this study showed evidence of an illusion of universality. The students failed to appreciate the extent to which others have different comfort levels with hooking-up behaviors. That is, students wrongly assumed that the attitudes of others about hooking up were more homogenous than they actually were.

20   Similar to other researchers (Cohen & Shotland, 1996; Knox & Wilson, 1981; Oliver & Hyde, 1993), we found that men expressed greater comfort than did women with sexually intimate hooking-up behaviors. In the context of hooking up, this could lead to serious consequences. Our study suggests that men believe women are more comfortable engaging in these behaviors than in fact they are, and also that women believe other women are more comfortable engaging in these behaviors than they are themselves. As a consequence, some men may pressure women to engage in intimate sexual behaviors, and some women may engage in these behaviors or resist only weakly because they believe they are unique in feeling discomfort about engaging in them. In this context it is possible for a woman to experience sexual assault but not interpret the behavior as such, believing it to be normative behavior with which her peers are comfortable.

21   "Most of Us" is a campaign implemented on many college campuses in an attempt to reveal pluralistic ignorance about alcohol consumption among college students (DeJong & Langford, 2002; Haines, 1998). The campaign is based on providing students with statistical evidence about actual student attitudes and behaviors regarding alcohol consumption. The goal of the campaign is to show that pluralistic ignorance exists regarding college students'

heavy alcohol consumption, and that most students prefer to drink less than what is commonly perceived to be the norm. Considering the results of this study, we propose that a similar campaign highlighting students' beliefs about and comfort levels with sexual behaviors while hooking up might help reduce pluralistic ignorance about hooking up.

Tracy A. Lambert is now at the University of Georgia.

This paper is based on an honors thesis by the first author under the direction of the second author. We wish to thank Steven Wise for his statistical assistance.

Address correspondence to Arnold S. Kahn, School of Psychology, MSC 7401, James Madison University, Harrisonburg, VA 22807: e-mail: kahnas@jmu.edu.

References

Allport, F. H. (1924). *Social psychology.* Boston: Houghton Mifflin.

Allport, F. H. (1933). *Institutional behavior.* Chapel Hill: University of North Carolina Press.

Boswell, A., & Spade, J. (1996). Fraternities and collegiate rape culture. *Gender and Society, 10,* 133–147.

Byers, S., & Lewis, K. (1988). Dating couples' disagreements over the desired level of sexual intimacy. *The Journal of Sex Research, 24,* 15–29.

Clark, R. D., & Hatfield, E. (1989). Gender differences in receptivity to sexual offers. *Journal of Psychology and Human Sexuality, 2,* 39–55.

Cohen, L. L., & Shotland, R. L. (1996). Timing of first sexual intercourse in a relationship: Expectation, experiences, and perceptions of others. *The Journal of Sex Research, 33,* 291–299.

DeJong, W., & Langford, L. A. (2002). Typology for campus-based alcohol prevention: Moving toward environmental management strategies. *Journal of Studies on Alcohol Supplement, 14,* 140–147.

DeLamater, J. (1987). Gender differences in sexual scenarios. In K. Kelley (Ed.), *Females, males, and sexuality* (pp. 127–139). Albany, NY: SUNY Press.

Fields, J. M., & Schuman, H. (1976). Public beliefs and the beliefs of the public. *Public Opinion Quarterly, 40,* 427–448.

Gerrard, M. (1980). Sex guilt and attitudes towards sex in sexually active and inactive female college students. *Journal of Personality Assessment, 44,* 258–261.

Gerrard, M., & Gibbons, F. X. (1982). Sexual experience, sex guilt, and sexual moral reasoning. *Journal of Personality, 50,* 345–359.

Haines, M. (1998). Social norms: A wellness model for health promotion in higher education. *Wellness Management, 14(4),* 1–8.

James Madison University Office of Institutional Research. (2001–2002). Retrieved February 22, 2003, from http://www.jmu.edu/instresrch/statsum/2001_02/2001-02toc.htm

Kahn, A. S., Fricker, K., Hoffman, J., Lambert, T., Tripp, M., Childress. K., et al. (2000, August). Hooking up: Dangerous new dating methods? In A. S. Kahn (Chair), *Sex, unwanted sex, and sexual assault on college campuses.* Symposium conducted at the annual meeting of the American Psychological Association, Washington, DC.

(continued)

(continued)

Katz, E., & Lazarsfeld, P. F. (1955). *Personal influence: The part played by people in the flow of mass communication.* Glencoe, IL: Free Press.

Knox, D., & Wilson, K. (1981). Dating behaviors of university students. *Family Relations, 30,* 255–258.

Miller, T. D., & McFarland, C. (1987). Pluralistic ignorance: When similarity is interpreted as dissimilarity. *Journal of Personality and Social Psychology, 53,* 298–305.

O'Gorman, H. J., & Garry, S. L. (1976). Pluralistic ignorance: A replication and extension, *Public Opinion Quarterly,* 40, 449–458.

Oliver, M. B., & Hyde, J. S. (1993). Gender differences in sexuality: A meta-analysis. *Psychological Bulletin,* 114, 129–151.

Paul, E. L., McManus, B., & Hayes, A. (2000). "Hookups": Characteristics and correlates of college students' spontaneous and anonymous sexual experiences. *The Journal of Sex Research, 37,* 76–88.

Peplau, L. A., & Gordon, S. L. (1985). Women and men in love: Gender differences in close heterosexual relationships. In V. E. O'Leary, R. K. Unger, & B. S. Wallston (Eds.), *Women, gender, and social psychology* (pp. 257–292). Hillsdale, NJ: Lawrence Erlbaum Associates.

Perkins, H. W., & Berkowitz, A. D. (1986). Perceiving the community norms of alcohol use among students: Some research implications for campus alcohol education programming. *International Journal of the Addictions, 21,* 961–976.

Prentice, D. A., & Miller, D. T. (1993). Pluralistic ignorance and alcohol use on campus: Some consequences of misperceiving the social norm. *Journal of Personality and Social Psychology, 64,* 243–256.

Prentice, D. A., & Miller, D. T. (1996). Pluralistic ignorance and the perpetuation of social norms by unwitting actors. In M. P. Zanna (Ed.), *Advances in experimental social psychology* (Vol. 28, pp. 161–209). San Diego, CA: Academic Press.

Simpson, J. A., & Gangestad, S. W. (1991). Individual differences sociosexuality: Evidence for convergent and discriminant validity. *Journal of Personality and Social Psychology, 60,* 870–883.

Snyder, M., Simpson, J. A., & Gangestad, S. (1986). Personality and sexual relations. *Journal of Personality and Social Psychology, 51,* 181–190.

Manuscript accepted August 21, 2002

Inquiring into the Essay

Use all four ways of inquiring to think about your reaction to this essay.

1. If true, the idea of "pluralistic ignorance"—that we consistently behave in ways that make us uncomfortable because we want to conform to the norm—is pretty disturbing because it implies that we internalize a certain kind of social control over our behavior that may not be in response to something real. For instance, this study suggests that for women especially, hooking up

might not feel right, but they do it anyway because they don't think others feel as they do. Explore this in your own life. Fastwrite about whether "pluralistic ignorance" makes sense to you, and bend the writing, if you can, toward a story that might reveal your own experience with the idea.

2.   Using different color highlighters or pens, identify some of the following elements of an academic paper: review of the literature, hypothesis, purpose of the study, interpretation of data, and assertion about the significance of the findings.

3.   Are the findings of this study credible? Based on your own experience and observations, how would you evaluate them? If you were going to suggest an area for further research, what might that be?

4.   A common and perfectly understandable response to an initial encounter with academic discourse like this is to find it utterly boring. Why is this so? If it is important to learn to get past this initial response to do serious research, what strategies would you use?

SEEING THE FORM

Idaho State Penitentiary, Women's Prison

(continued)

Seeing the Form (*continued*)

I took the picture on page 415 on a ridge overlooking the valley where I live. It includes a lot of visual information: long shots of the city of Boise, the university, the state penitentiary, and in the far distance, the Owyhee Range, which was recently designated as a federal wilderness. But do you really get a good look at any of these subjects? I don't think so, which is why I don't think much of the photograph. My brother, a professional photographer, would probably consider this shot a throwaway—a kind of photographic "prewriting" activity that might help him discover the visual subject he *really* wants to work with.

At the bottom middle of the photograph is a small building surrounded by high stone walls. This was the women's prison, which was built in the 1920s. It's a fascinating place both visually and historically, and so I "revised" my photographic project to focus on the women's prison rather than attempting to capture the valley. I took a slew of shots of the women's prison, including the two pictures shown above—one of a small cell with the light streaming through the tiny window and another of a rusting iron door. They are hardly masterpieces, but I do like them a lot better than the landscape shot. Do you agree? If so, why?

If the process of taking these pictures is a good analogy for the process of writing research essays, what do the comparisons between the landscape shot and the women's prison photographs suggest to you about the qualities of a good paper? What do they imply about the research process?

THE WRITING PROCESS

INQUIRY PROJECT: WRITE A RESEARCH ESSAY

Develop a 2,000- to 3,000-word research essay on a topic of your choice. (Your instructor may present some broad subjects or other limitations on topic choice.) The most important quality of this research essay is that it be organized around your own questions or ideas about the topic; it should be an *essay*, not a *report*. The research question should also have a sufficiently narrow focus. Don't look at the entire landscape of a topic but focus instead on a specific feature in that landscape. Your essay should also do the following:

- Be based on a "researchable" question.
- Have a central thesis or claim that represents your answer to the question you pose, even if it's tentative.
- Use appropriate and relevant sources based on your own experiences, observations, interviews, and reading, or all four sources of information.
- Be cited using the conventions recommended by your instructor.
- Be written for an audience of peers rather than experts on the topic.

mycomplab

For additional reading, writing, and research resources, go to **www.mycomplab.com**

Thinking About Subjects

What are you going to write about? This choice may be wide open, or your instructor might ask you to focus on a broad theme, perhaps one on which your class is focused. Either way, the same principle applies.

There are no boring topics, only poor questions.

There is no topic—dust mites, fruit cake, Elvis, nuclear fusion, or basketballs—that won't yield to the right question. (We'll take up the characteristics of a good question later.) But there's another condition upon which the success of your research project depends: Your curiosity. Whatever the question that eventually becomes a focus for inquiry, it must be one that you find interesting. Typically, this means that you choose a topic because it holds the promise of discovery.

Ask yourself this: *What have I seen, read, experienced, or heard about that raises interesting questions that research might help answer?*

Approaching your research project this way is exactly the impulse that might have motivated you to write a personal essay on growing up with an autistic sibling or a persuasive essay on the downside of recruiting NCAA athletes at your school. It's the same motive that inspires all genuine inquiry: *How do I feel about this? What do I think about this? What do I want to know?*

Generating Ideas

Use your notebook to generate some material. As in previous inquiry projects, at this stage don't prejudge anything you come up with. Let yourself play around with possibilities.

Listing Prompts. Lists can be rich sources of triggering topics. Let them grow freely, and when you're ready, use an item as the focus of another list or an episode of fastwriting. The following prompts should get you started.

1. Inventory your interests by creating five separate lists on a page of your notebook. Choose among the following words as a general category for each of the five lists you will create: Places, Trends, Things, Technologies, People, Controversies, History, Jobs, Habits, Hobbies. In each of the five categories you choose, brainstorm a list of words or phrases that come to mind when you think about *what you know and what you might want to know.* For example, under Places I would put "pigeons in Florence" because I want to know more about their impact on Renaissance buildings. Under Hobbies, I would put "fly fishing" because that's something I know about. Spend about fifteen minutes building these lists.

2. Look over your lists and ask yourself, *Are there research topics implied by a few of the items on these lists?* In other words, what here raises questions that more research might answer? What is it about this item that I wonder about?

3. Finally, choose a promising item from one of the lists and generate questions about it that you'd love to have answered. Perhaps you already know something about the topic but would like to learn more. Don't worry yet whether all the questions are great.

Fastwriting Prompts. Remember, fastwriting is a great way to stimulate creative thinking. Turn off your critical side and let yourself write "badly."

1. Choose an item from your lists and use it as a prompt for a seven-minute fastwrite. Begin by telling yourself the story of when, where, and why you first got interested in the subject. When the writing stalls, write the following phrase, and follow it for as long as you can: Among the things I most want to learn about this are...

2. Get a copy of the daily newspaper. Read it quickly and then clip any articles that make you think or feel something, even if you can't quite say much more about your reaction. Choose one article and glue it into your notebook. Just below, use the article as a prompt for a "narrative of thought" response. Begin this way: When I first read this article, I thought (or felt)...And then I thought...And then...If the writing takes off in another direction, let it. End by finishing the following sentence: When I first started thinking about this I thought _____, but now I think _____.

ONE STUDENT'S RESPONSE

Julian's Journal

TOPIC: JAZZ

My dad was into jazz. Would listen to it all night long after working all day long. He listened to all kinds of jazz—Bird, Miles Davis, Billy Holiday, Monk. It took me years to really appreciate the music but now it's my favorite kind. **Among the things I most want to learn about** jazz is its connection to African music and slave songs. It makes me wonder whether the uniqueness of jazz, its spontaneity especially, has something to do with the hymns and spirituals of the slaves. **Among the other things I want to learn** is whether jazz was accepted in the early days. I seem to remember my dad saying that the...

Visual Prompts. Sometimes the best way to generate material is to see what we think represented in something other than sentences. Boxes, lines, webs, clusters, arrows, charts, and even sketches can help us to see more of the landscape of a subject, especially connections among fragments of information that aren't as obvious in prose.

1. Cluster the phrase, *I'm really curious about....* Put the phrase in the center of a blank page and build a web of associations, each of which might begin with the word *why.* Explore your curiosity about things in your personal life, in the community, in the region, the state, the country, the world.

2. Do an image search using Google on some person, place, thing, or event that interests you (see the accompanying photo). Might one of the pictures you find be the focus of an investigation? Who was that guy? What *was* going on when this happened? Why did it happen?

Research Prompts. Should you do some research before you begin your research? Absolutely. By exploring what others have said or done or wondered about, you might discover an interest in something you wouldn't have otherwise considered.

1. Surf the Net, perhaps beginning with a subject directory such as The Virtual Library (http://vlib.org). Start by clicking on a subject area that interests you. Keep following the links as you branch more deeply into the subcategories and subdisciplines of that area of knowledge. Look for specific subject areas that intrigue you. For example, you might have begun in the broad subject of history, clicked the link for medieval history (maybe you've always wondered what was dark about the Dark Ages), and ended up reading some fascinating articles on the home life of medieval women. Does it raise some questions you'd like to explore?

2. Study the local newspaper. Devote some time to reading the local paper to discover a local controversy that intrigues you. Say there was an article on the impact of Title IX on the university's athletic department, and you wonder, *Is the elimination of the men's wrestling team really the result of shifts in funding to women's sports?* Or perhaps there's a letter to the editor about the condition of housing for migrant workers in the valley. Are things really that bad?

Judging What You Have

The great thing about simply generating material is that you can turn off your critical mind and simply muck about all sorts of possible topics for your essay. But, as always, the process depends on taking a more analytical look at whether you've discovered anything genuinely useful. Remember your goal at this stage: You want

A Google image search on the "Harlem Renaissance" produced this 1936 painting, *Aspiration* by Aaron Douglas. The image depicts one reason for the African American artistic renaissance in many American cities back then—the migration of blacks from the South to places such as New York and Chicago. The image suggests a great focus for an investigation of the Harlem Renaissance: Why did this migration occur?

to identify a possible topic—and maybe, if you're lucky, a research question—that will move your investigation forward in the next few days. The following suggestions should help.

What's Promising Material and What Isn't? Do you have a researchable *question*? The topic itself may not be the problem at all. Wondering whether Elvis is really dead isn't really a very good research question because the answer is pretty simple: Yep. But wondering why certain people keep asking the question in the first place—why there's a need to maintain the fiction that the King is still around is an excellent opening question for a research project. I've read riveting books on the most common subjects—salt, for example—that succeeded because the writer found interesting questions to ask about them. This, by the way, is the key to writing strong research papers about assigned topics. Virtually any topic can be interesting to you if you find the question that makes you wonder.

Is It a Researchable Question? What is a researchable question? I've already mentioned the most important characteristic: The question interests you. But there are some other things to consider as well:

- *Is it the right size?* As illustrated in the earlier "Seeing the Form" feature, the quickest way to make any research project unmanageable is to ask a really, really big question: What were the causes of the Iraqi War? Why is there racism in America? At the other extreme is the question that is so limited, so small in scope, that it isn't enough to carry the weight of your investigation; but this is rarely a problem. The key is to find an opening question that isn't too broad and isn't too narrow, one that allows you to *exclude* aspects of the topic because they aren't relevant.

- *Has something already been said about it?* In other words, is information available that *is* relevant to the question you're asking? Have experts and others addressed the question in some way, perhaps indirectly or in other contexts? This may be hard to know until you look.

- *Does it raise more questions?* Some questions have pretty simple answers. For example, wondering why the sky is blue might be an interesting question, but it probably won't sustain any kind of extended inquiry because the reasons for blue skies are well known. A better research question raises more questions the more you think about it, or seems to lead to controversies, debates, or disagreements among knowledgeable people.

- *Does it matter?* It might matter to you, and it needs to. But the best research questions should be potentially interesting and relevant to other people, too. Doing research on how to deal with your messy boyfriend, for example, may not matter really to anyone but you. But it really depends on how you frame the research question. Do men and women in this culture see domestic spaces differently, use them for different reasons, and talk about them in different ways? That's probably too big a research question, but it certainly transcends your personal problem to address questions many of us find interesting and relevant to our lives.

Questions About Audience and Purpose. The best motive for writing a research essay about a particular topic is the same reason you might want to write about anything—it makes you curious. It could interest you for any number of reasons. Perphaps you want to research an illness because your mother has it; maybe you're an engineering major and you're interested in the early history of the computer; maybe you're a hunter and want to know the impact of gray wolf reintroduction on the elk herd; or maybe you're a single parent interested in the impact of divorce on very young children.

You already know what a huge difference audience makes in how you write something. This applies to research papers, too. Though it may seem that there's some standard Research Paper, there's actually quite a range of writing that uses research. One way to distinguish between these types of writing is to think about *for whom* they're written. Readers of research who are less knowledgeable about your topic have different expectations than those who know a lot. For one thing, a general audience might welcome a conversational tone and wouldn't necessarily see the absence of, say, MLA documentation as a problem. On the other hand, a research paper you write in an environmental history class for your professor will likely be documented and may not use "I." Your professor might also expect you to use certain types of evidence, maybe drawing heavily on original (or primary) historical documents and avoiding information from Wikipedia, *History Magazine,* and other sources that might be perfectly fine in an essay for less knowledgeable readers. Consequently, the most important question you can ask when you're given a research assignment is about audience. Is this written for more—or less—knowledgeable readers?

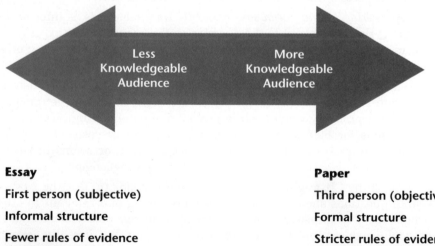

Essay	**Paper**
First person (subjective)	Third person (objective)
Informal structure	Formal structure
Fewer rules of evidence	Stricter rules of evidence
No peer review	Strong peer review
May document	Always documents
More conversational	More formal
Question-driven	Thesis-driven

For this assignment you'll likely be writing for a larger, less specialized audience—your peers and your instructor in this class. Learning to write about complex or technical subjects for a more general audience is enormously valuable, not only because you have to write papers in future classes. Much of the research-based writing you'll do after college will demand the ability to write clearly for readers who are less knowledgeable than you about a subject.

Practically speaking, then, this means choosing a topic that might interest other nonexperts. It also means choosing a good question to guide your investigation, one that people other than you might want to know the answer to. You can get some direction on this in class; also see the "Inquiring into the Details: Finding the Focusing Question" box below.

INQUIRING INTO THE DETAILS

Finding the Focusing Question

Once you tentatively settle on a topic, you're ready to do this in-class exercise. It should help you find questions that will help you focus your project.

1. Each student will take a piece of paper or a large piece of newsprint and post it on the wall. (In computer labs, students can use a word-processing program and move from station to station in the steps that follow.)

2. Write your topic at the very top of the paper (for instance, "hybrid cars").

3. Take a few minutes to briefly describe why you chose the topic.

4. Spend five minutes to briefly list what you know about your topic already (for instance, any surprising facts or statistics, the extent of the problem, important people or institutions involved, key schools of thought, common misconceptions, important trends, and controversies).

5. Now spend fifteen or twenty minutes brainstorming a list of questions about your topic that you'd love to learn the answers to. Make the list as long as you can.

6. Look around the room. You'll see a gallery of topics and questions on the walls. Now you can help each other. Move around the room, reviewing the topics and questions other students have generated. For each topic posted on the wall, do two things: Check the *one* question on the list you find most interesting, and add a question *you* would like answered about that topic.

7. Now you have long lists of questions about your topic. Is there one that you think might be researchable, using the criteria for such questions? Which questions seem to generate the most interest in the class? Do any of those interest you, too?

8. Pick one question from the list that could be your initial focusing question. Remember, you can change it later.

ONE STUDENT'S RESPONSE

Julian's Journal

FINDING THE FOCUSING QUESTION

1. The Blues

2. Chose this topic because I've listened to jazz and blues since I was a kid, but never really understood its origins.

3. Some famous blues singers: Robert Johnson, Blind Lemon Jefferson...Some qualities of blues: appeals more to the heart than the head, has a characteristic "bluesy" sound, early music in the South...

4. Questions:

    What's the relationship between blues and jazz?

    Who was the most influential blues musician in the early days?

    How is African music part of the blues?

    Did only blacks listen to blues in the beginning?

    How does the blues vary by region?

Writing the Sketch

The sketch for your research essay will be a little different from those you've written earlier. Rather than writing a "sketchy" draft of a possible essay, you'll develop a project narrative, one that summarizes your working knowledge of the topic and how your thinking about it has evolved so far. A working knowledge of your topic, according to William Badke, is achieved when you have enough information to be able to talk about it for five minutes without repeating yourself. You develop a working knowledge by conducting basic research on the Web and at the university library. (See Chapter 11 for details on how to develop working knowledge of a topic.)

Once you are ready, your project narrative should contain the following features:

- The title should be the tentative focusing question you've chosen on your topic.

- The piece itself should tell the story of your thinking about that question and topic from the beginning until now.

- This narrative of thought should discuss the ways in which your working knowledge of the topic has changed the way you think about it.

- The narrative should be about 500 words.

- Information, ideas, or quotations you borrow from outside sources should be cited. (See the "MLA Documentation Guidelines" and "APA Documentation Guidelines" sections in Chapter 12.)

▪ STUDENT SKETCH

It was spring and Amy Garrett-Brown began to imagine shorts and bathing suits, but then she took a look at her skin in the mirror. She looked pale and pasty. Wouldn't a nice tan be good about now? But would she be compromising her health for vanity, she wondered? Suddenly, Garrett had a research topic and an opening question. Here's her sketch on the topic.

Why Do People Tan?

Amy Garrett-Brown

This started as a simple question spurred by one of my occasional "people are so stupid" rants. I wondered who was to blame for this, who made it cool for white people to be tan? It seems completely asinine on the surface to waste money and time on a prepaid tan that will only result in prematurely leathered and wrinkled skin and a much higher risk of developing melanoma or other skin cancers. And then I looked down at my arms and noticed that I've managed to build up a decent tan this summer myself, not via lightbulb technology, but the old fashioned way, by playing in the sun. Hmmm...am I a hypocrite? 1

I wondered about that. As I researched sunbathing and the like I came across an interesting article in *The Atlanta Journal-Constitution* titled "The Rural South These Days Has More Tanning Salons Than John Deeres" by Rheta Grimsley Johnson. Johnson summarizes her point with a quote from E. B. White, "I am fascinated by the anatomy of decline...by the spectacle of people passively accepting a degenerating process which is against their own interests." She then explains, "He was writing about the redesign of the automobile— longer and lower with bigger fenders. He also objected to replacing the car window crank with a lazy push-button. If he could see us now, jumping into our foreign cars and speeding down to the tanning bed and nail art salon. Lost, buffed souls" (M1). 2

It struck me as I read the last lines of this sardonic critique of society that I don't necessarily wonder why people tan, but why they completely gyp themselves of the pleasures of the sun to be rewarded with a battle with cancer at worst and saggy skin at best. It seems like everyone wants to feel active, even if they aren't. 3

In a survey conducted by *Seventeen* magazine, "2/3 of the teens say they look better with a tan and feel healthier, more sophisticated and 50% say they looked more athletic" (qtd. in "Sun Tanning"). Somehow it seems that society has missed the forest for the trees. A nice tan once meant you spent your days on the beach playing volleyball and swimming, hiking in the mountains or riding a horse, riding a bike around town or jogging in the afternoons; it was usually accompanied by fit and trim bodies and healthy smiles. Now it means you spent $45 a month building a base tan. 4

But somehow the message isn't translating. People still feel healthy with a bastardized tan? So there must be something more to it all. Is the fashion industry that powerful? In her fashion column Patricia McLaughlin puts the fascination with a tan into perspective. 5

(continued)

(continued)

White people have it tough. At least the pale ones, whose skin is really a mottled, un-appetizing grayish-yellowish-pinkish off-white threaded with blue veins. Once, amazing as it may seem, it was actually cool to have skin this color. Then Coco Chanel came home with a tan from a cruise on the Duke of Westminster's yacht, and ever since, white people have preferred to be a biscuity golden color. (2)

6   So maybe that's it, people just like the way it looks to be tan. I know I feel better about putting on a bathing suit if I'm not so starkly white that I worry about blinding young children. I also know that it just feels good to be in the sun. The warm rays beating down on my back and shoulders as I work outdoors or go for a hike seem therapeutic and natural.

7   But the health industry sure doesn't like to condone it. In an article by Alexandra Greeley titled "No Tan Is a Safe Tan," she presents her case against spending time in the sun and especially tanning with facts and statistics, but I couldn't help but wonder if she ever has any fun after reading the closing lines to her article. "In the end, there really is nothing new under the sun, except that perhaps more people are staying out of it, heeding medical warnings such as Bergstresser's: 'Less sun is better. No sun is best of all'" (15).

8   I disagree. But I'm no expert, so I sought proof of my hunch that the sun is really our friend and found it. Of course, I'm not condoning the 1976 "Savage Tan" or complete ignorance of the dangers of a depleted ozone and proof that severe sunburns lead to cancers, but I think there must be some middle ground.

Works Cited

Greeley, Alexandra. "No Tan Is a Safe Tan." *Nutrition Health Review: The Consumer's Medical Journal* 59 (Summer 1991): 14–15. Print.

Johnson, Rheta Grimsley. "The Rural South These Days Has More Tanning Salons Than John Deeres." *The Atlanta Journal-Constitution* 23 Apr. 2000, home ed.: M1. Print.

McLaughlin, Patricia. "Dying for a Tan This Summer?" *St. Louis Post-Dispatch* 15 June 1995: 2.

"Sun Tanning." *Cool Nurse* 2000–2003 18 June 2003. Print.

Moving from Sketch to Draft

Your sketch may not really be an early draft of the essay you'll write later. It's probably more of a record of your thinking about your topic, perhaps leading you to a clearer idea about the best focusing question and perhaps a stronger sense of what you might want to say in the draft. Your sketch also gives you a chance to share what you've discovered so far with others in your class, but not in the usual way. Rather than workshopping your sketch, you'll use it to develop a brief presentation.

Evaluating Your Own Sketch. Follow the road map of the thinking present in your sketch to get a clearer sense of where you want to go in the draft.

1. What seemed to be the turning point in your own thinking about the topic? What caused it?

2. Is the focusing question you wrote at the beginning of the sketch still the right title? Does that question need to be revised or do you need to write a new one?

3. Based on what you know now, how would you answer the question you're asking?

Questions for Peer Review. Rather than workshopping your sketch, you will use it as the basis for a brief class presentation. Following a press conference format, you will speak for about five to ten minutes, highlighting some or all of the following:

- What focusing question did you start with? What question do you want to ask now?

- What is the most surprising thing you've learned so far?

- What do experts on the topic debate about?

- What are the most common misconceptions about the topic?

- What story can you tell about the topic—a case study, a telling event, a profile of the person involved?

Try to make this presentation lively and interesting. Your purpose, in part, is to get a sense of potential reader interest in your topic and the question you're pursuing. Students listening to the presentations should be encouraged to ask questions about what you've said—or haven't said. They also might have some suggestions of questions about your topic you hadn't considered, or tips on where to search for more information. Allow another five to ten minutes for this question-and-answer session.

Reflecting on What You've Learned. Following your presentation, spend a few minutes generating a list of everything you heard, and then begin a five-minute fastwrite that explores your reaction to these questions and suggestions and your tentative plan for revision. Did the class have a lot of questions about your topic following the presentation? What seems to have most piqued their interest? What questions or controversies seem to ignite the most discussion? What did the discussion suggest might be new avenues for research? End your fastwrite by writing about what you understand now about your topic and your initial beliefs about it that you didn't fully understand when you began writing.

Research and Other Strategies: Gathering More Information

Discovery is what drives inquiry-based research. This is why having a good question matters so much, and finding a good question for your project depends on knowing something about your topic. "Working knowledge" seeds this effort. (Chapter 11 provides some practical strategies for developing working knowledge on any topic). A working knowledge will give you an encyclopedia-like view of your topic—what is the terrain, what are the controversies or the questions, who is influential—and from this you can frame a question that interests you.

But this is just the beginning. As you explore your research question in the coming weeks, you'll go beyond working knowledge to "focused knowledge," finding information that drills down more deeply into your topic's terrain. Good questions are sharper drills. However, this is an open-ended process and your goal at this stage is to use what you discover to continually shape what you want to see. As you become more informed, you'll revise your approach: refining your question, developing ideas about what you think, and always searching for the answers to this simple question: *So what?*

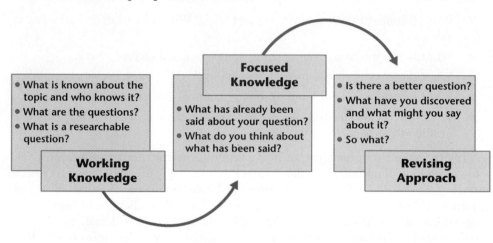

Writing *while you research* will help you figure this all out and even help you get a start on drafting your essay. I'm not talking about simply taking notes on the information that you find in the coming weeks. Writing about what you *think* about what you're reading or hearing is the best incubator of insight. The double-entry journal, which was introduced to you earlier in *The Curious Writer,* is one method that encourages this kind of writing. There are some other alternatives in Chapter 12.

Composing the Draft

Sara was a compulsive collector of information. She researched and researched, collecting more books and articles and Web sources until the desk in her apartment looked like a miniature version of downtown Chicago—towering piles of paper and books everywhere. She never felt as if she knew enough to begin writing her essay, and would only begin drafting when forced to—the paper was due tomorrow. Neal figured he could find most of what he needed pretty quickly on the Internet. He printed out a few articles and Web pages and felt confident he could write his paper using those. He didn't feel pressured to begin writing until the due date loomed. When Neal started writing and realized that he probably wouldn't be able to get the required page length, he widened the margins.

Sara and Neal obviously use different strategies for getting to the draft. Sara relies on accumulating great quantities of information, trusting that aggressively collecting sources will make the writing easier—the main source of anxiety for her—although she probably doesn't really believe that. On the other hand, Neal suffers from overconfidence. He figures he can make do with a few sources and doesn't look around much. Both Neal and Sara do what research paper writers have done forever: wait until the last minute. Neither of these writers will be happy with the result.

It's easy to avoid this situation if you begin the draft after you've accomplished the following:

- *You've done some writing before you start writing.* In other words, have you exploited the double-entry journal or an alternative notetaking method to both collect useful information and to explore your reaction to what it says?

- *You are working from abundance (but not overabundance).* Neal is much more typical than Sara. He is trying to compose his draft by drawing from a nearly empty well. Almost any writing—and particularly research writing—depends on working from abundance. You need to collect more information than you can use. But not too much. Don't let endless collecting become an avoidance tactic.

- *Your focusing question has helped you* exclude *information.* A good focusing question is a guide. It will help you see the relevance of certain portions of the sources you've collected and give you reason to ignore the rest. If you sense that this is happening consistently as you review your sources, you're probably ready to write.

- *You have a tentative idea about what you think.* By now, you know enough about your topic to have some feelings or ideas about a possible answer to the question behind your investigation. Remember the draft may make you change your mind—that's fine—but begin composing with at least a tentative point of view.

Methods of Development. The research essay is more likely than the previous essays to combine a range of methods of development. You can see that already from the professional essays earlier in this chapter. However, here are some more typical designs for research essays:

Narrative. We don't usually associate narrative structure with research papers, but research-based writing tells stories all the time. Perhaps one of the most common techniques is use of the case study, which can be an excellent way to begin your paper. Case studies or anecdotes about people involved or affected by a topic often bring that topic to life by moving it closer to the everyday *lives* of people. But narrative is also used as the backbone of a research essay. Sometimes an essay tells the story of what the writer wanted to know and what she found out, a kind of narrative of thought. The sketch you wrote earlier is an early project narrative that established your initial focusing question and some tentative clues about where it might lead. This structure could easily be imported into the final draft of your research essay, only it will be more developed and more insightful.

Question to Answer. Because much of the research process is devoted to developing a good question to drive the inquiry, it makes sense to consider organizing your essay around what that question is, where it came from, and what has already been said about it, and then reporting what you've discovered about possible answers to the question that triggered the investigation. A lot of formal academic research is organized this way, although there might be an added section about the methods the investigator chose to try to seek the answers.

Known to Unknown. This is a variation on the question-to-answer structure that might be particularly useful if you're writing about a complex topic about which much remains unknown. Your research might have led to the discovery that the question you're interested in is a question that has very speculative or limited answers. For example, Andy was writing about the use of psychiatric medicine such as antidepressants and antipsychotics on children because his family physician had recommended them for one of his own kids. Andy quickly discovered that this was a relatively new use for such drugs and that much mystery surrounded both the diagnosis and treatment of children with emotional problems. It became clear that the purpose of his essay was not to offer a definitive answer to his question, but to suggest areas that still needed further study.

Using Evidence. While every discipline has its own ideas about what counts as good research evidence, the research essay is a less specialized form with a more general audience. Therefore, the rules of evidence for a research essay aren't nearly as strict as they might be, say, in an academic article in psychology or biology. But that's not to say that anything goes. Research writing obviously depends mainly on sources outside the writer—published materials, interviews with people involved in the topic, and observations in the field—but the writer's personal experience can count if it's relevant. In some cases, you may want to cite your own experience as evidence that either supports or contradicts a claim made by someone else, but your experience alone probably isn't sufficient evidence. Find other voices that confirm it.

> Research writing obviously depends mainly on sources outside the writer...but the writer's personal experience can count if it's relevant.

Not all outside sources are equally convincing either. Figure 10.2 suggests a hierarchy that is one way of evaluating how "authoritative" a source might be. Notice that, generally speaking, the more specialized a publication's audience, the more likely the information in it will be valued. For example, an article on dream interpretation in the *Journal of American Psychology* is considered more authoritative than an article on the same subject in *Ladies' Home Journal*. The reasons for this are pretty obvious: When you write for experts in the field, you'd better know what you're talking about.

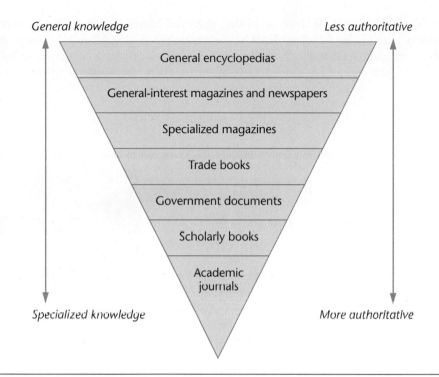

General knowledge   Less authoritative

General encyclopedias

General-interest magazines and newspapers

Specialized magazines

Trade books

Government documents

Scholarly books

Academic journals

Specialized knowledge   More authoritative

Figure 10.2   A hierarchy of sources places the most credible at the bottom of an inverted pyramid. For academic research, these are usually articles and books that are reviewed by other experts before they're published.

Finally, an important way to write authoritatively using outside sources is not only to use the right sources but to cite them carefully. It's crucial that you acknowledge those whose ideas have helped you see more deeply into your topic. In your draft, acknowledge your sources in two ways:

1. Mention them in your essay using attribution tags, such as *according to Jones*...or *Hill argues that*...or *Baraka said.*...

2. Cite borrowed information, quotations, and ideas using MLA or APA conventions. (See the "MLA Documentation Guidelines" and "APA Documentation Guidelines" sections in Chapter 12.)

Workshopping the Draft

Share your research essay in a small group workshop before you begin your final revision. Because of the length of these essays, you might want to allow more time for these discussions, or encourage group members to read the drafts before the group meets. Your instructor might also put you in smaller groups.

Reflecting on the Draft. A draft is a thing the wind blows through. That might be especially true of the full first draft of your research essay. After all, this project involves juggling a lot more than most other inquiry projects—controlling information and the ideas of a wide variety of sources, the challenge of trying to surround that outside material with your own ideas, worries about following citation conventions, and the struggle not to let the whole project get away from your own purposes and questions. Spend a little time reflecting on how all this went.

WRITING IN THE DISCIPLINES

Being a Stranger in the Village

As you do your research you might have some pretty heavy reading. Most things you encounter from the bottom of the pyramid of sources (see Figure 10.2) is pretty scholarly stuff. This might make you feel like a stranger in a faraway village. What language do these people speak? What are these odd customs? All communities have their own *discourses* or ways of talking and behaving that are familiar to insiders and make everyone else feel like outsiders. That's exactly how I might feel if I hung out with the "dudes" at the skateboard park in town.

Your frustration of trying to understand an article from the *Journal of Artificial Organs* (yes, there is one) when you're not a surgeon isn't that different from a surgeon's frustration at trying to understand an article in the *Journal of Bank Cost and Management Accounting*. In both cases, the readers are the village strangers.

Yet, if you're an undergraduate trying to do research, you've got to try to make sense of unfamiliar academic discourses. What can you do? Well, you can do what a visitor to a foreign land tries to do: Pay attention to the purposes of local customs, try to pick up some of the language, and figure out the minimum you need to know to get what you need.

While there are many different academic discourses, there are a few conventions that articles in many disciplines share. Knowing these will help you get what you need to do your research:

- **Read abstracts.** Journal articles in the social sciences and dissertations often include one-paragraph summaries of the investigator's findings, usually written by the investigator. Start with the abstracts to get a sense of whether it's worth your time to wade through the article.

- **Read conclusions.** The formally structured article in many disciplines has the following parts: abstract, introduction or literature review, methods, results or discussion, and conclusions. Skim the article to get a sense of the purpose of the study and then focus on the conclusion for more careful reading. There you should find the most important findings.

> ■ ***Go to the literature review***. For undergraduate research, sometimes the best part of any academic book or article isn't the findings, the claim, or the theory but the literature review. This is the part that appears in or immediately after an introduction where the author updates the reader on the current "conversation" on the topic, including prevailing findings, current theories, and important contributions to think about.
>
> ■ ***Mine the bibliography.*** The author of a book or article may have done some of your research for you. Even if you can't use much from a particular source for your paper, the bibliography can be invaluable, directing you to some of the best sources on your topic. The sources in the literature review section (see the preceding bullet point) are usually the best out there on that topic.

In your notebook or on a separate piece of paper you'll attach to the draft when you hand it in, answer the following questions:

■ What's the most important thing you learned about your topic after the research and writing you've just completed? Is this important understanding obvious in the draft?

■ Choose two paragraphs that incorporate outside sources—one that you think is written pretty well, and another less well. What differences do you notice between the two? Can you identify at least one problem you need to work on in the next draft that will help you improve the way you integrate sources?

■ What was your focusing question? How does the draft attempt to answer it?

Questions for Readers. Make sure that you have some specific questions you'd like to ask your workshop group about how the draft is working. Here are some others:

1. In your own words, what do you think is the main thing I'm trying to say in the draft? Where in the draft do you think I say it?

2. What was the most interesting part of the essay? What was the least interesting? Why?

3. After you read the first few paragraphs, did you have a clear sense of what my focusing question was?

4. Did any part of the draft seem to drift away from that focus?

5. Where do I need more information or more evidence?

Revising the Draft

As I discussed earlier in the book, one of the most common misconceptions about revision is that you do it only at the end of the writing process. In fact, up to this point, you should have been revising your work all along, from the first few journal exercises when you chose a topic and played with possible angles on it, to the journal work you might have done to prepare to write the sketch, and then again with your efforts to turn your sketch into a more developed draft. Revision is literally "re-seeing," and every time you create the conditions that allow you to discover something new about how you see or what you think about your subject, you are, in fact, engaged in the act of revision. In a sense, then, each writing assignment you undertake is one long act of revision, from start to finish.

But once you've completed a draft, the revision process becomes more focused. You are mostly working with material that should be somewhat settled, with purposes that might be clearer, and ideas that may have more shape. At this point, the biggest temptation is to tell yourself you are largely done and what revision remains is merely a matter of "fixing things"—tinkering with sentences, correcting typos, and running a spellchecker. In the survey from Chapter 1 (see page 19), 70 percent of students admitted as much. "I usually just tidy things up" was ranked first or second by students who were asked what they do most often when they revise an academic paper.

These activities are certainly an element of revision—and an important one—but as the word *revision* implies, it's important to "re-see" both what you are trying to say and how you try to say it, even at this stage in the process. Chapter 13, "Revision Strategies," is a useful introduction to the revision process for any essay, including the research essay. It emphasizes ways writers can break the bonds that limit their ability to find new ways of seeing the draft.

As you plan for revision, do any of the following problems typical of research essay drafts apply to yours?

- Is the essay sufficiently focused? Remember the photography metaphor from the "Seeing the Form" feature (page 415): you want to take closer pictures rather than landscape shots of your subject. Having too broad a focus is a particularly troublesome issue with research-based writing. You can fix this by refining your question and narrowing the scope of your project.

- Did you collect enough information? Drafts that work from scarcity typically run short, have too broad a focus, or suffer from vagueness. The solution? Go back to the library or the Web and collect more information.

- Is the essay organized around your research question from beginning to end? Do any paragraphs or passages strike off in irrelevant directions?

- Does the draft say too much? Remember that a strong research essay not only asks an interesting question about a topic but explicitly states what the writer thinks is the best answer, even if it's speculative. Is this thesis clear?

Refer to Chapter 13, "Revision Strategies," for ideas on how to revise your draft following your workshop. In particular, it would probably be useful to check your draft for logical fallacies, using the table on page 435. Because one of the challenges of a longer essay with sources is organizing all that information, consider some of the structure exercises in Chapter 13, particularly Revision Strategy 13.17, "The Frankenstein Draft." Use the following table to find other appropriate revision strategies. Remember that a draft may present problems in more than one category.

Everyday Research

Because of the Internet, people do everyday research more now than at any time in my lifetime. Online research skills are not only a key to academic success but will help keep you healthy, save money, and solve marital problems. A recent Pew study (2007) found that more people consult the Internet to solve problems than consult professionals who are experts on these problems. More surprising, though, was that people—particularly people aged 18 to 30—still go to libraries for a variety of purposes, including research.

"Information literacy" has long been a hot topic among librarians, but in recent years others—including business leaders—have called it one of "the basic skills sets of the twenty-first century." What exactly are we talking about here? Information literacy isn't just possessing the skills to use a computer to search for information, but knowing how to match appropriate information to solve a particular problem. People who are information literate can evaluate what they find, synthesize the information, and *use* it purposefully.

GUIDE TO REVISION STRATEGIES

Problems in the Draft (Chapter 13)	Page Number
Unclear purpose ■ Not sure what the paper is about?	551
Unclear thesis, theme, or main idea ■ Not sure what you're trying to say?	557
Lack of information or development ■ Need more convincing evidence? Need to check for logical fallacies?	564
Disorganized ■ Doesn't move logically or smoothly from paragraph to paragraph?	568
Unclear or awkward at the level of sentences and paragraphs ■ Seems choppy or hard to follow at the level of sentences or paragraphs?	577

Polishing the Draft

After you've addressed the more global problems in your draft, you should focus on more local matters, such as how effectively you integrate and cite sources, how successfully you've organized your paragraphs, and whether you've written the draft in a clear, lively style. Don't forget to use the handbook at the back of the book to help you with any grammatical and stylistic questions you might have; also use the guide to MLA or APA citations in Chapter 13 to check how well you've followed those conventions.

Before you finish your draft, work through the following checklist:

✓ Every paragraph is about one thing.

✓ The transitions between paragraphs aren't abrupt.

✓ The length of sentences varies in each paragraph.

✓ Each sentence is concise. There are no unnecessary words or phrases.

✓ You've checked grammar, particularly verb agreement, run-on sentences, unclear pronouns, and misused words (*there/their, where/were,* and so on).

✓ You've run your spellchecker and proofed your paper for misspelled words.

✓ You've double-checked your citations and Works Cited or References page to ensure that the formatting is correct.

■ STUDENT ESSAY

Gordon Seirup's essay "College Dating," which is formatted according to MLA documentation guidelines, is a great finale to this chapter's readings on the "hooking up" phenomenon on American college campuses. I like this essay because Seirup takes control of the information he gathered in his Web research by finding—and naming—the patterns he sees in college dating and using them to organize his essay. He does a great job of tapping a variety of sources and bringing in the voices of other students and experts who have something relevant to say. Also notice how well these quotations are embedded in Gordon's own prose.

Like any work, "College Dating" could be an even stronger essay. While the essay employs evidence from some of the professional readings in this chapter, most of these sources Seirup cites consist of informal quotations taken from the online versions of college newspapers and lack the authority of formal print sources. Though the research question is clear, Gordon's essay also isn't explicitly organized around a specific claim that arises from his research. What thesis about college romance would you advance after reading the essay?

Gordon E. Seirup

Professor Ballenger

English 101

6 October 2006

College Dating

First there was the passing notes, hand holding, and name-calling of middle school. Then you survived your first heartbreak when your high school sweetheart decided it would be best to "just be friends." Now swept away in college life you hardly take the time to step back and ask yourself, "What am I doing here? Whose bed did I just wake up in, and how the hell did I get here?!" If you have not yet taken the time to ponder what it is you plan to do with the so-called best four years of your life, besides studying and eating dorm food, perhaps it is about time you did. What do you want to be accomplishing in these prime dating years? More importantly, is that what you are accomplishing? In short, my purpose is to discuss the question: "What role should dating play in college students' lives?"

If you assume that most college students have thought how their dating decisions today might affect them tomorrow, think again. The students I spoke with informally here on the Colorado State University campus all hesitated when asked to simply "define dating." Once done struggling through that answer, they were asked, What is the purpose of dating in college?" These students' answers ranged from "getting laid!" to "discover more about yourself through others" to "find the person you want to marry" to "I have no clue." Are the college masses blissfully unaware of exactly what it is they are doing when they pursue relationships?

First, what is dating? For my purposes, dating is defined as seeing someone socially in a one-on-one setting. Other terms used within the following pages are "hooking up" and "courtship," defined as noncommittal sexual acts

1

2

3

Seirup 2

and nonserial exclusive dating with the intention of marriage, respectively. What I mean by "nonserial" dating is that when you choose to date someone, you intend to marry that person. While this may not work out, and might lead you to enter this process again, you sincerely choose each person you date as a potential spouse. While you may court more than one person, it isn't your intention to do so.

4   I have defined five major approaches to college dating based on their common purpose, values, and motivations, in addition to their general line of reasoning: Casual Dating, Exclusive Dating, Courting, Cannot Date, and Hooking Up.

5   Casual dating was popular during the American 1950s, although Beth Bailey notes that "between 1890 and 1925, dating—in practice and in name—had gradually, almost imperceptibly, become a universal custom in America" (19). The emergence of public dating rituals coincided with the emergence of mass media, especially TV and magazines that made dating a feature of the typical American romance (Bailey 9). Casual dating was modeled on popular TV shows, and analyzed in mostly women's magazines—where to go, how much to spend, when to allow a first kiss. A major motive for dating was, according to Bailey, public competition to spend the most, choose the best partner, and so on.

6   However, dating these days is much less ritualized. Rather than focusing on public display, these days casual daters value meeting new people, discovering and/or reinventing who you are as a person, and enjoying yourself. The original scenario for casual dating typically went something like this: Guy meets Girl, decides he would like to see her socially, and asks her to join him at the diner for hamburgers and a shared milkshake. If this date goes well, they may see each other again. After about three dates there is a good chance Guy would be graced with a goodnight kiss.

Seirup 3

These dates did not imply exclusivity or any concrete commitment at all. 7
While social enjoyment is the driving force behind the Casual Dating approach,
there are two other important aspects: meeting new people and discovering yourself. By the simple act of participating in these dates, each party naturally learns
more about himself and herself through their interaction. "Dating one-on-one
gives you a chance to become comfortable with new people," says Julie Baugher,
Georgetown University's premier relationship columnist (Baugher, "'Rules'").

The key to developing sufficient attachment for a couple to want to date 8
multiple times is that elusive quality called "chemistry." One study that
attempted to pin down exactly what college students mean by chemistry suggested that it involves similarity of interests and backgrounds, as well as
"reciprocity," or the feeling that both partners are giving something to each
other (Peretti and Abplanalp 5).

But chemistry isn't necessarily a scarce phenomenon, and it's possible to 9
find it with more than one person. According to Lee Ann Hamilton, a health
educator at the University of Arizona, "College is the time to re-invent yourself
and try new things; many people don't want to be tied down" (qtd. in Hill). It
is very important to keep in mind that not being "tied down," as Ms. Hamilton
put it, is a fundamental aspect of the Casual Dating approach.

Columnist Julie Baugher has laid out some guidelines helpful to circum- 10
venting our typical defensive maneuvers when it comes to dating. (It may be
useful to remember these next time you are asked out for a date.) "Don't
think about whether you want to Date him with an uppercase 'D' (meaning
exclusive dating). Don't conclude that he isn't 'Your type.' Don't assume this is
the beginning of a long-term relationship that you're not ready for" (Baugher,
"Dating"). Approaching it casually, couples may date as many people as there

Seirup 4

are nights available in the week, so long as all parties involved know the arrangement.

11   Similar to the Casual Dating approach is the Exclusive Dating approach. Both parties value dating as an activity for social enjoyment, as well as self-education. Exclusive dating may be thought of as the "next step" from casual dating, and indeed commonly tends to grow out of casual dating. When exclusively dating, you are not only learning more about yourself, but also consciously aware of what you are learning about your partner. Which characteristics can you see yourself living with for the rest of your life? Which make you want to run away and never date again? "Through several short-term relationships, students can find personalities with which they are most compatible," claims Matt West, a writer at the University of Virginia. "Relationships at this age allow you to explore what you like and don't like in a partner," agrees Mary Anne Knapp, a clinical social worker. Through a series of exclusive relationships, one forms a model of the ideal spouse (qtd. in Pleiss).

12   However, here is the crucial detail for this approach: This flirtation with long-term commitment is solely a mental exercise. Marriage is not a goal of the exclusive dating approach. Exclusively dating college students are aware of their proximity to marriage; however, they are not going to let that detail dominate their lives. The goal is gaining knowledge. This distinction is memorably worded by Jennifer Graham, a senior staff writer at Stanford University: "I think I'm going to put marriage on the backburner and, at least for the time being, refrain from appraising my peers' credentials for parenthood. There's no need to sap all the joy from life." Don't misinterpret Graham as saying she wishes to ignore completely her peers' credentials for parenthood; rather the issue is at which stage in the dating process qualifications for

Seirup 5

marriage become important. When making the choice of whether or not to date someone, these marriage-related thoughts are minimally important. However, while in a relationship, it would be wise to consider these credentials to learn what you are looking for when you are shopping for a spouse.

Expert testimony supports the Exclusive Dating approach. Clinical social worker Mary Anne Knapp says these exclusive relationships are healthy and "serve more of a purpose than just having a permanent date every Friday night," since "having a supportive partner, someone who knows you and is on your side, is good for a positive outlook on life" (qtd. in Pleiss 1).   13

The premise of the Courting approach is that dating should play no role in the lives of college students. Believers in courtship argue for a return to the practice of courtship rather than dating, and hold marriage absolutely paramount. Furthermore, proponents argue that this courtship should take place after college. In general, students who advocate the Courting approach share strong religious backgrounds, and actively use their faith to both justify their opinion and denounce others'. In fact, the approach is as much their adamant opposition to dating as it is their support of courtship, saying casual dating is "a bankrupt convention...a training ground for divorce [and]... a cheap imitation of the love and intimacy of a real marriage (Jensen)". Furthermore, they believe that the practice of casual dating is futile: "If the couple never intends to get married in the first place, then breaking up is a foregone conclusion, and their relationship is doomed" (Jensen).   14

Advocates of this approach value the unique bonds that are formed between husband and wife as well as purity upon entering marriage. Courtship "is the only way to date with true love, respect and honesty because it is rooted in a desire to take the relationship to its complete and glorious fulfillment"   15

Seirup 6

(Jensen). Those seeking courtship seek others who seek the same; assuming that if you have kept pure in pursuit of marriage, you should expect the same of your spouse to-be—though today the selection of potential partners may be slim. "It's hard enough to meet somebody who doesn't have a past relationship that is like a skeleton in her closet," says Matt Sweet, finance major at the University of Virginia (qtd. in Jensen). According to those who take the Courting approach, if more college students adopted their strategy, this wouldn't be a problem.

16   Believers in courtship share both a wholehearted commitment to a relationship that will lead to marriage and the best possible education while in college. Value is placed on the concept of college students being just that—students. During college they have neither the time nor energy to responsibly court a spouse. Therefore, it is best for people to engage in courtship only after graduation and they are settled into their careers.

17   Proponents of the Cannot Date approach also believe that dating should play no role in the lives of college students. They don't oppose dating, but these students have tried to date, or at least wanted to, but deemed it to be impossible. Like the Courting approach, these students value their standing as students and hold education as a very high priority. This approach is aptly described by a student at the University of Arizona: "While pursuing a double major, interning, working, maintaining a social life and attending school full time," Danielle Demizjian, a business economics and finance senior, finds "exclusive dating too much of a commitment" (qtd. in Hill). This is a common complaint among college students. Despite their desire to date, exclusively or casually, there just does not seem to be the time, though time alone is not the only issue. For those students advanced in their time management skills, the

Seirup 7

emotional burden may be too great. Jaime Dutton, a sophomore at Johns Hopkins University, says, "It's hard enough to have fun here with all the work you have to do, [and] there's no reason to have the extra drama in your life" (qtd. in Saxe). Nicole Kucewitz, a writer for the *Rocky Mountain Collegian*, agrees: "Relationships take time and patience, and in college, both of these can be very limited."

Finally, there is the Hooking Up approach. This last group has an alter-   18
nate social structure to replace traditional dating. Their philosophy is this: At the college level, formal dating is unnecessary. For social activities, in contrast with the one-on-one date, groups are ideal. As for sexual needs, noncommittal hooking up is not only acceptable, it's preferred. Common values amongst this group include enjoying yourself socially with friends, casually fulfilling sexual needs, and avoiding commitment. This "new age" form of dating is the solution that has flourished as a result of the gripes of the Cannot Date approach.

Many of the students who Hook Up see the dating arena as split into two dis-   19
tinct groups: "People are either single or practically married" (Burney). Hooking Up is the solution for those people who wish to largely retain their single status while still satisfying their social and sexual needs, and avoiding the "marriage-type" exclusive relationship. Dan, a student at Duke University, puts it this way: "In the real world, there is an expectation that after the third date, you might get a hookup. At Duke, there is the expectation that after the third hookup, you might get a date" (qtd. in Beckett). So perhaps once college students reach the "real world" this approach will fade away, but it remains wildly popular on campus.

One reason for its popularity is that Hooking Up avoids potential complica-   20
tions of exclusive dating or even casual dating. With this approach, future hookup partners spend time in groups and get to know each other in a friendlier

context first, avoiding the awkward chesslike strategies common to the predate period. Or even simpler, the story goes like this: "Now all a guy in a decent fraternity has to do to hookup on a Saturday night is to sit on the couch long enough at a party. It's slow at first, but eventually a girl will plop herself down beside him, they'll sit there drinking, he'll make a joke, she'll laugh, their eyes will meet, sparks will fly, and the mission is accomplished. And you want me to tell this guy to call a girl, spend $100 on dinner and hope for a goodnight kiss" (qtd. in Beckett)? This trend is perpetuated by "the beds [being] short walks from the parties. This increases the likelihood of the drunken hookup, while simultaneously decreasing the frequency of actual dates," according to Tom Burney, a columnist and student at Duke University (qtd. in Beckett).

21   With this tendency to go from partying to hooking up, a critic may be quick to draw the conclusion that sex is the driving force behind this approach. On the contrary, students' motives are often to get to know potential partners as friends (at least superficially) first. David Brunkow, computer science major at Colorado State University, attests to this: "Most of the people I've been with were already my friends...It's so much easier that way. You already know they're a good person and that they're not going to screw you over. Also, if things don't work out, you don't lose your friend" (qtd. in Borra).

22   Research seems to confirm Brunkow's contention. According to Paul and Hayes, the best hookups were more likely to be prefaced by hanging out, flirting, mutual attraction, and talking. The worst hookups often resulted from a friend's instigation (Paul and Hayes 648).

23   Of the five categories I've offered to describe college dating, Hooking Up is both the most common and the most controversial. In a recent study, three quarters of students interviewed reported that they had hooked up at least

Seirup 9

once and at least a third said this involved sex with a stranger or a new acquaintance (Paul, McManus, and Hayes 84). Students who choose Hooking Up may not believe that there are other, socially sanctioned choices, as this paper suggests. Do participants think Hooking Up is a good thing? One would assume so since it's so popular these days. But there is some evidence that the practice is driven by "pluralistic ignorance" or the mistaken assumption that their discomfort with the behavior is unique. This is particularly true of women (Lambert, Kahn, and Apple 132), a situation which could lead to abuses.

While no one approach is clearly ideal for all students, there seems to be one to suit everyone, despite a wide range of personal beliefs. Casual Dating, Exclusive Dating, Courting, Cannot Date, and Hooking Up represent distinct alternatives to college students, difficult choices that add to the complexities—both academic and non-academic—that college students find themselves caught up in every day. But it's crucial that students at least be aware that there are choices to make.

24

Works Cited

Bailey, Beth. "The Worth of a Date." *From Front Porch to Back Seat: Courtship in Twentieth-Century America*. 1998. Baltimore: Johns Hopkins University Press. Print.

Baugher, Julia. "Dating with a Lower Case 'd.'" *Hoya* 4 Oct. 2002. Web. 8 Oct. 2003.

Baugher, Julia. "'Rules' Teach Ladies Tricks to Winning Love." *Hoya* 15 Nov. 2002. Web. 7 Oct. 2003.

Beckett, Whitney. "What Lies Between the Hookup and Marriage?" *Chronicle* 5 Sept. 2003. Web. 13 Oct. 2003.

Borra, Jessup. "The 'He-Said-She-Said' on Dating." *Rocky Mountain Collegian* 17 Oct. 2002. Web. 19 Oct. 2003.

Seirup 10

Burney, T. "Dating Sea Nuggets." *Chronicle* 26 Mar. 2003. Web. 13 Oct. 2003.

Graham, Jennifer. "Graduation Time: Cap and Gown or Wedding Gown?" *Stanford Daily* 17 July 2003. Web. 13 Oct. 2003.

Hill, Tessa. "UA students Have Lost That Lovin' Feeling." *Arizona Daily Wildcat* 30 Jan. 2003. Web. 8 Oct. 2003.

Jensen, Mark. "A Return to Courtship." *Cavalier Daily* 26 Apr. 2002. Web. 19 Oct. 2003.

Kucewicz, Nicole. "Ins and Outs of the College Dating Game: Fun or Forever?" *Rocky Mountain Collegian* 15 Aug. 2001. Web. 19 Oct. 2003.

Lambert, Tracy, Arnold Kahn, and Kevin Apple. "Pluralistic Ignorance and Hooking." *Journal of Sex Research* 40.2 (2003): 129–33. Print.

Paul, Elizabeth, Brian McManus, and Allison Hayes. "Hookups: Characteristics and Correlates of College Students' Spontaneous and Anonymous Sexual Experiences." *Journal of Sex Research* 37.1 (2000): 76–88. Print.

Paul, Elizabeth, and Kristen Hayes. "The Casualities of Casual Sex: A Qualitative Exploration of the Phenomenology of College Student Hookups." *Journal of Social and Personal Relationships* 19 (2002): 639–61. Print.

Peretti, Peter, and Richard Abplanalp, Jr. "Chemistry in the College Dating Process: Structure and Function." *Social Behavior and Personality* 32.2 (2004): 147–54. Print.

Pleiss, Carissa. "Couples Can Offer Support, Comfort." *Collegian* 11 Feb. 2003. Web. 17 Oct. 2003.

Saxe, Lindsay. "Books before Relationships?" *Johns Hopkins News–Letter* 28 Mar. 2003. Web. 8 Oct. 2003.

West, Matt. "Steering clear of marriage until after College." *Cavalier Daily* 26 Apr. 2001. Web. 19 Oct. 2005.

Evaluating the Essay

1. Choose a page of Seirup's research essay and, using a highlighter, mark every line or passage in which he actually *does* something with information rather than simply explain or report what he found. In other words, where does he interpret, argue, analyze, assert, speculate, or evaluate? How much of the page is covered with color when you're done highlighting? Do the same thing with your own essay draft. Do you do more than report? Do you control information as well as Seirup did here?

2. Using Seirup's essay as a model, identify at least one question you have about the proper way to cite sources in a research essay.

3. If you were going to suggest that the writer revise "College Dating" around a particular assertion or thesis, what would it be? After reading the essay, what are your conclusions about the dating scene at American universities?

4. Identify at least two places where you might use other information from the professional reading in this chapter in "College Dating." Exactly what information would you use? How would you cite it?

USING WHAT YOU HAVE LEARNED

You've been involved in writing your own research essay and reading published and student essays that use research. What have you learned about the research process and the research essay that you can apply in other writing situations?

1. Explore how your thinking about research writing might have changed by completing the following sentence at least five times in your journal: Before I worked through this chapter I thought writing research essays involved _____, but now I think _____.

2. In this chapter you were introduced to a range of research-based work, from an undocumented essay to a formal academic paper. How will you use your understanding of academic research genres to prepare to write a research paper for another class? What information will you want to know before you start?

3. Writers of any academic essay must come across as authorities of sorts— credible and persuasive voices on whatever topics they choose to write about. This is particularly important in research-based writing. How exactly do you establish this authority?

Here's a formula for research twenty years ago:

- Take an upscale department store of information + store maps, clearly marked + helpful employees. Whip in reliability and strain out some accessibility.

I'm not that nostalgic about the old days when nearly all research was done in the university library. I will never miss the toil of thumbing through multiple volumes of bound indexes, trying to find a few articles located on another floor. And yet, it was awfully convenient to walk into a library, and like a customer in a big store, know where to find what I needed and get help from a reference librarian if I needed it. Best of all, because library specialists not only organize information but evaluate its quality, I could put some faith in the usefulness of what I found. The good news is that hasn't changed—the library still effectively organizes knowledge (see Figure 11.1 for how this is done using the Library of Congress system of letters and numbers) and makes the best of it available. What's more, even the online accessibility of information in the library has improved dramatically. The bad news is that Google is irresistibly convenient and can produce immediate results.

But this doesn't have to be bad news. The smart researcher knows that *both* the library and the Web are tremendous resources and always tries to combine them in the hunt for good information. In this chapter, you'll find out how you can do this. Maybe most important, you'll learn that one of the keys to efficient academic research is something most of us don't often think about much: crafting search terms.

LIBRARY OF CONGRESS SYSTEM

Organization of Books by Letter

A	General Works	L	Education
B	Philosophy, Psychology, Religion	M	Music
C	Auxiliary Sciences of History	N	Fine Arts
D	History: General and Europe	P	Language and Literature
E	History: America	Q	Science
F	History: America	R	Medicine
G	Geography, Anthropology, Recreation	S	Agriculture
H	Social Sciences	T	Technology
J	Political Sciences	U	Military Science
K	Law	Y	Naval Science
		Z	Library Science and Reference

Figure 11.1   Librarians categorize general areas of knowledge by letter, A–Z. These letters, used in combination with other letters and numbers, make up the "call numbers" that will help you locate a book.

Magic Words That Open Doors

One of the key electronic literacies is something that seems so simple you might wonder why I bring it up first: *the words you choose to search for information.* Consider that in 1850 the Harvard library, the first academic library in the nation, had only 84,200 volumes, and many of those were kept behind locked cabinets. To search these stacks, a student would plead with a librarian for a book. Today, my own university's library has more than a half million books and access to millions more through interlibrary loan. In addition, it has tens of thousands of periodicals on microfilm and access to millions more through electronic databases. Then there's the World Wide Web; it's impossible to know its actual size, but the number of pages is certainly in the billions. All this information can make a researcher giddy, except for this: How do you find your needle in that gargantuan haystack?

In 1850, the Harvard librarian was familiar with the books in the stacks and could lead you to what you wanted. Today, librarians must trust in the language systems and codes they've created to organize knowledge; to find anything, you have to know those language systems. And while information on the Web isn't nearly as organized as it is in the library—for one thing, there isn't any librarian in charge, although there are some Internet directories that librarians maintain—the software that searches the Web also uses a language logic. Using it well means the difference between getting 1 million "hits" on a topic search, which you will never be able to read through, or getting 300 hits, many of which will be relevant to your topic.

INQUIRING INTO THE DETAILS

The Big Red Books (Online)

We're all addicted to keyword searches when searching the Web. Often enough, just guessing what words will produce relevant results works okay. But the information in the library is *organized*, and that means that it really makes a difference if you know the subject terms librarians use to decide how library users can access information. The jargon for this is a "controlled language search." What this basically means is that if you know the right words to use when searching a library database, you'll get far better results. How would you know, for example, that if you want to find information on movies you should use the term "motion picture"? Before Internet searches became popular, you might have checked a couple of big red books in the library called *Library of Congress Subject Headings.* You still can. But an easier way is to visit an online site called "The Library of Congress Authorities" (see Figure 11.2). The term "authorities" is what librarians use to describe the word, or combination of words, they will use to make information accessible.

The site has some resources you'll never use. But if you want to know what terms to use in a library database search, something called the "subject authority
(continued)

Inquiring into the Details (*continued*)

headings" search is really useful. It will tell you what the preferred terms are for finding stuff on any subject. Interested in the history of chewing gum in the United States? You'll get better (though not necessarily more) information, says the Library of Congress Authorities site, if you use *chewing gum-America-history* when you do a "subject browse" on the library's book search page.

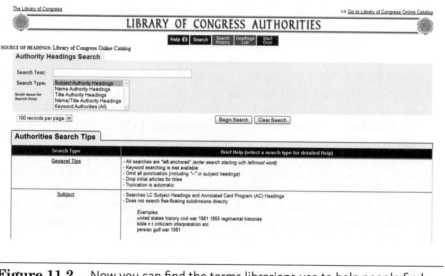

Figure 11.2   Now you can find the terms librarians use to help people find material on any subject online. The "Library of Congress Authorities" is a Web alternative to the bound *Library of Congress Subject Headings* in the reference room. Especially useful is the "subject authority headings" search.

Google Your Boole

George Boole was the eighteenth-century mathematician who came up with the system for using the words AND, OR, and NOT to help researchers design logical queries. Boole's professional legacy is something every modern college researcher should know. Consider Paul's situation. His grandmother has Alzheimer's disease, and his initial research question was, *What are the best therapies for treating Alzheimer's?* When Paul consulted PsycINFO, a popular database of citations from journals relating to psychology, his instinct was simply to enter the word *Alzheimer's* in the online search form. The result was 13,392 citations, and only a portion of these were relevant. But when Paul put the word AND between two key terms from his research question—*Alzheimer's AND therapy*—he managed to reduce his results to 1,955 more relevant citations (see Figure 11.3). As he was looking over his results, Paul became interested specifically in music therapies. His next search was even more focused when he typed in the words *Alzheimer's AND therapy AND music*. That produced 74 citations, and nearly all of these seemed promising (see Figure 11.4).

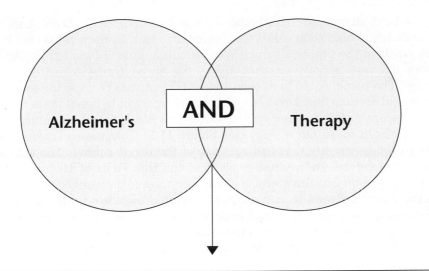

Figure 11.3   This query searches all documents that contain *both* words in the abstract or title. PsycINFO returned a list of 1,955 citations for *Alzheimer's AND therapy.*

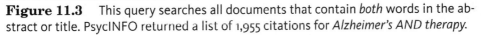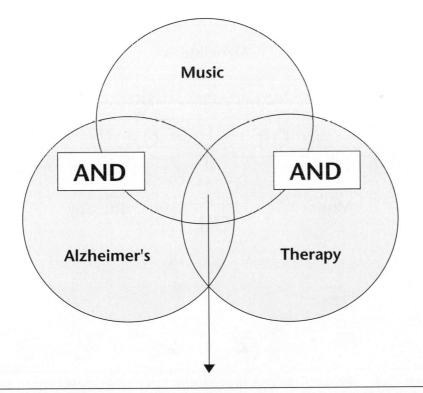

Figure 11.4   This focused query finds documents that include all the keywords. It generated a list of 74 citations, many of which were relevant and useful, for *Alzheimer's AND therapy AND music.*

The Boolean operator AND helped Paul search the PsycINFO database much more efficiently because it asked the computer to look for documents that had all three words in the title or abstract. What would happen if Paul left the AND operators out and simply searched using the three terms *Alzheimer's music therapy*? The result would have been 184,532 documents because the search software would assume that keywords with no operators in between them imply the Boolean operator OR. In other words, *Alzheimer's music therapy* is interpreted as *Alzheimer's OR music OR therapy* (see Figure 11.5). That means it would return citations for documents that had only one of the three words in the title or abstract. For a database of psychology publications, that's a lot of documents.

The only other Boolean operator you should know is the word NOT. This simply tells the search software to exclude documents that include a particular keyword. For example, if you were interested in finding information about environmental organizations in Washington State rather than Washington, D.C., you might construct a query like this: *environmental AND organizations AND Washington NOT D.C.*

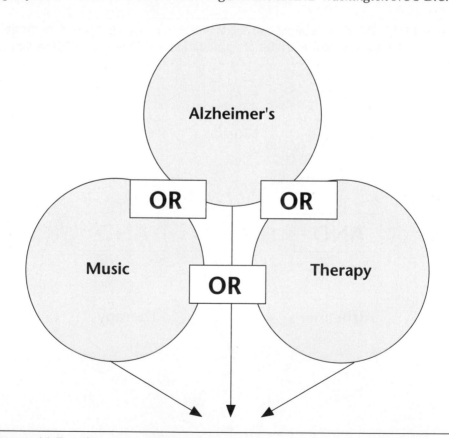

Figure 11.5 This query searches all documents that contain *any* of these three words in the abstract or title. PsycINFO returned an overwhelming list of 184,532 citations for *Alzheimer's music therapy*.

The real art of designing queries using the Boolean system is combining the operators to refine your search. For example, let's take the last search on environmental groups in Washington State. Suppose the previous query didn't produce enough results. Let's broaden it a bit: *(environmental OR conservation) AND organizations AND Washington NOT D.C.* This search would find documents that use either *environmental* or *conservation* in the title or abstract, probably returning a longer list. The parentheses simply group the keywords *environmental OR conservation* together as an expression that the search software evaluates first. You can use multiple parentheses in a query to control the order in which expressions are evaluated, beginning with the innermost parenthetical expressions. Librarians call the use of parentheses to group keywords in this manner *nesting*.

Increasingly, search pages for databases make it easy to exploit Boolean language in a search. For example, in the accompanying figure you can see how the advanced search page for Academic Search Premier, an EBSCOhost database, allows you to enter search terms and then use drop-down menus to add the Boolean connectors AND, OR, or NOT (see Figure 11.6). The search page adds even more refinement by allowing you to relate a particular term to a type or source or search. For example, you might want to search for Alzheimer's articles by a particular author whose work is relevant to your project. Using the advanced search page, you could simultaneously use *Alzheimer's* as a subject search, with *Smith* as an author search.

Knowing your Boolean operators will help you search library databases because most of the search software relies on the system. Some Web search

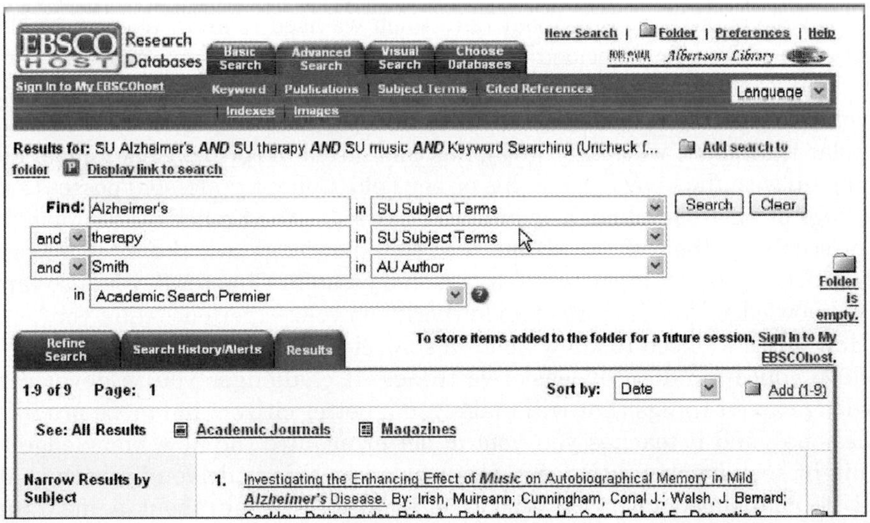

Figure 11.6   Advanced search pages such as the EBSCOhost database allow you to exploit Boolean terms using drop-down menus. Further refinements allow the researcher to link terms to different kinds of searches or sources.

engines do, too. But more often, search engines such as Google use a somewhat different language that accomplishes the same thing.

Today, search engines such as Google have an advanced search option that allows you to simply fill in a form if you want to search for certain keywords or phrases. I've found that, by far, the most useful syntax to use when searching the Web is quotation marks—an exact phrase search—and carefully ordered keywords, if possible more than three. For example, let's return to Paul's topic of Alzheimer's therapy. If he searched the Web using Google and the keywords *Alzheimer's therapy,* a syntax that implies an AND between the two words, Google would return about 9.9 million documents. But because the phrase *Alzheimer's therapy* or *therapies for Alzheimers* would likely appear in many relevant documents, Paul would be better off to try a phrase search. The result? Searching for *Alzheimer's therapy* produced 10,000 sites.

That's better, but Paul could further focus his research by querying Google with multiple terms, listed in order of importance because search engines usually evaluate keywords from left to right in level of importance. For example, Paul could try this: *+ Alzheimer's + research "music therapy,"* and this time focus the search on journal articles using Google Scholar. The results of this search were about 900 sites and a rich list of scholarly sources on his topic. There is much more to know about composing queries, but you now know enough to make a significant difference in the effectiveness of your searches.

DEVELOPING WORKING KNOWLEDGE

Every day we make decisions about how much we need to know about something. Twenty-five years ago, I decided to know enough to tune up my own car. Fifteen years ago I decided I wasn't interested in keeping up with the changes in electronic ignitions and fuel injection, so now I leave car repair to Davey at State Street Auto. A scholar is someone who, like Davey, has committed his or her professional life to keeping up with the knowledge in his or her field. College professors possess *expert knowledge* of their discipline. Five hundred years ago, the French writer Montaigne was a "scholar of the self," proposing that self-knowledge was the most important kind of knowing of all. If you wrote a personal essay in Chapter 3, you also tapped expert knowledge. Who is more of an authority on your experience than you?

How much we need to know about a subject is, in part, a personal choice, but a college education does at least two things: It challenges you to develop new knowledge about things that will make you a better citizen and more productive professional, and it teaches you *how* to better acquire the new knowledge that you might seek by choice. A research project like this is driven by both goals— you'll be challenged to go beyond superficial knowledge about a meaningful topic, and you'll learn some of the methods for doing that.

You will not end up a scholar on anorexia, college dating, the medical effects of music, or whatever topic you're researching. But you will go way beyond superficial knowledge of your subject, and when you do, it will be like opening a door and entering a crowded room of intelligent strangers, all deep in conversation about your

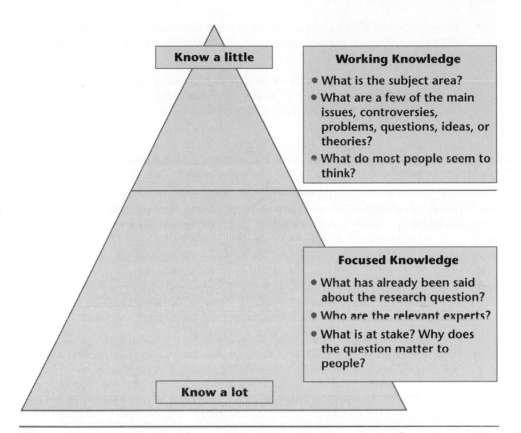

Figure 11.7   Working and focused knowledge. Inquiry projects often encourage you to choose a research topic you don't know much about. But you must quickly develop at least a *working knowledge* in order to come up with a good question. Guided by that question, you'll later develop a more *focused knowledge* of your topic and then discover what you have to say about it.

topic. At first you simply listen in before you speak, and that begins with a *working knowledge* (see Figure 11.7).

All of us know how to develop a working knowledge of something, especially when we need to. For example, I recently developed a working knowledge of podcasting software for a course I was teaching. Now I can knowledgeably talk about how to use Audacity to edit digital recordings for a few minutes without repeating myself. An audio expert would be unimpressed, but someone unfamiliar with the software might find it informative. As a researcher, you've got to know enough about your topic in order to come up with a research question. But how much knowledge is enough working knowledge? Here are some questions you need to ask:

- What are some people currently thinking about the topic? What are the controversies, problems, questions, or theories? (*Example: Some people who are interested in "green architecture" are enthusiastic about the energy savings but think the buildings are ugly. Can anything be done about that?*)

- Who are some of the individuals or groups that have a stake in the topic? *(Example: There's something called the "Sustainable Building Alliance" that seems influential.)*
- Is there a local angle? Are there people or organizations in the community who might have something to say? Are there local examples of the problem or solution? *(Example: There's a "certified" green building on campus.)*

A Strategy for Developing Working Knowledge

It's hard to beat the Internet as a quick-and-dirty way to develop working knowledge about nearly any topic. But the library can play an important role, too. While it's impossible to resist immediately firing up Google and trolling the Web, you are more likely to learn what's really important about your topic if you work systematically from general to more specialized sources. (See examples of these sources in Figure 11.8.) Here's a research sequence you might try:

1. **General encyclopedias.** These days many of us ignore encyclopedias in our rush to Google. Yet they are still wonderful ways to get a landscape picture of nearly any subject and they are also available online.

2. **Specialized encyclopedias.** But don't stop with a general encyclopedia. Next, search your library's database for the specialized encyclopedia offerings. You'd be amazed by how many there are on nearly any subject

Source	Examples
General Encyclopedias	Encyclopedia.com, Columbia Encyclopedia, Wikipedia, Oxford Reference, Encyclopedia Britannica
Specialized Encyclopedias	Encyclopedia of Psychology, Encyclopedia of World Art, Encyclopedia of Sociology, Encyclopedia of the Environment, Encyclopedia of Women and Sports, Encyclopedia of African-American Culture and History, Encyclopedia of Democracy, Encyclopedia of Science and Technology, Encyclopedia of Children, Adolescents, and the Media
Google (or other search engines)	www.google.com, www.mama.com, www.dogpile.com
Virtual Library or Internet Public Library	vlib.org, ipl.org
Google Scholar	google.scholar.com

Figure 11.8   Examples of sources that will help you develop a working knowledge of your topic

imaginable. (My favorite is the *Encyclopedia of Hell*). These reference works provide a more focused look at the subject area in which your topic falls. Writing about pigeons? There is an *Encyclopedia of Pigeon Breeds*. Writing something related to Islam? Look at the *Encyclopedia of Islam*.

3. **Google or other general search engines.** Google is, for many of us, the default choice. It's where we always start. There are other search engines, of course, including the so-called "metasearch" portals that will use multiple search engines at once and produce a combined result with the duplicates removed (e.g., www.mama.com and www.dogpile.com). These can complement Google because they increase the territory you cover.

4. **Virtual Library or Internet Public Library.** Fortunately, the Web isn't entirely information anarchy. People who have expertise on a subject may contribute or even manage content on reference sites. The two most popular of these is the Virtual Library (vlib.org) and the Internet Public Library (ipl.org). The Virtual Library is the "oldest catalog on the Web," and includes links on diverse subjects that are maintained by a worldwide network of expert volunteers. The Internet Public Library has more direct links to academic institutions in the United States. Both sites include subject directories that allow you to drill down from larger subjects to related smaller ones, an enormously useful method for discovering a topic or seeing an existing topic in a larger context.

5. **Google Scholar.** The emergence of Google Scholar in recent years has been a boon to academic researchers. While the search engine isn't nearly as good as a search of your university's library databases (a step you will take to develop focused knowledge on your topic), it's a wonderful resource to get a quick glimpse at information written by authorities.

DEVELOPING FOCUSED KNOWLEDGE

If working knowledge equips you to sustain a one-minute monologue on your topic, then focused knowledge is enough for you to make a fifteen-minute presentation to your class and to answer most of their questions. Knowing this much doesn't make you an expert, but it does make you far more informed than most people on your topic. Here are some questions you should be able to answer:

- Who are key people who have influenced the published conversation on your topic? (*Example: Among the key advocates for a playoff system in college football are long-time Penn State coach Joe Paterno and even President Barack Obama.*)

- What has already been said about the topic? Up until now, what are the major themes of the conversation? (*Example: Among the arguments against a playoff system is that student athletes will miss too much class. Others add that such a system will lead to the "NFL-ization" of college football, extending the season and compounding student athletes' academic problems, who already spend as many as 40 hours a week on football.*)

■ What is at stake for people? Why is the research question significant? (*Example: Thousands of student athletes in the United States are wedged between two conflicting goals for college football: the public hunger for big-time entertainment and the athletes' desire to complete a degree.*)

A Strategy for Developing Focused Knowledge

To move to this next level of knowing about your topic, launch your research on three fronts:

Library Research	> Online book catalog
	> Article databases
	  • General databases
	  • Specialized databases

Web Research	> General search engines > Metasearch engines > Specialized search engines

Living Sources	> Interview
	  • Subject
	  • Informant
	> Surveys

Library Research. While the Web is an intoxicating source of information, academic research still fundamentally depends on library work. Much of this work you can do online. Libraries offer database indexes to magazines, journals, and books that are accessible from your computer at home or at school, and in some cases you can retrieve and print out full-text articles.

But there are still reasons to walk into the university library. Here are six:

1. That's where the books are.
2. Some of the best articles on your topic aren't available as full-text PDFs.
3. Browsing the stacks in your topic's subject area will produce books you won't find any other way.
4. You can read current periodicals not yet online.
5. The reference room has books and other resources that aren't available anywhere else.
6. Reference librarians are irreplaceable.

So you'll want to go to the library—online and on foot—but you won't want to waste your time. The two best ways to avoid this are to have a good research question, one that will allow you to focus your efforts, and to have a handful of good search terms to try. In Chapter 10 we explored the characteristics of a good research question, and earlier in this chapter we discussed crafting search terms. Don't forget to use "controlled language searches," or searches that use the terms librarians have chosen

Laying some groundwork in the library at the start of your research will save you time later.

to organize access to materials on every subject. As you recall, you discover these terms using the big red books in the reference room, *Library of Congress Subject Headings*, or by going online to the "Library of Congress Authorities," a Web version of the *LCSH*.

Where should you begin? When you developed working knowledge, you started with more general sources like encyclopedias and then shifted to more specialized sources like Google Scholar, trying to drill down a little ways into your subject. Now it's time to drill more deeply. For focused knowledge, you can start anywhere, really, especially since you've already got some background knowledge on your research question. The key is to cover a lot of ground.

Searching for Books. Every library has an online index for books (also available at computers in the library, naturally), and using the right search terms you'll get an instantaneous list of relevant books on your topic and "call numbers" that will help you find them in the stacks. Your results will also tell you if the book is checked out, missing, or unavailable in your college library. If any of these apply to a book you're really hankering for, don't despair. You've got several options:

- *Recall.* Make an online request that the book is returned (usually in a few weeks) by the person who has checked it out.

- *Interlibrary loan.* This is a wonderful, underutilized service, often provided by campus libraries at no charge to students. You can request, usually online, a call-out to a large network of university libraries for the book (or article) you need. It is delivered to you, sometimes within days.

- *Check another library.* If the campus library doesn't have it, check the community library's index online.

The book search form on your university's Web site, like most search portals, has simple and advanced options. The advanced page is pretty cool because it makes it easy to do a Boolean search on your topic. You can also put "limiters" on the terms, allowing you to control the results for things like author, title, date, and so on. Learning to use the Advanced Search will really pay off after enduring the initial brief learning curve.

Searching for Periodicals and Newspapers. It's hard to imagine a research question or topic that isn't covered by periodicals. You'll want to check those databases, too. These are organized into four broad categories:

1. General subject databases, or indexes to periodicals across disciplines.
2. Specialized databases, or indexes that are discipline-specific.
3. Genre-specific databases like Newspaper Source.
4. Government document databases.

Quite often, general subject databases include periodicals that may not be considered scholarly, including magazines like *Discover, Newsweek*, or *Psychology Today*. These databases are a good place to start. To drill down further, use specialized databases, which are much more likely to produce the most interesting results on your research question because they are written by specialists in the field. They will also produce articles that can be a chore to understand if you don't know the jargon. That's when your working knowledge on your topic will really pay off. Also consider databases that warehouse certain types of content— plays, government documents, dissertations, and so on. You can see examples of all of these databases in the table that follows.

Web Research. "Google" is the new verb for research: "Did you Google it?" The consolidation in the last decade of public confidence in a single company's applications is remarkable, especially when there was once healthy competition between

Database Type	Examples
Interdisciplinary/general subject databases	Academic Search Premier, LexisNexis Academic, JSTOR, ArticleFirst, Project Muse, MasterFILE Premier, WorldCat
Discipline-specific databases	ABI/INFORM (business), AnthroSource, America: History and Life, ArtSTOR, Applied Science and Technology, Biography Index, BioOne, Communication and Mass Media, ERIC (education), MLA Bibliography (languages and literature), Philosopher's Index, PyscINFO, Sociological Abstracts, Worldwide Political Science Abstracts
Genre-specific databases	National Newspapers, Newspaper Source, New York Times Index, Dissertation Abstracts International, Book Review Digest, Literature Criticism Online, Play Index
Government documents	Fed in Print, GPO Monthly Catalog, LexisNexis Government Periodicals Index

companies with popular search portals like AltaVista and Excite. But that's another story. The point is this: Google is the dominant player in everyday research, but academic researchers shouldn't limit themselves to a single search service. Web research for inquiry projects should be motivated by the following principles:

1. Maximize coverage.
2. Maximize relevant results.
3. Find stable sources.
4. Find quality sources.

Later in this chapter, I'll elaborate on what I mean by stable, quality sources, but examples would include Web pages and documents with ".edu," ".gov," or ".org" domains, those that are routinely updated, and those that might include a bibliography of references that document claims.

On the other hand, depending on your topic you might seek a range of types of sources. For instance, suppose you're writing about green design and a blog from an architect in Texas has an interesting proposal for using turbines on a highway in Austin, powered by passing cars (see Figure 11.9). The proposal is interesting, and

Figure 11.9   A student architect in Texas published a wind power proposal on a blog that got the attention of professional architects. While a blog isn't a conventional academic source, depending on the quality of its content and the purpose of your essay, it might be a perfectly good source.

Search Type	Examples
General search engines	www.google.com, www.ask.com, www.yahoo.com
Metasearch engines	www.dogpile.com, www.clusty.com, www.surfwax.com, www.mamma.com
Subject directories	www.yahoo.com, www.about.com, directory.google.com, botw.org
Academic search engines or directories	google.scholar.com, infomine.ucr.edu, www.academicinfo.net, www.academicindex.net,
Search engines for particular content	www.videosurf.com, books.google.com, blogsearch.google.com, images.google.com, www.newslink.org, www.internetarchive .org (audio, video, education, etc.), www.usa.org (federal government)

other sites refer to the blogger's idea. While this isn't a conventional academic source, the architect's blog is certainly a relevant and useful one for your essay.

Consider other types of online content as well: images, video, podcasts, discussion boards, and so on. For example, iTunes includes iTunesU, a remarkable collection of lectures, interviews, and video clips on a range of subjects uploaded from universities around the United States.

The challenge is to find this stuff. Google is just the beginning. Try some of the alternative search portals or directories listed in the above table.

INQUIRING INTO THE DETAILS

Full-Text Articles and the Convenience Trap

We're spoiled by full-text articles that are served up by some databases. Not only do you get a citation, there is the huge bonus of actually looking at the article and printing it out. More and more indexes provide this service, and every database will allow you to filter your search so that you only get full-text results. This is all good except for one thing: Many articles still aren't available as instantly downloadable PDF or Web files. It's pretty common, in fact, to discover that the article you really need—the one that seems right on topic—isn't available online. That often means that student researchers ignore the really good article and just go for the one that's instantly available, even if it isn't quite right. Convenience isn't the highest value in academic research.

The commercial owners of periodical databases do not convert citations to include full-text articles on the basis of their significance to the subject. It's much more random than that. So you can't be sure, if you rely only on full-text versions, that you're getting the best information.

Finding those articles that aren't immediately available online requires a trip to the library where, armed with the citation information, you can find the piece in bound volumes of the journal or on microfilm. It might seem a bit old-fashioned, but that's the best way to get good information that isn't available digitally. Alternatively, you can order that article through the library's interlibrary loan service.

INQUIRING INTO THE DETAILS

Methods of Recording Information

The default mode for many student researchers is to simply quote information from a book, article, or Web page, writing down excerpts word for word. Jotting down quotations is fine. But it's often far more useful to summarize and paraphrase a source in your own words. Here's a brief description of each method.

1. *Summary.* One of the more useful ways of taking notes because it challenges you to condense, in your own words, a longer text, capturing key concepts or claims.

2. *Paraphrase.* This also tests your understanding of what you read, prompting you to translate a passage from a source into your own words; your paraphrase will be roughly the same length as the original.

3. *Quotation.* A perennial favorite approach to notetaking because it's mere transcription, ranging from a few key words to several paragraphs. Remember to always transcribe the words of the original source exactly.

EVALUATING LIBRARY SOURCES

One of the huge advantages of finding what you need at the campus library is that nearly everything there was chosen by librarians whose job it is to make good information available to academic researchers. Now that many of the university library's databases are available online, including full-text articles, there really is no excuse for deciding to exclusively use Web pages you downloaded from the Internet for your essays. But even in the campus library, some sources are more authoritative than others. The "Pyramid of Library Sources" (see Figure 10.1 in Chapter 10) gives you a general idea of the hierarchy of authority for most library sources.

In general, the more specialized the audience for a publication, the more authoritatively scholars view the publication's content. Academic journals are at the bottom of this inverted pyramid because they represent the latest thinking and knowledge in a discipline, and most of the articles are reviewed

INQUIRING INTO THE DETAILS

The Working Bibliography

A working bibliography lists sources you've collected that you think will be helpful when you draft your essay. These may include annotations or brief summaries of what the source says that you find relevant to your research question. Consider the following examples:

TOPIC: RELATIONAL AGGRESSION
PRINT SOURCES

Simmons, Rachel. *Odd Girl Out: The Hidden Culture of Aggression in Girls.* New York: Harcourt, 2002.

Simmons argues that the "secret world of girls' aggression"—the backstabbing, the silent treatment, the bartering of friendship for compliance to a group's "rules"—can be just as bad as the less subtle aggression of boys. Her basic thesis is that girls in American culture are supposed to be "nice," and therefore have no outlet for their anger except for exploiting the one thing they do covet: relationships. Because my essay focuses on the popularity phenomenon in high school—How does it affect girls when they become adults?—Simmons's chapter on parents of these girls seems particularly useful because it shows how the parents' responses are often shaped by their own experiences in school.

WEB SOURCES

"What Is Relational Aggression?" *The Ophelia Project.* 22 Sept. 2003 http://www.opheliaproject.org/issues/issues_RA.shtml.

The page defines relational aggression by contrasting it with physical aggression. It argues that most research, naturally, has focused on the latter because of need to limit physical injury between children. But girls tend to avoid physical aggression and instead indulge in actions that harm others by disrupting their social relationships, like giving someone the silent treatment. The Ophelia Project is a nonprofit group created in 1997 by parents who wanted to address the problem.

by specialists in the field before they are published. At the top of the inverted pyramid are general encyclopedias and general-interest magazines such as *Newsweek* and *Time.* These have broader audiences and feature articles that are written by nonspecialists. They are rarely peer-reviewed. As a rule, then, the lower you draw from this inverted pyramid, the more authoritative the sources are from an academic point of view. Here are some other guidelines to consider:

- *Choose more recent sources over older ones.* This is particularly good advice, obviously, if your subject is topical; the social and natural sciences also put much more emphasis on the currency of sources than humanities disciplines.

■ *Look for often-cited authors.* Once you've developed a working knowledge of your topic, you'll start noticing that certain authors seem to be mentioned or cited fairly frequently. These are likely to be the most listened-to authors, and may be considered the most authoritative on your topic.

■ *If possible, use primary sources over secondary sources.* In literary research, primary sources are the original words of writers—their speeches, stories, novels, poems, memoirs, letters, interviews, and eyewitness accounts. Secondary sources would be articles that discuss those works. Primary sources in other fields might be original studies or experiments, firsthand newspaper accounts, marketing information, and so on.

EVALUATING WEB SOURCES

One of the more amusing sites on the Web is titled "Feline Reactions to Bearded Men." At first glance, the site appears to be a serious academic study of the physiological responses of cats—heartbeat, respiration, and pupil dilation—to a series of photographs of men with beards. The researchers are listed with their affiliations to respected universities. The article includes an abstract, a methodology, and a results section, as well as a lengthy list of works cited.

The conclusions seem genuine and include the following:

1. Cats do not like men with long beards, especially long dark beards.
2. Cats are indifferent to men with shorter beards.
3. Cats are confused and/or disturbed by men with beards that are incomplete and, to a lesser degree, by men whose beards have missing parts.

The study is a hoax, a fact that is pretty obvious to anyone who critically examines it. For one thing, it was "published" in the *Annals of Improbable Research,* but I can usually fool about a third of my class with the site for five to ten minutes as I discuss the conventions of academic research, some of which are accurately reproduced in the "study."

Everyone knows to be skeptical of what's on the Web. But this is even more crucial when using Web sources for college writing. Because it's dominated by commercial sites, much of the World Wide Web has limited usefulness to the academic researcher, and although very few online authors are out to fool researchers with fake scholarship, many have a persuasive purpose. Despite its "educational" mission, for example, the purpose of the Web site ConsumerFreedom.com is to promote industry views on laws relating to food and beverages. That doesn't make the information it offers useless, but a careful researcher would be wary of the site's claims and critical of its studies. At the very least, the information on ConsumerFreedom.com should be attributed as a pro-industry view.

Imagine, as you're researching on the Web, that you've been dropped off at night in an unfamiliar neighborhood. You're alert. You're vigilant. And you're careful about whom you ask for directions. You can also be systematic about how you approach evaluating online sources. In general, follow these principles:

- *Favor governmental and educational sources over commercial ones.* These sites are more likely to have unbiased information. How can you tell which are institutional sites when it's not obvious? Sometimes the domain name—the abbreviation *.edu, .org,* or *.gov* at the end of an Internet address—provides a strong clue, as does the absence of ads on the site.

- *Favor authored documents over those without authors.* There's a simple reason for this: You can check the credentials of authors if you know who they are. Sometimes sites provide e-mail links so you can write to authors, or you can do a search on the Internet or in the library for other materials they've published.

- *Favor documents that are also available in print over those available only online.* Material that is published in both forms generally undergoes more

A cat reacts to a picture of a bearded man from the study "Feline Reactions to Bearded Men."

scrutiny. An obvious example would be newspaper articles, but also some articles from journals and magazines are available electronically and in print.

- *Favor Web sources that document their claims over those that don't.* This familiar academic convention is strong evidence that the claims an online author is making are supported and verifiable.

- *Favor Web pages that have been recently updated over those that haven't changed in a year or more.* Frequently at the bottom of a Web page there is a line indicating when the information was posted to the Internet and/or when it was last updated. Look for it.

An Evaluation Process for Web Sources

1. **Relevance.** Is this Web source relevant to my research question?
2. **Authors.** Are there any? If so, can I trust them? Are they recognized experts on the subject? Do they have a bias? Do they say sensible things? If there aren't authors, are there other things about the source that make it credible?

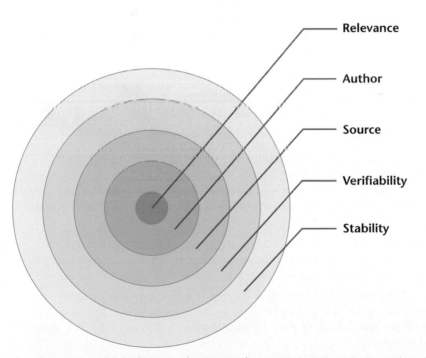

Relevance

Author

Source

Verifiability

Stability

Another way to think about evaluating Web sources is to imagine a series of questions you ask yourself beginning with the relevance of a site or document to your project and then working outward to some judgments about the author, the source, the verifiability of the information, and its stability.

3. **Source.** What's the domain: .edu, .gov, .org.? If it's a commercial site, is the content still useful because of its author, content, or relevance?

4. **Verifiability.** Can you contact the authors? Is there a bibliography of references? Do other credible sites refer to this one?

5. **Stability.** How long has the Web site been around and how often is it updated?

Writing in the Middle: Synthesizing Source Information and Your Own Ideas

It's not news that there is an epidemic of plagiarism, and it's not just a problem on the college campus. Recently, several well-known historians admitted to being a bit sloppy about giving their sources proper credit. Naturally, a lot of people assume that the problem of plagiarism has to do with ethics. Students cheat. They confuse means and ends. And so on. There's some truth to this, but I contend that the real cause of the problem comes not from what students do, but what they don't do—they don't "write in the middle."

The plagiarism problem usually surfaces when writers are rushed, madly composing drafts at the last minute, and they simply haven't made the time to make the information they've collected their own. As a result, they're controlled *by* the information rather than controlling it for their own purposes. "How can I improve on what this guy says?" The thinking goes, "I guess I should just get it

---

INQUIRING INTO THE DETAILS

How to Annotate a Book

The brevity of articles and most Web pages makes them much easier to annotate than a book. You can usually summarize the argument or relevant ideas of such sources fairly easily. But how do you do that with a book that may have hundreds of pages of information and an extended argument? Read strategically.

1. To summarize a book's approach or basic argument, skim the preface and introduction. Sometimes there's a concluding chapter that neatly summarizes things, too. Even the back cover or jacket flap can be helpful for this overview.

2. To explain the relevance of the book to your research question or topic, you may focus on a particular chapter or chapters. Again, at this point you can probably skim the text quickly to discover its relevance. Later, you may do a more careful reading.

3. Evaluate *part* of the author's treatment of your topic rather than the whole book. Search the table of contents for what you suspect are the most relevant chapters, and focus your reading on those.

down in my paper." The result is sometimes unintentional plagiarism—some quotation marks were omitted or the paraphrase was too close to the original—but more often the paper suffers from another problem: the absence of an author. The writer doesn't seem to be in charge of where the essay goes and what it says.

There's a solution to this that is really quite simple. Write about what you're reading *as you collect it.*

Note cards aren't what I have in mind unless you use them to do more than simply jot down what a source says. Instead, I strongly recommend that you keep a double-entry journal or a research log that will serve two purposes: collecting information and exploring your reactions to what you've found. This is merely an extension of what I've been suggesting from the beginning of *The Curious Writer*—that you can move dialectically from creative thinking to critical thinking and back again—but this time you'll be creatively exploring information and then reflecting on how it addresses your research question.

The suggestion that you take time to write about the information you have collected in the middle of the process may come across as needing a pretty tough sell. *Save the writing for the draft*, you're thinking. But you are essentially *beginning* your draft with thoughtful note taking, which will save you time later.

Double-Entry Journal. You already are familiar with the double-entry journal. This approach uses opposing pages of your notebook to encourage dialectical thinking. On the left page take notes—paraphrases, summaries, and quotations—as you might usually do with conventional note taking, and on the opposing right page *explore* your responses, reactions, and questions about the information you've collected on the left page (for a full description of the double-entry notebook method, see "Using the Double-Entry Journal" in Chapter 2).

Research Log. Another method of note taking that also exploits dialectical thinking is the research log. Rather than using opposing pages, you'll layer your notes and responses, one after another. This is a particularly useful method for those who would prefer to work with a keyboard rather than a pencil. Here's how it works:

1. Begin by taking down the full bibliographic information on the source, something you may already have in your working bibliography.

2. Read the article, book chapter, or Web page, marking up your personal copy as you typically do, perhaps underlining key facts or ideas or information relevant to your research question.

3. Your first entry in your notebook or on the computer will be a fastwrite, an open-ended response to the reading under the heading What Strikes Me Most. As the title implies, you're dealing with first thoughts here. Consider some of the following approaches to this initial response to the source:
   - First play the believing game, exploring how the author's ideas, arguments, or findings seem sensible to you. Then shift to the doubting

game, a more critical stance in which you look for gaps, raise questions, or express doubts about what the source says.

- What strikes you as the most important thing the author was trying to say?
- What do you remember best? What surprised you most after reading the source?
- What seemed most convincing? Least convincing?
- How does the source change your thinking on the topic? What do you understand better now than you did before you read the piece?
- How does it compare to other things you've read?
- What seems most relevant to your research question?
- What other research possibilities does it suggest?

4. Next, take notes on the source, jotting down summaries, paraphrases, quotations, and key facts you glean from it. Title this section Source Notes.

5. Finally, follow up with another episode of fastwriting. Title this The Source Reconsidered. This is a *more focused* look at the source; fastwrite about what stands out in the notes you took. Which facts, findings, claims, or arguments shape your thinking now? If the writing stalls, skip a line, take another look at your source notes, and seize on something else to write about.

ONE STUDENT'S RESPONSE

Claude's Research Log

SOURCE

Source Letawsky, Nicole R., et al. "Factors Influencing the College Selection Process of Student Athletes." *College Student Journal* 37.4 (2003): 604–11. *Academic Search Premier.* EBSCOhost Databases. Albertson's Lib. 5 Apr. 2004.

WHAT STRIKES ME MOST

Really interesting article that studied about 130 student athletes at a large 1-A university. Noted that there have been a lot of research studies on why students choose a particular school but not so much on why student-athletes choose a school. Everyone assumes, of course, that student-athletes go somewhere because they're wined and dined and promised national TV exposure. In other words, it all has to do with the glamour of playing 1-A, particularly the so-called revenue sports like basketball and football. But this study had some surprising findings. They found that the number one reason that student-athletes chose a school was the degree options it offers. In other words, the reasons student-athletes choose a school aren't that much different than the reason regular students choose one. The study also found that the glamour stuff—getting awards, getting on TV, and future professional possibilities—mattered the least to the student-athletes. This study challenges some of the myths about student recruiting, and should be read by recruiters especially. If you want to get a blue-ribbon player at your school, tell him or her about the academic opportunities there.

SOURCE NOTES (CUT-AND-PASTE FROM ELECTRONIC VERSION)

"This study found that the most important factor for student-athletes was the degree program options offered by the University. Other important factors were the head coach, academic support services, type of community in which the campus is located, and the school's sports traditions. Two of the top three factors were specifically related to the academic rather than athletic environment. This is a key finding and should be understood as recruiting efforts should be broad based, balancing academics and athletics if they are to be effective."

"A somewhat surprising result of the study concerned relatively low ratings associated with factors considered essential to 'Big-Time College Sports.' Television exposure, perceived opportunity to play immediately, and perceived future professional sporting opportunities were among the lowest-ranked factors. Furthermore, the participants rated athletic rewards (a 5-item survey scale containing these and other reward items) consistently lower than both the campus and athletic environment. These results may be due to the fact that respondents were from each of the sports offered by the University. Many of the sports (e.g., swimming, track), although funded and supported similar to the other sports, do not receive the national attention, large crowds, and television exposure."

SOURCE RECONSIDERED

This article did more than anything I've read so far to make me question my thesis that big-time college sports recruiting is way out of control. It's pretty convincing on the point that athletes care about the academic programs when they're choosing a school. But then the second quotation has an interesting part that I just noticed. This study surveyed athletes in all sports, not just the big-time sports like football and basketball at the university where the study was conducted. It seems to me that that would really skew the findings because someone participating in a sport like tennis that doesn't get a lot of attention and doesn't necessarily lead to professional opportunities after school *would* be more interested in academics. They're not dreaming of making a name for themselves, but getting a scholarship to pay for school. Seems like a better study would focus on the big-time sports...

Whichever note-taking method you choose—the double-entry journal or the research log—what you are doing is taking possession of the information and making it yours by evaluating it for your own purposes. One of the hardest parts of writing with outside sources is doing exactly that—using someone else's ideas or information in the service of your own questions. And that's why taking the time to write in the middle is so important: You're doing the most important intellectual work *as* you encounter the perspectives of others. This will make writing the draft much easier and will also, I believe, lower the risk of unintentional plagiarism, a mistake that often occurs in the mad rush to begin writing the draft the night before it's due.

INTERVIEWS

Tethered as we are these days to the electronic world of the Web and the increasingly digital university library, it's easy to forget an old-fashioned source for research: a living, breathing human being. People are often the best sources of information because you can have a real conversation rather than the imagined one simulated by the double-entry notebook. Some kinds of writing, such as the profile, fundamentally depend on interviews; with other genres, such as the personal essay or the research paper, interviews are one of several sources of information. But they can be central to bringing writing to life because when we put people on the page, abstract ideas or arguments suddenly have a face and a voice. People on the page make ideas matter.

> The principal advantage of doing interviews is that you ask the questions that you are most interested in learning the answers to.

Arranging Interviews

Whom do you interview? Basically, there are two kinds of interviews: (1) the interviewee is the main subject of your piece, as in a profile, and (2) the interviewee is *a source of information* about another subject.

The interviewee as a source of information is the far more common type of interview, and it usually involves finding people who either are experts on the topic you're writing about or have been touched or influenced in some way by it. For example, Tina was writing a research essay on the day-care crisis in her community. Among those affected by this issue were the parents of small children, their day-care teachers, and even the kids themselves; all were good candidates for interviews about the problem. Experts were a little more difficult to think of immediately. The day care teachers might qualify—after all, they're professionals in the area—but Tina also discovered a faculty member in the College of Health and Social Sciences who specialized in policies related to child care. Interviewing both types of people—experts and those influenced by the issue—gave Tina a much richer perspective on the problem.

How do you find experts in your topic? Here are a few strategies for locating potential interviewees:

- *Check the faculty directory on your campus.* Many universities publish an annual directory of faculty and their research interests, which may be online. In addition, your university's public information office might have a similar list of faculty and areas of expertise.

- *Cull a name from an online discussion group.* Use a specialized search engine like Google's group search (groups.google.com) to search by your topic and find someone interesting who might be willing to do an e-mail interview.

- *Ask friends and your instructors.* They might know faculty who have a research interest in your topic, or might know someone in the community who is an expert on it.

- *Check the phone book.* The familiar *Yellow Pages* can be a gold mine. Want to find a biologist who might have something to say about the effort to bring back migrating salmon? Find the number of the regional office of the U.S. Fish and Wildlife Service in the phone book and ask for the public information officer. He or she may help you find the right expert.

- *Check your sources.* As you begin to collect books, articles, and Internet documents, note their authors and affiliations. I get calls or e-mails from time to time from writers who came across my book on lobsters, posing questions I love to try to answer because no one in Idaho gives a hoot about lobsters. Google searches of authors who are mentioned in your sources may produce e-mail addresses or Web sites with e-mail links that you might query.

- *Check the* Encyclopedia of Associations. This is another underused book and database in your university's reference room that lists organizations in the United States with interests as varied as promoting tofu and saving salmon.

Conducting the Interview

The kinds of questions you ask fundamentally depend on what type of interview you're conducting. In a profile, your questions will focus on the interview subject (see Chapter 4). To some extent, this is also true when you interview nonexperts who are *affected* by the topic you're writing about. For example, Tina is certainly interested in what the parents of preschoolers *know* about the day-care crisis in her town, but she's also interested in the feelings and *experiences* of these people. Gathering this kind of information leads to some of the questions you may have used in a profile, but with more focus on the subject's experience with your topic:

- What was your first experience with _____? What has most surprised you about it?

- How does _____ make you feel?

- Tell me about a moment that you consider most typical of your experience with _____.

More often, however, your motive in an interview will be to gather information. Obviously, this will prompt you to ask specific questions about your topic as you try to fill in gaps in your knowledge. But some more general, open-ended questions may be useful to ask. For example:

- What is the most difficult aspect of your work?
- What do you think is the most significant popular misconception about _____?
- What are the significant current trends in _____?
- If you had to summarize the most important thing you've learned about _____, what would that be?
- What is the most important thing other people should know or understand?
- What do you consider the biggest problem?
- Who has the power to do something about it?
- What is your prediction about the future? Ten years from now, what will this problem look like?

Once you have a list of questions in mind, be prepared to ignore them. Good interviews often take turns that you can't predict, and these journeys may lead you to information and understandings you didn't expect. After all, a good interview is like a good conversation; it may meander, speed up or slow down, and reveal things about your topic and your interview subject that you don't expect. But good interviewers also attempt to control an interview when the turns it's taking aren't useful. You do this through questions, of course, but also more subtle tactics. For example, if you stop taking notes most interview subjects notice, and the astute ones quickly understand that what they're saying has less interest to you. A quick glance at your watch can have the same effect.

E-mail interviews produce a ready-made text with both your questions and the subject's answers. This is pretty wonderful. Live interviews, on the other hand, require more skill. It's usually a good idea to use a tape recorder (with your subject's permission), but never rely exclusively on it especially since machines can fail and batteries can expire unexpectedly. *Always take notes.* Your notes, if nothing else, will help you know where on the tape you should concentrate later, transcribing direct quotations or gathering information. Notetaking during interviews is an acquired skill; the more you do it, the better you get, inventing all sorts of shorthand for commonly occurring words. Practice taking notes while watching the evening news.

Most of all, try to enjoy your interview. After all, you and your interview subject have something important in common—you have an interest in your topic—and this usually produces an immediate bond that transforms an interview into an enjoyable conversation.

Using the Interview in Your Writing

Putting people on the page is one of the best ways to bring writing to life. This is exactly what information from interviews can do—give otherwise abstract questions or problems a voice and a face. One of the most common ways to use interview material is to integrate it into the lead or first paragraph of your essay. By focusing on someone involved in the research question or problem you're exploring, you immediately capture reader interest. For example, here's the beginning of a *Chronicle of Higher Education* essay, "What Makes Teachers Great?"[1] Quite naturally, the writer chose to begin by profiling someone who happened to be a great teacher, using evidence from the interviews he conducted.

> When Ralph Lynn retired as a professor of history at Baylor University in 1974, dozens of his former students paid him tribute. One student, Ann Richards, who became the governor of Texas in 1991, wrote that Lynn's classes were like "magical tours into the great minds and movements of history." Another student, Hal Wingo, the editor of *People* magazine, concluded that Lynn offered the best argument he knew for human cloning. "Nothing would give me more hope for the future," the editor explained, "than to think that Ralph Lynn, in all his wisdom and wit, will be around educating new generations from here to eternity."

This is a strong way to begin an essay because the larger idea—the qualities that make a great teacher—is grounded in a name and a face. But information from interviews can be used anywhere in an essay—not just at the beginning—to make an idea come to life.

Information from interviews can also provide strong evidence for a point you're trying to make, especially if your interview subject has expertise on the topic. But interviews can also be a *source* of ideas about what you might want to say in an essay. The essay on great teaching, for instance, offers seven qualities that great teachers embrace in their classrooms, things such as "create a natural critical learning environment" and "help students learn outside of class." All of these claims grew from interviews with sixty professors in a range of disciplines.

The principal advantage of doing interviews is that *you* ask the questions that you're most interested in learning the answers to. Rather than sifting through other sources that may address your research questions briefly or indirectly, interviews generate information that is often relevant and focused on the information needs of your essay. In other words, interviews are a source of data that can also be a *source* of theories or ideas on your topic. And this is often the best way to use interview material in your essay.

---

[1]Ken Bain, "What Makes Teachers Great?" *Chronicle of Higher Education* (April 9, 2004): B7–B9.

SURVEYS

The survey is a fixture in American life. We love surveys. What's the best economical laptop? Should the president be reelected? Who is the sexiest man alive? What movie should win Best Picture? Some of these are scientific surveys with carefully crafted questions, statistically significant sample sizes, and carefully chosen target audiences. In your writing class, you likely won't be conducting such formal research. More likely it will be like Mike's—fairly simple, and although not necessarily statistically reliable, your informal survey will likely be more convincing than anecdotal evidence or your personal observation, particularly if it's thoughtfully developed.

Defining a Survey's Goals and Audience

A survey is a useful source of information when you're making some kind of claim regarding "what people think" about something. Mike observed that his friends all seem to hate pennies, and he wanted to generalize from this anecdotal evidence to suggest that most people probably share that view. But do they? And which people are we really talking about? As we discussed this in his writing group, Mike pointed out that his grandfather grew up during the Great Depression, and that he has a very different perspective on money than Mike. "So your grandfather would probably pick up a penny in the parking lot, right?" I asked. Probably, Mike said.

Quickly, Mike not only had a survey question but began to think about qualifying his claim. Maybe younger adults—Mike's generation—in particular share this attitude about the lowly penny. To confirm this, Mike's survey had both a purpose (to collect information about how people view pennies) and an audience (students on his campus). If he had the time or inclination, Mike could conduct a broader survey of older Americans, but for his purposes the quad survey would be enough.

Types of Survey Questions

You can typically ask two types of questions on a survey: *open-ended questions* and *direct questions*. Open-ended questions often produce unexpected information, while direct questions are easier to analyze. Open-ended questions are like those on the narrative evaluations students might fill out at the end of the semester, such as, "What did you learn in this course?" and "What were the instructor's strengths and weaknesses?" Direct questions are the kind used on quizzes and tests, the kind that have a limited number of answers. The simplest, of course, would be a question or statement that people might agree or disagree with: "Would you pick up a penny if you saw it lying on the street?" Yes? No? You don't know?

How do you decide which types of questions to ask? Here are some things to consider:

- *How much time do you have to analyze the results?* Open-ended questions obviously take more time, while direct questions often involve mere tabulation of responses. The size of your sample is a big factor in this.

- *How good are you at crafting questions?* Direct questions need to be more carefully crafted than open-ended ones because you're offering limited responses. Are the responses appropriate to the question? Have you considered all the alternative ways of responding?

- *Do you want statistical or qualitative information?* Qualitative information—anecdotes, stories, opinions, case studies, observations, individual perspectives—are the stuff of open-ended questions. This can be wonderful information because it is often surprising, and it offers an individual's voice rather than the voiceless results of statistical data. On the other hand, statistical information—percentages, averages, and the like—is easily understood and can be dramatic.

Crafting Survey Questions

To begin, you want to ask questions that your target audience can answer. Don't ask a question about a campus alcohol policy that most students in your survey have never heard of. Second, keep the questions simple and easy to understand. This is crucial because most respondents resist overly long survey questions and won't answer confusing ones. Third, make sure the questions will produce the information you want. This is a particular hazard of open-ended questions. For example, a broad open-ended question such as, "What do you think of the use of animals in the testing of cosmetics?" will probably produce a verbal shrug or an answer of "I don't know." A better question is more focused: "What do you think about the U.S. Food and Drug Administration's claim that animal testing by cosmetic companies is 'often necessary to provide product safety'?"

Such a question could be an open-ended or direct question, depending on the kind of responses you're seeking. Focusing the question also makes it more likely to generate information that will help you compose your essay on the adequacy of current regulations governing animal testing. Also note that the question doesn't necessarily betray the writer's position on the issue, which is essential—a good survey question isn't biased or "loaded." Imagine how a less neutral question might skew the results: "What do you think of the federal bureaucrats' position that animal testing for cosmetics is 'often necessary to provide product safety'?" An even more subtle bias might be introduced by inserting the term *federal government* rather than *Food and Drug Administration* in the original question. In my part of the world, the Rocky Mountain West, the federal government is generally not viewed favorably, no matter what the issue.

Keep your survey questions to a minimum. It shouldn't take long—no more than a few minutes at most—to complete your survey, unless you're lucky enough to have a captive audience such as a class.

Finally, consider beginning your survey with background questions that establish the identity of each respondent. Typical information you might collect includes the gender and age or, with student-oriented surveys, the class ranking of the respondent. Depending on your topic, you might be interested in particular demographic facts, such as whether someone has children or comes from a particular part of the state. All of these questions can help you sort and analyze your results.

INQUIRING INTO THE DETAILS

Types of Survey Questions

These are a few of your options when deciding what type of questions to ask in a survey.

1. **Limited choice**

   Do you believe student fees should be used to support campus religious organizations?

   ☐   Yes

   ☐   No

   ☐   I'm not sure

   At what point in the writing process do you usually get stuck?

   ☐   Getting started

   ☐   In the middle

   ☐   Finishing

   ☐   I never get stuck

   ☐   Other_____.

2. **Scaled response**

   The Student Film Board should show more foreign films.

   ☐   Strongly agree

   ☐   Agree

   ☐   Neither agree or disagree

   ☐   Disagree

   ☐   Strongly disagree

3. **Ranking**

   Which of the following do you consider important in designing a classroom to be conducive to learning? Rank them from 1 to 5, with the most important a "1" and the least important a "5."

Comfortable seating	
Natural light from windows	
Carpeting	
Effective soundproofing	
Dimmable lighting	

4. Open-ended

Describe three things you learned in this course.

What steps do you think the university should take to increase attendance at women's soccer games?

Conducting a Survey

People who design surveys for a living always test them first. Invariably this turns up problems: A survey is too long, a question is poorly worded, the response rate to a particular question is low, and so on. You won't be able to test your draft survey nearly as thoroughly as the experts do, but before you put your faith in an untested survey, ask as many people as you can to try it out and describe their experience answering your questions. Was there any confusion? How long did it take? Is the survey generating relevant information?

Once you're confident in the design of your survey, plan how you'll distribute it. How do you reach the audience you've selected for your survey? Professional pollsters have all sorts of methods, including computerized dialing in some regions of the country and purchasing mailing lists. Your project is much more low tech. Begin by asking yourself whether your target audience tends to conveniently gather in a particular location. For example, if you're surveying sports fans, then surveying people by the main gate at the football stadium on Saturday might work. If your target audience is first-year college students and your university requires freshman English composition, then surveying one or more of those classes would be a convenient way to reach them.

In some situations, you can leave your survey forms in a location that might produce responses from your target audience. For example, a student at my university wanted to survey people about which foothill's hiking trails they liked best, and she left an envelope with the forms and a pencil at several trailheads.

A new possibility for tech-savvy students is the online survey. Software for designing online surveys is available now, but unless the survey is linked to a Web site that is visited by the target audience whose opinions you seek, the response rates will most likely be low. Telephone surveys are always a possibility, but they are often time consuming, and unless you can target your calls to a specific audience—say, people living in the dorms on your campus—it's hard to reach the people you most want to query. Postal mail is usually too slow and expensive, although intercampus mail can be an excellent option for distributing surveys. Response rates, however, may not meet your expectations.

Using Survey Results in Your Writing

The best thing about conducting an informal survey is that you're producing original and interesting information about your topic's local relevance. This can be an impressive element of your essay and will certainly make it more interesting.

Because analysis of open-ended questions can be time consuming and complicated, consider the simplest approach: As you go through the surveys, note which responses are worth quoting in your essay because they seem representative. Perhaps the responses are among the most commonly voiced in the entire sample, or they are expressed in significant numbers by a particular group of respondents. You might also quote a response because it is particularly articulate, surprising, or interesting.

In a more detailed analysis, you might try to nail down more specifically the *patterns* of responses. Begin by creating a simple coding system—perhaps numbers or colors—that represents the broadest categories of response. For example, perhaps you initially can divide the survey results into two categories: people who disagree with the university's general-education requirements and those who agree with it, Group 1 and Group 2. The next step might be to further analyze each of these groups, looking for particular patterns. Maybe you notice that freshmen tend to oppose the requirement in larger numbers than seniors and voice similar criticisms. In particular, pay attention to responses you didn't expect, responses that might enlarge your perspective about what people think about your topic.

Direct questions that involve choosing limited responses—true/false, yes/no, multiple choice, and so on—often involve tabulation. This is where knowledge of a spreadsheet program such as Microsoft Excel is invaluable.

Your analysis of the responses to direct questions will usually be pretty simple—probably a breakdown of percentages. What percentage of the sample, for example, checked the box that signaled agreement with the statement that their "main goal for a college education was to get a good job"? In a more sophisticated analysis, you might try to break the sample down, if it's large enough, to certain categories of respondents—men and women, class ranking, respondents with high or low test scores, and so on—and then see if any response patterns correlate to these categories. For example, perhaps a much higher percentage of freshmen than seniors sampled agreed that a good job was the most important reason to go to college.

What might this difference mean? Is it important? How does it influence your thinking about your topic or how does it affect your argument? Each of these questions involves interpretation of the results, and sample size is the factor that most influences the credibility of this kind of evidence. If you surveyed only five freshmen and three seniors about their attitudes toward your school's general-education requirements, then the comparisons you make among what they say are barely better than anecdotal. It's hard to say what the appropriate sample size for your informal survey should be—after all, you aren't conducting a scientific survey, and even a small sample might produce some interesting results—but, in general, the more responses you can gather the better.

USING WHAT YOU HAVE LEARNED

You will have countless opportunities, in school and out, to apply your research skills. But have you learned enough about research techniques to find good information efficiently? Consider the following situations. What would you suggest to the writer as a good research technique?

1. Casey is revising his essay on the effectiveness and accuracy of Internet voting. His workshop group says he needs more information on whether hackers might compromise the accuracy of computers used for voting. Casey says he's relied pretty heavily on Internet sources. Where else would you suggest he search for information? What search terms might he use?

2. Alexandra needs to find some facts on divorce rates in the United States. Where might she find them fairly easily?

3. The university is proposing to build a new parking lot on a natural area near the edge of campus. Sherry wants to investigate the proposal to write a paper on whether the parking lot might be built with minimal environmental damage. What steps might she take to research the topic? Where should she look for information first? And then?

Will you control the outside sources in your research essay, or will they control you? The appropriate use of sources is really a matter of control. Writers who put research information to work for them see outside sources as serving a clear purpose.

12

USING AND CITING SOURCES

CONTROLLING INFORMATION

The first college paper that really meant something to me was an essay on whaling industry practices and their impacts on populations of humpback and sperm whales. The essay opened with a detailed description of the exploding harpoon, a highly effective and dramatic method of subduing the animals, and was written at a time when the International Whaling Commission exerted little control over the whale harvests of the largest whaling nations. I never forgot that paper because it engaged both my heart and my head; I was intensely curious about the issue and felt strongly that this was a problem that needed to be solved.

Writing from the place of itchy curiosity and strong feelings is a wonderful thing. It will motivate you to read and learn about your topic, and when it comes to writing the draft you might find that you have little trouble enlisting the voices of your sources to make your point. More often, however, you've chosen a topic because you don't know what you think or feel about it—the inquiry-based approach—or you've been assigned a general topic that reflects the content of a course you're taking. In these cases, writing with sources is like crashing a party of strangers that has been going on for a long time. You shyly listen in, trying to figure out what everyone is talking about, and look for an opening to enter the conversation. Mostly you just feel intimidated, so you hang back feeling foolish.

This kind of writing situation is really a matter of control. Will you control the outside sources in your research essay, or will they control you? Will you enter the conversation and make a contribution to it, or will you let others do all the talking? The easiest way to lose control is simply to turn long stretches of your paper

What You'll Learn in This Chapter

- How to control sources so they don't control you.
- How to properly summarize, paraphrase, and quote source material.
- How to avoid plagiarism.
- Methods of citation in the MLA and APA systems.

over to a source, usually with long quotations. I've seen a quotation from a single source run more than a full page in some drafts. Another way to lose control is to do what one of my colleagues calls a "data dump." Fill the truck with a heavy load of information, back it up to the paper, and dump in as much as you can, without analysis, without carefully selecting what is relevant and what isn't, without much thought at all. The writer in this situation sees his or her essay as a hole that must be filled with information.

USING SOURCES

The appropriate use of sources is really a matter of control. Writers who put research information to work for them see outside sources as serving a clear purpose. There are at least five of these purposes:

1. To use information that provides useful background or a context for understanding the research question.
2. To use information that answers a relevant question.
3. To use information as evidence to support a claim or idea, or in some cases, evidence that seems *not* to support an assertion but might if seen a certain way.
4. To use information from a particular author who is influential in the debate about a topic.
5. To use information to *complicate* a writer's thesis, raising interesting questions.

Let's see how this works in an actual passage. In an essay that asks, "Why Did God Create Flies," writer Richard Conniff argues that the answer might be as a punishment for human arrogance. In the middle of the essay, he draws on research to provide some background for this claim by establishing the long and sometimes unhappy relationship between the housefly and human beings.

> The true housefly, *Musca domestica*, does not bite. (You may think this is something to like about it, until you find out what it does instead.) *M. domestica*, a drab fellow of salt-and-pepper complexion, is the world's most widely distributed insect species and probably the most familiar, a status achieved through its pronounced fondness for breeding in pig, horse, and human excrement. In choosing at some point in the immemorial past to concentrate on the wastes around human habitations, *M. domestica* made a major career move. Bernard Greenberg of the University of Illinois at Chicago has traced human representations of the housefly back to a Mesopotamian cylinder seal from 3000 B.C. But houseflies were probably with us even before we had houses, and they spread with human culture.

Here Conniff demonstrates exquisite control over outside sources, marshalling them in the service of his larger point. But he also does this by not simply quoting extensively or going on and on explaining the relevant information, but by *finding his own way of saying things.* Rather than writing that the housefly's fondness for associating with people had significant ecological implications for the insect, Conniff writes that it was "a major career move."

The sections that follow review the techniques of summarizing, paraphrasing, and quoting. You know these as the three horsemen of notetaking. But these should never be thoughtless activities; in fact, they're a great opportunity to exert control over your sources by doing two things:

1. *Taking notes with a particular purpose in mind.* How is the information you're writing about relevant to your purpose in your essay?

2. *Finding your own way of saying things.* By putting other people's words into your own voice, you take possession of the information.

Summarizing

"So basically what you're saying is that we can never win the war on terrorism because it isn't really a war in the conventional sense?"

Imagine that you're in the midst of a conversation with someone about the challenge of defeating terrorism. You've just listened for about a minute to a friend explain in some detail that the battle against terrorism isn't really a battle at all, but a series of surprise attacks that then provoke retaliation, with the two opponents blindly striking out at each other. Your friend adds that the terrorists' tactics are aimed at targets with symbolic rather than military value. Victory for terrorists is not measured in damage inflicted on military forces but in the terror provoked in the civilian population. You listen to all of this and summarize your friend's larger point: This isn't really war as we've historically understood it.

Summary is like making moonshine. You collect some ingredients and distill them into a more concise and powerful concoction, one that accurately captures the main idea of a book, an article, an argument, a chapter, or even a passage. The best summaries involve *thinking.* You're not just searching for a topic sentence somewhere in the source to copy down, but taking it all in as you would information and ideas in a conversation and then trying to find your own way of saying what seems to be at the heart of things.

A summary is usually much shorter than the original. For example, consider the following summary of the earlier extract paragraph about the relationship between houseflies and human beings:

> The common housefly is among the "most familiar" insects because it found its long partnership with human beings, one that goes back thousands of years, extremely beneficial.

Can you see how the summary captures the main idea of the longer paragraph? Also note that when the summary refers to identical language in the original—the phrase "most familiar"—the writer is careful to use quotation marks. Finally, the summary uses original language that breaks with the source, describing the relationship between people and flies as a "long partnership."

Reasons you would want to write a summary rather than quote directly or paraphrase a source include the following:

- Your essay needs not a longer explanation of what a source says but a nugget of an idea, one that might have more impact because of its brevity.
- The original source, while useful, doesn't say things in a particularly distinctive way. It isn't quotable, but when distilled it serves a purpose in your essay.
- The source is making an argument, and what matters most is the gist of that argument rather than a discussion of the details.

TIPS FOR CRAFTING A SUMMARY

1. If your aim is to summarize an entire work, and if the source isn't a book, read it all once through, marking what seem to be key claims or findings. Academic articles in the social sciences often include abstracts, or ready-made summaries of a study. Books frequently explain their purpose in a preface or introduction. Start there. Then check the concluding chapter.

2. If your aim is to summarize a passage of a longer work, remember to look for the author's most important ideas where he or she is most likely to put them: the first and last sentences of paragraphs or a concluding paragraph.

3. Summary has little to do with your opinion. Save that for the right side of your double-entry journal. Try, as best you can, to capture your understanding of the *source's* meaning or argument.

4. Typically, a summary includes the name(s) of the author or the title of the work, usually attached to a verb that characterizes its nature: so-and-so *argues, finds, explains, speculates, questions*, and so on.

Paraphrasing

Paraphrasing doesn't get any respect. It's like a difficult cousin that shows up at the family picnic and insists on enlisting everyone in a deep discussion. It's hard work, thinking that hard, particularly when there's beer and potato salad and Grandma's homemade chicken potpies. Of the three forms of note taking, paraphrasing requires the most attention and the greatest care. Your goal is to craft a restatement, in your own words, of what an original source is saying, in roughly the same length as the original.

Obviously, we don't paraphrase books or even entire articles. Paraphrasing usually involves closer work—examining a paragraph or a passage and then finding a way to accurately capture the original's ideas and information but in a fresh and original way. This demands not only faith in our own way of saying things—that's hard enough—but a pretty thorough understanding of what exactly the source is trying to say. You simply can't paraphrase a source you don't understand.

That's where the brain work comes in, and the payoff is significant. When you successfully paraphrase a source, you've written a part of your own essay. You've already done the work of comprehending what the source says, and found your own way of writing about it. This is the essence of using outside sources in your own work.

Here's a paraphrase of the earlier extract paragraph on houseflies.

Houseflies, according to Richard Conniff, have had "a long partnership with human beings." They are also among "the world's most widely distributed insect species," two factors that explain our familiarity with *Musca domesticus*, the housefly's Latin name. This partnership may have been cultivated for thousands of years, or certainly as long as humans—and their animal companions—produced sufficient excrement in which the flies can breed. Ironically, these pests have benefited enormously from their "fondness" for human and animal wastes, and unwittingly we have contributed to their success at our own expense.

A key element of the translation in a paraphrase is trying not to imitate the structure of the original passage. By deliberately setting out to reorganize the information, you'll find writing a paraphrase much easier. And you'll also find it much less likely that you unintentionally plagiarize the material. Notice as well that whenever the paraphrase borrows wording from the original, quotation marks are included. The very last line of the paraphrase seems to cross over into interpretation, pointing out an irony that the original passage may have only hinted at. This is fine. In fact, it's something that you should try to develop as a habit—don't just translate and transcribe the information, try to make something of it. This move is particularly important when quoting material.

Quoting

Jotting down exactly what a source says—word for word—is relatively mindless work. Beyond selecting *what* you'll write down—a choice that does involve some thought—quoting a source merely involves careful transcription. Is that why it's the most popular form of notetaking?

That's not to say that you should never quote a source. Not at all. If you jot down a passage from a source in the left page of your double-entry journal, and then use the right page to explore, analyze, question, and interpret what it says, you're doing the kind of work good research writing demands. Well-selected quotes in an essay can also be memorable. But too often writers turn to transcription alone, and this quoted material simply gets dropped into the draft with virtually no analysis or even explanation. Frequently, I notice a quoted sentence appearing in the middle of a paragraph simply because the writer was too lazy to paraphrase. Then there's the long quotation that's thrown in as an obvious ploy to make the paper longer.

When should you turn to quotation in your essay? There are two main situations:

1. When the source says something in a distinctive way that would be lost by putting it in your own words.

> ### TIPS FOR CRAFTING A PARAPHRASE
>
> 1. If a summary is a macroscopic look at a text, a paraphrase is microscopic, usually focusing on a brief passage. Consequently, the plagiarism danger goes from yellow to red (see "Avoiding Plagiarism" on page 493). Make sure to find your own way of saying things, quoting phrases that you borrow from the source.
>
> 2. Try the "look away" strategy. Carefully read the passage several times, then set it aside. Compose your paraphrase without looking at the source, trusting that you'll remember what's important. Then check the result against the passage, changing or quoting any borrowed language and refining your prose.
>
> 3. Like summary, introduce paraphrased material in your essay by attributing the author or the work.

2. When you want to analyze or emphasize a particular passage in the source, and the exact words of the author matter.

I like to tell the story of a moment in the thirteen-hour documentary *Shoah*, a film about the Holocaust. In one scene, the filmmakers are riding the train that took hundreds of Jews to their deaths in one of the concentration camps. Amazingly, the engineer who drove that train back then was still on the job, guiding the train on the same tracks past the ruins of the same camps. The filmmakers interviewed this man, and asked him the obvious question: *How does it feel to still be driving the train on which you led so many people to their deaths?* The engineer paused, and said quietly, "If you could lick my heart, it would poison you."

This is the kind of quotation that could never be paraphrased. To do so would be to rob what the man said of all its emotional power and truth. You will rarely find such a memorable quotation in your sources. Much more often, you encounter a voice in your reading that simply sounds interesting and has a nice way of putting things. For instance, the excerpt from "Why Did God Create Flies" is eminently quotable because Richard Conniff, its author, writes with such a lively voice. Consider his sentence:

> The true housefly is the world's most widely distributed insect species and probably the most familiar, a status achieved through its pronounced fondness for breeding in pig, horse, and human excrement.

When you introduce a voice other than your own, make it clear what this new voice adds to the conversation you have going about your topic.

What is it about this that seems quotable? Maybe the way it goes along with fairly straightforward exposition until the second half of the sentence, when suddenly the fly seeks status and feels fondness for you know what.

Academic writing also resorts to quotation when it's worthwhile to look more closely at what an author says. This is common in the critical essay when analyzing literature. But it's also a good move when working with other sources, perhaps excerpts from a transcript or in analyzing an expert's claim or a striking finding. The key is not just using such quotations sparingly—typically a research essay is no more than 20 percent quotation—but *working with them*.

When you bring someone else's voice into your own writing, it's usually a good idea to introduce the source and provide some justification for making such a move. For instance, you might introduce the preceding quote by saying something like this:

> Richard Conniff, whose popular studies of invertebrate animals have made even leeches lovable, observes that the familiarity of the house fly is no accident. He writes...

It's even more important in academic writing to follow up quoted text with your own commentary. What would you like the reader to notice about what the quotation says? What seems most relevant to your own research question or point? How does the quotation extend an important idea you've been discussing or raise an important question? What does it imply? What do you agree with? What do you disagree with? In other words, when you introduce a voice other than your own, make it clear what this new voice adds to the conversation you have going about your topic.

TIPS FOR HANDLING QUOTATIONS

Integrate quoted material in your essay in the following ways:

1. **Separate it.** There are two ways to do this. Provide an introductory tag that ends in a comma or a colon. *According to Carl Elliott (82), the new drug pushers "are officially known as 'pharmaceutical sales representatives' but everyone calls them 'sales reps.'"* Or, *Carl Elliott (82) observes that drug salespeople are easy to spot: "Drug reps today are often young, well groomed, and strikingly good looking. Many are women…"*

2. **Embed it.** Integrate quoted material in your own sentence something like this: *Carl Elliott calls drug reps "the best dressed people in the hospital."*

3. **Block it.** Extended quotations (more than 40 words in APA style and more than four lines in MLA) should be indented five spaces in APA style and ten spaces in MLA style in a block. Quotation marks, except those used in the source, are omitted. For instance:

   Carl Elliott, in "The Drug Pushers," highlights the perks doctors have historically received:

   > *Gifts from the drug industry are nothing new, of course. William Helfand, who worked in marketing for Merck for thirty-three years, told me that company representatives were giving doctors books and pamphlets as early as the late nineteenth century. "There is nothing new under the sun," Helfand says, "There is just more of it." The question is: Why is there so much more of it just now? And what changes occurred during the past decade to bring about such a dramatic increase in reps bearing gifts? (86)*

CITING SOURCES

Somewhere in the great hall at Mount Olympus, the mist obscuring his or her ankles, must have been an English teacher. Hardly the right hand of Zeus, this was a minor god. But there were important tasks for this god, for the mortals were careless with their language, running on their sentences and mistaking *their* for *there*. Nothing could make the god's anger flash more brilliantly than a missing citation. There was a special place in Hades reserved for the plagiarist, where the condemned spent eternity composing Works Cited pages of endless stacks of books whose title pages were unreadable.

Of all the rules some of my students believe were invented to torture composition students, requirements that they carefully cite their sources in research papers may cause the most anguish. They rarely question these requirements; they seem like divine and universal law. In fact, these aren't rules but conventions, hardly as old as the Greeks, and historically quite new. For many centuries, writers freely borrowed from others, often without attribution, and the appropriation of someone else's words and ideas was considered quite normal. This is still the view in some non-Western cultures; some students, for example, are quite puzzled in their English as a Second Language classes when they have to cite a source in their research essays.

This convention of explicitly acknowledging the source of an idea, quotation, piece of data, or information with a footnote or parenthetical citation and bibliography arose in the past 150 years. It began when mostly German universities began promoting the idea that the purpose of research was not simply to demonstrate an understanding of what already was known but to *make a contribution of new knowledge*. Researchers were to look for gaps in existing scholarship—questions that hadn't yet been asked—or to offer extensions of what had already been posed by someone else. Knowledge making became the business of the research writer, and, like gardeners, scholars saw themselves as tending a living thing, a kind of tree that grew larger as new branches were grafted onto existing limbs.

Just as a child clambering up a tree in the park is grateful for the sturdy limbs under his or her feet, research writers acknowledge the limbs they are standing on that have helped them to see a little more of their subjects. That's why they cite their sources. This is an act of gratitude, of course, but it also signals to readers on whose authority the writer's claims, conclusions, or ideas are based. Citation helps readers locate the writer's work on a specific part of the tree of knowledge in a discipline; it gives a useful context of *what has already been said* about a question or a topic.

> Citation helps readers locate the writer's work on a specific part of the tree of knowledge in a discipline; it gives a useful context of what has *already been said* about a question or a topic.

Student writers cite for exactly the same reasons. Not because it's required in most college research writing but because it makes their research writing more relevant and more convincing to the people who read it.

There are quite a few conventions for citing, and these conventions often vary by discipline. Humanities disciplines such as English often use the Modern Language Association (MLA) conventions, while the social sciences use the American Psychological Association (APA) methods. Both of these documentation styles are detailed later in this chapter. Although there are differences between the two styles, the purpose of each is the same: to acknowledge those from whom you have borrowed ideas and information.

Avoiding Plagiarism

Modern authors get testy when someone uses their work without giving them credit. This is where the concept of intellectual property comes from, an idea that emerged with the invention of the printing press and the distribution of multiple copies of an author's work. In its most basic form, plagiarism is stealing someone else's words, ideas, or information. Academic plagiarism, the kind that gets a lot of ink these days with the rise of the Internet, usually refers to more specific misdeeds. Your university probably has an academic honesty or plagiarism policy posted on the Web or in a student handbook. You need to look at it. But it probably includes most or all of the following forms of plagiarism:

1. Handing in someone else's work—a downloaded paper from the Internet or borrowed from a friend—and claiming that it's your own.

2. Using information or ideas that are not common knowledge from any source and failing to acknowledge that source.

3. Handing in the same paper for two different classes.

4. Using the exact language or expressions of a source and not indicating through quotation marks and citation that the language is borrowed.

5. Rewriting a passage from a source using minor substitutions of different words but retaining the same syntax and structure of the original.

Most plagiarism is unintentional. The writer simply didn't know or pay attention to course or university plagiarism policies. Equally common is simple carelessness. How can you avoid this trap? Check out the "Tips for Avoiding Plagiarism" box.

Intentional plagiarism, of course, is a different matter. Many Web sites offer papers on thousands of topics to anyone willing to pay for them. College instructors, however, have tools for identifying these downloaded papers. The consequences of buying and handing in online papers are often severe, including flunking the course and even expulsion, an academic Hades of sorts.

> Intentional plagiarism stems from an intellectual laziness and dishonesty that are bound to catch up with the person doing it sooner or later.

Moreover, even if a person is not caught committing this academic crime, intentional plagiarism stems from an intellectual laziness and dishonesty that are bound to catch up with the person doing it sooner or later. Just don't go there.

> ## TIPS FOR AVOIDING PLAGIARISM
>
> - **Don't procrastinate.** Many careless mistakes in citation or proper handling of source material occur in the rush to finish the draft in the wee hours of the morning.
> - **Be an active notetaker.** Work in the middle of the process to take possession of the material you read, especially exploring your responses to sources *in your own words* and *for your own purposes*.
> - **Collect bibliographic information first.** Before you do anything else, take down complete publication information for each source, including the page numbers from which you borrowed material.
> - **Mark quoted material clearly.** Whenever you quote a source directly, make sure that's obvious in your notes.
> - **Be vigilant whenever you cut and paste.** The great usefulness of cutting and pasting passages in electronic documents is also the downfall of many research writers. Is the copied material directly borrowed, and if so is it properly cited?

EXERCISE 12.1

The Accidental Plagiarist

Most plagiarism problems are accidental. The writer simply isn't aware that he or she has stumbled into the problem. Here's a low-stakes exercise that can test your understanding of how to avoid the simplest—and most common—types of accidental plagiarism. Get this wrong and the grammar police won't accost you in the middle of the night, throw you against the wall, and make you spell difficult words. You'll just learn something.

Using the words and ideas of others in your own writing is essential in most research essays and papers. Doing this without plagiarizing isn't exactly like walking through a minefield, but you do have to step carefully. For example, Beth is exploring the question, "What might explain the high rate of divorce in the early years of marriage?" She's interested in divorce because she just went through one. In her research, Beth encounters Diane Ackerman's book, *The Natural History of Love*, and Beth finds the following paragraph:

> "Philandering," we call it, "fooling around," "hanky-panky," "skirt chasing," "man chasing," or something equally picturesque. Monogamy and adultery are both hallmarks of being human. Anthropologist Helen Fisher proposes a chemical basis for adultery, what she calls "The Four-Year Itch." Studying the United Nations survey of marriage and divorce around the world, she noticed that divorce usually occurs early in marriage, during the couple's first reproductive and parenting years. Also, that this peak time for divorce coincides with the period in which infatuation normally ends, and a couple has to decide if they're going to

call it quits or stay together as companions. Some couples do stay together and have other children, but even more don't. "The human animal," she concludes, "seems built to court, to fall in love, and to marry one person at a time; then, at the height of our reproductive years, often with a single child, we divorce them; then, a few years after, we remarry once again."

Beth thought this was pretty interesting stuff, and in her draft she summarized the paragraph in the following way:

> According to Diane Ackerman, a hallmark of being human is "monogamy and adultery," and she cites the period right after infatuation subsides—about four years for most couples—as the time when they call it quits.

STEP ONE: In small groups, analyze Beth's summary. Does Beth plagiarize the original passage, and if so, do you have ideas about how she could fix it? Revise the summary on a piece of newsprint and post it on the wall.

STEP TWO: Discuss the proposed revisions. How well do they address any plagiarism problems you see in Beth's summary?

STEP THREE: Now compare the following paraphrases of the same Ackerman passage. Which has plagiarism problems and which seems okay?

PARAPHRASE 1

Divorce may have a "chemical basis," something that may kick in after four years of marriage and ironically when partners are reaching their highest potential for having children. Researcher Helen Fisher calls it "The Four-Year Itch," the time that often signals a shift from infatuation into a more sober assessment of the relationship's future: Are they going to stay together or "call it quits"? Most end up deciding to end the relationship.

PARAPHRASE 2

When infatuation fades and couples are faced with the future of their relationship, biochemistry may help them decide. According to researcher Helen Fisher, "divorce usually occurs early in marriage, during the couple's first reproductive and parenting years" (Ackerman 165). She suggests that this is often about four years into the relationship, and argues that humans may be designed to behave this way because the pattern seems so entrenched (Ackerman 166).

STEP FOUR: In class, discuss which paraphrase seems acceptable and which does not. Remember that the problems are pretty subtle.

STEP FIVE: Now practice your own *summary* of the following passage, applying what you've learned so far in the exercise about ways to avoid plagiarism when using the words and ideas of other people. This passage in Ackerman's book follows the passage you worked with earlier.

> Our chemistry makes it easy to follow that plan, and painful to avoid it. After the seductive fireworks of first attraction, which may last a few weeks or a few years, the body gets bored with easy ecstasy. The nerves no longer quiver with excitement. Nothing new has been happening for ages, why bother to rouse

oneself? Love is exhausting. Then the attachment chemicals roll in their thick cozy carpets of marital serenity. Might as well relax and enjoy the calm and security some feel. Separated even for a short while, the partners crave the cradle of the other's embrace. Is it a chemical craving? Possibly so, a hunger for the soothing endomorphins that flow when they're together. It is a deep, sweet river, just right for dangling one's feet in while the world waits.

Other people grow restless and search for novelty.

MLA DOCUMENTATION GUIDELINES

The professional organization in charge of academic writing in literature and languages, the Modern Language Association (MLA), uses one of the two methods of citing sources that you should know. The second, the American Psychological Association (APA) system, is described in the next section. Your English class will most likely use the MLA system.

In 2008, the MLA decided to spare us citation headaches by making some of its guidelines easier, including the move to no longer require that URLs be included in citations of online sources. Two other major changes were the shift to using italics instead of underlining titles and the addition of the publication medium to every citation (e.g., print Web, performance, and so on). This edition of *The Curious Writer* includes these updates.

Many things haven't changed. You must cite a source in your paper in the following situations:

1. Whenever you quote from an original source.
2. Whenever you borrow ideas from an original source, even when you express them in your own words by paraphrasing or summarizing.
3. Whenever you borrow factual information from a source that is not common knowledge (see the "Inquiring into the Details: The Common Knowledge Exception" box below).

INQUIRING INTO THE DETAILS

The Common Knowledge Exception

The business about *common knowledge* causes much confusion. Just what does this term mean? Basically, *common knowledge* means facts that are widely known and about which there is no controversy.

Sometimes, it's really obvious whether something is common knowledge. The fact that the Super Bowl occurs in late January and pits the winning teams from the American and National Football Conferences is common knowledge. The fact that former president Ronald Reagan was once an actor and starred in a movie with a chimpanzee is common knowledge, too. And the fact that most Americans get most of their news from television is also common knowledge, although this information is getting close to leaving the domain of common knowledge.

But what about a writer's assertion that most dreaming occurs during rapid eye movement (REM) sleep? This is an idea about which all sources seem to agree. Does that make it common knowledge?

It's useful to ask next, *How common to whom? Experts in the topic at hand or the rest of us?* As a rule, consider the knowledge of your readers. What information will not be familiar to most of your readers or may even surprise them? Which ideas might even raise skepticism? In this case, the fact about REM sleep and dreaming goes slightly beyond the knowledge of most readers, so to be safe, it should be cited. Use common sense, but when in doubt, cite.

Citing Sources

The foundation of the MLA method of citing sources *in your paper* is putting the last name of the author and the page number of the source in parentheses as closely as possible to the borrowed material. For example,

> Researchers believe that there is an "infatuation chemical" that may account for that
>
> almost desperate attraction we feel when we're near someone special (Ackerman 164).

The parenthetical citation tells a reader two things: the source of the information (for example, the author's name), and where in the work to find the borrowed idea or material. A really interested reader—perhaps an infatuated one—who wanted to follow up on this would then refer to the Works Cited at the back of the paper. This would list the work by the author's last name and all the pertinent information about the source:

> Ackerman, Diane. *A Natural History of Love.* New York: Vintage, 1994. Print.

Here's another example of parenthetical author/page citation from another research paper. Note the differences from the previous example:

> "One thing is clear," writes Thomas Mallon, "plagiarism didn't become a truly sore
>
> point with writers until they thought of writing as their trade. . . . Suddenly his
>
> capital and identity were at stake" (3–4).

The first thing you may have noticed is that the author's last name—Mallon—was omitted from the parenthetical citation. It didn't need to be included, because it had already been mentioned in the text. *If you mention the author's name in the text of your paper, then you only need to parenthetically cite the relevant page number(s).* This citation also tells us that the quoted passage comes from two pages rather than one.

Where to Put Citations. Place the citation as close as you can to the borrowed material, trying to avoid breaking the flow of the sentences, if possible. To avoid confusion about what's borrowed and what's not—particularly in passages longer than a sentence—mention the name of the original author *in your paper*. Note that in the next example the writer simply cites the source at the end of the paragraph, not naming the source in the text. Doing so makes it hard for the reader to figure out whether Blager is the source of the information in the entire paragraph or just part of it:

> Though children who have been sexually abused seem to be disadvantaged in
>
> many areas, including the inability to forge lasting relationships, low self-esteem,
>
> and crippling shame, they seem advantaged in other areas. Sexually abused chil-
>
> dren seem to be more socially mature than other children of their same age
>
> group. It's a distinctly mixed blessing (Blager 994).

In the following example, notice how the ambiguity about what's borrowed and what's not is resolved by careful placement of the author's name and parenthetical citation in the text:

> Though children who have been sexually abused seem to be disadvantaged in
>
> many areas, including the inability to forge lasting relationships, low self-esteem,
>
> and crippling shame, they seem advantaged in other areas. According to Blager,
>
> sexually abused children seem to be more socially mature than other children of
>
> their same age group (994). It's a distinctly mixed blessing.

In this latter version, it's clear that Blager is the source for one sentence in the paragraph, and the writer is responsible for the rest. Generally, use an authority's last name, rather than a formal title or first name, when mentioning him or her in your text. Also note that the citation is placed *inside* the period of the sentence (or last sentence) that it documents. That's almost always the case, except at the end of a blocked quotation, where the parenthetical reference is placed after the period of the last sentence.

INQUIRING INTO THE DETAILS

Citations That Go with the Flow

There's no getting around it—parenthetical citations can be like stones on the sidewalk. Readers stride through a sentence in your essay and then have to step around the citation at the end before they resume their walk. Yet citations are important in academic writing because they help readers know who you read or heard that shaped your thinking.

However, you can minimize citations that trip up readers and make your essay more readable by doing the following:

- Avoid lengthy parenthetical citations by mentioning the name of the author in your essay. That way, you usually have to include only a page number in the citation.

- Try to place citations where readers are likely to pause anyway—for example, the end of the sentence, or right before a comma.

- Remember that you *don't* need a citation when you're citing common knowledge, or referring to an entire work by an author.

- If you're borrowing from only one source in a paragraph of your essay, and all of the borrowed material comes from a single page of that source, don't bother repeating the citation over and over again with each new bit of information. Just put the citation at the end of the paragraph.

The citation can also be placed near the author's name, rather than at the end of the sentence, if it doesn't unnecessarily break the flow of the sentence. For example:

Blager (994) observes that sexually abused children tend to be more socially

mature than other children of their same age group.

When You Mention the Author's Name. It's generally good practice in research writing to identify who said what. The familiar convention of using attribution tags such as "According to Fletcher…" or "Fletcher argues that…" and so on helps readers attach a name to a voice, or an individual to certain claims or findings. When you mention the author of a source, you can drop his or her name from the parenthetical citation and just list the page number. For example,

Robert Harris believes that there is "widespread uncertainty" among students

about what constitutes plagiarism (2).

You may also list the page number directly after the author's name.

Robert Harris (2) believes that there is "widespread uncertainty" among students

about what constitutes plagiarism.

When There Is No Author. Occasionally, you may encounter a source in which the author is anonymous—the article doesn't have a byline, or for some reason the author hasn't been identified. This isn't unusual with pamphlets, editorials, government documents, some newspaper articles, online sources, and short filler articles in magazines. If you can't parenthetically name the author, what do you cite?

Most often, cite the title (or an abbreviated version, if the title is long) and the page number. If you choose to abbreviate the title, begin with the word under which it is alphabetized in the Works Cited. For example:

According to the Undergraduate Catalog, "the athletic program is an integral part

of the university and its total educational purpose" (7).

Here is how this publication would be listed at the back of the paper:

Works Cited

Undergraduate Catalog, Boise State University 2004–2005.

    Boise, ID: BSU, 2004. Print.

For clarity, it's helpful to mention the original source of the borrowed material in the text of your paper. When there is no author's name, refer to the publication (or institution) you're citing or make a more general reference to the source. For example:

An article in *Cuisine* magazine argues that the best way to kill a lobster is to

plunge a knife between its eyes ("How to Kill" 56).

or

According to one government report, with the current minimum size limit, most

lobsters end up on dinner plates before they've had a chance to reproduce ("Size

at Sexual Maturity" 3–4).

Works by the Same Author. Suppose you end up using several books or articles by the same author. Obviously, a parenthetical citation that merely lists the author's name and page number won't do, because it won't be clear *which* of several works the citation refers to. In this case, include the author's name, an abbreviated title (if the original is too long), and the page number. For example:

One essayist who suffers from multiple sclerosis writes that "there is a subtle

taxonomy of crippleness" (Mairs, *Carnal Acts* 69).

The Works Cited list would show multiple works by one author as follows:

Works Cited

Mairs, Nancy. *Carnal Acts*. Boston: Beacon, 1996. Print.

    – – –. *Voice Lessons*. Boston: Beacon, 1994. Print.

It's obvious from the parenthetical citation which of the two Mairs books is the source of the information. Note that in the parenthetical reference, no punctuation separates the title and the page number, but a comma follows the author's name. If Mairs had been mentioned in the text of the paper, her name could have been dropped from the citation.

Also notice that the three hyphens used in the second entry are meant to signal that the author's name in this source is the same as in the preceding entry.

When One Source Quotes Another. Whenever you can, cite the original source for material you use. For example, if an article on television violence quotes the author of a book and you want to use the quote, try to hunt down the book. That way, you'll be certain of the accuracy of the quote and you may find some more usable information.

Sometimes, however, finding the original source is not possible. In those cases, use the term *qtd. in* to signal that you've quoted or paraphrased a quotation from a book or article that initially appeared elsewhere. In the following example, the citation signals that Bacon's quote was culled from an article by Guibroy, not Bacon's original work:

Francis Bacon also weighed in on the dangers of imitation, observing that "it is hardly

possible at once to admire an author and to go beyond him" (qtd. in Guibroy 113).

Personal Interviews. If you mention the name of your interview subject in your text, no parenthetical citation is necessary. On the other hand, if you don't mention the subject's name, cite it in parentheses after the quote:

Instead, the recognizable environment gave something to kids they could relate

to. "And it had a lot more real quality to it than, say, *Mister Rogers...*," says one

educator. "Kids say the reason they don't like *Mister Rogers* is that it's unbeliev-

able" (Diamonti).

Regardless of whether you mention your subject's name, you should include a reference to the interview in the Works Cited. In this case, the reference would look like this:

Works Cited

Diamonti, Nancy. Personal interview. 5 Nov. 1999.

Several Sources in a Single Citation. Suppose two sources both contributed the same information in a paragraph of your essay. Or perhaps even more common is when you're summarizing the findings of several authors on a certain topic—a fairly common move when you're trying to establish a context for your own research question. You cite multiple authors in a single citation in the usual fashion, using author name and page number, but separating each with a semicolon. For example,

> A whole range of studies have looked closely at the intellectual development
>
> of college students, finding that they generally assume "stages" or
>
> "perspectives" that differ from subject to subject (Perry 122;
>
> Belenky et al. 12).

If you can, however, avoid long citations because they can be cumbersome for readers.

Sample Parenthetical References for Other Sources. MLA format is pretty simple, and we've already covered some of the basic variations. You should also know five additional variations, as follow:

AN ENTIRE WORK

If you mention the author's name in the text, no citation is necessary. The work should, however, be listed in the Works Cited.

> Leon Edel's *Henry James* is considered by many to be a model biography.

A VOLUME OF A MULTIVOLUME WORK

If you're working with one volume of a multivolume work, it's a good idea to mention which volume in the parenthetical reference. The following citation attributes the passage to volume 2, page 3, of a work by Baym and three or more other authors. The volume number always precedes the colon, which is followed by the page number:

> By the turn of the century, three authors dominated American literature: Mark
>
> Twain, Henry James, and William Dean Howells (Baym et al. 2: 3).

SEVERAL SOURCES FOR A SINGLE PASSAGE

Occasionally, a number of sources may contribute to a single passage. List them all in one parenthetical reference, separated by semicolons:

> American soccer may never achieve the popularity it enjoys in the rest of the
>
> world, an unfortunate fact that is integrally related to the nature of the game
>
> itself (Gardner 12; "Selling Soccer" 30).[1]

---

[1]Jason Pulsifer, University of New Hampshire, 1991. Used with permission

A LITERARY WORK

Because so many literary works, particularly classics, have been reprinted in so many editions, it's useful to give readers more information about where a passage can be found in one of these editions. List the page number and then the chapter number (and any other relevant information, such as the section or volume), separated by a semicolon. Use arabic rather than roman numerals, unless your teacher instructs you otherwise:

> Izaak Walton warns that "no direction can be given to make a man of a dull
>
> capacity able to make a Flie well" (130; ch. 5).

When citing classic poems or plays, instead of page numbers, cite line numbers and other appropriate divisions (book, section, act, scene, part, etc.). Separate the information with periods. For example, (*Othello* 2.3.286) indicates act 2, scene 3, line 286 of Shakespeare's work.

AN ONLINE SOURCE

Texts on CD-ROM and online sources frequently don't have page numbers. So how can you cite them parenthetically in your essay? You have several options.

Sometimes, the documents include paragraph numbers. In these cases, use the abbreviation *par.* or *pars.*, followed by the paragraph number or numbers you're borrowing material from. For example:

> In most psychotherapeutic approaches, the personality of the therapist can have
>
> a big impact on the outcome of the therapy ("Psychotherapy," par. 1).

Sometimes the material has an internal structure, such as sections, parts, chapters, or volumes. If so, use the abbreviation *sec., pt., ch.,* or *vol.* (respectively), followed by the appropriate number.

In many cases, a parenthetical citation can be avoided entirely by simply naming the source in the text of your essay. A curious reader will then find the full citation to the article on the Works Cited page at the back of your paper. For example:

> According to Charles Petit, the worldwide effort to determine whether frogs are
>
> disappearing will take somewhere between three and five years.

Finally, if you don't want to mention the source in text, parenthetically cite the author's last name (if any) or article title:

> The worldwide effort to determine whether frogs are disappearing will take some-
>
> where between three and five years (Petit).

Format

The Layout. A certain fussiness is associated with the look of academic papers. The reason for it is quite simple—academic disciplines generally aim for consistency in format so that readers of scholarship know exactly where to look to find what they want to know. It's a matter of efficiency. How closely you must follow the MLA's requirements for the layout of your essay is up to your instructor, but it's really not that complicated. A lot of what you need to know is featured in Figure 12.1.

Printing. Compose your paper on white, 8½" × 11" printer paper. Make sure the printer has sufficient ink or toner.

Margins and Spacing. The old high school trick is to use big margins. That way, you can meet your page length requirements with less material. Don't try that trick with this paper. Leave half-inch margins at the top and one-inch margins at the bottom and sides of your pages. Indent the first line of each paragraph five spaces and blocked quotes ten spaces. Double-space all of the text, including blocked quotes and Works Cited.

Title Page. Your paper doesn't need a separate title page. Begin with the first page of text. One inch below the top of the page, type your name, your instructor's name, the course number, and the date (see the following). Below that, type the title, centered on the page. Begin the text of the paper below the title.

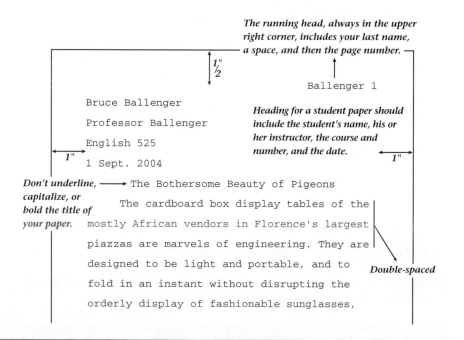

Figure 12.1   The basic look of an MLA-style paper

Julie Bird

Professor Ballenger

English 102

1 June 2004

Nature as Being: Landscape in Silko's 'Lullaby'

Leslie Marmon Silko, the author of "Lullaby," is a Native American writer from the

Laguna Pueblo culture...

Note that every line is double spaced. The title is not underlined (unless it includes the name of a book or some other work that should be underlined) or boldfaced.

Pagination. Make sure that every page including the first one is numbered. That's especially important with long papers. Type your last name and the page number in the upper right corner, flush with the right margin: Ballenger 3. Don't use the abbreviation *p.* or a hyphen between your name and the number.

Placement of Tables, Charts, and Illustrations. With MLA format, papers do not have appendixes. Tables, charts, and illustrations are placed in the body of the paper, close to the text that refers to them. Number illustrations consecutively (Table 1 or Figure 3), and indicate sources below them (see Figure 12.2). If you use a chart or illustration from another text, give the full citation. Place any table caption above the table, flush left. Captions for illustrations or diagrams are usually placed below them.

TABLE 1
PERCENTAGE OF STUDENTS WHO SELF-REPORT ACTS OF PLAGIARISM

Acts of Plagiarism	Never/ Rarely	Sometimes	Often/ Very Freq.
Copy text without citation	71	19	10
Copy paper without citation	91	5	3
Request paper to hand in	90	5	2
Purchase paper to hand in	91	6	3

Source: Scanlon, Patrick M., and David R. Neumann. "Internet Plagiarism Among College Students." *Journal of College Student Development* 43.3 (2002): 379.

Figure 12.2 Example of format for a table

Handling Titles. The MLA guidelines about handling titles are, as the most recent *Handbook* observes, "strict." The general rule is that the writer should capitalize the first letters of all principal words in a title, including any that follow hyphens. The exceptions are articles (*a, an*, and *the*), prepositions (*for, of, in, to*), co-ordinating conjunctions (*and, or, but, for*), and the use of *to* in infinitives. These exceptions apply *only if the words appear in the middle of a title*; capitalize them if they appear at the beginning or end.

The rules for underlining a title or putting it in quotation marks are as follows:

1. *Italicize the Title* if it is a book, play, pamphlet, film, magazine, TV program, CD, audiocassette, newspaper, or work of art.
2. "Put the Title in Quotes" if it is an article in a newspaper, magazine, or encyclopedia; a short story; a poem; an episode of a TV program; a song; a lecture; or a chapter or essay in a book.

Here are some examples:

The Curious Researcher (Book)

English Online: The Student's Guide to the Internet (CD-ROM)

"Once More to the Lake" (Essay)

Historic Boise: An Introduction into the Architecture of Boise, Idaho (Book)

"Psychotherapy" (Encyclopedia article)

Idaho Statesman (Newspaper)

"One Percent Initiative Panned" (Newspaper article)

Under the new MLA guidelines, the underlining of titles is out and the use of italics is in. Now, for instance, your Works Cited page would list the book title Bombproof Your Horse as *Bombproof Your Horse*. (And yes, that's horse not house.)

Language and Style

Names. Though it may seem as if you're on familiar terms with some of the authors you cite by the end of your research project, it's not a good idea to call them by their first names. Typically, initially give the full names of people you cite, and then only their last names if you mention them again in your essay.

Ellipsis Dots. Those are the three (always three) dots that indicate you've left out a word, phrase, or even whole section of a quoted passage. It's often wise to do this because you want to emphasize only certain parts of a quotation rather than burden your reader with unnecessary information, but be careful to preserve the basic intention and idea of the author's original statement. The ellipsis dots can come at the beginning of a quotation, in the middle, or at the end, depending where it is you've omitted material. The accepted format for using ellipsis dots is to enclose them in brackets. For example,

"After the publication of a controversial picture that shows, for example, either

dead or grieving victims..., readers, in telephone calls and in letters to the edi-

tor, often attack the photographer for being tasteless...."

Quotations. Quotations that run more than four lines long should be blocked, or indented ten spaces from the left margin. The quotation should be double-spaced and quotation marks should be omitted. In an exception from the usual convention, the parenthetical citation is placed *outside* the period at the end of the quotation. A colon is a customary way to introduce a blocked quotation. For example,

Chris Sherman and Gary Price, in *The Invisible Web*, contend that much of the

Internet, possibly most, is beyond the reach of researchers who use conventional

search engines:

  The problem is that vast expanses of the Web are completely invisible to

  general-purpose search engines like AltaVista, HotBot, and Google. Even

  worse, this "Invisible Web" is in all likelihood growing significantly

  faster than the visible Web that you're familiar with. It's not that search

  engines and Web directories are "stupid" or even badly engineered.

  Rather, they simply can't "see" millions of high quality resources that

  are available exclusively on the Invisible Web. So what is this Invisible

  Web and why aren't search engines doing anything about it to make it

  visible? (xxi)

Preparing the Works Cited Page

The Works Cited page ends the paper. Several other lists of sources may also appear at the end of a research paper. An Annotated List of Works Cited not only lists the sources used in the paper but also includes a brief description of each. A Works Consulted list includes sources that may or may not have been cited in the paper but shaped your thinking. A Content Notes page, keyed to superscript numbers in the text of the paper, lists short commentaries or asides that are significant but not central enough to the discussion to be included in the text of the paper.

The Works Cited page is the workhorse of most college papers. The other source lists are used less often. Works Cited is essentially an alphabetical listing of all the sources you quoted, paraphrased, or summarized in your paper. If you have used MLA format for citing sources, your paper has numerous parenthetical references to authors and page numbers. The Works Cited page provides complete information on each source cited in the text for the reader who wants

WHAT'S NEW WITH MLA CITATIONS?

The most important changes in the seventh edition of the *MLA Handbook* (2009) include the following:

- *No more URLs.* For the most part, it's no longer necessary to include the Web addresses of sources you found online.

- *Add medium of publication.* Now you need to indicate the form in which you found your source. In most cases, that will either be "Print" or "Web."

- *Italics instead of underlining.* Now the titles of independent works like books, magazines, and journals are italicized.

- *Include volume and issue numbers.* Whenever you cite a journal article, both should be included.

The New Look MLA Citation

Here's what a citation for an online document might look like:

Keim, Brandon. "Will Obama Save America's Giant, Smelly Worm?"

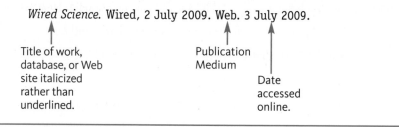

Wired Science. Wired, 2 July 2009. Web. 3 July 2009.

Title of work,
database, or Web
site italicized
rather than
underlined.

Publication
Medium

Date
accessed
online.

to know. (In APA format, this page is called References and is only slightly different in how items are listed.)

If you've been careful about collecting complete bibliographic information—author, title, editor, edition, volume, place, publisher, date, page numbers—then preparing your Works Cited page will be easy. If you've recorded that information on notecards, all you have to do is put them in alphabetical order and then transcribe them into your paper. If you've been careless about collecting that information, you may need to take a hike back to the library.

Format

Alphabetizing the List. Works Cited follows the text of your paper on a separate page. After you've assembled complete information about each source you've cited, put the sources in alphabetical order by the last name of the author. If the work has multiple authors, use the last name of the first listed. If the source has no author, then alphabetize it by the first key word of the title. If you're citing more than one source by a single author, you don't need to repeat the name for each source; simply place three hyphens followed by a period (- - -.) for the author's name in subsequent listings.

Indenting and Spacing.   Type the first line of each entry flush left, and indent subsequent lines of that entry (if any) five spaces. Double-space between each line and each entry. For example:

Works Cited

Greeley, Alexandra. "No Tan Is a Safe Tan." *Nutrition Health Review: The*

    Consumer's Medical Journal 59.3 (Summer 1991): 14–15. Print.

Hayes, Jean L. "Are You Assessing for Melanoma?" *RN* 66.2 (Feb. 2003): 36–40.

    Print.

Holick, Michael F. "Vitamin D—The Underrated Essential." *Life Extension* 9.4 (Apr.

    2003): 46–48. Print.

Johnson, Rheta Grimsley. "The Rural South These Days Has More Tanning Salons Than

    John Deeres." *Atlanta Journal-Constitution* 23 Apr. 2000, home ed.: M1. Print.

"Just the Facts Stats." *36 Expose* 17 Sept. 2003. Web. 6 Oct. 2005.

"The Light Touch." *Total Health* 14.3 (June 1992): 43. Print.

McLaughlin, Patricia. "Dying for a Tan This Summer?" *St. Louis Post-Dispatch* 15

    June 1995: 02. Print.

Reinhold, Vieth. "Vitamin D Nutrition and Its Potential Health Benefits for Bone,

    Cancer and Other Conditions." *Journal of Nutritional and Environmental*

    Medicine 11.5 (2001): 275–91. Print.

"Sun Tanning." *Cool Nurse 2000–2003* 18 June 2003. Web. 6 Oct. 2005.

Vid, Da. "Sound and Light: Partners in Healing and Transformation." *Share Guide*

    5.2 (Winter 1994): 20–21. Print.

Vogel, Phillip J. "A New Light on Vitamin D." *Life Extension* 9.4 (Apr. 2003):

    40–46. Print.

Citing Books.   You usually need three pieces of information to cite a book: the name of the author or authors, the title, and the publication information. Occasionally, other information is required. The *MLA Handbook*[2] lists this additional information in the order it would appear in the citation. Remember, any single entry will include a few of these things, not all of them. Use whichever are relevant to the source you're citing.

---

[2]Joseph Gibaldi, *MLA Handbook for Writers of Research Papers,* 7th ed. (New York: MLA, 2009).

1. Name of the author
2. Title of the book (or part of it)
3. Number of edition used
4. Number of volume used
5. Name of the series
6. Where published, by whom, and the date
7. Page numbers used
8. The publication medium, usually "Print."

Each piece of information in a citation is followed by a period and one space (not two).

Title. Titles of books are italicized, with the first letters of all principal words capitalized, including those in any subtitles. Titles that are not italicized are usually those of pieces found within larger works, such as poems and short stories in anthologies. These titles are set off by quotation marks. Titles of religious works (the Bible, the Qur'an, etc.) are neither underlined nor enclosed within quotation marks. (See the guidelines in the earlier "Handling Titles" section.)

Edition. If a book doesn't indicate an edition number, then it's probably a first edition, a fact you don't need to cite. Look on the title page. Signal an edition like this: *2nd ed., 3rd ed.*, and so on.

Publication Place, Publisher, and Date. Look on the title page to find out who published the book. Publishers' names are usually shortened in the Works Cited list: for example, *St. Martin's Press Inc.* is shortened to *St. Martin's*.

It's sometimes confusing to know what to cite about the publication place, because several cities are often listed on the title page. Cite the first.

The date a book is published is usually indicated on the copyright page. If several dates or several printings by the same publisher are listed, cite the original publication date. However, if the book is a revised edition, give the date of that edition. One final variation: If you're citing a book that's a reprint of an original edition, give both dates. For example:

Stegner, Wallace. *Recapitulation*. 1979. Lincoln: U of Nebraska P, 1986. Print.

This book was first published in 1979 and then republished in 1986 by the University of Nebraska Press.

Page Numbers. You don't usually list page numbers of a book. The parenthetical reference in your paper specifies that. But if you use only part of a book—an introduction or an essay—list the appropriate page numbers following the publication date. Use periods to set off the page numbers. If the author or editor of the entire work is also the author of the introduction or essay you're citing, list her by last name only the second time you cite her. For example:

> Lee, L. L., and Merrill Lewis. Preface. *Women, Women Writers, and the West*. Ed.
>
> > Lee and Lewis. Troy, MI: Whitston, 1980. v–ix. Print.

Publication Medium. A recent update to the MLA's guidelines now requires that you include the type of source. In most cases, a book citation will end with the word "Print." An online book would end with "Web."

Sample Book Citations
A BOOK BY ONE AUTHOR

> Keen, Sam. *Fire in the Belly*. New York: Bantam, 1991. Print.
>
> *In-Text Citation:* (Keen 101)

A BOOK BY TWO AUTHORS

> Ballenger, Bruce, and Barry Lane. *Discovering the Writer Within*.
>
> > Cincinnati: Writer's Digest, 1996. Print.
>
> *In-Text Citation:* (Ballenger and Lane 14)

A BOOK WITH MORE THAN THREE AUTHORS
If a book has more than three authors, list the first and substitute the term *et al.* for the others.

> Belenky, Mary Field, et al. *Women's Ways of Knowing*. New York: Basic Books,
>
> > 1973. Print.
>
> *In-Text Citation:* (Belenky et al. 21–30)

SEVERAL BOOKS BY THE SAME AUTHOR

> Baldwin, James. *Going to Meet the Man*. New York: Dell-Doubleday, 1948. Print.
>
> – – –. *Tell Me How Long the Train's Been Gone*. New York: Dell-Doubleday, 1968.
>
> > Print.
>
> *In-Text Citation:* (Baldwin, *Going* 34)

A COLLECTION OR ANTHOLOGY

> Crane, R. S., ed. *Critics and Criticism: Ancient and Modern*. Chicago: U of Chicago
>
> > P, 1952. Print.
>
> *In-Text Citation:* (Crane xx)

A WORK IN A COLLECTION OR ANTHOLOGY

The title of a work that is part of a collection but was originally published as a book should be italicized. Otherwise, the title of a work in a collection should be enclosed in quotation marks.

Bahktin, Mikhail. *Marxism and the Philosophy of Language*. *The Rhetorical Tradition*. Ed.

Patricia Bizzell and Bruce Herzberg. New York: St. Martin's, 1990. 928–44. Print.

In-Text Citation: (Bahktin 929–31)

Jones, Robert F. "Welcome to Muskie Country." *The Ultimate Fishing Book*. Ed. Lee

Eisenberg and DeCourcy Taylor. Boston: Houghton, 1981. 122–34. Print.

In-Text Citation: (Jones 131)

AN INTRODUCTION, PREFACE, FOREWORD, OR PROLOGUE

Scott, Jerie Cobb. Foreword. *Writing Groups: History, Theory, and Implications*. By

Ann Ruggles Gere. Carbondale: Southern Illinois UP, 1987. ix–xi. Print.

In-Text Citation: (Scott x-xi)

Rich, Adrienne. Introduction. *On Lies, Secrets,and Silence*. By Rich. New York:

Norton, 1979. 9–18. Print.

In-Text Citation: (Rich 12)

A BOOK WITH NO AUTHOR

American Heritage Dictionary. 3rd ed. Boston: Houghton, 1994. Print.

In-Text Citation: (*American Heritage Dictionary* 444)

AN ENCYLOPEDIA

"City of Chicago." *Encyclopaedia Britannica*. 1999 ed. Print.

In-Text Citation: ("City of Chicago" 397)

A BOOK WITH AN INSTITUTIONAL AUTHOR

Hospital Corporation of America. *Employee Benefits Handbook*. Nashville: HCA,

1990. Print.

In-Text Citation: (Hospital Corporation of America 5–7)

A BOOK WITH MULTIPLE VOLUMES

Include the number of volumes in the work between the title and publication information.

Baym, Nina, et al., eds. *The Norton Anthology of American Literature*. 5th ed.

2 vols. New York: Norton, 1998. Print.

In-Text Citation: (Baym et al. 2: 3)

If you use one volume of a multivolume work, indicate which one along with the page numbers, followed by the total number of volumes in the work.

Anderson, Sherwood. "Mother." *The Norton Anthology of American Literature*. Ed.

Nina Baym et al. 5th ed. Vol. 2. New York: Norton, 1998. 1115–31. 2 vols. Print.

In-Text Citation: (Anderson 1115)

A BOOK THAT IS NOT A FIRST EDITION

Check the title page to determine whether the book is *not* a first edition (2nd, 3rd, 4th, etc.); if no edition number is mentioned, assume it's the first. Put the edition number right after the title.

Ballenger, Bruce. *The Curious Researcher*. 6th ed. Boston: Longman, 2009. Print.

In-Text Citation: (Ballenger 194)

Citing the edition is necessary only for books that are *not* first editions. This includes revised editions (*Rev. ed.*) and abridged editions (*Abr. ed.*).

A BOOK PUBLISHED BEFORE 1900

For a book this old, it's usually unnecessary to list the publisher.

Hitchcock, Edward. *Religion of Geology*. Glasgow, 1851. Print.

In-Text Citation: (Hitchcock 48)

A TRANSLATION

Montaigne, Michel de. *Essays*. Trans. J. M. Cohen. Middlesex, England: Penguin,

1958. Print.

In-Text Citation: (Montaigne 638)

GOVERNMENT DOCUMENTS

Because of the enormous variety of government documents, citing them properly can be a challenge. Because most government documents do not name authors, begin an entry for such a source with the level of government (U.S. Government,

State of Illinois, etc., unless it is obvious from the title, followed by the sponsoring agency, the title of the work, and the publication information. Look on the title page to determine the publisher. If it's a federal document, then the *Government Printing Office* (abbreviated *GPO*) is usually the publisher.

United States. Bureau of the Census. *Statistical Abstract of the United States*.

Washington: GPO, 2005. Print.

In-Text Citation: (United States, Bureau of the Census 79–83)

A BOOK THAT WAS REPUBLISHED

A fairly common occurrence, particularly in literary study, is to find a book that was republished, sometimes many years after the original publication date. In addition, some books first appear in hardcover, and then are republished in paperback. To cite, put the original date of publication immediately after the book's title, and then include the more current publication date, as usual, at the end of the citation. Do it like so:

Didion, Joan. *Slouching toward Bethlehem*. 1968. New York: Farrar, 1992. Print.

In-Text Citation: (Didion 31)

AN ONLINE BOOK

Citing a book you found online requires more information than the usual citation for a book you can hold in your hands. As usual, include the author's name (if listed), an italicized title, and publication information. What you include in publication information depends on whether the text was published exclusively online or is also based in a print version. If it is only a digital book, include the date of electronic publication and the group or organization that sponsored it. If the book also appeared on paper, *you may* add the usual information (if provided) about the print version (city of publication, publisher, and date) if you think it would be helpful.

New MLA guidelines don't require you to include a URL for an online book. Instead, add the publication medium—"Web"— and end your citation with the date you accessed the work online.

Badke, William. *Research Strategies: Finding Your Way through the Information*

Fog. Lincoln, NE: Writers Club P, 2000. Web. 12 July 2009.

In-Text Citation: (Badke)

Citing Periodicals

Format. Citations for magazines, journals, newspapers, and the like aren't much different from citing books. MLA's 2009 update, however, introduced some significant changes in how you handle online periodicals (see the following table).

Print Periodical	Online Periodical
■ Name of author	■ Name of author
■ "Article title"	■ "Article title"
■ *Name of periodical*	■ *Name of Web site*
■ Volume (and issue number if a journal)	■ Publisher of Web site (if different from Web site name)
■ Date published	■ Date published
■ Publication medium: Print	■ Publication medium: Web
■ Page numbers	■ Page numbers (if available)
	■ Date of access

Author's Name. List the author(s) as you would for a book citation.

Article Title. Unlike book titles, article titles are usually enclosed in quotation marks.

Periodical Title. Italicize periodical titles, dropping introductory articles (Aegis, not The Aegis). If you're citing a newspaper your readers may not be familiar with, include in the title—enclosed in brackets but not italicized—the city in which it was published. For example:

Barber, Rocky. "DEQ Responds to Concerns About Weiser Feedlot." *Idaho*

 Statesman [Boise] 23 Apr. 2004: B1. Print.

Name of Web Site. If the name of the site is different from the title of the piece you're citing, include that name in italics.

Volume and Issue Numbers. Most scholarly journals have both. The latest MLA guidelines require that you include both in your citation. These will appear as weird decimals after the journal title. For example, the sixth volume and third issue of the journal *Diseases of the Dairy Cow* would be 6.3. Popular periodicals frequently don't have issue numbers and you're not required to use them.

Publisher of Web Site. Frequently, the publisher of a Web site is the same as its name. In that case, you can omit the publisher. But the name of the site's sponsor isn't always obvious. Try looking at the bottom of the page or click on the "About Us" link if there is one. If the publisher is unclear include *n.p.* (for "no publisher") in your citation. If you do include a publisher's name, don't italicize it.

Date. When citing popular periodicals, include the day, month, and year of the issue you're citing—in that order—following the periodical name. Academic journals are a little different. Because the volume number indicates when the journal was published within a given year, just indicate that year. Put it in parentheses following the volume number and before the page numbers (see examples following).

Page Numbers. Include the page numbers of the article at the end of the citation, followed by a period. Just list the pages of the entire article, omitting abbreviations such as *p.* or *pp.* It's common for articles in newspapers and popular magazines *not* to run on consecutive pages. In that case, indicate the page on which the article begins, followed by a " + " (*12+*).

Newspaper pagination can be peculiar. Some papers wed the section (usually a letter) with the page number (*A4*); other papers simply begin numbering anew in each section. Most, however, paginate continuously. See the sample citations for newspapers that follow for how to deal with these peculiarities.

Online sources, which often have no pagination at all, present special problems. For guidance on how to handle them, see the "Citing Online Databases" section.

Publication Medium. Indicate the form in which you found the periodical, usually either "Print" or "Web."

Date of Access. If you did find the journal or magazine online, end your citation with the date you first accessed it.

Sample Periodical Citations
A MAGAZINE ARTICLE

Elliot, Carl. "The New Drug Pushers." *Atlantic Monthly* Apr. 2006: 82–93. Print.

In-Text Citation: (Elliot 92)

Williams, Patricia J. "Unimagined Communities." *Nation* 3 May 2004: 14. Print.

In-Text Citation: (Williams 14)

Citations for magazines that you find online should also include the publication medium ("Web") and the date you accessed the material. For example,

Kaufman, Ken. "Stopover Country." *Audubon Magazine* May-June 2009.

Web. 1 July 2009.

In-Text Citation: (Kaufman)

Notice that both the Web site's name and its publisher are included in the online article below.

Schoen, John W. "Jobless Consumers Will Hold Up Recovery." *Msnbc.com.*

Microsoft, 2 July 2009. Web. 3 July 2009.

In-Text Citation: (Schoen)

A JOURNAL ARTICLE

There's a good chance that you found a journal article using your library's online database. If so, include the database name, italicized, in your citation. Remember to also include the volume and issue number whenever you cite any journal.

Here's an article from a library database.

Niservich, P. M. "Training Tips for Vegetarian Athletes." *IDEA Fitness Journal* 6.4

   (2009). *Physical Education Index.* Web. 2 July 2009.

In-Text Citation: (Niservich)

Here is sample citation for an article in print:

Allen, Rebecca E., and J. M. Oliver. "The Effects of Child Maltreatment on

   Language Development." *Child Abuse and Neglect* 6.1 (1982): 299–305. Print.

In-Text Citation: (Allen and Oliver 299–300)

A NEWSPAPER ARTICLE

Some newspapers have several editions (morning edition, late edition, national edition), and each may feature different articles. If an edition is listed on the masthead, include it in the citation.

Mendels, Pamela. "Internet Access Spreads to More Classrooms." *New York Times* 1

   Dec. 1999, morning ed.: C1+. Print.

In-Text Citation: (Mendels C1)

Some papers begin numbering pages anew in each section. In that case, include the section number if it's not part of pagination.

Brooks, James. "Lobsters on the Brink." *Portland Press* 29 Nov. 2005, sec. 2: 4. Print.

In-Text Citation: (Brooks 4)

The decline of print newspapers means you are more likely to find an article online. Since these often lack page numbers, you can omit them; but don't forget to include the Web site's name, publisher (if different), and the date you accessed the article.

Opel, Richard A. "U.S. Marines Try to Take Afghan Valley from Taliban."

   NYTimes.com. New York Times, 2 July 2009. Web. 3 July 2009.

In-Text Citation: (Opel)

AN ARTICLE WITH NO AUTHOR

"The Understanding." *New Yorker* 2 Dec. 1991: 34–35. Print.

In-Text Citation: ("Understanding" 35)

AN EDITORIAL

"Downward Mobility." Editorial. *New York Times* 27 Aug. 2006: 31. Print.

In-Text Citation: ("Downward" 31)

A LETTER TO THE EDITOR

Boulay, Harvey. Letter. *Boston Globe* 30 Aug. 2006: 14. Print.

In-Text Citation: (Boulay 14)

A letter to the editor you find online would be cited like this:

Willett, Catherine. "Go Ahead and Test but Spare the Animals." *NYTimes.com.*

New York Times, 2 July 2009. Web. 2 July 2009.

In-Text Citation: (Willett)

A REVIEW

Page, Barbara. Rev. of *Allegories of Cinema: American Film in the Sixties,* by

David E. James. *College English* 54 (1992): 945–54. Print.

In-Text Citation: (Page 945–46)

AN ABSTRACT

Edwards, Rob. "Air-Raid Warning." *New Scientist* 14 Aug. 1999: 48–49. Abstract.

MasterFILE Premier. Web. 1 May 2002.

In-Text Citation: (Edwards)

The following citation is from another useful source of abstracts, the *Dissertation Abstracts International.* In this case, the citation is from the print version of the index.

McDonald, James C. "Imitation of Models in the History of Rhetoric: Classical,

Belletristic, and Current-Traditional." U of Texas, Austin. *DAI* 48 (1988):

2613A. Print.

In-Text Citation: (McDonald 2613A)

Citing Nonprint and Other Sources
AN INTERVIEW

If you conducted the interview yourself, list your subject's name first, indicate what kind of interview it was (telephone, e-mail, or personal interview), and provide the date.

Kelley, Karen. Personal interview. 1 Sept. 2006.

In-Text Citation: (Kelley)

Or avoid parenthetical reference altogether by mentioning the subject's name in the text: According to Lonny Hall, . . .

If you're citing an interview done by someone else (perhaps from a book or article) and the title does not indicate that it was an interview, you should, after the subject's name, include *Interview*. Always begin the citation with the subject's name.

Stegner, Wallace. Interview. *Conversations with Wallace Stegner*. By Richard

Eutlain and Wallace Stegner. Salt Lake: U of Utah P, 1990. Print.

In-Text Citation: (Stegner 22)

If there are other works by Stegner on the Works Cited page.

(Stegner, *Conversations* 22)

As radio and TV interview programs are increasingly archived on the Web, these can be a great source of material for a research essay. In the following example, the interview was on a transcript I ordered from the Fresh Air Web site. Note that the national network, National Public Radio, *and* the local affiliate that produced the program, WHYY, are included in the citation along with the air date.

Mairs, Nancy. Interview by Terry Gross. *Fresh Air*. Radio. NPR. WHYY, Philadelphia.

7 June 1993.

In-Text Citation: (Mairs)

The following citation is for an interview published on the Web. The second date listed is the date of access.

Messner, Tammy Faye Bakker. Interview. *The Well Rounded Interview*. Well Rounded

Entertainment. Aug. 2000. 14 July 2002. Web.

In-Text Citation: (Messner)

SURVEYS, QUESTIONNAIRES, AND CASE STUDIES

If you conducted the survey or case study, list it under your name and give it an appropriate title.

Ball, Helen. "Internet Survey." Boise State U, 2006.

In-Text Citation: (Ball)

RECORDINGS

Generally, list a recording by the name of the performer and underline the title. Also include the recording company, catalog number, and year. (If you don't know the year, use the abbreviation *n.d.*)

Orff, Carl. *Carmina Burana*. Cond. Seiji Ozawa. Boston Symphony. RCA, 6533–2-RG,

n.d. CD.

In-Text Citation: (Orff)

TELEVISION AND RADIO PROGRAMS

List the title of the program (italicized), the station, and the broadcast date. If the episode has a title, list that first in quotation marks. You may also want to include the name of the narrator or producer after the title.

All Things Considered. Interview with Andre Dubus. NPR. WBUR, Boston. Radio.

12 Dec. 1990.

In-Text Citation: (All Things Considered)

ONLINE AUDIO OR VIDEO

Sarah Palin 20/20 Interview with Charlie Gibson, Part 2/4. YouTube. YouTube,

12 Sept. 2008. Web. 3 July 2009.

In-Text Citation: (Sarah Palin 20/20 Interview)

"Bad Bank." *This American Life*. Prod. Ira Glass. *NPR*. Chicago Public Radio,

27 Feb. 2009. Web. 3 July 2009.

In-Text Citation: ("Bad Bank")

BLOG

O'Brien, Terence. "EPA May Have Suppressed Global Warming Study." *Switched*.

AOL News, 2 July 2009. Web. 3 July 2009.

In-Text Citation: (O'Brien)

PODCAST

Kermode, Mark. "Drag Me to Hell." *5 Live*. BBC Radio, 12 May 2009. Web. 3 July 2009.

In-Text Citation: (Kermode)

WIKI

"Emily Dickinson." *Wikipedia*. Wikipedia Foundation, 2009. Web. 3 July 2009.

In-Text Citation: ("Emily Dickinson")

FILMS, VIDEOTAPES, AND DVD

Begin with the title (italicized), followed by the director, the distributor, and the year. You may also include names of writers, performers, or producers. End with the date and any other specifics about the characteristics of the film or videotape that may be relevant (length and size).

Saving Private Ryan. Dir. Steven Spielberg. Perf. Tom Hanks, Tom Sizemore, and

Matt Damon. Videocassette. Paramount, 1998. DVD.

In-Text Citation: (Saving)

You can also list a video or film by the name of a contributor you'd like to emphasize.

Capra, Frank, dir. *It's a Wonderful Life*. Perf. Jimmy Stewart and Donna Reed. RKO

Pictures, 1946. Film.

In-Text Citation: (Capra)

ARTWORK

List each work by artist. Then cite the title of the work (italicized) and where it's located (institution and city). If you've reproduced the work from a published source, include that information as well.

Homer, Winslow. *Casting for a Rise*. Hirschl and Adler Galleries, New York.

Ultimate Fishing Book. Ed. Lee Eisenberg and DeCourcy Taylor. Boston:

Houghton, 1981. Print.

In-Text Citation: (Homer 113)

LECTURES AND SPEECHES

List each by the name of the speaker, followed by the title of the address (if any) in quotation marks, the name of the sponsoring organization, the location, and the date. Only indicate what kind of address it was (*Lecture*, *Speech*, etc.) when no title is given.

Naynaha, Siskanna. "Emily Dickinson's Last Poems." Sigma Tau Delta, Boise, ID.

15 Nov. 1999. Lecture.

Avoid the need for parenthetical citation by mentioning the speaker's name in your text.

PAMPHLETS

Cite a pamphlet as you would a book.

New Challenges for Wilderness Conservationists. Washington, DC: Wilderness

Society, 2006. Print.

In-Text Citation: (New Challenges)

A Sample Paper in MLA Style. Most of the student essays in *The Curious Writer* use MLA style. For a fully documented research paper, see Gordon Seirup's essay, "College Dating," in Chapter 10.

APA DOCUMENTATION GUIDELINES

The American Psychological Association's (APA) citation conventions are the other dominant approach to acknowledging sources. If you're headed for courses in the social sciences, then this is the system you'll use. It's no harder than the MLA; in fact, the two systems are quite similar. Both use parenthetical citations. Both organize the bibliography (or References page) in very similar ways. But there are a few significant differences, some of which are summarized in the accompanying table. Detailed descriptions of the APA system then follow.

How the Essay Should Look

Page Format. Papers should be double spaced, with at least one-inch margins on all sides. Number all pages consecutively, beginning with the title page; put the page number in the upper right corner. Above or five spaces to the left of the page number, place an abbreviated title of the paper on every page, in case pages get separated. As a rule, the first line of all paragraphs of text should be indented five to seven spaces.

MLA VERSUS APA: SOME BASIC DIFFERENCES

MLA Approach	APA Approach
(Author page #)—Example:	**(Author, year)—Example:**
According to Ackerman, there is an infatuation chemical (164).	According to Ackerman (1994), there is an infatuation chemical.
Usually no title page.	Usually title page and abstract. An abstract is a short summary of the paper's content, always less than 120 words in APA style.
Pagination uses writer's last name and page number. For example:	Pagination uses running head and page number. A "running head" is the paper's abbreviated title. For example:
Smith 5	EXPORTING JOBS 5
Figures and tables included within the paper.	Figures and tables included in section at the end of the paper.
Bibliography called Works Cited page.	Bibliography called References page.

Title Page. Unlike a paper in MLA style, an APA-style paper has a separate title page, containing the following information: the title of the paper, the author, and the author's affiliation (e.g., what university she is from). Each line of information should be centered and double spaced. (See Figure 12.3.) At the top of the title page, flush left and in uppercase letters, you may also include a *running head*, or an abbreviation of the title (fifty characters or less, including spaces). A page header, which uses the first two or three words of the title followed by the page number, begins on the second page. This is different from the running head, which tends to be longer and appears only on the title page.

Abstract. Although it's not always required, many APA-style papers include a short abstract (no longer than 120 words) following the title page. (See Figure 12.4.) An abstract is essentially a short summary of the paper's contents. This is a key feature, because it's usually the first thing a reader encounters. The abstract should include statements about what problem or question the paper examines and what approach it follows; the abstract should also cite the thesis and significant findings. Type *Abstract* at the top of the page. Type the abstract text in a single block, without indenting.

Body of the Paper. The body of the paper begins with the centered title, followed by a double space and then the text. A page header (usually an abbreviated title and "3" if the paper has a title page and abstract) should appear in the upper right corner. (See Figure 12.5.)

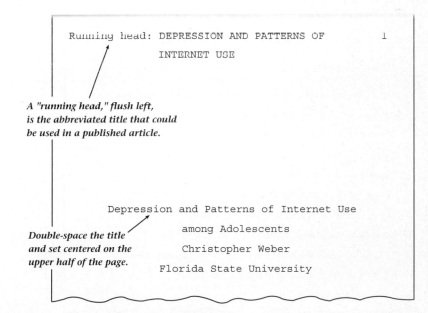

Figure 12.3   Title page in APA style

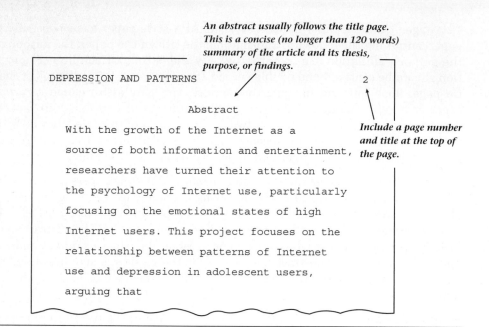

An abstract usually follows the title page. This is a concise (no longer than 120 words) summary of the article and its thesis, purpose, or findings.

DEPRESSION AND PATTERNS   2

Abstract

With the growth of the Internet as a source of both information and entertainment, researchers have turned their attention to the psychology of Internet use, particularly focusing on the emotional states of high Internet users. This project focuses on the relationship between patterns of Internet use and depression in adolescent users, arguing that

Include a page number and title at the top of the page.

Figure 12.4   The abstract page

You may find that you want to use headings within your paper. If your paper is fairly formal, some headings might be prescribed, such as *Introduction, Method, Results*, and *Discussion*. Or create your own heads to clarify the organization of your paper.

DEPRESSION AND PATTERNS   3

Depression and Patterns of Internet Use among Adolescents

Before Johnny Beale's family got a new computer in August 2002, the sixteen-year-old high school student estimated that he spent about twenty minutes a day online, mostly checking his e-mail. Within months, however, Beale's time at the computer tripled, and he admitted that he spent most of his time playing games. At first, his family noticed

Center the title of the paper and double-space to begin the body of the text.

Figure 12.5   The body of the paper in APA style

WHAT'S NEW WITH APA CITATIONS?

The publication of the sixth edition of APA's *Publication Manual* in 2009 featured some changes you should know about.

- A stronger emphasis on the Digital Object Identifier (DOI), instead of a URL, as a way for readers to retrieve cited documents (see a discussion of this on page 532).
- For documents with no DOI, include the URL but if you retrieved them from a database you no longer need to include its name.
- The hierarchy of headings is simpler (see below).
- Put two spaces, rather than one, following the period at the end of a sentence.

The New Look of APA Citations

The most significant changes are in references to electronic sources. For example,

King, L. A, Borton, C. M., Hicks, J. A., & Drigotas, S. M. (2007). Ghosts, UFOs, and

magic: Positive affect and the experiential system. *Journal of Personality and*

Social Psychology, 95(5), 905–919. doi: 10.1037/0022-3514.92.5.905.

Though this article is from the online database *PsychARTICLES,* it's no longer necessary to include the database name.

If present, the "Digital Object Identifier" (DOI) is now included instead of a URL for an online document.

If you use headings, the APA recommends a hierarchy like this:

Centered, Boldface, Uppercase and Lowercase

Flush Left, Boldface, Upper and Lowercase Heading

Indented, boldface, lowercase except first letter of first word

Indented, boldface, italicized, lowercase except first letter of first word

Indented, italicized, lowercase except first letter of first word.

Papers rarely use all five levels of headings; two or three is probably most common, particularly in student papers. When you use multiple levels, always use them consecutively. In other words, a Level 1 heading would always be followed by a Level 2 heading (if there is one).

For example,

The Intelligence of Crows

Current Understandings of Crow Intelligence

References Page. All sources cited in the body of the paper are listed alphabetically by author (or title, if anonymous) on the page titled References. See Figure 12.6. This list should begin a new page. Each entry is double spaced; begin each entry flush left, and indent subsequent lines five to seven spaces. Explanation of how to cite various sources in the references follows in the "Preparing the References List" section.

Appendix. This is a seldom-used feature of an APA-style paper, although you might find it helpful for presenting specific or tangential material that isn't central to the discussion in the body of your paper: a detailed description of a device described in the paper, a copy of a blank survey, or the like. Each item should begin on a separate page and be labeled *Appendix*, followed by *A, B*, and so on, consecutively, if there is more than one item.

Notes. Several kinds of notes might be included in a paper. The most common is *content notes*, or brief commentaries by the writer keyed to superscript numbers in the body of the text. These notes are useful for discussion of key points that are relevant but might be distracting if explored in the text of your paper. Present all notes, numbered consecutively, on a page titled Endnotes. Each note should be double spaced. Begin each note with the appropriate superscript number, keyed to the text. Indent each first line five to seven spaces; consecutive lines run the full page measure.

Tables and Figures. The final section of an APA-style paper features tables and figures mentioned in the text. Tables should all be double spaced. Type a table

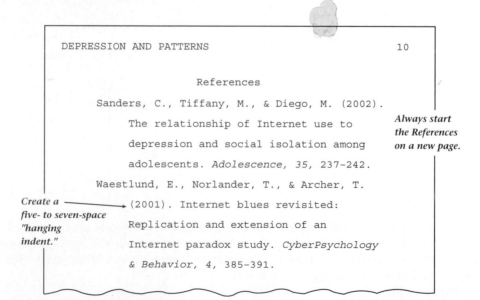

Figure 12.6   The References page

number at the top of the page, flush left. Number tables *Table 1, Table 2*, and so on, corresponding to the order in which they are mentioned in the text. A table may also include a title. Each table should begin on a separate page.

Figures (illustrations, graphs, charts, photographs, drawings) are handled similarly to tables. Each should be titled *Figure* and numbered consecutively. Captions may be included, but all should be typed on a separate page, clearly labeled *Figure Captions*, and listed in order. For example:

Figure Captions

Figure 1. A photograph taken in the 1930s by Dorothea Lange.

Figure 2. Edward Weston took a series of green pepper photographs like this. This

is titled "No. 35."

Language and Style. The APA is comfortable with the italics and bold functions of modern word processors, and underlining is a thing of the past. The guidelines for *italicizing* call for its use when writing the following:

- The title of books, periodicals, and publications that appear on microfilm.

- When using new or specialized terms, but only the first time you use them (e.g., "the authors' *paradox study* of Internet users...").

- When citing a phrase, letter, or word as an example (e.g., "the second *a* in *separate* can be remembered by remembering the word *rat*").

The APA calls for quotation marks around the title of an article or book chapter when mentioned in your essay.

Been nagged all your life by the question of whether to spell out numbers or use numerals in APA style? Here, finally, is the answer: numbers less than 10 that aren't precise measurements should be spelled out, and numbers 10 or more should be digits.

Citing Sources in Your Essay

When the Author Is Mentioned in the Text. The author/date system is pretty uncomplicated. If you mention the name of the author in text, simply place the year his work was published in parentheses immediately after his name. For example:

Herrick (1999) argued that college testing was biased against minorities.

When the Author Isn't Mentioned in the Text. If you don't mention the author's name in the text, then include that information parenthetically. For example:

A New Hampshire political scientist (Sundberg, 2004) recently studied the state's

presidential primary.

Note that the author's name and the year of her work are separated by a comma.

When to Cite Page Numbers. If the information you're citing came from specific pages, chapters, or sections of a source, that information may also be included in the parenthetical citation. Including page numbers is essential when quoting a source. For example:

The first stage of language acquisition is called "caretaker speech" (Moskowitz,

1985, pp. 50–51), in which children model their parents' language.

The same passage might also be cited this way if the author's name is mentioned in the text:

Moskowitz (1985) observed that the first stage of language acquisition is called

"caretaker speech" (pp. 50–51), in which children model their parents' language.

A Single Work by Two or More Authors. When a work has two authors, always mention them both whenever you cite their work in your paper. For example:

Allen and Oliver (1998) observed many cases of child abuse and concluded that

maltreatment inhibited language development.

If a source has more than two authors but less than six, mention them all the first time you refer to their work. However, any subsequent references can include the surname of the first author followed by the abbreviation *et al.* When citing works with six or more authors, *always* use the first author's surname and *et al.*

A Work with No Author. When a work has no author, cite an abbreviated title and the year. Place article or chapter titles in quotation marks, and *italicize* book titles. For example:

The editorial ("Sinking," 2006) concluded that the EPA was mired in bureaucratic

muck.

Two or More Works by the Same Author. Works by the same author are usually distinguished by the date; works are rarely published the same year. But if they are, distinguish among works by adding an *a* or *b* immediately following the year in the parenthetical citation. The reference list will also have these suffixes. For example:

Douglas's studies (1986a) on the mating habits of lobsters revealed that the

females are dominant. He also found that the female lobsters have the uncanny

ability to smell a loser (1986b).

This citation alerts readers that the information came from two studies by Douglas, both published in 1986.

An Institutional Author. When citing a corporation or agency as a source, simply list the year of the study in parentheses if you mention the institution in the text:

The Environmental Protection Agency (2000) issued an alarming report on ozone

pollution.

If you don't mention the institutional source in the text, spell it out in its entirety, along with the year. In subsequent parenthetical citations, you can abbreviate the name as long as the abbreviation will be understandable. For example:

A study (Environmental Protection Agency [EPA], 2000) predicted dire conse-

quences from continued ozone depletion.

And later:

Continued ozone depletion may result in widespread skin cancers (EPA, 2000).

Multiple Works in the Same Parentheses. Occasionally, you'll want to cite several works at once that speak to a topic you're writing about in your essay. Probably the most common instance is when you refer to the findings of several relevant studies, something that is a good idea as you try to establish a context for what has already been said about your research topic. For example,

A number of researchers have explored the connection between Internet use

and depression (Sanders, Field, & Diego, 2000; Waestlund, Norlander, & Archer,

2001).

When listing multiple authors within the same parentheses, order them as they appear in the references. Semicolons separate each entry.

Interviews, E-Mail, and Letters. Interviews and other personal communications are not listed in the references at the back of the paper, because they are not *recoverable data*, but they are parenthetically cited in the text. Provide the initials and surname of the subject (if not mentioned in the text), the nature of the communication, and the complete date, if possible.

Nancy Diamonti (personal communication, November 12, 1990) disagrees with

the critics of *Sesame Street*.

In a recent e-mail, Michelle Payne (personal communication, January 4, 2000)

complained that...

New Editions of Old Works. For reprints of older works, include both the year of the original publication and that of the reprint edition (or the translation).

Pragmatism as a philosophy sought connection between scientific study and real

people's lives (James, 1906/1978).

A Web Site. When referring to an *entire* Web site (see the following example), cite the address parenthetically in your essay. As for e-mail, it isn't necessary to include a citation for an entire Web site in your references list. However, you will cite online documents that contribute information to your paper (see the "Citing Electronic Sources" section).

One of the best sites for searching the so-called Invisible Web is the Librarians

Index to the Internet (http://www.lii.org).

Preparing the References List

All parenthetical citations in the body of the paper correspond to a complete listing of sources on the References page. The format for this section was described earlier (see the "References Page" section).

Order of Sources. List the references alphabetically by author or by the first key word of the title if there is no author. The only complication may be if you have several articles or books by the same author. If the sources weren't published in the same year, list them in chronological order, the earliest first. If the sources were published in the *same* year, include a lowercase letter to distinguish them. For example:

Lane, B. (1991a). Verbal medicine...

Lane, B. (1991b). Writing...

While the alphabetical principle—listing authors according to the alphabetical placement of their last names—works in most cases, there are a few variations you should be aware of.

- If you have several entries by the same author, list them by year of publication, beginning with the earliest.
- Because scholars and writers often collaborate, you may have several references in which an author is listed with several *different* collaborators. List these alphabetically using the second author's last name. For example,

Brown, M., & Nelson, A. (2002)

Brown, M., & Payne, M. (1999)

Order of Information. A reference to a periodical or book in APA style includes this information, in order: author, date of publication, article title, periodical title, and publication information.

Electronic sources include some additional information. If you're harvesting your books and articles online or from a library database, you need to cite in a way that makes it clear how readers can find the book or document. That seems simple, right? It isn't always. Typically, you include the URL for an online document in your citation, even if it's long and ugly. But URLs can change and they are vulnerable to transcription mistakes. To solve this problem, the APA created something call the Digital Object Identifier (see description on page 532). This is a number that is a permanent link to the document. But not all documents have them, and if not, use their URLs.

One other bit of information you usually include in a citation for an electronic document is the retrieval date, or exactly when you accessed the work online. This can be omitted, however, when the document you're citing is "archival." An archival copy is a final version, and it's usually the version that appeared in print.

Author. List all authors—last name, comma, and then initials. Invert all authors' names. Use commas to separate authors' names and add an ampersand (&) before the last author's name. When citing an edited book, list the editor(s) in place of the author, and add the abbreviation Ed. or Eds. in parentheses following the initials. End the list of names with a period.

Date. List the year the work was published, along with the date if it's a magazine or newspaper (see the following "Sample References" section), in parentheses, immediately after the last author's name. Add a period after the closing parenthesis.

Article or Book Title. APA style departs from MLA, at least with respect to periodicals. In APA style, only the first word of the article title is capitalized and appears without italics or quotation marks. Book titles are italicized; capitalize only the first word of the title and any subtitle. End all titles with periods.

Periodical Title and Publication Information. Italicize the complete periodical title; type it using both uppercase and lowercase letters. Add the volume number (if any), also italicized. Separate the title and volume number with a comma (e.g., *Journal of Mass Communication, 10,* 138–150). If each issue of the periodical starts with page 1, then also include the issue number in parentheses immediately after the volume number (see examples following). End the entry with the page numbers of the article. Use the abbreviation *p.* or *pp.* if you are citing a newspaper. Other APA-style abbreviations include the following:

chap	p. (pp.)
Ed./Eds. (Editor/Editors) ed. (edition)	Vol.
Rev. ed.	No.
2nd ed.	Pt.
Trans.	Suppl.

For books, list the city and state or country of publication (use postal abbreviations) and the name of the publisher; separate the city and publisher with a colon. End the citation with a period. The following cities do not require state or country abbreviations:

Baltimore	Amsterdam
Boston	Jerusalem
Chicago	London
Los Angeles	Milan
New York	Moscow
Philadelphia	Paris
San Francisco	Rome
	Stockholm
	Tokyo
	Vienna

Remember that the first line of each citation should begin flush left and all subsequent lines should be indented five to seven spaces. Double-space all entries.

Retrieval Date. If you're citing an electronic document, you often indicate when you accessed the book or article. This is important because online documents can change, and the retrieval date gives readers a "snapshot" of what version you were looking at when you did your research. Retrieval dates can be omitted when you're citing a permanent or "archival" version of the work.

DOI or URL. These are more ingredients for your alphabet soup. So readers can locate the electronic documents you're citing, you need to tell them where you found them. You frequently do this by including the URL. But more and more documents in the social sciences include something called the Digital Object Indentifier (DOI), a permanent link to the work. The DOI is often listed on the article's first page. It may also be hidden under the "Article" button that appears with the work on certain library databases.

Here's a summary of the similarities and differences in APA style when citing print and electronic journals and magazines:

Print Periodical	Electronic Periodical
■ Author(s)	■ Author(s)
■ (Date)	■ (Date)
■ Article title	■ Article title
■ Periodical title	■ Periodical title
■ Issue and volume number	■ Issue and volume number
■ Page numbers	■ Page numbers
	■ Retrieval date (unless archival)
	■ DOI (if available) or URL (if DOI unavailable)

Sample References: Articles

A JOURNAL ARTICLE

When citing an online article, include information about how readers can find it. Use the DOI, if available. For example,

> Mori, K., Ujiie, T., Smith, A., & Howlin P. (2009). Parental stress associated with
>
> caring for children with Asperger's syndrome. *Pediatrics International, 51*(3),
>
> 364–370. doi: 10.1111/j.1442-200X-2008.0278.x

In-Text Citation: (Mori, Smith, & Howlin, 2009) or (Mori et al., 2009) in subsequent citations. If authors are quoted, include page numbers.

If there is no DOI, include the document's URL.

> Wing, L. (1981). Asperger's syndrome: A clinical account. *Psychological Medicine*
>
> *11*(1), 115–129. Retrieved from http://search.ebscohost.com/login
>
> .aspx?direct=true&db=psyh&AN=1981-30537-001&site=ehost-live

In-Text Citation: (Wing, 1981)

Cite a print journal article like this:

> Blager, F. B. (1979). The effect of intervention on the speech and language of
>
> children. *Child Abuse and Neglect, 5,* 91–96.

In-Text Citation: (Blager, 1979)

If the author is mentioned in the text, just parenthetically cite the year: Blager (1979) stated that...

If the author is quoted, include the page number(s):

(Blager, 1979, p. 92)

A MAGAZINE ARTICLE

> Maya, P. (1981, December). The civilizing of Genie. *Psychology Today*, 28–34.

In-Text Citation: (Maya, 1981)

Maya (1981) observed that...

When citing a magazine article from a database, include the URL. Many databases include a "permanent link" to the article on the citation page. Use that if available. Notice also that the database name is no longer included.

> Horowitz, A. (July, 2008). My dog is smarter than your dog. *Discover magazine*
>
> 219(9), 71. Retrieved from http://search.ebscohost.com.libproxy.boisestate
>
> .edu/login.aspx?direct=true&db=aph&AN=32580478&site=ehost-live

In-Text Citation: (Horowitz, 2008). If quoting, include page numbers (Horowitz, 2008, p.71).

AN ARTICLE ON A WEB SITE
This article has no author so the citation begins with the title.

Enhancing male body image. (2006). *Nationaleatingdisorders.org.* Retrieved July 9, 2009, from http://www.nationaleatingdisorders.org/

In-Text Citation: ("Enhancing,"2006)

If quoting, include the page number(s): (Maya, 1981, p. 28)

A NEWSPAPER ARTICLE

Honan, W. (2004, January 24). The war affects Broadway. *New York Times,*

>   pp. C15–16.

In-Text Citation: (Honan, 2004)

Honan (2004) argued that...

Honan (2004) said that "Broadway is a battleground" (p. C15).

If there is no author, a common situation with newspaper articles, alphabetize using the first "significant word" in the article title. The parenthetical citation would use an abbreviation of the title in quotation marks, then the year.

There's a good chance that you'll find newspaper articles online. Here's how you cite them:

Jennings, D. (2009, July 7). With cancer, you can't hurry recovery. *The New York*

>   *Times.* Retrieved from http://www.nytimes.com

In-Text Citation: (Jennings, 2009)

Sample References: Books
A BOOK

Lukas, A. J. (1986). *Common ground: A turbulent decade in the lives of three*

>   *American families.* New York: Random House.

In-Text Citation: (Lukas, 1986)

According to Lukas (1986),...

If quoting, include the page number(s).

AN ONLINE BOOK
If you're citing an entire book you found online, include the URL. Sometimes, however, the Internet address may not lead to the work itself but information on

how to find it. In that case, use the phrase "Available from" rather than "Retrieved from." For example,

Suzuki, D. T. (1914). *A brief history of early Chinese philosophy.* Available from

http://www.archive.org/details/briefhistoryofea00suzuuoft

In-Text Citation: (Suzuki, 1914)

When citing a chapter from an online book, include a bit more information, including the name of the database (if any) from which you retrieved it.

Hollin, C.R. (2002). Criminal psychology. In Hollin, C.R., *Oxford handbook of*

criminology (pp. 144–174). Retrieved from Academic Research Premier database.

In-Text Citation: (Hollin, 2002)

A SOURCE MENTIONED BY ANOTHER SOURCE

Frequently you'll read an article that mentions another article you haven't read. Whenever possible, track down that original article and read it in its entirety. But when that's not possible, you need to make it clear that you know of the article and its findings or arguments indirectly. The APA convention for this is to use the expression *as cited in* parenthetically, followed by the author and date of the indirect source. For example, suppose you want to use some information from Eric Weiser's piece that you read about in Charlotte Jones's book. In your essay, you would write something like:

Weiser argues (as cited in Jones, 2002) that...

A BOOK OR ARTICLE WITH MORE THAN ONE AUTHOR

Rosenbaum, A., & O'Leary, D. (1978). Children: The unintended victims of marital

violence. *American Journal of Orthopsychiatry, 4,* 692–699.

In-Text Citation: (Rosenbaum & O'Leary, 1978)

Rosenbaum and O'Leary (1978) believed that...

If quoting, include the page number(s).

A BOOK OR ARTICLE WITH AN UNKNOWN AUTHOR

The politics of war. (2004, June 1). *New York Times,* p. 36.

In-Text Citation: ("Politics," 2004)

Or mention the source in the text:

In "The Politics of War" (2004), an editorialist compared Iraq to...

If quoting, provide page number(s) as well.

The Chicago manual of style (14th ed.). (1993). Chicago: University of Chicago
Press.

In-Text Citation: Chicago (Manual of Style, 1993)

According to the *Chicago Manual of Style* (1993),...

If quoting, include the page number(s).

A BOOK WITH AN INSTITUTIONAL AUTHOR

American Red Cross. (1999). *Advanced first aid and emergency care.* New York:
Doubleday.

In-Text Citation: (American Red Cross, 1999)

The book *Advanced First Aid and Emergency Care* (American Red Cross, 1999)
stated that...

If quoting, include the page number(s).

A BOOK WITH AN EDITOR

Crane, R. S. (Ed.). (1952). *Critics and criticism.* Chicago: University of Chicago Press.

In-Text Citation: (Crane, 1952)

In his preface, Crane (1952) observed that...

If quoting, include the page number(s).

A SELECTION IN A BOOK WITH AN EDITOR

McKeon, R. (1952). Rhetoric in the Middle Ages. In R. S. Crane (Ed.), *Critics and
criticism* (pp. 260–289). Chicago: University of Chicago Press.

In-Text Citation: (McKeon, 1952)

McKeon (1952) argued that...

If quoting, include the page number(s).

A REPUBLISHED WORK

James, W. (1978). *Pragmatism.* Cambridge, MA: Harvard University Press. (Original
work published 1907).

In-Text Citation: (James, 1907/1978)

According to William James (1907/1978), . . .

If quoting, include the page number(s).

AN ABSTRACT

The growth of online databases for articles has increased the availability of full-text versions or abstracts of articles. Although the full article is almost always best, sometimes an abstract alone contains some useful information. If the abstract was retrieved from a database or some other secondary source, include information about it. Aside from the name of the source, this information might involve the date, if different from the year of publication of the original article, an abstract number, or a page number. In the following example, the abstract was retrieved from an online database, Biological Abstracts.

Garcia, R. G. (2002). Evolutionary speed of species invasions. *Evolution, 56,*

661–668. Abstract retrieved from Biological Abstracts.

In-Text Citation: (Garcia, 2002), or Garcia (2002) argues that . . .

It isn't necessary to include information about the Weiser article in your references. Just cite the indirect source; in this case, that would be the Jones book.

A BOOK REVIEW

Dentan, R. K. (1989). A new look at the brain [Review of the book *The dreaming*

brain]. *Psychiatric Journal, 13,* 51.

In-Text Citation: (Dentan, 1989)

Dentan (1989) argued that . . .

If quoting, include the page number(s).

An online book review would include the same information below but with the review's URL and the phrase ("Retrieved from . . .").

ONLINE ENCYCLOPEDIA

Turner, B. S. (2007). Body and society. In G. Ritzer (Ed.), *Blackwell encyclopedia*

of sociology. Retrieved July 7, 2009, from http://blackwellreference.com

In-Text Citation: (Turner, 2007)

Since they are collaboratively written, Wikipedia articles have no single author. Usually, therefore, the citation will begin with the article title. For example,

Ticks (n.d.). Retrieved July 9, 2009 from Wikipedia: http://en.wikipedia.org/wiki/Ticks

In-Text Citation: ("Ticks," n.d.)

Sample References: Other
A GOVERNMENT DOCUMENT

> U.S. Bureau of the Census. (2004). *Statistical abstract of the United States*
>
> (126th ed.). Washington, DC: U.S. Government Printing Office.

> *In-Text Citation:* (U.S. Bureau of the Census, 2004)

> According to the U.S. Census Bureau (2004),...

> If quoting, include the page number(s).

A LETTER TO THE EDITOR

> Hill, A. C. (2006, February 19). A flawed history of blacks in Boston [Letter to
>
> the editor]. *The Boston Globe*, p. 22.

> *In-Text Citation:* (Hill, 2006)

> Hill (2006) complained that...

> If quoting, include page number(s).

A PUBLISHED INTERVIEW
Personal interviews are not cited in the References section of an APA-style paper, unlike published interviews. Here is a citation for a published interview:

> Cotton, P. (2004, April). [Interview with Jake Tule, psychic]. *Chronicles Magazine*,
>
> 24–28.

> *In-Text Citation:* (Cotton, 2004)

> Cotton (2004) noted that...

> If quoting, include the page number(s).

A FILM OR VIDEOTAPE

> Hitchcock, A. (Producer & Director). (1954). *Rear window* [Motion Picture].
>
> Los Angeles: MGM.

> *In-Text Citation:* (Hitchcock, 1954)

> In *Rear Window*, Hitchcock (1954)...

PODCAST, VIDEO, AND AUDIO

Shier, J. (Producer and Director). (2005). Saving the grizzly: One hair at a time. *Terrra:*

The nature of our world. Podcast retrieved from http://www.lifeonterra.com/

episode.php?id=1

In-Text Citation: (Shier, 2005)

Uhry, A. (2009, July 6). Private education in America. The economist. Podcast

retrieved from http://podcast.com/episode/40782102/5356/

In-Text Citation: (Uhry, 2009)

A TELEVISION PROGRAM

Burns, K. (Executive Producer). (1996). *The west* [Television broadcast]. New York

and Washington, DC: Public Broadcasting Service.

In-Text Citation: (Burns, 1996)

In Ken Burns's (1996) film, . . .

For an episode of a television series, use the scriptwriter as the author, and
provide the director's name after the scriptwriter. List the producer's name after
the episode.

Hopley, J. (Writer/Director), & Shannon, J. (Writer/Director). (2006). Buffalo

burrito/Parkerina [Television series episode]. In J. Lenz (Producer),

Mr. Meaty. New York: Nickelodeon.

In-Text Citation: (Hopley & Shannon, 2006)

Fans were appalled by the second episode, when Hopley and Shannon (2006) . . .

A MUSICAL RECORDING

Wolf, K. (1986). Muddy roads [Recorded by E. Clapton]. *On Gold in California* [CD].

Santa Monica, CA: Rhino Records. (1990).

In-Text Citation: (Wolf, 1986, track 5)

In Wolf's (1986) song, . . .

A COMPUTER PROGRAM

OmniPage Pro 14 (Version 14) [Computer software]. (2003). Peabody, MA: Scansoft.

In-Text Citation: (OmniPage Pro, Version 14, 2003)

Scansoft's new software, OmniPage Pro, (2003) is reputed...

DISCUSSION LISTS

Discussion lists abound on the Internet. They range from groups of flirtatious teenagers to those with a serious academic purpose. Although virtually all of these discussion lists are based on e-mail, they do vary a bit. The most useful lists for academic research tend to be e-mail discussion lists. Newsgroups, or Usenet groups, are extremely popular among more general Internet users. Various search engines can help you find these discussion groups on your topic. You can join or monitor the current discussion or, in some cases, search the archives for contributions that interest you. Google is a great search tool for newsgroups and includes an archive for many of them. *If there are no archives, don't include the citation in your references because the information isn't recoverable.* However, you may still cite these in your essay as personal communications.

The method of citation varies slightly if it's a newsgroup, an online forum, or an electronic mailing list. For example, a newsgroup posting would be cited like this:

Hord, J. (2002, July 11). Why do pigeons lift one wing up in the air? [Msg 5].

   Message archived at rec.pets.birds.pigeons

In-Text Citation: (Hord, 2002), or Hord asks (2002)...

Note that the citation includes the subject line of the message as the title, and the message number of the "thread" (the particular discussion topic). The prefix for this newsgroup is *rec*, which indicates the list is hobby oriented.

Electronic mailing lists would be cited this way:

Cook, D. (2002, July 19). Grammar and the teaching of writing. Message posted

   to the CompTalk electronic mailing list, archived at http://listserv.comptalk

   .boisestate.edu

In-Text Citation: (Cook, 2002), or According to Cook (2002)...

E-MAIL

E-mail is not cited in the list of references. But you should cite e-mail in the text of your essay. It should look like this:

In-Text Citation: Michelle Payne (personal communication, January 4, 2000) believes that PDAs are silly...

BLOG
Notice in the example that the blogger uses a screen name.

Rizaro. (7 July, 2009). Anxiety and suicide. Message posted to *HelptoHealth.co.cc*

A Sample Paper in APA Style. To see a documented student research paper in APA style, go to Kersti Harter's ethnographic essay "Beyond 'Gaydar' " on pages 378–387 in Chapter 9. Professional essays formatted using APA style include "Why Bother?" by Michael Pollan in Chapter 6 and "Pluralistic Ignorance and Hooking Up" by Tracy Lambert, Arnold Kahn, and Kevin Apple in Chapter 10.

USING WHAT YOU HAVE LEARNED

The main message you should take from this chapter is that if you don't make the effort to control your sources, your sources will control you, with results ranging from writing that fails to deliver on its promise to accidental plagiarism.

1. List three ways that you can control sources in a research essay so that they don't control you.

2. The concern about plagiarism is growing, and most blame the Internet. Do you agree with both of those premises—that plagiarism is a bigger problem today than ever before and that the Internet is the cause?

3. You won't always be required to cite sources for papers in other classes. In fact, you've probably noticed that some articles in more popular periodicals don't cite information at all, even though the work is clearly a product of research. How do you explain this?

Revision is work. But it's also an opportunity for surprise. The trick is to see what you have written in ways you haven't seen it before.

REVISION STRATEGIES

RE-SEEING YOUR TOPIC

"I don't really revise," Amy told me the other day. "I'm usually pretty happy with my first draft."

Always? I wondered.

"Well, certainly not always," she said. "But I know I work better under pressure, so I usually write my papers right before they're due. There usually isn't much time for revision, even if I wanted to do it, which I don't, really."

Amy is pretty typical. Her first-draft efforts usually aren't too bad, but I often sense tentativeness in her prose, endings that seem much stronger than beginnings, and promises that aren't really kept. Her essay promises to focus on the dangers of genetically engineered foods to teenagers who live on Cheeze-Its and Cheetos, but she never quite gets to saying much about that. The writing is competent—pretty clear and without too many awkward passages—but ultimately it's disappointing to read.

You can guess what I'm getting at here—Amy's work could be much stronger if it were rewritten—but the logic of last-minute writing is pretty powerful: "I really think I need to bump up against a deadline."

The writing process has three phases: prewriting, drafting, and rewriting. Prewriting refers to a range of activities writers might engage in before they attempt to compose a first draft, including fastwriting, listing, clustering, rehearsing lines or passages, preliminary research, conversations, or even the kind of

What You'll Learn in This Chapter

- How genuine revision involves exactly that: revision, or *re-seeing* your topic.
- Basic revision strategies for "divorcing the draft."
- How to become a reader of your own work.
- The five categories of revision.
- Advanced revision strategies.

deep thought about a topic that for some of us seems to occur best in the shower. The drafting stage is hardly mysterious. It often involves the much slower, much more focused process of putting words to paper, crafting a draft that presumably grows from some of the prewriting activities. Rewriting is a rethinking of that draft. Although this typically involves tweaking sentences, it's much more than that. Revision, as the name implies, is a *re-seeing* of the paper's topic and the writer's initial approach to it in the draft.

DIVORCING THE DRAFT

Sometimes I ask my students to generalize about how they approach the writing process for most papers by asking them to divide a continuum into three parts corresponding to how much time, roughly, they devote to prewriting, drafting, and rewriting. Then I play "writing doctor" and diagnose their problems, particularly resistance to revision. Figure 13.1 depicts a typical example for most of my first-year writing students.

> Revision, as the name implies, is a *re-seeing* of the paper's topic and the writer's initial approach to it in the draft.

The writing process shown in Figure 13.1 obviously invests lots of time in the drafting stage and very little time in prewriting or rewriting. For most of my students, this means toiling over the first draft, starting and then starting over, carefully hammering every word into place. For students who use this process, strong resistance to revision is a typical symptom. It's easy to imagine why. If you invest all that time in the first draft, trying to make it as good as you can, you'll be either too exhausted to consider a revision, delusional about the paper's quality, or, most likely, so invested in the draft's approach to the topic that revision seems impossible or a waste of time.

There also is another pattern among resistant revisers. Students who tend to spend a relatively long time on the prewriting stage also struggle with revision. My theory is that some of these writers resist revision as a final stage in

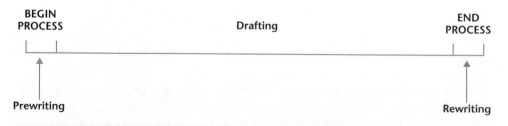

Figure 13.1   How some writers who resist revision typically divide their time between the three elements of the writing process: prewriting, drafting, and rewriting. The most time is devoted to writing the first draft, but not much time is given to prewriting and rewriting.

the process because *they have already practiced some revision at the beginning of the process*. We often talk about revision as occurring only after you've written a draft, which of course is a quite sensible idea. But the process of revision is an effort to *re-see* a subject, to circle it with questions, to view it from fresh angles; and many of the open-ended writing methods we've discussed in *The Curious Writer* certainly involve revision. Fastwriting, clustering, listing, and similar invention techniques all invite the writer to re-see. Armed with these discoveries, some writers may be able to write fairly strong first drafts.

What is essential, however, whether you revise at the beginning of the writing process or, as most writers do, after you craft the draft, is achieving some separation from what you initially thought, what you initially said, and how you said it. To revise well, writers must divorce the draft.

STRATEGIES FOR DIVORCING THE DRAFT

You can do some things to make separation from your work easier, and spending less time on the first draft and more time on the revision process is one of them. But aside from writing fast drafts, what are other strategies for re-seeing a draft that already has a hold on you?

1. **Take some time.** Absolutely the best remedy for revision resistance is setting the draft aside for a week or more. Professional writers, in fact, may set a piece aside for several years and then return to it with a fresh, more critical perspective. Students simply don't have that luxury. But if you can take a week or a month—or even a day—the wait is almost always worth it.

2. **Attack the draft physically.** A cut-and-paste revision that reduces a draft to pieces is often enormously helpful because you're no longer confronted with the familiar full draft, a version that may have cast a spell on you. By dismembering the draft, you can examine the smaller fragments more critically. How does each piece relate to the whole? Might there be alternative structures? What about gaps in information? (See Revision Strategy 13.18 later in this chapter for a useful cut-and-paste exercise.)

3. **Put it away.** Years ago I wrote a magazine article about alcoholism. It was about twenty-five pages long and it wasn't very good. I read and reread that draft, completely puzzled about how to rewrite it. One morning, I woke up and vowed I would read the draft just once more, then put it away in a drawer and start all over again, trusting that I would remember what was important. The result was much shorter and much better. In fact, I think it's the best essay I've ever written. Getting a troublesome draft out of sight—literally—may be the best way to find new ways to see it.

4. **Ask readers to respond.** Bringing other people's eyes and minds to your work allows you to see your drafts through perspectives other than your own. Other people have a completely different relationship with your writing

than you do. They will see what you don't. They easily achieve the critical distance that you are trying to cultivate when you revise.

5. **Write different leads.** The nonfiction writer John McPhee once talked about beginnings as the hardest thing to write. He described a lead as a "flashlight that shines down into the story," illuminating where the draft is headed. Imagine, then, the value of writing a new beginning, or even several alternative beginnings; each may point the next draft in a slightly different direction, perhaps one that you didn't consider in your first draft.

6. **Conduct research.** One of the central themes of *The Curious Writer* is that research isn't a separate activity but a source of information that can enrich almost any kind of writing. Particularly in genres such as the personal essay, in which the writer's voice, perspective, and experience dominate the draft, listening to the voices and knowledge of others about a topic can deepen and shift the writer's thinking and perspectives.

7. **Read aloud.** I always ask students in workshop groups to read their drafts aloud to each other. I do this for several reasons, but the most important is the effect that *hearing* a draft has on a writer's relationship to it. In a sense, we often hear a draft in our heads as we compose it or reread it, but when we read the words aloud the draft comes alive as something separate from the writer. As the writer listens to herself—or listens to someone else read her prose—she may cringe at an awkward sentence, suddenly notice a leap in logic, or recognize the need for an example. Try reading the work aloud to yourself and the same thing may happen.

8. **Write in your journal.** One of the strategies you can use to divorce the draft is to return to your notebook and fastwrite to yourself about what you might do to improve the piece. You can do this by asking yourself questions about the draft and then—through writing—attempt to answer them. The method can help you see a new idea that may become key to the structure of your next draft. Too often we see the journal exclusively as a prewriting tool, but it can be useful throughout the writing process, particularly when you need to think to yourself about ways to solve a problem in revision.

Later in this chapter, we'll build on some of these basic strategies with specific revision methods that may work with particular kinds of writing and with drafts that have particular problems. All of these methods encourage a separation between the writer and his or her draft or rely on that critical distance to be effective.

PHOTOGRAPHY AS A METAPHOR FOR REVISION

For several years, I taught composition by asking students to bring along a camera. The idea grew out of an experience I had in a graduate seminar with my friend and mentor Donald Murray, in which we were asked to apprentice to a creative activity and then write about how the process seemed to compare to the ways we write. I chose photography. It became clear almost immediately that there were dramatic parallels between the composing processes in each; the most striking was how much taking pictures taught me about revision.

What does it really mean to revise, or put another way, to *re-see*? What might be rewarding about such an effort? For many, revision may involve little more than proofreading a first draft. But when most experienced writers imagine revision, they mean something much less superficial (not that proofreading is unimportant!). Rewriting may involve adding or cutting information, reorganizing the draft, or even rebuilding around a new angle or purpose. This kind of revision grows from the conviction that when we first look at a topic there is much we don't notice, and this is a lesson photography teaches as well.

When I first ask my students to go out and take pictures, the only instruction I provide is that they must shoot an entire roll of film. I don't suggest photographic subjects, and I don't offer tips on technique. "Just go out and take a roll of pictures," I say, "and bring back the slides next week." The results are almost always the same: Every student in the class takes one photograph of every subject, a shot that usually captures it in the most familiar angle and light conditions—the school building from across the street, the roommate or friend squinting into the sun, the long shot down the beach at midday. Rarely were these particularly interesting pictures.

The same might be said of first drafts, especially those written in a rush the night before the paper is due. The writer pretty much goes with the first picture of his topic that he sees, and revision is pretty limited to "fixing" things here and there at the last minute. One common characteristic of these one-draft papers is that they often seize on the most obvious point or idea about their topics. A paper on the accuracy of "smart bombs" argues that they aren't always smart. Or a personal essay on fading friendships concludes that "true friends are hard to find." There isn't anything wrong with stating the obvious in a first draft *if* in a revision you plan to dig more deeply, working toward a fresher argument, a better insight, a less familiar way of seeing.

My students' first roll of film makes this point really well. When you take only one picture of a subject, you're not likely to see beyond what you've already seen. Our first look at almost anything is likely to reveal only what's most obvious about it. If we *really* want to see, if we really want to learn something we don't already know, we have to look and then look again. Speaking photographically, deep revision requires that we take more than one picture.

The value of taking more than one picture becomes apparent to my students when I ask them to complete a second assignment with their cameras. This time, I say, choose only two subjects from the first roll and take twelve shots of each one. Make every shot different by varying distance, angle, and light conditions. By composing multiple "drafts" of their subjects, even novice photographers discover new ways of seeing things they've seen before. They see the pattern of three kinds of stone that come together on the corner of Thompson Hall—something they never really noticed before although they walk by the building every day. They see the way the fire escapes cling like black iron insects to the west side of the building, its bricks bloodied by the setting sun. They see the delicate structure of a tulip or their best friend's hand, roughened by a summer of carpentry. Once my students get past the first few pictures of a subject, they really begin to see it freshly. More often than not, the twelfth picture is much more interesting than the fifth or sixth. The principle is simple: *The more you look, the more you see.*

Although the Greek meaning of the word is "light writing," photography, of course, is *not* writing. It really isn't hard to look through a camera, take a bunch of pictures, and re-see a subject. Doing this in writing is more difficult, because we must "see" through language. Words often get in the way. Yet the motive for revision in writing isn't much different from a photographer's inclination to take more than one shot—both writer and photographer know not to trust their first look at something. They know they won't see it well enough, so both writers and photographers use a process that helps them to see their subjects in new ways. The rewards for doing this are similar, too: the pleasure of surprise and discovery, of learning something new about their subjects and about themselves.

> The motive for revision is like a photographer's inclination to take more than one shot—both writer and photographer know not to trust their first look at something.

FIVE CATEGORIES OF REVISION

The following kinds of writers are typically ones who most need to revise:

1. Writers of fast drafts
2. Writers who compose short drafts
3. Writers who indulge in creative, but not critical, thinking
4. Writers who rarely go past their initial way of seeing things
5. Writers who have a hard time imagining a reader other than themselves
6. Writers who rely on limited sources of information
7. Writers who still aren't sure what they're trying to say
8. Writers who haven't found their own way of saying what they want to say
9. Writers who haven't delivered on their promises
10. Writers who think their draft is "perfect"

These are the usual suspects for revision, but there are many more. In general, if you think there's more to think about, more to learn, more to say, and better ways to say it, then revision is the route to surprise and discovery. Most writers agree that rewriting is a good idea, but where should they start?

Problems in drafts vary enormously. But the diagnosis tends to involve concerns in five general areas: purpose, meaning, information, structure, and clarity and style. Here are some typical reader responses to drafts with each kind of problem:

1. **Problems with Purpose**
   - "I don't know why the writer is writing this paper."
   - "The beginning of the essay seems to be about one thing, and the rest of it is about several others."
   - "I think there are about three different topics in the draft. Which one do you want to write about?"
   - "So what?"

2. **Problems with Meaning**
   - "I can't tell what the writer is trying to say in the draft."
   - "There doesn't seem to be a point behind all of this."
   - "I think there's a main idea, but there isn't much information on it."
   - "I thought the thesis was saying something pretty obvious."

3. **Problems with Information**
   - "Parts of the draft seemed really pretty vague or general."
   - "I couldn't really *see* what you were talking about."
   - "It seemed like you needed some more facts to back up your point."
   - "It needs more detail."

4. **Problems with Structure**
   - "I couldn't quite follow your thinking in the last few pages."
   - "I was confused about when this happened."
   - "I understood your point but I couldn't figure out what this part had to do with it."
   - "The draft doesn't really flow very well."

5. **Problems with Clarity and Style**
   - "This seems a little choppy."
   - "You need to explain this better. I couldn't quite follow what you were saying in this paragraph."
   - "This sentence seems really awkward to me."
   - "This doesn't have a strong voice."

PROBLEMS WITH PURPOSE

A draft that answers the *So what?* question is a draft with a purpose. Often enough, however, writers' intentions aren't all that clear to readers and they don't have a strong reason to keep reading.

It's a little like riding a tandem bike. The writer sits up front and steers while the reader occupies the seat behind, obligated to pedal but with no control over where the bike goes. As soon as the reader senses that the writer isn't steering anywhere in particular, then the reader will get off the bike. Why do all that pedaling if the bike seems to be going nowhere?

Frequently, when you begin writing about something, you don't have any idea where you're headed; that's exactly *why* you're writing about the subject in the first place. When we write such discovery drafts, revision often begins by looking for clues about your purpose. What you learn then becomes a key organizing principle for the next draft, trying to clarify this purpose to your readers. The first question, therefore, is one writers must answer for themselves: "Why am I writing this?" Of course, if it's an assignment it's hard to get past the easy answer—"Because I have to"—but if the work is going to be any good, there must be a better answer than that. Whether your topic is open or assigned, you have to find your own reason to write about it, and what you discover becomes an answer to your bike partner's nagging question, yelled into the wind from the seat behind you: "If I'm going to pedal this hard, you better let me know where we're going."

In general, writers' motives behind writing often involve more than one of these following four purposes.

1. **To explore.** One way to handle complicated questions is to approach the answers in an open-ended way; the writer writes to discover what he thinks or how he feels and reports to the reader on these discoveries.

2. **To explain.** Much of the writing we encounter in daily life is meant simply to provide us with information: This is how the coffeemaker works, or this is the best way to prepare for a trip to New Zealand. Expository writing frequently explains and describes.

3. **To evaluate.** In a sense, all writing is evaluative because it involves making judgments. For instance, when you explain how to plan a New Zealand vacation, you're making judgments about where to go. But when the explicit purpose is to present a judgment about something, the writer encourages readers to see the world the way the writer does. He or she may want the reader to think or behave a certain way: It makes sense to abolish pennies because they're more trouble than they're worth, or you should vote for the bond issue because it's the best way to save the foothills.

4. **To reflect.** Less frequently, we write to stand back from what we're writing about and consider *how* we're thinking about the subject, the methods we're using to write about it, and what we might learn from this writing situation that might apply to others.

Revision Strategy 13.1: The Motive Statement

It may help to begin a revision by attempting to determine your *primary motive* for the next draft. Do you want to explore your topic, explain something to your readers, offer a persuasive judgment, or step back and reflect on what you're saying or how you're saying it? The genre of writing has a great deal to do with this (see the following table). If you're writing a personal essay, your purpose is likely to be exploratory. If you're writing a review, a proposal, a critical essay, or an argument essay, it's likely your primary motive is to evaluate. One way, then, to get some basic guidance for the next draft is to carefully craft the second half of the following sentence: My primary motive in writing this paper is to explore/evaluate/explain/reflect about _____.

Genre	Primary Motive
Personal essay	Explore
Profile	Explore or explain
Review	Evaluate
Proposal	Evaluate
Argument	Evaluate
Critical essay	Evaluate
Ethnographic essay	Explore or evaluate
Research essay	Explore or evaluate
Reflective essay	Reflect

Of course, any one essay may involve all four motives, but for the purpose of this exercise, choose your *main* purpose in writing the essay. Composing the second half of the sentence may not be so easy because it challenges you to limit your subject. For instance, the following is far too ambitious for, say, a five-page essay: My main motive in writing this paper is to evaluate the steps taken to deal with terrorism and judge whether they're adequate. That's simply too big a subject for a brief persuasive paper. This is more reasonable: My main motive in writing this paper is to evaluate passenger screening procedures in Europe and decide whether they're better than those in the United States.

Since largely exploratory pieces often are motivated by questions, a writer of a personal essay might compose the following sentence: My main motive in writing this essay is to explore why I felt relieved when my father died.

After you craft your motive sentence, put it on a piece of paper or index card and post it where you can see it as you revise the draft. Periodically ask yourself, *What does this paragraph or this section of the draft have to do with my main motive?* The answer will help you decide what to cut and what needs more development in the next draft. Remember, the essay should be organized around this motive from beginning to end.

Revision Strategy 13.2: What Do You Want to Know About What You Learned?

Because inquiry-based writing is usually driven by questions rather than answers, one way to discover your purpose in a sketch or draft is to generate a list of questions it raises for you. Of course, you hope that one of them might be

ONE STUDENT'S RESPONSE

Julia's Draft

What do I understand about this topic now that I didn't understand before I started writing about it?

After writing this essay, I understand more clearly that there's a relationship between a girl's eating disorders and how her father treats her as a child.

LIST OF QUESTIONS

- Why the father and not the mother?

- What is it about father/daughter relationships that make them so vulnerable to feminine body images?

- Is the father's influence on a girl's body image greater at certain ages or stages in her life?

- How can a father be more informed about his impact on a daughter's body image?

behind your purpose in the next draft. Try the following steps with a draft that needs a stronger sense of purpose.

1. Choose a draft or sketch you'd like to revise, and reread it.

2. On the back of the manuscript, craft an answer to the following question: *What do I understand about this topic now that I didn't understand before I started writing about it?*

3. Next, if you can, build a list of questions—perhaps new ones—that this topic still raises for you. Make this list as long as you can, and don't censor yourself (see "One Student's Response" above).

4. Choose one or more of the questions as a prompt for a fastwrite. Follow your writing to see where it leads and what it might suggest about new directions for the revision.

5. If you can't think of any questions, or find you didn't learn much from writing about the topic (step 2), you may have several options. One is to abandon the draft altogether. Is it possible that this topic simply doesn't interest you anymore? If abandoning the draft isn't possible, then you need to find a new angle. Try Revision Strategy 13.3.

Revision Strategy 13.3: Finding the Focusing Question

The best topics, and the most difficult to write about, are those that raise questions for you. In a sketch or first draft, you may not know what these questions are. But if your subsequent drafts are going to be purposeful and focused, then discovering the main question behind your essay is essential. This is particularly important in essays that are research based because the drafts are longer and you're often trying to manage a lot of information. This revision strategy works best when it's a class activity.

1. Begin by simply putting your essay topic on the top of a large piece of paper such as newsprint or butcher paper. If yours is a research topic—say, Alzheimer's disease—jot that down. Post your paper on the classroom wall.

2. Spend a few minutes writing a few sentences explaining why you chose to write about this topic in the first place.

3. Make a quick list of everything you *already know* (if anything) about your topic—for instance, surprising facts or statistics, the extent of the problem, important people or institutions involved, key schools of thought, common misconceptions, familiar clichés that apply to the topic, observations you've made, important trends, and typical perspectives. Spend about five minutes on this.

4. Now spend fifteen or twenty minutes brainstorming a list of questions about your topic that you'd love to learn the answers to. Make this list as long as possible.

5. As you look around the room, you'll see a gallery of topics and questions on the walls. You can help each other. Circulate around the room and do two things: add a question that you're interested in about a particular topic, and check the question (yours or someone else's) that seems most interesting.

When you return to your newsprint or butcher paper, it should be covered with questions. How will you decide which of them might provide the best focus for the next draft? Consider the following criteria as you try to make this decision:

- **What question do you find most intriguing?** After all, it's your essay, and it should be driven by your own interests in the subject.

- **Which question seems most manageable?** This mostly has to do with the level of generality or specificity of the question. You want a focusing question that isn't too general or too specific. For example, a question such as *What causes international terrorism?* is a landscape question—it contains so much possible territory that you'll never get a close look at anything. But a question such as *How effective has the Saudi royal family been in limiting terrorist activities?* is a much more focused, and therefore manageable, question.

- **What question seems most appropriate for the assignment?** For example, if you're assigned a research essay, certain questions are more likely than others to send you to the library. If you're writing a persuasive essay, gravitate toward a question that might point you toward a claim or thesis.

- **What seems most relevant to the information you've already collected?** It would be convenient if information from your research or first draft is relevant to the question that's behind the next draft. While this might make the revision go more quickly, always be open to the possibility that a question that takes you in new directions might simply be more interesting to you.

- **What question is likely to yield answers that interest your readers?** You already have a sense of this from the questions that students in your class added to your newsprint about your topic. The challenge in any piece of writing, of course, is to answer the *So what?* question. Does your focusing question promise to lead you somewhere that readers would care to go?

Revision Strategy 13.4: What's the Relationship?

One of the more common purposes for all kinds of essays is to explore a relationship between two or more things. We see this in research all the time. What's the relationship between AIDS and IV drug use in China? What's the relationship between gender and styles of collaboration in the workplace? What's the social class relationship between Huck and Tom in *The Adventures of Huckleberry Finn*?

One way, then, to clarify your purpose in revision is to try to identify the relationship that may be at the heart of your inquiry. Relationships between things can be described in a couple different ways.

- **Cause and effect.** What is the relationship between my father's comments about my looks and my eating disorder when I was a teenager? What is the relationship between the second Iraqi war and destabilization in Saudi Arabia? What is the relationship between the decline of the Brazilian rain forest and the extinction of the native eagles? What is the relationship between my moving to Idaho and the failure of my relationship with Kevin?

- **Compare and contrast.** How is jealousy distinguished from envy? How might writing instruction in high school be distinguished from writing instruction in college? What are the differences and similarities between my experiences at the Rolling Stones concert last month and my experiences at the Stones concert fifteen years ago?

Review your sketch or draft to determine whether what you're really trying to write about is the relationship between two (or more) things. In your journal, try to state this relationship in sentences similar to those listed here. With this knowledge, return to the draft and revise from beginning to end with this purpose in mind. What do you need to add to the next draft to both clarify and develop the relationship you're focusing on? What should you cut that is irrelevant to that focus?

PROBLEMS WITH MEANING

Fundamentally, most of us write something in an attempt to say something to someone else. The note my wife Karen left for me yesterday said it in a sentence: "Bruce—could you pick up some virgin olive oil and a loaf of bread?" I had no trouble deciphering the meaning of this note. But it isn't always that easy. Certain poems, for example, may be incredibly ambiguous texts, and readers may puzzle over them for hours, coming up with a range of plausible interpretations of meaning. (See Figure 13.2.)

Where Does Meaning Come From?

Depending on the writing situation, you may know what you want to say from the start or you may *discover* what you think as you write and research. Inquiry-based projects usually emphasize discovery, while more conventional argument papers may rely on arriving at a thesis earlier in the process. It's something like the difference between sledding with a saucer or a flexible flyer. The saucer is likely to veer off course and you might find yourself somewhere unexpected, yet interesting.

TERMS TO DESCRIBE DOMINANT MEANING

- Thesis
- Main point
- Theme
- Controlling idea
- Central claim or assertion

No matter what you think about a topic when you start writing—even when you begin with a thesis to which you're committed—you can still change your

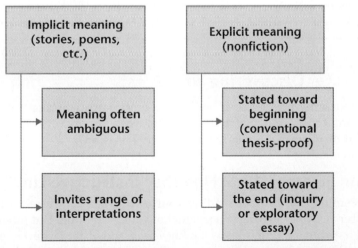

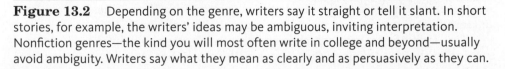

Figure 13.2 Depending on the genre, writers say it straight or tell it slant. In short stories, for example, the writers' ideas may be ambiguous, inviting interpretation. Nonfiction genres—the kind you will most often write in college and beyond—usually avoid ambiguity. Writers say what they mean as clearly and as persuasively as they can.

mind. You *should* change your mind if the evidence you've gathered leads you away from your original idea. Unfortunately, writers of thesis-driven papers and other deductive forms are far more resistant to any change in their thinking. In some writing situations—say, essay exams—this isn't a problem. But it's often important in academic writing, including arguments, to always be open to new insight.

Ideas about what we want to say on a writing topic grow from the following:

1. **Thesis.** This is a term most of us know from school writing, and it's most often associated with types of writing that work deductively from a main idea. Here's a sample thesis:

   The U.S. Securities and Exchange Commission is incapable of regulating an increasingly complex banking system.

2. **Theory.** We have strong hunches about how things work all the time, but we're not certain we're right. We test our theories and report on the accuracy of our hunches. Here's an example of a theory:

   Certain people just don't have a "head" for math.

3. **Question.** In a question-driven process, the emphasis is on discovery and you might work more inductively. You see or experience something that makes you wonder. Here's a question that led a writer to ideas about girls, advertising, and sexuality.

   Why does my ten-year-old want to dress like a hooker?

The revision strategies that follow assume either that you've got a tentative thesis and want to refine it or that you're still working on discovering what you want to say.

Methods for Discovering Your Thesis

Use the following strategies if you're not quite sure whether you know what you're trying to say in a sketch or draft. How can you discover clues about your main point or meaning in what you've already written?

Revision Strategy 13.5: Find the "Instructive Line"

It may seem odd to think of reading your own drafts for clues about what you mean. After all, your writing is a product of your own mind. But often a draft can reveal to us what we didn't know we knew—an idea that surfaces unexpectedly, a question that we keep asking, or a moment in a narrative that seems surprisingly significant. Part of the challenge is to recognize these clues to your own meanings, and understand what they suggest about the revision.

This isn't always easy, which is one reason it's often so helpful to share your writing with other readers; they may see the clues that we miss. However, this revision strategy depends on reading your own drafts more systematically for clues about what your point might be. What do you say in this draft that might suggest what you really want to say in the next one?

1. **Find the "instructive line."** Every draft is made up of many sentences. But which of these is *the most important sentence or passage*? What do I mean by *important*? Which line or passage points to a larger idea, theme, or feeling that seems to rise above much of the draft and illuminates the significance or relevance of many other lines and passages? The writer Donald Murray calls this the "instructive line," the sentence that seems to point upward toward the meaning of what you've set down. Underline the instructive line or passage in your draft. It may be subtle, only hinting at larger ideas or feelings, or quite explicitly stated. In a narrative essay, the instructive line might be a moment of stepping back to reflect—"As I look back on this now, I understand that..." In a review or persuasive essay, it might be an assertion of some kind—"American moviegoers are seduced by the 'twist' at the end of a film, and learn to expect it."

2. **Follow the thread of meaning.** If the instructive line is a ball of string, tightly packed with coils of meaning that aren't readily apparent, then to get any guidance for revision you need to try to unravel it. At the top of a journal page, write the line or passage you selected in your draft as most important. Use it as a prompt for five minutes of exploratory writing, perhaps beginning with the following seed sentence: I think/feel this is true because...and also because...and also...and also...

3. **Compose a thesis.** Reread your fastwriting in the preceding step and, keeping your original passage in mind, craft a single sentence that best captures the most important idea or feeling you'd like to bring into the next draft. For example, *Because of the expectation, encouraged by Hollywood, that every good movie has a surprise ending, American moviegoers often find even superior foreign films a disappointment.*

4. **Post it.** Put this thesis on the wall above your computer, or use a Post-it note and place the thesis on your computer screen. Revise with the thesis in mind, from beginning to end. Add information that will *illustrate, extend, exemplify, complicate, clarify, support, show, provide background,* or *prove* the thesis. Cut information from the draft that does none of these things.

Revision Strategy 13.6: Looping Toward a Thesis

I've argued throughout *The Curious Writer* for a dialectical approach to writing, moving back and forth between creative and critical modes of thinking, from your observations of and your ideas about, from generating and judging, from specifics and generalities. This is how writers can make meaning. The approach can also be used as a revision strategy, this time in a technique called *loop writing*. When you loop write, you move back and forth dialectically between both modes of thought—opening things up and then trying to pin them down. I imagine that this looks like an hourglass.

1. Reread the draft quickly, and then turn it upside down on your desk. You won't look at it again but trust that you'll remember what's important.

2. Begin a three-minute fastwrite on the draft in which you tell yourself the story of your thinking about the essay. When you first started writing it, what did you think you were writing about, and then what, and then…Try to focus on your ideas about what you were trying to say and how it evolved.

3. Sum up what you said in your fastwrite by answering the following question in a sentence: *What seems to be the most important thing I've finally come to understand about my topic?*

4. Begin another three-minute fastwrite. Focus on scenes, situations, case studies, moments, people, conversations, observations, and so on that stand out for you as you think about the draft. Think especially of specifics that come to mind that led to the understanding of your topic that you stated in the preceding step. Some of this information may be in the draft, but some may *not* yet be in the draft.

5. Finish by restating the main point you want to make in the next draft. Begin the revision by thinking about a lead or introduction that dramatizes this point. Consider a suggestive scene, case study, finding, profile, description, comparison, anecdote, conversation, situation, or observation that points the essay toward your main idea (see the "Inquiring into the Details: Types of Leads" box on page 574). For example, if your point is that your university's program to help second-language learners is inadequate, you could begin the next draft by telling the story of Maria, an immigrant from Guatemala who was a victim of poor placement in a composition course that she was virtually guaranteed to fail. Follow this lead into the draft, always keeping your main point or thesis in mind.

Revision Strategy 13.7: Reclaiming Your Topic

When you do a lot of research on your topic, you may reach a point when you feel awash in information. It's easy at such moments to feel as if you're losing control of your topic, besieged by the voices of experts, a torrent of statistics and facts, and competing perspectives. Your success in writing the paper depends on making it your own again, gaining control over the information for your own purposes, in the service of your own questions or arguments. This revision strategy, a variation of Revision Strategy 13.6, should help you gain control of the material you collected for a research-based inquiry project.

1. Spend ten or fifteen minutes reviewing all of the notes you've taken and skimming key articles or passages from books. Glance at your most important sources. If you have a rough draft, reread it. Let your head swim with information.

2. Now clear your desk of everything but your journal. Remove all your notes and materials. If you have a rough draft, put it in the drawer.

3. Now fastwrite about your topic for seven full minutes. Tell the story of how your thinking about the topic has evolved. When you began, what did you think? What were your initial assumptions or preconceptions? Then what happened, and what happened after that? Keep your pen moving.

4. Skip a few lines in your notebook, and write Moments, Stories, People, and Scenes. Now fastwrite for another seven minutes, this time focusing more on specific case studies, situations, people, experiences, observations, facts, and so on that stand out in your mind from the research you've done so far, or perhaps from your own experience with the topic.

5. Skip a few more lines. For another seven minutes, write a dialogue between you and someone else about your topic. Choose someone who you think is typical of the audience you're writing for. If it helps, think of someone specific—an instructor, a fellow student, a friend. Don't plan the dialogue. Just begin with the question most commonly asked about your topic, and take the conversation from there, writing both parts of the dialogue.

6. Finally, skip a few more lines and write these two words in your notebook: So what? Now spend a few minutes trying to summarize the most important thing you think your readers should understand about your topic, based on what you've learned so far. Distill this into a sentence or two.

As you work your way to the last step, you're reviewing what you've learned about your topic without being tyrannized by the many voices, perspectives, and facts in the research you've collected. The final step, Step 6, leads you toward a thesis statement. In the revision, keep this in mind as you reopen your notes, reread your sources, and check on facts. Remember in the rewrite to put all of this information in the service of this main idea, as examples or illustrations, necessary background, evidence or support, counterexamples, and ways of qualifying or extending your main point.

Revision Strategy 13.8: Believing and Doubting

In persuasive writing such as the argument, review, proposal, or research paper, we often feel that a thesis involves picking sides—"the play was good" or "the play was bad," "the novel was boring" or "the novel was fun to read." Instead of *either/or*, consider *both/and*. This might bring you to a more truthful, more sophisticated understanding of your subject, which rarely is either all bad or all good. One way to do this is to play Peter Elbow's doubting game and believing game.

1. Set aside ten to twelve minutes for two episodes of fastwriting in your journal or on the computer. First, spend a full five minutes playing the "believing game" (see the following prompts), exploring the merits of your subject even

if (and especially if) you don't think it has any. Then switch to the "doubting game." Write fast for another five minutes using a skeptical mind.

THE BELIEVING GAME	THE DOUBTING GAME
Give the author, performer, text, or performance the benefit of the doubt. Suspend criticism.	Adopt a critical stance. Look for holes, weaknesses, omissions, problems.
1. What seems true or truthful about what is said, shown, or argued?	1. What seems unbelievable or untrue?
2. How does it confirm your own experiences or observations of the same things?	2. What does it fail to consider or consider inadequately?
3. What did you like or agree with?	3. Where is the evidence missing or insufficient, or where do the elements not work together effectively?
4. Where is it strongest, most compelling, most persuasive?	4. How does it fail to meet your criteria for good in this category of thing?
5. How does it satisfy your criteria for being good, useful, convincing, or moving?	5. Where is it the least compelling or persuasive? Why?

2. From this work in your notebook, try to construct a sentence—a thesis— that is more than a simple statement of the worth or worthlessness of the thing you're evaluating, but an expression of *both* its strengths and weaknesses: Although _____ succeeds (or fails) in _____, it mostly _____. For example: Although reality television presents viewers with an often interesting glimpse into how ordinary people handle their fifteen minutes of celebrity, it mostly exaggerates life by creating drama where there often is none.

Methods for Refining Your Thesis

You may emerge from writing a draft with a pretty clear sense of what you want to say in the next one. But does this idea seem a little obvious or perhaps too general? Does it fail to adequately express what you really feel and think? Use one or more of the following revision strategies to refine a thesis, theme, or controlling idea.

Revision Strategy 13.9: Questions as Knives

Imagine that your initial feeling, thesis, or main point is like an onion. Ideas, like onions, have layers, and to get closer to their hearts you need to cut through the most obvious outer layers to reveal what is less obvious, probably more specific, and almost certainly more interesting. Questions are to ideas as knives are to onions: They help you slice past your initial impressions. The most important question—the sharpest knife in the drawer—is simply *Why? Why* was the Orwell essay interesting? *Why* do you hate foreign films? *Why* should the university do more for second-language speakers? *Why* did you feel a sense of loss when the old cornfield was paved over for the mall?

Why may be the sharpest knife in the drawer, but there are other W questions with keen blades, too, including *What?, Where?, When?,* and *Who?* In Figure 13.3 you can see how these questions can cut a broad thesis down to size. The result is a much more specific, more interesting controlling idea for the next draft.

1. Subject your tentative thesis to the same kind of narrowing. Write your theme, thesis, or main point as a single sentence in your notebook.
2. Slice it with questions and restate it each time.
3. Continue this until your point is appropriately sliced; that is, when you feel that you've gone beyond the obvious and stated what you think or feel in a more specific and interesting way.

As before, rewrite the next draft with this new thesis in mind, reorganizing the essay around it from beginning to end. Add new information that supports the idea, provides the necessary background, offers opposing views, or extends it. Cut information that no longer seems relevant to the thesis.

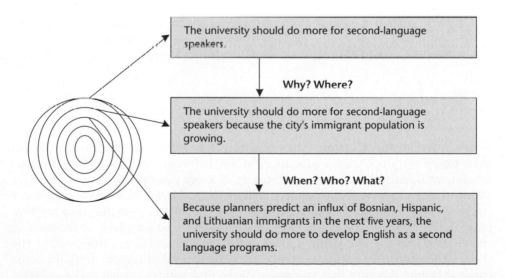

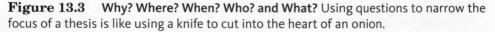

Figure 13.3   Why? Where? When? Who? and What? Using questions to narrow the focus of a thesis is like using a knife to cut into the heart of an onion.

Revision Strategy 13.10: Qualifying Your Claim

In your research you discovered that, while 90 percent of Americans think that their fellow citizens are too "fat," only 39 percent would describe themselves that way. This evidence leads you to make the following claim: *Although Americans agree that obesity is a national problem, their response is typical: it's somebody else's problem, an attitude that will cripple efforts to promote healthier lifestyles*. This seems like a logical assertion if the evidence is reliable. But if you're going to try to build an argument around it, a claim should be rigorously examined. Toulmin's approach to analyzing arguments provides a method for doing this.

1. Toulmin observes that sometimes a claim should be *qualified* to be more accurate and persuasive. The initial question is simple: *Is what you're asserting always or universally true?* Essentially, you're being challenged to examine your certainty about what you're saying. This might lead you to add words or phrases to it that acknowledge your sense of certainty: *sometimes, always, mostly, in this case, based on available evidence,* and so on. In this case, the claim is already qualified by specifying that it is limited to Americans, but it is also based on evidence from a single source. The claim, therefore, might be qualified to say this: *Although one survey suggests that Americans agree that obesity is a national problem, their response is typical: it's somebody else's problem, an attitude that will cripple efforts to promote healthier lifestyles.*

2. Imagining how your claim might be rebutted is another way to strengthen it. How might someone take issue with your thesis? What might be the exceptions to what you're saying is true? For example, might someone object to the assertion that Americans "typically" respond by putting their heads in the sand when personally confronted with problems? You must decide then whether this clever aside in your claim is something you're prepared to support. If not, cut it.

PROBLEMS WITH INFORMATION

Writers who've spent enough time generating or collecting information about their topics can work from abundance rather than scarcity. This is an enormous advantage because the ability to throw stuff away means you can be selective about what you use, and the result is a more focused draft. But as we revise, our purpose and point might shift, and we may find ourselves in the unhappy position of working from scarcity again. Most of our research, observation, or fastwriting was relevant to the triggering subject in the initial sketch or draft, not to the generated subject we decide is the better direction for the next draft. In some cases, this might require that you research the new topic or return to the generating activities of listing, fastwriting, clustering, and so on that will help provide information for the next draft.

More often, however, writers don't have to begin from scratch in revision. Frequently, a shift in the focus or refining a thesis in a first draft just means emphasizing different information or perhaps filling in gaps in later drafts. The strategies that follow will help you solve this problem.

Revision Strategy 13.11: Explode a Moment

The success of personal essays that rely on narratives frequently depends on how well the writer renders an important scene, situation, moment, or description. When you're telling a story from experience, not all parts of the story are equally important. As always, emphasis in a narrative depends on the writer's purpose in the essay. For example, Matt's essay on the irony of the slow poisoning of Butte, Montana, his home town, by a copper mine that once gave the city life would emphasize those parts of the story that best highlight that irony. Or a description of the agonizing death of the snow geese that unwittingly landed on the acid pond—their white beauty set against the deadly dark water—might be an important scene in Matt's next draft; it nicely portrays life and death, beauty and ugliness in much the same way the town and the mine might be contrasted. Matt should "explode that moment" because it's an important part of the story he's trying to tell about his Montana home town.

If you're trying to revise a draft that relies on narratives, this revision strategy will help you first identify moments, scenes, or descriptions that might be important in the next draft, and then develop these as more important parts of your story.

1. Choose a draft that involves a story or stories.

2. Make a list in your journal of the moments (for example, scenes, situations, and turning points) that stand out in the narrative.

3. Circle one that you think is most important to your purpose in the essay. It could be the situation that is most telling, a dramatic turning point, the moment of a key discovery that is central to what you're trying to say, or a scene that illustrates the dilemma or raises the question you're exploring in the draft.

4. Name that moment at the top of a blank journal page (for example, the snow geese on the acid pond, when the ice broke, or when I saw my grandfather in his coffin).

5. Now put yourself back into that moment and fastwrite about it for seven full minutes. Make sure that you write with as much detail as possible, *drawing on all your senses*. Write in the present tense if it helps.

6. Use this same method with other moments in the narrative that might deserve more emphasis in the next draft. Remember that real time means little in writing. An experience that took seven seconds can easily take up three pages of writing if it's detailed enough. Rewrite and incorporate the best of the new information in the next draft.

Revision Strategy 13.12: Beyond Examples

When we add information to a draft we normally think of adding examples. If you're writing a research essay on living with a sibling who suffers from Down syndrome, you might mention that your brother typically tries to avoid certain cognitive challenges. Members of your workshop group wonder, "Well, what kind of challenges?" In revision, you add an example or two from your own experience to clarify what you mean. This is, of course, a helpful strategy; examples of what you mean by an assertion are a kind of evidence that helps readers more fully understand your work. But also consider other types of information it might be helpful to add to the next draft. Use the following list to review your draft for additions you might not have thought of for revision.

- **Presenting counterarguments.** Typically, persuasive essays include information that represents an opposing view. Say you're arguing that beyond "avoidance" behaviors, there really aren't personality traits that can be attributed to most people with Down syndrome. You include a summary of a study that says otherwise. Why? Because it provides readers with a better understanding of the debate, and enhances the writer's ethos because you appear fair.

- **Providing background.** When you drop in on a conversation between two friends, you initially may be clueless about the subject. Naturally, you ask questions: "Who are you guys talking about? When did this happen? What did she say?" Answers to these questions provide a context that allows you to understand what is being said and to participate in the conversation. Background information like this is often essential in written communication, too. In a personal essay, readers may want to know when and where the event occurred or the relationship between the narrator and a character. In a critical essay, it might be necessary to provide background on the short story because readers may not have read it. In a research essay, it's often useful to provide background information about what has already been said on the topic and the research question.

- **Establishing significance.** Let's say you're writing about the problem of obesity in America, something that most of us are generally aware of these days. But the significance of the problem really strikes home when you add information from research suggesting that 30 percent of American adults are overweight, up from 23 percent just six years ago. It is even more important to establish the significance of a problem about which there is little awareness or consensus. For example, most people don't know that America's national park system is crumbling and in disrepair. Your essay on the problem needs to provide readers with information that establishes the significance of the problem. In a profile, readers need to have a reason to be interested in someone—perhaps your profile subject represents a particular group of people of interest or concern.

- **Giving it a face.** One of the best ways to make an otherwise abstract issue or problem come to life is to show what it means to an individual person. We can't fully appreciate the social impact of deforestation in Brazil without being introduced to someone such as Chico Mendes, a forest defender who was murdered for his activism. Obesity might be an abstract problem until we meet Carl, a 500-pound 22-year-old who is "suffocating in his own fat." Add case studies, anecdotes, profiles, and descriptions that put people on the page to make your essay more interesting and persuasive.

- **Defining it.** If you're writing about a subject your readers know little about, you'll likely use concepts or terms that readers will want you to define. What exactly do you mean, for example, when you say that the Internet is vulnerable to cyberterror? What exactly is cyberterror anyway? In your personal essay on your troubled relationship with your mother, what do you mean when you call her a narcissist? Frequently your workshop group will alert you to things in the draft that need defining, but also go through your own draft and ask yourself, *Will my readers know what I mean?*

Revision Strategy 13.13: Research

Too often, research is ignored as a revision strategy. We may do research for the first draft of a paper or essay, but never return to the library or search the Web to fill in gaps, answer new questions, or refine the focus of a rewrite. That's crazy, particularly because well-researched information can strengthen a draft of any kind. That has been one of the themes of *The Curious Writer* since the beginning of the book: Research is not a separate activity reserved only for the research paper, but a rich source of information for any type of writing. Try some of these strategies:

1. For quick facts, visit http://www.refdesk.com. This enormously useful Web site is the fastest way to find out the exact height of the Great Wall of China or the number of young women suffering from eating disorders in America today.

2. Return to the *Library of Congress Subject Headings*, the reference mentioned in Chapter 11 that will help you pinpoint the language you should use to search library databases on your topic. Particularly if the focus of your next draft is shifting, you'll need some fresh information to fill in the gaps. The *LCSH* will help you find more of it, more quickly.

3. To maximize Web coverage, launch a search on at least three different search engines (for example, Google, MSN Search, and Yahoo!), but this time search using terms or phrases from your draft that will lead you to more specific information that will fill gaps in the draft.

4. Interview someone relevant to your topic. (See Chapter 11.)

5. To ferret out some new sources on your topic, search library databases under author rather than keyword. Focus on authors that you know have something to say on your topic.

6. Return to any of the steps in Chapter 11 that involve developing deep knowledge about your topic.

Revision Strategy 13.14: Backing Up Your Assumptions

Targeted research is particularly important when you're making an argument. In addition to providing evidence that is relevant to your thesis, frequently an argument rests on the assumptions behind that assertion. Stephen Toulmin calls these assumptions *warrants* (see Chapter 8). For example, suppose your claim is the following: *Although most Americans agree that obesity is a national problem, most don't describe themselves as fat, an attitude that will cripple efforts to promote healthier lifestyles*. Every claim rests on assumptions, or warrants. In other words, what do you have to believe is true to have faith in the accuracy of the claim?

1. Write your claim on the top of a journal page, and then list the assumptions or warrants on which it seems to rest. For example, the claim about obesity includes an assumption that most Americans equate the words *obesity* and *fat*. Also there's an assumption that public attitudes—particularly the view that there is a problem but it isn't my problem—hinder progress on public policy.

2. Which of the warrants behind your claim would be stronger if there were "backing" or evidence to support them? This will give you new direction for research. It might strengthen the argument on the obesity problem, for example, to draw on evidence from the civil rights struggle. Is there any evidence that attitudes toward personal responsibility for racism lagged behind acknowledgment of racial inequality as a national problem? Was progress finally made when this gap narrowed?

PROBLEMS WITH STRUCTURE

When it's working, the structure of a piece of writing is nearly invisible. Readers don't notice how the writer is guiding them from one piece of information to the next. When structure is a problem, the writer asks readers to walk out on a shaky bridge and trust that it will help them get to the other side, but the walkers can think of little else but the shakiness of the bridge. Some professional writers, such as John McPhee, obsess about structure, and for good reason—when you're working with a tremendous amount of information, as McPhee often does in his research-based essays, it helps to have a clear idea about how you'll use it.

It's helpful to distinguish two basic structures for writing. One typically organizes the information of experience, and one organizes our thinking so that it's clear and convincing. Typically, we use narrative, and especially chronology, to organize our experiences, though how we handle time can vary considerably. Writing that presents information based on the writer's reasoning—perhaps making an argument or reporting on an experiment—is logically structured. The most common example is the thesis-example, or thesis-proof, paper. Much formal academic writing relies on logical structures that use deduction or induction.

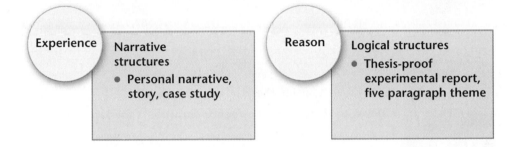

And yet some kinds of writing, like the researched essay or ethnography, may *combine* both patterns, showing how the writer reasoned through to the meaning of an experience, observation, reading, and so on. These essays tell a "narrative of thought."

Experience and reason | Story of what happened *and* story of writer's thinking about it
● Researched essay, ethnography, personal essay, reader response

Formal Academic Structures

In some academic writing, the structure is prescribed. Scientific papers often have sections—Introduction, Methodology, Results, Discussion—but within those sections writers must organize their material. Certain writing assignments may also require you to organize your information in a certain way. The most common of these is the thesis/support structure. In such essays you typically establish your thesis in the first paragraph, spend the body of the paper assembling evidence that supports the thesis, and conclude the essay with a summary that restates the thesis in light of what's been said.

Thesis/support is a persuasive form, so it lends itself to arguments, critical essays, reviews, proposals, and similar pieces. In fact, you may have already structured your draft using this approach. If so, the following revision strategy may help you tighten and clarify the draft.

Beginning

- Establishes purpose (answers *So what?* question)
- Introduces question, dilemma, problem, theory, thesis, claim (sometimes dramatically)
- Helps readers understand—and feel—what's at stake for them

Middle

- Tests theory, claim, thesis against the evidence
- Develops reasons, with evidence, for writer's thesis or claim
- Tells story of writer's inquiry into question, problem, or dilemma

End

- Proposes answer, even if tentative, for writer's key question
- Revisits thesis or claim, extending, qualifying, contradicting, or reconfirming initial idea
- Raises new questions, poses new problems, or offers new understanding of what is at stake for readers

Revision Strategy 13.15: Beginnings, Middles, Ends, and the Work They Do

Stories, we are often told, always have a beginning, middle, and end. This may be the most fundamental structure of all, and it doesn't just apply to narratives. The figure above explains what a beginning, middle, and end might contribute to making nearly any piece of writing coherent and convincing. Apply some of these ideas to your draft.

1. Divide a draft you'd like to revise into three parts—beginning, middle, and end—by drawing lines in the paper to distinguish each section. Where you decide to divide the draft is entirely up to you; there's no formula to this. But you may change your mind as you go along.

2. Now use the figure above to analyze your beginning, middle, and end. Does each section do at least *one* of the listed tasks? If not, revise that section

so that it does. This may involve adding one sentence or possibly paragraphs of new information, perhaps moving some from elsewhere in the draft.

3. Generally speaking, the middle of an essay does the most work, and so proportionally it should have the most information. For example, many essays look like this:

If you find, for example, that your beginning takes three pages of a five-page essay, then you might want to cut away at the first few pages and concentrate on developing the body of your essay.

Revision Strategy 13.16: Reorganizing Around Thesis and Support

Because the thesis/support structure is fairly common, it's useful to master. Most drafts, even if they weren't initially organized in that form, can be revised into a thesis/support essay. (Personal essays would be an exception.) The order of information in such an essay generally follows this design:

■ **Lead paragraph:** This paragraph introduces the topic and explicitly states the thesis, usually as the last sentence in the paragraph. For example, a thesis/support paper on the deterioration of America's national parks system might begin this way:

> Yellowstone National Park, which shares territory with Idaho, Montana, and Wyoming, is the nation's oldest park and, to some, its most revered. Established on March 1, 1872, the park features the Old Faithful geyser, which spouts reliably every 76 minutes on average. What isn't nearly as reliable these days is whether school groups will get to see it. Last year 60% of them were turned away because the park simply didn't have the staff. <u>This essay will argue that poor funding of our national parks system is a disgrace that threatens to undermine the Park Service's mission to preserve the areas "as cumulative expressions of a single national heritage" ("Famous Quotes")</u>.

The thesis (underlined) is the final sentence in the paragraph, for emphasis.

- **Body:** Each succeeding paragraph until the final one attempts to prove or develop the thesis. Often each paragraph is devoted to a single *reason* why the thesis is true, frequently stated as the topic sentence of the paragraph. Specific information then explains, clarifies, and supports the reason. For example, here's a typical paragraph from the body of the national parks essay:

> <u>One aspect of the important national heritage at risk because of poor funding for national parks is the pride many Americans feel about these national treasures.</u> *Newsweek* writer Arthur Frommer calls the national park system among the "crowning glories of our democracy." He adds, "Not to have seen them is to have missed something unique and precious in American life" (12). To see the crumbling roads in Glacier National Park, or the incursion of development in Great Smoky Mountains National Park, or the slow strangulation of the Everglades is not just an ecological issue; it's a sorry statement about a democratic nation's commitment to some of the places that define its identity.

The underlined sentence is the topic sentence of the paragraph and is an assertion that supports and develops the thesis in the lead of the essay. The rest of the paragraph offers supporting evidence of the assertion, in this case a quotation from a *Newsweek* writer who recently visited several parks.

- **Concluding paragraph:** This paragraph reminds the reader of the central argument, not simply by restating the original thesis from the first paragraph but by reemphasizing some of the most important points. This may lead to an elaboration or restatement of the thesis. One common technique is to find a way in the end of the essay to return to the beginning. Here's the concluding paragraph from the essay on national park funding:

> We would never risk our national heritage by allowing the White House to deteriorate or the Liberty Bell to rust away. <u>As the National Park Service's own mission states, the parks are also "expressions" of our "single national heritage," one this paper contends is about preserving not only trees, animals, and habitats, but our national identity.</u> The Old Faithful geyser reminds Americans of their constancy and their enduring spirit. What will it say about us if vandals finally end the regular eruptions of the geyser because Americans didn't support a park ranger to guard it? What will we call Old Faithful then? Old Faithless?

Note that the underlined sentence returns to the original thesis but doesn't simply repeat it word for word. Instead, it amplifies the original thesis, adding a definition of "national heritage" to include national identity. It returns to the opening paragraph by finding a new way to discuss Old Faithful. Revise your draft to conform to this structure, beginning with a strong opening paragraph that explicitly states your thesis and with an ending that somehow returns to the beginning without simply repeating what you've already said.

Revision Strategy 13.17: Multiple Leads

A single element that may affect a draft more than any other is the beginning. There are many ways into the material, and of course you want to choose a beginning or lead that a reader might find interesting. You also want to choose a beginning that makes some kind of promise, providing readers with a sense of where you intend to take them. But a lead has less obvious effects on both readers and writers. How you begin often establishes the voice of the essay; signals the writer's emotional relationship to the material, the writer's ethos; and might suggest the form the essay will take.

   This is, of course, why beginnings are so hard to write. But the critical importance of where and how we begin also suggests that examining alternative leads can give writers more choices and more control over their essays. To borrow John McPhee's metaphor, if a lead is a "flashlight that shines down into the story," then pointing that flashlight in four different directions might reveal four different ways of following the same subject. This can be a powerful revision strategy.

1. Choose a draft that has a weak opening, doesn't have a strong sense of purpose, or needs to be reorganized.

2. Compose four *different* openings to the *same* draft. One way to generate ideas for this is to cluster your topic, and write leads from four different branches. Also consider varying the type of lead you write (see the "Inquiring into the Details: Types of Leads" box on the following page).

3. Bring a typed copy of these four leads (or five if you want to include the original lead from the first draft) to class and share them with a small group. First simply ask your classmates to choose the beginning they like best.

4. Choose the lead *you* prefer. It may or may not be the one your classmates chose. Find a partner who was not in your small group and ask him or her the following questions after sharing the lead you chose:

    ■ Based on this lead, what do you predict this paper is about?

    ■ Can you guess the question, problem, or idea I'm writing about in the rest of the essay?

    ■ Do you have a sense of what my thesis might be?

    ■ What is the ethos of this beginning? In other words, how do I come across to you as a narrator or author of the essay?

INQUIRING INTO THE DETAILS

Types of Leads

Writer John McPhee says beginnings—or leads—are "like flashlights that shine down into the story." If you imagine that information about your topic is collected in a darkened room, then where and how you choose to begin an essay will, like a flashlight, illuminate some aspect of that room. Different beginnings point the flashlight in different directions and imply the different directions the essay might develop. Consider a few types of leads:

1. *Announcement.* Typical of a thesis/support essay, among others. Explicitly states the purpose and thesis of the essay.

2. *Anecdote.* A brief story that nicely frames the question, dilemma, problem, or idea behind the essay.

3. *Scene.* Describe a situation, place, or image that highlights the question, problem, or idea behind the essay.

4. *Profile.* Begin with a case study or description of a person who is involved in the question, problem, or idea.

5. *Background.* Provide a context through information that establishes the significance of the question, problem, or idea.

6. *Quotation or Dialogue.* Begin with a voice of someone (or several people) involved or whose words are relevant.

7. *Comparison.* Are there two or more things that, when compared or contrasted, point to the question, problem, or idea?

8. *Question.* Frame the question the essay addresses.

If the predictions were fairly accurate using the lead you preferred, this might be a good alternative opening to the next draft. Follow it in a fastwrite in your notebook to see where it leads you. Go ahead and use the other leads elsewhere in the revision, if you like.

If your reader's predictions were off, the lead may not be the best choice for the revision. However, should you consider this new direction an appealing alternative for the next draft? Or should you choose another lead that better reflects your current intentions rather than strike off in new directions? Either way, follow a new lead to see where it goes.

Revision Strategy 13.18: The Frankenstein Draft

One way to divorce a draft that has you in its clutches is to dismember it; that is, cut it into pieces and play with the parts, looking for new arrangements of information or new gaps to fill. Writing teacher Peter Elbow's cut-and-paste revision can be a useful method, particularly for drafts that don't rely on narrative structures (although sometimes playing with alternatives, particularly if the draft is strictly chronological, can be helpful). Research essays and other pieces that attempt to corral lots of information seem to benefit the most from this strategy.

1. Choose a draft that needs help with organization. Make a one-sided copy.

2. Cut apart the copy, paragraph by paragraph. (You may cut it into smaller pieces later.) Once you have completely disassembled the draft, shuffle the paragraphs to get them wildly out of order so the original draft is just a memory.

3. Now go through the shuffled stack and find the *core paragraph*. This is the paragraph the essay really couldn't do without because it helps answer the *So what?* question. It might be the paragraph that contains your thesis or establishes your focusing question. It should be the paragraph that explains, implicitly or explicitly, what you're trying to say in the draft. Set this aside.

4. With the core paragraph directly in front of you, work your way through the remaining stack of paragraphs and make two new stacks: one of paragraphs that don't seem relevant to your core (such as unnecessary digressions or information) and those that do (they support the main idea, explain or define a key concept, illustrate or exemplify something important, or provide necessary background).

5. Put your reject pile aside for the moment. You may decide to salvage some of those paragraphs later. But for now focus on your relevant pile, including the core paragraph. Now play with order. Try new leads, ends, and middles. Consider trying some new methods of development as a way to organize your next draft (see the "Methods of Development" box). As you spread the paragraphs out before you and consider new arrangements, don't worry about the lack of transitions; you can add those later. Also look for gaps, places where more information might be needed. Consider some of the information in the reject pile as well. Should you splice in *parts* of paragraphs that you initially discarded?

6. As a structure begins to emerge, begin taping together the fragments of paper. Also splice in scraps in appropriate places and note what you might add in the next draft that is currently missing.

Now you've created a Frankenstein draft. But hopefully this ugly mess of paper and tape and scribbled notes holds much more promise than the

METHODS OF DEVELOPMENT

- Narrative
- Problem to solution
- Cause to effect, or effect to cause
- Question to answer
- Known to unknown, or unknown to known
- Simple to complex
- General to specific, or specific to general
- Comparison and contrast
- Combinations of any of these

monster. On the other hand, if you end up with pretty much the original organization, perhaps your first approach wasn't so bad after all. You may at least find places where more information is needed.

Revision Strategy 13.19: Make a PowerPoint Outline

While outlines can be a useful tool for planning a formal essay, they can also help writers revise a draft. One of the best tools for doing this is a program such as PowerPoint that challenges you to develop brief slides in sequence. The ease of moving the slides around, the imperative to be brief and to the point, and the visual display of your logic all combine to make the program an ideal medium for playing with the order of information. This is often helpful even if you don't ever make a presentation.

Your goal in creating a PowerPoint outline isn't to transfer all your text to slides and then move it around, though you could do that if you thought it helpful. Your aim is to exploit the software to help you develop a logical outline. You have several options for doing this. One is to title separate slides using some of the conventional structures of academic essays, and then make bulleted lists of the information you might include in each (see the sample slide). For example, these could be slide titles:

- Abstract, Introduction, Literature Review, Thesis/Purpose, Methods, Results, Discussion, Conclusion
- The Problem/Question, Purpose of the Essay, Claim, Reasons and Evidence (separate slide for each reason), Conclusion

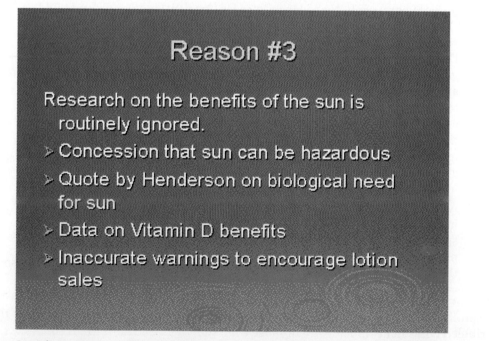

Sample PowerPoint slide outlining a plan for an essay.

- Introduction, Thesis, Example 1, Example 2, Example 3, etc., Conclusion
- Lead/Introduction, Background, Research Question, Significance of the Problem or Question, Other Voices on the Question, Thesis, Conclusion

Alternatively, you might use less formal methods of parsing the information in the draft onto slides. For example, can you label categories of information? In a narrative essay, it might be a particular scene, description, or reflection. In an argument it might be claims, warrants or assumptions, evidence, and counterarguments. A literary essay might be grouped on slides using key passages, the main idea, textual background, information on the author, and so on.

Whichever method you use, once you are able to disassemble your draft onto PowerPoint slides using some logic, don't just play with the order. Consider moving some of the information from slide to slide, too.

PROBLEMS WITH CLARITY AND STYLE

One thing should be made clear immediately: Problems of clarity and style need not have anything to do with grammatical correctness. You can have a sentence that follows all the rules and still lumbers, sputters, and dies like a Volkswagen bug towing a heavy trailer up a steep hill. Take this sentence, for instance:

> Once upon a point in time, a small person named Little Red Riding Hood initiated plans for the preparation, delivery, and transportation of foodstuffs to her grandmother, a senior citizen residing at a place of residence in a wooded area of indeterminate dimension.

> Strong writing at the sentence and paragraph levels always begins with clarity.

This beastly sentence opens Russell Baker's essay "Little Red Riding Hood Revisited," a satire about the gassiness of contemporary writing. It's grammatically correct, of course, but it's also pretentious, unnecessarily wordy, and would be annoying to read if it wasn't pretty amusing. This section of the chapter focuses on revision strategies that improve the clarity of your writing and will help you consider the effects you want to create through word choice and arrangement. Your questions about grammar and mechanics can be answered in the handbook at the back of the book.

Maybe because we often think that work with paragraphs, sentences, and words always involves problems of correctness, it may be hard to believe at first that writers can actually manage readers' responses and feelings by using different words or rearranging the parts of a sentence or paragraph. Once you begin to play around with style, however, you will discover that it's much more than cosmetic. In fact, style in writing is a lot like music in movies. Chris Douridas, a Hollywood music supervisor who picked music for *Shrek* and *American Beauty*, said recently that he sees "music as an integral ingredient to the pie. I see it as helping to flavor the pie and not as whipped cream on top." Certainly people don't pick a movie for its music, but we know that the music is central to our experience of a film. Similarly, *how* you say things in a piece of writing powerfully shapes the reader's experience of *what* you say.

But style is a secondary concern. Strong writing at the sentence and paragraph levels always begins with clarity. Do you say what you mean as directly and economically as you can? This can be a real problem, particularly with academic writing, in which it's easy to get the impression that a longer word is always better than a shorter word, and the absence of anything interesting to say can be remedied by sounding smart. Nothing could be further from the truth.

Solving Problems of Clarity

Begin by revising your draft with one or more revision strategies that will make your writing more direct and clear.

Revision Strategy 13.20: The Three Most Important Sentences

Writers, like car dealers, organize their lots to take advantage of where readers are most likely to look and what they're most likely to remember. In many essays and papers, there are three places to park important information and to craft your very best sentences. These are,

- the very first sentence
- the last line of the first paragraph
- the very last line of the essay

The First Sentence. Obviously, there are many other important places in a piece of writing—and longer essays, especially, have more and different locations for your strongest sentences. But in an informal piece of modest length, the first sentence not only should engage the reader, it should, through strong language and voice, introduce the writer as well. For example, here's the first line of Richard Conniff's researched essay, "Why God Created Flies": "Though I've been killing them for years now, I have never tested the folklore that, with a little cream and sugar, flies taste very much like black raspberries." In more formal writing, the first line is much less about introducing a persona than introducing the subject. Here's the first line of an academic piece I'm reading at the moment: "Much of the international debate about the relationship between research and teaching is characterized by difference." This raises an obvious question—"What is this difference?"—and this is exactly what the author proposes to explore.

The Last Line of the First Paragraph. The so-called "lead" (or "lede" in journalism speak) of an essay or article does three things: It establishes the purpose of the work, raises interesting questions, and creates a register or tone. A lead paragraph in a shorter essay is just that—the first paragraph—while a lead in a longer work may run for paragraphs, even pages. Whatever the length, the last sentence of the lead launches the work and gets it going in a particular direction. In conventional thesis-proof essays, then, this might be the sentence where you state your main claim. In inquiry-based forms like the essay, this might be where you post the key question you're exploring or illuminate the aspect of the problem you want to look at.

The Last Line of the Essay. If it's good, this is the sentence readers are most likely to remember.

Try this revision strategy:

1.   Highlight or underline each of these three sentences in your draft.
2.   Ask yourself these questions about the first line and, depending on your answers, revise the sentence:
     - Is the language lively?
     - Does it immediately raise questions the reader might want to learn the answers to?
     - Will they want to read the second sentence, and why?
3.   Analyze the last sentence of your "lead" paragraph for ideas about revision. Ask yourself this:
     - Is the sentence well-crafted?
     - Does it hint at or explicitly state your motive for asking readers to follow along with you in the paragraphs and pages that follow?
4.   Finally, scrutinize your last sentence:
     - Is this one of the best-written sentences in the piece?
     - Does it add something?

Revision Strategy 13.21: Untangling Paragraphs

One of the things I admire most in my friends David and Margaret is that they both have individual integrity—a deep understanding of who they are and who they want to be—and yet they remain just as profoundly connected to the people close to them. They manage to exude both individuality and connection. I hope my friends will forgive the comparison, but good paragraphs have the same qualities: Alone they have their own identities, yet they are also strongly hitched to the paragraphs that precede and that follow them. This connection happens quite naturally when you're telling a story, but in expository writing the relationship between paragraphs is more related to content than time.

The following passage is the first three paragraphs from Paul de Palma's essay on computers, with the clever title "www.when_is_enough_enough?.com." Notice the integrity of each paragraph—each is a kind of mini-essay—as well as the way each one is linked to the paragraph that precedes it.

A paragraph should be unified, focusing on a single topic, idea, or thing. It's like a mini-essay in that sense.

Note how the first sentence in the new paragraph links with the last sentence in the preceding one.

As before, the first sentence links with the last sentence in the previous paragraph.

The final sentence is the most important one in a paragraph. Craft it carefully.

In the misty past, before Bill Gates joined the company of the world's richest men, before the mass-marketed personal computer, before the metaphor of an information superhighway had been worn down to a cliché, I heard Roger Schank interviewed on National Public Radio. Then a computer science professor at Yale, Schank was already well known in artificial intelligence circles. Because those circles did not include me, a new programmer at Sperry Univac, I hadn't heard of him. Though I've forgotten details of the conversation, I have never forgotten Schank's insistence that most people do not need to own computers.

That view, of course, has not prevailed. Either we own a personal computer and fret about upgrades, or we are scheming to own one and fret about the technical marvel yet to come that will render our purchase obsolete. Well, there are worse ways to spend money, I suppose. For all I know, even Schank owns a personal computer. They're fiendishly clever machines, after all, and they've helped keep the wolf from my door for a long time.

It is not the personal computer itself that I object to. What reasonable person would voluntarily go back to a typewriter? The mischief is not in the computer itself, but in the ideology that surrounds it. If we hope to employ computers for tasks more interesting than word processing, we must devote some attention to how they are actually being used, and beyond that, to the remarkable grip that the idol of computing continues to exert.

Well-crafted paragraphs like these create a fluent progression, all linked together like train cars; they make readers feel confident that this train is going somewhere. This might be information that clarifies, extends, proves, explains, or even contradicts. Do the paragraphs in your draft work well on their own and together?

1. Check the length of every paragraph in your draft. Are any too long, going on and on for a full page or more? Can you create smaller paragraphs by breaking out separate ideas, topics, discussions, or claims?

2. Now examine each paragraph in your draft for integrity. Is it relatively focused and unified? Should it be broken down further into two or more paragraphs because it covers too much territory?

3. In Figure 13.4, note the order of the most important information in a typical paragraph. Is each of your paragraphs arranged with that order in mind? In particular, how strong is the final sentence in each paragraph? Does it prepare readers to move into the next paragraph? In general, each paragraph adds some kind of new information to the old information in the paragraphs preceding it. This new material may clarify, explain, prove, elaborate on,

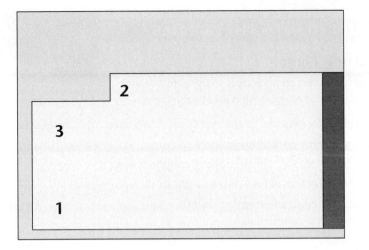

Figure 13.4 Order of important sentences in a paragraph. Often the first sentence is the second most important sentence in a paragraph. The third most important sentence follows immediately thereafter. The most important sentence usually comes at the end of the paragraph.

contrast, summarize, contradict, or alter time. Sometimes you should signal the nature of this addition using transition words and phrases (see the "Inquiring into the Details: Transition Flags" box). Are there any awkward transitions? Should you smooth them using transition flags?

Revision Strategy 13.22: Cutting Clutter

Russell Baker's overinflated version of "Little Red Riding Hood" suffered from what writer and professor William Zinsser called "clutter." This disease afflicts much writing, particularly in academic settings. Clutter, simply put, is saying in three or four words what you might say in two, or choosing a longer word when a shorter one will do just as well. It grows from the assumption that simplicity means simplemindedness. This is misguided. Simplicity is a great virtue in writing. It's respectful of the readers, for one thing, who are mostly interested in understanding what you mean without unnecessary detours or obstacles.

In case Russell Baker's tongue-and-cheek example of cluttered writing isn't convincing because it's an invention, here's a brief passage from a memo I received from a fellow faculty member some years ago. I won't make you endure more than a sentence.

While those of us in the administration are supporting general excellence and consideration of the long-range future of the University, and while the Faculty Senate and Caucus are dealing with more immediate problems, the Executive Committee feels that an ongoing dialogue concerning the particular concerns of faculty is needed to maintain the quality of personal and educational life necessary for continued educational improvement.

INQUIRING INTO THE DETAILS

Transition Flags

One way to connect paragraphs is to signal to a reader with words what the relationship is between them.

- **Clarifying:** *for example, furthermore, specifically, also, to illustrate, similarly*
- **Proving:** *in fact, for example, indeed*
- **Time:** *first…second…finally, subsequently, following, now, recently*
- **Cause or effect:** *therefore, consequently, so, accordingly*
- **Contrast or contradiction:** *on the other hand, in contrast, however, on the contrary, despite, in comparison*
- **Summarizing:** *finally, in the end, in conclusion, summing up, to conclude*

That's a 63-word sentence, and while there is nothing inherently wrong with long sentences, I'm pretty sure that at least half of the words are unnecessary. For the fun of it, see if you can cut at least thirty words from the sentence without compromising the writer's intent. Look for ways to say the same things in fewer words, and look for shorter words that might replace longer ones. What kinds of choices did you make to improve the clarity of the sentence?

Now shift your attention to one of your own drafts and see if you can be as ruthless with your own clutter as you were with the memo writer's.

1. One of the most common kinds of clutter is stock phrases, things we mindlessly say because we've simply gotten in the habit of saying them. *Due to the fact that…* is the one that drives me most crazy. Why not the simpler word *Because*? The following table lists some of the most common stock phrases used in student writing. Read your draft from beginning to end and when you see one of these, cut it down to size.

STOCK PHRASE	SIMPLER VERSION
Due to the fact that…	Because
At the present time…	Now
Until such time as…	Until
I am of the opinion that…	I think
In the event of…	When
This is an appropriate occasion to…	It's time
Proceed with the implementation of…	Begin
Referred to as…	Called
Totally lacked the ability to…	Couldn't
A number of…	Many
In the event of…	If
There is a need for…	Must

2. Another thing to consider is choosing a shorter, simpler word rather than a longer, more complicated word. For example, why not say *many* rather than *numerous*, or *ease* rather than *facilitate*, or *do* rather than *implement*, or *found* rather than *identified*. Go through your draft and look for opportunities such as these to use simpler, more direct words.

3. In his book *Style: Ten Lessons in Clarity and Grace*, Joseph Williams cleverly calls the habit of using meaningless words "verbal tics." These are words, he writes, that "we use unconsciously as we clear our throats." My favorite verbal tic is the phrase *in fact*, which I park at the front of a sentence when I feel like I'm about to clarify something. Mostly I can do without it. In fact, most of us have verbal tics, and we should learn to recognize them. Williams mentions a few common ones, including *kind of, actually, basically, generally, given, various,* and *certain*. For example, *It's generally assumed that certain students have various reasons for being apolitical these days.* A better version would be, *Students have reasons for being apolitical these days.*

Go through your draft and search for words and phrases that you use out of habit, and cut them if they don't add meaning.

Revision Strategy 13.23: The Actor and the Action Next Door

I live in a relatively urban neighborhood, and so I can hear Kate play her music across the street and Gray powering up his chainsaw to cut wooden pallets next door. I have mixed feelings about this. Kate and I have different taste in music and Gray runs the saw at dusk. But I am never confused about who is doing what. That's less obvious in the following passage:

> A conflict that was greeted at first with much ambivalence by the American public, the war in Iraq, which caused a tentativeness that some experts call the "Vietnam syndrome," sparked protests among Vietnam veterans.

The subject or actor of the sentence (*the war in Iraq*) and the action (*sparked protests*) are separated by a few city blocks. In addition, the subject is buried behind a long introductory clause. As a result, it's a bit hard to remember who is doing what. Putting actor and action next door to each other makes the writing livelier, and bringing the subject up front helps clarify who is doing what.

> The war in Iraq sparked protests among Vietnam veterans even though the conflict was initially greeted with public ambivalence. Some experts call this tentativeness the "Vietnam syndrome."

Review your draft to determine whether the subjects in your sentences are buried or in the same neighborhood as the verbs that modify them. If not, rewrite to bring the actors up front in your sentences and to close the distance between actors and actions.

Improving Style

These revision strategies will improve the style of your writing. In the same way that a John Williams score can make movies such as *Indiana Jones and the Temple of Doom* and *Star Wars* more memorable and moving, style in writing can add to readers' experiences of a text. These are often calculated moves. Writers adopt a style because it serves a purpose, perhaps encouraging a certain feeling that makes a story more powerful, enhancing the writer's ethos to make an essay more convincing, or simply giving certain information particular emphasis. For example, here's the beginning of an article about Douglas Berry, a Marine drill sergeant.

> He is seething, he is rabid, he is wound up tight as a golf ball, with more adrenalin surging through his hypothalamus than a cornered slum rat, he is everything these Marine recruits with their heads shaved to dirty nubs have ever feared or ever hoped a drill sergeant might be.

The style of this opening is calculated to have an obvious effect—the reader is pelted with words, one after another, in a breathless sentence that almost simulates the experience of having Sgt. Douglas Berry in your face. There's no magic to this. It is all about using words that evoke action and feeling, usually verbs or words based on or derived from verbs.

Revision Strategy 13.24: Actors and Actions

My favorite verb yesterday was *shattered*. I often ask my writing students to come to class and share their favorite verb of the day; last spring, my senior seminar consistently selected *graduate* as their favorite.

As you know, verbs make things happen in writing, and how much energy prose possesses depends on verb power. Academic writing sometimes lacks strong verbs, relying instead on old passive standbys such as *it was concluded by the study* or *it is believed*. Not only are the verbs weak, but the actors, the people or things engaged in the action, are often missing completely from the sentences. *Who* or *what* did the study? *Who* believes?

This is called *passive voice*, and while it's not grammatically incorrect, passive voice can suck the air out of a room. While reasons exist for using passive voice (sometimes, for instance, the writer wants the reader to focus on the action, not the actor), you should avoid it in your own writing. One of the easiest ways to locate passive voice in your drafts is to conduct a *to be* search. Most forms of the verb *to be* (see the Forms of *To Be* box on the next page) usually signal passive voice. For example,

> It is well known that medieval eating habits were unsavory by contemporary health standards. Cups were shared, forks were never used, and the same knives used to clean under fingernails or to gut a chicken were used to cut and eat meat.

What is missing, of course, are the actors. To revise into active voice you simply need to add the actors, whenever possible:

> Medieval diners had unsavory eating habits by contemporary health standards. They shared cups with friends, they never used forks, and they used their knives, the same ones they used to clean under their fingernails or gut a chicken, to cut and eat their meat.

1. Conduct a *to be* search of your own draft. Whenever you find passive construction, try to put the actor into the sentence.

2. Eliminating passive voice is only one strategy for giving your writing more energy. Try to use lively verbs as well. Can you replace weak verbs with stronger ones? How about *discovered* instead of *found*, or *seized* instead of *took, shattered* instead of *broke.* Review every sentence in the draft and, when appropriate, revise with a stronger verb.

FORMS OF *TO BE*

- Is
- Are
- Was
- Were
- Has been
- Have been
- Will be

Revision Strategy 13.25: Smoothing the Choppiness

Good writing reads like a Mercedes drives—smoothly, suspended by the rhythms of language. One of the most important factors influencing this rhythm is sentence length, or, more precisely, pauses in the prose that vary as the reader travels from sentence to sentence and paragraph to paragraph. We rarely notice either the cause or the effect, but we certainly notice the bumps and lurches. Consider the following sentences, each labeled with the number of syllables:

> When the sun finally rose the next day I felt young again.(15) It was a strange feeling because I wasn't young anymore.(15) I was fifty years old and felt like it.(10) It was the smell of the lake at dawn that thrust me back into adolescence.(19) I remembered the hiss of the waves.(9) They erased my footprints in the sand.(9)

This really isn't awful; it could pass as a bad Hemingway imitation. But do you notice the monotony of the writing, the steady, almost unvarying beat that threatens to dull your mind if it goes on much longer? The cause of the plodding rhythm is the unvarying length of the pauses. The last two sentences in the passage each have 9 syllables, and the first two sentences are nearly identical in length as well (15 and 15 syllables, respectively).

Now notice how this choppiness disappears by varying the lengths of the pauses through combining sentences, inserting other punctuation, and dropping a few unnecessary words.

When the sun finally rose the next day I felt young again,(15) and it was a strange feeling because I wasn't young.(13) I was fifty years old.(6) It was the smell of the lake at dawn that thrust me back into adolescence and remembering the hiss of the waves as they erased my footprints in the sand.(39)

The revision is much more fluent and the reason is simple: The writer varies the pauses and the number of syllables within each of them—15, 13, 6, 39.

1. Choose a draft of your own that doesn't seem to flow or seems choppy in places.

2. Mark the pauses in the problem areas. Put slash marks next to periods, commas, semicolons, dashes, and so on—any punctuation that prompts a reader to pause briefly.

3. If the pauses seem similar in length, revise to vary them, combining sentences, adding punctuation, dropping unnecessary words, or varying long and short words.

Revision Strategy 13.26: Fresh Ways to Say Things

It goes without saying that a tried-and-true method of getting to the heart of revision problems is to just do or die. Do you know what I mean? Of course you don't, because the opening sentence is laden with clichés and figures of speech that manage to obscure meaning. One of the great challenges of writing well is to find fresh ways to say things rather than relying on hand-me-down phrases that worm their way into our speech and writing. Clichés are familiar examples: *home is where the heart is, hit the nail on the head, the grass is greener*, and all that. But even more common are less figurative expressions: *more than meets the eye, rude awakenings, you only go around once, sigh of relief*, and so on.

Removing clichés and shopworn expressions from your writing will make it sound more as if you are writing from your own voice rather than someone else's. It gives the work a freshness that helps readers believe that you have something interesting to say. In addition, clichés especially tend to close off a writer's thoughts rather than open them to new ideas and different ways of seeing. A cliché often leaves the writer with nothing more to say because someone else has already said it.

1. Reread your draft and circle clichés and hand-me-down expressions. If you're not sure whether a phrase qualifies for either category, share your circled items with a partner and discuss them. Have you heard these things before?

2. Cut clichés and overused expressions and rewrite your sentences, finding your own way to say things. In your own words, what do you really mean by "do or die" or "striking while the iron is hot" or becoming a "true believer"?

USING WHAT YOU HAVE LEARNED

Take a few moments to reflect on what you learned in this chapter and how you can apply it.

1. Which revision strategy has proved most helpful to you so far? Does it address one of your most common problems in your drafts?

2. Here's a common situation: You're assigned a paper for another class and the professor doesn't require you to hand in a draft. She's just interested in your final version. What incentive do you have to work through a draft or two?

3. If revision is rhetorical, then the kinds of revision strategies you need to use depend on the particular situation: to whom you're writing and why, and in what form. The kind of writer you are—and the kinds of problems you have in your drafts—also matters. Consider the following forms: the essay exam, the review, the annotated bibliography, the letter, the formal research paper, and the reading response. Which of the five revision strategies would probably be most important for each form?

1. By talking with other students about writing, you get practice using the language you're learning in the writing classroom, language that helps you describe important features of your own work.

2. Because writing is about making choices among a range of solutions to problems in a draft, workshop groups are likely to surface possibilities that never occurred to you (and perhaps wouldn't occur to the instructor, either).

3. Your peers are also student writers and because they come from similar circumstances—demands of other classes, part-time jobs, and perhaps minimal experience with college writing—they are in a position to offer practical and realistic revision suggestions.

4. Finally, in most writing courses, the students in the class are an important audience for your work. Getting firsthand responses makes the rhetorical situation real rather than imagined.

Will you get bad advice in a peer workshop? Of course. Your group members will vary in their experience and ability to read the problems and possibilities in a draft. But in the best writing workshops, you learn together, and as time goes by the feedback gets better and better. Paradoxically, it pays off in your own writing to be generous in your responses to the work of others.

MODELS FOR WRITING WORKSHOPS

The whole idea of peer review workshops in writing classes has been around for years. Collaboration is hardly a novelty in the professional world, but small-group work in academia is a relatively recent alternative to lecture and other teaching methods in which the student listens to a professor, takes notes on what is said, and later takes a test of some kind. You won't learn to write well through lecture, although it may be a perfectly appropriate approach for some subjects. Because collaboration in the writing classroom fits in perfectly with the class's aim of generating knowledge about the many ways to solve writing problems, peer review of drafts in small groups is now fairly common. You'll find workshops in writing classes ranging from first-year composition to advanced nonfiction writing.

What will workshops be like in your course? Your instructor will answer that question, but the workshop groups will likely reflect one or more of the following models.

Full-Class Workshops

Sometimes you may not work in small groups at all. Depending on the size of your class and your instructor's particular purposes for using peer review, you may share your work with everyone in a full-class session. This approach is popular in creative writing classes, and it's typically used in composition classes to introduce students to the process of providing responses to other students' work. It also can work nicely in small classes with ten students or fewer.

In a full-class workshop, you'll choose a draft to share, and you (or your instructor) will provide copies for everyone either a few days before the workshop or at the beginning of the workshop session. On drafts you receive days ahead of the session, you're often expected to read and bring written comments to class with you. If you receive the draft at the beginning of the workshop session, you might make notes while the draft's author reads the piece aloud, or take some time to write some comments either immediately after the draft is read or following the group discussion.

Reading your draft aloud to your workshop group is a common convention in all kinds of workshop groups, large or small. This might be something you resist at first. It will quickly become apparent, however, how useful it is to read your own work aloud. It's an entirely different reading to literally give voice to your words. You'll stumble over passages in your draft that seemed fine when you read them silently, and you may notice gaps you glossed over. You'll hear what your writing voice sounds like in this particular essay, and whether it works for you and your readers.

Your instructor may lead the discussion in a full-class workshop, or she may sit back and wait while students share their responses. There may be guidelines and ground rules for responses as well (for some examples of these, see "The Reader's Responsibilities" section later in the chapter). If your draft is being discussed, your instructor may ask you to simply listen. Sometimes it's best to avoid defending certain choices you made in a draft and simply take in the range of responses you receive to what you have done. In other cases, you may be asked to present the large group with questions to consider. It certainly can be scary sharing your work with twenty or twenty-five people, but imagine the range of perspectives you'll get!

Small-Group Workshops

Far more typical is the workshop group of between three and seven members, either chosen randomly by your instructor or self-selected. These groups may stay together all semester or part of the semester, or you may find yourself working with fresh faces every workshop session. Each of these alternatives has advantages and disadvantages, all of which your instructor has considered in making a choice.

Ideally, your workshop group will meet in a circle, because when everyone, including the writer presenting a draft, is facing each other you'll have more of a conversation and be able to engage each other directly (see Figure 14.1). Like so many writing group methods, this is a basic principle of teamwork borrowed from the business world.

Some of the methods of distributing drafts apply to the small group as well as to the full-class workshop discussed earlier: Writers will distribute copies of their drafts either a few days before their workshops or at the beginning of the sessions. You will provide written comments to each writer either before or after the workshop.

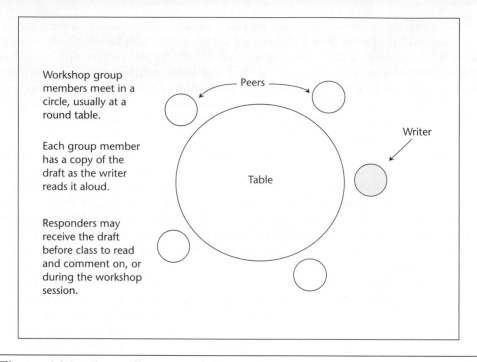

Workshop group members meet in a circle, usually at a round table.

Each group member has a copy of the draft as the writer reads it aloud.

Responders may receive the draft before class to read and comment on, or during the workshop session.

Peers

Writer

Table

Figure 14.1   The small-group workshop

One-on-One Peer Review

Your instructor also may ask you to work with a partner, exchanging drafts and discussing them with each other. While you lose some of the range and quantity of feedback by working with a single reader, this conversation is often richer because each of you is reading the other's work with particular care and attention. You'll probably also have more time to talk because you'll be discussing only two rather than four or five drafts.

One variation of this kind of one-on-one peer review is the draft exchange. Your instructor will ask you to make a pile of drafts at the front of the room and ask you to take a draft from the pile, comment on it, return it, and then take another. You may return multiple times to collect, comment on, and return a draft, and the result is that each draft may have three or four readers during the class session.

THE WRITER'S RESPONSIBILITIES

No matter what model your instructor chooses, the success of the workshop depends largely on the writers themselves. Sure, it can be harder to get what you need from some groups, but in the end, you can always get *some* help with a draft if you ask the right questions and seek certain kinds of responses.

How should you prepare for a workshop to make the most of it, and what are your responsibilities during the workshop? Here's a list you might find helpful:

- Make sure everyone in the group gets a copy of the draft in a timely way.

- Reread and reflect on the draft before the workshop session. What kinds of responses would be most helpful from your group? What questions do you have about the draft's possible problems?

- Time the discussion so that your draft gets the allotted time and no more, particularly if there are other drafts to discuss.

- Avoid getting defensive. Listen to comments on your work in an open-minded way. Your obligation is simply to listen, not to take all the advice you're offered.

- Take notes. There are two reasons for this. First, it will help you remember other students' comments and, second, it will signal that you take those comments seriously. This increases everyone's engagement with your work.

THE READER'S RESPONSIBILITIES

Tina poured her heart and soul into her personal essay draft, and she was eager to get some response to it. When it was her turn to workshop the piece, however, one of the group's members was absent, and two others failed to write her the required response. "It was so lame," she told me. "It was as if no one cared about my essay. It sure makes me feel less inclined to read their stuff carefully." If this workshop group were at Hewlett-Packard or any of the thousands of businesses that encourage teamwork, the slackers would be in trouble. But teamwork in the writing class depends more on internal motivation—a sense of responsibility to others—than any external reward or punishment. There is some external motivation: It pays to be generous with your responses to others' work because you'll learn more about your own.

You can increase your own learning in a workshop and contribute to a writer's positive experience by taking the following responsibilities seriously:

- Always read and respond to a writer's draft in a timely way. The writer may suggest the type of response that would be most helpful; if so, always keep that in mind.

- Whenever possible, focus your responses on particular parts or passages of the draft but, except in an editorial workshop, avoid a focus on grammar or mechanics.

- Offer suggestions, not directives. The word *could* is usually better than *should*. Remember that the purpose of the workshop is to help identify the range of choices a writer might make to improve a draft. There is almost always more than one.

- Identify strengths in the draft. This is often a good place to begin because it sets writers at ease, but, more important, writers often build on strengths in revision.

- Consider varying the roles you play in conversation with your group (see the "Inquiring into the Details: Finding a Role" box). It's easy to fall into a rut in group work, pretty much sticking to saying the same kinds of things or developing certain patterns of response. Stay vigilant about this and try deliberately shifting the role you play in the workshop group.

WHAT CAN GO WRONG AND WHAT TO DO ABOUT IT

Lana is not a fan of workshops. In an argument essay, she complained that they "lack quality feedback," and sometimes workshop groups encourage "fault finding" that can hurt the writer and the writing. Things can go wrong in workshops, of course, and when they do students like Lana feel burned. Typically, unsuccessful

---

INQUIRING INTO THE DETAILS

Finding a Role

"Slacker" is a role that's easy to slide into in small-group work. It's completely passive, and it's really pretty selfish. Active roles ask more of you, but they pay off big because you learn more about your own writing. You might assume any of several active roles in a workshop group. Try them out.

ROLES THAT HELP GROUPS GET THINGS DONE

Initiators: "Here's how we might proceed with this."
Information seekers: "What do we need to know to help the writer?"
Information givers: "This seems to be an important example."
Opinion seekers: "What do you think, Al?"
Opinion givers: "I think this works."
Clarifiers: "We all seem to be saying that the lead doesn't deliver, right?"
Elaborators: "I agree with Tom, and would add..."
Summarizers: "I think we've discussed the thesis problem enough. Should we move on to the evidence?"

ROLES THAT HELP MAINTAIN GROUP HARMONY

Encouragers: "I love that idea, Jen."
Expressivists: "My silence isn't because I'm not moved by the essay, but I'm still trying to figure out why. Is that why you're quiet, Leah?"
Harmonizers: "I think we disagree about this, but that's okay. Let's move on to discussing this next page."
Compromisers: "Maybe both Richard and Joseph are right, particularly if we look at it this way..."
Gatekeepers: "Jon, we haven't heard anything from you yet."

workshop groups suffer from two major problems: lack of commitment by group members and lack of clarity about the process of giving feedback. It's like a cold and a runny nose—when a group is afflicted with one problem it usually suffers from the other.

Lack of commitment is easy to see. The writer whose draft is to be discussed forgets to make copies for the rest of her group. Members who were supposed to provide written responses to a writer's draft before class hastily make notes on his manuscript as it's being discussed. The group is supposed to allot fifteen minutes to discuss each draft but finishes in five. Members are frequently absent and make no effort to provide responses to drafts they missed. Discussion is limited to general, not particularly thoughtful, compliments: "This is really good. I wouldn't change a thing," or "Just add a few details."

This lack of commitment is contagious and soon infects nearly every group meeting. Things rarely improve; they frequently get worse. Part of the problem may be that workshop participants are not clear on what is expected of them, a problem that should be minimized if you reviewed the checklists about the writer's and reader's responsibilities in workshop, discussed in the preceding sections. A solution that is beyond your control is that the instructor evaluates or even grades workshop participation, but a group can evaluate itself, too. Questions members should ask when evaluating their group can include: How effectively does your group work together? How would you evaluate the participation of group members? How do you feel about your own performance? How satisfied were you with the responses to your draft?

Groups that work together over a period of time should always monitor how things are going, and the group evaluations can be particularly helpful for this. If problems persist, the instructor may intervene or the group might consider intervention of its own (consider Exercise 14.1 as one option). Remember, the best workshops have a simple but powerful effect on writers who share their work: *It makes them want to write again.*

EXERCISE 14.1

Group Problem Solving

If group evaluations reveal persistent problems, devote ten minutes to exploring possible solutions.

STEP ONE: Choose a facilitator and a recorder. The facilitator times each step, directs questions to each participant, and makes sure everyone participates. The recorder takes notes on newsprint.

1. Discuss the patterns of problems identified by group members. Do writers seem dissatisfied? Do readers feel like they're performing poorly?

2. What is behind these problems? Brainstorm a list.

3. What might be done to change the way the group operates? You must come up with *at least* one concrete idea that you agree to try.

STEP TWO: After the next workshop session, set aside five minutes at the end to discuss whether the change improved the group's performance. Is there something else you should try?

ONE STUDENT'S RESPONSE

Amy's Perspective On Workshops

WHEN THINGS GO RIGHT

In both small and large workshops things are most productive when the conversation delves deep into a couple of issues instead of skimming the surface on a broad range of topics. My best experiences have been in small workshops because the groups were willing to get more deeply involved in a piece. It probably helps that there aren't too many ideas in a small group and the ones that get thrown out for debate are well considered. I always appreciate it when the group writes notes on my paper for future reference and my absolute best workshops have been multiple sessions with the same small group. Assessing each other's progress really helps in the revision stages.

WHEN THINGS GO WRONG

Especially in a small workshop people can take things too personally and ruin the objective atmosphere, letting their own agenda take precedence over progression. In one of the worst workshops I've been a part of, we were assessing an essay by a writer who chose to write about her relationship with God. The essay had many problems, she used very vague metaphorical language, and the attempted symbolism didn't really work. It was a bit hard to read because of the overly sentimental tone of the piece. Instead of discussing these points, though, the workshop turned into an argument about outside topics and became pretty vicious. The writer was very open to most of the comments I made about some major changes that needed to happen in the piece, but very defensive (understandably) to the personal attacks. The communication simply broke down due to varying personal beliefs when they could have been a strength of the group.

In a large group a fine balance must be achieved. It is important that the conversation runs deep, but also that it covers more than one topic. Because of the multitude of opinions in a large group, the entire workshop can get stuck on one topic or section of the piece. Not only is it unproductive when the debate gets stuck, but it's also really hard to sit through.

METHODS OF RESPONDING

One thing I don't need with an early draft is someone telling me that I misspelled the word *rhythm*. It is a word I'll never be able to spell, and that fact makes me eternally grateful for spellcheckers. I do like to know whether an early draft delivers on its implied promises to the reader, and especially whether there is another angle or another topic lurking there that I might not have noticed. But I don't want my wife, Karen, to read my stuff until I have a late draft to show her because I sometimes find her comments on early drafts discouraging.

The *kinds* of responses we seek to our writing in workshops depend on at least two things: where we are in the writing process and how we feel about the work in progress. This is not particularly surprising. After all, certain kinds of problems arise during different stages of the writing process, and sometimes what we really need from readers of our work is more emotional than practical. We want to be motivated, encouraged, or validated, or feel any number of things that will help us work well.

> The kinds of responses we seek to our writing in workshops depend on at least two things: where we are in the writing process and how we feel about the work in progress.

Experiential and Directive Responses

It makes sense, then, to invite certain kinds of readings of your work that you'll find timely. In general, these responses range from experiential ("this is how I experienced your draft") to more directive ("this is what you could do to make it better"). Which of these two forms would make reader comments on your work most helpful? For example, depending on who you are and how you work, it may be most helpful to get less directive responses to your work early on. Some people feel that very specific suggestions undermine their sense of ownership of rough drafts. They don't want to know what readers think they should do in the revision but how readers experienced their draft. What parts were interesting? What parts were confusing? On the other hand, other writers feel particularly lost in the early stages of the writing process; they could use all the direction they can get. You decide (or your instructor will make suggestions), choosing from the following menu of workshop response methods. These begin with the most experiential methods of response to those that invite your readers to offer quite specific suggestions about the revision.

Response Formats

The following formats for responding to workshop drafts begin with the least directive, most experiential methods and move to the more directive approaches.

THE ETHICS OF RESPONDING

- Respect the writer.
- Everyone contributes.
- Say "could" rather than "should."
- Say "I" rather than "you," as in "I couldn't follow this" rather than "You weren't very clear."

While many of these formats feature some particular ways of responding to drafts, remember that the writer's and reader's responsibilities described earlier apply to all of them. Participate thoughtfully and ethically (see the box "The Ethics of Responding") and you'll be amazed at what you learn about your own writing from talking with other writers about theirs.

The No-Response Workshop. Sometimes the most useful response to your work comes from simply reading it aloud to your group and asking them to just listen—nothing more. Why? You may not be ready for comments because the work is unformed and you're confident that'll you discover the direction you want to go in the next draft. Comments may confuse or distract you. It's always helpful to read your work aloud to yourself, but it's also valuable to read to an audience even if you don't invite a response. You will read with more attention and awareness. Finally, you may simply feel unprepared for a response because your confidence is low.

The method couldn't be simpler. You read your draft with little or no introduction while your group quietly listens. They will not comment unless they want you to repeat something because it was inaudible. Remember to read slowly and clearly.

The Initial-Response Workshop. Robert Brooke, Ruth Mirtz, and Rick Evans[1] suggest a method that is useful for "maintaining your motivation to write while indirectly learning what to improve in your text." It might also be appropriate for an early draft.

They suggest that you invite three kinds of responses to your work: a "relating" response, a "listening" response, and a "positive" response. These three types of response to a draft could be made in writing, in workshop discussion, or both.

- **Relating response.** As the name implies, group members share what personal associations the writer's topic inspires. Perhaps they've had a similar or a contradictory experience. Maybe they've read something or seen something that is relevant to what the writer is trying to do in the draft.

---

[1]Robert Brooke, Ruth Mirtz, and Rick Evans, *Small Groups in Writing Workshops* (Urbana, IL: NCTE, 1994).

- **Listening response.** This is much like the "say back" method some therapists use with patients. Can you summarize what it is that you hear the writing saying in the draft? Is this something that is helpful to know?

- **Positive response.** What parts of the draft really work well and why? Might these be things the writer could build on in the next draft?

The Narrative-of-Thought Workshop. A writer who hears the story of readers' thinking *as they experienced the draft* can get great insight about how the piece shapes readers' expectations and how well it delivers on its promises. This method borrows a term from Peter Elbow— "movie of the mind"—to describe the creation of such a narrative response to a piece of writing.

The easiest way to create stories of your readers' experiences is to prepare your draft ahead of time to accommodate them. Before you make copies for your workshop group, create 2- to 3-inch white spaces in the manuscript immediately after the lead or beginning paragraph, and then again in the middle of the essay. Also leave at least that much white space after the end of the piece.

You will read your draft episodically, beginning by just reading the lead or introductory paragraph, then allowing three or four minutes for your group's members to respond in writing in the space you provided for some of the following questions. The writer should time this and ask everyone to stop writing when it's time to read the next section of the draft. Repeat the process, stopping at the second patch of white space after you've read roughly half of the essay. Give your group the same amount of time to respond in writing and then finish the essay to prompt the final episode of writing.

- **After hearing the lead:** What are your feelings about the topic or the writer so far? Can you predict what the essay might be about? What questions does the lead raise for you that you expect might be answered later? What has struck you?

- **After hearing half:** Tell the story of what you've been thinking or feeling about what you've heard so far. Has the draft fulfilled your expectations from the lead? What do you expect will happen next?

- **After hearing it all:** Summarize your understanding of what the draft is about, including what it *seems* to be saying (or not quite saying). How well did it deliver on its promises in the beginning? What part of your experience of the draft was most memorable? What part seemed least clear?

Discuss with your group each of the responses—after the lead, after the middle, and at the end of the draft. This conversation, and the written comments you receive when you collect their copies of your draft, should give you strong clues about how well you've established a clear purpose in your essay and sustained it from beginning to end. The responses also might give you ideas about directions to take the next draft that you hadn't considered.

The Instructive-Lines Workshop. Most essays balance on a thesis, theme, question, or idea. Like the point of a spinning top, these claims, ideas, or questions are the things around which everything else revolves. Essay drafts, however, may easily topple over because they lack such balance—there is no clear point, or there are too many, or some of the information is irrelevant. In discovery drafts especially, a writer may be seeking the piece's center of gravity—or *centers* of gravity—and a useful response from a workshop group is to help the writer look for the clues about where that center might be.

This format for a workshop invites the members to try to identify the draft's *most important lines and passages,* by clearly marking them with underlining or highlighting. What makes a line or passage important? *These are places where writers explicitly or implicitly seem to suggest what they're trying to say in a draft,* and they may include the following:

- A line or passage where the writer seems to state his or her thesis.
- A part of a narrative essay when the writer adopts a critical stance and seems to be trying to pose a question or speculate about the meaning of an experience or some information.
- A part of the draft in which the writer seems to make an important claim.
- A scene or comparison or observation that hints at the question the writer is exploring (or could explore).
- A comment in a digression that the writer didn't seem to think was important, but you think might be.

These portions of the text become the subject of discussion in the workshop session. Questions to consider include the following: Why did this particular line seem important? What does it imply about what you think is the meaning of the essay? Do the different underlined passages speak to each other—can they be combined or revised into a controlling idea or question for the next draft—or do they imply separate essays or treatments? Would the writer underline something else? How might the different interpretations of the draft be reconciled?

The Purpose Workshop. Sometimes writers know their purpose in a draft: "I'm trying to argue that the Enron collapse represented the failure of current methods of compensating CEOs," or "I'm proposing that having vegetarian fast-food restaurants would reduce American obesity," or "This essay explores the question of why I was so relieved when my father died." What these writers may need most from their workshop groups is feedback on how well the draft accomplishes particular purposes.

Before the workshop session, the writer crafts a statement of purpose similar to those in the preceding paragraph—a sentence that clearly states what the writer is trying to do in the draft. This statement of purpose should include a verb that implies what action the writer is trying to take—for example, *explore, argue, persuade, propose, review, explain,* or *analyze.* As you probably guessed, these verbs are usually associated with a particular form of inquiry or genre.

The writer should include this sentence *at the end* of the draft. It's important that you make group members aware of your purpose only after they've read the entire piece and not before. Discussion and written responses should then focus on some of the following questions:

- Were you surprised by the stated purpose, or did the essay prepare you for it?

- If the stated purpose did surprise you, what did you think the writer was trying to do in the draft instead?

- Does the lead explicitly state or hint at the stated purpose?

- What parts or paragraphs of the draft seemed clearly relevant to the stated purpose, and which seemed to point in another direction?

- Did the draft seem to succeed in accomplishing the writer's purpose?

If more directive responses would be helpful to you, consider also asking some questions such as whether there might not be a stronger beginning or lead buried elsewhere in the draft, or soliciting suggestions about which parts or paragraphs should be cut or what additional information might be needed. Which parts of the draft seemed to work best in the context of the writer's stated purpose, and which didn't work so well?

The Graphing-Reader-Interest Workshop. What commands readers' attention in a draft and what doesn't? This is useful to know, obviously, because our overall aim is to engage readers from beginning to end—which is difficult to do, particularly in longer drafts, and reader attention often varies from paragraph to paragraph in shorter drafts. But if three or four paragraphs or a couple of pages of your draft drone on, then the piece isn't working well and you need to do something about it in revision.

One way to know this is to ask your workshop group members to graph their response to your essay, paragraph by paragraph, and then discuss what is going on in those sections that drag.

For this workshop, consecutively number all the paragraphs in your draft. You or your instructor will provide each member of your group with a "reader interest chart" (see Figure 14.2), on which the corresponding paragraph numbers are listed. On the vertical axis is a scale that represents reader interest, with 5 being high interest and 1 being low interest in that particular paragraph. As you slowly read your draft aloud to your group's members, they mark the graph after each paragraph to roughly indicate their interest in what the paragraph says and how it says it.

When you're finished, you'll have a visual representation of how the essay worked, paragraph by paragraph, but the important work is ahead. Next, you

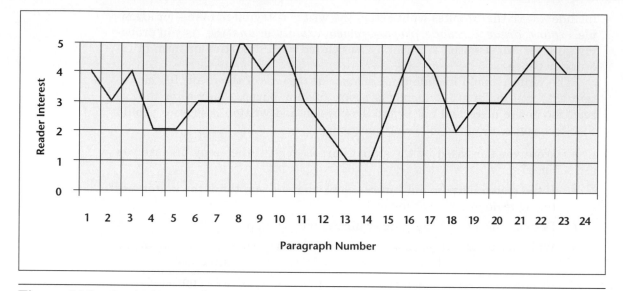

Figure 14.2   Reader interest chart

need to discuss with your group *why* a paragraph or section of the draft failed to hold some readers' attention. What is going on in those parts of the draft?

- Are they confusing?
- Do they needlessly digress?
- Is the prose awkward?
- Is there too much or too little explanation?
- Are they too loaded with facts and not enough analysis?
- Does the writer seem to lose his voice?

One way to find out what's going on with the weaker parts of your essay is to look at the stronger ones. What do you notice about those paragraphs that were rated 4 or 5 by your group members? What are the particular strengths of these sections? Can you do more of that in other, less lively sections of the draft?

The Sum-of-the-Parts Workshop. Like a watch, a well-written essay moves fluently forward because all of its parts work together. In workshops you can never talk about all those parts; there is too little time, and often it's hard to tease apart all the gears and the springs that make an essay go. But you can try to be as thorough as you can during a workshop, essentially running through a checklist of some of the most important elements, including purpose, theme, structure, information, and style. In this workshop, you attempt to cover as much territory as possible, so the responses you get will have breadth but not depth. You also invite some directive responses from your readers—suggestions for the revision and specific areas of confusion—as well as their interpretation of your purpose and theme.

One of the best ways to solicit this information is to use a worksheet like the one that follows. Typically, this worksheet would be filled out by your group's members outside class and before you workshop the draft. It would then be attached to the copies of your draft and returned to you after the group discusses the work. If your peers respond thoughtfully to the worksheet, it can generate a wealth of information for you about your draft.

The Thesis Workshop. An alternative to the sum-of-all-parts format is to focus on a single element of the draft that you are particularly concerned about, and no part is more important than the thesis. An essay without an implicit theme or an explicit thesis is an essay without meaning. No one is particularly interested in reading a pointless story or research essay, nor are most readers interested in points that seem unrelated to the information in the draft or that are painfully obvious. For example, the idea that the death of your Aunt Trudy was sad for you is a much less compelling theme to build an essay around than the idea that her death—and the deaths of family members generally—upset the family system in ways that helped you to take on new roles, new identities.

A thesis workshop will help you make sure there is a controlling idea or question behind the draft, and help you think more deeply about what you're trying to say. Your workshop members can help with this because they bring a range of perspectives and experiences to a conversation about your theme that might make it richer and more informative for you.

WORKSHOP WORKSHEET

Purpose: In your own words, what is the writer's motive in the draft? Use one of the following verbs to describe this in a sentence: *explore, explain, argue, analyze, review, report, propose, persuade, reflect.*

Theme: State in your own words what you think the thesis, main point, or central question is in this draft. What question does this idea or question raise for you?

Information: Name at least two specific places in the draft where you wanted more information to fully appreciate what the writer was trying to say. What kind of information do you suggest (anecdote, story, fact, detail, background, example, interview, dialogue, opposing perspective, description, case study, etc.)?

Design: Identify *at least* one paragraph or passage that seemed out of place. Any suggestions about where it belongs?

Style: Place brackets [ ] around several sentences or passages in the draft that seemed awkward or confusing to read.

In this workshop, group members receive the drafts ahead of time. Before the workshop session they should underline the thesis, main idea, theme, or question that seems to be behind the draft. This will be the *main thing* the writer seems to be saying or exploring. This isn't particularly difficult in essays with explicit thesis statements, such as arguments or proposals, but in personal essays and other more literary pieces, the theme may not be so explicit. In that type of essay, they should underline the passage that seems central to the meaning of the essay. This may be a reflective passage or it might be a scene or moment.

Second, at the top of a piece of paper, they should write down in a sentence or two—at most—the thesis or theme as they understand it. This may involve simply copying it down from the draft. However, if the thesis or theme is not that clear or explicit, each reader should write it down in his or her own words, trying to capture the main point of the draft.

Then members should fastwrite for five minutes about their own thoughts and experiences about the writer's thesis or theme, constantly hunting for questions it raises for them. Say the draft's thesis is that the university athletic programs have become too powerful and have undermined the university's more important academic mission. In the fastwrite, explore what you've noticed about the football team's impact on the school. Where does the football program get funds? Does it compete with academic programs? Then fastwrite about what you've heard—for instance, that athletics have strong alumni support. Keep the fastwrite focused on the thesis; if it helps, stop and reread it for another prompt.

The workshop session that follows will be a conversation largely focused on what people thought was the point of the draft, and their own thoughts and feelings about it. The writer should facilitate the conversation without comment and make sure the following two things are discussed in this order:

1. What seems to be the thesis, theme, or question behind the essay? Is it clear? Are there alternative ideas about what it might be?

2. What does each group member think or feel about what the writer seems to be saying? How do the reader's experiences and observations relate to the writer's main point or question? And especially, what questions should the writer consider in the next draft?

Although it may be hard to keep quiet if your draft is being discussed, the conversation will probably surprise you. You may discover that several of your group members either failed to understand what you were trying to say in the draft or give you a completely new idea about what you were up to. At its best, the thesis workshop inspires you to think more deeply about your theme or main idea as you consider the range of experiences and questions that other people have about it. Take lots of notes.

The Editing Workshop. In a late draft, the larger issues—for example, having a clear purpose, focus, and point, as well as appropriate information to support it—may be resolved to your satisfaction, or you may feel that you already have some pretty good ideas about how to deal with them. If so, what you may need most from your workshop group is editorial advice: responses to your work at the sentence and paragraph levels.

In the editing workshop, you invite your group members to focus on style and clarity (and perhaps grammar and mechanics). The questions that direct the reading of the draft might include some or all of the following:

- Did you stumble over any awkward passages that seemed to interrupt the fluency of the writing?

- Were there any sentences or passages that you had to read a few times to understand?

- Could any long paragraphs be broken down into smaller ones? Did any paragraphs seem to be about more than one thing?

- Are the first and last lines of the essay well crafted? Are the last lines of paragraphs strong enough?

- Were there any abrupt transitions between paragraphs?

- Was the voice or tone of the draft consistent?

- (Optional) Did you notice any patterns of grammatical problems, including run-on sentences, unclear pronoun references, or lack of subject–verb agreement?

Group members who see any of these problems should bracket [ ] the sentence or passage and refer to it when discussing the editorial issue with the group. The workshop discussion has the following ground rules:

- Be respectful of the writer's feelings. Some of us feel that style is a very personal issue, and that grammar problems are related somehow to our self-worth.

- Don't have arguments about editorial judgments. Group members don't have to agree. In fact, you probably won't agree about a lot of things. Offer your comments on style as suggestions and then move on, although don't hesitate to offer a differing opinion.

- Make sure to identify places in the draft where the writing is working just fine. Editorial workshops need not focus exclusively on problems. Sentences, paragraphs, or passages that work well stylistically can often help the writer see how to revise the less effective parts.

- If readers have some comments about larger issues in the draft, things such as purpose or theme, ask the writer first if he or she welcomes that kind of feedback. Otherwise, keep the workshop focused on editorial matters.

An editing workshop may sound a little harrowing. It really isn't, particularly if the group knows the ground rules. My students often tell me that these conversations about style are some of the best workshops they have had.

Everybody learns something—not just the writer—a principle that applies to many workshop formats and another reason that peer review is such a useful practice in the writing classroom.

Reflecting on the Workshop

The real work follows the workshop. Then you have the task of mulling over the things you've heard about your draft and deciding how you're going to rewrite it. This calls for a way of inquiring—reflection—that you've already practiced. As soon as possible after your workshop session, reread your notes and your readers' comments, then go to your journal and fastwrite for five minutes. Choose one of the following prompts to get—and keep—you going.

- What did I hear that seemed most useful? What did I hear that I'm not sure about?
- What responses to my draft do I remember most? Why?
- What did I think I needed to do to revise the draft before the workshop? Did my peer review experience change my mind? Did it reinforce my initial plans?
- What do I plan to do to revise this draft to make it stronger?

USING WHAT YOU HAVE LEARNED

The writing workshop is just one of many forms of collaboration that you'll likely experience both during and after college. Even unsuccessful workshops are instructive because they help you understand how groups work and what roles you can play to make them function better. Consider your experience so far.

1. What is the best workshop group experience you've had in this class? What made it so good? What was the worst experience? What made it so bad?

2. As you reflect on your own performance in groups, what have you learned about yourself as a collaborator? How would you describe yourself as a group member? How would you *like* to describe yourself?

3. If you're currently involved in a group project in another class, how would you compare your writing workshop with that other group project? Can what you've learned in one provide useful guidance for the other?

APPENDIX A

THE WRITING PORTFOLIO*

What Is a Portfolio?

You've probably heard about stock portfolios and artist portfolios, but the term *writing portfolio* may be something new. *Portfolio* in these three examples means a collection of stocks, photographs or paintings, or writings that represent something about the compiler: for example, if you have a stock portfolio in which 75 percent of your money is invested in high risk growth funds and the other 25 percent is in safe bond funds, then you might be showing that you're a risk taker. If you are an artist and you select a range of photographs taken over a long period of time, you might be showing how you've developed and changed as a photographer.

Writing portfolios can reflect similar things about their authors. As a collection of the work you've done for a writing class, a portfolio can demonstrate how you've developed as a writer, it can show specific writing principles you've learned, or it can illustrate the range of genres you have worked with (to name a few). Often it will be a large percentage of your course grade, so the work you submit will have been revised several times and you might be asked to reflect on your assembled work, exploring what you want the portfolio to illustrate. In fact, the whole idea of using a portfolio to evaluate your work emphasizes the principles of inquiry and reflection at the heart of this book.

Instructors use portfolios in different ways: Some require certain essays and assignments to be included, some allow *you* to choose what to include, others ask that you choose according to particular guidelines (for example, pieces that demonstrate your ability to conduct research, to put a lesson plan together if it's a teaching portfolio, or to revise). It's important that you understand what kind of portfolio your instructor is requiring and why. We'll talk about why later—let's look first at the different kinds of portfolios you might be asked to assemble.

---

*Appendixes A, B, C, and D were written by Dr. Michelle Payne, English Department Chair at Boise State University.

Types of Portfolios

It's important here to distinguish between *unevaluated* and *evaluated* portfolios. An unevaluated portfolio would be one in which you are collecting all your work for the course, like a journal or working folder, but your instructor will not be evaluating the material. You keep class notes, doodles, drafts of essays, exercises, and anything else that relates to the course. From that folder, you then might be asked to *choose specific assignments*, continue working on them, and turn them in for your final portfolio. A final portfolio is one type of evaluated portfolio. Your instructor either gives you the evaluation criteria for it or helps the class develop those criteria with him or her. You turn in selected pieces from the course, either freely chosen by you or required by your instructor. The work is "final" in that you have stopped revising, done your best to make it as effective an essay as possible, and are ready to have it graded. Unevaluated portfolios, then, are places in which you experiment with, collect, and play around with your ideas and your writing, not worrying about evaluation as much as you would when you assemble an evaluated portfolio. All the activities in this book, for example, would be part of a writing journal or working folder that your instructor might not evaluate. Then, as you develop essays from those exercises, you revise them into final products that your instructor can grade.

Unevaluated Portfolios

The unevaluated portfolios you are most likely to encounter in your college writing are as follows:

- *A journal or working folder.* In this type of unevaluated portfolio, keep all your work for your writing course—everything that you do in and out of class, all your assignments and drafts. It's a place where you can track your progress as a writer because you have everything there. Some instructors ask you to turn this type of portfolio in for a holistic grade (that is, the entire body of work is evaluated, not individual pieces), based on criteria that are different from the criteria used for evaluating a portfolio of final drafts (for example, in evaluating a writing journal, your instructor might consider whether you've completed all the assignments, taken risks in your writing, and experimented).

- *A learning portfolio.* For this type of unevaluated portfolio, you collect materials from your course and possibly other places that reflect something about your learning process. Let's say your writing instructor wants you to keep a record of your learning in another course, such as sociology. You might include class notes that changed the way you understood a concept, restaurant napkins scribbled with conversations you've overheard, a paper you are assigned to write, and some reflections on how the theories you've been learning affect how you perceive your world. You can include both print and nonprint materials, such as photos or music. Learning portfolios often allow for free choice, so you have to carefully select what you will include and why. This type of portfolio may be helpful as you apply the concepts you learn in this course—about inquiry, essay writing, and reflection—to another course.

Evaluated Portfolios

Evaluated portfolios include the following types:

- A *midterm portfolio*. As the name suggests, this portfolio is assembled at midterm. Your instructor might ask you to include particular assignments—such as your two best reading responses and a revised essay— and write a cover letter that explains, for example, what you've learned about writing that is reflected in these pieces. You might also be asked to evaluate the portfolio yourself and discuss your goals for the rest of the course. A midterm portfolio might be evaluated, but it might also be used as a practice run for the final portfolio at the end of the course and not be evaluated.

- A *final portfolio—limited choice*. Your instructor may require you to include specific assignments and essays in the portfolio you turn in at the end of the course. Let's say your university's writing program requires all students to write a research essay in their first-year writing course and to demonstrate that they can use documentation effectively, support their claims with evidence, and do more than simply string information together. Your instructor, then, would ask you to include one or more research essays in the final portfolio so he or she can assess whether you have learned what is required. That might be the only required essay and you would have some choice about what else to include. Or you might be required to include a profile, an argument, and an ethnographic essay, as well. In addition, instructors might ask you to include a reflective essay with your final portfolio (explained in more detail next). In general, a final portfolio emphasizes the final products of the course, the revised and polished work that shows what you've learned for the entire term.

- A *final portfolio—open choice*. While all your work will be revised and polished, your instructor may ask you to choose your best writing for the course and not require particular essays. She might ask that you choose only from the essays you've written or that you choose from the informal writing you've done, as well (such as the writing exercises in this book). She may require a certain number of pages (say, twenty to twenty-five pages) or a certain number of assignments (three out of the five essays required in the course) or leave the length and number of assignments open. Here are a couple of examples: If you feel your research essay is better than your ethnographic essay, then you might include it and not work any further on your ethnographic essay. You might also include your personal essay, an argument, and your response to a particular writing exercises. You would include these pieces because you believe they are your best work, but you want to be sure you can talk specifically about *why* they are the best and *what* they show your instructor about what you've learned. For instance, do you want to show your growth, your success in using writing as inquiry, or what you've learned about crafting paragraphs?

Why Require a Portfolio?

Before we talk more about how to choose the materials to include in your portfolio, we should talk about why you will be expected to assemble one. If you are keeping an unevaluated portfolio, your instructor wants to emphasize your learning process at least as much as your final product. We rarely take the time to reflect on how we learn, but doing so can help you learn better in your other courses. Are you a visual learner? Do you learn best when you have a relationship with your teacher or when the teacher is more removed? If you learn more outside school, why? Learning portfolios enable you to develop even better learning strategies and understand why you might struggle with certain learning situations. The same is true for a writing journal or working folder. As you collect everything you do in a writing course, you can pause periodically and reflect on which writing strategies seem to sabotage your efforts, which seem to work well, how you might work through writer's block, or what principles about writing you've been learning. Many of the exercises in this book prompt you to reflect on your writing process, your reading strategies, and your learning and thinking, so if you've been doing them, you have already seen the benefits of reflecting on your process.

In both kinds of unevaluated portfolios, the *process* of whatever you're doing is being emphasized and valued. You don't have to worry about writing beautifully styled sentences the first time around or having a complicated reading all figured out the first time through. An unevaluated portfolio allows for—in fact encourages—the messiness of writing and thinking instead of focusing only on polished work. These kinds of portfolios emphasize risk, experimentation, and reflection on the process of writing and learning, all of which are central to the ideas in this book. These types of portfolios, then, reflect and reinforce what you've been learning about writing so far.

Evaluated portfolios are important for very similar reasons. In order to get your drafts to the point that they are ready to be evaluated, you are encouraged all term to experiment, rewrite, and critique them. In fact, most of the term you are working in your writing journal, exploring ideas, commenting on peers' drafts in workshop, revising your own drafts, and taking them apart again, all in an effort to learn more about writing and make your essays more effective.

Portfolios allow you to do all that over a long period of time and in a relatively "evaluation-free" zone, so you are graded based on your final product at the end, not in the middle, of the process.

Your final product, though, is the result and reflection of all that work you did throughout the semester. In addition, the reflection exercises in this book have had you thinking about your learning all term. You will be more conscious of the writing and reading strategies that work best for you, and so will be better prepared to write the reflective essay that your instructor may require in the portfolio.

Of course, the final product is what is evaluated in a final portfolio, so while this kind of portfolio reinforces the process of inquiry and reflection, it also emphasizes the way a sentence is crafted, the way an essay is organized, and the way a writer explores an idea. A portfolio, then, allows an instructor to evaluate *both* the process of writing and the quality of the final product.

Organizing Portfolios

Because a writing portfolio emphasizes the *process* of writing and learning as much as the final product, you'll want to keep your course materials organized— that is, the materials that reflect your process. Whether or not your instructor assigns a journal or working folder, it's a good idea to keep one yourself. You can do this on the computer or in a notebook. You can organize your writing journal or working folder in several ways, including these options:

1. **Organize by chronological order.** Keep everything that you do in the course in the order you complete it.
2. **Organize by assignments.** Within each category, include all the writing you've done (fastwriting, drafts, exercises), peer and teacher responses, notes, research materials, and so on. As an example, your portfolio might be broken out into the following categories:
   - Profile
   - Ethnographic essay
   - Review
   - Argument
   - Reflective exercises
   - Reading responses
   - Essay exam
3. **Organize by subjects.** Here you place your writing into categories defined by the subject or theme of the writing. For example:
   - Racism (profile, research essay)
   - Italy trip (personal essay, review, argument)

With this approach, you have a better sense of how you've explored a topic through different genres, comparing what you've learned about the subject as well as about the form.

4. **Organize by stage of process.** Here you place your writing into categories based on what place in the writing process it falls, starting with your fastwriting and journal writing and ending with your final drafts and reflective writing. For example:

- Fastwriting/journal writing
- Exercises
- Sketches
- Early drafts
- Peer responses
- Instructor responses
- Revisions
- Final drafts
- Reflective writing

You can also create your own categories to organize your class work. However you choose to organize your writing, be sure to keep everything you write for the course; don't throw anything away. If you are using a computer, *save all of your writing files and keep a separate backup copy.*

If you are expected to include a reflective letter or essay as a preface to your portfolio, it's a good idea to create a separate section in your journal or folder for all the reflective writing you've done in the class. You can do all the reflective exercises in that separate section, or you can include them for each separate assignment. However you do it, keeping your reflective writing in one place will make it easier to compose your reflective letter or essay.

Writing a Reflective Letter or Essay

You may have to preface your final portfolio with a letter or essay that introduces the pieces you've included and reflect on what you've learned about writing, reading, and inquiry. For some instructors, this letter or essay becomes crucial in evaluating the whole portfolio because it gives coherence and purpose to the material and articulates what you've learned. In my own classes, the reflective essay can make the difference of half a letter grade in the overall evaluation of the portfolio. As always, clarify with your instructor what is expected in the reflective letter or essay and how it will be weighed in the portfolio grade. While some instructors require a five- to seven-page essay or letter that begins the portfolio, others may require a prefatory letter for *each piece* you include in the portfolio. Some want only a reflection on the writing process for each essay; others may want only a narrative of how your thinking changed about each subject you wrote about. Regardless, you'll want to spend some time going through your writing journal or folder and reflecting on what you notice. Here are some questions that might help:

- **Patterns.** As you flip through the pages of your writing journal or folder, what patterns do you notice? What seems to happen frequently or stand out to you? For example, you might notice that you always begin your essays the same way, or you ended up writing about the same subject the whole semester without realizing it, or you got better at organizing your essays and using significant detail.

- **Reflective writing.** As you look only at the reflective writing you've done throughout the course (and the reflective exercises in this book), what do you notice? What five things have you learned about writing, reading, and inquiry based on that early reflective writing?

- **Change over time.** How did you describe your writing process (and/or reading process) at the beginning of the course? How would you describe it now? If it has changed, why and how?

- **Writing principles.** List five to seven principles about writing that you have learned in this course, the five to seven most important things you've learned about writing, reading, and inquiry. Or, list five to seven strategies for writing and reading that you will take with you into other writing situations.

- **Revision.** For each of the essays you are including in your portfolio, what would you do differently if you had more time?

- **Writing processes.** For each of the essays in your portfolio, describe the writing and thinking process that led to the final product. Emphasize the most important changes you made and why you made them.

- **Most and least effective writing.** Which essay in the portfolio is your strongest? Your weakest? Why?

- **Effect of peer response.** How have your peers and other readers of your work affected the revisions you've made?

- **Showing what you've learned.** What does your portfolio demonstrate about you as a writer, a student, a reader, a researcher? How? Be as specific as possible.

- **What's missing.** What is *not* reflected in your portfolio that you believe is important for your instructor to know?

- **Expectations.** How does your portfolio meet the expectations for effective writing defined in your class?

- **Applying the textbook.** How have you applied the principles about each essay form that are outlined in this textbook?

- **Personal challenge.** In what ways did you challenge yourself in this course?

> ## TYPICAL PROBLEMS IN REFLECTIVE ESSAYS/LETTERS
>
> - Use of overly general and vague comments.
> - Not enough specific details.
> - Giving the teacher only what you think he or she wants whether it's true or not.
> - Critiquing the course (usually this is reserved for end-of-term evaluations that are confidential and anonymous); it's not wise to risk criticizing the person who is evaluating you.
> - Comments that suggest you don't take the assignment seriously.

Your instructor might ask you to address only three or four of these questions in the letter or essay itself, but it's a good idea to do some fastwriting on all of them. Doing so will help your essay or letter be more specific, thoughtful, and persuasive.

As with any essay, you'll want to take this one through several revisions and get feedback from readers before you include it in the portfolio. Your instructor might even ask you to workshop a draft of this with your group. If you've done some fastwriting on the preceding questions, you are in good shape to compose a first draft of your reflective letter or essay. Keep in mind who your audience is—your teacher, teachers unknown to you, and/or your peers—and address what that audience expects. Be as specific as possible, citing examples from your work and drawing on the terms and principles you've discussed in class and read about in this book.

If you've been doing reflective writing all term, you will have plenty of material to draw from to make your reflective essay or letter concrete, substantive, and as honest as it can be (given the circumstances). You'll probably surprise yourself with all that you've learned.

Final Preparations

Before you turn your portfolio in, take time to proofread it carefully, possibly asking one of your peers for help. Check again to be sure you've met all the criteria for the portfolio, including what is required, assembling it appropriately, and formatting it as required. This is work that you are proud of, so the way you present it should reflect that pride. It should meet high standards for presentation and quality.

APPENDIX B
THE LITERATURE REVIEW

What Is a Literature Review?

Have you ever wondered why those academic articles you read for your research projects seem to begin with a list of the other people who've talked about the same ideas? Somewhere in the first few pages you find a section that seems to list everyone who's ever had anything to say about the subject of, say, Charlotte Brontë or quantum physics. This "who's who" list, though, is actually a common academic convention called the *literature review*. In it a writer reviews or summarizes what has already been said about his or her research question and then analyzes it.

An explicit example of giving this kind of background is the opening to "Is the Medium the Message?" by Ellen M. Bennet, et al. As you read it, notice the way the writers acknowledge the specific people who are a part of this conversation and try to accurately summarize their contributions (I've italicized some of the phrases these writers use to signal this summary). Imagine this as the writers' way of introducing us to the conversation that we've just walked into. The article begins:

> When Pennsylvania official Budd Dwyer committed suicide during a press conference in January 1987, television coverage of the incident was criticized sharply, although most stations cut the tape before the shot was fired. Somehow, coverage of this event by print reporters and photojournalists did not stir the same scorn from the critics or the public that TV news accounts evoked.
>
> The "bad news" bias of journalism professionals has been of increasing concern generally, and much of the criticism has been leveled specifically at television news. Both *practitioners of the profession and news consumers* have complained that TV news exploits graphic and grotesque news events for the purpose of increasing ratings in the competitive race for profits. *Two common responses* to these criticisms are that, first, the morbid event is newsworthy and, second, that this is what the audience wants.
>
> *A common criticism* leveled at television is that it is excessively morbid in its presentation of news. Even *those who have pioneered the field of television news* identify the medium as uniquely able to portray tragedy because it is so visual.

Researchers have also noted the near universal appeal of stories about disturbing, unpleasant, tragic events. *Haskins* has observed that "throughout history humans have been drawn to public spectacles involving bloody death and disfigurement, to helpless victims, to public hangings and crucifixions and decapitation." The purpose of the present study…

Although this introduction doesn't cover a wide range of specific experts in the field, it does summarize what most people in the field have said—or what people *outside* have said. It gives us an overview, a brief summary with background on the issue so we all know why it is important and what has been said about it already. After all, how can we determine how significant someone's research is unless they tell us how it compares with the work of other people in the same field?

So in a literature review, a writer gives readers an overview of the conversation that other scholars, writers, or researchers have been having over the years so they will understand why his question is important and where it comes from. But he also gives us this critical overview to signal that he's done his research, he knows who has said what and why it's important, and therefore he has credibility to write about the subject, too. A literature review, then, does at least three things:

1. **Summarizes the established knowledge** on a particular subject and **analyzes it** within the context of the writer's overall thesis or research question.

2. **Establishes why the writer's question is significant,** given what has already been said, and how it emerged as an important subject for further study.

3. **Establishes the writer's ethos or credibility,** signaling membership in a particular community (such as the field of biology or engineering) and demonstrating thoroughness in researching.

As you might guess, writing a literature review means you will focus on the two ways of inquiring we've discussed in this book: *explanation* and *evaluation*. The thinking and reading you do *before* you write the review, however, will demand that you use all four ways of inquiring, including reflection and exploration.

How to Write the Literature Review

The easiest and most efficient way to write a literature review is to approach its composition systematically. This will include gathering materials, reading strategies, organizing, and drafting processes.

Gathering Materials

First, you have to conduct some research: Do a thorough search for materials related to your research question and sort out which are most relevant and most important in the field. Often you can discover who the important researchers and scholars are in an area by looking at the bibliographies of the articles and books you have found. Whose name seems to occur frequently? Who seems to be cited quite often? Whose work seems to be central to the ideas you're talking about?

Sorting out what is relevant to your question all depends on your question and the scope of your research.

- If your research question hasn't been explored by others yet, then you need to look at material that helps you discuss *why* it hasn't been researched before.

- If you are using a particular theory or approach to your research—such as feminist literary theory to interpret *Jane Eyre* or an ethnographic approach to understand reading skills in third graders—you will need to discuss that particular theory or approach. What has been argued about this theory or approach? What are the key principles and arguments that will be relevant to your own work?

- If your research question touches on an area that has been written about a great deal—let's say Shakespeare or World War II—then you need to narrow your overview to the particular issue about that subject you are focusing on—say, gender in Shakespeare's tragedies or military strategies during the invasion of Normandy. Then you have to choose the sources that are most relevant and significant in the conversation that has been going on about the particular subject you're researching.

You cannot cover everything that has been said in the last seventy-five years—nor should you. You have to have criteria for deciding what you will include in your literature review. How many sources you discuss is often dependent on how long your project is (for a thesis or dissertation, a literature review is a chapter of about thirty pages; for a ten- to fifteen-page research paper, the review might be several paragraphs).

Reading Strategies

Like any other assignment, the reading strategies you use for this assignment will have a particular purpose. Your main task will be to understand well the argument each source is making, and then to judge its conclusions, methods of research, evidence, and relevance to your overall question or purpose. Most important, when you get ready to write your literature review, you need to have made connections among all the materials you've read, not only evaluating them against each other, but showing how each is related to the other. The following are some questions you should keep in mind as you read individual texts:

- What is the author's overall question and her conclusions? What argument is she making?

- What research methods does she use (for example, empirical, ethnographic, theoretical, case study)? What are the strengths and limitations of this method? Has she addressed them? How reliable are her conclusions?

- How well does she review the literature relevant to her subject?

- How effectively does she argue her case? Are her conclusions logical? Is her evidence relevant, specific, and substantial? Are her emotional appeals effective? Does she include counterarguments?

- What seem to be the gaps or unanswered questions in her research and/or conclusions? In other words, what does she not address or seem to dismiss or ignore that you think is relevant?

- What other approach might she have taken to this issue?

- How does this particular article/review/book/study fit into what has already been said? What is its relationship to other studies? For example, does it build on the work of another scholar, does it refute a long-standing theory, does it critique the research methods used, does it answer a question raised at the end of an earlier study?

After you finish reading individual texts, you will want to ask some broader questions:

- As you read all the material you've gathered, what overall patterns seem to emerge? For example, what seems to be common knowledge among the people in this area?

- Do the studies share similar research methods?

- Do they address different perspectives on the same question?

- Do they come to similar conclusions?

- Do they all seem to ignore similar assumptions or limitations?

- In other words, what kind of picture can you get about this conversation?

Finally, before you begin writing your literature review, use this seed sentence to help you summarize the material and articulate how your question is related to what you've read: *When most people think about/study/write about_____, they say/assert/argue _____ . However, what they don't address is _____ .*

Organizing

Once you have a sense of the conversation going on about your subject and you've carefully read and evaluated your sources, you need to figure out how you will organize your review. What you don't want to do is simply list all the relevant sources like a grocery list or a list of summaries, beginning each paragraph with "According to..." Although you'll want to introduce the authors using this kind of signal phrase, you don't want to organize your literature review by author. Instead, you need to organize the material around each source's *relationship* to the others and its significance to your project. That's what you've begun to do by answering the preceding questions about the patterns you see among all the sources you've read.

When you focus on the relationship among sources, you will be comparing, contrasting, and evaluating them based on particular criteria. You might, for example, want to focus on the trends in the research or compare the various conclusions of researchers. You need an organizing strategy. The following strategies are only a few of the possibilities:

- Trends in current research.
- Types of research methods used (quantitative, qualitative).
- Theoretical approaches.
- Specific purposes for the research/arguments.
- Conclusions reached.
- Gaps in the literature, questions not answered, and/or conflicts among theories, conclusions, evidence, or research methods.
- Chronology, or a history of how one idea led to the next.

The organizational strategy you choose will also be related to the question you're pursuing in your own research, especially if your literature review is part of a longer essay. If you are writing an essay about the medical uses of leeches, for example, you probably won't focus on the types of research methods used or the theoretical approaches. You might write a narrative of how leeches have been used in history, you might focus on what is known and what is not, or you might look at conflicting studies on the effectiveness of using leeches in medicine. The literature review should offer the reader context for your own question, reasons why it's important, and your own approach to the subject compared to that of others in the field.

You can use these organizational strategies to create sections in your literature review or to organize by paragraph. It all depends on the number of sources you plan to study and the length of your essay.

APPENDIX C

THE ANNOTATED BIBLIOGRAPHY

What Is an Annotated Bibliography?

You've had experience putting together a Works Cited or References page for your research essays, but you may not have had experience writing an annotated bibliography, which includes descriptions and comments about each of your sources. It is a list in which each citation is followed by a short descriptive and sometimes evaluative paragraph or annotation. Many scholars use published annotated bibliographies during their research to help them narrow down the material that seems most relevant to their work, but you might be asked to write one as part of a larger project for a class, sometimes in preparation for a literature review or a research proposal. Annotated bibliographies, then, can serve a lot of different purposes, so if you are assigned one, you want to be sure you understand your role as a researcher and writer.

We will examine four types of annotated bibliographies in this appendix.[1] Their purposes include indicating content and coverage, describing thesis and argument, evaluating the work, and a combination of these three. If you have looked at published annotated bibliographies, you have probably seen one of these types. When you are assigned to write an annotated bibliography, you'll need to decide which of the following four forms is the most appropriate, but you can also consider using these at various stages of your own research process.

Indicative Bibliography. Are you being asked to *indicate* what the source contains or simply identify the topic of the source, but *not evaluate or discuss the argument and evidence*? If so, explain what the source is about ("This article explores gender in Shakespeare's tragedies."). List the main ideas it discusses—this may include chapter titles, a list of authors included if the source is an anthology, or the main ideas included in the subsections if it's an article ("Topics covered include male homosocial desire, women as witches, and conceptions of romantic love."). Usually, in a descriptive annotation, you don't evaluate the source's argument or relevance, nor do you describe its overall thesis.

---

[1] The four forms discussed are found on the Writing Center Web site for the University of Wisconsin–Madison (http://www.wisc.edu/writing/Handbook/AnnBib_content.html).

WHY WRITE AN ANNOTATED BIBLIOGRAPHY?

- It can help you compile a list of sources on your subject that will need to be sorted through later. It can also help you decide if you want to return to a source later in your process.
- If you have been keeping a dialogue journal for your research project, you can refer to it in composing these annotations. This type of bibliography can help you further think through your own developing thesis or conclusions.
- This type of bibliography will also help you develop your own thesis, and it will help you write a literature review, as well.

Informative Bibliography. Are you being asked *to summarize the argument* for each source? If so, briefly state each work's thesis, the primary assertions and evidence that support the main argument, and any conclusions the author makes. You are not evaluating the effectiveness of the argument, nor are you delineating the content of the source (as you would in an indicative form); instead, you are informing your audience about the works' arguments and conclusions.

Evaluative Bibliography. Are you being asked *to evaluate the sources* you find? If so, your annotations will include a brief summary of the argument and conclusions and then move on to critically evaluate it: How useful is the source to your particular project? What are the limitations of the study or argument? What are the strengths? How reliable are the conclusions? How effective are the research methods? The criteria you use for evaluating each source depend on the purpose of the bibliography, whether you are compiling one to help focus your research project and sort out the most important articles or you are writing one to help others decide what is most relevant in the subject area. Be sure you are clear about the evaluation criteria.

Combination of Types. Are you being asked to be *both informative and evaluative*? Many annotated bibliographies have multiple purposes, so you will be combining the preceding forms. Because most annotations can be up to 150 words, you need to devote only a sentence or two for each purpose—in other words, a few lines to summarize and describe, a few to evaluate and comment. However, you may be told exactly what to include in the annotations and how many words or sentences to use. Your instructor might, for example, ask that you write one sentence summarizing each work's argument and then another sentence describing how the work relates to your own developing thesis.

How to Write an Annotated Bibliography

Before you can begin writing an annotated bibliography you must choose a subject on which to focus. From there you will move to gathering materials, applying reading strategies, and finally writing the annotated bibliography.

Gathering Materials

See Chapter 11, "Research Techniques," to help you find material relevant to your subject. Are you supposed to find a wide range of materials, such as reviews, scholarly articles, and books? Are you to focus only on materials from the last five years? What are the parameters for your researching? Be sure to clarify these issues with your instructor.

Reading Strategies

You'll again use the critical reading strategies you've learned as you read the sources you've decided to include in your bibliography. If the materials you've gathered will later become part of a research essay, then you will be taking notes and writing about them as discussed in Chapter 11. But to create your annotated bibliography, you'll have an additional purpose for reading your sources. If you simply need to describe the content of the sources (indicative form), you will do little critical evaluation; instead, you'll focus on explanation. Once you determine the focus for your annotations, use the following questions (which apply primarily to evaluative forms of annotation, but also can help with informative and indicative forms) to guide your reading.

- Who is the intended audience for this article, review, or book?

- What central research question or claim does the material address? Write it out in one or two sentences.

- What kind of evidence is used to support the conclusions, argument, and thesis? How valid is it, given what the intended audience values? For example, literary examples wouldn't be taken seriously as evidence in a biology paper, nor would anecdotal evidence about an experiment.

- How effectively has the author addressed the central question or claim?

- Sketch out the main argument in a brief outline. Note the main subjects covered, the authors listed (if it's a collection of articles), and the general organization of the work.

- What is known about the credibility of this author(s)? Have you seen her name appear in other works on this subject? Is she publishing in her area of expertise?

- Note the dates of publication, usually on the copyright page. Is the material current? Does it need to be? Is this a revised edition?

- Compare the source to others on the same subject. Are the ideas similar enough to suggest that this author is working with accepted knowledge?

- If they aren't, do you find them valid, significant, or well researched? Is one source on this subject better than another, and why or why not? Does the source build on the ideas of others, critique them, and add new knowledge?

- How effectively is the source written?
- If you can, try to find reviews of the material or commentaries from other scholars in the area. This will give you a sense of how the work was received, what (if any) controversy it has generated, and what about it has been lauded and/or criticized.

Writing the Annotated Bibliography

Because annotations are so brief, it's tempting to think that they are easy to write. But as in any writing project, you need to have a lot of material to draw from—in this case, substantive notes and reflective writing about each work. It is better to work from abundance than from scarcity—remember, you need material to work with if you are going to identify what's worth keeping and what should be dropped.

Length. Depending on the requirements for and purposes of the annotations, they could be one paragraph or only a few sentences, so you have to choose your words carefully and use specific details judiciously. Clarify with your instructor the kind of writing style he expects; that is, does he want brief phrases, almost like a bulleted list of main points, or full sentences and paragraphs?

Content. Begin with the proper citation form for the source, following the guidelines for the specific documentation style your instructor requires (APA or MLA). Organize this list alphabetically. After each source, compose a paragraph or two that addresses your purpose for the bibliography. That purpose, again, will depend on the requirements your instructor has given you. If you are describing the content of the source, for example, begin with an overview of the work and its thesis, then select the specific points you want to highlight about it (such as chapter titles, subjects covered, authors included). If you are explaining the main argument of the work, begin with the central thesis and then include the main claims, evidence, research methods, and conclusions. Finally, if you are evaluating the source, add comments that summarize your critique.

Sample Student Annotated Bibliography

In the example that follows, Lauren Tussing wanted to apply what she's learned about feminist theory to the film *Lost in Translation*, and her annotated bibliography helped her focus her research question and decide which of the sources would be most useful in composing her essay. Notice that she has written an annotated bibliography that combines the informative and evaluative forms—she primarily summarizes the main argument of each source and then discusses its relevance to her research project.

Lauren Tussing

Instructor Michelle Payne

Engl 497

18 April 2004

Annotated Bibliography

Doane, Mary Ann. "Film and the Masquerade: Theorising the Female Spectator."

Feminism and Film. Ed. E. Ann Kaplan. Oxford: Oxford, 2000. 418–36. Print.

This is an article in a collection of articles on feminist film theory. In the essay, Doane works to create a theory for the female spectator, moving away from prior focus on the male spectator. Doane does, however, reintroduce the idea of Laura Mulvey's binary opposition of passive/female and active/male that she introduced in her essay "Visual Pleasure and Narrative Cinema." Doane applies the notion of distance to Mulvey's binary opposition.

This essay, written for an academic audience, is esoteric and sometimes difficult to understand, but it might be helpful for my paper if I decide to talk about the female spectator. Despite my difficulty with this essay, Doane did give me some ideas about how to think about *Lost in Translation,* the film that I discuss in my essay. A woman directs this film, so I wonder how her direction affects the gaze. Is there a uniquely female gaze for this film? Or does the film conform to the male gaze? How might viewers, both male and female, gaze upon this film?

Gaines, Jane. "White Privilege and Looking Relations: Race and Gender." *Feminism and Film*. Ed. E. Ann Kaplan. Oxford: Oxford, 2000. 336–55. Print.

This essay, also included in the same collection as the above essay, argues that psychoanalysis isn't a good way to critique films, particularly because it overlooks racial and sexuality issues. Even when theorists use psychoanalysis to describe black family interaction, they impose "an erroneous universalisation and inadvertently reaffirm white middle-class norms" (337). When feminist theory uses gender first and foremost in discussing oppressions, it "helps to reinforce white middle-class values" (337). Also, Gaines argues, because feminist theory universalizes white middle-class values, it ideologically hides other forms of oppression from women.

This essay has given me new ideas about how to read *Lost in Translation*. Although I wasn't initially going to talk about issues of race, I might want to. Race actually plays a big role in the movie because it is about white people in an Asian country. Also, I think this essay is helpful in its critique of psychoanalysis. In my research of feminist film theory, I have found that you can't escape psychoanalysis. I don't particularly like psychoanalysis, but I realize that it is an important theory to understand. It is at the basis of many articles on feminist film theory. However, I don't think I will be discussing psychoanalysis in my essay.

Jayamanne, Laleen, ed. *Kiss Me Deadly: Feminism and Cinema for the Moment.*
    Sydney: Power Institute of Fine Arts, 1995. Print.

This is a collection of articles about feminism and film. The articles in this book focus mostly on directors, such as Kathryn Bigelow, Rainer Werner Fassbinder, Alexander Kluge, and Nicolas Roeg. Before looking at this book, I had never heard of any of these directors. I didn't find this book particularly helpful, especially because, as Jayamanne notes in the introduction, some of the directors and films discussed are "foreign to the semi-official canons of feminist film theory" (14).

Johnston, Claire. "Dorothy Arzner: Critical Strategies." *Feminism and Film.* Ed.
    E. Ann Kaplan. Oxford: Oxford, 2000. 139–50. Print.

In this essay, Johnston discusses Dorothy Arzner, a director from the 1920s to the 1940s who was nearly the only woman during her time to create a lucid bulk of work in Hollywood. Because not many studies have been written about Arzner—especially in male-dominated film studies—Johnston's purpose is to explore various approaches to Arzner's work and to discuss how her films are important for contemporary feminists.

This essay also gave me a new idea about how to look at the film I will be discussing in my paper. I'd like to discuss the director of *Lost in Translation.* Are her films, particularly *Lost in Translation,* important for contemporary feminists?

Kaplan, E. Ann, ed. *Women in Film Noir.* London: British Film Institute, 1978. Print.

This book is a collection of articles about film noir. Because the book is aimed at scholars who are educated in feminist film theory, it does not actually give a definition of film noir, and I didn't know what film noir was, so I looked it up in the Oxford English Dictionary. According to the Oxford English Dictionary, film noir is "a cinematographic film of a gloomy or fatalistic character." I don't think the film I will be discussing falls into this category, so I don't think I will be using this source for my essay.

———. *Feminism and Film.* Oxford: Oxford University Press, 2000. Print.

This is a collection of articles on feminist film theory. Many of the essays in this book are esoteric and difficult to understand, but I think this is an invaluable resource to my research essay because of the range of essays it includes. The book is split into four phases: (1) Pioneers and Classics, (2) Critiques of Phase 1 Theories: New Methods, (3) Race, Sexuality, and Postmodernism in Feminist Film Theory, and (4) Spectatorship, Ethnicity, and Melodrama. By employing these different "phases" of feminist film theory, the book allows the reader to see the conversations within feminist film theory and its subsequent evolutions. I have summarized a few of the articles contained in this collection above.

Kuhn, Annette. *Women's Pictures: Feminism and Cinema.* London: Verso, 1994. Print.

In this book, Kuhn argues that "feminism and film, taken together, could provide the basis for new forms of expression, providing the opportunity for a truly feminist alternative cinema in terms of film language, of reading that language and of representing the world." The book provides a systematic view of film. First, Kuhn discusses the dominant cinema. Then, she explores "rereading dominant cinema" from a feminist stance. Finally, she discusses "replacing dominant cinema" with feminist film.

I think this book will be helpful when I attempt to understand where *Lost in Translation* fits into film culture. Is the film part of dominant cinema? How can it be read from a feminist viewpoint? How is it a feminist film? How isn't it a feminist film?

APPENDIX D
THE ESSAY EXAM

The following table explains the differences between essay exams and the essays you write for class assignments. From this we can figure out which writing and reading strategies will be most useful when you're sitting in a classroom with only fifty minutes to craft an argument on one of Shakespeare's plays or apply an economic theory to a specific scenario.

	Essay Exam	Essay for Class Assignment
Time	Usually limited to a class period (60–75 minutes), within which time you have to generate ideas, focus, plan, draft, and revise.	Usually several days to several weeks to generate ideas, explore and focus them, draft, workshop, and revise.
Purpose	To show your instructor how well you know class material and how well you can *analyze and apply it.*	Depending on subject, genre, and focus of the class, this can vary from demonstrating competency at certain writing strategies to mastering a particular genre to making a persuasive argument.
Choice	While you may have a choice of which essay questions you'll respond to, often your choice of subject is limited by the question. Within the question you might have some choice over texts or materials to which you will refer.	Often students have a wider range of choices for subjects when writing for a class assignment.

(continued)

(continued)

	Essay Exam	Essay for Class Assignment
Process	Your writing process is truncated into a shorter period, so you might go right to drafting an outline, drafting the response to the question, and then revising; you won't have time to experiment or explore ideas; your goals are to demonstrate your knowledge, not explore it.	More time to explore ideas, experiment, revise, and get feedback from other writers.
Methods of Inquiry	You will have little if any time for reflecting or even exploring ideas; instead, you will have to focus on explaining and evaluating, stating a claim, and providing explanation and evidence.	At various times you will use all the methods of inquiry: exploring, reflecting, explaining, and evaluating. The methods used in a particular paper depend on the assignment, the audience, the form, and the subject.
Form	Depending on the nature of the exam question, the form expected is something similar to a five-paragraph thesis essay: an introduction that states your thesis; supporting paragraphs that "prove" it using details from class materials; and a conclusion that wraps everything up (this is not true for short-answer essay questions). Essay exams are often expected to be close-ended forms.	Depending on the subject and audience: from narrative to thesis-example structure, open-ended to closed-ended form. Much more flexibility in choosing a form that fits the material than in an essay exam.
Thesis	Many instructors expect a thesis statement in the first paragraph.	Some instructors expect a thesis to be implied (as in the personal essay and the profile); others expect it to be explicit (as in the critical essay). How explicit it is depends on the genre, purpose, audience, and subject.

How to Write Essay Exams

Given the difference between essay exams and the essays you write for class assignments, you should employ very specific strategies when writing in this form.

Gathering Materials

Because the purpose of an essay exam is different from that of a regular essay, the sources of information are going to be different. This may seem obvious, but it's crucial to understanding how to prepare for the exam. For a research essay, textbooks are rarely considered good reference sources, and while class lectures can be used in a course paper, they cannot form the basis of the paper. Yet these sources are often the sole basis for essay exams, and you usually can't have these sources open at your side as you write. So how do you figure out what is important to focus on in this rhetorical context?

Let's talk first about the purposes of essay exams. For many instructors, the essay exam offers a forum for students to demonstrate one or more of the following achievements.

- Students *understand* the main course concepts.
- Students can *apply* those concepts to other kinds of information, situations, or problems.
- Students can *evaluate and support* that evaluation with relevant evidence and criteria.
- Students can *analyze* a subject; this includes *synthesizing and summarizing* a range of information, as well as *making connections* among that information by considering cause/effect and using comparison and contrast.

Anticipating the Exam

If you've been paying attention to the main ideas of the course and the methods of inquiry your instructor seems to value, then you are in good shape to anticipate the questions that might be on the exam. One of the best ways to prepare for an exam is to play the role of your instructor.

- What does she want you to learn and why?
- What kinds of questions has she asked on previous exams?
- What kinds of questions would best show how you've met the course goals?

After you've thought about these questions, generate a good list of possible exam questions and then answer them, either alone or in a small study group. You'll quickly learn what you need to go back and learn in more depth because you will be in a group reflecting on your learning process. And you may just find some version of those questions on the exam.

Because your instructor is your only audience and will be forming the questions, you might ask about the kinds of questions you can anticipate: How long will they be? What kinds of questions will there be? What criteria will be used for evaluating the answers? And, if they are available, look over previous exams from the same course and instructor.

If you've been engaging in inquiry throughout the course, then you will most likely have a good grasp of the main ideas in the course and your judgments about them. Inquiry can reduce the amount of time you spend memorizing the course material. You will have already been doing more than simply collecting facts and theories while your instructor lectures; you will have been posing questions, making connections, evaluating, and exploring, then reflecting on what you know and what more you need to know. You will, in short, understand the material. By the time you sit down to commit some key concepts and details to memory, you'll remember them better because you understand their purpose and their relationship to each other.

Analyzing Essay Questions

When you get the exam, read through all of it before you do anything else, and consider the following factors before you start writing your answers:

Time. Make some choices about how much time you will spend on each question based on:

- *Point value.* How many points is each question assigned? Prioritize them based on how much they are worth so you spend more time on those questions that are worth more. If you run out of time, then the questions you haven't responded to won't hurt you quite as much.

- *Priorities.* Based on your priorities, divide the time up for each question. Spend more time on questions worth more points. Try to stick to the time limits you've given yourself.

- *Ability to answer the question.* If you have a choice of questions, consider carefully which one you will answer. To decide, quickly brainstorm in the margins your ideas for each question. That will tell you how much you know about each and whether you can do what the question asks. For example, you might be able to explain a concept, but not compare it to something else, which is what the exam question actually demands that you do.

Key Phrases/Verbs. Once you've tentatively decided which questions you'll answer and how much time you'll devote to each, analyze the questions as quickly as you can. Your first step is to figure out what a question is asking you to *do*. Circle the key verbs that indicate your purpose when writing your answer. One way to understand what an essay question is asking you to do is to think of it in terms you already know: the ways of inquiring. In general, essay exams ask you to evaluate or explain. The accompanying table lists some of the verbs that imply one or the other way of inquiring.

Verbs of Evaluation	Required Action
Prove/justify/support	Offer reasons and evidence in support of a position.
Argue	Like *prove* and *justify*, this verb demands that you present an argument with reasons and evidence, but often the essay question gives you a position to take or asks you to choose a particular position.
Evaluate/assess	Make a judgment about the value or importance of a particular idea or subject, being clear about the criteria you're using for evaluation and supporting your claim with reasons and evidence.
Analyze	Usually this means you examine the parts of something—such as an argument—breaking it into sections and discussing the relationships among them; sometimes it may mean assessing those parts, or explaining your response. The rest of the question should indicate how much you should describe the parts and how much you should judge them.
Critique	To analyze and evaluate the subject in the essay question (an idea, argument, or theory).
Respond	Often this verb means that you must evaluate or justify your response to whatever the question asks of you.
Synthesize	Bring together two or more ideas/subjects/concepts that haven't been considered together and do more than simply summarize and compare them; explain why you have brought them together and what new understanding emerges from that.

Verbs of Explanation (Information)	Required Action
Define	Describe and give the meaning of the idea presented, using authoritative sources, comparing and contrasting it to other ideas that are related.
Enumerate	Present the steps, sequence, or events involved in a particular process in some detail.
Trace	Like *enumerate*, trace asks you to describe a series of events, but in chronological order.

(continued)

(continued) Verbs of Explanation (Information)	Required Action
List	Like *enumerate,* this verb asks you to name several things that are connected to a main idea presented in the question.
Review	Quickly summarize something.
Summarize	Present the main ideas of an argument or concept in an organized way.
Explain why/how	Offer reasons and examples of why and/or how something happened or relates to a larger idea.
Illustrate	Describe specific examples of something and their relationship to each other and the larger subject given in the question.
Identify	Like *illustrate,* this verb asks you to describe something and show its relationship to a larger idea, but often it implies looking at just one or two things.
Discuss	At length and from different perspectives, describe and analyze the idea presented in the question, using specific examples and evaluating the strengths and weaknesses.
Research	Just as it implies, gather sources and analyze what you've found.

Verbs of Explanation (Relationships and Connections)	Required Action
Compare	Illustrate the similarities of two or more things.
Contrast	Illustrate the differences of two or more things.
Relate	Show the relationships among various things.
Cause	Illustrate how various events relate to each other and resulted in a particular effect.
Apply	Illustrate how a theory or concept works in another situation.
Construct	Sometimes asks you to create a model or diagram through which to present your ideas.

Noun Phrases. Now that you know you need to contrast two different ideas, you need to be sure you know what to contrast. Some essay questions are rather long and it may be hard to decipher what, exactly, the subject of your answer should be. Usually the clues are in the noun phrases ("parts of the cell," "factors that led to the Civil War," "three influences on Sylvia Plath's poetry"). If the question begins with a quotation, read the question carefully to see whether it's background information for the question, or something you need to address in your answer. Underline all the key noun phrases that indicate the ideas/concepts you are expected to discuss.

Organizational Clues. Based on the subject and purpose of your answer, how might you best organize it? You may need to use a cause-effect, step-by-step, or thesis/support structure. Sometimes the question itself implies a structure. For example, if you are asked to analyze the cause and effect of the Great Depression, you'll use a cause-effect structure. If you are asked to identify three influences on Sylvia Plath's poetry and argue which is most significant, you'll name those three, then devote a separate paragraph for each one to discuss in more detail, ending with the one you believe is most significant. Before you begin writing, sketch an outline that seems appropriate for the question.

Planning and Drafting

Once you have analyzed the exam question and you have a good sense of what you are being asked to do, you need to draft an answer in a very short period of time. Before you begin writing your response, jot down a rough outline of what you'll say and the supporting details and examples you'll use. Put your points in the order of most to least important in case you run out of time. That way you know you've touched on the most important ideas before time is up. Then draft an introductory paragraph that summarizes your argument and gets right to your thesis statement at the end. Your lead doesn't need an attention grabber as much as it needs a clear direction for the essay and a clear statement of your answer in one or two sentences.

Focus your writing on the body of the essay, developing your points as fully as you can. Keep in mind what your instructor will value the most, and use the key terms that are used in the exam question to show how you are directly addressing it. Essay exams necessarily demand clear, simple, and direct writing. Leave some time at the end to reread your answer, editing it carefully and considering which sections need more information. Sometimes it helps to write on every other line of notebook or blue-book paper so you have space to write in when you revise. If you don't finish your answer in time, briefly describe for your instructor what you would do if you had more time. Write as legibly as you can, minimizing scratch-outs and keeping in mind how many exams your instructor will have to read.

When you analyzed the essay question, you paid some attention to the kind of structure the question was probably demanding. You may need to use a cause-effect pattern, a step-by-step pattern, or a thesis/support structure. Within the body of that structure, though, keep each paragraph to one main idea, using specific details to illustrate or support your main assertions. Then try to connect the idea in the paragraph back to your main thesis, explaining why it's important to what you are trying to say ("Another example of this phenomenon is _____ or "An additional factor that complicates this process is _____"). Your conclusion, then, will tie the essay together with a sentence or two restating your main claim and telling your instructor what all this information means.

HANDBOOK

This guide assumes that you, like other writers, sometimes have problems getting your sentences to come out right. These are problems in *usage*: how to use verbs, modifiers, and pronouns, for example. This discussion focuses on those problems, explaining the *how* more than the *what*, treating those problems as matters of writing, not of grammar. It avoids grammatical jargon as much as possible but defines terms where necessary for understanding the problem. This guide also gives you a quick review of punctuation, mechanics, spelling, style, and basic grammar. It also offers tips for ESL writers. Refer to this guide while writing and when your instructor suggests sections for you to study.

Here's how the sections are arranged:

1 Sentence Boundaries

Sentence boundaries are marked by end punctuation (7A): periods, question marks, or occasionally exclamation points. Because they mark the ends of sentences, each mark of end punctuation must be preceded by at least one independent clause (a complete statement containing a subject and a verb and not beginning with a subordinating word). Errors in sentence boundaries involve inappropriate punctuation: periods where commas or no punctuation should go, and commas or no punctuation where periods or semicolons should go. To develop your own **sense** of which marks to use, think of periods, semicolons, and commas as *strongest* to *weakest*. The weakest mark, the comma, is not interchangeable with the strongest mark, the period, and usually not with the semicolon. But periods and semicolons, depending on the writer's choice, *are* often interchangeable. The following discussions regarding sentence boundary errors are based on this reasoning.

1A Fragments

Sentence fragments are errors in which partial sentences are treated as sentences—begun with a capital letter and ended with a period. The fragment may be a subordinate clause, a phrase, or a combination of subordinate elements. What makes each a fragment is that it lacks a subject or a verb, or that it begins with a subordinating word. Only independent clauses can make independent statements.

Subordinate Clause Fragment

Recognition. A subordinate clause has a subject and a verb but cannot make an independent statement because of the connector that implies it is only part of a sentence. Here are two lists of the most common subordinating connectors.

Subordinating conjunctions, arranged by function

Time	Place
after	where
before	wherever
once	
since	Cause
until	as
when	because
whenever	since
while	
	Condition
Contrast	even if
although	if
even though	

though	Result
while	in order that
	so
Alternative	so that
than	that
whether	

Relative pronouns

who (whom, whose)	whoever (whomever, whosever)
which	whichever
that	
what	whatever
where	wherever
when	whenever
why	
unless	
whereas	

Any clause beginning with one of these words is *subordinate* and should not be written as a sentence. Here are examples of clause fragments (italicized):

The Vikings revolutionized shipbuilding with the keel. *Which allowed their ships to go faster and farther without stopping for supplies.*

Norway's Lapps are believed to be a nomadic people of Asian heritage. *Who follow reindeer herds through Norway's cold, rugged land.*

Because the northern part of Norway is so far north. It has long periods during the summer when the sun shines 24 hours a day.

Correction. There are mainly two ways of correcting clause fragments: (1) attaching them to the preceding or following sentence and (2) removing or changing the subordinating connector. These sentences illustrate both types of correction:

The Vikings revolutionized shipbuilding with the keel. *This innovation* allowed their ships to go faster and farther without stopping for supplies. The subordinating word of the fragment is changed.

Norway's Lapps are believed to be of Asian heritage—nomadic people who follow reindeer herds through Norway's cold, rugged land. The fragment is connected to the preceding sentence with a dash.

Because the northern part of Norway is so far north, it has long periods during the summer when the sun shines 24 hours a day. The fragment is connected to the following sentence with a comma.

Phrase Fragment

Phrase fragments lack a subject, a verb, or both. The most common phrases written as fragments are *verbal phrases* and *prepositional phrases*.

Recognition. A *verbal phrase* is a word group made up of a verb form and related modifiers and other words. As opposed to *verb phrases,* which are made up of verb parts (such as *has been gone*), a verbal phrase is constituted with a *verbal,* a word formed from a verb but not functioning as a verb. *Going,* for example, is a verbal, as is *gone*. You probably wouldn't write "Charles going to St. Louis" or "Charles gone to St. Louis." Instead, you would add helping verbs: "Charles *is going* to St. Louis" and "Charles *has gone* to St. Louis."

There are three kinds of verbals: gerunds, participles, and infinitives. Gerunds end in *-ing*; participles end in either *-ing* (present) or *-ed* (regular past); infinitives have no ending but are usually introduced by *to*. Here are a few examples of how verbals are formed from verbs:

Verb	Present participle and gerund	Past participle	Infinitive
snap	snapping	snapped	to snap
look	looking	looked	to look
want	wanting	wanted	to want
go	going	gone	to go
has	having	had	to have

Verbals function primarily as adjectives and nouns, most often in verbal phrases.

In the following examples, the italicized verbal phrases are fragments because they are written as sentences:

Eero Saarinen designed the 630-foot Gateway Arch for the St. Louis riverfront. *Imagining a giant stainless steel arch.* Participial phrase modifying *Eero Saarinen.*

Critics said that cranes could not reach high enough. *To lift the steel sections into place.* Infinitive phrase modifying *high.*

Under Saarinen's plan, a derrick would creep up the side of each leg of the arch *Lifting each plate into position.* Participial phrase modifying *derrick.*

Saarinen knew that precision was of utmost importance. In *building the arch.* Gerund phrase as object of preposition *In.*

Correction. Verbal phrase fragments can be corrected in one of two ways: (1) by connecting them to a related sentence or (2) by expanding them to a sentence. Both ways are illustrated next.

Eero Saarinen designed the 630-foot Gateway Arch for the St. Louis riverfront. *He imagined a giant stainless steel arch.* The verbal fragment is expanded to a sentence.

Critics said that cranes could not reach high enough *to lift the steel sections into place.* The verbal fragment is connected to a related sentence.

Under Saarinen's plan, a derrick would creep up the side of each leg of the arch, *lifting each plate into position.* The verbal fragment is connected to a related sentence.

Saarinen knew that precision was of utmost importance in *building the arch.* The gerund phrase, object of the preposition *In,* is connected to a related sentence.

Recognition. A *prepositional phrase* is a word group made up of a preposition and its object. Together they contribute meaning to a sentence, usually modifying a noun or a verb. Like subordinating conjunctions, prepositions show relationships, such as time, place, condition, cause, and so on. Here are some of the most common prepositions:

about	concerning	onto
above	despite	out
according to	down	out of
across	during	outside
after	except	over
against	except for	past
along	excepting	regarding
along with	for	since
among	from	through
around	in	throughout
as	in addition to	till
at	in back of	to
because of	in place of	toward
before	in spite of	under
behind	inside	underneath
below	instead of	unlike
beneath	into	until
beside	like	up
between	near	up to
beyond	next	upon
but	of	with
by	off	within
by means of	on	without

In the following examples, prepositional phrases have been written as sentences and are therefore fragments:

The Vikings were descendents of Teutonic settlers. *Like most of today's Norwegians.*

Norway is a land of natural beauty. *From its fjord-lined coast to frigid Lapland.*

Correction. Preposition phrase fragments also can be corrected (1) by connecting them to a related sentence or (2) by expanding them to a sentence.

The Vikings were descendents of Teutonic settlers, *like most of today's Norwegians.* **or** *Like most of today's Norwegians*, the Vikings were descendents of Teutonic settlers. The prepositional phrase is connected to a related sentence.

Norway is a land of natural beauty. *Its charm extends from its fjord-lined coast to frigid Lapland.* The prepositional phrase is expanded to a sentence.

Incomplete Thoughts

Sometimes fragments are simply errors in punctuation: The writer uses a period when a comma or no punctuation would be correct. A more difficult type of fragment to correct is the incomplete thought, such as this one:

> A large concrete dock 50 feet short of a wooden platform anchored in the middle of the bay.

In this fragment, something is missing, and, as a result, a reader doesn't know what to make of the words "large concrete dock." With fragments of this sort, the writer needs to insert the missing information. The fragment might be revised like this:

> A large concrete dock juts out, stopping 50 feet short of a wooden platform anchored in the middle of the bay.

Acceptable Fragments

You probably encounter fragments every day. Titles are often fragments, as are answers to questions and expressions of strong emotion.

Titles. *The Curious Writer,* "A Fire in the Woods"

Answer to question: "How many more chairs do we need?" "Fifteen."

Expression of strong emotion: "What a great concert!"

And much advertising utilizes fragments:

> Intricate, delicate, exquisite. Extravagant in every way.

> Another successful client meeting. Par for the course.

Common as they are in everyday life, fragments are usually unacceptable in academic or business writing. Even though professional writers and advertising writers sometimes use them for emphasis, there are rarely cases when you will need intentional fragments for effective expression of your thoughts in school or business.

1B Comma Splices

Comma splices consist of two independent clauses (clauses that can stand alone as sentences) improperly joined together by a comma in the same sentence. Here are two examples:

> The economy of Algeria is in trouble, many citizens blame the government.

> The death of any soldier is tragic, however, death by friendly fire is particularly disturbing.

Recognition. The first step in avoiding comma splices is to identify them. Because they happen only in sentences with at least two independent clauses, you can test your sentences by substituting periods for your commas. If you end up with complete sentences, you probably have a comma splice.

In testing the first of the two preceding examples we come up with the following result:

The economy of Algeria is in trouble.

Many citizens blame the government.

Both of these clauses obviously qualify as complete sentences, so they must be independent clauses. They therefore cannot be connected with a comma. Remember this simple rule of punctuation: *Periods and commas are not interchangeable.* If a period is correct, a comma is not.

Correction. You can revise comma splices using five different strategies.

1. Separate the independent clauses using a comma and a *coordinating conjunction*. The list of coordinating conjunctions is short:

   and   or   for   yet
   but   nor   so

   To correct a comma splice, begin the second independent clause with one of these conjunctions preceded by a comma. For example:

   The economy of Algeria is in trouble, *and* many citizens blame the government.

2. Separate the independent clauses using a semicolon (with or without a transitional adverb). Semicolons are often interchangeable with periods and therefore can be used to separate independent clauses. For example:

   The economy of Algeria is in trouble; many citizens blame the government.

   The death of any soldier is tragic; *however,* death by friendly fire is particularly disturbing.

In the second example, *however* is a transitional adverb. Unlike coordinating conjunctions, *transitional adverbs* are not conjunctions and so do not join sentence elements. They do, however, connect ideas by showing how they relate to one another. Like conjunctions, they can show addition, contrast, result, and other relationships. Here are some of the common transitional adverbs, arranged by function:

Addition	Examples
in addition	for example
also	for instance
moreover	in fact
next	specifically
then	
finally	
	Contrast
	however
Comparison	nevertheless
likewise	on the contrary
similarly	on the other hand
in comparison	otherwise

Result	Time
therefore	meanwhile
consequently	subsequently
then	finally
as a result	then

A semicolon should always precede the transitional adverb that begins the second independent clause. A comma usually follows the transitional adverb, although in some instances, as in the following example, the comma is omitted:

> Air bags deflate within one second after inflation; *therefore* they do not interfere with control of the car.

Some comma splices result when writers use transitional adverbs as if they were coordinating conjunctions. If you have trouble distinguishing transitional adverbs from coordinating conjunctions, remember that none of the coordinating conjunctions is longer than three letters, and all of the transitional adverbs are four letters or longer. Also, keep in mind that transitional adverbs are movable within the sentence while coordinating conjunctions are not; for example, the preceding example could be rewritten as:

> Air bags deflate within one second after inflation; they do not *therefore* interfere with control of the car.

3. Make one of the independent clauses subordinate to the other by inserting a subordinating conjunction. When one of the clauses explains or elaborates on the other, use an appropriate subordinating conjunction to make the relationship between the two clauses more explicit (see 1A Fragments for a list of subordinating conjunctions). Consider the following comma splice and its revision:

> Henry forgot to fill in his time card on Friday, he is going to have a hard time getting paid for the overtime he put in last week.

> *Because* Henry forgot to fill in his time card on Friday, he is going to have a hard time getting paid for the overtime he put in last week.

4. Rewrite one of the independent clauses as a modifying phrase. A *modifying phrase* serves as an adjective or adverb within a sentence. By rewriting one of the independent clauses as a phrase you can eliminate unneeded words. For example, consider the following comma splice and its revision:

> The celebrity couple smiled for the cameras, they were glowing of wealth and fame.

> The celebrity couple smiled for the cameras, glowing of wealth and fame. Here *glowing of wealth and fame* acts as an adjective modifying the noun *couple*.

5. Punctuate each independent clause as a separate sentence. No law of grammar, punctuation, or style says you must present the two independent clauses together within one sentence, so you won't be cheating if you write

them as two separate sentences. The example from before is perfectly acceptable written as follows:

The economy of Algeria is in trouble. Many citizens blame the government.

It may be to your advantage to divide long and/or complex independent clauses into separate sentences—doing so may help convey your meaning to readers more clearly.

1C Fused Sentences

Fused sentences, sometimes called *run-on sentences,* are similar to comma splices. However, instead of a comma between the two independent clauses, there is no punctuation; the two independent clauses simply run together. For example:

The United States has 281 lawyers per 100,000 people Japan has only 11 attorneys per 100,000.

The World Cup is the most popular sporting event in the world you would never know it based on the indifferent response of the average American.

Recognition. Unlike the comma splice, there is no punctuation in the fused sentence to guide you to the end of the first independent clause and the beginning of the second. As a result, it can be more challenging to identify independent clauses within fused sentences, particularly if the sentence also contains modifying phrases or dependent clauses set off by commas. The best way to do this is to read from the beginning of the sentence (reading aloud may help) until you have found the end of the first independent clause. Consider the following example:

Even though I was still sick with the flu, I attended the awards banquet as my family watched, the coach presented me with the trophy for most valuable player.

This fused sentence contains two subordinate clauses (*Even though I was still sick with the flu* and *as my family watched*), each one attached to one of the two independent clauses (*I attended the awards banquet* and *the coach presented me with the trophy*).

Correction. Revise fused sentences using any one of the same five strategies employed for correcting comma splices (see 1B Comma Splices for more information on each strategy).

1. Separate the independent clauses using a comma and a coordinating conjunction. For example:

   The United States has 281 lawyers per 100,000 people, *but* Japan has only 11 attorneys per 100,000.

2. Separate the independent clauses using a semicolon (with or without a transitional adverb). For example:

   The United States has 281 lawyers per 100,000 people; Japan has only 11 attorneys per 100,000.

The World Cup is the most popular sporting event in the world; *however,* you would never know it based on the indifferent response of the average American.

3. Make one of the independent clauses subordinate to the other by inserting a subordinating conjunction. The newly formed dependent clause should explain the remaining independent clause. For example, consider the following fused sentence and its revision:

I run a marathon my feet get sore.

Whenever I run a marathon, my feet get sore.

4. Rewrite one of the independent clauses as a modifying phrase. Remember, modifying phrases act as adjectives or adverbs. Consider the following fused sentence and its revision:

Last night the tomcats fought outside my window they were crying and hissing for what seemed like hours.

Last night the tomcats fought outside my window, crying and hissing for what seemed like hours. Here *crying and hissing* acts as an adjective modifying the noun *tomcats*.

5. Punctuate each independent clause as a separate sentence. As with comma splices, you can write the independent clauses (and their related phrases and dependent clauses) as separate sentences. Indeed, this is often the easiest way to handle fused sentences. For example:

I attended the awards banquet even though I was still sick with the flu. As my family watched, the coach presented me with the trophy for most valuable player. Here the subordinate clause attached to the first independent clause *even though I was still sick with the flu* was also moved to the back of the first sentence for the sake of greater readability.

2 Sentence Inconsistencies

Sentences pose difficulties for readers when the grammar is confused or inconsistent. Such problems happen when writers pay attention to what they are saying and not to how they are saying it. Such attention is a natural condition of writing, and careful revision usually takes care of any problems.

2A Parallelism

Parallelism results when two or more grammatically equivalent sentence elements are joined. The sentence elements can be nouns, verbs, phrases, or clauses. (See 2B Coordination and Subordination.) Here is a sentence with parallel elements:

In a country where college education becomes increasingly everybody's chance, where executives and refrigerator salesmen and farmers play golf together, where a college professor may drive a cab in the summertime to keep his family alive, it becomes harder and harder to guess a person's education, income, and social status by the way he talks. —Paul Roberts

Here is the same sentence with the parallel elements arranged to be more visually accessible:

In a country

{where college education becomes increasingly everybody's chance,

{where {executives

and {refrigerator salesmen

and {farmers play golf together,

{where a college professor may drive a cab in the summertime to keep

his family alive,

it becomes {harder

and {harder to guess a person's {education

{income,

and {social status

by the way he talks.

This sentence has parallel clauses (each beginning *where*), parallel subjects (*executives, refrigerator salesmen,* and *farmers*), parallel adverbs (*harder* and *harder*), and parallel direct objects (*education, income,* and *social status*). As this sentence illustrates, the principle of parallelism does not require that elements be alike in every way. Some of these nouns have modifiers, for example, and the clauses have different structural patterns.

Parallelism becomes a problem when dissimilar elements are joined in pairs, in series, in comparisons using *than* or *as,* or in comparisons linked by correlative conjunctions. Consider the following examples of faulty parallelism:

She did not like rude customers or taking orders from her boss. The two elements in the pair are not parallel.

We were having a hard time deciding what to do in the afternoon: go snorkeling, go fishing, or swim out to the sand bar. The last of the three elements in the series is not parallel.

Michael decided to complete his degree next semester rather than studying abroad for another year. The two elements compared using *than* are not parallel.

My sister not only lost the race but also her leg got hurt. The two elements compared by the correlative conjunction *not only...but also* are not parallel. Other correlative conjunctions include *both...and, either...or, neither...nor, whether...or,* and *just as...so.*

Faulty parallelism can be corrected in various ways:

> She did not like *dealing with* rude customers or taking orders from her boss. Words were added to the first element to make it parallel to the second.

> We were having a hard time deciding what to do in the afternoon: go snorkeling, go fishing, or *go swimming*. The last element was rewritten to make it parallel with the others in the series.

> Michael decided to complete his degree next semester rather than *to study* abroad for another year. The verb form of the second element is changed from a participle to an infinitive to make it parallel with the verb form in the first element.

> My sister not only lost the race but also *hurt her leg*. The second element was rewritten to make it parallel with the first element.

Revision of faulty parallelism is usually fairly easy to achieve. What is difficult is recognizing it, and unfortunately there are no tricks to easy recognition. Even experienced writers find that in their own writing they need to make an editing trip through their drafts looking just at their parallel structures. The absence of faulty parallels is a sign of careful writing.

2B Coordination and Subordination

Most sentence relationships embody either coordination or subordination. That is, sentence elements are either grammatically equal to other elements (coordination) or grammatically dependent on other parts (subordination). For example, two independent clauses in a sentence are coordinate; but in a sentence containing an independent clause and a dependent clause, the dependent clause is subordinate (indeed, dependent clauses are also called subordinate clauses).

Coordination

When two or more equivalent sentence elements appear in one sentence they are coordinate. These elements can be words, phrases, or clauses. Only parallel elements can be coordinated: verbs linked with verbs, nouns with nouns, phrases with phrases, and clauses with clauses. (See 2A Parallelism.) For example:

> *Broccoli* and *related vegetables* contain beta-carotene, a substance that may reduce the risk of heart attack. Two nouns are joined by a coordinating conjunction.

> We *ran, swam,* and *cycled* every day while we were at the fitness camp. Three parallel verbs are joined in a series with commas and a coordinating conjunction.

> American medical devices are equally remarkable, *giving life to those with terminally diseased organs, giving mobility to those crippled with arthritic joints and deadened nerves,* and even, miraculously, *restoring the sense of hearing to those deprived of it.—Atlantic.* The participial (verbal) phrases are joined by commas and a final coordinating conjunction. Also, embedded in the second participial phrase, two coordinate noun phrases are joined by a coordinating conjunction: *arthritic joints and deadened nerves.*

The term "Big Bang" is common usage now with scientists, but it originated as a sarcastic rejection of the theory. Two independent clauses are joined by a comma and a coordinating conjunction.

Subordination

Subordination is an essential aspect of sentence relations. If all sentence elements were grammatically equivalent, the sameness would be tedious. Subordinate elements show where the emphasis lies in sentences and modify elements with independent clauses. A subordinate element—be it a phrase or clause—is dependent on the element it modifies for its meaning. At the same time, it often provides a fuller meaning than could be achieved exclusively through the use of independent elements.

For example:

For walking and jogging, the calorie expenditure is greater for people of greater body weight. The subordinate element is a prepositional phrase, modifying *is greater*.

Increasing both speed and effort in aerobic activities, the exerciser burns more calories. The subordinate element is a verbal phrase, modifying *exerciser*.

Because sedentary people are more likely to burn sugar than fat, they tend to become hungry sooner and to overeat. The subordinate clause modifies the verb *tend*.

People *who exercise on a regular basis* change certain enzyme systems *so that they are more likely to burn fat than sugar*. There are two subordinate clauses, one beginning with *who* and modifying *People*, and one beginning with *so that* and modifying the verb *change*.

Effective writing has both coordination and subordination—coordination that sets equivalent elements side by side, and subordination that makes some elements dependent on others. Both are useful writing tools.

2C Mixed Sentences

In mixed sentences, called faulty predications when they involve the mismatching of subject and predicate, two or more parts of a sentence do not make sense together. Like other inconsistencies, this kind of problem usually occurs when writers concentrate harder on meaning than on grammar.

The following mixed sentences are common in everyday speech and may not seem inconsistent to you. Indeed, in casual speech they are usually accepted. In standard written English, however, they qualify as grammatical errors.

By driving to the movie was how we saw the accident happen. The prepositional phrase *By driving to the movie* is treated as the subject for the verb *was*. Prepositional phrases cannot serve as subjects.

Just because the candidate once had a drinking problem doesn't mean he won't be a good mayor now. The adverb clause *because the candidate once had a drinking problem* is treated as the subject of the verb *doesn't mean.* Adverbs modify verbs and adjectives and cannot function as subjects.

A CAT scan is when medical technicians take a cross-sectional X-ray of the body. The adverb clause *when medical technicians take a cross-sectional X-ray of the body* is treated as a complement of the subject *CAT scan*—another function adverbs cannot serve.

The reason I was late today is because my alarm clock broke. The subject, *reason,* is illogically linked with the predicate, *is because. Reason* suggests an explanation, so the predicate, *is because,* is redundant.

Revise mixed sentences by ensuring that grammatical patterns are used consistently throughout each sentence. For cases of faulty predication either revise the subject so it can perform the action expressed in the predicate or revise the predicate so it accurately depicts an action performed by the subject. Also avoid using *is when* and *is where* to explain an idea and *The reason . . . is because* constructions in your writing.

There are often many ways to revise mixed sentences. In each of the following revisions the grammatical patterns are consistent and the subjects and predicates fit together logically:

While driving to the movie, we saw the accident happen.

Just because the candidate once had a drinking problem, we can't conclude that he won't be a good mayor.

A CAT scan is a cross-sectional X-ray of the body.

The reason I was late today is that my alarm clock broke.

2D Shifts

Shifts occur when writers lose track of their sentence elements. Shifts occur in a variety of ways:

In person

In music, where left-handed people seem to be talented, the right-handed world puts *you* at a disadvantage. Shift from *people,* third person, to *you,* second person.

In tense

Even though many musicians *are* left handed, instruments *had been designed for right handers.* Shift from present tense to past perfect.

In number

A left-handed *violinist* has to pay extra to buy *their* left-handed violin. Shift from singular to plural.

In mood

Every time the *violinist played, she could always know* when her instrument was out of tune. Shift from the indicative mood, *violinist played,* to the subjunctive mood, *she could always know.*

In voice

The sonata *was being practiced* by the violinists in one room while the cellists *played* the concerto in the other room. Shift from the passive voice, *was being practiced,* to active voice, *played.*

In discourse type

She said, *"Your violin is out of tune,"* and that *I was playing the wrong note.* Shift from the direct quotation, *Your violin is out of tune,* to indirect quotation, that *I was playing the wrong note.*

Once you recognize shifts, revise them by ensuring that the same grammatical structures are used consistently throughout the sentence:

In music, where left-handed *people* seem talented, the right-handed world puts *them* at a disadvantage.

Even though many musicians *are* left handed, instruments *have been designed* for right handers.

Left-handed *violinists* have to pay extra to buy *their* left-handed violins.

Every time the violinist *played,* she *knew* when her instrument was out of tune.

The violinists *practiced* the sonata in one room while the cellists *played* the concerto in the other room.

She said, *"Your violin is out of tune and you are playing the wrong note."*

3 Problems with Modification

One part of a sentence can be *modified* by another part. A part that is modified is changed in some way: limited or broadened, perhaps, or described, defined, identified, or explained. Adjectives and adverbs always serve modifying functions, but phrases and subordinate clauses also can be modifiers. This section deals with problems in modification. (See 2B Coordination and Subordination.)

3A Dangling and Misplaced Modifiers

Dangling and misplaced modifiers are words and word groups that, because of their position or the way they are phrased, make the meaning of a sentence unclear and sometimes even ludicrous. These troublesome modifiers are most commonly verbal phrases, prepositional phrases, and adverbs. Here are examples:

Reaching to pick up the saddle, the obnoxious horse may shake off the blanket. The dangling verbal phrase appears to relate to *horse.*

To extend lead out of the eversharp pencil, the eraser cap is depressed. The dangling verbal phrase implies that *the eraser cap* does something.

> The eversharp pencil is designed to be used permanently, *only periodically replacing the lead.* The dangling verbal phrase implies that the pencil replaces the lead.

> Dick *only* had to pay ten dollars for his parking ticket. The misplaced adverb should immediately precede *ten*.

> Theodore caught a giant fish in the very same spot where he had lost the ring *two years later.* The misplaced adverb phrase confusingly appears to modify the last part of the sentence instead of, correctly, the first part.

Errors of this type are difficult for writers to recognize because to the writers they are not ambiguous.

Recognition. Verbal phrases always have implied subjects; in other words, somebody is performing the action. For clarity, that implied subject should be the same as the subject of the sentence or clause. To recognize your own dangling verbal modifiers, make sure that the implied subject of the verbal phrase is the same as the subject of the sentence. In the first example above, the implied subject of *Reaching* is not *the horse*. In the second example, the implied subject of *To extend* is not *the eraser cap*. And in the third example, the implied subject of *replacing* is not *the pencil*. Also check passive voice, because in a passive sentence the subject is not the doer of the action. In the second example, the dangler can be corrected when the verb, changed from passive to active voice, tells who should depress the eraser (see correction that follows).

Correction. Correcting dangling and misplaced modifiers depends on the type of error. Misplaced modifiers can often be moved to a more appropriate position:

> Dick had to pay *only* ten dollars for his parking ticket.

> *Two years later,* Theodore caught a giant fish in the very same spot where he had lost the ring.

Dangling modifiers usually require some rewording:

> *As you reach to pick up the saddle,* the obnoxious horse may shake off the blanket. The dangling verbal phrase is converted to a clause.

> To extend lead out of the eversharp pencil, *depress the eraser cap.* The main clause is revised so that *you* is the implied subject of *depress* (as it is for *To extend*).

> The eversharp pencil is designed to be used permanently, *only periodically needing the lead replaced.* The dangling verbal phrase is revised so that the implied subject of *needing* is *pencil*.

3B Restrictive and Nonrestrictive Modifiers

Some modifiers are essential to a sentence because they *restrict,* or limit, the meaning of the words they modify; others, while adding important information, are not essential to the meaning of a sentence. The first type is called restrictive and the second nonrestrictive. The terms usually refer to subordinate clauses and phrases. Here are examples of restrictive and nonrestrictive modifiers:

Restrictive

People *who plan to visit Europe* should take time to see Belgium. Relative clause modifying and identifying *People*.

The industrialized country *between the Netherlands and France on the North Sea* is constitutionally a kingdom. Prepositional phrases modifying and identifying *country*.

The Kempenland was thinly populated *before coal was discovered there*. Subordinate clause modifying *was populated* and giving meaning to the sentence.

Language and cultural differences have created friction *that has existed for centuries*. Relative clause modifying and identifying *friction*.

Nonrestrictive

Belgium has two major populations: the Flemings, *who live in the north and speak Flemish,* and the Walloons, *who live in the south and speak French*. Two relative clauses, the first modifying *Flemings* and the second modifying *Walloons*.

With Brussels in the middle of the country, both groups inhabit the city. Prepositional phrases, together modifying *inhabit*.

NATO's headquarters is in Brussels, *where it has been since its beginning in 1950*. Subordinate clause modifying *Brussels*.

Covering southeastern Belgium, the sandstone Ardennes mountains follow the Sambre and Meuse rivers. Participial (verbal) phrase modifying *mountains*.

These examples illustrate several aspects of restrictive and nonrestrictive modifiers:

1. They *modify* a word in the clause or sentence; they therefore function as adjectives or adverbs.
2. They can appear at the beginning, somewhere in the middle, or at the end of a sentence or clause.
3. Most types of subordinate elements can be restrictive and nonrestrictive.
4. Whether a clause or phrase is restrictive or nonrestrictive depends on its function in the sentence.
5. Restrictive elements are not set off with punctuation; nonrestrictive elements are set off with commas (and sometimes dashes).

If you think the distinction between restriction and nonrestriction is not worth making, consider the following sentences, the first restrictive and the second nonrestrictive:

People who wear braces on their teeth should not eat caramel apples.

People, who wear braces on their teeth, should not eat caramel apples.

Set off with commas, the nonrestrictive *who* clause implies that all people wear braces on their teeth and should not eat caramel apples, which is clearly not the case. It does not *restrict,* or limit, the meaning of *people*. In the first sentence, however, the *who* clause does restrict, or limit, the meaning of *people* to only those who wear braces on their teeth. Often only the writer knows the intended meaning and therefore needs to make the distinction by setting off, or not setting off, the modifier.

Here are a few guidelines that might help you in making this fine distinction:

1. A modifier that modifies a proper noun (one that names a person or thing) is usually nonrestrictive, because the name is sufficient identification. Notice *Flemings* and *Walloons* in the previous example.

2. A *that* clause is almost always restrictive.

3. Adverbial subordinate clauses (those beginning with subordinating conjunctions such as *because* and *when*; see list on page 641) are almost always restrictive and usually not set off with commas when they appear at the end of their sentences. If they appear at the beginning of sentences, they are almost always set off with commas.

4. A nonrestrictive modifier at the beginning of a sentence is followed by a comma, one at the end is preceded by a comma, and one in the middle is enclosed with two commas.

3C Adjectives and Adverbs

Adjectives and adverbs, often called *modifiers,* describe nouns and verbs (see 9A Parts of Speech). Adjectives modify nouns; that is, they describe, limit, explain, or alter them in some way. By modifying, they *limit* the meaning of the nouns: *red car* is narrower in meaning than *car,* and *fast red car* is narrower than *red car.* Adverbs modify verbs, adjectives, and other adverbs, telling more than the words by themselves would tell: drive *carefully* (adverb modifying a verb), *unexpectedly* early (adverb modifying an adjective), drive *very* carefully (adverb modifying an adverb). Adverbs usually tell how, where, when, and how much.

Adjectives and adverbs occasionally present some problems for writers. Be careful not to use adjectives when adverbs are needed, as in this sentence:

The governor suspected that the legislators were not taking him *serious*. The sentence element receiving modification is the verb *were not taking* yet the modifier *serious* is an adjective, which can only modify nouns. The correct modifier for this sentence is the adverb *seriously*. (If you are not sure whether a word is an adjective or an adverb, check your dictionary, which should identify parts of speech.)

Another problem in form concerns the *comparative* and *superlative* degrees. The comparative form of adjectives and adverbs shows a greater degree between two things:

Your luggage is *stronger* than mine. Adjective comparing *your luggage* and *mine*.

Your luggage survives airport baggage handling *better* than mine does. Adverb comparing how the two *survive* handling.

The comparative degree is formed by adding *-er* to shorter adjectives and adverbs (*strong, stronger, hard, harder*); longer words are preceded by *more* (*beautiful, more beautiful; seriously, more seriously*). Do not use *-er* with *more* (not *more harder*).

The superlative form shows a greater degree among three or more things:

This is the *strongest* luggage I have ever seen. Adjective comparing the present luggage to all other luggage the writer has seen.

Your luggage survives airport baggage handling *best* of all luggage I've seen. Adverb comparing how all luggage the writer has seen survives handling.

The superlative degree is formed by adding *-est* to shorter adjectives and adverbs (*strong, strongest; hard, hardest*); longer words are preceded by *most* (*beautiful, most beautiful; seriously, most seriously*). Do not use *-est* with *most* (not *most strongest*).

Do not use adjectives and adverbs gratuitously, just to fill space or because you think you ought to. They are effective only when they add meaning to a sentence.

4 Verbs

Verbs are the central core of a sentence; together with subjects, they make statements. Verbs often tell what the subject is doing:

The company *agreed* to plead guilty to criminal charges.

Nearly every miner *can name* a casualty of black lung disease.

Another common function of verbs is to link subjects to complements:

Logan *is* an isolated county in the corner of the state.

Sometimes the verb tells something about the subject, as the following passive verb does:

Casualties of mining *cannot be measured* only by injuries.

Through changes in form, verbs can tell the time of the action (past, present, future), the number of the subject (singular or plural), and the person of the subject (first person, *I, we*; second person, *you*; third person, *he, she, it, they*).

4A Tense

The problems that writers sometimes encounter when using verbs in writing result from the fact that verbs, unlike most other words in English, have many forms, and a slight shift in form can alter meaning. Notice how the meanings of the following pairs of sentences change as the verbs change:

The fish *has jumped* into the boat.

The fish *have jumped* into the boat.

The concert *starts* at 8:15 p.m.

The concert *started* at 8:15 p.m.

In the first pair, the meaning changes from one fish to more than one fish jumping into the boat. In the second pair, the first verb implies that the concert has not yet begun; the second, that it had already begun. It is important, therefore, to use the verb form that conveys the intended meaning. Observe how the verb *vanish* changes in the following sentences to indicate differences in time, or *tense*:

Present:	Many agricultural jobs *vanish*.
Past:	Many agricultural jobs *vanished*.
Future:	Many agricultural jobs *will vanish*.
Perfect:	Many agricultural jobs *have vanished*.
Past Perfect:	Many agricultural jobs *had vanished*.
Future Perfect:	Many agricultural jobs *will have vanished*.

To omit an *-ed* ending or use the wrong helping verb gives readers a false message.

Helping (Auxiliary) Verbs. It is also important to use a form that is a *finite,* or an actual, verb. In the following example, the word that appears to be a verb (italicized) is not a finite verb:

The fish *jumping* into the boat.

The word *jumping* does not have one of the primary functions of verbs—telling time of the action, called *tense*. The time of the occurrence could have been the past (*the fish were jumping*), present (*the fish are jumping*), or the future (*the fish will be jumping*). We also don't know whether the writer meant one fish or many. The *-ing* form is a *verbal* and requires a helping, or auxiliary, verb to make it finite, or able to tell time: words such as *am, is, are, was, were* (forms of *be*). Other helping verbs are *do* (*Do* you *want* the paper? She *doesn't want* the paper) and *have* (I *haven't seen* the paper; *has* she *seen* it?).

Irregular Verbs. Most verbs change forms in a regular way: *want* in the present becomes *wanted* in the past, *wanting* with the auxiliary *be* (i.e., *is wanting*), and *wanted* with the auxiliary *have* (i.e., *have wanted*). Many verbs change irregularly, however—internally rather than at the ending. Here are a few of the most common irregular verbs:

Base form	Past tense	Present participle	Past participle
be (is, am, are)	was, were	being	been
come	came	coming	come
do	did	doing	done
drink	drank	drinking	drunk
give	gave	giving	given
go	went	going	gone
grow	grew	growing	grown
lie	laid	lying	lain
see	saw	seeing	seen
take	took	taking	taken
teach	taught	teaching	taught
throw	threw	throwing	thrown
wear	wore	wearing	worn
write	wrote	writing	written

Check your dictionary for the forms of other verbs you suspect may be irregular.

The verb form that is perhaps the most troublesome is the *-s* form in the present tense. This form is used for all singular nouns and the pronouns *he, she,* and *it*. (See 4D Subject–Verb Agreement.)

4B Voice

English sentences are usually written in the active voice, in which the subject of the sentence is the doer of the action of the verb:

> Scott misplaced the file folder. *Scott*, the subject of the sentence, performed the action, *misplaced*.

With the passive voice, the doer of the action is the object of a preposition or is omitted entirely:

> The file folder was misplaced by Scott. *File folder* is now the subject of the sentence.

> The file folder was misplaced. The person doing the action is not named.

At best, the passive voice is wordier than the active voice; at worst, it fails to acknowledge who performs the action of the verb. Use the passive voice when you do not know or want to name the doer or when you want to keep the subjects consistent within a paragraph.

To avoid the passive voice, look for *by* phrases near the ends of your sentences; if you find any, see if the subject of your sentence performs the action of your verb. If not, revise the sentence so that it does. Another way to find occurrences of the passive voice is to look for forms of *be*: *am, is, are, was, were, been, being*. Not all these verbs will be passive, but if they function as part of an action verb, see if the subject performs the action. If it does not, and if your sentence would be clearer with the subject performing the action, revise to the active voice.

4C Mood

Mood refers to the writer's attitude toward the action of the verb. There are three forms: indicative, imperative, and subjunctive. Verbs in the *indicative mood* are used to make statements, to ask questions, and to declare opinions. For example:

> Not many people today *think* the world *is* flat. Makes a statement.

> *Does* anybody today *think* the world is flat? Asks a question.

> Members of the Flat Earth Society *should reevaluate* their thinking. Declares an opinion.

Verbs in the *imperative mood* issue commands, requests, or directions. Imperative verbs never change form. When the subject of an imperative verb is not explicitly identified it is understood to be *you*.

Julia, *stop* teasing your baby brother. Issues command.

Please *complete* this report by tomorrow morning. Issues request.

Turn right at the light and *drive* for another two blocks. Issues directions.

Verbs in the *subjunctive mood* communicate wishes, make statements contrary to fact, list requirements and demands, and imply skepticism or doubt. They usually appear in clauses introduced by *if, that, as if,* and *as though.* Use the base form of the verb for the present tense subjunctive. For the past tense subjunctive of the verb *be,* use *were* for all subjects.

She wishes that her son's best friend *were* more responsible. Communicates wish.

If the world *were* to end tomorrow, we would not have to pay taxes anymore. Makes statement contrary to fact.

The jury summons requires that your cousin *arrive* punctually at 8:00 a.m. and *sign* in with the court clerk. Lists requirements.

His girlfriend talks as if she *were* a pop music diva. Implies skepticism.

Be sure to select the correct verb forms to express indicative, imperative, and subjunctive moods.

4D Subject–Verb Agreement

Clauses are made of subjects and verbs plus their modifiers and other related words. A fundamental principle of usage is that verbs agree with their subjects. In most cases, this principle presents no problem: You say "Birds *have* feathers," not "Birds *has* feathers." But not all sentences are this simple. Before getting into the problem areas, consider first that errors in subject–verb agreement occur only with present-tense verbs and the verb tenses that use present tense forms of helping verbs (such as *have* and *be*). And, except for the irregular verb *be* (with its forms *am, is, are, was, were*), the problem centers on third-person singular verbs with their *-s* ending. Here is the problem illustrated. Notice that only the verbs in the third-person singular are different. The unfortunate thing is that all nouns are third person and, when singular, require this form in the present tense.

	Present		Present Perfect	
	singular	plural	singular	plural
first person	I work	we work	I have worked	we have worked
second person	you work	you work	you have worked	you have worked
third person	he works (she, it)	they work	he has worked (she, it)	they have worked

It is the *-s* form, then, that you need to watch for to avoid errors in subject–verb agreement. Here are some situations that may cause problems.

Intervening Subordinate Element

When a subject and a verb are side by side, they usually do not present a problem. Often, however, writers separate them with subordinate elements, such as clauses, prepositional or verbal phrases, and other elements. The result may be a verb error. The following sentence illustrates this problem:

> The realization that life is a series of compromises never occur to some people. The subject is *realization*, a singular noun, and should be followed by the singular verb *occurs*. The corrected sentence would read "The realization that life is a series of compromises never occurs to some people."

Subject Complement

Subject complements follow some verbs and rename the subject, although they are not always in the same number as the subject. Because a singular subject may have a plural complement, and vice versa, confused writers might make the verb agree with the complement instead of the subject. Here's an example:

> The result of this mistake are guilt, low self-esteem, and depression. The subject is *result*, not *guilt, low self-esteem*, and *depression*; the singular subject should be followed by the singular verb *is*. The corrected sentence would read "The result of this mistake is guilt, low self-esteem, and depression."

Compound Subject

Two or more words may be compounded to make a subject. Whether they are singular or plural depends on their connector. Subjects connected by *and* and *but* are plural, but those connected by *or* and *nor* are singular or plural depending on whether the item closer to the verb is singular or plural. Here are examples:

> The young mother and the superior student *are* both candidates for compulsive perfectionism. Two subjects, *mother* and *student*, are joined by *and* and take a plural verb.

> Promotions or an employee award *tells* the perfectionist he or she is achieving personal goals. When two subjects, *promotions* and *award*, are joined by *or*, the verb agrees with the nearer one; in this sentence a singular verb is required.

> An employee award or promotions *tell* the perfectionist he or she is achieving personal goals. Here the plural verb, *tell*, agrees with *promotions*, the closer of the two subjects.

Indefinite Pronoun as Subject

Indefinite pronouns are defined and listed under 5C Pronoun Agreement. Although these words often seem plural in meaning, most of them are singular grammatically. When indefinite pronouns are the subjects of sentences or clauses, their verbs are usually singular. Here are examples:

> Everyone *has* at some time worried about achieving goals. The singular indefinite pronoun *everyone* takes a singular verb, *has*.

> Each car and truck on the highway *was* creeping along on the icy pavement. The singular indefinite pronoun *each* requires a singular verb, *was*.

> Neither of us *is* going to worry about being late. The singular indefinite pronoun *neither* takes a singular verb, *is*.

Nevertheless, some of us *are* going to be very late. The indefinite pronoun *some* (like *all*, *any*, and *none*) is singular or plural depending on context; compare "Some of the book *is* boring."

Inverted Sentence Order

Inverted sentence order can confuse your natural inclination to subject–verb agreement. Examples of inverted order are questions, plus sentences beginning with *there*. Sentences like these demand closer attention to agreement.

Have the results of the test come back yet? The plural subject, *results*, takes a plural verb, *have*.

There *are* many special services provided just for kids at hotels, ski lodges, and restaurants. The plural subject, *services*, takes a plural verb, *are*. *There* is never a subject; it only holds the place for the subject in an inverted sentence.

Intervening Relative Clause

Subordinate clauses that begin with the relative pronouns *who*, *which*, or *that* present special problems in subject–verb agreement. Their verbs must agree with their own subjects, not with a word in another clause. These subordinate clauses demand special attention because whether the pronouns are singular or plural depends on their antecedents. These sentences illustrate agreement within relative clauses:

Every person who *attends* the baseball game will receive a free cap. *Who*, the subject of *attends*, means "person," a singular noun.

John is one of the few people I know who *care* about frogs. *Who*, the subject of *care*, means "people," a plural noun.

John is the only one of all the people I know who *cares* about frogs. *Who* in this sentence means "one."

5 Pronouns

Pronouns can have all the same sentence functions as nouns; the difference is that pronouns do not have the meaning that nouns have. Nouns name things; a noun stands for the thing itself. Pronouns, however, refer only to nouns. Whenever that reference is ambiguous or inconsistent, there is a problem in clarity.

5A Pronoun Case

Case is a grammatical term for the way nouns and pronouns show their relationships to other parts of a sentence. In English, nouns have only two case forms: the regular form (the one listed in a dictionary, such as *year*) and the possessive form (used to show ownership or connection, such as *year's*; possessive nouns are discussed in 8C Apostrophe).

Pronouns, however, have retained their case forms. Here are the forms for personal and relative pronouns:

	Subjective	Objective	Possessive
Personal	I	me	my, mine
	you	you	your, yours
	he	him	his
	she	her	her, hers
	it	it	its
	we	us	our, ours
	they	them	their, theirs
Relative	who	whom	whose
	whoever	whomever	whosever

Notice, first, that possessive pronouns, unlike possessive nouns, do not take apostrophes—none of them. Sometimes writers confuse possessive pronouns with contractions, which do have apostrophes (such as *it's,* meaning *it is* or *it has*; and *who's,* meaning *who is*; for a further discussion, see 8C Apostrophe).

Another problem writers sometimes have with pronoun case is using a subjective form when they need the objective or using an objective form when they need the subjective.

Subjective Case. Use the subjective forms for subjects and for words referring to subjects, as in these examples:

Among the patients a nutritionist sees are the grossly overweight people *who* have tried all kinds of diets. *Who* is subject of the verb *have tried* in its own clause.

They have a life history of obesity and diets. *They* is the subject of *have*.

He and *the patient* work out a plan for permanent weight control. *He* and *the patient* are the compound subjects of *work*.

The patient understands that the ones who work out the diet plan are *he* and *the nutritionist*. *He* and *the nutritionist* refer to *ones*, the subject of the clause.

Notice that pronoun case is determined by the function of the pronoun in its own clause and that compounding (*he and the patient*) has no effect on case.

Objective Case. Use the *objective* forms for objects of all kinds:

"Between *you* and *me*," said the patient to his nutritionist, "I'm ready for something that works." *You* and *me* are objects of the preposition *between*.

An exercise program is usually assigned the patient for *whom* diet is prescribed. *Whom* is the object of the preposition *for*.

The nutritionist gives *her* a suitable alternative to couch sitting. *Her* is the indirect object of *gives*.

Modest exercise combined with modest dieting can affect *him or her* dramatically. *Him or her* is the direct object of *can affect*.

Having advised *them* about diet and exercise, the nutritionist instructs dieters about behavioral change. *Them* is the object of the participle *having advised.*

Notice again that the case of a pronoun is determined by its function in its own clause and is not affected by compounding (*you and me*).

Possessive Case. Use the possessive forms to indicate ownership. Possessive pronouns have two forms: adjective forms (*my, your, his, her, its, our, their*) and possessive forms (*mine, yours, his, hers, its, ours, theirs*). The adjective forms appear before nouns or gerunds; the possessive forms replace possessive nouns.

The patient purchased *his* supplements from the drug store *his* nutritionist recommended. Adjective form before nouns.

His swimming every day produced results faster than he anticipated. Adjective form before gerund.

His was a difficult task to accomplish, but the rewards of weight loss were great. Possessive form replacing possessive noun.

5B Pronoun Reference

Personal and relative pronouns (see the list in section 5A Pronoun Case) must refer to specific nouns or antecedents. By themselves they have no meaning. As a result, they can cause problems in clarity for writers. If you were to read "She teaches technical writing at her local technical college," you would know only that *someone*, a woman, teaches technical writing at the college. But if the sentence were preceded by one like this, "After getting her master's degree, my mother has achieved one of her life goals," the pronoun *she* would have meaning. In this case, *mother* is the antecedent of *she*. The antecedent gives meaning to the pronoun. For this reason, it is essential that pronouns refer unambiguously to their antecedents and that pronouns and antecedents agree.

Ambiguous pronoun reference may occur in various ways:

- More than one possible antecedent.
- Adjective used as intended antecedent.
- Implied antecedent.
- Too great of a separation between antecedent and pronoun.

Here are sentences in which the pronouns do not clearly refer to their antecedents:

The immunologist refused to admit fraudulence of the data reported by a former colleague in a paper *he* had cosigned. More than one possible antecedent. *He* could refer to *immunologist* or to *colleague.*

In Carolyn Chute's book *The Beans of Egypt, Maine*, **she** treats poverty with concern and understanding. Adjective used as intended antecedent (possessive nouns function as adjectives). In this case, *Carolyn Chute's* modifies *book* and cannot serve as an antecedent of the pronoun *she*.

It says in the newspaper that the economy will not improve soon. Implied antecedent. There is no antecedent for it.

At Ajax *they* have tires on sale till the end of the month. Implied antecedent. There is no antecedent for *they*.

This only reinforces the public skepticism about the credibility of scientists. Implied antecedent. There is no antecedent for *This*.

One of the primary rules for using humor in advertising is often broken, *which* is that the ad doesn't make fun of the product. Too great a separation between antecedent and pronoun. The antecedent of *which* is *rules*, but its distance from the pronoun makes reference difficult.

Faulty pronoun reference is corrected by clarifying the relationship between the pronoun and its intended antecedent. Observe how the example sentences have been revised:

The immunologist refused to admit fraudulence of the data reported by a former colleague in a paper *the immunologist* had cosigned. *The immunologist* replaces the unclear pronoun *he*.

In **her** book *The Beans of Egypt, Maine*, **Carolyn Chute** treats poverty with concern and understanding. The possessive pronoun *her* replaces the possessive noun and refers to the noun subject, *Carolyn Chute*.

The newspaper reports that the economy will not improve soon. The unclear pronoun *it* is replaced by its implied antecedent, *the newspaper*.

Ajax has tires on sale till the end of the month. The unclear pronoun *they* is replaced by *Ajax*.

This *kind of waffling* only reinforces public skepticism about the credibility of scientists. The unclear pronoun *this* is replaced by the adjective *this* modifying the intended antecedent *kind of waffling*.

That the ad doesn't make fun of the product is an often-broken primary rule for using humor in advertising. Parts of the sentence are moved around until they are clear.

Revising unclear pronoun reference is sometimes like working a jigsaw puzzle: finding and adding a missing piece or moving parts around to achieve the best fit. Often only the writer can make the right connections.

5C Pronoun Agreement

Some pronoun errors result because the pronoun and its antecedent do not agree. In the sentence, "When a student is late for this class, they find the door locked," the plural pronoun *they* refers to a singular antecedent, *a student*. There is no agreement in *number*. In this sentence, "When a student is late for this class, you find the door locked," again the pronoun, this time *you,* does not agree with the antecedent. This time the problem is *person*. Pronouns must agree with their antecedents in number, person, and gender. (See the list of pronouns in 5A Pronoun Case.)

Compound Antecedents

Problems sometimes occur with compound antecedents. If the antecedents are joined by *and,* the pronoun is plural; if joined by *or,* the pronoun agrees with the nearer antecedent. Here are examples of correct usage:

> In the pediatric trauma center, the head doctor and head nurse direct *their* medical team. The pronoun *their* refers to both *doctor* and *nurse*.

> The head doctor or the head nurse directs *his or her* team. The pronouns *his or her* refer to the closer antecedent, *nurse* (because the gender of the nurse is not known, the neutral alternatives are used).

> The head doctor or the other doctors give *their* help when it is needed. The pronoun *their* agrees with the closer antecedent, *doctors*.

Indefinite Pronouns as Antecedents

A particularly troublesome kind of agreement is that between personal or relative pronouns and *indefinite pronouns*. As their name implies, indefinites do not refer to particular people or things; grammatically they are usually singular but are often intended as plural. Here are the common indefinite pronouns:

all	every	none
any	everybody	nothing
anybody	everyone	one
anyone	everything	some
anything	neither	somebody
each	no one	someone
either	nobody	something

Like nouns, these pronouns can serve as antecedents of personal and relative pronouns. But because most of them are grammatically singular, they can be troublesome in sentences. Here are examples of correct usage:

> Everyone in the trauma center has *his or her* specific job to do. **or** *All* the personnel in the trauma center have *their* specific jobs to do. The neutral, though wordy, alternative *his or her* agrees with the singular indefinite *everyone*. The second sentence illustrates the use of plural when gender is unknown.

> *Each* of them does *his or her* job efficiently and competently. **or** *All* of them do *their* jobs efficiently and competently. *Each* is singular, but *all* is either singular or plural, depending on context (compare "*All* literature has *its* place").

Shifts in Person

Agreement errors in *person* are shifts between *I* or *we* (first person), *you* (second person), and *he, she, it,* and *they* (third person). These errors are probably more often a result of carelessness than of imperfect knowledge. Being more familiar with casual speech than formal writing, writers sometimes shift from *I* to *you,* for example, when only one of them is meant, as in these sentences:

> Last summer *I* went on a canoeing trip to northern Manitoba. It was *my* first trip that far north, and it was so peaceful *you* could forget all the problems back home. The person represented by *you* was not present. The writer means *I*.

See also 2D Shifts.

5D Relative Pronouns

Use relative pronouns to introduce clauses that modify nouns or pronouns. Personal relative pronouns refer to people. They include *who, whom, whoever, whomever,* and *whose*. Nonpersonal relative pronouns refer to things. They include *which, whichever, whatever,* and *whose*.

  Most college writers know to use *who* when referring to people and *which* or *that* when referring to things, but sometimes carelessness or confusion can lead to errors. Many writers assume that *which* and *that* are interchangeable when they are not. Use *which* to introduce nonrestrictive clauses and *that* to introduce restrictive clauses (see 3B Restrictive and Nonrestrictive Modifiers). Another problem area concerns the correct use of *who* and *whom*. Use *who* to refer to the subject of the sentence and *whom* to refer to an object of the verb or preposition. Following are examples of common errors:

> The lawyer *that* lost the case today went to law school with my sister. Uses impersonal relative pronoun *that*.

> Conflict between the two parties led to the lawsuit *that* was finally settled today. The relative pronoun *that* introduces a nonrestrictive clause that modifies *lawsuit*. Nonrestrictive clauses supply extra information to the sentence, not defining information.

> The case resulted in a ruling, *which* favored the plaintiff. The relative pronoun *which* introduces a restrictive clause that modifies *ruling*. Restrictive clauses supply defining information.

> Later, the lawyer *whom* lost the case spoke with the jurors *who* we had interviewed. The first relative pronoun *whom* refers to the subject *lawyer* while the second relative pronoun *who* refers to the object of the verb *had interviewed*.

Once you recognize relative pronoun errors it is usually easy to fix them:

> The lawyer *who* lost the case today went to law school with my sister.

> Conflict between the two parties led to the lawsuit, *which* was finally settled today.

> The case resulted in a ruling *that* favored the plaintiff.

> Later, the lawyer *who* lost the case spoke with the jurors *whom* we had interviewed.

6 Style

Style in writing, like style in clothes, art, or anything else, is individual and develops with use and awareness. But even individual writers vary their style, depending on the situation. At school and work, the preferred style tends to be more formal and objective. The readings in this book provide abundant examples of this style. It is not stuffy, patronizing, or coldly analytical. It is simply clean, direct, and clear. This handbook section treats a few of the obstacles to a good writing style.

6A Conciseness

Nobody wants to read more words than necessary. When you write concisely, therefore, you are considerate of your readers. To achieve conciseness you do not need to eliminate details and other content; rather, you cut empty words, repetition, and unnecessary details.

In the following passage, all the italicized words could be omitted without altering the meaning.

> *In the final analysis, I feel that* the United States should have converted to the *use of the* metric system *of measurement* a long time ago. *In the present day and age,* the United States, except for Borneo and Liberia, is the *one and* only country in the *entire* world that has not yet adopted this measurement system.

Repetition of key words is an effective technique for achieving emphasis and coherence, but pointless repetition serves only to bore the reader.

Follow these guidelines to achieve conciseness in your writing:

1. **Avoid redundancy**. Redundant words and expressions needlessly repeat what has already been said. Delete them when they appear in your writing.

2. **Avoid wordy expressions**. Phrases such as *In the final analysis* and *In the present day and age* in the preceding example add no important information to sentences and should be removed and/or replaced with less wordy constructions.

3. **Avoid unnecessary intensifiers**. Intensifiers such as *really, very, clearly, quite,* and *of course* usually fail to add meaning to the words they modify and therefore are often unnecessary. Deleting them does not change the meaning of the sentence.

4. **Avoid excess use of prepositional phrases**. The use of too many prepositional phrases within a sentence makes for wordy writing. Always use constructions that require the fewest words.

5. **Avoid negating constructions**. Negating constructions using words such as *no* and *not* often add unneeded words to sentences. Use shorter alternatives when they are available.

6. **Avoid the passive voice**. Passive constructions require more words than active constructions (see 4B Voice). They can also obscure meaning by concealing the sentence's subject. Write in the active voice whenever possible.

Following are more examples of wordy sentences that violate these guidelines:

If the two groups *cooperate together,* there will be *positive benefits* for both. Uses redundancy.

There are some people *who* think the metric system is un-American. Uses wordy expression.

The climb up the mountain was *very* hard on my legs and *really* taxed my lungs and heart. Uses unnecessary modifiers.

On the day of his birth, we walked *to the park down the block from the house of his mother*. Uses too many prepositional phrases.

She *did not like* hospitals. Uses negating construction when a shorter alternative is available.

The door *was closed* by that man over there. Uses passive voice when active voice is preferable.

Corrections to the previous wordy sentences result in concise sentences:

If the two groups cooperate, both will benefit. This correction also replaces the wordy construction *there will be…for both* with a shorter, more forceful alternative.

Some people think the metric system is un-American.

The climb up the mountain was hard on my legs and taxed my lungs and heart.

On his birthday, we walked to the park near his mother's house.

She hated hospitals.

That man over there closed the door.

6B Appropriate Language

Effective writers communicate using appropriate language; that is, language that:

1. Suits its subject and audience.
2. Avoids sexist usage.
3. Avoids bias and stereotype.

Suitability

The style and tone of your writing should be suitable to your subject and audience. Most academic and business contexts require the use of *formal language.* Formal language communicates clearly and directly with a minimum of stylistic flourish. Its tone is serious, objective, and detached. Formal language avoids slang, pretentious words, and unnecessary jargon. *Informal language,* on the other hand, is particular to the writer's personality and also assumes a closer and more familiar relationship between the writer and the reader. Its tone is casual, subjective, and intimate. Informal language can also employ slang and other words that would be inappropriate in formal language.

As informal language is rarely used within an academic setting, the following examples show errors in the use of formal language:

The director told the board members to *push off*. Uses informal language.

Professor Oyo *dissed* Marta when she arrived late to his class for the third time in a row. Uses slang.

The *aromatic essence* of the gardenia was intoxicating. Uses pretentious words.

The doctor told him to take *salicylate* to ease the symptoms of *viral rhinorrhea*. Uses unnecessary jargon.

Employing formal language correctly, these examples could be revised as follows:

The director told the board members to leave.

Professor Oyo spoke disrespectfully to Marta when she arrived late to his class for the third time in a row.

The scent of the gardenia was intoxicating.

The doctor told him to take aspirin to ease his cold symptoms.

Sexist Usage

Gender-exclusive terms such as *policeman* and *chairman* are offensive to many readers today. Writers who are sensitive to their audience, therefore, avoid such terms, replacing them with expressions such as *police officer* and *chairperson* or *chair*. Most sexist usage in language involves masculine nouns, masculine pronouns, and patronizing terms.

Masculine Nouns. Do not use *man* and its compounds generically. For many people, these words are specific to men and do not account for women as separate and equal people. Here are some examples of masculine nouns and appropriate gender-neutral substitutions:

Masculine Noun	Gender-Neutral Substitution
mailman	mail carrier
businessman	businessperson, executive, manager
fireman	firefighter
man-hours	work hours
mankind	humanity, people
manmade	manufactured, synthetic
salesman	salesperson, sales representative, sales agent
congressman	member of Congress, representative

Using gender-neutral substitutions often entails using a more specific word for a generalized term, which adds more precision to writing.

Masculine Pronouns. Avoid using the masculine pronouns *he, him,* and *his* in a generic sense, meaning both male and female. This can pose some challenges, however, because English does not have a generic singular pronoun that can be used instead. Consider the following options:

1. Eliminate the pronoun.

   Every writer has an individual style. Instead of Every writer has his own style.

2. Use plural forms.

   Writers have their own styles. Instead of A writer has his own style.

3. Use *he or she, one,* or *you* as alternates only sparingly.

   Each writer has his or her own style. Instead of Each writer has his own style.

   One has an individual writing style. Instead of He has his own individual writing style.

   You have your own writing style. Instead of A writer has his own style.

Patronizing Terms. Avoid terms that cast men or women in gender-exclusive roles or that imply that women are subordinate to men. Here are some examples of biased or stereotypical terms and their gender-neutral substitutions:

Biased/Stereotypical Term	Gender-Neutral Substitution
lady lawyer	lawyer
male nurse	nurse
career girl	professional, attorney, manager
coed	student
housewife	homemaker
stewardess	flight attendant
cleaning lady	housecleaner

Biases and Stereotypes

Biased and stereotypical language can be hurtful and can perpetuate discrimination. Most writers are sensitive to racial and ethnic biases or stereotypes, but writers should also avoid language that shows insensitivity to age, class, religion, and sexual orientation. The accepted terms for identifying groups and group members have changed over the years and continue to change today. Avoid using terms that have fallen into disuse such as *Indian* or *Oriental*; instead, use accepted terms such as *Native American* or *Asian*.

7 Punctuation

Punctuation is a system of signals telling readers how the parts of written discourse relate to one another. They are similar to road signs that tell the driver what to expect: A sign with an arrow curving left means that the road makes a left curve, a "stop ahead" sign that a stop sign is imminent, a speed limit sign what the legal speed is. Drivers trust that the signs mean what they say. Readers, too, expect punctuation marks to mean what they say: A period means the end of a sentence, a colon that an explanation will follow, a comma that the sentence is not finished. Punctuation is a way for writers to help readers understand their words in the intended way.

Punctuation corresponds roughly to intonations and other physical signals in speech. When you speak, you use pitch levels, pauses, hand signals, head movements, and facial expressions to make sure your audience understands you. At the end of a sentence, you unconsciously let your voice drop—not just pause but decidedly drop in pitch. With some questions, your voice rises at the end, as in "Do you want to go?" With other questions, the pitch drops, as in "Do you want to go or not?" You can have brief pauses, or you can lengthen them to increase the drama of what you are saying. You can increase or decrease the sound volume of your words. None of these signals are available to writers. To make their situation even more difficult, writers do not have their audience right in front of them to look puzzled or to question them when meaning is unclear. So writers use punctuation.

Ends of sentences are punctuated with periods, question marks, or exclamation points. Semicolons function as "soft" periods, usually marking the end of independent clauses (as periods do) but not of complete thoughts. Commas show relationships within sentences, as do colons, dashes, quotation marks, parentheses, brackets, and ellipsis dots. These marks are explained in the sections that follow. Other marks, those used within words (apostrophes, hyphens, italics, and slashes), are explained in Section 8, Mechanics and Spelling.

Figure H-1 serves as a quick guide to sentence punctuation. For explanations, refer to the relevant entry.

7A End Punctuation

A period is the normal mark for ending sentences. A question mark ends a sentence that asks a direct question, and an exclamation point ends forceful assertions.

Period

Sentences normally end with a period.

> Studies suggest that eating fish two or three times a week may reduce the risk of heart attack. Statement.

> Eat two or three servings of fish a week. Mild command.

> The patient asked whether eating fish would reduce risk of heart attack. Indirect question.

Avoid inserting a period before the end of a sentence; the result will be a fragment (see 1A Fragments). Sentences can be long or short; their length does not determine their completion. Both of the following examples are complete sentences.

> Eat fish. Mild command; the subject, *you*, is understood.

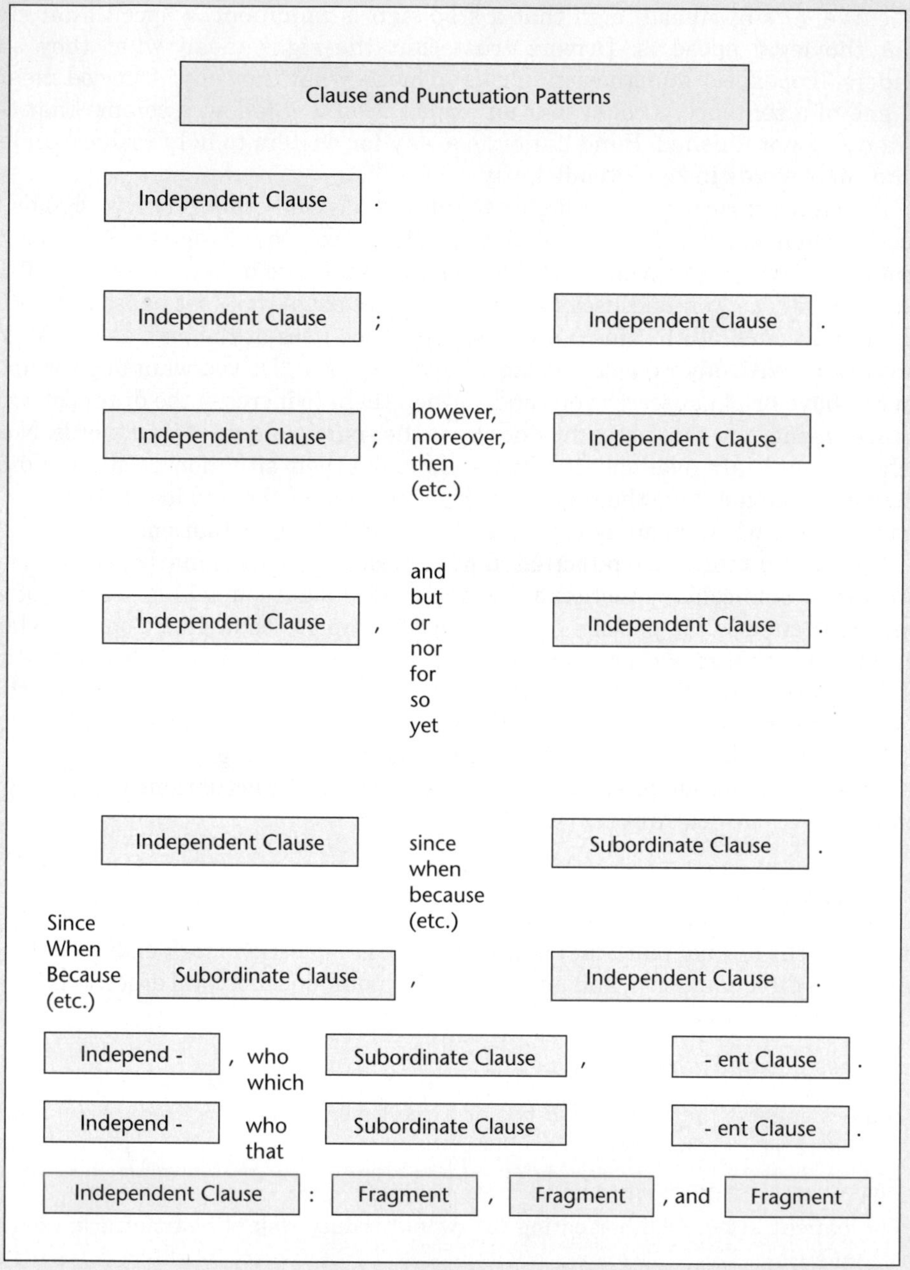

| Clause and Punctuation Patterns |

Independent Clause .

Independent Clause ;   Independent Clause .

Independent Clause ;   however, moreover, then (etc.)   Independent Clause .

Independent Clause ,   and but or nor for so yet   Independent Clause .

Independent Clause   since when because (etc.)   Subordinate Clause .

Since When Because (etc.)   Subordinate Clause ,   Independent Clause .

Independ -   , who which   Subordinate Clause ,   - ent Clause .

Independ -   who that   Subordinate Clause   - ent Clause .

Independent Clause :   Fragment ,   Fragment , and   Fragment .

Figure H-1

In a two-year study of 1,000 survivors of heart attack, researchers found a 29 percent reduction in mortality among those who regularly ate fish or took a fish oil supplement. Statement; one sentence.

Question Mark

A sentence that asks a direct question ends in a question mark:

How does decaffeinated coffee differ from regular coffee?

Do not use a question mark to end an indirect question:

The customer asked how decaffeinated coffee differs from regular coffee.

With quoted questions, place the question mark inside the final quotation marks:

The customer asked, "How does decaffeinated coffee differ from regular coffee?"

Exclamation Point

The exclamation point ends forceful assertions:

Fire!

Shut that door immediately!

Because they give the impression of shouting, exclamation points are rarely needed in formal business and academic writing.

7B Semicolon

The main use for a semicolon is to connect two closely related independent clauses:

Dengue hemorrhagic fever is a viral infection common to Southeast Asia; it kills about 5,000 children a year.

Sometimes the second clause contains a transitional adverb (see 1B Comma Splices):

Dengue has existed in Asia for centuries; *however,* it grew more virulent in the 1950s.

Do not use a comma where a semicolon or period is required; the result is a comma splice (see 1B Comma Splices). In contrast, a semicolon used in place of a comma may result in a type of fragment (see 1A Fragments):

In populations where people have been stricken by an infectious virus, survivors have antibodies in their bloodstreams; *which prevent or reduce the severity of subsequent infections*. The semicolon makes a fragment of the *which* clause.

Do not confuse the semicolon with the colon (see 7D Colon). While the semicolon connects independent clauses, a colon ordinarily does not. The semicolon is also used to separate items in a series when the items contain internal commas:

Scientists are researching the effects of staphylococcus bacteria, which cause infections in deep wounds; influenza A virus, which causes respiratory flu; and conjunctivitis bacteria, which have at times caused fatal purpuric fever.

7C Comma

The comma is probably the most troublesome mark of punctuation because it has so many uses. It is a real workhorse for punctuation within a sentence. Its main uses are explained here.

Compound Sentences. A comma joins two independent clauses connected with a coordinating conjunction (see 1B Comma Splices):

> Martinique is a tropical island in the West Indies, *and* it attracts flocks of tourists annually.

Do not use the comma between independent clauses without the conjunction, even if the second clause begins with a transitional adverb:

> Faulty: Martinique is a tropical island in the West Indies, it attracts flocks of tourists annually. Two independent clauses with no conjunction; it is a comma splice.

> Faulty: Martinique is a tropical island in the West Indies, consequently it attracts flocks of tourists annually. Two independent clauses with transitional adverb; it is a comma splice.

Introductory Sentence Elements. Commas set off a variety of introductory sentence elements, as illustrated here:

> *When the French colonized Martinique in 1635,* they eliminated the native Caribs. Introductory subordinate clause.

> *Choosing death over subservience,* the Caribs leaped into the sea. Introductory participial (verbal) phrase.

> *Before their death,* they warned of a "mountain of fire" on the island. Introductory prepositional phrase.

> *Subsequently,* the island's volcano erupted. Introductory transitional adverb.

Short prepositional phrases sometimes are not set off:

> *In 1658* the Caribs leaped to their death.

Sometimes, however, a comma must be used after a short prepositional phrase to prevent misreading:

> *Before,* they had predicted retribution. Comma is required to prevent misreading.

Nonrestrictive and Parenthetical Elements. Words that interrupt the flow of a sentence are set off with commas before and after. If they come at the end of a sentence, they are set off with one comma.

   In this class are nonrestrictive modifiers (see 3B Restrictive and Nonrestrictive Modifiers), transitional adverbs (see 1B Comma Splices), and a few other types of interrupters. Here are examples:

> This rugged island, *which Columbus discovered in 1502,* exports sugar and rum. Nonrestrictive *which* clause; commas before and after.

A major part of the economy, *however,* is tourism. Interrupting transitional adverb; commas before and after.

Tourists, *attracted to the island by its climate,* enjoy discovering its culture. Interrupting participial (verbal) phrase (see 1A Fragments); commas before and after.

A popular tradition in Martinique is the Carnival, *which occurs just before Lent each year*. Nonrestrictive *which* clause; one comma.

Martinique is an overseas department of France, *a status conferred in 1946*. An absolute, ending the sentence (participial phrase plus the noun it modifies).

Series

Commas separate items in a series:

Martiniquans dance to *steel drums, clarinets, empty bottles, and banjos*. Four nouns.

Dressing in colorful costumes, dancing through the streets, and thoroughly enjoying the celebration, Martiniquans celebrate Carnival with enthusiasm. Three participial (verbal) phrases.

Martinique has a population of over 300,000, its main religion is Roman Catholicism, and its languages are French and Creole dialect. Three independent clauses.

Various sentence elements can make up a series, but the elements joined should be equivalent grammatically (see 2A Parallelism, which discusses faulty parallelism). Common practice calls for a comma before the conjunction joining the last item in the series.

Quotations

Commas set off quoted sentences from the words that introduce them:

"A wise man," says David Hume, "proportions his belief to the evidence."

According to Plato, "Writing will produce forgetfulness" in writers because "they will not need to exercise their memories." The second clause is not set off with a comma.

"*X* on beer casks indicates beer which paid ten shillings duty, and hence it came to mean beer of a given quality," reports *The Dictionary of Phrase and Fable*.

Quotations introduced with *that* and other connectors (such as *because* in the second sentence here) are not set off with commas. Commas at the end of quotations go inside the quotation marks.

Coordinate Adjectives

Commas separate adjectives that equally modify a noun:

The "food pyramid" was designed as a *meaningful, memorable* way to represent the ideal daily diet. Two adjectives modify the noun *way* equally.

When you're not sure about using a comma, try inserting the coordinating conjunction *and* between the two adjectives to see if they are truly coordinate (*meaningful and memorable*). Another test is to reverse the order of the adjectives (*memorable, meaningful*). Do not use a comma between adjectives that are not coordinate or between the last adjective and the noun being modified. (See also 3C Adjectives and Adverbs.)

Addresses and Dates

Use a comma to separate city and state in an address, but do not set off the zip code:

Glen Ridge, New Jersey 07028 *or* Glen Ridge, NJ 07028

In a sentence, a state name is enclosed in commas:

The letter from Glen Ridge, New Jersey, arrived by express mail.

Dates are treated similarly:

January 5, 1886 *but* 5 January 1886

The events of January 5, 1886, are no longer remembered. When other punctuation is not required, the year is followed by a comma.

Commas to Avoid

Some people mistakenly believe that commas should be used wherever they might pause in speech. A comma does mean pause, but not all pauses are marked by commas. Use a comma only when you know you need one. Avoid the following comma uses:

1. To set off restrictive sentence elements:

   People, *who want a balanced diet,* can use the food pyramid as a guide. The restrictive *who* clause is necessary to identify *people* and should not be set off with commas.

2. To separate a subject from its verb and a preposition from its object:

   People who want a balanced diet, can use the food pyramid as a guide. The comma following the *who* clause separates the subject, *people*, from its verb, *can use*.

   The bottom level of the food pyramid contains food from grains, *such as,* bread, cereals, rice, and pasta. The preposition *such as* should not be followed by a comma.

3. To follow a coordinating conjunction (see 1B Comma Splices):

   The food pyramid describes a new approach to a balanced diet. But, the meat and dairy industries opposed it. The coordinating conjunction *but* should not be set off with a comma.

4. To separate two independent clauses (see 1B Comma Splices) not joined with a coordinating conjunction:

   The pyramid shows fewer servings of dairy and meat products, therefore consumers would buy less of these higher-priced foods. The comma should be replaced with a semicolon (7B).

5. To set off coordinate elements joined with a coordinating conjunction:

   Vegetables and fruits are near the bottom of the pyramid, *and should be eaten several times a day*. The coordinating conjunction *and* joins a second verb, *should be eaten*, not a second independent clause; therefore no comma is needed.

7D Colon

The colon is used most often to introduce an explanatory element, often in the form of a list:

> The space shuttle *Challenger* lifted off on January 28, 1986, with a seven-member crew: Francis R. Scobee, Michael J. Smith, Ronald E. McNair, Ellison S. Onizuka, Judith A. Resnik, Gregory B. Jarvis, and Christa McAuliffe. The list explains *crew*.

> A twelve-member investigating team discovered the cause of the disaster: a leak in one of the shuttle's two solid-fuel booster rockets. The phrase explains the *cause of the disaster*.

Do not use colons interchangeably with semicolons (see 7B Semicolon). Semicolons separate two independent clauses (see 1B Comma Splices); colons ordinarily are followed by a phrase or phrases. Also avoid using colons after verbs and prepositions (see 1A Fragments):

> The two causes of the O-ring failure were cold temperatures and design deficiencies. No colon after *were*.

> The commission investigating the disaster noted a number of failures in communication, such as one within the National Aeronautics and Space Administration. No colon after *such as*.

Colons have a few other set uses:

Time:	10:15 a.m.
Salutation in a business letter:	Dear Patricia Morton:
Biblical reference:	Genesis 2:3

7E Dash

The dash separates sentence elements with greater emphasis than a comma:

> In *The War of the Worlds* (1898), science fiction writer H. G. Wells described an intense beam of light that destroyed objects on contact—the laser.

It is also used to set off a nonrestrictive sentence element (see 3B Restrictive and Nonrestrictive Modifiers) that might be confusing if set off with commas:

> A number of medical uses—performing eye surgery, removing tumors, and unclogging coronary arteries—make the laser more than a destructive weapon. The three explanatory items separated by commas are set off from the rest of the sentence with dashes.

Like commas that set off nonrestrictive elements within a sentence, dashes often are used in pairs—at the beginning of the interruption and at the end.

A dash is sometimes used in place of a colon when a colon might seem too formal:

> Besides its medical uses, the laser serves many other functions—reading price codes, playing compact audio disks, and sending telephone messages.

Use the dash with caution; overuse gives the impression that you aren't familiar with alternative means of punctuation.

7F Quotation Marks

The main use for quotation marks is to set off direct quotations:

> Professor Charlotte Johnson announced, "Interdisciplinary science is combining fields of scientific knowledge to make up new disciplines."

> "Biochemistry," she went on to say, "combines biology and chemistry."

Quotations within quotations are marked with single quotation marks:

> "The term 'interdisciplinary science' thus describes a change in how processes are investigated," she concluded.

Use quotation marks correctly with other punctuation marks. Periods and commas (see 7C Comma) always go inside the end quotation marks; colons and semicolons almost always go outside the quotation. Dashes, question marks, and exclamation points go inside or outside depending on meaning—inside if the mark applies to the quotation and outside if it applies to the surrounding sentence:

> "Do you know the various branches of the physical sciences?" asked Professor Johnson. Question mark goes inside quotation marks because it applies to the quotation.

> Did the professor say, "Histology deals with tissues and cytology with the fine structures of individual cells"? Question mark goes outside quotation marks because it applies to the surrounding sentence, not the quotation.

Do not use quotation marks to set off indirect quotations:

> The professor said that histology and cytology are different branches of study.

Another use for quotation marks is to enclose titles of works that are not published separately, including short stories, poems, and essays:

> "You Are a Man," by Richard Rodriguez

> "The Incident," by Countee Cullen

Do not enclose titles of your own essays in quotation marks when they are in title position. (See 8D Italics for treatment of titles of works that are published separately.)

Quotation marks are sometimes used to enclose words used in a special sense, but be careful not to abuse this function:

> The "right" way to do a thing is not always the best way.

> See Chapter 12 for more details on using quoted material in your writing.

7G Other Marks

Parentheses

Parentheses enclose interrupting elements, setting them off from the rest of the sentence or discourse with a greater separation than other enclosing marks such as commas and dashes. They usually add explanatory information that might seem digressive to the topic.

> The Particle Beam Fusion Accelerator *(PBFA II)* is a device designed to produce energy by fusion. Parentheses set off an abbreviation that will henceforth be used in place of the full term.

> The PBFA II stores up to 3.5 million joules of energy. *(One joule is the amount of energy expended by a one-watt device in one second.)* Parentheses set off an explanation framed as a complete sentence.

Parentheses are always used in pairs. They might have internal punctuation (as in the second example), but marks related to the sentence as a whole go outside the parentheses. Parentheses are almost never preceded by a comma. Note the following example:

> During fusion *(joining of two atomic nuclei to form a larger nucleus),* mass is converted to energy. Parenthetical element is followed by a comma, showing that it relates to *fusion*. If it had been preceded by a comma, it would appear, illogically, to relate to *mass*.

Brackets

Square brackets have limited uses and are not interchangeable with parentheses. Their most common use is to mark insertions in quoted material:

> Describing the Great Depression, Frederick Lewis Allen says, "The total amount of money paid out in wages *[in 1932]* was 60 percent less than in 1929." The words *in 1932* were not part of the original text.

Some writers use brackets to enclose brief parenthetical material within parentheses:

> Jules Verne *(Journey to the Center of the Earth* [1864]) described giant apes and a vast subterranean sea at the core of the earth. The date of publication is parenthetical to the title of the book.

Ellipsis Dots

Ellipsis dots (spaced periods) are used in quotations to indicate where words have been omitted. Three spaced dots mark omissions within a sentence. If the omission comes at the end of your sentence but not at the end of the original sentence, use four spaced periods.

> One of the legacies of the Great Depression, says Frederick Lewis Allen, is that "if individual Americans are in deep trouble,...their government [should] come to their aid." Words following a comma in the original sentence are omitted within the sentence. The brackets enclose an inserted word.

This idea, adds Allen, "was fiercely contested for years...." Allen's sentence did not end at *years*, where the quoted sentence ends.

When using ellipsis dots, be careful not to distort the meaning of the original by your selection of what to include and what to omit (see also Chapter 12).

8 Mechanics and Spelling

Some "rules" of writing are flexible, allowing choices, but this is not the case with spelling. With the invention of the printing press in the fifteenth century and the publication of dictionaries in the eighteenth century, flexibility in spelling all but vanished. Dictionaries spell almost all their words in exactly the same way as other dictionaries, and readers expect writers to do likewise. We have expectations about the way hyphens are used in compound words, the way apostrophes show possession or contraction, the way suffixes are added to root words, and so on. This section treats the formation of words—capitalizing, abbreviating, punctuating (apostrophes, italics, and hyphens), and spelling.

8A Capitalization

The rules for capitalization are relatively fixed. Following are examples of situations calling for capitalization.

Beginning of a sentence

In 1929, the whole credit structure of the American economy was shaken.

Proper names or nouns

With the onset of the *Great Depression, President Hoover* at first tried to organize national optimism. Historical period or event; person.

Bankers on *Wall Street,* manufacturers in *Detroit,* and legislators in *Washington* all had an effect on the economy. Place.

The Great Depression was part of a worldwide collapse, ending only with *World War II*. Historical period or event.

President Hoover set up the *Reconstruction Finance Corporation* to aid banks and businesses. Person; institution.

In 1900, most of the *African Americans* in this country lived in the *South*. Race and nationality; geographical region.

Jell-O, Pepsi, Rice Krispies Trade names.

Aunt Beatrice, Grandmother Dietz, Dad Relationships when they are part of the name; but not *my dad* and *my aunt and uncle.*

Titles

Death at an Early Age, by Jonathan Kozol; *The Dancing Wu Li Masters: An Overview of the New Physics,* by Gary Zukav. Capitalize first and last words, words following colons, and all other words except articles (*a, an,* and *the*) and conjunctions and prepositions of fewer than five letters (*and, but, in, by,* etc.).

Avoid capitalizing common nouns; for example:

For many people, the *winter* of 1902 was bleak. Seasons.

Many people moved *south* to a warmer climate. Compass directions.

My *great-grandparents* were among those who moved. Relationships.

Simon Waterson was a *professor of history* at the time. Titles that are not part of proper names.

8B Abbreviation

While abbreviations are part of the language, not all are acceptable in all circumstances. A general guideline is that they are less common in formal prose than in less formal circumstances.

Titles with proper names

Dr. Paul Gordon   Paul Gordon, Ph.D.
George Grossman, Jr.

Times and dates

11:15 A.M. *or* 11:15 a.m.   53 B.C.   A.D. 371

Names of organizations and countries

NATO   CIA   NBC

Use *U.S.* as an adjective (*in a U.S. city*) and *United States* as a noun (*a city in the United States*)

Latin abbreviations (write out except in source citations and parenthetical comments)

etc.   and so forth (*et cetera*—applies to things)
i.e.   that is (*id est*)
e.g.   for example (*exempli gratia*)
cf.   compare (*confer*)
et al.   and others (*et alii*—applies to people)
N.B.   note well (*nota bene*)

Abbreviations to be avoided in most prose

The school board not bd. met on Tuesday not Tues. February 3 not Feb.

William not Wm. Townsend was a guest lecturer in the economics not econ. class.

Townsend arrived from Pittsburgh, Pennsylvania not *PA* or *Penn.* late last night. For letters and envelopes, use the U.S. Postal zip codes, such as PA for *Pennsylvania* and IL for *Illinois*. Note that both letters are capitalized and are not followed by periods.

Consult your dictionary when you have questions about specific abbreviations.

8C Apostrophe

The apostrophe has two main uses in English—to mark possessive nouns and to show contractions—plus a few specialized uses. Avoid all other uses.

Possessive Nouns

Ownership or connection is marked on nouns with apostrophes:

Norton's resume is short and concise. The resume belongs to Norton.

This week's newsletter will be a little late. The newsletter of this week.

The article's title is confusing. The title of the article.

To make nouns possessive, follow one of these steps:

1. For singular nouns, add *'s* (*nature* + *'s* = *nature's*; *Tess* + *'s* = *Tess's*).
2. For plural nouns ending in *s,* add *'* (*strangers* + *'* = *strangers'*).
3. For plural nouns not ending in *s,* add *'s* (*men* + *'s* = *men's*).

Do not use apostrophes to make nouns plural. (See 8G Spelling.) And do not use apostrophes with possessive and relative pronouns. (See 5A Pronoun Case and the Contractions section that follows.)
    For example:

The *Harris's* are in Florida. Incorrectly uses apostrophe to make the noun *Harris* plural.

The family lost *it's* home in the fire. Incorrectly uses apostrophe with the pronoun *it* to make it possessive.

Contractions

Apostrophes stand in place of omitted letters in contractions:

doesn't	does not
isn't	is not
I'd	I would
you've	you have
it's	it is *or* it has
who's	who is *or* who has
let's	let us
we'll	we will

Because contractions reflect a casual style, they are usually not acceptable in formal writing. Do not confuse the contracted *it is* (*it's*) and *who is* (*who's*) with the possessive pronouns *its* and *whose*. (See 5A Pronoun Case.)

Special Uses

Plurals of letters, numbers, and words used as terms

I am hoping to get all *A*'s this year.

The memo had four misspelled *there*'s. See 8D Italics, which discusses underlining words used as terms.

All the *7*'s are upside down in the 1990s catalog. The plural for years is usually formed without apostrophes.

Omitted letters or numbers

We'll never forget the summer of *'78*. Restrict to informal writing.

"Be *seein'* ya," Charlie said. Dialect in quoted speech.

8D Italics (Underlining)

Italic type slants to the right and is used in printed material in the same way that underlining is used in handwritten or typed copy. It has specialized uses.

Titles of works published independently

The Atlantic Monthly (magazine)

A Farewell to Arms (book)

The Wall Street Journal (newspaper)

Desperate Housewives (television program)

Cats (play)

Ships, aircraft, spacecraft, and trains

Challenger (spacecraft)

Leasat 3 (communications satellite)

San Francisco *Zephyr* (train)

Words, letters, and numbers used as themselves

The process of heat transfer is called *conduction*.

The Latin words *et cetera* mean "and other things."

The letter *e* is the most commonly used vowel.

Many people consider *13* to be an unlucky number.

Emphasis

"I said, '*Did* you buy the tickets?' not '*Would* you buy the tickets?' "

Many people writing with computers use italics instead of underlining. If you are writing a documented paper for class, find out if your teacher approves of italics for titles.

8E Hyphens

Hyphens have three main uses: to divide words at the ends of lines, to form compound words, and to connect spelled-out numbers.

Dividing Words

There are three general rules to remember when using hyphens to divide words at the ends of lines: (1) always divide between syllables, (2) don't divide one-syllable words, and (3) don't divide words so that only two letters carry over to the second line. Consider the following examples:

After the results came back, the doctor sat me down and explained my *condition*.

While they could not cure the condition, at least they could alleviate its *symptoms*.

In the end, after months of waiting and mountains of legal fees, the court *ruled* against him. Incorrectly divides the one-syllable word *ruled*.

Needless to say, when the court ruled against him, he was not *particularly* pleased. Incorrectly divides the word *particularly* so that only the last two letters carry over to the second line.

Forming Compound Words

Knowing when to hyphenate compound words can be tricky. This is because some compound words can be written as single words (for example, *graveyard* or *postmaster*) while others can be written as two separate words (for example, *place kick* or *executive secretary*). Complicating matters further, compound adjectives take hyphens when they precede nouns but not when they follow nouns. Here are some examples of the correct and incorrect use of hyphens:

My *ex-husband* is a *pro-Communist* crackpot. Use hyphens after the prefix *ex-* and any prefix placed before a proper name, in this case *pro-* before *Communist*. In general, though, most words formed with prefixes are written as one word; for example, *antisocial* or *multicultural*.

The *post-mortem* revealed that her *brother in law* died of natural causes. This sentence contains two hyphenation errors. First, the compound word *post-mortem* should be written as a single word, *postmortem* (see comment on prefixes in the preceding example). Second, the compound noun *brother in law* should be hyphenated as *brother-in-law*.

Twentieth-century fiction is notable for its experimentation. **or** The fiction of the *twentieth century* is notable for its experimentation. In the first sentence *Twentieth-century* functions as a compound adjective modifying the noun *fiction* and so requires a hyphen. In the second sentence, *twentieth century* functions as a compound noun (specifically an object of the preposition *of*) and does not require a hyphen.

The *secretary treasurer* discouraged the group from making *highly-risky* investments. This sentence contains two hyphenation errors. First, the compound noun *secretary treasurer* requires a hyphen. Second, *-ly* adverbs such as *highly* are written as separate words when they precede adjectives such as *risky*.

Connecting Spelled-Out Numbers

Use hyphens to link compounds of spelled out numbers and to link numbers to nouns. For example:

twenty-fifth time

nine-page letter

132-page report

six-year-old

35-year-old

Whenever you have a question about dividing words and hyphenating compound words, use your dictionary. Dots usually mark syllables, and hyphens mark hyphenated compounds.

8F Numbers

Numbers can be spelled out or written as numerals. When to employ one style or the other depends on the writing context. In most academic writing in the humanities, and indeed in most writing geared for a general audience, numbers are usually spelled out as discussed next. In the sciences, however, numbers are usually written as numerals.

Unless you are asked to follow different conventions, use the following guidelines to handle numbers in writing:

1. Spell out numbers requiring two words or less and write numerals for numbers requiring three or more words. In practice, this means you will write out numbers *one* to *ninety-nine* and write numerals for *100* and above.

2. Spell out numbers that begin sentences. For long numbers this can lead to awkward sentences. In such instances, you should consider revising the sentence to move the number away from the beginning of the sentence so it can be written in numerals.

3. Make exceptions for numbers used in special figures. In these instances, numbers are usually written as numerals. Special figures of this type include days and years; pages, chapters, and volumes; acts, scenes, and lines; decimals, fractions, ratios, and percentages; temperatures; addresses; statistics; and amounts of money.

Consider the following examples:

The company mailed *twenty-one* parcels yesterday.

She bought *2,200* acres of ranch land with her lottery winnings.

One hundred and fifty-two cows drowned in the flood.

The Japanese attacked Pearl Harbor on December *7, 1941*.

You will find the answer on page *87* in chapter *5*.

The famous "To be, or not to be" soliloquy appears in act *3*, scene *1* of *Hamlet*.

The temperature reached *105*°F yesterday.

The suspect resided at *221* Dolores Street, apartment *3B*.

The winning margin was *2* to *1*.

With tax, the umbrella cost *$15.73*.

8G Spelling

One of the unfair facts of life is that the ability to spell is not equally distributed: Some people spell easily and some don't. If you're one of the latter, you'll need to put more time into getting your words right. A spellchecker is helpful, because it flags most misspelled words and suggests alternatives. If you are using one of these aids, however, be especially careful to look for misspelled homonyms. Rules of spelling sometimes help, though too many of them are probably a hindrance. Therefore only the most useful and dependable ones are included here.

Doubling a Final Consonant

When adding a suffix such as *-ing* or *-ed* to a word that ends in a consonant, double the final consonant to keep the internal vowel short; for example, *permit, permitted; stop, stopped*. Double the final consonant when all three of the following are true:

1. The word ends in a consonant preceded by a vowel.
2. The word is one syllable or the accent is on the final syllable.
3. The suffix begins with a vowel.

Here are some other examples:

hop	hopped	begin	beginning
sit	sitting	prefer	preferred
put	putting	occur	occurrence
win	winner	recap	recapped

Words Containing *ie* or *ei*

The familiar rhyme about using *ie* or *ei* is true most of the time—enough times that it is worth remembering: *i* before *e* except after *c* when the sound is long *e*. Thus words such as these follow the rule:

receive	believe	weight
ceiling	chief	beige
conceited	siege	eight

There are a few common exceptions: *caffeine, either, neither, seize,* and *weird*. Another common word that the rule does not address is *friend* (spelled *i* before *e*, but the sound is not long *e*).

Final *e*

To add an ending to a word that ends in a silent *e,* drop the *e* when the ending begins with a vowel:

believe + able = believable	believe + ed = believed
move + able = movable	move + ment = movement
hope + ing = hoping	hope + ful = hopeful

When the consonant preceding the final *e* is a soft *c* or *g,* the *e* is dropped only when the ending begins with *e* or *i*:

change + ing = changing	change + able = changeable
notice + ing = noticing	notice + able = noticeable
manage + er = manager	manage + ment = management
nice + er = nicer	nice + ly = nicely

Final *y*

To add an ending to a word with a final *y* preceded by a consonant, change the *y* to *i* except when your ending is *-ing*:

happy + ly = happily	study + ing = studying
apply + s = applies	apply + ing = applying
vary + ous = various	vary + ing = varying
try + ed = tried	try + ing = trying

When the final *y* is preceded by a vowel, keep the *y*:

play + ed = played	play + ful = playful
employ + ed = employed	employ + ment = employment

but

say + s = says	say + d = said
pay + ment = payment	pay + d = paid

Never change the *y* when adding an ending to a proper noun: *the Barrys*.

Plurals

Plural nouns ordinarily have an *s* ending:

boy + s = boys	car + s = cars

Words that end in *ch, s, sh, x,* or *z* require *-es*:

box + es = boxes	church + es = churches

Words ending in *o* are a little more troublesome. If the *o* is preceded by a vowel, add *s*:

radio + s – radios	video + s – videos

If the *o* is preceded by a consonant, ordinarily add *-es*:

hero + es = heroes	potato + es = potatoes

A few common words take either *s* or *-es*:

tornados, tornadoes	zeros, zeroes	volcanos, volcanoes

Some words form their plurals internally or do not have a plural form. Do not add an *s* to these words:

child, children	deer, deer
man, men	fish, fish
mouse, mice	moose, moose

Compound words ordinarily have an *s* at the end of the compound:

textbook, textbooks	snowshoe, snowshoes
text edition, text editions	snow goose, snow geese

But when the first word of the compound is the main word, add the *s* to it:

sisters-in-law   attorneys-general

Whenever you are in doubt about the correct plural ending, check your dictionary.

Homonyms

Some of the most troublesome words to spell are homonyms, words that sound alike but are spelled differently. Here is a partial list of the most common ones:

accept, except	maybe, may be
affect, effect	of, 've (have)
already, all ready	passed, past
cite, sight, site	than, then
forth, fourth	their, there, they're
it's, its	to, too, two
know, no	whose, who's
lead, led	your, you're

A few other words, not exactly homonyms, are sometimes confused:

breath, breathe	lightning, lightening
choose, chose	loose, lose
clothes, cloths	precede, proceed
dominant, dominate	quiet, quite

Check the meanings of any sound-alike words you are unsure of in your dictionary.

9 Review of Basic Grammar

Grammar is the set of rules used for communicating in a language. Words are the basic units of grammar, which classifies them by their function into the *parts of speech*. In English, grammar determines the form words take and the order in which they can be combined into *phrases, clauses,* and *sentences*. Sentences, unlike phrases and clauses, must represent complete thoughts and to do so each must contain at least one *subject* and one *predicate*. Sentences can also include *objects* and *complements*.

9A Parts of Speech

This section examines nine parts of speech: verbs, nouns, pronouns, adjectives, adverbs, prepositions, conjunctions, articles, and interjections. Some words can function as more than one part of speech. For example, the word "crow" can function as a noun (The *crow* stole food from our table) and a verb (The fans *crow* insults at the referee). For such words, determine the function the word plays within a sentence before you identify the part of speech it constitutes.

Verbs

Verbs express action (She *ran* for the senate) or a state of being (I *am* sick). Through changes in *form,* verbs can indicate *tense* (present, past, future, etc.);

person (first person, second person, or third person); *number* (singular or plural); *voice* (active or passive); and *mood* (indicative, imperative, and subjunctive). Other classifications of verbs include *linking verbs, transitive and intransitive verbs, helping verbs,* and *verbals.*

Form. Verbs have five primary forms:

Base	Present + *s*	Present Participle	Past	Past Participle
ask	asks	asking	asked	asked
climb	climbs	climbing	climbed	climbed
jump	jumps	jumping	jumped	jumped
move	moves	moving	moved	moved
reach	reaches	reaching	reached	reached
vanish	vanishes	vanishing	vanished	vanished
walk	walks	walking	walked	walked

The *base form* is used to indicate present tense action in the first-person singular (*I*) and plural (*we*), the second person (*you*), and the third-person plural (*they* or a plural noun).

We *hope* that you *drive* safely.

The hikers *vanish* into the fog.

The *present + s form* is made by adding an *-s* or *-es* to the base form and is used only to indicate present tense action in the third-person singular (*he, she, it,* or a singular noun).

She *walks* up the stairs.

The voter *reaches* for the ballot.

The *present participle form* is created by adding *ing* to the base form. When used as a participle, this form functions as an adjective.

The *dripping* faucet kept him up all night.

When used as a *gerund,* the form functions as a noun.

Dancing was her favorite activity.

When joined with the verb *be* and helping verbs, the present participle form indicates the ongoing action of the progressive tense.

He *is studying* at the moment. Present progressive tense.

They *have been listening* to music. Past perfect progressive tense.

The *past form* is made by adding a *-d* or *-ed* to the base form. This form is used to indicate past action.

The committee *waited* for our answer.

He *moved* with the beat.

Verbs that express past action without adding a *-d* or *-ed* to the base form are known as *irregular verbs* (see the list below).

The *past participle form* is also made by adding a *-d* or *-ed* to the base form. In fact, for regular verbs, the past participle form and the past form are identical. When used as a participle, this form functions as an adjective.

The *wilted* flowers lay on the table.

When joined with the helping verbs *have* and *will* the past participle form indicates the perfect tenses.

We *have waited* for a long time. Present perfect tense.

She *will have finished* her paper by noon. Future perfect tense.

When joined with the verb *be,* the past participle form is used to indicate *passive voice*.

The guests *were escorted* to their table.

The plan *was approved* unanimously.

Just as they do in the past form, irregular verbs do not add *-d* or *-ed* to make the past participle form. Irregular verbs often change internally to indicate their past and past participle forms. Common irregular verbs and their past and past participle forms include the following:

Base	Past	Past Participle
be (is, am, are)	was, were	been
come	came	come
do	did	done
drink	drank	drunk
eat	ate	eaten
give	gave	given
go	went	gone
grow	grew	grown
see	saw	seen
take	took	taken
throw	threw	thrown
write	wrote	written

Tense. A verb's tense indicates when its action occurred. The *simple tenses* are used the most frequently. They depict action in a straightforward manner in the present, past, and future.

Present	The children *kiss* their grandmother.
Past	The children *kissed* their grandmother.
Future	The children *will kiss* their grandmother.

The *perfect tenses* express action that has been completed by a specific time or action that has already been completed before another action begins.

Present Perfect	The children *have kissed* their grandmother.
Past Perfect	The children *had kissed* their grandmother.
Future Perfect	The children *will have kissed* their grandmother.

The *progressive tenses* express ongoing actions.

Present Progressive	The children *are kissing* their grandmother.
Past Progressive	The children *were kissing* their grandmother.
Future Progressive	The children *will be kissing* their grandmother.
Present Perfect Progressive	The children *have been kissing* their grandmother.
Past Perfect Progressive	The children *had been kissing* their grandmother.
Future Perfect Progressive	The children *will have been kissing* their grandmother.

Person and Number. The relationship between person and number is intertwined so the two need to be discussed together. The subject's connection to the verb *as a speaker* is expressed through person. In the first person, the subject does the speaking (*I, we*); in the second person, the subject is spoken to (*you*); and in the third person, the subject is spoken about (*he, she, it, they*).

A verb's number can be either singular or plural and is determined by its subject. Singular verbs show the action of an individual subject (*I, you, he, she, it*) while plural verbs show the action of a collective subject (*we, you, they*). The verb form is the same for the singular and the plural in all of the tenses with the exception of present tense in the third-person singular, which adds an *-s* or *-es* to the base form (see *present + s* form on p. 691).

	Singular	Plural
First Person	*I forgive* the debt.	*We forgive* the debt.
Second Person	*You forgive* the debt.	(All of) *You forgive* the debt.
Third Person	*He (she, it) forgives* the debt.	*They forgive* the debt.

Voice. In a sentence written in the *active voice,* the subject is the doer of the verb's action. In a sentence written in the *passive voice,* the subject is not the doer of the verb's action. Instead, the doer of the verb's action is the object of a preposition or is not stated at all. Because the active voice is clearer, more direct, and less wordy than the passive voice, you should strive to write in the active voice whenever possible. Reserve use of the passive voice only for instances in which you do not know or want to name the doer of the verb's action.

Susan lost the car keys. Active voice: Here the subject, *Susan*, performs the action of the verb *lost*.

The car keys were lost by Susan. Passive voice: The information communicated in this example is the same as that expressed in the previous example, but now *car keys* have become the subject and the doer of the verb's action, *Susan,* is the object of the preposition *by.*

The car keys were lost. Passive voice: Here the subject remains *car keys* but the doer of the verb's action is not stated.

Mood. Mood expresses the writer's attitude toward the action of the verb. There are three forms of mood: indicative, imperative, and subjunctive. Verbs in the *indicative mood* make statements, ask questions, and declare opinions. For example:

He *said* that your argument *is* wrong. Makes a statement.

Did he really *say* that? Asks a question.

He *should rethink* his objection to my argument. Declares an opinion.

Verbs in the *imperative mood* issue commands, requests, or directions. When the subject of an imperative verb is not explicitly identified, it is understood to be *you.*

Don't touch the hot plate. Issues a command.

Class, please *read* the essays tonight. Issues a request.

Turn right at the next intersection. Issues directions.

Verbs in the *subjunctive mood* communicate wishes, make statements contrary to fact, list requirements and demands, and imply skepticism or doubt. They usually appear in clauses introduced by *if, that, as if*, and *as though*. Use the base form of the verb for the present tense subjunctive. For the past tense subjunctive of the verb *be*, use *were* for all subjects.

He wishes that he *were* a movie star. Communicates wish.

If I *were* to live for a thousand years, think of all that I would see. Makes statement contrary to fact.

The day care center requires that your sister *sign* a consent form and *provide* proof of immunization for her daughter. Lists requirements.

The lawyer acts as if his client *were* a saint. Implies skepticism.

Linking Verbs. Verbs that link the subject to a subject complement (see 9C Objects and Complements) are called linking verbs. These verbs commonly express states of being rather than action. Common linking verbs include *be, look, sound, taste, smell, feel, grow, appear, seem, become, remain,* and *get.*

I *am* tired.

You *look* thirsty.

Things *sound* grim over there.

She *felt* happy.

Your neighbors *seem* angry.

Helping Verbs. Some verbs require the addition of helping verbs (or auxiliary verbs) to communicate their meaning. The combination of a main verb and a helping verb forms a *verb phrase*. The most frequently used helping verbs are *be, do,* and *have.* These three helping verbs can also stand alone as main verbs: I *am* hungry; She *did* her chores; You *have* won. Other helping verbs, however, cannot stand alone as main verbs and can only be used in verb phrases. These helping verbs include *can, could, may, might, should, will,* and *would.* Helping verbs are often required to indicate tense, voice, and mood.

Mr. Nguyen *will* call you tomorrow. Future tense.

The students *have* completed the test. Present perfect tense.

Next month I *will have been* living here for three years. Future perfect progressive tense.

The report *was* delivered early. Passive voice.

We *can* help you. Indicative mood.

Did you leave the door open? Indicative mood.

Transitive and Intransitive Verbs. Transitive verbs express action at objects, which receive that action (see 9C Objects and Complements). Intransitive verbs do not express action at objects.

She *mailed* the letter to me. Transitive: the direct object *letter* receives the action of the transitive verb *mailed.*

The children *slept* peacefully. Intransitive: the verb *slept* does not express its action at an object—the adverb *peacefully* functions only to modify the verb.

Many verbs can function as both transitive and intransitive verbs.

The athlete *ate* the roast turkey. Transitive: the direct object *roast turkey* receives the action of the transitive verb *ate.*

The athlete *ate* like a pig. Intransitive: the verb *ate* does not express its action at an object—the adverbial phrase *like a pig* only modifies the verb.

Verbals. Verb forms that function as nouns, adjectives, or adverbs in sentences are known as *verbals.* There are three kinds of verbals: participles, gerunds, and infinitives. *Participles* function as adjectives. The present participle form adds *-ing* to the base form. The past participle form adds a *-d* or *-ed* to the base form of regular verbs (irregular verbs are often conjugated internally).

The *howling* wolf startled the hunters. The present participle *howling* modifies the subject *wolf.*

She threw the *chipped* vase into the trash. The past participle *chipped* modifies the direct object *vase.*

Gerunds function as nouns and use the present participle form, that is, *-ing* added to the base form of the verb.

Fishing takes patience.

The consequences of *drinking* and *driving* are often tragic.

Infinitives can function as nouns, adjectives, or adverbs. Infinitives begin with the word *to* followed by the base form of the verb.

Everyone wants *to fall in love*. The infinitive *to fall in love* acts as a direct object and so functions as a noun.

They had nothing *to eat* today. The infinitive *to eat* modifies the noun *nothing* and so acts as an adjective.

You must persevere *to succeed* in life. The infinitive *to succeed* modifies the verb phrase *must persevere* and so acts as an adverb.

Nouns

Nouns include people (ice skater, Malcolm X), places (playground, Grand Canyon), things (bicycle, Empire State Building), and concepts (happiness, liberty). *Common nouns* refer to people, places, things, or concepts that are representative of groups or classes (mechanic, colleges, keys, hardness). *Proper nouns* refer to specific people, places, things, or concepts (*President Chirac, Tokyo, the Titanic, Marxism*). Common nouns may be either concrete or abstract in character. *Concrete nouns* refer to things that have a tangible existence in the world (tears, lawyer, roast beef). *Abstract nouns,* on the other hand, refer to ideas and feelings that do not exist outside of our thoughts or emotions (sadness, justice, hunger). *Count nouns* can be counted and have singular (cat, cookie, bike) and plural forms (cats, cookies, bikes). *Noncount nouns* (or mass nouns) cannot be counted and do not possess plural forms (violence, copper, stability). *Collective nouns* refer to groups; although they are frequently used in the singular, they also possess plural forms (people, family, crowd, party, horde). Nouns may indicate possession by adding an apostrophe and -*s* to singular forms (Michael's car, cat's meow) and an apostrophe to the plural forms (dancers' clothes, birds' feathers). Nouns are often preceded by articles (*a, an, the*) or quantifiers (*one, many, some, a few, several*). They may also be modified by adjectives (*black* cat), adjective phrases (keys *on the table*), or adjective clauses (car *that was stolen last night*).

Pronouns

Pronouns act as substitutes for nouns. They perform the same functions as nouns, but whereas nouns actually name people, places, things, and concepts, pronouns only stand in for nouns. The noun to which a pronoun refers is known as the pronoun's *antecedent*.

Mrs. Ghatta had a nightmare while *she* slept on the couch. The subject *Mrs. Ghatta* is the antecedent of the pronoun *she*.

While *she* slept on the couch, *Mrs. Ghatta* had a nightmare. The subject *Mrs. Ghatta* remains the antecedent of the pronoun *she* even though the pronoun now precedes the subject in the sentence.

Pronouns are classified by function into the following groups: personal, relative, interrogative, reflexive/intensive, indefinite, and demonstrative. Personal, relative, and interrogative pronouns possess subjective, objective, and possessive case forms.

Personal Pronouns. These replace nouns that name people or things and possess subjective, objective, and possessive case forms.

Subjective	Objective	Possessive
I	me	my, mine
you	you	your, yours
he	him	his
she	her	hers
it	it	its
we	us	our, ours
they	them	their, theirs

The *subjective case form* stands in for nouns that function as subjects or subject complements.

They crossed the street. The pronoun *they* serves as the sentence's subject.

The fool is *he* who turns his back on wisdom. The pronoun *he* serves as the subject complement.

The *objective case form* stands in for nouns that function as objects of verbs or prepositions.

Ms. Lin paid *us* in cash. The pronoun *us* serves as an indirect object.

Their grievances seemed petty to *me*. The pronoun *me* serves as an object of the preposition *to*.

The *possessive case form* shows ownership. This form can function as a possessive adjective (*my, your, his, her, its, our, their*) or as both a possessive adjective and the noun or gerund it modifies (*mine, yours, his, hers, its, ours, theirs*).

Your cat ate *my* canary. The pronouns *Your* and *my* function as adjectives indicating ownership.

Theirs was an unhappy fate. The pronoun *Theirs* functions as both the possessive adjective *their* and the noun *fate*.

Relative Pronouns. These pronouns introduce adjective clauses. Relative pronouns that refer to people possess subjective, objective, and possessive case forms.

Subjective	Objective	Possessive
who	whom	whose
whoever	whomever	whosever

Relative pronouns that do not refer to people (*that, what, whatever, which, whichever, whose*) do not possess subjective, objective, and possessive case forms.

Ahmed, *who* lives next door, was promoted today. The pronoun *who* is the subject of *lives*.

She hung up on her boyfriend, *whom* she despised. The pronoun *whom* is the object of *despised*.

We greeted our friends, *whose* home we had watched for the last two weeks. The pronoun *whose* indicates ownership.

They bought a car *that* was within their price range. The pronoun *that* indicates ownership.

Interrogative Pronouns. These pronouns take the same forms as relative pronouns, including subjective, objective, and possessive case forms when they refer to people.

Interrogative pronouns, however, do not introduce adjective clauses. Instead, they introduce questions.

Who lost the argument?

To *whom* did the prize go?

Whose car is that?

What questions did he ask you?

Whatever happened to her?

Reflexive/Intensive Pronouns. Reflexive pronouns refer to subjects or objects introduced earlier in the same clause. Their function is to show action directed by the antecedent at itself. Reflexive pronouns include *myself, yourself, himself, herself, itself, oneself, ourselves, yourselves,* and *themselves*.

She asked me how I managed to keep cutting *myself* while shaving.

Please make *yourself* at home. The unstated subject of this sentence is understood to be *you*.

We tell *ourselves* the same stories over and over again.

The campers washed *themselves* in the river.

Intensive pronouns take the same forms as reflexive pronouns but are used only to emphasize the action of the antecedent, not to show action directed by the antecedent at itself.

She fixed the flat tire by *herself*.

It is surprising the resources one finds inside *oneself*.

Indefinite Pronouns. These pronouns refer to quantities or unspecified people and things. Indefinite pronouns include *a few, a lot, all, another, any, anybody, anyone, anything, anywhere, both, each, either, enough, everybody, everyone, everything, everywhere, few, many, more, most, much, neither, nobody, none, no one, nothing, one, several, some, somebody, someone, something,* and *somewhere*.

Anybody caught shoplifting will be prosecuted.

Few have sacrificed as much as we have.

One good deed deserves *another*.

I have called *everyone* together today to say *a few* words about *something* very important.

Demonstrative Pronouns. These pronouns (*this, that, these, those*) point to antecedents in such a way as to hold them up for special scrutiny or discussion.

That was a spectacular meal.

I will take *these* shoes, please.

Adjectives

Adjectives modify nouns and pronouns. They answer questions such as *How many? What kind? Which?* and *Whose?*

She bought *five jumbo-sized* platters of appetizers for *tomorrow's* party at *Ken's* house. How many platters? *Five.* What kind of platters? *Jumbo-sized.* Which party? *Tomorrow's.* Whose house? *Ken's.*

Adjectives usually precede the words they modify but they can follow after words, or, as subject complements, even after the verb.

The ocean, *cool* and *inviting,* lapped at our feet.

The movie was *boring.*

Nouns and pronouns often function as adjectives, in both their subjective case forms and possessive forms. Indeed, a word may function as a noun in one part of a sentence and as an adjective elsewhere in the same sentence.

Some children attend *summer* school; *some* do not. The word *some* functions as an adjective in its first instance and as a noun in its second instance. The word *summer,* frequently used as a noun, functions as an adjective modifying *school.*

Adjectives have positive, comparative, and superlative forms.

Their house is *big.* Positive form.

Their house is *bigger* than mine. Comparative form.

Theirs is the *biggest* house on the block. Superlative form.

Adverbs

Adverbs modify verbs, adjectives, and other adverbs. They answer questions such as *How? How often? When?* and *Where?*

Yesterday, we *narrowly* won the championship game. How did we win? *Narrowly.* When did we win? *Yesterday.* Both adverbs modify verbs.

Our rivals play *nearby* and had beaten us *frequently.* Where do the rivals play? *Nearby.* How often had they beaten us? *Frequently.* Both adverbs modify verbs.

It was a *desperately* needed victory. The adverb *desperately* modifies the adjective *needed.*

The losing team left the field *very* quietly. The adverb *very* modifies the adverb *quietly.*

Adverbs can come before or after the words they modify. Sometimes, for the sake of rhythm or emphasis, adverbs can be placed at the beginning or end of the sentence.

The detective *slowly* opened the door.

Slowly, the detective opened the door.

The detective opened the door *slowly.*

Adverbs, like adjectives, have positive, comparative, and superlative forms. For adverbs that end in *-ly,* the comparative adds the word *more* to the positive form while the superlative adds the word *most.*

She sings *beautifully*. Positive form.

She sings *more beautifully* than I do. Comparative form.

She sings *most beautifully* of us all. Superlative form.

Prepositions

Prepositions introduce *prepositional phrases* and show the relationship (place, desti-nation, possession, time, cause, movement, purpose, etc.) between the *object of the preposition,* which is always a noun or pronoun, and another word or group of words. Common prepositions include *about, above, after, around, at, before, behind, below, be-neath, between, beyond, by, down, for, from, in, inside, into, like, of, off, on, onto, out, over, past, since, through, to, toward, under, until, up, with,* and *without.*

The police car parked *in* our driveway. Place.

The protestors marched *toward* city hall. Destination.

This is the home *of* a World War II veteran. Possession.

We will arrive *at* 8:00 p.m. Time.

The water is dripping *from* the leak. Cause.

She walked *into* the theater. Movement.

The students studied *for* the final exam. Purpose.

Conjunctions

Conjunctions link one or more words, phrases, or clauses within a sentence. There are three types of conjunctions: coordinating, subordinating, and correlative.

Coordinating Conjunctions. These conjunctions join parallel words, phrases, and clauses (see 2A Parallelism). Coordinating conjunctions include *and, but, for, nor, or, so,* and *yet.*

The pitcher *and* the hitter confronted each other.

She wanted to go to the beach, *but* she had to stay home instead.

You can have orange juice *or* lemonade.

Subordinating Conjunctions. These conjunctions introduce subordinate (dependent) clauses. Subordinating conjunctions include *after, although, as, because, before, even if, even though, if, once, since, so, so that, than, that, unless, until, when, whenever, where, whereas, wherever, whether,* and *while.*

After she won the race, Robin celebrated with her family and friends.

We will not leave *until* Jim returns.

I was on the phone *when* the earthquake struck.

Correlative Conjunctions. Like coordinating conjunctions, correlative conjunctions join parallel words, phrases, and clauses. Correlative conjunctions, however, only occur in pairs. They include *both...and; either...or; just as...so; neither...nor; not only...but also;* and *whether...or.*

She wanted *both* to have a career *and* to start a family.

We will visit *either* the museum *or* the park this afternoon.

Articles

Articles introduce nouns. The word *the* is a *definite article* and it introduces nouns whose specific character is known (*The* cat walked down *the* path). The words *a* and *an* are *indefinite articles* and they introduce nouns whose specific character is not known (*A* cat walked down *a* path). *A* precedes words that begin with consonants; *an* precedes words that begin with vowels or a silent *h* (*an* hour).

Interjections

Interjections are words that express strong feelings, alarm, or surprise. They are common in speech and may be used in personal or informal writing, but are generally inappropriate for formal and academic writing. When they do appear in writing they typically stand alone as fragments. Common interjections include *boo, cool, oh, oh no, ouch, shhh, uh-oh, wow, yea,* and *yikes.* Profanity is often used as an interjection, particularly in speech, but it is considered offensive in most academic and professional settings.

9B Subjects and Predicates

The *subject* of a sentence is its main topic. The subject is always a noun, pronoun, noun phrase, or noun clause. The *predicate* makes a statement or asks a question about the subject. The predicate must always contain a verb but it can also contain adjectives, adverbs, nouns, pronouns, and other words.

Subjects

The simple subject is the noun or pronoun that represents the sentence's main topic. It is usually a single word, although proper nouns can run to two or more words (*General George Washington*). The complete subject contains the simple subject and any words or phrases that modify it.

Subject	Predicate
He	slept.
The man	had terrible nightmares that night.
The wearied, defeated prime minister	tossed fitfully in his bed.

Most of us at dinner that evening got sick the next day. The pronoun *Most* is the sentence's simple subject and *Most of us at dinner that evening* is the complete subject.

Compound subjects are two or more parallel nouns or pronouns linked by commas and coordinating conjunctions or correlative conjunctions.

Mishal, Zanab, and Amir swam out to the sailboat.

Playing to win and playing fair are not mutually exclusive concepts.

Neither you nor I will win the lottery.

Predicates

The simple predicate is the sentence's main verb. The complete predicate contains the simple predicate and any words or phrases that modify it.

> The strikers *picketed outside the factory's main gate despite the wind and rain*. The verb *picketed* is the sentence's simple predicate; the simple predicate and all of the words that follow after it represent the complete predicate.

Compound predicates represent two or more main verbs linked by commas and coordinating conjunctions or correlative conjunctions.

> We *laughed, ate, and drank* our way through the evening.

> He *tiptoed* to the door *and pressed* his ear up against its cold, hard wood.

> That afternoon she *not only aced* the exam *but* she *also submitted* her final paper to her instructor.

9C Objects and Complements

Objects are nouns or pronouns that appear within a sentence's predicate and complete its meaning. *Complements* are nouns or adjectives that rename or describe the sentence's subject or direct object.

Objects

There are three types of objects: direct objects, indirect objects, and objects of prepositions.

Direct Objects. These are nouns or pronouns that accept the action of *transitive verbs* (see 9A Parts of Speech). Direct objects answer questions such as *What?* or *Whom?* about their verbs.

> She kissed *her children* good night. Kissed whom? *Her children*.

> He wrote *the essay* on sustainable growth. Wrote what? *The essay*.

> The teacher gave *them* to us. Gave what? *Them*.

Indirect Objects. These are nouns or pronouns for which the action of the transitive verb is performed. Direct objects answer questions such as *For what? To what? For whom?* or *To whom?* about their verbs. Because indirect objects never appear without direct objects, one way to avoid confusing the two is to identify the direct object (DO) first and then the indirect object (IO).

> We mailed *them* the invitations. Mailed what? The invitations (DO). To whom? *Them* (IO).

> The county clerk issued *Michael and Caitlin* a marriage license. Issued what? A marriage license (DO). To whom? *Michael and Caitlin* (IO).

> Her father gave *their union* his blessing. Gave what? His blessing (DO). To what? *Their union* (IO).

Objects of Prepositions. These are nouns or pronouns that complete the meaning of *prepositional phrases* (see 9A Parts of Speech). When they appear in sentences with direct objects, objects of prepositions convey the same meaning as indirect objects. Objects of prepositions, however, can also appear in sentences that do not contain direct objects.

> We mailed the invitations to *them*.
>
> I left the keys in *the ignition*.
>
> For *the older couple,* the hike would be long and hard.

Complements

There are two types of complements: subject complements and object complements.

Subject Complements. These are nouns or adjectives that follow after a *linking verb* (see 9A Parts of Speech) and rename or describe the subject. Subject complements that are nouns rename their subjects and those that are adjectives describe their subjects.

> Margaret is *a lawyer*. The subject complement *a lawyer* is a noun.
>
> My grandfather is *ill*. The subject complement *ill* is an adjective.

Object Complements. These are nouns or adjectives that rename or describe the direct object. Object complements that are nouns rename their direct objects and those that are adjectives describe their direct objects.

> The panel voted Sogiko *the winner*. The object complement *the winner* is a noun.
>
> Many people consider travel *pleasurable*. The object complement *pleasurable* is an adjective.

9D Phrases

A *phrase* is a group of related words that lack a subject or a predicate or both. A phrase, then, can never express a complete thought as a sentence and independent clause can. Phrases modify words, groups of words, or the entire sentence. There are six types of phrases: prepositional phrases, participial phrases, gerund phrases, absolute phrases, infinitive phrases, and appositive phrases.

Prepositional Phrases

Prepositional phrases begin with a *preposition* (see 9A Parts of Speech) and contain a noun or pronoun and its modifiers, if any. Prepositional phrases act as adjectives and adverbs.

> The neighbors *across the street* own a speedboat. The prepositional phrase functions as an adjective modifying the noun *neighbors*.
>
> The satellite burned up *in the upper atmosphere*. The prepositional phrase functions as an adverb modifying the verb *burned up*.

Participial Phrases

Participial phrases contain *present* or *past participles* (see 9A Parts of Speech) and their modifiers or complements. Participial phrases act as adjectives.

The man *arrested yesterday* was an industrial spy. The participial phrase modifies the noun *man*.

The dancers *demonstrating the tango right now* are my friends. The participial phrase modifies the noun *dancers*.

Gerund Phrases

Gerund phrases contain *gerunds* (see 9A Parts of Speech) and their modifiers, objects, and complements. Gerund phrases function as nouns and therefore can serve as a subject, direct object, object of the preposition, object complement, and subject complement.

Dating over the Internet has become popular. The gerund phrase serves as the subject.

The children love *playing computer games*. The gerund phrase serves as the direct object.

He was exhausted from *running under the hot sun*. The gerund phrase serves as the object of the preposition.

We wished them luck *climbing the mountain*. The gerund phrase serves as an object complement.

Her favorite pastime is *knitting wool sweaters*. The gerund phrase serves as the subject complement.

Absolute Phrases

Absolute phrases contain a noun or pronoun, a present or past participle, and any modifiers. Absolute phrases modify an entire sentence, not just one word or group of words within the sentence. Whether they appear at the beginning, middle, or end of a sentence, absolute phrases are always set off with a comma.

Its whistle blowing, the ferry pulled away from the dock.

The patient, *his body convulsed with fever,* slipped into unconsciousness.

He stepped on the gas, *his heart racing with adrenaline.*

Infinitive Phrases

Infinitive phrases contain *infinitives* (see 9A Parts of Speech) and their modifiers, objects, or complements. Infinite phrases function as adjectives, adverbs, and nouns.

He wanted his son *to help him fix the leak*. The infinitive phrase modifies the noun *son* and so acts as an adjective.

She studied *to pass the exam*. The infinitive phrase modifies the verb *studied* and so acts as an adverb.

Before I made a decision, I needed *to think things over thoroughly*. The infinitive phrase acts as a direct object and so functions as a noun.

Appositive Phrases

Appositive phrases are nouns and their modifiers that rename the nouns or pronouns that immediately precede them. They are often set off with commas.

My neighbor, *a doctor,* is a very kind woman.

He has an engineering degree from Caltech, *one of the most prestigious universities in the country.*

9E Clauses

A clause is a group of words containing both a subject and a predicate. An *independent clause* can function on its own as a sentence.

Subject	Predicate
She	wept.
The woman who lives next door	personally delivered the letter to me today.

A *subordinate clause* (dependent clause) cannot function on its own as a sentence and must be linked to an independent clause by a subordinating conjunction or relative pronoun. There are three types of subordinate clauses: adjective clauses, adverb clauses, and noun clauses.

Adjective Clauses

Adjective clauses modify nouns or pronouns in an independent clause or in another subordinate clause. Adjective clauses begin with *relative pronouns* (see 9A Parts of Speech) such as *who, whom, whose, which,* and *that.*

The doctor *who delivered our baby* is from India.

She wrote a letter *that explained how she felt.*

Adverb Clauses

Adverb clauses usually modify verbs in an independent clause or in another subordinate clause, but on occasion they may also modify adjectives and adverbs. Adverb clauses begin with *subordinating conjunctions* (see 9A Parts of Speech) such as *after, although, as, because, before, if, since, so, than, that, unless, until, when, where,* and *while.*

After the movie was over, we strolled through the mall.

They planned to travel the world *until they ran out of money.*

She left the party *when her ex-boyfriend* arrived.

Noun Clauses

Noun clauses serve as a subject, object, or complement. They can begin with relative pronouns or subordinating conjunctions.

Where the ship sank no one knows. The noun clause serves as the subject.

She asked him *when he would be leaving.* The noun clause serves as the direct object.

I will not run from *what is coming.* The noun clause serves as the object of the preposition.

Their complaint was *that the contract had not been fulfilled.* The noun clause serves as the subject complement.

9F Basic Sentence Patterns

A sentence must contain a subject and a predicate. The complexity of predicates, however, means that sentences can follow one of five basic patterns:

Subject + Intransitive verb

Subject + Transitive verb + Direct object

Subject + Linking verb + Subject complement

Subject + Transitive verb + Indirect object + Direct object

Subject + Transitive verb + Direct object + Object complement

These five patterns form the foundation on which all sentences in the English language are written. The following examples show only the simplest uses of these patterns. Because all of the elements that make up these patterns can be modified by other words, phrases, and clauses, these sentence patterns can assume much more complicated forms in everyday writing.

Subject	Intransitive verb		
We	won.		

Subject	Transitive verb	Direct object	
Our team	defeated	our rivals.	

Subject	Linking verb	Subject complement	
My teammates	were	ecstatic.	

Subject	Transitive verb	Indirect object	Direct object
They	gave	us	the trophy.

Subject	Transitive verb	Direct object	Object complement
Our coach	declared	the game	a milestone.

9G Types of Sentences

Sentences are also classified by the way in which they use *clauses* (see 9E Clauses) into four categories: simple sentences, compound sentences, complex sentences, and compound-complex sentences.

Simple Sentences

A simple sentence is made up of one *independent clause*. The independent clause may contain compound *subjects,* compound *predicates,* and modifying *phrases,* but must not be linked with other clauses.

Some professional athletes are poor role models for children. Single subject and single predicate.

Some professional athletes and movie stars are poor role models for children. Compound subject and single predicate.

Some professional athletes lack social responsibility and are poor role models for children. Single subject and compound predicate.

Some professional athletes, *their interests focused exclusively on themselves,* lack social responsibility. Single subject, with modifying phrase (in italics) and single predicate.

Compound Sentences

A compound sentence is made up of two or more independent clauses (IC) linked by a semicolon or a comma and a *coordinating conjunction*. Each clause may contain compound subjects, compound predicates, and modifying phrases, but must not be linked with a subordinate clause.

———— IC ————   ———————— IC ————————

John was uneasy, but he didn't believe in werewolves. The two independent clauses are linked by a comma and the coordinating conjunction *but*.

———————————— IC ———————————   ——————————— IC ———————————

He *checked the lock and stood motionless;* there was someone or something growling on the other side of the door. The two independent clauses are linked with a semicolon.

Complex Sentences

A complex sentence is made up of one independent clause (IC) and one or more *subordinate clauses* (SC). Both the independent and subordinate clause(s) may contain compound subjects, compound predicates, and modifying phrases. Subordinate clauses always begin with *subordinating conjunctions* or *relative pronouns* (see 9A Parts of Speech).

———— IC ————   ———————— SC ————————

The lawyer laughed when my wife told the joke. The subordinate clause begins with the subordinating conjunction *when*.

———————————— IC ———————————   ——————————— SC ———————————

I reluctantly shook the hand of the lawyer who was representing my wife in the divorce. The subordinate clause begins with the relative pronoun *who*.

Compound-Complex Sentences

A compound-complex sentence contains two or more independent clauses (IC) and at least one subordinate clause (SC). The independent clauses must be linked by a semicolon or a comma and a coordinating conjunction. Each clause may contain compound subjects, compound predicates, and modifying phrases.

———— IC ————   ———— SC ————   ——————— IC ———————

They won't believe me until they see you, for you have completely changed. The first independent clause and its subordinate clause are linked to the second independent clause with a comma and the coordinating conjunction *for*.

10 Tips for ESL Writers

Many non-native writers of English find it challenging to master the language's complicated grammatical rules. This section offers advice in traditional problem areas for writers of English as a second language (ESL).

10A Articles

Articles introduce nouns, but the rules for determining how they do so are complex. *The* is the *definite article* that introduces nouns whose specific character is known (*The* cat), while *a* and *an* are *indefinite articles* that introduce nouns whose specific character is not known (*A* cat). To use definite and indefinite articles correctly, however, you also need to know whether the noun under consideration is a *count noun,* a *noncount noun,* or a *proper noun*.

Count Nouns

Count nouns can be counted and have singular forms (*cat, cookie, bike*) and plural forms (*cats, cookies, bikes*). Singular count nouns whose specific character is not known take the indefinite articles *a* and *an*; those whose specific character is known take the definite article *the*. Plural count nouns whose specific character is not known, that is, nouns that are referred to in general, do not take articles. Plural count nouns whose specific character is known take the definite article *the*.

> *An aardvark* turned up in my backyard. Singular count noun of unknown specific character—use the appropriate indefinite article, *a* or *an*.

> *The aardvark* befriended us. Singular count noun of known specific character—use the definite article *the*.

> *Aardvarks* are interesting animals. Plural count noun of unknown specific character—do not use an article.

> *The aardvarks* moved to our neighbor's backyard. Plural count noun of known specific character—use the definite article *the*.

Noncount Nouns

Noncount nouns (or mass nouns) cannot be counted and do not possess plural forms (*violence, copper, stability*). Noncount nouns whose specific character is not known, that is, nouns that are referred to in general, do not take articles. Noncount nouns whose specific character is known take the definite article *the*.

> *Peace* is universally valued around the world. Noncount noun of unknown specific character—do not use an article.

> *The peace* held while the negotiations dragged on. Noncount noun of known specific character—use the definite article *the*.

Proper Nouns

Proper nouns refer to specific people, places, things, or concepts (*President Chirac, Tokyo, the Titanic, Marxism*). Singular proper nouns generally do not take definite articles with the exception of the following: noun phrases (*the* Man in the Moon); geographic features (*the* Himalayas); architectural landmarks (*the* Brooklyn Bridge); titles of ships, aircraft, spacecraft, and vehicles (*the* Challenger); titles of political and religious institutions (*the* Senate, *the* Episcopalian Church); titles of political and religious leaders (*the* prime minister, *the* pope); titles of documents (*the* Emancipation Proclamation); and titles of periods and events (*the* Middle

Ages, *the* Great Depression). Plural proper nouns take definite articles with the exception of the titles of companies (General Mills).

President Bush spoke at the commencement. The singular proper noun *President Bush* does not take a definite article.

The president spoke at the commencement. The singular common noun *president* is the title of a political leader and so does take a definite article.

The De Beers are a very wealthy family. The plural proper noun *De Beers* takes a definite article.

De Beers is a very wealthy company. The plural proper noun *De Beers* is the title of a company and so does not take a definite article.

10B Verbs

The common verb errors and the basic functions and forms of verbs are discussed elsewhere in this handbook (see 4 Verbs and 9A Parts of Speech). Challenging areas for ESL writers can include the helping verbs *be*, *do*, and *have*; modal auxiliaries; phrasal verbs; and gerunds and infinitives.

Helping Verbs *be*, *do*, and *have*

Helping verbs (or auxiliary verbs) join with main verbs to create verb phrases. The most frequently used helping verbs are *be*, *do*, and *have*, which can also stand alone as main verbs. How to use these three helping verbs with main verbs can sometimes be confusing.

The Helping Verb *be*. Use the present forms of *be* (*am*, *is*, *are*) with the present participle (base form + *-ing*) to make the present progressive tense. Use the past forms of *be* (*was*, *were*) with the present participle to make the past progressive tense. The other progressive tenses require the addition of the helping verbs *have* and *will* (see the following examples) along with the forms of *be* and the present participle.

She *is working* at the moment. Present progressive.

I *was calling* overseas when the doorbell rang. Past progressive.

They *will be sailing* tomorrow. Future progressive.

Larry *has been sulking* since last night. Present perfect progressive.

We *had been skiing* for three hours when your brother showed up. Past perfect progressive.

You *will have been barbecuing* chicken all day long before the party is over. Future perfect progressive.

Use the present forms of *be* (*am*, *is*, *are*) with the past participle (base form + *-ed*) to create the present tense in the passive voice. Other tenses in the passive voice require the addition of the other helping verbs *will* and *have* along with the forms of *be* and the past participle.

The car *is stopped* at the light.

In some countries, the local elections *have been rigged* for many years.

The Helping Verb *do*. Use forms of *do* (*do, does, did*) with the base form of the verb to create a verb phrase. Use verb phrases of this sort to add emphasis or to restate a claim that provokes doubt or disbelief. Add the modal auxiliary *not* to make negative claims.

We *do believe* in the judicial system.

She *does drive* carefully.

I *did mail* the letter to you.

He *does not know* the answer.

The Helping Verb *have*. Use the present forms of *have* (*have, has*) with the past participle (base form + *-ed*) to make the present prefect tense. Use the past forms of *have* (*had*) with the past participle to make the past perfect tense. The future perfect tense requires the addition of the helping verb *will* along with the present form of *have* and the past participle.

She *has purchased* a new car. Present perfect.

We *had vacationed* at the Grand Canyon before we went to Monument Valley. Past perfect.

They *will have painted* the house by this evening. Future prefect.

Modal Auxiliaries

Modal auxiliaries are helping verbs that cannot stand alone as main verbs. Joined with a main verb, modals express ability, intention, necessity, permission, possibility, or prohibition. Modals include *can, cannot, could, have to, may, might, must, must not, not, should,* and *would*. These modals do not change form, regardless of the main verb's tense or whether the main verb is singular or plural. They only have one form. When joining modals with main verbs, use the base form of the main verb immediately after the modal. Never use more than one modal with one main verb.

We *can* reach the stars if we try. Expresses ability.

We *cannot* get there tomorrow. Expresses prohibition.

I *have* to wash the dishes. Expresses necessity.

I *might* even clean out the refrigerator. Expresses possibility.

You *should* forget the past. Expresses advisability.

You *would* have a great time in Italy. Expresses probability.

Phrasal Verbs

A phrasal verb is an idiomatic verb phrase that contains a verb and one or two prepositions or adverbs. The meaning of the two- or three-word phrasal verb generally cannot be understood by combining the literal meanings of its words. For example, the phrasal verb *turn down* does not mean "to turn downward" but rather "to reject or refuse." Common phrasal verbs include the following:

act up	run into
break down	stay up
call on	step in
catch on	take off
cut in	throw away
figure out	turn down
hang on	turn on
look into	walk out on
look out for	watch out for

Phrasal verbs are informal and often are inappropriate for academic and professional writing. If you do choose to use them in your writing, be sure you understand their correct meaning.

Gerunds and Infinitives

Gerunds function as nouns and use the present participle form (base form + *-ing*). Infinitives usually function as nouns but can also function as adjectives or adverbs. They begin with the word *to* followed by the base form of the verb. Gerunds and infinitives that follow after main verbs function as objects. Keep the following guidelines in mind when using gerunds and infinitives with main verbs.

1. **Verbs that do not change meaning whether followed by gerunds or infinitives:**

attempt	like
begin	love
can't stand	omit
continue	prefer
hate	start

   In the following examples, below the meaning of the verb *hated* and the gerund *losing* is the same as the verb *hated* and the infinitive *to lose*.

   > We hated *losing* the game.

   > We hated *to lose* the game.

2. **Verbs that change meaning when followed by gerunds or infinitives:**

forget	stop
remember	try

   In the following examples, notice how the meaning of the first sentence differs from the second.

   > I forgot *practicing* the piano yesterday. Forgot the subject of *practicing* yesterday.

   > I forgot *to practice* the piano yesterday. Forgot actually *to practice* yesterday.

3. **Verbs that can precede gerunds but not infinitives:**

admit	keep
appreciate	miss
avoid	postpone
cannot help	practice
consider	put off
delay	quit
deny	recall
discuss	resist
enjoy	risk
finish	suggest
imagine	tolerate

In the following examples, the gerund in the first sentence is correct and the infinitive in the second sentence represents an error.

She enjoys *painting* watercolors. Gerunds may be used after the verb *enjoy*.

She enjoys *to paint* watercolors. Infinitives may not be used after the verb *enjoy*.

4. **Verbs that can precede infinitives but not gerunds:**

agree	mean
ask	need
beg	offer
choose	plan
claim	pretend
decide	promise
expect	refuse
fail	venture
have	wait
hope	want
manage	wish

In the following examples, the infinitive in the first sentence is correct and the gerund in the second sentence represents an error.

They decided *to climb* the mountain. Infinitive may be used after the verb *decide*.

They decided *climbing* the mountain. Gerund may not be used after the verb *decide*.

10C Adjectives and Adverbs

The correct use of adjectives and adverbs can present challenges for all writers; however, for ESL writers in particular, the placement and word order of these modifiers can be troublesome.

Adjectives

Adjectives modify nouns and pronouns (see 9A Parts of Speech). Other words such as articles and pronouns can also act as adjectives and modify nouns and pronouns. When using multiple adjectives to modify one or more words in the sentence, use the word order listed here:

1. **Article, pronoun, and possessive noun:** *a, an, the, his, my, our, your, a lot, many, some, that, their, those, Steve's, the neighbor's,* etc.

2. **Adjectives indicating number or order:** *one, two, three, one hundred, one thousand, first, second, third, last, final,* etc.

3. **Adjectives indicating judgment, opinion, or evaluation:** *awful, astonishing, beautiful, excellent, evil, good, faithful, ugly, wicked,* etc.

4. **Adjectives indicating size:** *big, diminutive, giant, large, little, long, massive, minuscule, short,* etc.

5. **Adjectives indicating shape:** *boxy, circular, loose, rectangular, round, snug, square, tight, triangular, wide,* etc.

6. **Adjectives indicating condition:** *broken, damaged, fixed, functional, operating, repaired, reconditioned, running, undamaged, whole, working,* etc.

7. **Adjectives indicating age:** *aged, ancient, antique, fresh, immature, mature, new, old, young,* etc.

8. **Adjectives indicating color:** *black, blue, green, mauve, orange, purple, violet, white, yellow,* etc.

9. **Adjectives indicating nationality, ethnicity, and religion:** *African American, Anglo, Arabic, Armenian, Brazilian, Canadian, Chinese, Kenyan, Latin American, Mandarin, Buddhist, Catholic, Hindu, Presbyterian,* etc.

10. **Adjectives indicating material:** *aluminum, birch, copper, cotton, gold, iron, oak, metal, pine, plastic, platinum, polyester, silk, steel, wood,* etc.

11. **Nouns used as adjectives:** *bird* (brain), *dog* (house), *car* (park), *floor* (mat), *mosquito* (net), etc.

12. **The noun being modified.** Examples:

> His last undamaged birch-bark canoe sank yesterday.

> She found *some beautiful little green turquoise* beads at the flea market.

> My grandmother gave *that antique black Chinese silk* dress to my sister as a birthday gift.

Adverbs

Adverbs modify verbs, adjectives, and other adverbs (see 9A Parts of Speech). Adverbs can come before or after the words they modify. Sometimes, for the sake of rhythm or emphasis, adverbs can be placed at the beginning or end of the sentence. Although there is considerable flexibility in where you can place most adverbs, there are also some limitations. Use the following guidelines:

1. **Place adverbs indicating the author's or speaker's *perspective* at the front of the sentence:**

   Thankfully, I had recovered from the flu by then.

   Unfortunately, we won't be able to make your party tonight.

2. **Place adverbs indicating *order* at the front or end of the sentence:**

   First, we will consider the results of our fund-raising efforts.

   Proposals for overhauling the department will be discussed *last.*

3. **Place adverbs indicating *manner* immediately before the words they modify or at the end of the sentence:**

   They *softly* entered the room.

   She answered my questions *sheepishly.*

4. **Place adverbs indicating *time* immediately after any adverbs indicating *manner* or *place* or, if none exist, at the front or end of the sentence:**

   The earth shook *ferociously here yesterday.*

   Tomorrow, I am leaving for California.

   He writes reports *slowly.*

10D Prepositions

Prepositions introduce *prepositional phrases* and show the relationship (place, destination, possession, time, cause, movement, purpose, etc.) between the *object of the preposition,* which is always a noun or pronoun, and another word or group of words. The prepositions used to show place and time can be troublesome for non-native speakers of English.

Place

The prepositions showing place include *in, on,* and *at.* Use the preposition *in* to refer to an established physical, geographic, or political space (*in* the garage, *in* the Amazon, *in* Egypt). Use the preposition *on* as a synonym for *on top of* (*on* the coffee table, *on* the roof) and to indicate location on mass transportation, streets, book pages, building floors, and land (*on* the bus, *on* 114th Street, *on* page 177, *on* the eleventh floor, *on* the field). Use the preposition *at* to refer to specific locations, general locations, and addresses (*at* the Museum of Modern Art, *at* my mother's house, *at* the beach, *at* 23349 Westwood Boulevard).

The Band-Aids are *in* the medicine box.

Her apartment is *on* the fourth floor.

You are welcome to stay *at* my house.

Time

The prepositions showing time also include *in, on,* and *at.* Use the preposition *in* to refer to general time of day (except *night*), months, seasons, and years (*in* the afternoon, *in* December, *in* spring, *in* 1983). Use the preposition *on* to refer to days of the week and dates (*on* Friday, *on* the 28th, *on* July 4, 1770). Use the preposition *at* to refer to specific time of day and with *night* (*at* 1:15, *at* noon, *at* night).

I will see her *in* the evening.

We will see them *on* Friday.

He will see you *at* noon.

10E Participles

Present participles (base form of the verb + *-ing*) and *past participles* (base form of the verb + *-d* or *-ed*) can both function as adjectives in sentences. Their meanings are different, however, and they cannot be used interchangeably. In particular, participles that describe feelings and mental states can sometimes be troublesome for ESL writers. These participles include the following:

amazing / amazed	fascinating / fascinated
annoying / annoyed	frightening / frightened
boring / bored	interesting / interested
confusing / confused	pleasing / pleased
depressing / depressed	satisfying / satisfied
disappointing / disappointed	surprising / surprised
exciting / excited	terrifying / terrified
exhausting / exhausted	tiring / tired

To avoid errors with these participles and others, only use present participles to describe nouns and pronouns that *cause* a feeling or mental state. Similarly, only use past participles to describe nouns and pronouns that *experience* a feeling or mental state.

The lecture was *fascinating*. The noun being modified, *lecture,* causes the mental state, so the present participle *fascinating* is required.

We were *fascinated* by the lecture. The pronoun being modified, *We,* experiences the mental state, so the past participle *fascinated* is required.

The news is filled with *depressing* events. The noun being modified, *events,* causes the mental state, so the present participle *depressing* is required.

Julia was *depressed* by events in the news. The noun being modified, *Julia,* experiences the mental state, so the past participle *depressed* is required.

CREDITS

Text Credits

Page 13B. Andreas Von Einsiedel © Dorling Kindersley

Page 40. Getty Images–Stockbyte.

Page 45. © John M. Greim/Mira.com

Page 48. © Dorling Kindersley

Page 54. © Tate London/Art Resource

Page 62. Edward Weston, "Pepper #30," 1930. Photograph by Edward Weston. Collection Center for Creative Photography, The University of Arizona. © 1981 Arizona Board of Regents.

Page 74. Photofest NYC

Page 78. Bruce Ballenger

Page 90. Craig Lupien/Laura Zazulak

Page 95. © Roderick Chen/Alamy

Page 118. Jacques Jangoux/Photo Researchers, Inc.

Page 127. Research Division of the Oklahoma Historical Society

Page 136. Courtesy of the Library of Congress Prints and Photographs

Page 155. Yoav Levy/Phototake NYC

Page 160. WALT DISNEY/THE KOBAL COLLECTION

Page 169. Lotus Cars USA, Inc. Photo by Rick Dole.

Page 177TL. © The Dorothea Lange Collection, Oakland Museum of California, City of Oakland.

Page 177TR. Courtesy of the Library of Congress

Page 177ML. Courtesy of the Library of Congress

Page 177MR. Dorothea Lange/CORBIS–NY

Page 177BL. Courtesy of the Library of Congress

Page 177BR. © Dorothea Lange/CORBIS All Rights Reserved

Page 198. Craig Lovell/Stock Connection

Page 218 All: Benjamin Damm http.//dammfine.com

Page 240. Christinne Muschi/CORBIS–NY

Page 265. © Photo B.D.V./ CORBIS. All Rights Reserved

Page 277. Courtesy National Eating Disorders Association. www.nationaleatingdisorders.org

Page 288. Richard Megna/Fundamental Photographs, NYC

Page 317. Wyeth, Andrew (1917–2009), "Christina's World." 1948. Tempera on gessoed panel, 32 1/4 X 47 3/4". Purchase. The Museum of Modern Art, New York, NY, U.S.A. Digital Image © The Museum of Modern Art/Licensed by SCALA / Art Resource, NY

Page 343. © Greg Smith/CORBIS All Rights Reserved

Page 338. Corbis RF

Page 390. Viesti Associates, Inc.

Page 420. Aaron Douglas, American, 1899–1979, "Aspiration," 1936. Oil on canvas. 60 x 60" (152.4 x 152.4 cm). Fine Arts Museums of San Francisco. Museum purchase, the estate of Thurlow E. Tibbs Jr., The Museum Auxiliary, American Art Trust Fund, Unrestricted Art Trust Fund, partial gift of Dr. Ernest A Bates, Sharon Bell, Jo-Ann Berverly, Barbara Carleton, Dr. & Mrs. Arthur H. Coleman, Dr. & Mrs. Coyness Ennix, Jr., Nicole Y. Ennix,

INDEX

REVISION SYMBOLS

ab	faulty abbreviation	pron	incorrect pronoun form
ad	faulty use of adjective/adverb	ref	unclear pronoun reference
agr	error in agreement	rep	unnecessary repetition
appr	inappropriate word	sp	spelling error
awk	awkward diction or construction	shift	shifted sentence
ca	faulty case	sub	faulty subordination
cap	error in capitalization	t	verb tense error
coh	problem with coherence	trans	transition needed
coord	faulty coordination	var	sentence variety needed
cs	comma splice	vb	verb form error
d	problem with diction or word choice	w	wordy
dm	dangling modifier	ww / wc	wrong word / word choice
dev	development needed	/ /	faulty parallelism
doc	problem with documentation	.?!	faulty end punctuation
emph	emphasis needed	:	colon
frag	sentence fragment	'	apostrophe
fs	fused sentence	—	dash
hyph	hyphen	( )	parentheses
inc	incomplete sentence	[ ]	brackets
ital	italics	...	ellipsis dots
lc	lower-case letter	/	slash
log	faulty logic	;	semicolon
mm	misplaced modifier	" "	quotation marks
mix	mixed sentence	,	comma
no ¶	no new paragraph needed	#	add space
num	number	⌒	close up space
¶	new paragraph needed	∧	insert
prep	inappropriate preposition	ℓ	delete
		X	transpose order